THE IMPACT OF USA PATRIOT ACT ON AMERICAN SOCIETY:
AN EVIDENCE BASED ASSESSMENT

THE IMPACT OF USA PATRIOT ACT ON AMERICAN SOCIETY:
AN EVIDENCE BASED ASSESSMENT

KAM C. WONG

Nova Science Publishers, Inc.
New York

For permission to use material from this book please contact us:
Telephone 631-231-7269; Fax 631-231-8175
Web Site: http://www.novapublishers.com

NOTICE TO THE READER

The Publisher has taken reasonable care in the preparation of this book, but makes no expressed or implied warranty of any kind and assumes no responsibility for any errors or omissions. No liability is assumed for incidental or consequential damages in connection with or arising out of information contained in this book. The Publisher shall not be liable for any special, consequential, or exemplary damages resulting, in whole or in part, from the readers' use of, or reliance upon, this material.

Independent verification should be sought for any data, advice or recommendations contained in this book. In addition, no responsibility is assumed by the publisher for any injury and/or damage to persons or property arising from any methods, products, instructions, ideas or otherwise contained in this publication.

This publication is designed to provide accurate and authoritative information with regard to the subject matter cover herein. It is sold with the clear understanding that the Publisher is not engaged in rendering legal or any other professional services. If legal, medical or any other expert assistance is required, the services of a competent person should be sought. FROM A DECLARATION OF PARTICIPANTS JOINTLY ADOPTED BY A COMMITTEE OF THE AMERICAN BAR ASSOCIATION AND A COMMITTEE OF PUBLISHERS.

Library of Congress Cataloging-in-Publication Data

Wong, Kam C.
 The impact of USA Patriot Act on American society : an evidence based assessment / Kam C. Wong..
     p. ; cm.
 Includes bibliographical references and index.
 ISBN-13: 978-1-60021-840-8 (hardcover : alk. paper)
 ISBN-10: 1-60021-840-7 (hardcover : alk. paper)
 1. United States. Uniting and Strengthening America by Providing Appropriate ToolsRequired to Intercept and Obstruct Terrorism (USA PATRIOT ACT) Act of 2001.
2 Terrorism-United States- -Prevention, 3. Terrorism- -Government policy- -United States Psychological aspects. 4. Terrorism- -Government policy- -United States- -Social aspects.
5. Muslims- -Civil rights- -United States. 6. Civil rights- -United States. 1. Title.
 KF9430.A316W66 2006
 345.73'02--dc22
                                    2007023789
            Published by Nova Science Publishers, Inc. ✤*New York*

CONTENTS

PREFACE

Much has been written about the USA Patriot Act, and the controversy that surrounds this far-reaching legislation has also generated a great deal of confusion and uncertainty about its impact and importance in the war on terrorism. As Professor Kam C. Wong notes in this important contribution to the literature: "There is little scholarly research on the legislation, implementation and impact of the Act."

Undoubtedly, few Americans are actually aware of most of the details in the Act, or its implications in a free society. The events of September 11, 2001 in attacks on the World Trade Center and the Pentagon prompted a unique response by Congress in passing a series of wide reaching laws, expanding the powers of law enforcement and the judiciary. Of particular concern to many are the requirements of public and private organizations to provide information in connection with homeland security that is considered intrusive and in violation of privacy rights. Ultimately, it will be many years before the actual impact of the Patriot Act can be assessed. In this treatise Professor Wong provides a critical analysis of the legislation and its capacity for abuse.

From the perspective of civil libertarians the Patriot Act has been viewed as a direct attack on democratic freedoms, and a litany of cases involving individuals and organizations that have been harmed by overzealous agents have been covered widely in the media. The conflicts in Iraq and Afghanistan have contributed in no small measure to the fear of another terrorist attack on American soil, fueling what many view as the government's knee-jerk reaction to homeland security.

Stalwart proponents of the Patriot Act argue that all means necessary must be used to protect the American public from what they perceive as the radical Muslim threat. If it means giving up civil liberties and permitting wide-spread "fishing" expeditions, so be it. In the middle of the debate are the vast numbers of Americans who recognize that homeland security is necessary in a turbulent world, but the response must be measured, and based upon the principles by which America was founded.

Professor Wong, a lawyer and a PhD, American educated and a former police officer in Hong Kong, brings a wealth of experience and insight into issues of civil liberties. His descriptive analysis of the historical background and political climate surrounding the passage of the Act in 2001, less than two months after 9/11, raises some interesting questions. Chapters concerning the impact of the Act on the Muslim community in the United States, on libraries, and on immigrant students display some of the author's major concerns. A case study of the Student Exchange and Visitor Information System (SEVIS) is revealing, and exposes many of the problems associated with recruiting students and visiting scholars to American universities.

Given the rapid developments in technology and communication issues of privacy, freedom of speech, and the investigative tactics of the government have contributed to an ongoing debate. In his final chapter the author addresses what he terms the "grassroots resistance" to the Patriot Act, and in doing so offers an important "starting point" for exploring many of the criticisms associated with the legislation and its interpretation. Of particular importance for the future will be a better understanding of the strengths and weaknesses of the more controversial aspects of the ACT, and how it has been used in the war on terrorism. There are strong differences between errors of judgment in a small number of cases and interpretations that may impact thousands of innocent persons. As Rolando del Carmen, a noted legal scholar points out: "The USA Patriot Law is one of the most controversial laws ever passed by the United States Congress and is considered in some quarters to have the potential to modify current court decisions on the Fourth Amendment if most of its provisions are upheld."[1] Professor Wong's treatise will contribute greatly to the ongoing debate, and also serve as a primer for those who are all too unfamiliar with the Act and its impact on American society.

Richard H. Ward

Sam Houston State University
Huntsville, Texas

---

[1] Del Carmen, Rolando (2004). Criminal Procedure: Law and Practice. US: Thomson Wadsworth.

Chapter 1

INTRODUCTION

Almost two years after passage of the USAPA,
little is known about how the law is being used to track terrorists or
innocent Americans.

Nancy Kranich (August 27, 2003)[2]

On September 11, 2001, terrorists attacked America without warning, killing 2752 in New York City alone.[3] On the same day, the President of the United States promised that: "The United States will hunt down and punish those responsible for these cowardly acts." [4] A day later, on September 12, 2001, the President declared war on terrorism, pledging: "United States of America will use all our resources to conquer this enemy." [5] Two more days later, on September 14, 2001, the President, pursuant to National Emergencies Act (50 U.S.C. 1601 et seq.), declared that the nation was in a state of emergency.[6] On September 19, 2001, the President lobbied the Congress for war powers to invade Iraq to fight a war on terror.[7] Meantime, on September 20, 2001, the President declared war on Afghanistan.[8] The first

---

[2] Nancy Kranich, "Commentary: The Impact of the USAPA: An Update," (August 27, 2003)The Free Expression Policy Project, NYU Law School http://www.fepproject.org/commentaries/patriotactupdate.html

[3] See "2,752: World Trade Center Death Toll Shrinks By 40," WNBC.com October 30, 2003. http://www.wnbc.com/wtc/2590013/detail.html The FBI reported 3,047 victims resulting from the terrorist attacks on September 11, 2001. Uniform Crime Reports: Crime in the United States 2001 (Washington DC: U.S. Department of Justice, 2002).

[4] "Remarks by the President Upon Arrival at Barksdale Air Force Base." (September 11, 2001). http://www.whitehouse.gov/news/releases/2001/09/20010911-1.html

[5] "Remarks By The President In Photo Opportunity With The National Security Team." (9/11/01) The White House. http://usinfo.state.gov/topical/pol/terror/01091208.htm

[6] "Declaration of National Emergency by Reason Of Certain Terrorist Attacks," By the President of the United States of America, A Proclamation. (9/14/2003). White House. http://www.whitehouse.gov/news/releases/2001/09/20010914-4.html

[7] "Bush To Congress: Give Me Force," CBS September 19, 2001. (President Bush: "If you want to keep the peace, you've got to have the authorization to use force.") http://www.cbsnews.com/stories/2002/09/20/world/main522673.shtml

[8] Transcript of President Bush's address, September 21, 2001. Posted: 2:27 AM EDT (0627 GMT) (To avoid war with America, Afghanistan must: "Deliver ...all of the leaders of Al Qaeda ...; Release all foreign nationals...; Protect foreign journalists...; Close immediately and permanently every terrorist training camp...; And hand over every terrorist and every person and their support structure to appropriate authorities; Give the United States full access to terrorist training camps...) http://archives.cnn.com/2001/US/09/20/gen.bush.transcript/

salvo on the global war on terror was fired on October 7, 2001.[9] Domestically, the first major piece of anti-terrorism legislation is that of USAPA (USAPA), passed on October 26, 2001.[10]

NATIONAL SECURITY STRATEGY AND WAR ON TERROR

The Bush administration advanced three major objectives in fighting terrorists at home and defeating terrorism abroad.[11] They included disrupting terrorist networks;[12] protecting the homeland; [13]and prevailing over terrorism[14] ideology.[15] In order to achieve these goals and objectives, the Bush administration proposed a six prong strategies:

First, to preemptively attack terrorists;[16] i.e., stopping the terrorists before they can strike and attacking them wherever they can be found.[17] In this regard, the National Security Strategy of the United States (2002) [18] provides in pertinent part:

> "The United States has long maintained the option of preemptive actions to counter a sufficient threat to our national security. The greater the threat, the greater is the risk of inaction— and the more compelling the case for taking anticipatory action to defend ourselves, even if uncertainty remains as to the time and place of the enemy's attack." [19]

Second, to engage and cooperate with other nations in neutralizing terrorism threats[20] and creating favorable conditions for lasting peace.[21] In this regard the National Security Strategy of the United States (2002) provides:

---

[9] "Operation Enduring Freedom – Operations." GolbalSecurity.org. http://www.globalsecurity.org/military/ops/ enduring-freedom-ops.htm

[10] USAPA of 2001 stands for: `Uniting and Strengthening America by Providing Appropriate Tools Required to Intercept and Obstruct Terrorism (USAPA) Act of 2001'. The stated legislative purpose of the Act is to: "To deter and punish terrorist acts in the United States and around the world, to enhance law enforcement investigatory tools, and for other purposes."

[11] National Strategy for Combating Terrorism (The White House, September 2006). http://hosted.ap.org/specials/ interactives/wdc/documents/wh_terror060905.pdf This study references the original National Strategy for Combating Terrorism (2003).

[12] Id. p. 15. (Goal: Defeat Terrorists and Their Organization.)

[13] Id. p. 17. (Goal: Deny Sponsorship, Support and Sanctuary to Terrorists.)

[14] Under Secretary of Defense for Policy Douglas J. Feith, "U.S. Strategy for the War on Terrorism." Speech at Political Union University of Chicago, Chicago, Illinois , Wednesday, April 14, 2004. http://www.defenselink. mil/speeches/2004/sp20040414-0261.html

[15] National Strategy for Combating Terrorism (2003) p. 23. (Objective: Wing the War of Idea)

[16] Christopher Greenwood, "International Law and the Pre-emptive Use of Force: Afghanistan, Al-Qaida, and Iraq," 4 San Diego Int'l L.J. 7 (2003).

[17] The National Security Strategy of the United States of America. The White House (2002). Peter Baker, "Bush to Restate Terror Strategy 2002 Doctrine of Preemptive War To Be Reaffirmed," Washington Post Thursday, March 16, 2006; Page A01

[18] "Bush reaffirms first-strike policy, calls Iran biggest possible threat," CNN.COM Thursday, March 16, 2006; Posted: 7:19 p.m. EST (00:19 GMT) (National Security Adviser Hadley: "If necessary, the strategy states, under longstanding principles of self defense, we do not rule out the use of force before attacks occur, even if uncertainty remains as to the time and place of the enemy's attack.") http://www.cnn.com/2006/POLITICS/ 03/16/bush.security.ap/index.html

[19] "V. Prevent Our Enemies from Threatening Us, Our Allies, and Our Friends with Weapons of Mass Destruction." The pre-emption doctrine was re-affirmed in "V. Prevent Our Enemies from Threatening Us, Our Allies, and Our Friends with Weapons of Mass Destruction" The National Security Strategy of the United States of America. (The White House (2006). http://www.whitehouse.gov/nsc/nss/2006/sectionV.html

[20] Fighting global terrorism requires global solutions. "I. Overview of America's International Strategy" in *The National Security Strategy of the United States of America*. The White House (2002) (To "strengthen alliances

"Wherever possible, the United States will rely on regional organizations and state powers to meet their obligations to fight terrorism. Where governments find the fight against terrorism beyond their capacities, we will match their willpower and their resources with whatever help we and our allies can provide." [22]

Third, to deny terrorists and terrorist organization of the necessary support, i.e., state sanctuary and economic maintenance, e.g., through sanctioning of terrorist states such as Libya [23] or freezing economic assets of terrorist organizations such as Hamas.[24] In this regard, the President said:

"We will starve terrorists of funding, turn them one against another, drive them from place to place, until there is no refuge or no rest. And we will pursue nations that provide aid or safe haven to terrorism. ... From this day forward, any nation that continues to harbor or support terrorism will be regarded by the United States as a hostile regime."[25]

Fourth, to neutralize fanatic Islamic fundamentalism, through constructing civil society as a matter of choice, and by use of military force if necessary, e.g., invading Afghanistan and liberating Iraq.[26]

Fifth, to reorganize the counter-terrorism and homeland security functions in one super ordinary national security body with the establishment of the Homeland Security Department.[27] In this regard, the President said:

---

to defeat global terrorism and work to prevent attacks against us and our friends"). More specifically, see "III. Strengthen Alliances to Defeat Global Terrorism and Work to Prevent Attacks Against Us and Our Friends" (The engagement of and cooperation with other nations occurred at multiple levels (strategic vs. tactical) and in different areas (institution building and defense fortification). To win the war on terror, the United States must work "closely with allies and friends, to make clear that all acts of terrorism are illegitimate so that terrorism will be viewed in the same light as slavery, piracy, or genocide... supporting moderate and modern government, especially in the Muslim world, to ensure that the conditions and ideologies that promote terrorism do not find fertile ground in any nation ... diminishing the underlying conditions that spawn terrorism by enlisting the international community to focus its efforts and resources on areas most at risk...) See also "VIII. Develop Agendas for Cooperative Action with the Other Main Centers of Global Power" (In the post 9/11 world, the U.S. must stay engaged with other global powers (China, Russia, Japan) and regional alliances (NATO, ASEAN to promote peace and provide for join security.)

[21] *Id.* (To "work with others to defuse regional conflicts.")

[22] *Id.* "III. Strengthen Alliances to Defeat Global Terrorism and Work to Prevent Attacks Against Us and Our Friends".

[23] Ken Silverstein, "How Kadafi Went From Foe to Ally: Common cause against Islamic radicals has woven U.S. intelligence ties with Libya, whose secular regime is still listed as a state sponsor of terrorism," *L.A. Times* September 4, 2005. (Libya was considered by the U.S. as a terrorist state and rogue regime, until it redeemed itself and turned over suspects of the 1999 Pan Am bombing and renounced its WMD program in 2004. Since then it has worked with the U.S. in outlawing Islamic extremism as a common enemy.) http://www.latimes.com/news/printedition/la-fg-uslibya4sep04,1,6796656,full.story

[24] Juan Carlos Zarate, "Bankrupting Terrorists," *e-journalUSA* (See U.N. Security Council Resolution 1373 and the eight Special Recommendations on Terrorist Financing by the 33-member Financial Action Task Force on money laundering (FATF). http://usinfo.state.gov/journals/ites/0904/ijee/zarate.htm

[25] Address to a Joint Session of Congress and the American People. White House. Office of the Press Secretary. September 20, 2001. http://www.whitehouse.gov/news/releases/2001/09/20010920-8.html

[26] *National Strategy for Victory in Iraq.* The White House, November 30, 2005. (Executive Summary: "Iraq is the central front in the global war on terror. Failure in Iraq will embolden terrorists and expand their reach; success in Iraq will deal them a decisive and crippling blow.") For an opposing view, see Andrea Mitchell, "CIA insider says U.S. fighting wrong war: Anonymous career officer makes bold claims in book about U.S. war on terror," *NBC News* Updated: 9:03 a.m. ET June 24, 200 (Interview with veteran CIA officer suggested that invasion of Iraq has the opposite effect. Iraq is the second holiest place of Islam. By invading it, America because the enemy of Islam, breeding more terrorism in turn.) http://www.msnbc.msn.com/id/5279743

"The Department of Homeland Security will be charged with four primary tasks. This new agency will control our borders and prevent terrorists and explosives from entering our country. It will work with state and local authorities to respond quickly and effectively to emergencies. It will bring together our best scientists to develop technologies that detect biological, chemical, and nuclear weapons, and to discover the drugs and treatments to best protect our citizens. And this new department will review intelligence and law enforcement information from all agencies of government, and produce a single daily picture of threats against our homeland. Analysts will be responsible for imagining the worst, and planning to counter it."[28]

Sixth, to secure the homeland [29] by providing law enforcement and national security officials with broad powers, and with little oversight from the Congress and supervision by the courts.[30]

NATIONAL STRATEGY FOR HOMELAND SECURITY AND USAPA

On October 26, 2001, President Bush signed into law the USAPA.[31] The USAPA gave the law enforcement officials expansive powers and security agencies increased resources to fight terrorism, at home and abroad.[32] USAPA powers and related counter-terrorism measures were fashioned to alleviate problems besetting US security system, then, as revealed by prior commissioned terrorism studies and uncovered by government audit offices.[33] It also resonant with the National Strategy for Homeland Security[34] promulgated nine months later and

---

[27] See "Organizing for a Secure Homeland" in *The National Strategy For Homeland Security* (2002), p. 13. http://www.whitehouse.gov/homeland/book/sect2-2.pdf

[28] Remarks by the President in Address to the Nation. White House. Office of the Press Secretary. June 6, 2002. http://www.whitehouse.gov/news/releases/2002/06/20020606-8.html

[29] See also Geov Parrish, "The Police State Enhancement Act of 2003: Bush Administration begins work on secretive sequel to the USAPA," *workingforchange.com* Feb. 10, 2003. http://foi.missouri.edu/domsecenhanceact/policestate.html (In the name of fighting a war on terror, President Bush and AG Ashcroft sought to introduced USAPA II. The Act, if passed, would: (1) allow the federal government to declare citizens as enemies of the states, and deny them of their endowed and entrenched Constitutional rights of citizenship; (2) define liberally, expansively and vaguely what constitute "espionage" or "enemy" activities such that lawful activities are implicated, e.g. providing legal advice to terrorists; (3) punish people for releasing information on government detainees; (4) create a DNA database of suspected "terrorists" detainees without due process; (5) over-ride all state ban on law enforcement surveillance activity; (6) make capital punishment applicable to "terrorism" and "espionage"-related offenses; (7) provide draconian punishment for routine immigration violations.) Rep. Ron Paul, "Is America Becoming a Police State?" http://www.conspiracyplanet.com/channel.cfm?channelid=90andcontentid=1729

[30] "Editorial: Big Brother Bush / The president took a step toward a police state," *Pittsburgh Post-Gazette*, Sunday, December 18, 2005. (NSA is listening on thousands of people without legal authority and Pentagon is keeping Threat and Local Observation Notice, or TALON, database of protesters.) http://www.post-gazette.com/pg/05352/623818.stm

[31] USAPA, October 26, 2001, P. L.107-056; 115 STAT. 272.

[32] For legal analysis, see Charles Doyle, "The USAPA: A Legal Analysis," *Congressional Research Service*, April 15, 2002.

[33] Through the years GAO (Government Accounting Office) has repeated pointed to major structural and operational deficiencies with America's homeland security system or counter-terrorism readiness. As of March 28, 2007, GAO has published 488 items on terrorism. See "Terrorism Products since April 1979." Of those, about 18% were conducted before 9/11. http://www.gao.gov/docsearch/featured/terrorism.html For a representative study conducted before 9/11 and published afterward, see "Combating Terrorism: Selected Challenges and Related Recommendations," GAO-01-822, September 20, 2001.

[34] *The National Strategy For Homeland Security* The White House (June 2002).

anticipated 9/11 Commission recommendations two years hence,[35] e.g. need to coordinate and integrate disparate government efforts in fighting terrorism. For example, coordinating domestic (CIA) vs. global (State Department – Diplomatic Security) vs. international (M16) activities, federal (FBI and Customs) vs. locally (local sheriffs vs. state police), executive (NSC vs. FBI) vs. legislative (Judicial Committee vs. Intelligence Committee vs. Foreign relations Committees) vs. judicial branches, and between (FBI vs. CIA vs. INS) and within agencies (policy vs. administration vs. operations). There is a dire need for a nation-wide homeland security agency that is internationally linked and intra – governmental connected with operations informed by up to the minute tactical intelligence embedded in a just in time security – terrorist screening warning system, to provide for visa validation, for airport screening, for security clearance, and more.

The Nation Strategy for Homeland Security was promulgated by the President on July 2002. The expressed homeland security strategic objectives, as prioritized are: secure the homeland from attack; reduce the Nation's vulnerability from attack; minimize the damage from attack and recover from an attack quickly.[36] The objectives are refined into six mission critical areas: intelligence and warnings, border and transportation security, domestic counterterrorism, protecting critical infrastructure and key assets, defending against catastrophic terrorism, and emergency preparedness and response.[37]

The USAPA is designed to shift criminal justice paradigm, fix security lapse and otherwise enhance law enforcement – intelligence capacities. These include:

From crime to war metaphor. Shifting counter-terrorism from "crime" suppression to "war" fighting.[38] Terrorists are no longer treated as criminals entitled to civil liberties but enemies deprived of human rights. The shift in paradigm has come to affect every aspects of our democratic form of government, from Constitutional jurisprudence to law enforcement operations to judicial process.

From liberty to security. Underscoring the above shift of paradigm is a shift from a concern with Constitutional rights and civil liberties of citizens to a concern with the security and survival of the state. This is justified two ways: (1) There is no liberty without security. (2) Liberty is not absolution, but contingent entitlement.

From reaction to pre-emption. Shifting counter-terrorism strategy from a reactive crime fighting mentality to a pro-active terrorism reduction/prevention/interdiction mindset. This allows the administration to take pre-emptive actions to neutralize the terrorism threats through breaking up the organization or disrupting the operations of the terrorists, instead of conducting after the fact crisis management, investigation and prosecution.

From collecting evidence to collecting intelligence. In order to accurately predict, effectively prevent and timely interdict terrorist subterranean and subversive activities, information of every kind is necessary. This requires law enforcement agencies and

---

[35] "9-11 Commission Report Recommendations" Chapters 12 and 13 of the *Final Report of the National Commission on Terrorist Attacks Upon the United States* (2004) Official Government Editionhttp://grumet.net/911/recommendations.html

[36] *The National Strategy For Homeland Security* The White House (June 2002). p. vii.

[37] *Id.* p. viii. (Critical Missions Area)

[38] Mark Riebling, "Counter-Counterterrorism: The debacle pre-9/11,". *National Review.* Nov. 25, 2002. (First, law enforcement reacts to crime after the fact, counter-terrorism requires preemptive attack on terrorists. Second, criminals are processed in accordance with the rule of law. But terrorists respect no rule. Third, law enforcement agents gather identifiable evidence for prosecution. Counter-terrorism operatives require intelligence to ascertain the intent and capacity of terrorists.) http://www.nationalreview.com/flashback/riebling200404130920.asp

intelligences communities to conduct data mining, community surveillance and personal monitoring.

From competition to collaboration. Breaking down the intelligence wall between law enforcement (FBI) and intelligence community (CIA), so that they can pool investigative resources, e.g. conducting joint task, and share intelligence data, e.g. releasing grand jury testimonies, and be able to connect the dots to discern what the terrorists are doing.

In so doing, according to some critics, the U.S. is moving closer and closer to being a police state.[39]

IMPACT OF THE USAPA[40] ON SOCIETY:
THE ILLUSTRATIVE CASE OF THE UNIVERSITY

As it turned out, the USAPA, in design and as applied, with intent and by default, has come to impact on many aspect of American society, e.g. air travel, immigration, library, higher education, scientific research and banking; issues that were avoided by the Bush administration and escape the attention the Congress, in their haste to fight terrorism and in defense of the nation. One of the social institutions that is most seriously impacted by the USAPA is the nation's university system as a place of scholarly research, intellectual discourse and higher learning. This is so for a number of reasons.

The primary mission of the university is to discover and distribute ideas, in the process preserves and advance our civilization through questioning conventional wisdom and embracing new ideas. The provost of Columbia University observed thusly:

> The mission of a great university in our society is to create and disseminate new knowledge through research and teaching—and to lead debates that have broader implications for peoples' values, ethics, and behavior…In our society the high calling of intellectuals and scholars is to challenge received wisdom, political correctness, and intellectual complacency; to be skeptical about claims of "fact" and "truth"; to question presuppositions and biases of others as well as their own…Truth rests less in product than in process.[41]

As such, the universities conduct research, explore ideas, encourage free speech, promote diversity of ideology, facilitate exchange of scholarship and foster academic freedom.

---

[39] Sean Gonsalves, "Is U.S. Becoming a Police State?" *Cape Cod Times* (Massachusetts) Tuesday, December 20, 2005.

[40] While the main focus of this research is on USAPA, the impact of the ACT on universities cannot be discerned, analyzed, and discussed independent of and separate from other integrally related and closely associated post 9/11 anti-terrorism legislation and measures, including: Illegal Immigration Reform and Responsibility Act of 1996 (IRRA) that authorized the Student Exchange Visa Information System (SEVIS). The USAPA of 2001 that increased foreign student monitoring and Internet surveillance. The Public Health Security and Bioterrorism Preparedness and Response Act of 2002 (P.L. 107-188) (June 12, 2002) that expanded upon the Antiterrorism and Death Penalty Act of 1996 in calling for the reporting and registration of all facilities and individuals in possession of biological agents and toxins. The Enhanced Border Security and Visa Entry Reform Act of 2002 (P.L. 107-173) (May 14, 2002) that required that Student Exchange Visa Information System be fully operational by January 30, 2003.

[41] Jonathan R. Cole, "The Patriot Act on Campus: Defending the university post–9/11," *Boston Review* (A talk presented at "The Futures of Higher Education," University of Chicago, Graham School of General Studies, May 9, 2003. Jonathan R. Cole has been provost and dean of faculties at Columbia University since 1989.) http://www.bostonreview.net/BR28.3/cole.html

On the other hand, the USAPA, in the name of security, restricts sensitive research, frowns on controversial ideas, regulates provocative speech, advocates political correctness, retard intellectual exchange and attack academic freedom. This is particularly so with respect to research universities.

Impact on Universities

The USAPA has come to affect every members of the university community: school administrators, teaching faculty, international students, foreign visitors, and research scientists. It implicates every aspect of university activities, i.e. university administration, foreign student counseling, information technology, library services, academic research, scientific communication and scholarly exchange. For example, the USAPA affects the university, institutionally and operationally, in a number of significant ways, from what biological agents a university is allowed to possess [42] to who is allowed to conduct sensitive research,[43] from what the students can read in the library[44] to who they can associate with on the internet,[45] from which international scholars to invite to which foreign students to recruit.[46]

Ultimately, the USAPA radically transforms the role and function, administration and operation of the university,[47] calling for self examination and objective assessment. [48] In this regard, the USAPA raises controversial philosophical issues as it attracts heated policy debates for the university community:

> "Are we prepared to relinquish personal privacy and academic freedom to secure some vaguely articulated increase in national security? Do these new laws and regulations accomplish that? What effect will they have on the growth of knowledge and on the intellectual environment at universities? What, in fact, is the threat to national security that is posed by students and faculty at our universities? What evidence is there that select agents and

---

[42] Section 817 of the USAPA; "Expansion of the Biological Weapons Statute," amends Chapter 10 of title 18, United States Code and prohibits the possession of a biological agent, toxin, or delivery system "...of a type or in a quantity that, under the circumstances, is not reasonably justified by a prophylactic, protective, bona fide research, or other peaceful purpose."

[43] "Restricted persons" who are not allowed to handle "select agents" include: (A) an indicted criminal; (B) a convicted person; (C) a fugitive; (D) a drug user; (E) an illegal alien; (F) a mentally defective person (G) is an alien who is a national of Cuba, Iran, Iraq, Libya, North Korea, Sudan or Syria, or from country which supported international terrorism; and (H) a dishonorable discharged soldier.

[44] Section 215 of the Act gives law enforcement the power to apply for a court order requiring the librarian to surrender "any tangible thing" including books, records, papers, documents, and anything else which is "relevant" to anti-terrorist investigation.

[45] Section 216 of the Act gives law enforcement the power to capture "routing, addressing, and signaling" information in any electronic communication media.

[46] "AACRAO Position Letter to INS on SEVIS Implementation," American Association of Collegiate Registrars and Admissions Officers (AACRAO) – Federal Relations (June 17, 2002). http://www.aacrao.org/federal_relations/cipris/SEVIS.htm The INS has authority to deny visa to foreign student for failing to SEVIS requirements.

[47] Kyna Rubin, ""Keeping the Door Open", *International Educator* Spring 2003 ((Louisiana University Chancellor Mark Emmert observed: "Legislative bodies think that universities should be in a position to better control students, but we don't play the role of policeman very well ... It's inappropriate to expect universities to do this alone-we don't have the authority or the resources...") http://www.udel.edu/iepmedia/article_rubin.html

[48] See discussion on "The Patriot Act," in "University Council Meeting Coverage," *Almanac*, Vol. 49, No. 31, April 29, 2003. (University of Pennsylvania). http://www.upenn.edu/almanac/v49/n31/council_coverage.html

toxins used in American scientific laboratories for legitimate purposes pose a real threat to national security and require that we deny students access to that research opportunity because of where they were born? Are there students with links to terrorist organizations studying at our universities? What evidence is there to support such a claim and do the probabilities of a vague potential threat warrant the types of measures being taken to limit free inquiry, open communication, and individual privacy?[49]"

Of all the people within the university community, the foreign students are most affected. The USAPA places foreign students under close observation.[50] It calls for intense scrutiny of visiting scholars[51] and strict monitor of foreign students to the U.S, e.g. students must keep INS informed at all times of their education status and progress.[52] Such security measures affect the foreign students in many ways, including:[53]

(1) It is now more difficult to apply for a visa to study in the United States.[54] Many scholars and students are denied admission or delayed re-entry. This is particularly so with applicants from black listed countries or those who are pursuing study in a sensitive subject. [55] First, the Technology Alert List (TAL) has been expanded to include biological sciences and urban planning as Critical Fields of Study, off limited to many nations' foreign students. Second, export controlled goods and technologies (under TAL) are now restricted to all nationals. Third, the consular officers are not expected to be familiar with TAL during visa interviews. They only have to "listen for key words or phrases from the Critical Fields list" while interviewing applicants. Fourth, the Department of State has eliminated time limitations for processing of a

---

[49] Jonathan R. Cole, "The Patriot Act on Campus: Defending the university post–9/11," *Boston Review*, Vol. 28, Nos. 3–5, Summer 2003. http://www.bostonreview.net/BR28.3/cole.html

[50] "Patriot Act puts foreign students under scrutiny," *INDYSTAR.COM*, December 21, 2003, http://www.indystar.com/articles/8/104335-1688-009.html (Foreign students, particularly those from the Middle East or those who look like Middle Eastern, were being placed under strict scrutiny by federal officials. According to individual experience, some visas were denied or delayed. All of them worried that they might not be able to find a job. Many of them worried that their family members might not be able to come to their graduation)

[51] Olivier Guitta, "Danger: Tariq Ramadan is coming to the US," *American Thinker* May 03, 2004. (Ramadan is the grandson of Hassan Al Banna, the founder of the Muslim Brotherhood, an Islamist terrorist organization. " Ramadan wants to lift up the Muslim community by telling them that they are superior beings, because Islam is beyond and above everything." He is an Anti—Semite and has links to terrorists in Switzerland. He should not be allowed to teach at University of Notre Dame)

[52] For a security measures adopted since 9/11 affecting students, see Summary of Major Federal Regulation Changes that Impact International Students, December 28, 2002. http://international.tamu.edu/iss/regulations/INSSummaryDec182002.doc

[53] For statistics and case study of how new visa requirements adversely affect Chinese students in the US, see http://www.columbia.edu/cu/cucssa/news/visa/visa_appendix.htm

[54] For a statement of the problems, see "International Student Visa Processing: Will Students be here in time for fall classes," AACRAO Transcript. July 14, 2003. http://www.aacrao.org/transcript/index.cfm?fuseaction=show_viewanddoc_id=1445
For a public hearing on the problems and issues of visa delay, see "Hearing on the Impact of the Visa Process on Foreign Travel in the U.S.," July 10, 2003, House Government Reform and Oversight Committee. For the need to strengthen visa requirements, see General Accounting Office, Report No. GAO-03-132NI, "Border Security: Visa Process Should Be Strengthened as an Antiterrorism Tool" (Oct. 21, 2002).

[55] "The University Responds: The Impact of the USAPA and Other Legislation on International GSAS Students bout one month after the 9/11 attacks in 2001," *GSAB Bulletin*, Vol. XXXIII (2), October 2003. http://www.gsas.harvard.edu/pdfs/bulletin_oct03.pdf

student visa request. All these changes raise the threshold and complicate the process for visa approval.[56]

(2) It is now more time consuming to apply for a visa.[57] The application process is much lengthened because: (a) Effective August 1, 2003 onward, the State Department requires that all applicants be interviewed, with few exceptions.[58] This caused length delay, e.g. six months of more delay in Korea[59] and London.[60] Rome, Paris, Tokyo, and Taipei[61] are particularly hard hit. [62] (b) There are more documents to file, and still more steps to go through, e.g., consulate officials have to screen applicants according to three check lists: Consular Lookout Automated Support System (CLASS).[63] CONDOR[64] and MANTIS.[65][66] (C) Applications are often routed through

---

[56] See diplomatic cable concerning: Using the Technology Alert List: Update.

[57] Dan Eggen, "Tougher Rules On U.S. Visas Bring Fears of Long Backlogs," *Washington Post*, May 24, 2003.

[58] Fed. Reg. 40,127 (July 7, 2003) (amending 22 C.F.R. § 41.102). Under the new rule a consular officer may waive a visa interview only for: (1) individuals under the age of 16 or over 60; (2) diplomats and government officials; (3) individuals who are seeking a timely revalidation of their visa; and (4) limited emergency circumstances. 68 Fed. Reg. at 40,128-29. There are only 843 consular officers processing over 8 million visa applications a year. General Accounting Office, Report No. GAO-03-132NI, Border Security: Visa Process Should Be Strengthened as an Antiterrorism Tool 7 (Oct. 21, 2002).

[59] Stanley Mailman and Stephen Yale-Loehr, "Visa Worries, Visa Delays," *New York Law Journal* August 20, 2003. Reprint at http://www.twmlaw.com/index.php?this_cat=1andthis_sub_cat=1andarticle_id=213and keyword=patriot%20act (According to immigration specialists: "Analyzing data from the U.S. embassy in Seoul, the American Chamber of Commerce in Korea estimates that the added interviews will mean about a six-month wait for a visa appointment in Seoul".)

[60] *Id.* Testimony of Janice L. Jacobs, Deputy Assistant Secretary for Visa Services, Department of State, before the House Committee on Government Reform, July 10, 2003. Immigration lawyers report that nonimmigrant visa applicants must now wait about six weeks for an appointment at the U.S. embassy in London.

[61] *Id.* Testimony of Randel K. Johnson, Vice President of Labor, Immigration and Employee Benefits, U.S. Chamber of Commerce, before the House Committee on Government Reform, July 10, 2003. Consular posts in Rome, Paris, Tokyo, and Taipei are also expected to be hit particularly hard.

[62] To ameliorate the backlog resulting from new visa interview requirements after 9/11. Secretary of State Powell has asked consulate officers to give priority to certain visa applications, such as exchange students and visiting scholars, so as not to disrupt their study plan. See State Department diplomatic cable, R181803Z, "RE: Priority for Student and Exchange Visa Processing" (June 3, 2003)

[63] CLASS now contains more than 15 million records on people ineligible to receive visas, more than double the number available before 9/11. See U.S. Dep't of State, 9 Foreign Affairs Manual (FAM), Part IV Appendix D section 200.

[64] Visas Condor was started in January 2002 checks the applicant's identification information against as many as 20 U.S. security databases, such as CLASS (Consular Lookout and Support System). Before 9/11/2001, the six million or so records in CLASS were entered because of previous visa denials or other immigration law infractions. After 9/11, another six million or so records were added from FBI files. The Visas Condor program requires consular officers to obtain security clearances for all male visa applicants between the ages of 6 and 45 from any of 26 countries, mostly in the Middle East. The Visas Mantis program requires security clearances for people studying or working in sensitive areas identified on the Technology Alert List.

[65] Mantis is used to determine an applicant's visa eligibility under Section 212(a)(3)(A)(i)(II) of the Immigration and Nationality Act: "Any alien who a consular officer or the [Secretary of Homeland Security] knows, or has reasonable ground to believe, seeks to enter the United States to engage solely, principally, or incidentally in - (i) any activity . . . (II) to violate or evade any law prohibiting the export from the United States of goods, technology, or sensitive information . . . . is ineligible to receive a visa." The Visas Mantis program is an effective tool for U.S. intelligence and law enforcement agencies to support consular officers in screening individuals and entities that seek to gain controlled goods, technology and sensitive information in violation of US export laws.

[66] John Marburger, Director of the White House Office of Science and Technology Policy, American Association for the Advancement of Science, Colloquium on Science and Technology Policy, Washington, D.C., April 10, 2003. (The top two reasons for visa application failure are: (a) failure to establish "intent to return to home country" and (b) failure to provide for necessary documentation.) http://www.ostp.gov/html/jhmAAASvisas.pdf

many different agencies and departments.[67] Each with its own data requirements and approval process. (D) Before 9/11 visa are cleared if on objection is forthcoming. Now affirmative clearance is required.[68] (E) It takes a longer time to process an application background investigation, especially from less developed countries with poor record keeping system and dysfunctional/corrupt/inefficient government bureaucracy. [69] (c) It takes time to perfect the Student and Exchange Visitor Information System (SEVIS) process. [70] DHS experienced technical delays in uploading SEVIS information into its database. (d) SEVIS requires the payment of SEVIS fees to DHS before visa application are to be filed at the US Consulate.[71] DHS accepts two forms of payment, i.e. by e-mail or by mail.[72] If mail is used, it "will likely result in significant delays to an already lengthy visa application and review process. One could easily envision adding four to six weeks to the process for mail delivery and return." [73] The lengthy and cumbersome visa process affects visitors and students alike.[74]

(3) It is now more costly to apply for a visa.[75] 'In some countries, students are expected to have a personal interview. In Brazil [for example], some students have to fly to

---

[67] Before 9/11 consular officers submitted SAOs to the State Department headquarters in Washington, DC and then waited for 30 days, before proceeding. . Now consular officers must wait for an affirmative response from relevant agencies (usually the FBI) before approving a visa. FBI processes approximately 200,000 visa check, including 75,000 Visa Condor and 25,000 Visa Mantis checks. In calendar year 2002, consular affairs conducted 50,000 visas condor and about 14,000 visas mantis checks. Consular affairs officers have stated that such checks represent about a three-fold increase in the number of cases referred to Washington D.C. Testimony of Robert J. Garrity, Jr., Acting Assistant Director, Records Management Division, Federal Bureau of Investigation, before the House Committee on Government Reform, July 10, 2003.

[68] U.S. Department of State Office of Inspector *General Review of Nonimmigrant Visa Issuance Policy and Procedures Memorandum* Report ISP-I-03-26, December 2002. http://oig.state.gov/documents/organization/16215.pdf

[69] John Marburger, Director of the White House Office of Science and Technology Policy, American Association for the Advancement of Science, Colloquium on Science and Technology Policy, Washington, D.C., April 10, 2003. (The top two reasons for visa application failure are: (a) failure to establish "intent to return to home country" and failure to provide for necessary documentation.) http://www.ostp.gov/html/jhmAAASvisas.pdf

[70] Letter Regarding Proposed SEVIS FEE Collection Process (December 10, 2003) (To Regulations and Forms Service Division, Department of Homeland Security). http://www.aacrao.org/federal_relations/position/sevis_fee.htm

[71] Department of Homeland Security's (DHS) Proposed Rule No. 2297-03, published in the Federal Register on October 27, 2003. The collection of fees, currently set at $100 to finance the setting up, maintainance of SEVIS is mandated by Section 647 (e) of Illegal Immigration Reform and Immigrant Responsibility Act of 1996 (IIRIRA), 8 U.S.C. 1372. The proposed rule by DHS: "Authorizing Collection of the Fee Levied on F, J, and M Nonimmigrant Classifications Under Public Law 104-208" can be found at Federal Register: October 27, 2003 (Volume 68, Number 207), Proposed Rules, Page 61148-61158, accessible from the Federal Register Online via GPO Access [wais.access.gpo.gov] [DOCID:fr27oc03-20]

[72] "SEVIS Student User Fee Announced," AACRAO, 10/27/03 ("If the visa applicant remits payment via mail the payment would be processed by DHS within three days of receiving it and a paper receipt would returned to the applicant via the same method. Students that seek F, M or J status while living abroad will be required to remit payment prior to applying for a visa. The applicant would be required to submit the receipt of payment to the appropriate U.S. Consulate or Embassy abroad at which the alien submits his F, M or J visa application.") http://www.aacrao.org/transcript/index.cfm?fuseaction=show_viewanddoc_id=1674

[73] Letter Regarding Proposed SEVIS FEE Collection Process (December 10, 2003) (To Regulations and Forms Service Division, Department of Homeland Security). http://www.aacrao.org/federal_relations/position/sevis_fee.htm

[74] Abraham McLaughlin, Foreign Visits to US Drop Sharply, Christian Science Monitor, July 30, 2003.

[75] Natalie J. Mikhail, "Federal fee for SEVIS," *Badger Herald* (UW) December 08, 2003. UW currently has about 4,600 foreign students, including 1,000 researchers and teaching scholars. This number has fallen by only 35 students since last year. http://www.badgerherald.com/vnews/display.v/ART/2003/12/08/3fd4145914471.

where they have to have the interview, which might cost them US$700 before they've even got their visa."[76]

Some Cases of Impact

Some examples of how USAPA impacted the universities are helpful to illustrate the problems on hand:

(1) *Workload problem for school administrators.* Many schools reported difficulties in operating the untested SEVIS system. For example, confidential *SEVIS* forms requested by the Jet Propulsion Laboratory - a secure government installation - were printed at a proprietary school in San Francisco. And batch processing of data at schools worked intermittently, if at all.[77]

(2) *Visa problems for foreign students.* In December of 2002, Zhirong Li, a second-year pant biology Ph.D. student at UC Berkeley went home to visit with her family in China. She planned to return January 23, 2003 but was denied a re-entry visa by the U.S. Embassy in Beijing on account of the sensitive subject she was studying. She was held up for eight months while waiting for a new security check. She suffered much uncertainty, anxiety and financial loss in the process, e.g. Li had to postpone her PhD. qualifying exams for nearly a year.[78] A Columbia Chinese doctoral student of physics was not able to return to defend her dissertation after she returned to China to bury her parents who died in a car accident.[79] Similarly, a fourth-year University of Washington pharmacy student, Adrian Natawidjaja was not able to return to the United States to finish his study after leaving for his mother's funeral.[80]

(3) *Censorship problem for students.* In September of 2002, the University of California at San Diego ordered Che Cafe Collective,[81] an anarchistic student organization, to remove the web link to Revolutionary Armed Forces of Colombia (FARC) on

---

[76] Jennifer Jacobson, "Foreign-Student Enrollment Stagnates," *The Chronicle of Higher Education* 11/7/2003 http://opendoors.iienetwork.org/?p=36997 (Irving Lerch, director of international affairs at the American Physical Society, says that current visa difficulties have put a damper on some graduate programs and do not bode well for scientific enterprises in this country, especially "when you realize that 35 percent of all students in the sciences -- math, technology, and engineering -- are foreign." First-rate Chinese students are applying to German schools instead.)

[77] Testimony of Dr. David Ward, President American Council before the U.S. House of Representatives Committee on Science in regard to "Dealing with Foreign Students and Scholars in the Age of Terrorism: Visa Backlogs and Tracking Systems." March 26, 2003.

[78] "TOEFL sees sharp drop in attendees," *China Daily* November 18, 2003. http://www1.chinadaily.com.cn/en/doc/2003-11/18/content_282343.htm

[79] Brian Braiker, "The Long Wait," *Newsweek.* December 15, 2003.

[80] Susan Paynter, "Patriot Act proves an insecurity measure for foreign students," SEATTLE *POST-INTELLIGENCER*, November 3, 2003, http://seattlepi.nwsource.com/paynter/146390_paynter03.html

[81] This is not the first time UCSD has tried to de-link an organization from student organization web site on grounds that the student organization has supported terrorists organization. In April 2002, the university has asked another study organization the Groundwork Books collective, to de-link from the Kurdistan Workers Party (PKK), which is also on the State Department's "Designated Foreign Terrorist Organization (FTO)" list. See letter of September 20, 2002, outline factual and legal bases for disciplinary action from UCSD Student Services to Groundwork Books http://checafe.ucsd.edu/correspondence/groundwork-2.html

grounds that it might violate USAPA, or face disciplinary action.[82] Specifically, the university was afraid of being charged with providing "material support or resources" to foreign terrorists. Under USAPA material support is defined as providing money, lodging, training or "communications equipment."[83] The Che Café Collective members asserted that they did not offer financial, training or housing support for FARC, only a hyperlink to the FARC site.[84] UCSD finally backed down.

(4) *Violation of students' privacy.* According to the American Association of Collegiate Registrars and Admissions Officers, immediately after 9/11, FBI, INS and other federal, state and local law enforcement agencies have asked more than 200 colleges and universities to turn over student information which is protected by Family Educational Rights and Privacy Act (FERPA) which protected students' educational records from unauthorized disclosure, without parental consent.[85] The USAPA (Section 507)[86] amends FERPA by including a terrorism investigation exception.[87] The terrorism investigation exception allows the Attorney General to apply for and be granted an *ex parte* order by certifying to the court that "there are specific and articulable facts giving reason to believe that the education records are likely to contain information" that is relevant to the investigation and prosecution of terrorism offences.[88]

(5) *Violations of students First Amendment rights.* In Minnesota, student groups such as Anti-Racist Action and Students Against War were labeled as potential terrorist threats.

A Summary of Impact and Concerns

Columbia provost and dean of faculties best summarize university community concerns with USAPA:

"First, as some of you know, provisions of the Patriot Act hold that …foreign students from about 25 nations must now be denied access to scientific research laboratories that use

---

[82] "UC San Diego OK's Web site link to Revolutionary Armed Forces of Colombia Administrators back down from claims link violates U.S.A. Patriot Act," *Student Press Law Center* October 8, 2002

[83] Declan McCullagh, "University Bans Controversial Links," *CNET News.com*, September 26, 2002. In context, the university has a right to be concerned. First, the student group was organized by radical students seeking radical social changes. Second, the university was of the opinion that the display of link was more than a neutral gesture. It was meant to be an active endorsement of the cause and affirmative support for the promotion of the organization. Third, another link of the organization - Raise the Fist – was recently raided by the FBI in January 2002.

[84] "UC San Diego OK's Web site link to Revolutionary Armed Forces of Colombia Administrators back down from claims link violates U.S.A. Patriot Act," *Student Press Law Center* October 8, 2002

[85] For a legislative history and content analysis, see "Legislative History of Major FERPA Provisions" (June 2002), Department of Education http://www.ed.gov/policy/gen/guid/fpco/pdf/ferpaleghistory.pdf

[86] SEC. 507. Disclosure of Educational Records. [115 Stat. 367-68]

[87] "Recent Amendments to Family Educational Rights and Privacy Act Relating to Anti-Terrorism Activities" (April 22, 2002) Department of Education, http://www.ifap.ed.gov/eannouncements/attachments/412FERPA.pdf

[88] As specified in 2332b(g)(5)(B) and 2331 of title 18, U.S. Code or related to domestic or international terrorism, i.e. offenses calculated to influence the conduct of government such as destruction of aircraft, assassination, arson, hostage taking, destruction of communications lines or national defense premises, and use of weapons of mass destruction.

"select agents" (biological agents and certain toxins)…And if a faculty member permits a prohibited student to enter a laboratory that is using select agents, that faculty member, too, is open to criminal penalties.

Second, in addition to classified research …the federal government has created a new category: "sensitive but unclassified research." There is significant concern that federally funded research so designated may be subject to government scrutiny, and that publication of research findings obtained under such contracts could be impeded or prevented. A number of research universities, including MIT, have refused to accept government contracts designated as "sensitive but unclassified." Other universities have accepted these contracts despite the inclusion of provisions for funding-agency review of findings prior to publication…

The Patriot Act also modifies the Family and Educational Rights Privacy Act and requires that educational institutions disclose educational records to federal law enforcement agents without notifying students that they are doing so and without the students' consent. In fact, the government—particularly Attorney General John Ashcroft and his office—has been employing what are known as "national security letters" that authorize the Attorney General or a delegate, with no judicial approval, to compel production of substantial amounts of relevant information. The government at this time refuses to give us information about how extensively these "letters" are being used on university campuses.

Under provisions of these laws the government can now investigate library records (to learn who is taking out books from various libraries) without informing individuals, as well as examine the content of e-mail records. Librarians who are required to release this information may not report on these activities to the people whose records are being identified.

The new legislation places most foreign students under a microscope when they request student visas. Continuing students in good standing at their universities are fearful of returning home for holidays and summer breaks for fear of not being permitted reentry into the United States. The Enhanced Board of Security and Visa Entry Reform Act of 2002 requires that entering students be scrutinized through a system called SEVIS, which is supposed to have been put in place several months ago and which would gather information that would enable the government to track these individuals. But this system is not fully operational and is preventing students from getting visas or delaying them to the point that they either miss their time in school or must cancel their visits. It also is limiting access to universities by scholars who are traveling to the United States to take part in university activities.

I am also hearing about intrusions on privacy, increased surveillance, and personal intimidation in the name of national security. For example, I have now received several calls from Columbia faculty members—some are American citizens of Iraqi or Middle Eastern descent—reporting visits to their homes by FBI agents who are conducting investigations. While there have been no reports that the agents have acted improperly, these faculty members express fear and apprehension—fear about their privacy, apprehension that they may be under surveillance, and concern that they may be subjected to continuing visits from the FBI.

If these new laws and regulations stand up to judicial review, university faculty and students will have lost some of the degrees of personal privacy and intellectual liberty we now enjoy...At the least, the academic community should not allow these measures to be put into place in silence." [89]

These comments while concisely and clearly summarize the impact of and concern with USAPA on the university community in broad terms, they fail to address the disparate impact felt by different university/department, [90] e.g. MIT vs. Columbia or research v. vocational schools.

University Reactions

Overall, the reaction of the universities, individually and as a group, has been very much muted:

> "Since the events of September 11, 2001, and the close-on-its-heels passage of the USAPA and subsequent presidential directives, I have been struck by (and dismayed at) the near-deafening silence of the expected voices of dissent on the great university campuses, and by the absence of a sustained debate over the fundamental issues and tension—the balancing act—between the needs for national security and the protection of basic, individual, constitutional liberties." [91]

The universities muted reaction was hard to explain and difficult to justify given the philosophy, mission and culture of the university. University is a powerful social institution. Faculty members are independent minded individuals. College students take pride in being radical. They are given to debate controversial ideas and issues by professional creed and training. Historically, the university community considers itself as a public (brain) trust, providing leaders for the community, especially in time of crisis. Morally, the university community considers itself to have an affirmative obligation to investigate and advocate unpopular, but worthy, ideas and ideals. Culturally, the university community prides itself on its readiness to "speak truth to power."

As times goes by, the university community shows increasingly signs of discontent. The AAUP Special Committee: Academic Freedom and National Security observed in its Special Report:

---

[89] Jonathan R. Cole, "The Patriot Act on Campus: Defending the university post–9/11.," *Boston Review* (A talk presented at "The Futures of Higher Education," University of Chicago, Graham School of General Studies, May 9, 2003. Jonathan R. Cole has been provost and dean of faculties at Columbia University since 1989.) http://www.bostonreview.net/BR28.3/cole.html

[90] "The Patriot Act and Higher Education: How should colleges respond to the USAPA? Will the new law force colleges to compromise their principles?," *Chronicle of Higher Education* Wednesday, February 27, at 1 p.m. U.S. Eastern time. http://chronicle.com/colloquylive/2002/02/patriot/

[91] Jonathan R. Cole, "The Patriot Act on Campus: Defending the university post–9/11.," *Boston Review* (A talk presented at "The Futures of Higher Education," University of Chicago, Graham School of General Studies, May 9, 2003. Jonathan R. Cole has been provost and dean of faculties at Columbia University since 1989.) http://www.bostonreview.net/BR28.3/cole.html See also "Report of an AAUP Special Committee: Academic Freedom and National Security in a Time of Crisis" The American Association of University Professors (October 2003) ("There was also a realization that many organizations that should have been vigilant then (the AAUP among them) were regrettably slow to respond." Executive Summary, p. 1. http://www.aaup.org/statements/REPORTS/911report.htm

"This report rests on the premise that freedom of inquiry and the open exchange of ideas are crucial to the nation's security, and that the nation's security and, ultimately, its well-being are damaged by practices that discourage or impair freedom."[92]

In time, AAUP starts to take issue with USAPA, i.e. academic freedom vs. individual privacy vs. national security with the support of the general public[93] and other powerful interest groups.[94] For example, AAUP argued against the false dichotomy of security vs. liberty choice within the context of the university:

It has become something of a commonplace to assume that security and freedom exist in an inherent and therefore ineluctable tension. This report questions that assumption. The free exchange of scientific data—for example, a component of a deadly toxin—may well help to equip a terrorist group with a means of mass destruction. But that same openness may better equip researchers to produce the means of preempting or neutralizing that very threat. Secrecy can impede the pace of scientific discovery for good as well as for ill. We are not alone in observing that freedom is often a critical component of security; it is not invariably inimical to it.[95]

More significantly, the AAUP went on the offensive in putting the burden of proof on the government to justify in specific terms and concrete ways how various provisions of USAPA might enhance national security without infringing civil liberties:

The government must demonstrate the particular threat to which the measure is intended to respond, not as a matter of fear, conjecture, or supposition, but as a matter of fact …
The government must demonstrate how any proposed measure will effectively deal with a particular threat…
The government must show why the desired result could not be reached by means having a less significant impact on the exercise of our civil or academic liberties….[96]

AAUP rightful insists that the USAPA must understood and debated in a larger historical,[97] cultural,[98] ideological or political context the USAPA finds itself.

---

[92] Report of an AAUP Special Committee: Academic Freedom and National Security in a Time of Crisis" (2003). *Id.*

[93] "Remind those outside the academic world of the imperative values of academic freedom and free inquiry." *Id.*

[94] "Collaborate with national associations in advancing the collective interests in academic freedom and free inquiry." *Id.*

[95] *Id.* note 5. Citing Thomas Blanton, "National Security and Open Government in the United States: Beyond the Balancing Test," in *National Security and Open Government: Striking the Right Balance* (Syracuse, N.Y.: Campbell Public Affairs Institute, 2003).

[96] "Report of an AAUP Special Committee: Academic Freedom and National Security in a Time of Crisis" (2003)

[97] "Even at the height of the Cold War, when we faced the prospect of nuclear annihilation, the government did not institute security measures as far reaching as some now proposed." Report of an AAUP Special Committee: Academic Freedom and National Security in a Time of Crisis" (2003).

[98] The university community's response to the USAPA cannot be understood away from the long running and bitterly contested cultural war fought over the hearts and mind of America in classrooms of higher learning, all over the nation. Mark S. Hamm, "The USAPA and the Politics of Fear." In Jeff Ferrell et al., eds. *Cultural Criminology Unleashed.* (London: Glasshouse Press, 2004), especially section on "Cultural Conflict". http://www.indstate.edu/crim/terrorism/hamm.pdf

DEBATE OVER THE USAPA

A cursory inspection of the legislative history[99] shows that the USAPA was "rushed" passed Congress by the Bush administration without following the usual legislative procedure, e.g. public hearings, mark up, floor debate, and conference report, in both chambers. As observed by C. William Michaels and Jennifer Van Bergen:

> "The USAPA ...was enacted by Congress virtually without significant debate, without detailed committee reports, without a conference committee, and with little floor commentary. Submitted just several days after the September 11 (2001) attacks, it was rushed through Congress at lightning speed for a statute of its size and complexity. It passed the House on October 24, 2001 by a vote of 357 to 66, and passed the Senate the next day, October 25, 2002, by a vote of 98 to 1."[100]

Throughout the entire USAPA legislative process, neither the Congress nor the Administration has systematically investigated, judiciously examined, openly debated, and comprehensively considered the relative utilities – necessity and efficacy, costs and benefits, and long term impact - on the Constitution, on the society, of the Act.

Five years after it's passage, the USAPA continues to draw vociferous criticism and fiery protests[101] Intellectuals, scholars and professors spared no time in attacking the ACT as undemocratic and unconstitutional. The liberals and activists called it un-American.[102] Concerned citizens labeled it unpatriotic.[103] Many legal,[104] commercial[105] and political[106]

---

[99] See James Bovard, *Terrorism and Tyranny: Trampling Freedom, Justice, and Peace to Rid the World of Evil* (Palgrave Macmillan, 2003) Chapter 4: "Patriot Railroad." See also Beryl A. Howell, Seven Weeks: The Making of the PATRIOT Act, 72 *Geo. Wash. L. Rev.* 1145 (2004).

[100] See C. William Michaels and Jennifer Van Bergen, "The USAPA: One Year Later," Parts I and II, *truthout* Nov. 14, 2002. http://www.truthout.org/docs_02/11.15D.jvb.cm.usapa.1.htm

[101] The latest professional group to challenge the Patriot Act includes the medical profession. Arthur J. Pais, "New York City physician joins rights groups in challenging Patriot Act clause," *India Abroad*, 29 August 2003

[102] *Steve Bonta*, "The Un-American Patriot Act," *The New American*, Volume 18, Number 01 January 14, 2002.

[103] Michelle Garcia, "N.Y. City Council Passes Anti-Patriot Act Measure," *The Washington Post* Thursday, February 5, 2004; Page A11.

[104] Letter of President Michael Gresco, American Bar Association, Conference Report Re: H.R. 3199. Nov. 5, 2005. (ABA wrote in support of the Senate on requiring more restrictions and added supervision over USAPA, in particularly FISA powers, on the eve of its re-authorization on December 31, 2005, e.g. Attorney General should be required to report to Congress statistically on how the FSIA powers were used and business and legal communities should have rights to challenge the government's exercise of power under FISA powers.) http://www.epic.org/privacy/terrorism/usapatriot/aba_letter1105.pdf

[105] Letter from the Business Community (United States Chamber of Commerce) to Congress (Senate Judiciary Committee), October 4, 2005. (The Chamber called for reform to Section 215 and 505 of the USAPA. Specifically, it is concerned with the cost of compliance and release of secret information. With respect to Section 215 the Chamber wants to limit its exercise to demonstrated need in investigation of suspected spies or terrorists and fortified rights to challenge unreasonable and oppressive order. With respect to Section 505 (National Security Letters), the Chamber asked that it be restricted and given right to challenge its abusive exercise.) http://www.checksbalances.org/busletter.pdf

[106] Patriots to Restore Checks and Balances (Conservatives have five compelling reasons to reject the USAPA. (1. Provisions of the Act challenged the US Constitution - The Fourth Amendment - Search and seizure clause (Ratified December 15, 1791); 2. Section 213 of the Patriot Act allows the government to obtain court authorization to secret search and seizure of a person's home or office, without due notice before and after. This should not be allowed except under the most dire circumstances. 3. Section 215 of the Patriot Act enables the government to obtain a rubber stamp secret court order to collect medical, financial, library, and other personal records without any suspicion of wrong doing. 4. The ACT punished patriots for being critical of government. Section 802 defines domestic terrorism as "any act that is dangerous to human life" and involves

associations and myriads of special interest groups[107] have joined hands in calling for more stringent oversight on the implementation and reauthorization of the ACT. Finally, grassroots resistance, ad hoc or organized, grew by the day. As of April 1, 2007, there were 410 resolutions upholding civil liberties and rights and against aspects of the USAPA across the Country, representing 8 states and 402 communities, affecting 85,104,445 people.[108]

The issues that should and could have been rationally discussed in the corridors of Congress, such as the impact and implications of the USAPA, are now being emotionally challenged in the streets of American heartland. The zealous implementation of the ACT by the Justice Department attracted loud protests[109] and quiet resistant[110] across the United States. The inept defense of the Attorney General further infuriated the Act's opponents and alienated its supporters.[111] Not one day goes by without witnessing a litany of victimized individuals, affected communities, afflicted organizations, impacted agencies, concerned citizens, flanked by testy NGOs, partisan politicians, adversarial advocates, and opportunistic political pundits speaking up against the ACT. Not a moment was spared by organized dissenters – ACLU, ALA – in seeking the dissolution of the Act.

JUSTIFICATION AND FOCUS OF THIS STUDY

Given mass disaffection, pervasive discontent and growing resistance with the USAPA, there is a dire need to provide for a systematic, comprehensive, and scientific evaluation of the process, outcome, and impact of the USAPA as it relates to various aspects of American society that are afflicted by it, e.g. Muslim community, immigration,[112] library,[113] higher

---

a violation of any state or federal law. This covers any violent political protests. 5. "The extraordinary powers granted to law enforcement by the Patriot Act can and will be used by subsequent administrations, including those with which we may disagree.") http://www.checksbalances.org/topfive.php

[107] Bill Wallace, "The Patriot Act Reconsidered: Next round of antiterrorist legislation seeks to balance privacy and security," *PC World magazine* (December 2003) ("The shift in congressional opinion seems largely due to the coalition of organizations that oppose the Patriot Act--disparate interest groups that agree on little else. As a result, legislators in favor of various reform measures come from both sides of the aisle.") http://www.pcworld.com/news/article/0,aid,113247,00.asp

[108] Bill of Rights Defense Committee, http://www.bordc.org/.

[109] José A. Cruz, "Protesters assail Ashcroft, Patriot Act," *People's Weekly World Newspaper*, 09/13/03 (Thousands of Bostonian turned out to protect against the Attorney General's nationwide tour in defense of the USAPA.) http://host10.cpusa.org/article/view/4047/1/180/

[110] In New Advertisement, ACLU Calls for Stop to Attorney General's Assault on Civil Liberties ACLU.com (2/6/2003) (32 communities and 4.5 million people adopted resolutions in to stop implementation of objectionable provisions of USAPA. "And since the attacks of 9/11, the ACLU's membership has surged by 15 percent, to 378,000 members and supporters nationwide.") http://www.aclu.org/safefree/general/7156prs20030206.html

[111] See Eric Lichtblau, "Ashcroft Mocks Librarians and Others Who Oppose Parts of Counterterrorism Law," *New York Times*, September 16, 2003. http://www.nytimes.com/2003/09/16/politics/16LIBR.html Specifically, the Attorney General described librarian's concerns with the USAPA "breathless reports and baseless hysteria." See Prepared Remarks of Attorney General John Ashcroft "The Proven Tactics in the Fight against Crime" Washington, D.C., September 15, 2003. http://www.usdoj.gov/ag/speeches/003/091503nationalrestaurant.htm

[112] Rosemary Jenks, "The USAPA of 2001: A Summary of the Anti-Terrorism Law's Immigration-Related Provisions." (December 2001) The Center for Immigration Studies (A number of USAPA provisions might have a bearing on immigrants: Section 412 requires the Attorney General to detain any alien "where there are reasonable grounds to believe that he is affiliated with a designated terrorist organization or engaged in terrorist activities. ...It authorizes the Attorney General to detain certified terrorists for additional periods of up to six months if their removal is unlikely in the near future and if the alien's release will threaten national security or public safety. It limits judicial review of such detention to *habes corpus* proceedings."); "America's

education, and financial services. Some of the more salient issues to be studied include: how many times and under what circumstances has the USAPA been invoked, a process question? [114] Is the USAPA effective in achieving its intended objectives, i.e. fighting terrorism, an outcome evaluation question?[115] What are the impact and implications of the Patriot Act, e.g. on civil liberties, an impact evaluation question?[116] The book attempted to fill his literature gap.

This chapter is organized into the following sections. Section II provides a brief "Literature Review" for this research project. This then is followed by Section III detailing the "Research need, focus and difficulties". The chapter concludes with Section IV: "Organization of the book" which provides an outline of the chapters as an overview of the content and structure of the book.

LITERATURE REVIEW

There are many published work on the subject matter of USAPA.[117] Most of them are properly classified as populist readings, [118] not specialized treatises. [119] Many of the publication are reports commissioned by the government, e.g. Congressional Research

---

Disappeared: Seeking International Justice for Immigrants Detained after September 11," (1/26/2004). ACLU – Safe and Free Publication. (Documenting cases of arbitrary arrest, prolonged detention, and abusive treatments of immigrants by FBI, INS and law enforcement officials immediately after 9/11 and calling for investigation by the U.N. Working Group on Arbitrary Detention for violation of Universal Declaration of Human Rights and International Covenant on Civil and Political Rights.) http://www.aclu.org/safefree/resources/16911pub20040126.html

[113] Susan Nevelow Mart, "Protecting the Lady from Toledo: Post-USAPA Electronic Surveillance at the Library," 96 *LAW LIBR. J.* 449 (2004)

[114] There is little objective and verifiable data on USA PATRIOT implementation. The Attorney General would not disclose how USAPA was implemented. Congressional oversight shows that there is no systemic abuse of powers by FBI or gross violation of Constitutional rights of librarians, see "Sensenbrenner Statement and Release of Justice Department's Answers to USA-PATRIOT Act Oversight Questions," U.S. House of Representatives, Committee on the Judiciary, F. James Sensenbrenner, Jr., Chairman, Press Release, October 17, 2002. ("The Committee's review of classified information related to FISA orders for tangible records, such as library records, has not given rise to any concern that the authority is being misused or abuse")

[115] See "Fighting Terrorism, Preserving Civil Liberties," *CATO, POLICY FORUM,* Tuesday, October 2, 200. 4:00 p.m. (Featuring Rep. Bob Barr (R - Ga.), with commentary by Solveig Singleton, Senior Analyst, Competitive Enterprise Institute; Stuart Taylor, Senior Writer, National Journal; Jonathan Turley, Professor of Law, George Washington University), p. 16. http://www.cato.org/events/transcripts/011002et.pdf

[116] Gary Strong, University Librarian, University of California, Los Angeles, "Patriot Act Strikes at Heart of Library," *UCLA Today* 24:5 (11/4/03) (The USAPA discourages library use, violates professional ethics and betrays shared American ideals, just when the citizens need to resort to library for more information.) http://www.today.ucla.edu/html/031104voices_patriot.html

[117] For representative bibliographies, see "USAPA," Santa Clara County Library http://www.santaclaracountylib.org/about/patriot_act.html; "The U.S.A. PATRIOT Act: A Selected Bibliography." Prepared By Kate Dixon, Research Librarian, Western New England College School of Law Library. Prepared: April 2005. http://www1.law.wnec.edu/library/index.cfm?selection=doc.3759; Select Bibliogrpahy: USA PATRIOT Act and Related Issues, Arizona School of Law http://www.law.arizona.edu/Library/Research/Guides/Patriotactbibliography.pdf?page=research

[118] These include such titles as: Dahlia Lithwick and Julia Turner, "Guide to the Patriot Act, parts 1-4. "Should you be scared of the Patriot Act," *Slate,* September, 2003. http://slate.msn.com/id/2087984/ ; Nancy Kranich, "The Impact of the USAPA on Free Expression," Free Expression Policy Project.

[119] For specialized repots, see Congressional Research Services series on USAPA, at http://www.au.af.mil/au/awc/awcgate/crs/#patriotact

Service[120] and IGO reports,[121] sponsored by think tanks, e.g. Heritage Foundation[122] and CATO Institute,[123] advocacy materials distributed by interests groups, e.g. ALA conference materials[124] and ACLU position papers.[125]

Over all there is only a handful of scientific investigation into and scholarly report on the impact of the USAPA. [126] An electronic search of Pro-Quest – Criminal Justice Periodicals data base (with 215 journals) for "Scholarly journals, including peer-reviewed" articles returned 39 items, 12 of which are on money laundering.[127] These 39 scholarly articles, including the following (selected 27):

---

[120] "Terrorism: Section by Section Analysis of the USAPA," (December 10, 2001) (CSR Report RL31200); ˜ "The USAPA: A Legal Analysis," (April 15, 2002) (CRS Report RL31377); The USAPA: A Sketch," (April 18, 2002) (CRS Report RL 21203); "USAPA Sunset: Provisions That Expire on December 31, 2005," (June 10, 2004) (CRS Report RL32186); "USAPA Reauthorization Proposals and Related Matters in Brief, (July 15, 2005) (CSR Report RS22196) "Arrest and Detention of Material Witnesses: Federal Law In Brief and Section 12 of the USA PATRIOT and Terrorism Prevention Reauthorization Act (H.R. 3199)," (September 8, 2005) (CRS Report RL33077); "USAPA: Background and Comparison of House- and Senate-approved Reauthorization and Related Legislative Action," (August 9, 2005) (CRS Report RL33027) "USAPA Reauthorization in Brief,"(August 10, 2005) (CRS Report RS22216); "USA PATRIOT Improvement and Reauthorization Act of 2005 (H.R. 3199): A Brief Look," (December 9, 2005) (CRS Report RS22348); "USA PATRIOT Improvement and Reauthorization Act of 2005 (H.R. 3199): A Side-by-Side Comparison of Existing Law, H.R. 3199 (Conference), and H.R. 3199 (Senate Passed)" (December 28, 2005) (CSR Report RL33210). "USA PATRIOT Improvement and Reauthorization Act of 2005 (H.R. 3199): A Legal Analysis of the Conference Bill" (January 17, 2006) (CRS Report RL33239);

[121] Section 1001 of the Patriot Act directs the Office of the Inspector General (OIG) in the U.S. Department of Justice (DOJ) to file semiannual reports to Congress concern actions taken with respect claims of civil rights or civil liberties violations against DOJ employees. See Office of Inspector General, "Report to Congress on Implementation of Section 1001 of the USAPA." (as required by Section 1001(3) of Public Law 107-56), July 15, 2002; January 22, 2003; July 17, 2003. See also, The Office of the Inspector General, "September 11 Detainees: A Review of the Treatment of Aliens Held on Immigration Charges in Connection with the Investigation of the September 11 Attacks." (June 2003). http://www.usdoj.gov/oig/special/03-06/index.htm

[122] See for example, Michael Scardaville and Jack Spencer, "9/11 One Year Later: Progress and Promise," Backgrounder #1584, September 10, 2002. Heritage Foundation Research – Homeland Security. http://www.heritage.org/Research/HomelandDefense/bg1584.cfm

[123] See Timothy Lynch, "Breaking the Vicious Cycle Preserving Our Liberties While Fighting Terrorism," Cato Policy Analysis No. 443, June 26, 2002.

[124] Safeguarding Our Patrons' Privacy: What Every Librarian Needs to Know about the USAPA and Related Anti-Terrorism Measures Videotape (120 minutes) and manual (27 pp.), December 2002. (The teleconference on USAPA framed the issues as: "What do the PATRIOT Act, the revised FBI Guidelines, and other Homeland Security measures mean for all types of librarians and library patrons? How should librarians respond to requests from law enforcement for patron information? What policies and procedures should be implemented at libraries? What tools or resources are available to help librarians understand the changing landscape and respond with confidence to law enforcement requests?")

[125] See "Insatiable Appetite: The Government's Demand for New and Unnecessary Powers After September 11" (10/15/2002); "Civil Liberties After 9-11: The ACLU Defends Freedom," (09/20/2002); "PATRIOT Propaganda: Justice Department's PATRIOT Act Website Creates New Myths About Controversial Law," (8/26/2003); "Unpatriotic Acts: The FBI's Power to Rifle Through Your Records and Personal Belongings Without Telling You," (07/30/2003); "Seeking Truth From Justice: PATRIOT Propaganda - The Justice Department's Campaign to Mislead The Public About the USAPA," (07/09/2003); "Freedom Under Fire: Dissent in Post-9/11 America," (05/08/2003). ACLU – Safe and Free Publications. http://www.aclu.org/safefree/relatedinformation_publications.html

[126] For organization purpose, this review is organized by sources of authorship and sponsorship, i.e. journalistic accounts, official publications, commissioned reports, and scholarly studies. This approach is taken because the objectivity and orientation of reports or studies often, though not always, hinges on authorship and purposes, e.g. ACLU is ultra liberal in defending civil liberties and Heritage Foundation is very conservative in defending the security. Similarity, official publications are supportive of the USAPA. ACLU reports are anti-Patriotic Act. For example, both DOJ and ACLU accused each other of not telling the truth about the implementation and reception of the USAPA.

[127] A manual review of Crime, Law and Social Change index from Oct.. 2001 (Vol. 36 (4) to Dee. 2003 (Vol. 4) confirm the reliability of Pro-Quest reliability search system.

Scholarly articles on USAPA – October 2001 to October 2003

No.	Title, Summary	Remark
1	Robert Kennedy, Kasey Wertheim, Peter Striupaitis, Lloyd Josey Jr, et al., "2002 - 2003 report from the Science and Practice committee," *Journal of Forensic Identification*. Vol. 53, Iss. 5. Sep/Oct 2003; p. 603 (5 pages) (The impact of USAPA on biometric standards is discussed.)	Brief discussion – implications for Forensic professional practices
2	Ruth Plato-Shinar, "Israel: The impact of the anti-money laundering legislation on the banking system," *Journal of Money Laundering Control*. Vol. 7, Iss. 1, Summer 2003; p. 18 (USAPA is cited in footnote 31 but never discussed.)	Citation in support
3	Stefan D Cassella, "Reverse money laundering," *Journal of Money Laundering Control. London: Journal of Money Laundering Control*. Vol. 7, Iss. 1, Summer 2003; p. 92 (A brief discussion of USAPA as relates to transfer of money to support future criminality.)	Brief discussion – implications on international money transfer
4	Trifin J Roule, Michael Salak, "The anti-money laundering regime in the Republic of Nauru," *Journal of Money Laundering Control*. Vol. 7, Iss. 1; Summer 2003; p. 75 (Brief reference to the impact of proposed regulations (April 15, 2003) of US Department of Treasury to impose 'special measures' against Nauru under s. 311 of the USAPA.)	Brief discussion – impact on a foreign country
5	Rachel S Martin, "Watch what you type: As the FBI records your keystrokes, the fourth amendment develops carpal tunnel syndrome," *The American Criminal Law Review*. Vol. 40, Iss. 3; Summer 2003; p. 1271 (Reference in passing (text to notes 214, 222) to Section 216 of USAPA for the proposition that legislation is better than judicial order in regulating electronic surveillance.)	Brief discussion – implications for electronic surveillance
6	Michael Welch, "Ironies of social control and the criminalization of immigrants," *Crime, Law and Social Change*. Vol. 39, Iss. 4; Jun 2003; p. 319. (The author is concerned with "court stripping" under the USAPA and the use of racial profiling of aliens and mass detention immigrants in secret in fighting terrorism after 9/11.)	Brief discussion - impact on immigrants
7	Marvin Zalman, Elsa Shartsis, "A roadblock too far?" *Journal of Contemporary Criminal Justice*. Vol. 19, Iss. 2; May 2003; p. 182 (Mention in passing USAPA in the study of Justice O'Connor's Fourth Amendment jurisprudence.)	Citation in support
8	Elizabeth Chadwick, "It's War, Jim, But Not As We Know It: A ``Reality-Check'' for International Laws of War?" *Crime, Law and Social Change*. Dordrecht: Vol. 39, Iss. 3; Apr 2003; p. 233 (Mention in passing USAPA in discussing the applicability of International Humanitarian Laws of Armed Conflict to war on terror.)	Citation in support
9	Deborah Wilkins Newman, "September 11: A societal reaction perspective," *Crime, Law and Social Change*. Vol. 39, Iss. 3; p. 219. Apr 2003. (How labeling affected post 9/11 public reaction and social change, including the USAPA.)	Brief discussion – effect of 9/11 on USAPA
10	David D Aufhauser, "Analysis: Terrorist financing: Foxes run to ground," *Journal of Money Laundering Control* Vol. 6, Iss. 4; Spring 2003; p. 301 (Briefly discuss how the USAPA compels the fiduciaries of US financial institutions to know with whom they are doing business and monitor the transfer of fund across border.)	Brief discussion – implications of Title III of USAPA for banks

No.	Title, Summary	Remark
11	Robert Ditzion, Elizabeth Geddes, Mary Rhodes, "Computer crimes," *The American Criminal Law Review* Vol. 40, Iss. 2; Spring 2003; p. 285 (Analyzed how US PAPA amended National Information Infrastructure Protection Act of 1996 (NIIPA) in offense, jurisdiction, defense and sentencing. In the main the USAPA lowers the threshold requirements for the prosecution of computer crime (hacking) under NIIPA (Section 1030(a)(5)(A) - criminalizes knowingly causing the transmission of a program, code, or command, and as a result, intentionally causing damage to a protected computer) from $5000 to "any impairment to the integrity or availability of data, a program, a system, or information." The USAPA extends the jurisdiction of Secret Service to all violations of Section 1030(a). It gives FBI express jurisdiction over offenses involving espionage, foreign counterintelligence, unauthorized access to national defense information or restricted data. (Section under 1030(a)(1) The USAPA increased the maximum prison sentence for first offenses under 1030(a)(A)(i) to ten years, and set a maximum sentence of twenty years for repeat offenders who violate subsections (a)(5)(A)(i) or (a)(5)(A)(ii).)	Detail legal analysis of USAPA – implications for computer crime
12	Tiffany Britton Constantin, "Editor's note," *The American Criminal Law Review* Spring 2003. Vol. 40, Iss. 2; p. 217 ("The Articles in this Survey have been updated from the prior edition to reflect changes in the law, most notably changes with regard to the USAPA of 2001 and the Sarbanes-Oxley Act of 2002.")	Editor's note on content
13	Christopher Boran, "Money laundering," *The American Criminal Law Review*. Vol. 40, Iss. 2; Spring 2003; p. 847 (Legal analysis of the Money Laundering Control Act of 1986, with a brief reference to Title III of USAPA, entitled "International Money Laundering Abatement and Anti-Terrorist Financing Act of 2001" ("IMLAFA"), as "RECENT DEVELOPMENTS" (text to note 162). Observing IMLAFA significantly expands the responsibilities of U.S. financial institutions with regard to combating money laundering.)	Brief discussion – legal analysis of Title III of USAPA
14	Jerry Berman, Lara Flint, "Guiding lights: Intelligence oversight and control for the challenge of terrorism," *Criminal Justice Ethics*. Vol. 22, Iss. 1; Winter 2003; p. 2 (There are many walls separating FBI (law enforcement) and CIA (foreign intelligence). These walls serve vital functions. In the haste to fight terrorism, the USAPA hastily breaks down the wall between FBI and CIA without thinking about the historical reasons and functional purpose(s) of the existing walls into account, nor trying to provide for their absence.)	Brief discussion – impact of USAPA on Legislative wall between CIA – FBI
15	Stephanos Bibas, "The real-world shift in criminal procedure," *Journal of Criminal Law and Criminology*. Vol. 93, Iss. 2/3; Winter 2003; p. 789 (USAPA was mentioned in one footnote, note 22, with no substantive discussion).	Citation in support
16	Mariano-Florentino Cuellar, "The tenuous relationship between the fight against money laundering and the disruption of criminal finance," *Journal of Criminal Law and Criminology*. Vol. 93, Iss. 2/3; Winter 2003; p. 311 (How Title III of USAPA RIOT Act changes the traditional money laundering legal and regulatory framework. Observing that the USAPA has expanded the investigative powers of the regulators, the duties and responsibilities of the banks, and number of unlawful activities.)	Detail discussion – legal analysis Title III of USAPA and impact on traditional money laundering

Scholarly articles on USAPA (Continued)

No.	Title, Summary	Remark
17	Anonymous, "International legal developments," *Journal of Money Laundering Control*. Vol. 6, Iss. 3; Winter 2003; p. 201 (An analysis of Title III of the USAPA, entitled the International Money Laundering Abatement and Anti-Terrorist Financing Act of 2001; its statutory provisions and compliance implications.)	Brief discussion – legal analysis Title III of USAPA
18	Anonymous, "The law: An overview," *Journal of Money Laundering Control*. Vol. 6, Iss. 3; Winter 2003; p. 217 (A brief discussion of the impact and implications of Title III of the USAPA, the International Money Laundering Abatement and Anti-Terrorist Financing Act of 2001 (the 'IMLA') on banking activities.)	Brief discussion – implications of Title III of USAPA for banks
19	Lori A Johnson, "Creating rules of procedure for federal courts: Administrative prerogative or legislative policymaking?" *Justice System Journal*. Denver: 2003. Vol. 24, Iss. 1; p. 23 (The USAPA is referenced in the text once, with no substantive discussion)	Citation in support
20	Anonymous, "Overview: Race, security, and social movements," *Social Justice*. Vol. 30, Iss. 1; p. 1 (2003) (Introduction to articles appears in the volume, including "Patriot Acts," by Tony Platt and Cecilia O'Leary.)	Editorial comments
21	Tony Platt, Cecilia O'Leary, "Patriot acts," *Social Justice*. Vol. 30, Iss. 1; 2003; p. 5 (How 9/11 hysteria and patriotism converged to give the government more powers to conduct searches, deport suspects, eavesdrop on Internet communications, monitor financial transactions, and crack down on immigrant violations.)	Detail discussion – 9/11 and USAPA
22	Barry A K Rider, "Editorial: Time for reflection!" *Journal of Money Laundering Control*. Vol. 6, Iss. 2; Autumn 2002; p. 103 (1 page) (The use of USAPA powers to fight terrorism without seeking political accommodation and social adjustment may be counter-productive.)	Editorial comments – long term implications of speedy passage of USAPA
23	Giannis Keramidas, "International cooperation and mutual assistance under the proceeds of crime bill 2001." *Journal of Money Laundering Control*. London: Autumn 2002. Vol. 6, Iss. 2; p. 141 (10 pages) (Analysis of UK's new Proceeds of Crime Bill 2001. Compared to USAPA in terrorists financing and money laudering.)	Citation to USAPA in support
25	Trifin J Roule, Jeremy Kinsell, "Legislative and bureaucratic impediments to suspicious transaction reporting regimes," *Journal of Money Laundering Control*. London: Autumn 2002. Vol. 6, Iss. 2; p. 151 (6 pages) (Compare the enforcement of SAR regiment in 20 jurisdiction, including USAPA SAR requirement. Conclude the successful implementation of USAPA – SAR requirement "routinely impeded by significant legislative and bureaucratic deficiencies." Legislative deficiencies discussed included lack of SAR reporting requirement and lack of FIU (Financial Investigation Unit) to analyze the SAR data collected. Administrative deficiencies include lack of resources to process the SAR. SAR filed under USAPA to FinCEN received 86,000 SAR before 9/11 and 125,000 SARA from 1st October, 2001 to 31st March, 2002.)	Brief discussion – implementation issues of USAPA – SAR provisions.

No.	Title, Summary	Remark
26	Fletcher N Baldwin Jr., "Money laundering countermeasures with primary focus upon terrorism and the USAPA 2001," *Journal of Money Laundering Control*. London: Autumn 2002. Vol. 6, Iss. 2; p. 105 (32 pages) (A detail section by section analysis of USAPA with particular attention to Title III.)	Legal analysis of USAPA, Title III.
27	Jeffrey Toobin, "The USA-Patriot Act and the American response to terror: Can we protect civil liberties after September 11?"*The American Criminal Law Review*. Chicago: Fall 2002. Vol. 39, Iss. 4; p. 1501 (33 pages) (A Panel Discussion on the "USAPA and the American response to terror" with Congressman Barney Frank, Assistant Attorney General Michael Chertoff, Professor David Cole, Mr. Stuart Taylor, Jr., and Ms. Beth Wilkinson, sponsored by the American Criminal Law Review, George Town Law Center and Moderated by Mr. Jeffrey Toobin)	A forum discussion of the meaning and impact of USAPA.

The bulk of materials – books, articles, reports – published after 9/11 on the subject matter of USAPA were legal analysis or policy commentary. Nearly all of them focused on the social impact and political implications of giving the government too much power, particularly how USAPA affected personal psychology, group identity or organizational operations.

Many of such books are written by established experts in security vs. civil liberties debate: Professor David Cole from Georgetown Law School, Anthony Romero from ACLU, Nancy Chang from Center for Constitutional Rights, James Demsey from Center for Democracy and Technology, Net Hantoff from Village Voice.[128] A majority of the reports were sponsored by civil liberties interest groups, e.g. ACLU, CDT, Electronic Frontier Foundation, or liberal think thanks, e.g. CATO. The issues discussed, perspective adopted, views espoused, and positions taken have been developed over time and fortified after repeated engagements with adversaries, e.g. ACLU's position on the USAPA is no different than its position to Anti-terrorism Death Penalty Act of 1996.[129] 9/11 and USA PATRIOT offers another opportunity to revisit past issues and reiterate old arguments,[130] and re-ignite long time ideological differences.

Looking at USAPA literature in this light, there is nothing new to report; reading representative past literature is as pertinent.

A majority of the published work, especially books, is against the USAPA. Pro-Patriot Act materials remain to be in the minority. A sampling of 9/11 books bearing upon USAPA

---

[128] Nat Hentoff is a columnist with the *Village Voice*, a progressive magazine. He has won the National Press Foundation Award for Distinguished Contributions to Journalism, the American Bar Association Certificate of Merit for Coverage of the Criminal Justice System, and Thomas Szasz Award for Outstanding Contribution to the Cause of Civil Liberties.

[129] "Upsetting Checks and Balances: Congressional Hostility to Courts in Times of Crisis," Statement of Ronald Weich, Partner, Zuckerman Spaeder LLP, Nov. 1, 2001, ACLU Press Release (President Clinton, much like Bush, enacted draconian measures, e.g. Antiterrorism and Effective Death Penalty Act, of dubious utilities to fight terrorism; trampling over civil rights and denying check and balance of the court in the process.) http://archive.aclu.org/news/2001/n110101d.html

[130] "New Anti-Terrorism Law Continues Dangerous Trend Of Stripping Federal Judiciary Of Authority," ACLU Features ("In treating the judiciary as an inconvenient obstacle to executive action rather than an essential instrument of accountability, the recently passed USAPA builds on the dubious precedent Congress set five years ago when it enacted a trilogy of laws [Anti-Terrorism and Effective Death Penalty Act, Illegal Immigration Reform and Immigrant Responsibility Actand the Prison Litigation Reform Act] that, in various ways, deprive federal courts of their traditional authority to enforce the Constitution of the United States.") http://archive.aclu.org/features/fl10101b.html

shows that while they all frowned upon the 9/11 attack, a majority of them insist that civil liberties need not or should not be sacrificed in the name of national security. A brief review of a few of the more representative anti-terrorism – anti-Patriot books suffice to demonstrate the general orientation and overall arguments of this genre of scholarship.

Terrorism and Tyranny: Trampling Freedom, Justice and Peace to Rid the World of Evil[131] is a book about Bush administration's anti-terrorism policies and practices after 9/11. The book started with the author observing that: ""The war on terrorism is the first political growth industry of the new Millennium," suggesting that while the devastating impact of 9/11 attack is real, the subsequent mass panic was exploited and terrorism war was manufactured for political reasons. He concluded by observing the Bush administration has no coherent plan or comprehensive strategy to fight terrorism effectively, beyond putting up an "aura of righteousness." In the book, the author systematically and meticulously documented the Bush administration's mishandling of the war on terror, resulting in the destruction of our Constitution, erosion of our civil liberties and undermining our national security. For example, in the name of fighting terror the USAPA was passed without scrutiny and the FBI "treats every citizen like a suspected terrorist."

In *Lost Liberties: Ashcroft and the Assault on Personal Freedom*[132] Cynthia Brown[133] invited 13 civil rights experts, including law professor David Cole, human rights lawyer Nancy Chang and civil liberties advocate Anthony Romero, to render their assessment of Attorney General's effort to fight terrorism. The consensus is that Attorney General Ashcroft, with the complicity of Congress, acquiescence of the Judiciary, and support of the public was able to systematically undermine the freedom and liberties of the American people in the name of fighting terrorism[134] by means of racial profiling,[135] surreptitious surveillance,[136] warrantless arrest,[137] and secret detention.[138]

Terrorism and the Constitution: Sacrificing Civil Liberties in the Name of National Security[139] was written by Georgetown University Law professor David Cole and Senior Counsel of Center for Democracy and Technology, James Dempsey. Both are liberal. Both are foremost experts on anti-terrorism and civil liberties. The book is an update of version of

---

[131] James Bovard, *Terrorism and Tyranny: Trampling Freedom, Justice and Peace to Rid the World of Evil* (Palgrave Macmillan, 2003)

[132] Cynthia Brown (Editor) *Lost Liberties: Ashcroft and the Assault on Personal Freedom* (W W Norton and Co Inc, 2003).

[133] Cynthia Brown is a former Human Rights Watch program director.

[134] Relevant chapters on the implications of USAPA on civil liberties included: David Cole, "The Course of Least Resistance: Repeating History in the War on Terrorism," (pp. 13-32); Nancy Chang, "How Democracy Dies: The War on Our Civil Liberties," (pp. 33-52); and others. The chapter succinctly summarizes the contributing authors' respective positions on the USAPA, more elaborated elsewhere. For example, David Cole repeated his long held conviction that we should learn from history – Palmer's raid, Japanese internment – and not over-react to security threat with giving up of liberties. A position he elaborate at length in his book with James X. Dempsey, *Terrorism and the Constitution: Sacrificing Civil Liberties in the Name of National Security* (New Press, 2002), first published in 1999 as a commentary on Clinton administration's Antiterrorism and Effective Death Penalty Act of 1996'.

[135] Tanya E. Coke, "Racial Profiling Post--9/11: Old Story, New Debate," (pp. 91-112).

[136] Reg Whitaker, "After 9/11: A Surveillance State?" (pp. 53-75).

[137] Anthony Romero, "Living in Fear: How the U.S. Government's War on Terror Impacts American Lives," (pp.112-131).

[138] Kate Martin, "Secret Arrests and Preventive Detention," (pp. 75-91).

[139] David Cole and James X. Dempsey, *Terrorism and the Constitution: Sacrificing Civil Liberties in the Name of National Security* (New Press, 2002). For a review, see "Anti-Terrorism's lengthy history and current abuses: A Review of Terrorism and the Constitution," By Elaine Cassel FindLaw October 11, 2002. http://writ.news.findlaw.com/books/reviews/20021011_cassel.html#bio

Terrorism and the Constitution: Sacrificing Civil Liberties in the Name of National Security (1999) by the same two authors. The 1999 book traced the nation's past effort in dealing with threat of political violence - Civil war, WWI, WWII, Cold war - ending with the enactment of the 1996 Antiterrorism and Effective Death Penalty Act in response to 1995 Oklahoma bombing of Murray Federal Building. The current edition brings the book up to date with an analysis of the promulgation of USAPA after 9/11. The authors stated the thesis of the book on the first page: "The record of our nation's response to the threat of political violence is unfortunately one of repeated infringements on the First Amendment and other constitutional principles....With confounding regularity, our government has, in the name of protecting national security, subverted the very rights and liberties "which make the defense of the Nation worthwhile." Looking back in history, more often than not, stringent security measures failed to make the nation more safe but resulted in suppressing political dissenters and infringing civil liberties instead.

The book *The War on Our Freedoms: Civil Liberties in an Age of Terrorism*[140], as the title suggests, is an edited volume of essays on the impact of 9/11 on civil liberties. The book offers 14 chapters, including:

Introduction: "The Quiet Republic: The Missing Debate About Civil Liberties After 9/11," by Richard C. Leone. (There is little reflection and deliberation of 9/11 before the nation reacted with radical and draconian measures.);

Chapter One: "A Familiar Story: Lessons from Past Assaults on Freedoms," by Alan Brinkley, Provost, Columbia University (History informs that government habitually reacted to emergencies without care and thought. They pursued political agendas in the name of national security. They often pacified alarmist at the expense of vulnerable minority rights or unpopular causes. The Bill of Rights is not effective in protecting civil liberties of citizens, especially minorities, in time of national emergencies. The public, government, and judiciary need to be vigilant against such challenges.);

Chapter Two: "Security and Liberty: Preserving the Values of Freedom," Anthony Lewis, former columnist, New York Times (The war on terrorism is a special kind of war, with no fix battle ground, no end in sight, and no rules. We must be careful not to sacrifice our freedom in order to win the war on terrorism. "If we are to preserve constitutional values- the values of freedom- understanding and resistance must come now").

Chapter Three: "No Checks, No Balances: Discarding Bedrock Constitutional Principles," by Stephen Schulhofer, Professor of Law, New York University (Bush's anti-terrorism measures and programs violated three fundamental principles underscoring Constitutional democracy, i.e. legal accountability, checks and balances, and narrow tailoring of government's power to reach evil without unduly and unnecessarily violating citizens rights. The Bush administration has violated all three principles. In its haste to advance its political agenda and administrative priority, the Bush administrative failed to pursue the least intrusive alternatives in fighting terrorism)[141]

Chapter Four: "'The Least Worst Place': Life in Guantanamo," by Joseph Lelyveld, former Executive Editor, New York Times (Guantanamo Bay detainees are beyond the reach of international human rights convention and U.S. domestic Constitutional law. It is a place

---

[140] Richard C. Leone and Greg Anrig, Jr., eds., *The War on Our Freedoms: Civil Liberties in an Age of Terrorism* (New York: Public Affairs, 2003)

[141] The article was published in different form elsewhere, see Stephen J. Schulhofer, "At War With Liberty," *The American Prospect* Vol 14, Iss. 3. March 1, 2003.

where the executive order of President of United States becomes the law and the final arbiter of justice.)

Chapter Five: "Under a Watchful Eye: Incursions on Personal Privacy," by Kathleen Sullivan, Dean, Stanford School of Law (The USAPA compromised personal privacy without building in check and balance, e.g. judicial supervision. "In the absence of self-restraint within the Department of Justice, it will be up to Congress and the courts to ensure that even during the war on terrorism law-abiding citizens retain the right to be let alone")

Chapter Six: "Who Are 'We' Now? The Collateral Damage to Immigration," by Roberto Suro, Executive Director, Pew Hispanic Center (Post 9/11 immigration reform scheme enhances law enforcement powers at the expense of immigrants rights. The new immigrant screening and surveillance scheme is not able to screen out small number of potential terrorists.)

Chapter Seven: "The New American Dilemma: Racial Profiling Post-9/11," by Christopher Edley, Jr., Professor, Harvard Law School (Post 9/11 racial profiling fractures society's bonding and accentuatez racial and ethnic conflicts, without contributing to the nation's overall security. For example, alienated ethnic minority (Muslim) are less likely to help with the nation's anti-terrorism efforts by supplying information)

Chapter Eight: "From Saviors to Suspects: New Threats to Infectious Disease Research," by Patricia Thomas, Visiting Scholar, Knight Center for Science and Medical Journalism, Boston University (Academic researchers have a hard time adjusting to government post 9/11 infectious disease research regulatory paradigm. Viewing bio-organisms as potential weapons, graduate students as possible spies, and scientific publications as possible recipes for bioterrorism is incompatible with research community culture and university ethos)

Chapter Nine: "Need to Know: Governing in Secret," by John Podesta, Professor, Georgetown University Law Center (President Bush's "culture of secrecy" will hurt the country's democratic institutions and make the nation less secure)

Chapter Ten: "Watchdogs on a Leash: Closing Doors on the Media" by John Stacks, former Executive Editor, Time Magazine (Bush administration officials are into using the media to send their rehearsed messages. The media is being denied access to information about how government works or decision made. The media is not allowed to perform its traditional watchdog functions on government activities)

Chapter Eleven: "The Fog of War: Covering the War on Terrorism," by Stanley Cloud, former Editor, Time Magazine (The effect of reporting as embedded journalists with U.S. and allied forces in Iraq is too early to tell. In the ultimate analysis, the American people will be among the last to know about the progress and prospect of the war)

Chapter Twelve: "The Go-for-Broke Presidency: Can National Unity and Partisanship Coexist?," by E.J. Dionne, Columnist, Washington Post ("Here is the central contradiction of George W. Bush's presidency: He can be a commanding and unifying leader who rallies the country behind the war on terrorism and foreign policy endeavors aimed at transforming the world. Or he can be a partisan and ideological leader who tries to radically alter domestic policy and politics. Bush, however, sees no contradiction. He has decided that his will be a go-for-broke presidency, an administration in which no priority will give way to any other priority")

Chapter Thirteen: "On the Home Front: A Lawyer's Struggle to Defend Rights After 9/11," by Ann Beeson, Staff Counsel, National Legal Department, American Civil Liberties Union (Muslim students were being singled out by the FBI for surveillance and intimidation.

They were subjected to 'intrusive and humiliating "voluntarily" interview. Many feared about continuing their student/resident status in the U.S. Some feared that they would be arrested for donating to charities from home. All were afraid of expressing their true feeling and free opinion about the government for fear of retaliation)

The War on Our Freedoms: Civil Liberties in an Age of Terrorism.[142] The editors of the book Richard C. Leone and Greg Anrig, Jr started off by observing that America has reacted to 9/11 with "Disturbing absence of information and debate about the genuine and imagined trade-offs between liberty and security." (p. ix) For example, Americans were willing to give up freedom without asking whether that would make them safer, or whether, the government was asking for national sacrifice to advance its own political agenda. They suggested that while America cannot stop 9/11 from happening, it certainly can control its impact and consequences. In this regard Leone writes, prophetically:

> "The struggle against terrorism could continue for generations, and we run the risk of finding ourselves on a slippery slope, making decisions in which freedoms that are set aside for the 'emergency' become permanently lost to us. In the end, the freedoms we abridge in the interests of security will be largely the result of choices that we, not the terrorists, make." (p. 6).

The book is devoted to promoting "real understanding, open debate, and informed consensus" in order to sustain trustworthy government in time of crisis.

Three chapters (out of 14) sum up much of the main observations, key arguments and major themes of the book, as it relate to USAPA and civil liberties.[143]

Richard C. Leone in "The Quiet Republic: The Missing Debate about Civil Liberties after 9/11" (1-22) raised one of the central issues to the USAPA debate: the problem with lack of information and debate over anti-terrorism measures. The central thesis of the chapter is that our reaction to 9/11 is not tampered with reflection or deliberation, e.g. 9/11 Commission came one year after 9/11 while in WWII it was three weeks; $3 millions were budgeted for the 9/11 Commission when $60-80 millions were budgeted for Columbia disaster; the USAPA passed Congress without debate and within 6 weeks; the public media was not interested in secret detentions; politicians were more interested in debating the workers' right in setting up Department of Homeland Security than USAPA control over people's access to information. He suggested that we should investigate into the questions of - Why 9/11 happened before reacting? Deciding who are the terrorists and how to stop them taking drastic and draconian measures to curtail our freedom in the name of security. The key lessons Leone's article impart is that knee jerk reaction to 9/11, when so much (civil liberties) is at stake, is both unconscionable and non-functional. In the short run, it does not make us safer. In the long run, it detracts people's support for anti-terrorism efforts and erodes our confidence in the government.

---

[142] *The War on Our Freedoms: Civil Liberties in an Age of Terrorism* (Public Affairs, 2003)

[143] Not all the articles are about USAPA. For example, John Podesta, "Need to Know: Governing in Secret" discusses how Bush administration's policy on executive and administrative secrecy comes to hurt America's democracy and war on terror. Joseph Lelyveld, "'The Least Worst Place': Life in Guantanamo" and Christopher Edley, Jr., "The New American Dilemma: Racial Profiling Post-9/11" are not about USAPA at all. Chapter Twelve, "The Go for Broke Presidency: Can National Unity and Partisanship Coexist" has nothing to do with civil liberties.

In the chapter on "A Familiar Story: Lessons from Past Assaults on Freedoms" (chapter 2) Alan Brinkley put anti-terrorism measures (including the USAPA) in a broader historical perspective. In so doing, he instructed as to the true value and strength behind our Constitutional democracy, namely ultimately it is the people, institutions and judiciary which keep the Bill of Rights vibrant. Like most commentators, Professor Brinkley observed that:

> "The history of civil liberties in times of emergency in government suggests that governments seldom react to crises carefully or judiciously. They acquiesce to the most alarmist proponents of repression. They pursue preexisting agendas in the name of national security. They target unpopular or vulnerable groups in the population less because there is clear evidence of danger than because there is little political cost."

Unlike most commentators, the likes of ACLU, he cautioned the readers that the Bill of Rights, as designed and in practice, is not sufficient to protect civil liberties, in peace as with war. The Bill or Rights can only be sustained with public awareness, institutional assertiveness (ACLU), and judiciary supervision (Abraham). [144] Brinkley's chapter offers hope in the midst of darkness after 9/11 attack on civil liberties. Brinkley's reading of history is that 9/11, just like the Palmer raid in WWI, Japanese internment in WWII, and anti-Communist purge in Cold War, will in time creates countervailing force in defense of civil liberties; in the process and with each successful challenge to civil liberties, the attack on civil liberties serves to renew our understanding and rekindle our commitment to the importance of Bill of Rights. Afterall the meaning and significance of the Constitution in general and the Bills of Rights in particularly must be found in the living history of human progress as exhibited in the dynamism of the a living political compact.

In "No Checks, No Balances: Discarding Bedrock Constitutional Principles," Professor Stephen Schulhofer provided a trenchant analysis and no holds bar critique of Bush's anti-terrorism measures and programs. His major contribute to the USAPA debate is to make explicit what lies underneath the surface: the debate over Bush's post 9/11 anti-terrorism measures and program is not about means but about ends, i.e. disagreement over direction and priority, not legality and constitutionality. For example, he observed: "Never before in American history has an administration stinted on many homeland- and national-security expenditures and made tax cuts its top priority at a time of war."

As evidence, he observed that the Bush administration has failed to make a convincing case for the increased power to fight terrorism, across the board. Instead the newly minted anti-terrorism powers were mostly used to fight conventional crime, not catastrophic terrorism. The Administration has also failed to take steps to improve upon the existing anti-terrorism capacity, e.g. making rules for more accountable surveillance of e-mails.

In *The War on the Bill of Rights and the Gathering Resistance* [145] Nat Hentoff observed that the Bush administration, especially Attorney General John Ashcroft, and the DOJ, have used September 11, 2001 as a pretext to expand the power of the executive to create an imperial presidency. In the name of fighting a war on terror, the Bush administration was able to curtail personal rights and civil liberties of the citizens without close scrutiny of the Congress and proper supervision of the judiciary. The central thesis of Hentoff's book can be summed up in this quote by Lance Morrow: "If Americans win a war (not just against

---

[144] "The Silver lining" pp. 32-39.
[145] Nat Hentoff , *The War on the Bill of Rights and the Gathering Resistance* (Seven Story Press, 2003).

Saddam Hussein but the longer-term struggle) and lose the Constitution, they will have lost everything." In the book Nat Hentoff described how the government established a surveillance society with Patriot I, Patriot II, Operation TIPs, and the Total Information Awareness System. Hentoff also chronicled the rise of grassroots movement, e.g. "Bill of Rights Defense Committees", against government encroachment.

No Greater Threat: America After September 11 And The Rise Of A National Security State[146] is about the demise of democratic state and the rise of a national security state in the aftermath of 9/11.

No Greater Threat is one of the few 9/11-USAPA books with a central thesis supported by empirical (personal) observations. This sets it apart from other 9/11 books which argued from received value postulates, e.g. freedom of speech and privacy rights are inviolable, accepted factual assumptions, e.g. liberties and security cannot co-exist in a war time polity, and pre-conceived ideological positions, e.g. the Constitution prefers liberties over security, anytime.[147]

The book contributed to our understanding of the impact and implications of USAPA by introducing the idea of "national security state."

In the book, Michaels analyzed the USAPA in great depth and minute details in order to show how America is increasing becoming a national security state. The central message being:

> "Indeed there is no greater threat to the security of this country than a systematic dismantling of civil liberties and the rule of law with a dramatic shift of political will and resources to investigate, surveillance, and prosecution, coupled with the almost uncanny ability of the American public to place too much faith in government at the precise time when just the opposite approach is required." (Italic is in the original).[148]

According to Michaels, a "national security state" is a State which "believes it is under constant siege by malevolent forces both within and without." It "is beset by internal strife and even armed conflict aimed at the ruling government." It "usually believes it is on a special mission to avenge its national pride abroad or to maintain social order within."[149] In essence, a threatened state with a siege mentality and a propensity for revenge and order.

In one of the biggest led down in the book, the author failed to explain how those national security "ratings" – 12 in all, were systematically observed, objectively measured and independently verified; inviting the readers to come up with their own "rating" scheme and process. For example, how to measure "media in the service or the state", starting with a theoretical and operational definition of what "service" means? As a result, in spite of the authors' confidence of the utility of the scoreboard, the national security state measures speaks to subjective valuation of observations and arbitrary assessment of indicators, as reflecting individual judgment and personal preference. As frankly admitted to by the author:

---

[146] C. William Michaels, *No Greater Threat: America After September 11 And The Rise Of A National Security State* (Algora Publishing 2002). For a review, see Mark S. Zaid, "Was September 11, 2001 actually a prelude to 1984?: A Review of A New Book Forecasting The Possible Rise Of A National Security State," FindLaw's Writ, Jan. 24, 2003. http://writ.news.findlaw.com/books/reviews/20030124_zaid.html

[147] David Cole and James X. Dempsey, *Terrorism and the Constitution: Sacrificing Civil Liberties in the Name of National Security* (New Press, 2002).

[148] *No Greater Threat*, p. 8.

[149] *No Greater Threat*, pp. 6-7.

"Any "rating of national security state characteristics is inexact and subjective. The ratings presented here are meant to encourage further discussion. Nevertheless, it reasonably can be argued that some of the 12 characteristics have been fulfilled and others are closed to that point." [150]

As a one time law professor, Michaels writes in terse, lucid, clear and organized prose. As expected he is at his best when he is conducting legal analysis of the USAPA (which is the first half of the book (pp. 33-180) and marshalling support for the existence of a "national security state (pp. 185 to 312). However, he is not as thoughful in theoretical development, beyond making bold assertions. For example, he described causally[151] but did not articulate formally[152] how a national security state operates in theoretical terms, e.g. what are the necessary and sufficient conditions for the emergency and desistance of a national security state? What is the theoretical relationship between "internal strife", "siege mentality" and "national security characteristics"? What is the theoretical relationship between one national security state characteristics and another? Michaels tempted us with titillating potentialities of looking at post 9/11 world in a new light but never satisfied us with substantive actualities of observing USAPA in action.

No Greater Threat informs us that we, as a nation, as a people and lastly as individuals, should never take our Constitution, freedom and liberties for granted. It warns that the "big brother" state envisioned by *1984* might be just around the corner, if not here already, to stay, perhaps forever.[153] "By these scores, America is close to being a national security state. The score is at or above 50 in 8 of the 12 characteristics, and 90 or above in 2 of those 8 (characteristics 1 and 9)." [154]

Finally, the book *Its a Free Country: Personal Freedom in America After September 11* [155] edited by Danny Goldberg, [156] Victor Goldberg [157] and Robert Greenwald, [158] with

[150] *No Greater Threat*, pp. 299.

[151] Some of the description of what counts as evidence of a national security state do not hold up to scrutiny. For example, in "lack of accountability in law enforcement" the author discussed in great detail how law enforcement in the past has not been amenable to control. But he did not provide an empirical or logical linkage between past police accountability problems and post 9/11 accountability issues. This is not to suggest that the author is wrong. This is to say that the author has failed affirmatively to demonstrate his case. The same kind of lose description happens elsewhere.

[152] See "Theory Construction from Empirical Observations, B Wright," ("Scientific understanding of a phenomenon requires the construction of a theory. This theory is the basis for predicting, manipulating, controlling and counteracting the phenomenon, and also for relating the phenomenon to other phenomena...A strong theory implies structure in data despite the inevitable vagaries inherent in all observations," http://www.rasch.org/rmt/rmt82h.htm

[153] "Throughout this discussion ....a national security state, if it occurs, could be permanent." *No Greater Threat*, p. 299.

[154] No Greater Threat, p. 300.

[155] *Its a Free Country: Personal Freedom in America After September 11* (Akashic Books , 2002). (*It's a Free Country*)Some of the contributing authors, included: U.S. Rep. Bob Barr, Republican legislator from Georgia; U.S. Rep. Barney Frank, Democratic legislator from Massachusetts; Ani DiFranco, singer/songwriter who formed her own record label; Steve Earle, singer/songwriter whose song about "American Taliban" John Walker Lindh sparked controversy; Tom Hayden, California state senator and leader of the civil rights and anti-war movements in the 1960s and 70s; Asma Hasan, author of a book on being a young American Muslim; Michael Isikoff, Newsweek investigative correspondent; Andrew Kirkland, Assistant Police Chief in Portland Oregon who refused the Justice Department's demand that he ignore Oregon state law and investigate Middle Eastern individuals not suspected of any crime; Michael Moore, best selling author and documentary filmmaker; U.S. Rep. Maxine Waters, Democratic legislator from California; Cornel West, professor of African-American studies at Princeton University

[156] President of ACLU Foundation of Southern California.

contributions from law makers,[159] public intellectuals,[160] political activists,[161] civil liberties lawyers,[162] human rights workers,[163] and afflicted persons[164] conveniently sums up the varieties of felt impact and disparate perceived implications of the USAPA from the vantage point of progressive anti-PATRIOT Act community:

First, the USAPA is not required. Procedurally, the case for the USAPA has not been made by the administration. Substantively, the sacrifice of civil liberties does not make us more secure.

Second, given the impact on the USAPA on civil rights, it should be studied more before passage. The USAPA powers are not fine tuned to meet the 9/11 crisis.

Third, the USAPA is destructive of the Constitution that it purports to protect.

Fourth, as a "war" time legislation, the USAPA is an authoritarian legislation. "It elevates executive action beyond accountability of the judiciary" and oversight of the legislature.[165] By design, the USAPA purposely breaks down the check and balance system conjured by the Founding fathers and ordained by the Constitution. In effect, this concentration of powers in the executive branch of government invites indiscretion action and invites abuse of power.

Fifth, as a "protective" measure, the USAPA sacrifices rights and liberties to achieve security. This means that citizens are vulnerably exposed to government oppression and police suppression. It further means that the minorities are subjected to the tyranny of the majority.

Sixth, the USAPA ignored hard learned lessons from history in breaking the legislative wall between FBI (law enforcement) and CIA (foreign intelligence), thereby legalizing CONINTELPRO type of government surveillance of public dissent and threatening every citizens' First Amendment rights in the process.

Seventh, the USAPA can be used to investigate and prosecute common criminal.[166] In effect, the USAPA federalize many local offense, subjecting them federal jurisdiction and enhanced punishment.

---

[157] Life time civil liberties activists.

[158] Public interest TV/Movie producer.

[159] See "Congressional Commentaries" from Congressman Jerrold Nadler (D.-NY), Bob Barr, Barney Frank (D-MA), Maxine Walters (D-CA), Dennis Kucinich (D-OH), *It's a Free Country,* pp. 89-118.

[160] See for example, Hoard Zinn, "A Primer: Wartime Erosion of Civil liberties," *It's a Free Country,* pp. 25-28.

[161] See for example, Tom Hadden, "It's Empire Versus Democracy," *It's a Free Country,* p. 42-51.

[162] See for example David Cole, "The Ashcroft raids," *It's a Free Country,* p. 280-284.

[163] See for example, "Human Rights Violations and Discrimination in San Francisco in the Wake of September 11," *It's a Free Country,* p. 293 – 302.

[164] See "Personal Testimony" in *It's a Free Country,* p. 303 – 359.

[165] Cornel West, "Forward: Lift every Voice," *It's a Free Country,* p. 2.

[166] Three cases support this observation:

(1) "USAPA charges against two brothers in firebomb at congressional office," *LA Times,* June 19, 2003. (Hai Duc Le, 34, was prosecuted under USAPA for possessing WMD a pipe bomb in his car exploded outside a congresswoman's office. They might have been trying to bomb a cafe patronised by fellow Vietnamese nearby. Instead of being charged with a local offense with a maximum of seven years, he was then facing a minimum of 35 years under the USAPA.) http://groups.yahoo.com/group/stop-polabuse/message/12839 Hai Duc Le could have been more appropriately charged and convicted under a state criminal law, if his intent was not political in nature but criminal in origin. See also "Brothers charged in connection with pipe bomb explosion in Santa Ana," FBI *LA Division,* Press Release, June 17, 2003.

(2) Mike Gordon, "Traveler on cruise ship charged with terrorism," *Honolulu Adviser,* April 29, 2003 (Ms. Kelley Marie Ferguson, 20, was charted with USAPA related terrorism charge (terrorist threats on mass transport systems) for leaving notes threatening to kill passengers on a cruise ship to Hawaii so that she could be with

There are a minority, but strong, position that the war on terror is on the right track, and the USAPA is a balanced and appropriate measure for the day. The arguments for and against the USAPA was best captured by the Fifteenth "The Great Debates" entitled: "Are we sacrificing civil liberties to the war against terrorism?" at Boston University on November 5, 2003.[167]

In the above overview of the literature, the case in support of the USAPA can be summed up as following:[168]

(1) The threat of terrorism is real, and not likely to disappear soon, if at all. The Constitution requires the government to secure life, before liberties. The USAPA provides the necessary power to secure the nation against the terrorists who are bent on destroying us.

(2) The USAPA does not give the government any more new powers[169] than they already possess and use against conventional criminals in other quarters, e.g. grand jury order, 'pen registration" surveillance order and "sneak and peek" search warrant in organized crime investigation.[170]

(3) The USAPA updates law to meet technological challenges

(4) The USAPA powers are necessary to fight terrorism, e.g. making possible information sharing between FBI and CIA.

(5) The USAPA powers have not been abused, e.g. Section 215 has not been used.

(6) The USAPA powers have been granted by the Congress, e.g. USAPA passed the Senate by 96-1, and supervised by the Courts, e.g. Section 215 powers can only be exercised with court authorization.

(7) The USAPA works. USAPA powers have been successfully used in detecting terrorism and deterrent terrorists.[171]

---

her boyfriend. USAPA permits 20 years sentence. She could have been charged with non-USAPA offenses which would spare her imprisonment.) http://the.honoluluadvertiser.com/article/2003/Apr/29/ln/ln24a.html

[167] The debate was sponsored by the College of Communication. The Affirmative case was argued by Nadine Strossen, Professor of Law at New York Law School; President of the American Civil Liberties Union; Andrew Good, Partner in the Boston offices of Good and Cormier, LLP; President-elect of the Massachu-setts Association of Criminal Defense Lawyers and Matt Brown, SMG '04, School of Management Finance Major. The Negative case was defended by Viet Dinh, Professor of Law at Georgetown University Law Center; U.S. Assistant Attorney General for Legal Policy from May 2001-2003; Alice Fisher, Partner in litigation department of the Washington, D.C. offices of Lathem and Watkins, LLP; Deputy Assistant Attorney General of Criminal Division from July 2001-2003; Kenny St. Onge, COM '05, College of Communication Graduate Student of Journalism. See also American Criminal Law Review's seventh annual debate at Georgetown University Law Center and reported in Jeffrey Toobin, "The USA-Patriot Act and the American response to terror: Can we protect civil liberties after September 11?," *The American Criminal Law Review*. Chicago: Fall 2002. Vol. 39, Iss. 4; p. 1501 (33 pages) (Speakers included Attorney, Michael Chertoff, the Assistant Attorney General in charge of the [United States Department of Justice] Criminal Division, Professor David Cole, Professor of Law from Georgetown Law Center, Congressman Bary Frank (R-Mass.), Mr. Stuart Taylor, Legal Journalist and Ms. Beth Wilkinson, partner at Latham and Watkins.)

[168] "In defense of the PATRIOT ACT, "Pittsburgh Post - Gazette. Pittsburgh, Pa.: Aug 31, 2003. p. B.1; Heather Mac Donald, "Anti-Patriot Games *New York Post*, August 31, 2003.

[169] Attorney General Ashcroft has acknowledged that the USAPA provide FBI with sweeping powers to investigate and deter terrorists.

[170] "Don't deny government useful anti-terror tools," USA TODAY. McLean, Va.: Sep 23, 2003. p. A.22

[171] The Justice Department has provided the following data to show the following kinds of activities after the passage of USAPA. (1) Help identified many suspected terrorists; (2) Led to increased (double) anti-terrorism investigations and intelligence sources – 1,000 FBI. 337% staffing of joint terrorism task force; (3) Resulted in more than 18,000 subpoenas and search warrants being issued; (4) Conviction (and PG) of 100 people for

RESEARCH FOCUS, CONTRIBUTION AND DIFFICULTIES

The Focus of Research

This study is a "program evaluation" of the USAPA, loosely defined. Particularly this book is about documenting the impact and implications of USAPA on aspects of American society. Program evaluation has been defined as "the systematic collection of information about the activities, characteristics, and outcomes of programs to allow informed judgments about program improvement, program effectiveness, and decisions about future programming."[172] Traditionally program evaluation has been conducted to facilitate program planning, development, and/or accountability. Evaluation studies can be of three kinds, i.e. "process" evaluation which investigate how a program actually functioning; "normative" evaluation which investigate how the program is achieving its goals and objectives; and "outcome" or "impact" evaluation investigates the consequences or effect the program had, intended or otherwise.

This study is an evaluative research of USAPA's process, outcomes and impact, especially with reference to the implementation of SEVIS and impact on Muslims and library. The three research questions being posed are:

(1) *Evaluating process*: How did the USAPA "rushed" past Congress? Why was it possible? How was the Act, e.g. SEVIS - implemented?

(2) *Evaluating impact:* What has been the impact of the USAPA on segments of society? How was the USAPA greeted by the grassroots?

(3) *Evaluation implication*: What are the long term implications of the USAPA on the Muslim community and library system? For example, how might the USAPA change forever the role, functions and image of library in our society from liberator of information to guardian of secrets? How might the USAPA - SEVIS electronic tracking process affects the immediate interaction pattern and long term relationship between university and students, university and government? How might the USAPA changes the symbolic status and cultural standing of the library in our society? How might the USAPA alters permanently our fundamental valuation of and balance between security and liberty?[173]

---

federal offenses; (5) Allowed 1,000 suspected international terrorists targeted.) "Don't deny government useful anti-terror tools," *USA TODAY*. McLean, Va.: Sep 23, 2003. p. A.22.

[172] See "Program Evaluation," *Program Evaluation and Improvement Staff http://www.fsis.usda.gov/oppde/peis/ Evaluation/Types.htm*

[173] It was Senator Russ who warned against tipping the Constitutional balance between security vs. liberty in favor of the former in time of crisis and forever: "Of course, there is no doubt that if we lived in a police state, it would be easier to catch terrorists. If we lived in a country that allowed the police to search your home at any time for any reason; if we lived in a country that allowed the government to open your mail, eavesdrop on your phone conversations, or intercept your email communications; if we lived in a country that allowed the government to hold people in jail indefinitely based on what they write or think, or based on mere suspicion that they are up to no good, then the government would no doubt discover and arrest more terrorists. But that probably would not be a country in which we would want to live. And that would not be a country for which we could, in good conscience, ask our young people to fight and die. In short, that would not be America." Statement of Senator Russ Feingold on Anti-Terrorism Legislation, October 25, 2001.

This book aims to provide the citizens and policy makers with a detail description and in-depth analysis of the various impact and implications of the Patriot Act on the U.S. five years after its passage (9/11/01 – 9/11/06).

The main focus of the investigation is on how the original design and later implementation of the USAPA affected the routine functioning and entrenched values in American society.

THE CONTRIBUTION OF THIS RESEARCH

The process, impact and implications of the USAPA, in general terms, such as its direct impact on civil liberties, and with specific case, such as its long term implications on higher education or financial institutions, is not fully investigated and completely understood. Particularly, the question of how the USAPA was implemented and impact upon the library's role and functions, operations and institution, has not been systematically documented, much less comprehensively examined.

A systematic and comprehensive review of literature informs that there is a dearth of research literature on this subject matter. While there are many journalistic accounts, a number of commissioned reports, and a few scientific surveys describing how the USAPA has affected various aspects of the public institutions, e.g. university and library, there is as yet no scholarly study of the *overall* impact and *long term* implications of USAPA on American society as a whole. This study is a first attempt to fill such a literature gap.

This study makes two kinds of contribution, one on data, the other on policy.

Contribution to Data Collection

Lack of reliable and valid data inhibits scholarly research and distorts policy making. Currently, there is a gross lack of data on all aspects of the USAPA – from drafting to legislating to implementation to impact. For example, until recently (September 16, 2003), the extent to which Section 215 powers were employed by federal or state law enforcement agencies to investigate libraries has not been officially acknowledged nor properly documented.

This study contribute to future research by conducting a systematic examination of all available data source – government releases, library reports, scholarly researches, newspaper accounts – on the passage, implementation and impact of the USAPA on various aspects of American society.

Contribution to Policy Analysis

The USAPA has been reauthorized in March 2006. Now the legislature, advocates and public needs reliable data and accessible information to make critical policy choices, e.g. to ascertain the strength and weakness, cost and benefits of the USAPA. The data collected and analysis performed in the study should help in facilitating the ongoing assessment of the utility and effectiveness of the USAPA.

RESEARCH DIFFICULTIES: THE LACK OF RESEARCH DATA

"I will continue to consult with Congress so that you may fulfill your constitutional responsibilities. In some areas, however …I cannot and will not divulge information, nor do I believe that anyone here would wish me to divulge information, that will damage the national security of the United States, the safety of its citizens or our efforts to ensure the same in an ongoing investigation."[174]

Attorney General John Ashcroft, Senate Committee on the Judiciary, December 6, 2001.

Introduction

Data collection – obtaining valid and reliable information – is one of the more challenging aspects of conducting any research. This is particularly so when researching into the USAPA. The data collection difficulties resulted from two factors: secrecy of the Bush administration and the confidentiality in law enforcement operations, now war on terrorism.

The Secrecy of the Bush Administration

The Bush administration has been considered as one of the more, if not most, secretive administrations in recent times.[175] Professor Alan Brinkley, a Columbia University historian, observed that "while secrecy has been increasingly attractive to recent administrations, "this administration has taken it to a new level …instinct is to release nothing." The Bush administration exhibited a propensity to keep government records secret in a number of high profile case before and after 9/11:

(1) Vice Cheney Refused to Turn over Energy Task Force Records to GAO

On January 29, 2001 President Bush established the National Energy Policy Development Group (NEPDG) chaired by Vice President Dick Cheney. Congressman Henry Waxman (D. CA), the ranking member on the Committee on Government Reform, and John Dingell (D. MI), the ranking member on the Energy and Commerce Committee requested information from NEPDG concerning its composition, process and activities. The request was declined. Waxman and Dingell asked GAO to investigate whether NEPDG was required by the Federal Advisory Committee Act (FACA) to make full public disclosure of how NEPDG

---

[174] Testimony of Attorney General John Ashcroft, Senate Committee on the Judiciary, December 6, 2001. http://judiciary.senate.gov/te120601f-ashcroft.htm

[175] "Bush administration the most secretive ever" *New York Times* January 3, 2003. Baker, N.V. "The Law: The Impact of Antiterrorism Policies on Separation of Powers: Assessing John Ashcroft's Role," *Presidential Studies Quarterly* v. 32 no. 4 (December 2002) p. 765-78, 769-770 (The Bush administration is one of the most secretive even before 9/11. After 9/11 Bush's secretive policy is justified on the need to fight terrorism.) http://villagenews.weblogger.com/stories/storyReader$7006.

worked. Cheney claimed "executive privileges" and refused to cooperate. GAO finally has to file suit in U.S. District Court on February 22, 2002 to obtain the requisite information to fulfill its statutory function (U.S.C. sections 712, 716 and 717).[176]

(2) President Bush Bared Access to Presidential Papers

In the year ending Sept. 30, 2001, the Bush presidency re-classified more than 260,978 documents that were made available to the public; an 18 percent increase over that of 2000. On March 23, 2001, Mr. Gonzales, the White House counsel, barred the public release of 68,000 pages of President Ronald Reagan papers as requested by scholars under the Presidential Records Act of 1978. The Act made Reagan's Presidential documents available after 12 years, i.e. Jan. 20, 2001.[177] President Bush further signed Executive Order 13233 barring all future public access to Presidential papers.[178]

(3) Commerce Secretary Evans Refused to Turn over Adjusted Census Data

On April 16, 2001 Representative Waxman, the ranking minority member of Government Reform Committee, and 18 other Congressional members requested the Commerce Secretary Evans to release adjusted 2000 Census data for audit. There were claims that the 2000 Census data has reported 4.3 million people and over counted one million people. The request was submitted under the "seven member rule" (5 U.S.C. § 2954), i.e., "an Executive agency, on request of the Committee on Government Operations of the House of Representatives, or of any seven members thereof . . . shall submit any information requested of it relating to any matter within the jurisdiction of the committee." The Secretary of Commerce declined to compile with request. On May 21, 2001, 16 members of the House Government Reform Committee, led by Reps. Waxman filed suit in United District Court of Central District of California[179] Finally on Jan. 18, 2002, the federal court ruled in favor of the 16 minority members of the Government Reform Committee in a "Summary Judgment Ordering the

---

[176] See David W. Walker, Comptroller General of the United States, Plaintiff, vs. Richard Cheney, Vice President of the United States and Chair, National Energy Policy Development Group, Defendant (U.S. District Court for the District of Columbia, Civil Action No. 02-0340 (JDB) For a chronology of GAO investigation of NEPDG, see "Investigation of the Energy Task Force" The Committee on Energy and Commerce (Democrats). http://www.house.gov/commerce_democrats/EnergyTaskForce/energytaskforce.shtml

For a legal and political analysis of the case, see John Dean, "GAO V. Cheney is Big-Time Stalling: The Vice President Can Win Only If We Have Another Bush v. Gore -like Ruling," *Findlaw* Feb. 01, 2002. http://writ.news.findlaw.com/dean/20020201.html

[177] Attorney General Ashcroft notified Representative James F. Sensenbrenner Jr. (R-WI), Chairman of House Judiciary Committee (which has oversight responsibility of DOJ and FBI) less than two hours before he changed the Levi guidelines (1976) which allow FBI to conduct surveillance of Internet, church, library and bookstores. The Levi guidelines required the FBI to show evidence of a crime before engaging in domestic spying. The restrictions grew out of the FBI's civil rights abuses under Director J. Edgar Hoover in the 1960s and 1970s. See Joyce Howard Price, "Scrapping domestic-spying restrictions 'goes too far' ; GOP representative speaks against new Bush administration policy," *Washington Times.* Jun 2, 2002. p. A.04 http://80-proquest.umi.com.www.remote.uwosh.edu:2048/pqdweb?index=385anddid=000000122336611 andSrchMode=1andsid=1andFmt=3andVInst=PRODandVType=PQDandRQT=309andVName=PQDandTS=1 064916115andclientId=3849

[178] See "Presidents Bush Protect America with Executive Order 13233" White House News Room, November 5, 2001. http://www.whitehouse.org/news/2001/110501.asp

[179] For the 'Civil Complaint for Declaratory and Injunctive Relief' of Henry A. Waxman, et al., Members of Congress, Plaintiffs, v. DONALD L. EVANS, Secretary of Commerce, Defendant. Civil Action No. 01-04530. http://www.house.gov/reform/min/pdfs/pdf_inves/pdf_other_census_comp_rep.pdf

Release of Census Data".[180] This was followed up by a March 25, 2002 District Court decision rejecting a reconsideration filed by Commerce Secretary Evans.[181]

(4) Attorney General, Ashcroft Restrictive Interpretation of the FOIA

On October 12, 2001, Attorney General Ashcroft promulgated an administrative guideline instructing federal employees not to honor FOIA requests, if legally defensible.[182] The "Memorandum on FOIA" to Heads of all Federal Departments effectively superseded the October 1993 Reno memorandum on the same subject which called for maximum public disclosure, if at all possible. [183] The Ashcroft memorandum called for a much more restrictive interpretation of the FOIA:

> "As you know, the Department of Justice and this Administration are committed to full compliance with the Freedom of Information Act (FOIA), 5 U.S.C. § 552 (2000)... The Department of Justice and this Administration are equally committed to protecting ...our national security, enhancing the effectiveness of our law enforcement agencies, protecting sensitive business information and, not least, preserving personal privacy...Any discretionary decision by your agency to disclose information protected under the FOIA should be made only after full and deliberate consideration of the institutional, commercial, and personal privacy interests that could be implicated by disclosure of the information...When you carefully consider FOIA requests and decide to withhold records, in whole or in part, you can be assured that *the Department of Justice will defend your decisions unless they lack a sound legal basis* or present an unwarranted risk of adverse impact on the ability of other agencies to protect other important records."[184] (Underline supplied)

---

[180] "Order Denying Defendnat's Motion to Dismiss, or in the Alternation, Defendant's Motion for Summary Judgement; order granting defendant's motion for summary judgement," January 18, 2002. http://www.house.gov/reform/min/pdfs/pdf_inves/pdf_other_census_judgment.pdf

[181] For a detail discussion of the case, see "Committee Members Sue for Adjusted Census Data" Government Reform Committee, Minority Office. http://www.house.gov/reform/min/inves_other/other_census.htm

[182] *United States Department of Justice, Office of Information and Privacy* http://www.usdoj.gov/oip/foiapost/2001foiapost19.htm For a discussion of the effect of change of FOIA policy, see "Freedom of information" *Homefront Confidential* http://www.rcfp.org/ homefrontconfidential/foi.html

[183] See "Memorandum for Heads of Departments and Agencies, Subject: The Freedom of Information Act," The White House Washington, October 4, 1993 ("The Freedom of Information Act, moreover, has been one of the primary means by which members of the public inform themselves about their government...I therefore call upon all Federal departments and agencies to renew their commitment to the Freedom of Information Act, to its underlying principles of government openness, and to its sound administration.... Further, I remind agencies that our commitment to openness requires more than merely responding to requests from the public. Each agency has a responsibility to distribute information on its own initiative, and to enhance public access through the use of electronic information systems.") and "Memorandum for Heads of Departments and Agencies, Subject: The Freedom of Information Act," Office of the Attorney General Washington, D.C. 20530 October 4, 1993. ("In short, it shall be the policy of the Department of Justice to defend the assertion of a FOIA exemption only in those cases where the agency reasonably foresees that disclosure would be harmful to an interest protected by that exemption. Where an item of information might technically or arguably fall within an exemption, it ought not to be withheld from a FOIA requester unless it need be.") http://www.fas.org/sgp/clinton/reno.html

[184] See "Memorandum for Heads of all Federal Departments and Agencies; From: John Ashcroft, Attorney General; Subject: The Freedom of Information Act" (October 12, 2001). For reactions to Ashcroft memo, see Tom Beierle and Ruth Greenspan Bell, "Don't let 'right to know' be a war casualty," *Christian Science Monitor*, December 20, 2001. ("Years of hard-won battles that turned FOIA into a fundamental routine bulwark against government secrecy were undermined in a day. The memo ushered out the principle of "right to know" and replaced it with "need to know." Now, the presumption is that information is inherently risky.") See also, Rebecca Daugherty, "Ashcroft's FOI Act memo prompts concerns," *The News Media and the Law*, Vol 26 (1), Winter 2001, p. 25. (The Gannett News Service described it as "ignorance is bliss policy ... "the less

In effect, Ashcroft preferred withholding of information unless required by law ("sound legal basis") and Reno preferred release of information subject to demonstration of harm ("foreseeable harm.")[185]

(5) DOJ Officials Refused to Release Information of on 9/11 Detainee

On Nov. 8, 2001, DOJ officials declined to release information on 9/11 anti-terrorism investigation detainees. Up until two weeks before, DOJ provided for a running account of the number of people under 9/11 detention.

The Lack of Cooperation with the Congress

The Bush administration reluctance to release information extended to Congressional oversight. Bush officials have refused to share information with the Congress to discharge its oversight responsibilities and 9/11 Commission charged with investigating 9/11:

(1) On October 21, 2003, Attorney General, Ashcroft has refuses to address Senate Judiciary Hearings in spite of repeated requests[186] to discuss the USAPA. He sent two deputies instead.

(2) On October 26, 2003, Senator John D. "Jay" Rockefeller IV (D- WV), Senate Select Committee on Intelligence, complained publicly on "Meet the Press" that his committee has difficulty in getting documents from the administration: "We're going through some of the same problems — a lot of the documents that we've requested from the Department of Defense, from the White House and the National Security Agency, we do not yet have."

(3) In April of 2003, the Bush administration refused to declassify information and allow the REPORT OF THE JOINT INQUIRY INTO THE TERRORIST ATTACKS OF SEPTEMBER 11, 2001 (July 24, 2003) compiled by the House Permanent Selected Committee on Intelligence and Senate Select Committee on Intelligence to be made public. Senator Graham, the immediate past Senate Intelligence Committee chairman, [187] was "increasingly frustrated" by the administration's "unwillingness to release what he regards as important information the public should have about 9-11." House Intelligence Committee Chairman Goss, a staunch Republican (and former CIA officer) who had consistently defended the administration's handling of 9-11 issues, was compelled to observe:

Americans know about how our government works, the better off we are." The *San Francisco Chronicle* wrote "without fanfare, the attorney general simply quashed the FOIA")

[185] Successive Attorney Generals have issued FIOA policy memos. In 1977, then-Attorney General Griffin Bell (appointed by President Carter) told agencies that government officials should "not withhold documents unless it is important to the public interest to do so." In 1981, William French Smith (appointed by President Regan) reversed the Bell policy and called for the withholding of information unless there is no substantial legal basis to do so. The Ashcroft memorandum reinstated the Smith memo.

[186] David Sarasohn, 'A Patriot Act's chief backer is a no-show," *Washington Post*, 10/22/03.

[187] Michael Isikoff and Mark Hosenball, "The Secrets of September 11: The White House is battling to keep a report on the terror attacks secret. Does the 2004 election have anything to do with it," MSNBC April 30, 2002. (Bush administration refused to declassify inform in Joint Senate and House Committee Report) http://stacks.msnbc.com/news/907379.asp?0cv=kb10

"I find this process horrendously frustrating ... Senior intelligence officials said things in public hearings that they [administration officials] don't want us to put in the report ... That's not something I can rationally accept without further public explanation."

(4) On June 13, 2002 the House Judiciary Committee sent a letter to Attorney General Ashcroft and FBI Director Robert F. Mueller requesting information "concerning the Department of Justice's use of these new [Patriot Act enforcement] tools and their effectiveness." On July 26, 2002, the Justice Department belatedly responded, answering only 34 of the 50 questions posed. Of those six answers were classified[188] and five were answered in a perfunctory manner, e.g., the Justice Department did not keep the records or statistics needed to answer the question.[189]

(5) Finally, the Bush's administration has refused to cooperate with the National Commission on Terrorist Attacks Upon the United States (9/11 Commission) in providing documents it needed to investigate into the cause of 9/11. Key members from both parties on the 9/11 Commission faulted the Bush administration for refusing to turn over classified intelligence documents requested.[190] More specifically, on May 7, 2003 the Commission requested all information and documents related to 9/11 hijacking. In early September, the Commission was assured by the FAA that all information had been supplied, only to find out later that substantial amount of tapes, interview reports and self-assessment studies were not turned over. The Commission was forced to issue a subpoena.[191] In the process, the Commission made the following critical observation: "The FAA ...serious deficiencies in ... production of critical documents....The FAA's delay has significantly impeded the progress of our investigation and undermined our confidence in the completeness of the FAA's production." On October 15, 2003, the 9/11 Commission issued a public statement complaining that the FAA has not been forthcoming with information requested, but to no avail.

Comptroller General David M. Walker, who headed the GAO, has also complained that the Bush administrative was one of the least cooperative n sharing information.[192] This led Stephen Cribari to observe: "What you've got now is an administration that is anti-[freedom of information], anti-open records, and at the same time, it wants enhanced authority to investigate..."[193]

---

[188] Answers to 8 (on implementation of Section 206 – "roving order"),10 (on implementation of Section 214 – "pen registers and trap and trace", 11 (on implementation of Section 215), 12 (on implementation of Section 215), 15 (on FSIA surveillance order) and 27 (on implementation of Section 206 – "roving order") will be sent to the House Permanent Select Committee on Intelligence or appropriate channels under separate cover.

[189] See Justice Department's reply to the June 13, 20002 letter from House Judiciary Chairman F. James Sensenbrenner, Jr. and Ranking Minority Member John Conyers, Jr. of July 26, 2002.

[190] "Congress Presses White House for 9/11 Papers," *LA Times*, October 27, 2003. http://www.latimes.com/news/printedition/asection/la-na-commish27oct27,1,5391529.story?coll=la-news-a_section

[191] "Statement by the 911 Commission," National Commission on Terrorist Attacks Upon the United States http://www.9-11commission.gov/press/statement_2003-10-15.pdf

[192] "Justice Dept. Balk at Study of Anti-terror Power," *Whywar.com* August 14, 2002 http://www.whywar.com/news/2002/08/14/justiced.html.

[193] John Yaukey, "Domestic spy network feared; Post-Watergate era saw tighter limits on FBI's power," *Chicago Sun – Times* Jun 2, 2002. p. 30.3.x

Why is the Bush administration so secretive? Some suggested that it reflects Bush's personality, philosophy and style of governance.[194] Others observed that it is necessary,[195] especially in fighting terrorism.[196]

The Confidentiality of Law Enforcement

After 9/11, Bush administration secrecy in government - non-disclosure to the public and un-cooperation with Congress - on anti-terrorism grounds.[197] Successful anti-terrorists investigations requires the protection of "source and methods" from would be enemies.[198]

The FOIA specifically exempts sensitive law enforcement data from public release:[199]

---

[194] According to some accounts, Bush is not intellectual curiosity nor opened. minded. He sees the world in black and white terms. He does not read the newspapers and rarely read books lest they contradict his personal judgment and challenge his own world view. He makes decision intuitively, not reflectively. He seeks input a few trusted cabinet members, come to be known as his "war cabinet." Once a decision is made, he never relents or reconsiders. Bush was questioned once about the soundness of his judgment, Bush asserted that he is the President who gives order. For a full analysis of President George W. Bush's personality and decision making style, see Frum, *The Right Man* (N.Y.: Random House, 2002). For a more scholarly treatment, see William Crotty, "Presidential Policymaking in Crisis Situations: 9/11 and Its Aftermath," *Policy Studies Journal* Vol. 31(3): 451-64 (2003), especially p. 60.

[195] Concern with keeping classified information secret afflicted all administrations, Republican as well as Democrat, see "Rumsfeld on Leaks of Classified Information," Press briefing, September 12, 2001 (Defense Secretary Rumsfeld was concerned with the leakages of classified information.) and "SECDEF Perry Memo on Unauthorized Disclosure of Intelligence," 31 July 1996 (Secretary Perry called for tighter control over unauthorized release of classified information by DOD employees to the press). See Memo on "Unauthorized Disclosure of Classified Information" 31 July 1996, Secretary of Defense.

[196] "Operations Security Throughout the Department of Defense," Memo from Deputy Defense Secretary Wolfowitz, October 18, 2001. (DOD personnel should be careful not to discuss work related matters in public place or via unsecured electronic media. Sensitive but not classified information should also be withheld from public.) http://www.fas.org/sgp/bush/wolfowitz.html

[197] N.V. Baker, "The Law: The Impact of Antiterrorism Policies on Separation of Powers: Assessing John Ashcroft's Role," *Presidential Studies Quarterly* Vol. 32 (4):765-78 (2002)

[198] See "White House Memorandum for Heads of Executive Departments and Agencies Concerning Safeguarding Information Regarding Weapons of Mass Destruction and Other Sensitive Documents Related to Homeland Security" (Mar. 19, 2002) [hereinafter White House Homeland Security Memorandum], reprinted in *FOIA Post* (posted 3/21/02) (directing agencies to consult Information Security Oversight Office and Office of Information and Privacy to ensure that they have properly applied FOIA exemptions liberally, including following Exemption 2 strictly in withhold information that is unclassified but nevertheless sensitive).

[199] THE FREEDOM OF INFORMATION ACT, 5 U.S.C. 552, As Amended by Pub. L. No. 104-231, provides for the following exemptions to public disclosure: "Section 552 (b) This section does not apply to matters that are- - (1)(A) ... Executive order to be kept secret in the interest of national defense or foreign policy ...(2) ... internal personnel rules and practices of an agency; (3) ... exempted from disclosure by statute ... (4) trade secrets and commercial or financial information ... (5) inter-agency or intra-agency memorandums or letters which would not be available by law to a party ... (6) personnel and medical file ...constitute a clearly unwarranted invasion of personal privacy; (7) records or information compiled for law enforcement purposes ... (A) could reasonably be expected to interfere with enforcement proceedings, (B) would deprive a person of a right to a fair trial or an impartial adjudication, (C) could reasonably be expected to constitute an unwarranted invasion of personal privacy, (D) could reasonably be expected to disclose the identity of a confidential source ... (E) would disclose techniques and procedures for law enforcement investigations or prosecutions ... or (F) could reasonably be expected to endanger the life or physical safety of any individual; (8) ...reports prepared by ,,, an agency responsible for the regulation or supervision of financial institutions; or (9) geological and geophysical information and data, including maps, concerning wells."

FOIA Exemption 2 – Law Enforcement Manuals and Guidelines

Section 552 (b) provides in pertinent part: "This section does not apply to matters that are-- (2) related solely to the internal personnel rules and practices of an agency;[200]

In interpreting FOIA Exemption 2, the Supreme Court in *Department of the Air Force v. Rose*[201] has excluded from disclosure matters of some substantial public interest "where disclosure may risk circumvention of agency regulation."[202] Since then *Crooker v. ATF*[203] a case involving a law enforcement agents' training manual, has articulated the follow test for Exemption 2: (1) "predominantly internal" test, and (2) that its disclosure "significantly risks circumvention of agency regulations or statutes" test.[204]

Courts have since found the following as materials properly exempted under Section 552(b) (2):[205]

(1) general guidelines for conducting investigations;[206]
(2) guidelines for conducting post-investigation litigation;[207]
(3) guidelines for identifying law violators;[208]
(4) study of agency practices and problems pertaining to undercover agents;[209]
(5) Bureau of Prisons manual that summarize procedures for security of prison control centers;[210]
(6) vulnerability assessments.[211]

---

[200] Exemption 2 (Section 552(b) (2) has been interpreted to include internal law enforcement guidelines and manuals. See "Freedom of Information Act Guide, May 2002: Exemption 2 http://www.usdoj.gov/oip/exemption2.htm In Department of the Air Force v. Rose, 425 U.S. 352 (1976). The Supreme Court construed Exemption 2 to exclude trivial or routine internal agency matters, i.e. information requested must be "subject to . . . a genuine and significant public interest." 425 U.S. 352, 369 (1976).

[201] 425 U.S. 352 (1976).

[202] 425 U.S. 352, 369 (1976).

[203] 670 F.2d 1051, 1074 (D.C. Cir. 1981) (en banc).

[204] 670 F.2d 1051, 1074 (D.C. Cir. 1981) See also Inst. for Policy Studies v. Dep't of the Air Force, 676 F. Supp. 3, 5 (D.D.C. 1987) (notwithstanding significant public interest, classification procedures can be withheld because of risk of circumvention).

[205] Extracted from "Freedom of Information Act Guide, May 2002: Exemption 2," text to footnotes 66-71.

[206] PHE, Inc. v. United States Dep't of Justice, 983 F.2d 248, 251 (D.C. Cir. 1993) ("[R]elease of FBI guidelines as to what sources of information are available to its agents might encourage violators to tamper with those sources of information and thus inhibit investigative efforts.");

[207] Silber v. United States Dep't of Justice, No. 91-876, transcript at 21 (D.D.C. Aug. 13, 1992) (bench order) (deciding that disclosure of agency's fraud litigation monograph would allow access to strategies and theories of government litigation and its efforts to enforce False Claims Act);

[208] Church of Scientology Int'l v. IRS, 845 F. Supp. 714, 723 (C.D. Cal. 1993) (protecting "information about internal law enforcement techniques, practices, and procedures used by the IRS to coordinate the flow of information regarding Scientology");

[209] Cox v. FBI, No. 83-3552, slip op. at 1 (D.D.C. May 31, 1984) (holding that report concerning undercover agents had no effect on public and contained no "secret law"), appeal dismissed, No. 84-5364 (D.C. Cir. Feb. 28, 1985).

[210] Linn v. United States Dep't of Justice, No. 92-1406, 1995 WL 417810, at *19 (D.D.C. June 6, 1995) (protecting numerical symbols used for identifying prisoners, because disclosure could assist others in breaching prisoners' security).

[211] Schwarz v. United States Dep't of Treasury, 131 F. Supp. 2d 142, 150 (D.D.C. 2000) (finding Secret Service evaluations of personal characteristics and threat potential of individuals "clearly exempt from disclosure" under both Exemptions 2 and 7(E)), summary affirmance granted, No. 00-5453, 2001 WL 674636 (D.C. Cir. May 10, 2001)

Any other sensitive information that has been found likely to result in circumvention of the law:

(1) information that would reveal the identities of informants;[212]
(2) information that would reveal the identities of undercover agents;[213]
(3) sensitive administrative notations in law enforcement files;[214]
(4) security techniques used in prisons;[215]
(5) agency audit guidelines;[216]
(6) agency testing or employee rating materials;[217]
(7) codes that would identify intelligence targets;[218]
(8) agency credit card numbers;[219] and
(9) agency classification of information manual.[220]

FOIA Exemption 2 – Law Enforcement Practice and Process

Section 552 (b) provides in pertinent part: "This section does not apply to matters that are--

(1) records or information compiled for law enforcement purposes, but only to the extent that the production of such law enforcement records or information (A) could reasonably be expected to interfere with enforcement proceedings, (B) would deprive a person of a right to a fair trial or an impartial adjudication, (C) could reasonably be expected to constitute an unwarranted invasion of personal privacy, (D) could reasonably be expected to disclose the identity of a confidential source...(E) would disclose techniques and procedures for law enforcement investigations or prosecutions, or would disclose guidelines for law enforcement investigations or

---

[212] Davin v. United States Dep't of Justice, 60 F.3d 1043, 1065 (3d Cir. 1995) (upholding protection for informant codes); Jones v. FBI, 41 F.3d 238, 244 (6th Cir. 1994) (same); Massey v. FBI, 3 F.3d 620, 622 (2d Cir. 1993) (finding that disclosure of informant symbol numbers and source-identifying information "could do substantial damage to the FBI's law enforcement activities"); Shores v. FBI, 185 F. Supp. 2d 77, 83 (D.D.C. 2002) (recognizing that disclosing "informant symbol and file numbers," and thereby "compromising the identities of government informants," readily "could deter individuals from cooperating with the government");

[213] Cox v. FBI, No. 83-3552, slip op. at 2 (D.D.C. May 31, 1984) (protecting report concerning FBI's undercover agent program because of potential for discovering identities of agents).

[214] Cappabianca v. Comm'r, United States Customs Serv., 847 F. Supp. 1558, 1563 (M.D. Fla. 1994) (protecting Customs Service file numbers "containing information such as the type and location of the case" because "if the code were cracked, [it] could reasonably lead to circumvention of the law"); Curcio v. FBI, No. 89-941, slip op. at 5 (D.D.C. Nov. 2, 1990) (protecting expense accounting in FBI criminal investigation).

[215] Jimenez v. FBI, 938 F. Supp. 21, 24 (D.D.C. 1996) (approving nondisclosure of criteria for classification of prison gang member

[216] Dirksen v. HHS, 803 F.2d 1456, 1458-59 (9th Cir. 1986) upholding protection of internal audit guidelines in order to prevent risk of circumvention of agency Medicare reimbursement regulations)

[217] Patton v. FBI, 626 F. Supp. 445, 447 (M.D. Pa. 1985) (testing materials withheld because release would impair effectiveness of system and give future applicants unfair advantage), aff'd, 782 F.2d 1030 (3d Cir. 1986) (unpublished table decision); Oatley v. United States, 3 Gov't Disclosure Serv. (P-H) ¶ 83,274, at 84,065 (D.D.C. Aug. 16, 1983) (civil service testing materials satisfy two-part Crooker test);

[218] Tawalbeh v. United States Dep't of the Air Force, No. 96-6241, slip op. at 13 (C.D. Cal. Aug. 8, 1997) (finding that disclosure of Air Force internal intelligence collection codes "would allow unauthorized persons to decode classified . . . messages")

[219] Judicial Watch, Inc. v. United States Dep't of Commerce, 83 F. Supp. 2d at 110 (upholding protection of government credit card numbers based upon "realistic possibility of . . . misuse and fraud").

[220] Inst. for Policy Studies, 676 F. Supp. at 5.

prosecutions if such disclosure could reasonably be expected to risk circumvention of the law, or (F) could reasonably be expected to endanger the life or physical safety of any individual; …(c)(1) Whenever a request is made which involves access to records described in subsection (b)(7)(A) and-- the investigation or proceeding involves a possible violation of criminal law; and (B) There is reason to believe that (i) the subject of the investigation or proceeding is not aware of its pendency, and (ii) disclosure of the existence of the records could reasonably be expected to interfere with enforcement proceedings, the agency may, during only such time as that circumstance continues, treat the records as not subject to the requirements of this section.

(2) Whenever informant records maintained by a criminal law enforcement agency under an informant's name or personal identifier are requested by a third party according to the informant's name or personal identifier, the agency may treat the records as not subject to the requirements of this section unless the informant's status as an informant has been officially confirmed.

(3) Whenever a request is made which involves access to records maintained by the Federal Bureau of Investigation pertaining to foreign intelligence or counterintelligence, or international terrorism, and the existence of the records is classified information as provided in subsection (b)(1), the Bureau may, as long as the existence of the records remains classified information, treat the records as not subject to the requirements of this section.

Thus in spite of repeated requests by Congressional oversight committees[221] and human rights organizations,[222] the government (Department Justice, FBI) has steadfastly refused to release any data on the use of Section 215 and related counter-terrorism powers on national security grounds[223] and for executive privileges reasons.

The open resistance of the executive branch to Congressional oversight efforts[224] has led some lawmakers, such as Senator Patrick J. Leahy (D-VT), to observe in frustration: "Since

---

[221] See June 13, 2002 letter sent by Committee Chairman Rep. James Sensenbrenner Jr. and Ranking Member John Conyers Jr. of House Judiciary Committee, seeking answers from Attorney General Ashcroft and FBI Director Robert F. Mueller to 50 questions on matters "concerning the Department of Justice's use of these new tools and their effectiveness." http://www.house.gov/judiciary/ashcroft061302.htm

[222] See "Freedom of Information Request" to Office of Information and Privacy, Department of Justice and FBI, Letter dated September 24, 2002. Center for Cognitive Liberty and Ethics. http://www.cognitiveliberty.org/pdf/FOIA1.pdf

[223] See Section II. "Overview of FBI Oversight in the 107th Congress …. B. Judiciary Committee FBI Oversight Activities in the 107th Congress.. 3. DOJ and FBI Non-Responsiveness." Senator Patrick Leahy, Senator Charles Grassley, and Senator Arlen Specter, "Interim Report on FBI Oversight in the 107th Congress by the Senate Judiciary Committee: FISA Implementation Failures," (February 2003). See also Adam Clymer, "Justice Dept. Balks At Effort to Study Antiterror Powers," *New York Times*. Aug. 14, 2002.(The Justice Department has refused House Judiciary Committee requests for information about conduct of "roving surveillance"; calls to and from telephone numbers; bookstore, library and newspaper records; and subpoenas served on Americans or permanent US residents.) http://www.nytimes.com/2002/08/15/politics/15PATR.html?ex=1064376000anden=cfeff6942d197054andei=5070

[224] *Dan Eggen*, "Ashcroft Assailed On Policy Review: Lawmakers Say Oversight Is Blocked," *Washington Post* August 21, 2002; Page A02 ("Lawmakers on the House and Senate judiciary committees are complaining that Attorney General John D. Ashcroft is blocking attempts to review Justice Department counterterrorism policies.")

I've been here, I have never known an administration that is more difficult to get information from that the oversight committees are entitled to."[225]

The administration's repeated refusal to make public information available to public interest organizations led to the filing of many FOIA law suits against the Department of Justice, including bookstores and libraries investigative policies, activities and records. The law suit was joined by American Booksellers Foundation for Free Expression, the American Library Association's Freedom to Read Foundation, the American Civil Liberties Union and the Electronic Privacy Information Center.

In the end, the public, as with researchers, have to reply on government releases (including Congressional hearings, GAO reports, 9/11 Commissions' findings), journalistic reports, library accounts, think tank investigation, interest groups advocacy papers and scholarly studies to gain some idea on how the USAPA has been enforced and received.

ORGANIZATION OF THE BOOK

This book resulted from a five years (2002 – 2007) research project entitled: "The Impact and Implications of USAPA on American Society." The ambit of the project is to investigate into the historical context, legislative process, implementation problems, social impact and political undoing of the USAPA. The study conveniently on December 31, 2006, the year end the USAPA was due for renewal.

This book is organized into the following chapters.

Chapter Two: "Legislative Process" investigated into the legislative history of the USAPA. It examined the Congressional records, tracked the floor debates and monitored newspaper accounts to document the process and detail the dynamics as to how the USAPA was passed.

Chapter Three: "Legislative Climate" investigated into *why* the USAPA was adopted without any serious contest and effective challenge by exploring the public sentiments, legislative climate, political gamesmanship and media patriotism attending to and accounting for USAPA's speedy and uncritical passage.

The main thesis of this chapter is that we cannot begin to understanding the Nation's reaction to 9/11 in general and the passage of USAPA in particular without first documenting how 9/11 changed American people's ways and means, psyche and ethos; specifically how Americans as citizens, law makers, President and journalists react to 9/11.

Chapter Four: "Implementation of USAPA" investigated into how the USAPA - Student and Exchange Visitor Information System (SEVIS) originated, developed and launched. It seeks to answer the research question: what were the implementation problems and resulting impact of SEVIS on university administration, particularly at international offices of higher learning all over the nation.

The contribution of this study is in providing useful data to help with our understanding of problems and issues associated with the implementation of SEVIS. Specifically, it allows us to have a better understanding of the impact and implication of SEVIS on university administration.

---

[225] Adam Clymer, "Justice Dept. Balks At Effort to Study Antiterror Powers," *New York Times*. Aug. 14, 2002.

Chapter Five: "Impact on Muslim Community" investigated the impact of USAPA and related anti-terrorism measures on the Muslim community in the U.S, and with it the implications of the USAPA on American society.

The research concludes with the observation that 9/11 and related anti-terrorism measures, including the USAPA, provided a call to arms to the Muslim and immigrants communities, making them aware of their plight and motivating them to take steps to get unified and organized in championing for their own interests, welfare, and in time securing their collective identity and status in American society. In terms of long term implications to America, America is increasingly becoming a national security state.

Chapter Six: "The Impact on Library" investigated the impact of the USAPA on the library. Library is chosen as a research site in part because it is one of the most conspicuous victims of war on terror. The main focus of the investigation is thus on how the original design and later implementation of the USAPA affected the traditional role, routine operations, altered expectations of library, communities and government.

This "impact study" calls for two kinds of investigations: (1) what is the impact of Section 215 on daily operations of a library; (2) what is the implication of USAPA on the traditional role and functions of library in our society.

Chapter Seven: "Grassroots Resistance" observed that soon after USAPA passage, the Bill of Rights Defense Committee (BRDC) launched a grassroots anti USAPA ("anti-Patriot" for short) movement to defeat the USAPA, one community at a time. All told, from October 2001 to April 9 2006, there were 406 anti-Patriot Resolutions nationwide, make up of 8 State Resolutions and 398 Community Resolutions, covering a total of 84,617,547 people in America.

This chapter is devoted to studying the Bill of Rights Defense Committee; its origination and development, charter and strategy, and finally impact and effect, with archived data at the BRDC web site and contemporary news paper accounts – report, comments, analysis - all over the nation. From such an inquiry, it is discovered that "civil liberties free zone" (anti-Patriot) movement represents a one of a kind emerging grassroots social qua political movement seeking to repeal the USAPA with the passage of anti-Patriot resolutions.

Chapter Eight: "USAPA: A Preliminary Assessment" provided a preliminary assessment of the USAPA, in its totality: how could the USAPA legislative process be satisfactory explained, whether the Act is effective in dealing with terrorism, and what are the costs of the Act to our constitutional democracy, social and political life? In so doing the book takes issue with both the efficacy and utility of the Act, in securing the nation and protecting the civil rights, intimating at the ultimate question: "Is it worth the cost?"

Finally, this book closed with the observation that there are more questions to answer, and more questions than answers. More research is required to address some of these troubling questions, and raises new one. Hopefully, this remains to be the first impression and a lasting contribution of this scholarship.

Chapter 2

THE LEGISLATIVE PROCESS

*"Those who would give up essential liberty to purchase a little temporary safety
deserves neither liberty nor safety."*

Benjamin Franklin

I. INTRODUCTION

There is little research on USAPA legislative process.[226] Existing research shows that the USAPA was "rushed" passed Congress by the Bush administration without following the formal legislative procedure,[227] i.e., agency review,[228] public hearings,[229] mark up,[230] floor

---

[226] A recent law librarian biographic search uncovered only one entry having to do with the legislative history of USAPA, i.e. Beryl A. Howell, "Seven Weeks: The Making of the USAPA," 72 *Geo. Wash. L. Rev.* 1145 (2004). See Kate Dixon, "The U.S.A. PATRIOT Act: A Selected Bibliography," Research Librarian Western New England College School of Law Library. April 2005. Dixon's findings is confirmed by Kam C. Wong, "The making of the USA PATRIOT ACT I: "Legislative Process and Dynamics" *International Journal of the Sociology of Law* Vol. 34 (3): 179 – 219 (2006). For USAPA legislative activities, see Robert O' Harrow Jr., "Six Weeks in Autumn," *Washington Post.* Sunday, October 27, 2002; W06 (The USAPA was rushed through Congress by the administration under the stewardship of Ashcroft.) See also Morton H. Halperin, "Less Secure, Less Free," *The American Prospect* Vol. 12 (20) November 19, 2001 (hereinafter "Less Secure, Less Free") (http://www.prospect.org/print/V12/20/halperin-m.html For a day to day account of anti-terrorism legislative activities in the Congress, see *Tech Law Journal Daily E-Mail Alert* http://www.techlawjournal.com/welcome.htm For a detail description of the passage of the USAPA, see James Bovard, *Terrorism and Tyranny: Trampling Freedom, Justice, and Peace to Rid the World of Evil* (Palgrave Macmillan, 2003), esp. Chapter 4: "Patriot Railroad." For legislative materials, see Bernard D., Jr. Reams and Christopher Anglim (Editors), *USAPA: A Legislative History of the Uniting and Strengthening America by Providing Appropriate Tools Required to Intercept and Obstruct Terrorism Act* (Fred B Rothman and Co, 2002). For a summary of the process, see "Introduction", *Id.* For an inside the beltway account of the legislative process, see "USAPA: A Summary of ALA Activities," ALA Washington Office, Jan.19, 2002. For an electronic library of key legislative documents, consult "Legislative History of the USAPA," Center for Democracy and Technology. For critical events in the passage of the USAPA, see Steven Brill, "What Price Freedom? The day the Constitution died," *Capitol Hill Blue* March 3, 2003. http://chblue.com/artman/publish/printer_1865.shtml

[227] See "Legislative procedure is not flawed" (text to notes 63 – 72) in Kam C. Wong, "USA PATRIOT ACT: Some Unanswered Questions," *International Journal of the Sociology of Law* 43(1): 1 - 41 (2006).

[228] "Less Secure, Less Free," *supra*, note 1. (The Administration's original anti-terrorism measures (Combating Terrorism Act (CTA) – Anti-Terrorism Act (ATA) – Mobilization Anti-Terrorism (MTA) was the handmaiden

debate,[231] and conference report,[232] in both chambers.[233] For example, floor debate was limited to four hours for USA ACT. The debate was less a real debate as it was an opportunity for respective senators to put statements on the record, i.e. to detail the content and describe the process (e.g., Senator Leahy started by observing that the Bill was not to anyone's liking); list the concessions and catalogue the (negotiated) achievements made (e.g., Senate Leahy spent most of the time allotted explaining various technical provisions to the Act); leave a legislative record anticipating Supreme Court challenges ahead (Senate Specter (R-PA).[234] From the beginning to the end, the anti-terrorism legislation was orchestrated for passage by the Administration, not open for input by the public or subject to scrutiny of the Congress. In the final USA ACT debate, the Senate leadership from both parties made it known that that the USA ACT was not to be changed. No floor amendments were allowed, except for three by Senator Feingold. Dissenters were shunned, lest they would undo the hard fought compromised bill.

More significantly, throughout the entire USAPA legislative process, neither the Congress nor the Administration has systematically investigated, judiciously examined, openly debated, and comprehensively considered the relative merits and utilities – necessity and efficacy, costs and benefits – and the impact and implications – long and short, direct and indirect - of the USAPA on the Constitution,[235] on the society, and on the people. A few vocal Senators, e.g. Leahy, Feingold, and a coalition of interested groups, e.g. ACLU and EFF, did raise objections over the dire consequences of the USAPA on civil liberties. But these voices were intentionally suppressed and conveniently ignored. As a result, there was no serious consideration given to the long term impact and implications of the USAPA on our Constitutional form of government and democratic governance, e.g. how USAPA might

---

of the Attorney General staff, alone. The Office of Budget Management (OBM) was intentionally bypassed to deny input and avoid comments from affected agencies.)

[229] There were a total of two hearings being held before the passage of USAPA, one on September 25, 2001 when Attorney General Ashcroft was invited to answer questions on Administration's anti-terrorism proposals (MATA – ATA). Senate Committee on the Judiciary Hearing, Tuesday, September 25, 2001, on "Homeland Defense." Presided by Chairman Leahy. The other public hearing was called by Senator Feingold on October 3, 2001 to discuss civil liberties implications of the USAPA and related anti-terrorism measures. The Senate Judiciary Committee's Subcommittee on the Constitution, Federalism, and Property Rights held a hearing titled "Protecting Constitutional Freedoms in the Face of Terrorism." Presided by Sen. Russ Feingold (D-WI)

[230] Morton H. Halperin, "The Liberties We Defend," *American Prospect* Vol. 12 (18) Oct. 22, 2001. http://www.prospect.org/print/V12/18/halperin-m-2.html ("Four key Republicans on the House Judiciary Committee wrote to their chairman questioning the rush to mark up a bill (MATA) after only one hearing with the Attorney General on 9/25/01. "What we must avoid ... is the impulse to hastily approve wholesale changes to search and seizure, surveillance, immigration and other laws in an understandable but misguided attempt to thwart future attacks.")

[231] "Seven Weeks", note 1, *supra*.

[232] *Ibid.* (House and Senate Conference on PATRIOT ACT and USA ACT was done away with because the Bush Administration in general and Attorney General Ashcroft in particular was afraid that the conference leadership (as then constituted) might jeopardize the chance of quick passage.).

[233] For process in the Senate, see "Guide to Senate Legislative Processes." (Congressional Research Service, Feb. 2002). For process in the House, see HOW OUR LAWS ARE MADE, Revised and Updated by Charles W. Johnson, Parliamentarian, United States House of Representatives (Last update: Thu, 06 Jan 2005 18:49:22 GMT).

[234] "Seven Weeks", note 1, *supra*.

[235] Andrew Kohut and Bruce Stokes, *America Against the World: How We Are Different and Why We Are Disliked* (Times Book, 2006) (Pew Global Attitudes Project interviewed 91,00o in fifty nations from 2002 through 2005 and come to the conclusion that after 911 and as a result of Bush administration, anti-Americanism is on the rise world-wide.)

affect the constitutional structure, process and culture, in historical terms or international arena.

As it turned out and with hindsight, 9/11 was a watershed event. It has changed international opinion about US democratic institutions and domestic attitude towards law and order.[236] Increasingly the world – friends and foes alike – from Europe to Asia, from South America to Africa - have a negative image of America. For example, in terms of favorable ratings of America, Britain went from 75% (summer 2002) to 58% (Mar. 2004) and Jordon went from 25% to 5% in the same period. The sincerity of US war on terrorism was widely questioned in 2004: Britain (41%), France (61%), Russia (48%), Germany (65%), Turkey (64%), Morocco (66%), Jordon (58%) and Pakistan (58%). Most significantly, world public opinion about US's commitment to democracy has slipped in 2004 survey: Britain (45% less committed), France (79%), Russia (53%), Germany (70%), Turkey (73%), Morocco (66%), Jordon (56%) and Pakistan (57%).[237] Domestically, by a margin of 52% vs. 38%, US public surveyed observed that the remove of (Constitutional) limitations on government has gone too far. Contrary to Bush government policy, a majority of the public in the U.S. believed that U.S. citizens detained as terrorists should be given rights (80%) and afforded lawyers (78%).

Knowledgeable insiders observed that the USAPA was entirely a Bush administration brainchild, conceived by the Attorney Generation,[238] imposed on the Congress[239] and fed to the American people in a time of crisis[240] and with the use of high handed tactics.[241] To date, no serious attempt has been made to understand how and why the USAPA was able to rush through Congress without serious contest and effective challenge.[242] This is a first attempt to do so.

This chapter investigated into the legislative history of the USAPA. This chapter is organized into the following parts. After this "Introduction," Part II: "The Legislative Process" traced the origin and followed the development of the USAPA. It observed that the USAPA was rushed through the Congress with few consultations with the public and virtually no participation by the legislators, individually. Part III: "Conclusion" summarized the chapter's major findings as it discussed the implications of a such a flawed legislative process. The reasons why the legislative process was compromised is a subject matter to be dealt with at length and in more detail in Chapter Three.

---

[236] For international opinion, see "Global Opinion: The Spread of Anti-Americanism A review of Pew Global Attitudes Project findings," January 24, 2005.

[237] For domestic opinion, see "Americans on Terrorism: Two Years After 9/11," *Program on International Policy Attitudes* and *Knowledge Networks* (2003)

[238] See text to notes 68 – 71, *infra*.

[239] "Less Secure, Less Free." *Supra*, note 1 (Even the Attorney general did not read the ATA.). See also "Seven Weeks", note 1, *supra*.

[240] The Bush Administration has rejected this charge, emphatically. Viet Dinh "A White Paper: How Does the USAPA defends democracy." The Foundation for the Defense of Democracies, June 1, 2004. (During the drafting of the anti-terrorism measures, the Administration has listened to and took suggestions from a coalition of concerned people and interested parties. (p. 3) http://www.defenddemocracy.org/usr_doc/USA_Patriot_Act.pdf

[241] See also "Seven Weeks", not 1, *supra*. (Attorney General Ashcroft repeatedly demanded the quick passage of the Administration's proposals without debate and with no revisions, with threats of political fallouts of yet another terrorist attack.) See Chapter 2, *infra*.

[242] The two exceptions being "Seven Weeks" note 1, *supra*. (an insider account of the legislative process) and Robert O' Harrow Jr. (with assistance from the *Center for Investigative Reporting*) "Six Weeks in Autumn," note 1, *supra*. (The USAPA was rushed through Congress by the administration under the stewardship of Attorney General staff.) There were suggestions that the President Bush was personally involved by giving the matching order, i.e. Attorney General Ashcroft acted only as a loyal foot soldier.)

II. THE LEGISLATIVE PROCESS

There were many legislative measures – Acts, Bills, Resolutions - introduced during the first two week after 9/11 including: Victims of Terrorism Tax Relief Act of 2001, Public Law No: 107-134 (introduced 9/13/2001) ("Exempts from income taxes any individual who dies as a result of wounds or injury incurred from the terrorist attacks against the United States on April 19, 1995, or September 11, 2001, or who dies as a result of illness incurred from a terrorist attack involving anthrax occurring on or after September 11, 2001, and before January 1, 2002 (such attacks)."); Public Safety Officer Benefits Bill, Public Law No: 107-37 (introduced 9/13/2001) ("To provide for the expedited payment of certain benefits for a public safety officer who was killed or suffered a catastrophic injury as a direct and proximate result of a personal injury sustained in the line of duty in connection with the terrorist attacks of September 11, 2001."); Intelligence Authorization Act for Fiscal Year 2002 ("To authorize appropriations for fiscal year 2002 for intelligence and intelligence-related activities of the United States Government, the Community Management Account, and the Central Intelligence Agency Retirement and Disability System, and for other purposes."); 2001 Emergency Supplemental Appropriations Act for Recovery from and Response to Terrorist Attacks on the United States, Public Law No: 107-38 (introduced 9/14/2001) ("Making emergency supplemental appropriations for the fiscal year 2001 for additional disaster assistance, for anti-terrorism initiatives, and for assistance in the recovery from the tragedy that occurred on September 11, 2001, and for other purposes."); Air Transportation Safety and System Stabilization Act, Public Law No: 107-42 (introduced on 9/21/2001) ("To preserve the continued viability of the United States air transportation system."); Freedom Bonds Act of 2001, H.R.2899 (introduced 9/17/2001) ("To authorize the Secretary of the Treasury to issue Freedom Bonds in response to the September 11, 2001, hijackings and attacks on the Pentagon and the World Trade Center, and for other purposes").[243]

Combating Terrorism Act of 2001 - Amendment No. 1562[244]

The first comprehensive and significant post 9/11 anti-terrorism legislative measure[245] introduced was in the form of an amendment attached to a budget appropriation bill, "DEPARTMENTS OF COMMERCE, JUSTICE, AND STATE, THE JUDICIARY, AND RELATED AGENCIES APPROPRIATIONS ACT, 2002" (HR 2500), in the Senate on September 13, 2001,[246] i.e. AMENDMENT NO. 1562, entitled: "Combating Terrorism Act of 2001." (CTA) [247]

---

[243] For a summary of existing terrorism federal law provisions as of October 2001, see "Terrorism Legislation Comparison," http://www.netcaucus.org/books/surveillance2001/docs/EFF_Leg_Compare_Chart.pdf

[244] *Combating Terrorism Act of 2001*, S. Amdt. 1562, 107th Cong. (2001), http://www.cdt.org/security/ 010913senatewiretap2.shtml. (last visited November 16, 2003).

[245] For a list of 9/11 legislations, see "LEGISLATION RELATED TO THE ATTACK OF SEPTEMBER 11, 2001," http://thomas.loc.gov/home/terrorleg.htm

[246] See Congressional Record, September 13, 2001, at pages S9401-4.

[247] For a discussion, see "Liberty for Security," *Duke L. and Tech. Rev.* 0036 (2001), esp. "Combating Terrorism Act of 2001." For a copy of the CTA text, see http://msbnetworks.net/~hillct/cta/ For Senate floor debate, see "Senate debate on wiretap and anti-terrorism proposals," Sept. 13, 2001 (Hereinafter "Combating Terrorism Act of 2001 debate") http://www.cdt.org/security/010913senatewiretap.shtml

The Original Ideas

The professed purpose of the CTA was: "To enhance the capability of the United States to deter, prevent, and thwart domestic and international acts of terrorism against United States nationals and interests."[248] In layman's terms and as Senator Hatch put it: "It is essential that we give our law enforcement authorities every possible tool to search out and bring to justice those individuals who have brought such indiscriminate death into our backyard."[249]

The CTA was cosponsored by Senators Hatch (R-Utah), Feinstein (D-CA), and Kyl (R-Arizona). Senators Dewine (R-OH), Session (R-AL), Thompson (R-TN), Thurmond (R-SC), McCain (R-AZ), and Schumer (D-NY) also joined.[250] The CTA passed the Senate two days after 9/11, with about 30 minutes of floor debate and one lone dissenting voice, i.e. that of Sen. Patrick Leahy (D-VT). Leahy wanted more time to study the bill.[251] This was an all too familiar pattern with post 9/11 legislative measures,[252] to be repeated again with the USAPA.[253]

The CTA was intended to provide law enforcement officials with the necessary resources and added legal authority to fight terrorism, particularly in the investigation of 9/11 terrorists and to bring them to justice.[254] As observed by Senator Hatch in introducing the CTA: "we, as lawmakers, must take every step possible to ensure, in addition to adequate financial resources, that the law enforcement community has the proper investigative tools at its disposal to track down the participants in this evil conspiracy and to bring them to justice."[255]

Facing a national crisis of yet untold proportions, the Congressional leadership had other contingency plans to secure the nation, should CTA failed to materialize.[256] For example, on September 20, 2001, Representative Lamar Smith circulated a bill - Public Safety and Cyber Security Enhancement Act (PSCSEA) – similar to the CTA as a backup for S.A. 1562 should H.R. 2500 failed to pass. Senator Patrick Leahy was also working on his own anti-terrorism bill, later passed as the USA ACT.

---

[248] See Combating Terrorism Act of 2001 debate.

[249] Declan McCullagh, "Senate OKs FBI Net Spying," *WIRED NEWS* 12:55 PM Sep. 14, 2001 PT http://www.wired.com/news/politics/0,1283,46852,00.html

[250] Senators Kyl, Hatch, and Feinstein were all members of the Subcommittee on Technology, Terrorism, and Government Information and Terrorism, (106th Congress), and later the Technology and Homeland Security (107th and 108th Congress) which was responsible for "Oversight of anti-terrorism enforcement and policy". Senator Feinstein was the Democratic Chairman of Subcommittee on Technology, Terrorism, and Government Information (106th Congress) in 2001 with Senator Kye acting as the Ranking Republican. Senator Kyl was the Chairman and Senator Feinstein was the Ranking Democrat on the Terrorism, Technology and Homeland Security (107th and 108th Congress).

[251] See Senate Leahy floor speech, Combating Terrorism Act of 2001 debate.

[252] "USAPA: More Questions than Answers," note 2, *supra*, esp. "Table 2: The number of 9/11 legislative actions acted upon within six (6) months," referencing Margaret F. Klemm and Albert C. Ringelstein, "Congressional Response to the September 11, 2001 Terrorist Attacks," *extensions. A Journal of Carl Albert Center* (Fall 2002).

[253] *Id.*

[254] At this juncture, the traditional law and order paradigm in dealing with terrorism and terrorists still applies, i.e. reactive and punitive (terrorism as crime), not pre-emptive and destructive (terrorists as enemies). In this regard, the CTA diverges from USAPA, philosophically, in substantial and material ways.

[255] See Combating Terrorism Act of 2001 debate.

[256] It also registers a starch reality, everyone America is trying to find a way to express their anger, stamp their anxiety and "do something" about 9/11. View this way, the USAPA is a must pass legislation.

The CTA was demanded by the public (to track down the culprits, to secure the nation)[257] and required by the situation (in fighting an illusive enemy).[258] Above all else it reflected and reinforced the nation's sober mood and crisis mentality. The political climate of the time was in seeking security at all costs.[259] Most of the provisions have been recommended by former anti-terrorism commissions, e.g. National Commission on Terrorism[260] and requested by law enforcement officials for years. As Senator Kye observed when speaking in support of the bill: "the Director of the FBI and other U.S. Government officials all imploring us to do some things to help in this battle against terrorism."[261] Nearly half of the provisions have passed the Senate one and half year before.[262]

CTA Substantive Provisions

The "Combating Terrorism Act of 2001 was "sought to for improve upon current counter-terrorism readiness:

(i) *Assessment of readiness* The Comptroller General was asked to conduct "an assessment of the capabilities of the National Guard to preemptively disrupt a terrorist attack within the United States involving weapons of mass destruction, and to respond to such an attack" (Section 811 (a).[263]

(ii) *Scientific and technology research* The President was asked to establish a comprehensive long- term scientific and technology research program to prevent, preempt, detect, interdict, and respond to catastrophic terrorist attacks (Section 812 (b).[264]

(iii) *Legal authority* The Attorney General was asked to conduct a review of the legal authority of the Federal government agencies to adequately respond to and prevent, preempt, detect, and interdict – "catastrophic terrorist attacks." (Section 813(a)[265]

(iv) *Intelligence agent recruitment* The Director of Central Intelligence was asked to rescind the 1995 CIA guidelines relating to "the recruitment of persons who have

---

[257] Senator Kye: "But, as policymakers, we have also been asked some hard questions by our constituents and those questions include things such as: Why can't our Government do something about these horrible crimes?" *Id.* See "USAPA supported by the public" (text to notes 35 to 37). In "USAPA: More Questions than Answers" *International Journal of the Sociology of Law* (In print, March 2006).

[258] "On the Importance of Anti-terrorism Legislation," ("Viet Dinh: I think the American people have made their preferences very clear in their public statements expressed to the various news agencies, not only with respect to the fight against terrorism, but on this package in particular.") http://www.aclj.org/news/nf_011004_viet_dinh_interview.asp

[259] "The making of the USA PATRIOT ACT II: Public Sentiments, Legislative Climate, Political Gamesmanship, Media Patriotism," *International Journal of the Sociology of Law* 34 (2): 105-140 (2006).

[259] *Combating Terrorism Act of 2001*, S. Amdt. 1562, 107th Cong. (2001).

[260] See testimony of Senator Kyle, Combating Terrorism Act of 2001 debate. ("We implement one of the recommendations of the Bremer commission, which said there is a lot of illicit fundraising for terrorist organizations going on in the United States. ") Bremer and Sonnenberg, "Countering the Changing Threat on International Terrorism," National Commission on Terrorism. http://www.fas.org/irp/threat/commission.html

[261] *Id.*

[262] See testimony of Senator Kyle, Combating Terrorism Act of 2001 debate. ("In fact, we incorporated some of the provisions of these commission recommendations in the bill that passed the Senate a year and a half ago.")

[263] SEC. 811. ASSESSMENT OF NATIONAL GUARD CAPABILITIES TO PREEMPTIVELY DISRUPT DOMESTIC TERRORIST ATTACKS INVOLVING WEAPONS OF MASS DESTRUCTION.

[264] SEC. 812. LONG-TERM RESEARCH AND DEVELOPMENT TO ADDRESS CATASTROPHIC TERRORIST ATTACKS.

[265] SEC. 813. REVIEW OF AUTHORITY OF FEDERAL AGENCIES TO ADDRESS CATASTROPHIC TERRORIST ATTACKS.

access to intelligence related terrorist plans, intentions and capabilities." (Section 814)[266]

(v) *Sharing of intelligence* The President was asked to report on "legal authorities that govern the sharing of criminal wiretap information under applicable Federal laws, including section 104 of the National Security Act of 1947 (50 U.S.C. 403-4)(Section 815 (a)[267] and made recommendations for sharing intelligence between DOJ and intelligence community (Section 815 (b) (2).[268]

(vi) *Terrorism financing* The Federal Government was asked to use all the tools available to prevent, deter, or disrupt the fundraising activities of international terrorist organizations. (Section 816 (2)[269]

(vii) *Controls of biological pathogens* The Attorney General was asked to report upon "the means of improving United States controls of biological pathogens and the equipment necessary to develop, produce, or deliver biological weapons" (Section 817 (a).[270] The President was asked to adopt measures "to enhance the standards for the physical protection and security of the biological pathogens ... from illegal theft or other wrongful diversion" (Section 817 (b).[271]

(viii) *Reimbursing employee liability insurance* The Head of Federal agencies were to reimburse law enforcement agents and intelligence employees for professional liability insurance covering counterterrorism duties (Section 818 (a)[272]

(ix) *Authorizing the use of a pen register or trap and trace device* Federal and State investigative or law enforcement officers are authorized to use a pen register or trap and trace device to obtain "dialing, routing, addressing" information by certifying "to the court that the information likely to be obtained by such installation and use is relevant to an ongoing criminal investigation." (Section.832 (b).[273] It also authorized the emergency installation of such devices without a court order by U.S. Attorneys if there is a certified immediate threat to "national security", "public health or safety", "attack on the integrity or availability of a protected computer" (Section.832 (c)[274]

(x) *Authority to intercept wire, oral and electronic communications* Law enforcement officials are authorized to intercept wire, oral and electronic communications in the investigation of terrorism (Section 833)[275] and computer fraud and abuse (Section 834) offenses.[276]

---

[266] SEC. 814. GUIDELINES ON RECRUITMENT OF TERRORIST INFORMANTS
[267] SEC. 815. DISCLOSURE BY LAW ENFORCEMENT AGENCIES OF CERTAIN INTELLIGENCE OBTAINED BY INTERCEPTION OF COMMUNICATIONS.
[268] *Ibid.*
[269] SEC. 816. JOINT TASK FORCE ON TERRORIST FUNDRAISING.
[270] SEC. 817. IMPROVEMENT OF CONTROLS ON PATHOGENS AND EQUIPMENT FOR PRODUCTION OF BIOLOGICAL WEAPONS
[271] *Ibid.*
[272] SEC. 818. REIMBURSEMENT OF PERSONNEL PERFORMING COUNTERTERRORISM DUTIES FOR PROFESSIONAL LIABILITY INSURANCE
[273] SEC. 832. MODIFICATION OF AUTHORITIES RELATING TO USE OF PEN REGISTERS AND TRAP AND TRACE DEVICES.
[274] *Ibid.*
[275] SEC. 833. AUTHORITY TO INTERCEPT WIRE, ORAL, AND ELECTRONIC COMMUNICATIONS RELATING TO TERRORISM OFFENSES.
[276] SEC. 834. AUTHORITY TO INTERCEPT WIRE, ORAL, AND ELECTRONIC COMMUNICATIONS RELATING TO COMPUTER FRAUD AND ABUSE.

As it turned out, the process and debate over AMENDMENT NO. 1562 served as a dry run for the USAPA. Specifically, it anticipated many of the substantive issues that were raised, e.g. roving wiretap as threatening civil liberties, and rehearsed most of process related arguments that were made, e.g. Congress should not rush to judgment without proper notice and public hearing. For example, much like the USAPA, the Senators were given the CTA bill only 30 minutes before the floor debate.[277] In this regard, Senator Leahy floor speech on CTA was instructive on things to come:

> "Unfortunately, because this is something that we have had no hearings on, we haven't had the discussions in the appropriate committees--Intelligence, Armed Services, and Judiciary--we are somewhat limited in opposition... I would feel far more comfortable voting on something like this if these various committees not only had a chance to look at it but that President Bush's administration--the Attorney General, the Director of CIA, the Secretary of Defense--would have the opportunity to let us know their views on it. I would feel far more comfortable with that."[278]

Muted Public Awareness, Vocal Special Concerns

The CTA did not attract much media attention nor generate any public concerns.[279] The nation was still taken back over the aftermath of 9/11 attack and struggling to deal with many of its unforeseen consequences.

There were however some very serious concerns over the vagueness of many of its provisions form some quarters, such as America Civil Liberties Union (ACLU), and (civil rights) advocacy coalitions, such as Electronic Frontier Foundation (EFF).[280] What is the exact meaning of "addressing" and "routing" data?[281] How might the CTA impact on

---

[277] Morgan Streetman, "Liberty for Security," 2001 *The Duke Law and Technology Review* (DLTR) 0036, para. 8 http://www.law.duke.edu/journals/dltr/articles/2001dltr0036.html

[278] See Combating Terrorism Act of 2001 debate.

[279] There were occasional constituent letters to the law-makers. There was no systematic counting or analysis of such letters. See letter of Mike Perry (505 E. White St #4, Champaign, Il, 61820) to Senators Durbin and Fitzgerald, and Representative Johnson ("All post 9/11 anti-terrorism legislations – Attorney General Ashcroft's Anti-Terrorism Act (ATA); Sen. Leahy's Uniting and Strengthening of America Act (USAA); Rep. Smith's Public Safety and Cyber Security Enhancement Act (PSCSEA, H.R. 2915); Sen. Hatch's Combating Terrorism Act (CTA, amendment S.A. 1562 to bill H.R. 2500); and Sen. Graham's Intelligence to Prevent Terrorism Act (IPTA, S. 1448), and Sen. Gregg's draft anti-encryption legislation - were ill advised. Instead of catching hard core terrorists, they would only affect innocent citizens. For example by declaring computer crime terrorism acts, it resulted in serving up extensive and severe punishments for unsuspecting and not deserving "young, curious programmers, essentially pranksters" who, who left alone, might one day "grow up to be accomplished security professionals.") http://fscked.org/rants/letters/Repletter

[280] The Electronic Frontier helped to keep track of the impact of anti-terrorism measures (not all of them related to terrorism law or USAPA) from day one: "Chilling Effects of Anti-Terrorism "National Security" Toll on Freedom of Expression, including: Websites Shut Down by US Government; Websites Shut Down by Other Governments; Websites Shut Down by Internet Service Provider; Websites Shut Down or Partially Removed by Website Owner; US Government Websites That Shut Down or Removed Information; US Government Requests to Remove Information Media Professionals Terminated or Suspended; Other Employees Terminated or Suspended; Related Incidents." http://www.eff.org/Censorship/Terrorism_militias/antiterrorism _chill.php#websiteshutdownusgov

[281] "Senate OKs FBI Net Spying," *Wired*, September 11, 2001 ("Nobody really knows what routing and addressing information is.... If you're putting in addressing information and routing information, you may not just get (From: lines of e-mail messages), you might also get content," the source said.) http://www.wired.com/news/politics/0,1283,46852,00.html

liberties, e.g. how intrusive is electronic surveillance on web based activities?[282] For example, the EFF was critical of various aspects of CTA, mostly because CTA intrudes into computer users' privacy with very little safeguards: [283]

(1) CTA expands "traditional" wiretap authority beyond recognition. Before CTA, wiretap orders were authorized for a few well defined predicated offences. Now, the CTA allows for wiretapping based on loosely copulated terrorism crime (Section 833)[284] and computer offenses (Section 834).[285]

(2) CTA allows for application of "pen register" and "track and trace" to electronic communication, e.g. e-mail, web surf, URL search. The definition of pen register under the amended (18 U.S.C. § 3127(3) now reads: "a device or process which records or decodes dialing, routing, addressing, or signaling information transmitted by an instrument or facility from which a wire or electronic communication is transmitted ..." Similarly, 18 U.S.C. § 3127(4) defines "trap and trace device" as "a device or process which captures the incoming electronic or other impulses which identify the originating number or other dialing, routing, addressing, and signaling information reasonably likely to identify the source of a wire or electronic communication, provided, however, that such information shall not include the contents of any communication.." In this way, the CTA allows "pen register" to go beyond merely capturing phone numbers [286] to capture routing and addressing information, which is revealing of message content and threatening personal privacy.

(3) CTA allows for multi-jurisdiction "pen register" and "trap and trace" order. Whereas before CTA "pen register" and "trap and trace" order only apply "within the jurisdiction of the court." The CTA makes "pen register" and "trap and trace" orders applicable nation wide: "The order shall, upon service of the order, apply to any entity providing wire or electronic communication service in the United States whose assistance is required to effectuate the order." (Section 832 (b) (1).

(4) CTA lowers the threshold of court approval (i.e. based on *relevant* to ongoing criminal investigation) and minimizes judicial supervision (i.e. based on *certification* of law enforcement officials) in the application for "pen register" and "trap and trace" orders in electronic surveillance cases. Section 832 (b) (1) reads in pertinent part: "Upon an application made under section 3122(a)(1) of this title, the court *shall* enter an *ex parte* order authorizing the installation and use of a pen register or trap and trace device if the court finds that the attorney for the Government has *certified* to the court that the information likely to be obtained by such installation and use is *relevant* to an ongoing criminal investigation." (Emphasis supplied) In so doing,

---

[282] See open web e-mail to Senator Feinstein "14-09-2001: Combating Terrorism Act of 2001," http://www.kocharhook.com/nick/letters/cta2001.html

[283] *EFF Analysis of SA 1562, Subtitle B* (Sept. 19, 2001), http://www.eff.org/ (last visited October 2, 2001).

[284] SEC. 833. AUTHORITY TO INTERCEPT WIRE, ORAL, AND ELECTRONIC COMMUNICATIONS RELATING TO TERRORISM OFFENSES.

[285] SEC. 834. AUTHORITY TO INTERCEPT WIRE, ORAL, AND ELECTRONIC COMMUNICATIONS RELATING TO COMPUTER FRAUD AND ABUSE.

[286] Under the former law "pen register" and "track and trace" devices only applied to "wire" communications. Thus, a "pen register" is "a device which records or decodes electronic or other impulses which identify the numbers dialed or otherwise transmitted on the telephone line to which such device is attached ..." UNITED STATES CODE, TITLE 18 - CRIMES AND CRIMINAL PROCEDURE, PART II - CRIMINAL PROCEDURE, CHAPTER 205 - SEARCHES AND SEIZURES. Section 3127. Definitions for chapter. (3).

CTA extends the old wiretap order application standard and procedures to electronic searches.[287]

There were also grave concerns with the legislative process:

"Perhaps extending the privileges of government to limit our privacy is something that should be done in half an hour in the middle of the night, as it was here, but then again, maybe Senators Carl Levin of Michigan and Patrick Leahy of Vermont were correct, that this was all being done far too quickly, with a speed in fact that prevented most of the senators to make a full review of the legislation which was presented to them a mere half hour before they were to vote on it."[288]

Some felt that the CTA provisions were more show than substance,[289] symbolic than real.[290]

The Bush administration in general, and Attorney General Ashcroft in particular, was universally condemned for using 9/11 to introduce draconian police powers and ushering in an Owellian state with the passage of CTA – MATA - ATA – Patriot Act.[291] As lamented by Al Gore: "They have taken us much farther down the road toward an intrusive, 'big brother'-style government - toward the dangers prophesied by George Orwell in his book '1984' - than anyone ever thought would be possible in the United States of America."[292]

While Ashcroft was responsible for initiating many of the post 9/11 counter-terrorism legislation, he did not, however, draft all of them out of clean cloth. A fair reading of historical records suggests that many of the counter- terrorism measures already existed on the book and were just being applied to new situations, e.g. extending and applying "pen register" and "track and trace" to search and seizure of electronic data.[293]

---

[287] 18 U.S.C. 3223 provides in pertinent parts "the court shall enter an *ex parte* order authorizing the installation and use of a pen register or a trap and trace device within the jurisdiction of the court if the court finds that the attorney for the Government or the State law enforcement or investigative officer has certified to the court that the information likely to be obtained by such installation and use is relevant to an ongoing criminal investigation."

[288] "Combating Terrorism Act of 2001 - Analyzed (Op-Ed),"Tue Sep 18th, 2001 at 12:24:17 PM EST http://www.kuro5hin.org/story/2001/9/17/22230/2697

[289] Bob Barr the maverick Republican Representative openly questioned the necessity and utility of the CTA. "Fighting Terrorism, Preserving Civil Liberties," CATO, POLICY FORUM, Tuesday, October 2, 200. 4:00 p.m. (Featuring Rep. Bob Barr (R - Ga.), with commentary by Solveig Singleton, Senior Analyst, Competitive Enterprise Institute; Stuart Taylor, Senior Writer, National Journal; Jonathan Turley, Professor of Law, George Washington University.)

[290] "SECRECY NEWS: from the FAS Project on Government Secrecy," September 14, 2001 (Most of the post 9/11 legislations only consisted of declaration of the sense of Congress and/or requests for reports, rather than providing for new powers to fight terrorism. The exception substantive policy change was the doing away with the 1995 CIA guidelines governing the recruitment of informants who have committed human rights violations or terrorism acts.) http://www.fas.org/sgp/news/secrecy/2001/09/091401.html

[291] "Gore: Bush Has Failed to Make U.S. Safer," *Earthlink*, November 10, 2003.

[292] *Id.*

[293] See "An Analysis of How the Events of September 11 May Change Federal Law," *Tech Law Journal*, September 17, 2001.

The MATA and ATA

The drafting of USAPA started with a simple instruction from President Bush [294] to the Attorney General Ashcroft immediately after the 9/11 attack: "John, make sure this (9/11 – terrorism) can't happen again."[295] The Attorney General took the charge seriously, [296] and zealously, and above all else personally.[297]

The Drafting Process

The Attorney General turned to Viet Dinh,[298] an Assistant Attorney General in charge of Department of Justice (DOJ),[299] Office of Legal Policy, to work on an anti-terrorism package on the same day.[300] On Thursday (September 13, 2001) Dinh told Ashcroft that the package – Mobilization Anti-Terrorism Act (MATA)[301] - would be ready by Friday (September 14,

---

[294] To date, there is no investigation into the role of President Bush in the drafting and passage of the USAPA and related anti-terrorist, measures. Was President Bush a hands-off manager, aloof and detached, as many observers made him out to be? To what extent and in what manner did Bush contributed – in content and process - to the passage of the USAPA? 9/11 was a defining moment for the Bush administration. How Bush handled 9/11, from talking to the crowd at ground zero to pushing the USAPA through Congress, unmistakably reflected Bush's governing philosophy and management style.

[295] The instruction was given in the White House in the afternoon of 9/11. Steven Brill, *After: How American Confronted the September 12 Era* (N.Y.: Simon and Shuster, 2003), p. 15. (Hereinafter "After 9/11")

[296] "Attorney General Ashcroft Announces the Formation of Anti-terrorism Task Forces in U.S. Attorney Offices," DOJ, Press release, September 18, 2001; Letter to Mayors from Attorney General Ashcroft (9/19/01) (on formation of anti-terrorism task force) (September 19, 2001); Attorney General Ashcroft Directs Law Enforcement Officials to Implement New Anti-Terrorism Act, DOJ, Press release, Friday, October 26, 2001; Dan Eggen, "Ashcroft champions Patriot Act Responding to critics, attorney general says law is linchpin of war on terrorism," *San Francisco Chronicle*, Wednesday, August 20, 2003 (The Attorney General took personal charge of a national campaign (18 cities) to drum up support for the USAPA). For an assessment of Ashcroft's tenure as Attorney General and his impact on war on terrorism, see "Controversial Tenure" *PBS-Online News-hour* November 11, 2004. http://www.pbs.org/newshour/bb/law/july-dec04/ashcroft_11-11.html

[297] In public service, officials are supposed to separate private preferences from public choices. In this case, Ashcroft not only failed to draw such a distinction but actively made his own ideology, values and interests to stand for the common good of the nation; from religious beliefs, to moral values to political ideology. JUDY BACHRACH, "John Ashcroft's Patriot Games," *Vanity Fair* Feb. 1, 2004. http://www.mindfully.org/Reform/2004/Ashcroft-Patriot-Games1feb04.htm ("There are only two things you find in the middle of the road, a moderate and a dead skunk" He believes that "you can legislate morality," and that any senator who suggests otherwise will simply be legislating "immorality, and we've done too much of that already." The attorney general invested his fight for the Patriot Act with a Crusader's fervor, "questioning his opponents' patriotism…")

[298] Viet Dinh was known as the "chief architect of the USAPA. "At Home in War on Terror: Viet Dinh has gone from academe to play a key behind-the scenes role. Conservatives love him; others find his views constitutionally suspect." *Los Angeles Times* September 18, 2002. http://www.asianam.org/viet%20dinh.htm In time, he becomes the USAPA chief spokesman and main defender. His rationale for the USAPA is security before freedom; one cannot enjoy the later without the guarantee of the former. Viet Dinh "A White Paper: How Does the USAPA defends democracy." The Foundation for the Defense of Democracies, June 1, 2004.

[299] OPIC: USAPA; Interview Subject: Viet Dinh; Film: The Cost of Freedom - Civil Liberties, Security and the USAPA; Interviewer: Alison Rostankowski/Chip Duncan; Transcripts: Troy Avdek. © 2004 The Duncan Group, Inc. http://www.duncanentertainment.com/interview_vietdinh.php (Viet Dinh Interview)

[300] Another account suggested that Dinh's marching order came on September 12, 2001 (Wednesday) indirectly and by way of Adam Ciongoli, Ashcroft's counselor. Robert O'Harrow Jr., "Six Weeks in Autumn," *Washington Post* Sunday, October 27, 2002; Page W06.

[301] The original draft of the anti-terrorism package released to the Congress on September 19, 2001 was a 31 page document entitled MATA. For the proposed text of the first draft of MATA, see http://www.eff.org/Privacy/Surveillance/20010919_mata_bill_draft.html For a fair and balance analysis of original draft to MATA, see DOJ http://www.eff.org/Privacy/Surveillance/20010919_doj_mata_analysis.html

2001).[302] Dinh was assisted by David Carp, a DOJ lawyer who helped drafted the Oklahoma City (1995) anti-terrorism legislative measures, [303] with input from John Yoo who later co-authored a report to the President arguing that Geneva Conventions do not apply to Taliban or Al Qaeda fighters as a matter of international law because Afghanistan was a "failed state", and "torture" can be used.[304]

In the course of a little over six weeks a 20 – 30 pages of MATA – ATA turned into a document which was 131 pages in length with 1016 different sections.

According to Dinh his first order of business was to consult law enforcement agents and prosecutors all over the nation for their ideas on how best to fight terrorism.[305] The three criteria for suggestions from the field were: operation necessity, civil rights impact, and constitutionality. All told, fifty legislative proposals were compiled and submitted. Most of them have been proposed and considered before.[306] In fact, many of the proposed provisions in the MATA of 2001 were just off the shelf items from the 1996 anti-terrorism legislation. These included roving wiretaps, obtaining customers' information from telephone and Internet companies, and seizing of personal property.[307] Additional provisions of the proposed MATA included measures which: allowing law enforcement officials to obtain e-mail message header information; allowing law enforcement officials to gather web browsing data; [308] diluting judicial supervision over roving wiretaps;[309] allowing law enforcement officials to share wiretap information with the Executive branch; [310] allowing FISA to be used domestically; [311] allowing grand jury evidence to be shared with the US intelligence community;[312] allowing the President to designate any "foreign-directed individual, group, or

---

The second draft of the MATA, a 21 pages bill, rendered on September 19, 2001 – 12.30 pm, was entitled ATA of 2001. For text of second draft of MATA a/k/a ATA, see http://www.cdt.org/security/010920bill_text.pdf

For DOJ analysis of second draft of MATA, i.e. ATA, see http://www.cdt.org/security/010919terror.pdf Draft 9/19 12:30 pm [ET] Since then MATA and ATA has been interchangeably used to refer to both drafts. As late as September 24, 2001, the Attorney General still referred to the second draft MATA, when people outside the administration have correctly identity it as ATA. See "Attorney General Ashcroft Outlines Mobilization Against Terrorism Act," USDOJ September 24, 2001. http://www.usdoj.gov/opa/pr/2001/September/492ag.htm

[302] "After 9/11," *supra* note 66, p. 52.

[303] *Ibid.* p. 53.

[304] "Application of Treaties and Laws to Al Qaeda and Taliban Detainees" (Jan. 9. 2002) (with Robert J. Delahunty). See "The Bush Administration Torture Memo Scandal," http://texscience.org/reform/torture/

[305] This consultation process (if substantiated) contradicted the common impression and repeated allegations that the Bush administration has not done enough to incorporate different ideas and opposing views in the drafting process. Alternative, the USAPA was an ideological statement, not a consultative or consultation document. A question still remains, why was the ATA – MATA – USAPA bill not distributed for comments through the proper channels, i.e. through OMB onto each and every related and affected agencies.

[306] This detracted from opponents' argument that the USAPA provisions need to be thoroughly researched and critically examined. See Viet Dinh Interview.

[307] There was an inconsistency in positions offered by the opponents to the Act, i.e. the USAPA contained new and radical provisions vs. USAPA contained old and tested rules. Jennifer Van Bergen, "The USAPA Was Planned Before 9/11," *Truthout.org*, 20 May, 2002 ("Many people do not know that the USAPA was already written and ready to go long before September 11th.") http://www.truthout.org/docs_02/05.21B.jvb.usapa.911.htm

[308] SEC. 103. MODIFICATION OF AUTHORITIES RELATING TO USE OF PEN REGISTERS AND TRAP AND TRACE DEVICES (2) (A) and 3 (B).

[309] SEC. 106. MULTI-POINT WIRETAPS.

[310] SEC. 108. AUTHORIZED DISCLOSURE.

[311] SEC. 157. PEN REGISTER AND TRAP AND TRACE AUTHORITY.

[312] SEC. 154. FOREIGN INTELLIGENCE INFORMATION SHARING.

entity, including any United States citizen or organization" as fitting for FISA surveillance;[313] preventing people from exercising their first amendment rights in discussing terrorism related matters;[314] establishing a DNA database for every criminals and certain sex offenders.[315]

Gathering Opposition

Meantime, the first attempt to organize different opposition interest groups into a viable political coalition started to take shape. It later became a thorn to Bush administration's effort in crating a garrison state. The impetus and agenda for the organization effort was bested summed up by Nat Hentoff, a longtime activities of civil rights causes and key members to the group:

> To save our liberties, we have to organize nationally—as was done effectively in the civil rights and antiwar campaigns of the 1960s. There are already a large number of groups that can and should form an *organizing* and educational network to put ads in newspapers and on radio and television, set up teach-ins on campuses and in town meetings around the country, and plan a March on Washington on the order of the 1963 assembly addressed by Martin Luther King ("I Have a Dream").[316]

On September 14, 2001 (Thursday), Halperin and ACLU called a meeting at the ACLU white townhouse in D.C. to discuss strategy in how to deal with 9/11 counter-terrorism measures. Participants came with different ideologies, interests, agenda and political affiliation. They come together to oppose ill advised 9/11 legislations. For example, People for the American Way was formed in the 1981 to fight right-wing extremist. The group joined to protect minority and civil rights and minorities rights. [317] Project on Government Accountability (at George Mason University) was formed to improve government policy and decision making. The group joined to promote government accountability.[318] The Free Congress Foundation was dedicated to preserving traditional American way of life. The group joined to check expansion of Federal power at the expense of the state and invididuals.[319] Finally, the Competitive Enterprise Institute was dedicated to advancing free market and limited government. The group joined to reduce government regulation in the name or as a result of war on terrorism.[320]

The coalition decided to issue a 10 points public statement calling for a more reflective and rational debate before adopting any anti-terrorism measures as follows:

---

[313] SEC. 156, DEFINITION.
[314] SEC.202. DEFINITIONS RELATING TO TERRORISM
[315] SEC.356. DNA IDENTIFICATION OF TERRORISTS
[316] Nat Hentoff, "Getting Back Our Rights Don't Brood and Despair. Organize!" *Village Voce*, December 7th, 2001 2:45 PM http://www.villagevoice.com/news/0150,hentoff,30634,6.html
[317] "Statement of People for the American Way President G Ralph Neas." September 20, 2001. http://www.indefenseoffreedom.org/statements/pfaw_release.pdf
[318] "Whistle Blowers are Modern Paul Reveres Against Terrorism," September 20, 2001 http://www.indefenseoffreedom.org/statements/gap_release.pdf
[319] "Free Congress: Established Online Petition" September 20, 2001http://www.indefenseoffreedom.org/statements /freecongress_release.pdf
[320] http://www.cei.org/pages/about.cfm

In Defense of Freedom[321]

1. On September 11, 2001 thousands of people lost their lives in a brutal assault on the American people and the American form of government. We mourn the loss of these innocent lives and insist that those who perpetrated these acts be held accountable.

2. This tragedy requires all Americans to examine carefully the steps our country may now take to reduce the risk of future terrorist attacks.

3. We need to consider proposals calmly and deliberately with a determination not to erode the liberties and freedoms that are at the core of the American way of life.

4. We need to ensure that actions by our government uphold the principles of a democratic society, accountable government and international law, and that all decisions are taken in a manner consistent with the Constitution.

5. We can, as we have in the past, in times of war and of peace, reconcile the requirements of security with the demands of liberty.

6. We should resist the temptation to enact proposals in the mistaken belief that anything that may be called anti-terrorist will necessarily provide greater security.

7. We should resist efforts to target people because of their race, religion, ethnic background or appearance, including immigrants in general, Arab Americans and Muslims.

8. We affirm the right of peaceful dissent, protected by the First Amendment, now, when it is most at risk.

9. We should applaud our political leaders in the days ahead who have the courage to say that our freedoms should not be limited.

10. We must have faith in our democratic system and our Constitution, and in our ability to protect at the same time both the freedom and the security of all Americans.

The "In Defense of Freedom statement" above was endorsed by more than 150 organizations, [322] 300 law professors, and 40 computer scientists.[323]

Explaining and Promoting the Law

On September 16, 2001, Attorney General John Ashcroft announced his intention to ask Congress for more powers to fight terrorism. Subsequently on Monday, September 17, 2001, Ashcroft discussed the details of an anti-terrorist package he intended to send to the Congress:

> "Yesterday I met with several members of the House and Senate leadership, including the leadership of the Intelligence and Judiciary Committees. FBI Director Mueller and I discussed with them the current threat assessment, including our belief that associates of the hijackers that have ties to terrorist organizations may be a continuing presence in the United States. This

---

[321] The statements in text is a verbatim account from http://www.indefenseoffreedom.org/

[322] Some of these included NAACP Board of Directors; National Association of Criminal Defense Lawyers; National Council of Churches of Christ, National Council of La Raza, National Gay and Lesbian Task Force, National Lawyers Guild, National Native American Bar Association, NOW Legal Defense and Education Fund, Physicians for Human Rights, Rutherford Institute; the American-Arab Anti-Discrimination Committee; American Federation of State, County, and Municipal Employees; Amnesty International USA; Baptist Joint Committee on Public Affairs; Center for Constitutional Rights; Free Congress Foundation; Gun Owners of America; Leadership Conference on Civil Rights.

[323] http://www.indefenseoffreedom.org/

threat assessment has helped us to identify several areas where we should strengthen our laws to increase the ability of the Department of Justice and its component agencies to identify, prevent and punish terrorism ...In the next few days, we intend to finalize a package of legislative measures that will be comprehensive. Areas covered include criminal justice, immigration, intelligence gathering and financial infrastructure..."[324]

The proposed anti-terrorists legislation substantially enhances the intelligence gathering capacity of law enforcement officials, including:

First, allowing wiretapping of persons, instead on just a phone number:
"And given the nature and availability of literally disposable telephones in modern society, we need to be able to have the court authority to monitor, not the phone, but the telephone communications of a person."[325]

Second, allowing for a nationally valid wiretapping order ("roving"):
"so that one wiretap approval can be obtained for all jurisdictions working on an investigation, particularly given the mobility of individuals and the capacity of individuals who are mobile to communicate."[326]

Third, making sure that terrorism offenses are treated the same as other serious crimes. "For example, we are identifying instances where the law currently makes it easier to prosecute drug trafficking and organized crime or espionage than it is to prosecute terrorism...We think this reflects an inadequate response to the kind of threat that terrorism poses to our culture." [327]

Finally, the proposed legislation makes: "providing material support or resources to a terrorist organization an offense that would enable us to prosecute someone under the money laundering statutes."[328]

On September 19, 2001 congressional members, White House and justice department leadership gathered formally to exchange proposals and informally to negotiate for a compromise. Attorney General John Ashcroft distributed the proposed MATA to members of Congress.[329] The Attorney General further "demanded" the MATA to be passed within the week, i.e. in two more days,[330] with a dire warning issued on September 24, 2001 at a Congressional hearing:

---

[324] Attorney General John Ashcroft Remarks, Press Briefing with FBI Director Robert Mueller, FBI headquarters, September 17, 2001. http://www.yale.edu/lawweb/avalon/sept_11/doj_brief002.htm

[325] *Id.*

[326] *Id.*

[327] *Id.*

[328] http://www.patriotresource.com/wtc/federal/0917/AGFBI.html

[329] "DOJ's Anti-Terrorism Law Would Dismantle Civil Liberties, Legislate to Improve Security Not Eliminate Freedoms," Electronic Frontier Foundation Media Release, September 19, 2001. http://peacenowar.net/Sep%2019%2001--EFF.htm

[330] http://www.patriotresource.com/wtc/federal/0917/AGFBI.html

"Everyday that passes with outdated statutes and the old rules of engagement, each day that so passes is a day that terrorists have a competitive advantage. Until Congress makes these changes we are fighting an unnecessary uphill battle." [331]

Running into Obstacles

While the MATA was not well received on the Hill, [332] the Congress nevertheless promised expedited action. House Judiciary Committee Chairman F. James Sensenbrenner, Jr. (R-Wis.) declared that the leadership: "intend to have the House Judiciary Committee hold a legislative hearing followed by a full committee markup as soon as possible once legislation is introduced."[333]

In the face of an imminent and oppressive MATA, EFF Executive Director Shari Steele sounded the all familiar alarm against emergence legislations: no trading of civil liberties for national security:

"One particularly egregious section of the DOJ's analysis of its proposed legislation says that "United States prosecutors may use against American citizens information collected by a foreign government even if the collection would have violated the Fourth Amendment." [334]

EFF Senior Staff Attorney Lee Tien followed with an ominous warning: Americans could be paying a high price in the war on terror if were to give up our liberties and dilute the nation's Constitution to fight terrorism. , another point of contention in the looming war of ideas (and works) over how to fight terror without (too much) sacrifice.[335] Finally, the EFF

---

[331] Such strong languages, while reflecting a sense of urgency and frustration in the face of crisis, was most unhelpful in promoting cooperation and between the two branches of government The ascendancy of the Executive branch of government and diminution of constitutional check and balance process in time of war has began. "Ashcroft Asks Congress for Anti-Terrorism Measures," *PBS* September 24, 2001, 5:45pm EST

[332] Brandon Spun, "Attorney General John Ashcroft Fails to Justify Encroachment of Civil Liberties," *Insight Magazine*, 9/25/01 (In spite of the Attorney General's plead for expedited action on MATA - "The American people do not have the luxury of unlimited time in erecting the necessary defenses to future terrorism attacks." The law makers were more reticent, preferring to take a more wait and see approach. The immigrant provisions in Part II were found to be most objectionable. "Reps. Steve Chabot (R-Ohio), John Conyers (D-Mich.) and Zoe Lofgren (D-Calif.) shared their concern that such stipulations may allow for the indefinite and discriminatory detainment of aliens…Rep. Jerrold Nadler (D-N.Y.) was unwilling to give an attorney general "carte blanche" in deciding whether an already detained alien posed a threat to national security and how long the detainment of such an individual, if determined dangerous, could last". While Rep. Barney Frank (D-Mass.) was concerned with "inappropriate release of information", Judiciary Committee members Reps. Maxine Waters (D-Calif.) and Bob Barr (R-Ga.) wanted more time to study the document.)

[333] "Sensenbrenner Statement on Bush Administration's Anti-terrorism "Working Draft" Legislation," U.S. House of Representatives Committee on the Judiciary, F. James Sensenbrenner, Jr., Chairman. September 19, 2001. http://www.house.gov/judiciary/news091901.htm

[334] *Id.*

[335] The security vs. liberty debate raised two kinds of issues. First, whether it is ever worth sacrificing liberty for security, as a proposition: Constitutional is not a suicide pack vs. "Those Who Sacrifice Liberty For Security Deserve Neither" (Benjamin Franklin). Richard A. Posner, *Not A Suicide Pact: The Constitution In A Time of National Emergency*, (New York: Oxford University Press, 2006) vs. Romero, "In Defense of Liberty at a Time of National Emergency," HUMAN RIGHTS MAGAZINE (Winter 2002). http://www.abanet.org/irr/hr/winter02/romero.html Second, whether sacrificing liberty can give us more security, empirically. Or conversely liberty is not incompatible with security. This in fact was the strategy taken by ACUL. ACLU's web site adopted the banner: "SAFE AND FREE". See also James Dempsey, "Preliminary Analysis: Anti-Terrorism Act Expands Government Surveillance Authorities, Weakens Privacy Protection with No Clear Benefit to Security," Center for Democracy and Technology, September 21, 2001. http://www.netcaucus.org/books/surveillance2001/docs/010921cdt.pdf

issued a call to arms, asking its member to protest against the impending anti-terrorism laws, starting with a nation wide write in campaign.[336]

Originally, Attorney General Ashcroft was counting on Rep. James Sensenbrenner (R-WI), Chairman of the House Judiciary Committee, for a speedy passage of this legislation. Rep. Sensenbrenner planned to hold hearings on Monday (9/24), conduct a mark up session on Tuesday (9/25), and then take the bill to the House floor for a final vote and (assured) passage before the House breaks for the Yom Kippur holiday on Thursday (9/27). However, at the Committee hearing on Monday afternoon all Democrats and a few Republicans expressed strong opposition to this expedited schedule. By the end of the hearing Rep. Sensenbrenner agreed to postpone mark up for another week, i.e. into October.

Meanwhile, Sen. Patrick Leahy (D-VT), Chairman of the Senate Judiciary Committee, has already indicated that his Committee might take weeks to pass a bill. The senate Judicial Committee was scheduled to hold a hearing on Tuesday, September 25, 2001.

Once tabled, ATA was widely attacked from liberals and conservatives alike. President George Bush has to come to its defense. On September 25, 2001, the President for the first time openly embraced the ATA and advocated for its passage in a policy speech at FBI:

> "I hope Congress will ... give the tools necessary to our agents in the field to find those who may think they want to disrupt America again. We're asking Congress for the authority to hold suspected terrorists who are in the process of being deported, until they're deported...And we're asking for the authority to share information between intelligence operations and law enforcement ..." [337]

On September 27, 2001, President Bush issued yet another statement in support at the CIA. Finally, on September 29, 2001, the President, frustrated by the delay, appealed directly to the people in his weekly radio address:

> "I'm asking Congress for new law enforcement authority, to better track the communications of terrorists, and to detain suspected terrorists until the moment they are deported. I will also seek more funding and better technology for our country's intelligence community." [338]

Meantime, on September 24, 2001, the House Judiciary Committee held a "briefing" for civil liberties groups regarding the ATA of 2001. [339] As expected, critics of the ATA raised substantial civil rights concerns,[340] including:

---

[336] "Cyber rights groups urges defeat of 'Anti-Terrorism" Act'http://groups.yahoo.com/group/portside/message/1413

[337] "President: FBI Needs Tools to Track Down Terrorists: Remarks by the President to Employees at the Federal Bureau of Investigation, FBI Headquarters," The White House. Office of the Press Secretary, September 25, 2000 http://www.whitehouse.gov/news/releases/2001/09/20010925-5.html

[338] Radio Address of the President to the Nation, The White House, September 29, 2001.

[339] Strategically, the Chairman of the House Judiciary Committee, Rep. Sensenbrenner, did not want to have Attorney General and the ACLU appearing on the same day as co-equal. Sensenbrenner also did not want to give ACLU and other civil liberties organizations a forum to argue their case and promote their cause at the risk of derailing the ATA passage. Tech Law Journal Daily E-Mail Alert, September 25, 2001, 9:00 AM ET, Alert No. 272. http://www.techlawjournal.com/alert/2001/09/25.asp

[340] For a Congressional reaction to the ATA, see Brandon Spun, "Judiciary Committee Balks at Proposed Antiterrorism Act," Insight Magazine (Sept. 25, 2001), at http://www.citizenreviewonline.org/sept_2001/judiciary_committee.htm. (Rep. Jerrold Nadler (D-N.Y.) was unwilling to allow the Attorney General to decide whether an alien should be detained indefinitely as a national security threat. Rep. Barney Frank (D-

James Dempsey[341] and Morton Halperin[342] both objected to the proposed changes to the FISA and associated electronic surveillance procedures. The CDT was also displeased with defining hacking as terrorism and allowing IPS to monitor clients account.[343]

While Greg Nojeim (ACLU) raised electronic surveillance issues, David Cole (Georgetown University Law Center) articulated immigration concerns. For Brad Jansen (Free Congress Foundation), he was concerned with money laundering and forfeiture issues and Rachel King (ACLU) was troubled over criminal law problems.[344]

Finally, People For the American Way had called for public hearings on the proposed 9/11 legislations. Legislations should only be passed if they adheres to three basic principles:

(1) The provisions should be carefully drafted to preserve constitutional liberties and to prevent abuse of power;
(2) There should be meaningful judicial review and strict congressional oversight;
(3) Anti-terrorism laws should be narrowly tailored to achieve clearly stated goals and objectives. [345]

The Attorney General's pushed for early adoption of ATA backfired for a number of reasons. First, the Attorney General has failed to discuss with the White House and consulted with key administrative officials before making the ATA public.[346] Under the leadership of Dinh, it was very much a DOJ production. For example, Joshua Bolten the deputy chief of staff of the White House was kept in the dark until the ninth hour. Likewise, the White House legal counsel's and legislative affairs office were not advised. None of the government departments were informed or consulted. They did not even have a copy of the proposal before Monday September 17, 2001. [347]

Second, the Attorney General has failed to sought support from key Congressional leadership, choosing instead to adopt an us (administration) vs. them (the world – court, Congress, interest groups, dissenters) attitude, and a "take it or leave it" approach. The Bush administration has decided early on the USAPA legislative process not to seek a negotiated bill (with Congress) but preferred to impose an all or nothing law. For example, the powerful

---

Mass.) objected to FBI spying on American, as in the case of Rev. Martin Luther King Jr. Judiciary Committee members Reps. Maxine Waters (D-Calif.) and Bob Barr (R-Ga.) did not want to rush the USAPA without the proper hearing and deliberation, since many of the provisions are very controversial (such as computer surveillance and data mining) and had been rejected by the committee before.)

[341] Statement of James X. Dempsey, Deputy Director, Center for Democracy and Technology, before the House Committee on the Judiciary on Legislative Measures to Improve America's Counter-Terrorism Programs, September 24, 2001. http://www.cdt.org/testimony/010924dempsey.shtml

[342] Statement of Morton H. Halperin, Chair, Advisory Board, and Kate Martin, Director, on behalf of the Center for National Security Studies. Before the Permanent Select Committee on Intelligence of the United States Senate on Legislative Proposals in the Wake of the September 11, 2001 Attacks. Including the Intelligence to Prevent Terrorism Act of 2001, S. 1448. September 24, 2001. http://www.cnss.org/mhtest0924.htm

[343] Declan McCullagh, "Anti-Terror Bill Not Done Yet," *Wired News* 02:00 AM Sep. 29, 2001 PT http://www.wired.com/news/conflict/0,2100,47199,00.html

[344] See, Rachel King, Legislative Counsel, American Civil Liberties Union, Washington National Office, Statement on Anti-Terrorism Act OF 2001, Before The House Judiciary Committee, September 24, 2001. http://www.aclu.org/natsec/emergpowers/14393leg20010924.html

[345] "Bipartisan Anti-Terrorism Bill Abandoned in House, Civil Liberties Protections Sacrificed to Administration Pressure," http://www.citizenreviewonline.org/oct_2001/bipartisan_antiterrorism_bill.htm

[346] The Bill was not vetted by respective agencies through MBO but instead drafted by the DOJ lawyers alone; a most unusual process.

[347] "After 9/11," *supra* note 66, p. 75. (Source Bolten, see p. 646).

Republic chairman of the Judiciary Committee, Sensenbrenner, only heard about the ATA package on the morning of September 16, 2001 at home while Ashcroft was making the announcement on TV in a talk show.[348] House Speaker Dennis Hasket was likewise not informed.[349] Sensenbrenner was finally given a fax copy of the proposed ATA in the evening.[350] In this regard, the Bush administration claimed (incorrectly) absolute President power to lead the nation in time of war[351] and relied (correctly) on total public support of the President in time of a national crisis.[352]

The first sign of trouble came when Sensenbrenner informed Ashcroft that while he was eager to work with Ashcroft his cooperation was not to be taken for granted. Still, Ashcroft was unyielding and unapologetic.[353] To demonstrate his resolve - seriousness and power, Sensenbrenner insisted upon having the Attorney General removed the suspension of habeas provision in the original ATA draft before reaching his committee.[354]

Third, the Attorney General underestimated the political resistant he was to encounter, particularly from members of his own party, such as Bob Barr. He certainly did not anticipate ACLU joining cause with Bob Barr in seeking the delay, if not derailment, of the ATA.[355] On September 21, 2001 (Friday), Bob Barr with four other members of the House Judiciary Committee sent a letter, drafted by ACLU, to Sensenbrenner listing their concerns with the ATA as proposed. The letter particularly listing ten provisions that required significant "further public debate" before final adoption.[356] The letter sealed the fate of an early passage of the ATA as planned. By September 25, 2001 ATA was dead on arrival.[357]

The USA ACT

The democratic response to ATA (later USAPA) was the USA ACT Senate bill 1510[358] Senator Leachy, Chairman of Senate Judiciary Committee along with the Democratic majority leader, Senator Daschle, and the Republican minority leader, Senator Lott, also the chairmen of the Banking and Intelligence Committees, Senators Sarbanes, Graham, Hatch, and Shelby introduced the USA ACT on October 4, 2001.

---

[348] After 9/11," *supra* note 71, p. 73. (Source Sensenbrenner, see p. 646).

[349] *Ibid.* p. 73. (Source Sensenbrenner, see p. 646). Hasket was unhappy at not being kept informed, and still less not being consulted, p. 74.

[350] *Ibid.* p. 74 (Source Sensenbrenner, see p. 646).

[351] John Dean, "PRESIDENTIAL POWERS IN TIMES OF EMERGENCY: Could Terrorism Result In A Constitutional Dictator?," *Finalw.com* Friday, Jun. 07, 2002. http://writ.news.findlaw.com/dean/ 20020607.html

[352] Brian J. Gaines, *"Where's the Rally? Approval and Trust of the President, Cabinet, Congress, and Government Since September 11,"* PS: Political Science and Poli*t*ics, *Volume 35 (3): 531-536 (2002). (President Bush popularity rating went up precipitously (in less than one week) and to unprecedented high level (90%) after 911. There it stayed for a long time.) http://www.apsanet.org/imgtest/Where'stheRally-Gaines.pdf*

[353] *Ibid.*

[354] *Ibid.*

[355] *Ibid.* p. 121.

[356] *Ibid.*

[357] *Ibid.*

[358] Senate Bill 1510 was introduced by Senator Daschle for himself and Senators Lott, Leahy, Hatch, Graham, Shelby and Sarbanes

Partisan Politics

Originally the USA ACT was to be tabled for a vote on October 9, 2004. But in the last minute, after an all-night negotiation by the Senate leadership the USA ACT was withdrawn. A brand new "bi-partisan" bill was introduced. The majority leader, Senator Daschle of South Dakota, called for unanimous consent to bring the bill to a floor vote without debate or amendment. This was postponed for two days to accommodate Senator Feingold's amendments.[359] The Senate finally passed the USA ACT on October 11th 2001 [360] after a brief (4 hours) of debate.[361]

For two weeks, the USA ACT became a tedious negotiation between Democratic Chairman Patrick Leahy and Republican Ranking Member Orrin Hatch in the Senate Judiciary Committee, as representing the legislative branch on the one hand, and the Department of Justice as representing the executive branch on the other. The negotiation was a difficult, tortuous and meandering one. The difficulties resulted as much from bitter partisanship in the Senate as it is from an overbearing Attorney General[362] and obstinate President.[363] After all, it was Ashcroft who made national and international news with this inflammatory statement which united the oppositions to the USAPA:

> "To those who pit Americans against immigrants, citizens against non-citizens, to those who scare peace-loving people with phantoms of lost liberty, my message is this: Your tactics only aid terrorists for they erode our national unity and diminish our resolve... They give ammunition to America's enemies and pause to America's friends. They encourage people of good will to remain silent in the face of evil"[364]

Thus observed, legislative conflicts resulted from disagreeable style rather than disagreeing positions. Impasses over policy were caused by clashes of ideology more so than parting of interests.

The USA Act having passed in the Senate was defeated in the House.[365]

Partisanship ruled the day. Senators were voting along party lines, not reason, logic, and most certainly not facts and evidence. For example, provisions that have been rejected by

---

[359] Senate Debate on The Uniting and Strengthening America Act of 2001, Congressional Record: October 11, 2001 (Senate), Page S10547-S10630, S10570http://www.fas.org/sgp/congress/2001/s101101.html

[360] While the final USAPA was much improved over the original (September 19, 2001 MATA aka ATA) draft, it did not go far enough in protecting citizens' rights. For example, the original Administration proposal allowed the use of foreign law enforcement agencies' wiretapped information in U.S. criminal proceedings as against U.S. citizens; the freezing of non-criminal assets before trial and conviction; and obtaining of educational records without a court order. All of these objectionable provisions were either removed nor revised in the final bill. "Statement of Senator Patrick Leahy The Uniting And Strengthening of America Act Of 2001 ("USA ACT")" (October 9, 2001) http://leahy.senate.gov/press/200110/100901a.html

[361] Senate Debate on The Uniting and Strengthening America Act of 2001, Congressional Record: October 11, 2001 (Senate), Page S10547-S10630 http://www.fas.org/sgp/congress/2001/s101101.html

[362] "The 9/11 Commission: Justice's Blind Spot," *MSNBC* April 2004. ("Ashcroft seemed at once overbearing and naive.") http://www.msnbc.msn.com/id/4711886/

[363] Mike Allen and David S. Broder, "Bush's Leadership Style: Decisive or Simplistic?" *Washington Post* Monday, August 30, 2004; Page A01. (Mitchell E. Daniels Jr., Bush's first budget director: "He would pick the basic trajectory, and he was pretty resolute then about sticking with the policies it required ...He never thought about reversing course." http://www.washingtonpost.com/wp-dyn/articles/A45277-2004Aug29.html

[364] "Ashcroft: Critics of new terror measures undermine effort," *CNN.com* December 7, 2001 Posted: 9:58 AM EST (1458 GMT). http://archives.cnn.com/2001/US/12/06/inv.ashcroft.hearing/

[365] Declan McCullagh, "USA Act Stampedes Through," *Wired News* 2001-10-25 14:00:00.0.

prior Republican Senators as an encroachment on liberty under the Clinton administration were now supported by the same Senators as promoting security of the nation post 9/11.

> "In fact, then Sen. Ashcroft voted to table that amendment, and my good friend from Utah, Senator Hatch, spoke against it and opined, "I do not think we should expand the wiretap laws any further. " I recall Senator Hatch's concern then that "We must ensure that in our response to recent terrorist acts, we do not destroy the freedoms that we cherish."[366]

An Overbearing Attorney General

An overbearing, and over-confident, Attorney General with an overwhelming public support was quick to browbeat meek (thoughtful?) opposing lawmakers into submission. Those who spoke up to the Administration were not only considered as weak and indecisive, but labeled as disloyal and unpatriotic. The Attorney General also demonstrated his contempt for Congress by not keep faith with negotiated anti-terrorism terms. Senator Leahy bitterly observed:

> "On several key issues that are of particular concern to me, we had reached an agreement with the Administration on Sunday, September 30. Unfortunately, within two days, the Administration announced that it was reneging on the deal. I appreciate the complex task of considering the concerns and missions of multiple federal agencies, and that sometimes agreements must be modified as their implications are scrutinized by affected agencies."[367]

For example, negotiated agreement to allow for judicial supervision of grand jury testimony released to executive branch for intelligence purposes was reneged within two days of September 30, 2001.[368]

The Content of USA ACT

The USA ACT was a collective effort of many Senators. Senator Leahy drafted the original USA ACT.[369] It included Intelligence Committee provisions sponsored by then Chairman Bob Graham;[370] Banking Committee money laundering provisions[371] and other provisions proposed by other Senators.

The USA ACT adopted a more balanced and integrated approach in providing security for the nation after 9/11. In terms of legislative process, USA ACT differed from ATA in one major respect, USA ACT was a bi-partisan and inter-branch legislation. As Senator Patrick Leahy put it:

---

[366] Statement of Senator Patrick Leahy The Uniting And Strengthening of America Act Of 2001. (October 9, 2001), para. 8.

[367] *Id.* para. 9.

[368] *Id.*

[369] Mainly on securing Northern border, providing for the needs of victims and State and local law enforcement, and criminal law improvements. Leahy initial proposals were given to the AG on September 19, 2001, the day the AG unveiled his ATA effort. *Id.* Para. 5.

[370] Senator Graham's Anti-Terrorism Bill: "Intelligence to Prevent Terrorism Act of 2001," Sept. 23, 2001. ttp://www.cdt.org/security/010923ipta.pdf

[371] Senator Levine (D-MI), Hearing of Committee on Banking, Housing and Urban Affairs on Money Laundering and Terrorism, September 26, 2001. http://levin.senate.gov/newsroom/release.cfm?id=211390 Terrorism was provided in Title III to USAPA.

"This is not the bill that I, or any of the sponsors, would have written if compromise were unnecessary. Nor is the bill the Administration initially proposed and the Attorney General delivered to us on September 19, at a meeting in the Capitol...

In negotiations with the Administration, I have done my best to strike a reasonable balance between the need to address the threat of terrorism, which we all keenly feel at the present time, and the need to protect our constitutional freedoms. Despite my misgivings, I have consented to some of the Administration's proposals because it is important to preserve national unity in this time of crisis and to move the legislative process forward."[372]

The USA ACT was sold as a work in progress. As it stood, the House version of the USA Act of 2001 as passed on October 12, 2001 (HR 3108) was a compromise between the House PATRIOT ACT (HR2975) and Senate USA ACT (S. 1510) (passed on October 11, 2001). The majority staff who prepared the House USA ACT of 2001 was instructed to start with the Senate version of USA ACT and jettison provisions that were not compatible with the House's version, e.g. adopted a 5 years instead of 2 years sunset clause for selected provisions. The Senate's USA ACT was used as the foundation for negotiation because it was already a work of compromise incorporating many of the Administration desired and Senate accepted provisions, during the last three weeks of negotiation. Some of the more significant provisions included, provisions providing for (1) modernization of pen register and trap and trap law, i.e. authority to capture address not content; (2) nation wide service of electronic warrant and terrorism warrant; (3) "roving wiretap" of target's phone; (4) FISA wiretap after showing that terrorist investigation is "a significant" reason of wiretap probe; (5) sharing of "foreign intelligence information", including grand jury testimony, between law enforcement and intelligence community, (6) expanded authority to obtain business information with FISA order by "certifying to the court that information is relevant to on going foreign intelligence investigation; (7) 5 years sunset on selected provisions with civil liberties implications.[373]

It was understood that US ACT would be most likely be subjected to future judicial scrutiny (on Constitutionality) and Congressional oversight hearings (on implementation).[374]

Substantively, the USA ACT was more comprehensive in scope, defined in focus, integrative in approach and broad in operations. For example, in terms of scope, the ACT did not stop at giving the federal government more power to fight terrorism. It also provided compensation for victims and liabilities for terrorism workers.[375] In terms of focus, the ACT protected civil liberties and individual rights by punishing "hate crime" (against Islamic people).[376] In terms of integration, the ACT invited and engaged the state and local law enforcement authorities to play a key role in fighting terrorism, alongside with the Federal government.[377] In terms of broadness, the ACT moved from reacting to terrorism to preemptively neutralize the terrorism threats.[378]

---

[372] "Statement of Senator Patrick Leahy The Uniting And Strengthening of America Act Of 2001 ("USA ACT")" (October 9, 2001) http://leahy.senate.gov/press/200110/100901a.html

[373] See Judiciary Committee Majority Staff Description of the House bill, as of Friday morning, Oct. 12, 2001. http://www.cdt.org/security/011012patriotinfo.pdf

[374] "Statement of Senator Patrick Leahy The Uniting And Strengthening of America Act Of 2001 ("USA ACT")" (October 9, 2001). para. 4.

[375] See "VICTIMS" *Id.* para.15 – 24, esp. 20.

[376] See "HATE CRME", para. 25 – 26, esp. 36.

[377] See "STATE AND LOCAL LAW ENFORCEMENT", para. 27 – 37.

[378] See "NORTHERN BORDERS" *Id.* para. 38 to 42, esp. 40 – 42.

The lone dissenter to the USA ACT was Senator Feingold (D-Wisconsin. His major concerns were four folds. First, the nation should not rush to judgment; haste makes waste.[379] Second, as a nation we should learn from history and not make the same mistakes we did when we passed the Alien and Sedition Acts and suspended habeas corpus during the Civil War, interned Japanese-Americans during World War II, blacklisted communist sympathizers during the McCarthy era, and harassed antiwar protesters during the Vietnam war.[380] We should secure the nation without losing sight of the nation's Constitution and the people's rights. Third, the Senate has an important Constitutional role to play in providing meaningful scrutiny for the bill.[381] Fourth, the Administration should not be allowed to use the (9/11) occasion to seek unlimited and unsupervised executive powers.[382] Fifth, the nation should fight security without destroying our treasured civil liberties.

Specifically, Feingold supported the idea of "roving wiretaps" but objected to its indiscriminate application, e.g., to permit eavesdrop when the targeted person is not the one using the phone. He objected to unsupervised police access to any electronic data - typed or stored, or "tangible" information just with an administrative order. He objected to "sneak and peek" which allowed the police to search people's place without notifying the person involved. He objected to allowing system administrators at universities or libraries to monitor private net activities of "computer trespasser."[383]

When USA ACT came to a floor vote, Senate Feingold negotiated for three amendments, all of them were defeated, though not without some consoling support and soul searching comments from Senate colleagues, afterward.

From PATRIOT ACT to USA PATRIOT ACT

The current USAPA found its genesis in the PATRIOT ACT, introduced as House bill 2975 on October 2, 2001.[384] The PATRIOT ACT incorporated most of the administration ATA provisions and expanded on them.[385]

---

[379] Senate Debate on The Uniting and Strengthening America Act of 2001, Congressional Record: October 11, 2001 (Senate), Page S10547-S10630, S10571 ("But I still believe we needed a more deliberative process on this bill, and more careful consideration of the civil liberties implication of it.") http://www.fas.org/sgp/congress/2001/s101101.html

[380] Id.

[381] Id. ("We took an oath to support and defend the Constitution of the United States. In these difficult times that oath becomes all the more significant.")

[382] Id. ("Why does the administration insist on leaving open the possibility that this provision will be abused to entirely eliminate the privacy of students' and library patrons' computer communications? Is there a hidden agenda here? ")

[383] "A Senator's Lonely Privacy Fight," Wired News: 06:08 AM Oct. 11, 2001 PT http://www.wired.com/news/conflict/0,2100,47490,00.html?tw=wn_story_related

[384] *Substantively*, the PATRIOT ACT (HR 2975) was based on Administrative anti-terrorism proposals contained in CTA, MATA, ATA. H.R. 2975 - Provide Appropriate Tools Required To Intercept and Obstruct Terrorism (PATRIOT) Act (Rep. Sensenbrenner (R) Wisconsin). Oct. 12, 2001. OBM. ("H.R. 2975 includes the provisions proposed by the Administration in three main areas: (1) information gathering and sharing; (2) substantive criminal law and criminal procedure; and (3) immigration procedures.") http://www.whitehouse.gov/omb/legislative/sap/107-1/HR2975-h.html. *Procedurally*: A version of H.R. 2975 was passed by the House Committee on the Judiciary unanimously, i.e. 36 to nothing. The House then passed H.R. 2975 by a vote of 337 to 79.

[385] R. 2975 was introduced by Representative Sensenbrenner for himself and Representatives Conyers, Hyde, Coble, Goodlatte, Jenkins, Jackson-Lee, Cannon, Meehan, Graham, Bachus, Wexler, Hostettler, Keller, Issa,

The Negotiated Settlement

The PATRIOT ACT was the negotiated product of Republican Congressman Jim Sensenbrenner of Wisconsin, Chairman of the Judiciary Committee, and John Conyers, Ranking Democrat from Michigan.

In the Senate "on October 12, 2001, after another all-night drafting session, a text was produced that had only minor changes from the Senate-passed bill. It was rushed to the floor and passed with only three Republican and 75 Democratic votes in opposition. Thus by Friday, October 12, both houses had passed nearly identical antiterrorism bills."[386]

House and senate leaders worked non-stop to resolve the differences between HR2975 and S1510. The work was interrupted by an anthrax attack on the Hill. Issues were unresolved for a week. The negotiation and compromise between the House (HR2975) and Senate (S1510) fell in the following areas:

Major compromise between House and Senate PATRIOT Bill

Provisions	Original House version	Senate version	Compromise
Sunset clause	5 years	None	4 years
McDades law[387]	None	Revisions to McDade	None
Money laundering provisions	None	None	Comprehensive Money laundering provisions
Information-sharing [388]provisions[389]	Sharing information subject to prior court authorization	Sharing information without notice to court	Sharing with notice to the court after disclosure.
Electronic surveillance note	None	None	*Ex parte* and in camera notice with the court when a lawful pen register or trap and trace order is installed on ISP.
Certification of alien as terrorists	Declaration of alien as terrorist limited to Deputy AG	Declaration of alien as terrorist limited to Commissioner of INS	Declaration of alien as terrorist limited to Deputy AG.

Hart, Flake, Schiff, Thomas, Goss, Rangel, Berman and Lofgren. S.1510 by Senator Daschle for himself and Senators Lott, Leahy, Hatch, Graham, Shelby and Sarbanes.

[386] "Less Secure, Less Free." *Supra*, note 1.
[387] The McDade law requires federal prosecutors to comply with state ethics laws.
[388] Sharing of grand jury information.
[389] Between law enforcement and intelligence community.

Provisions	Original House version	Senate version	Compromise
Revisit of alien terrorists certification	Revisit of alien terrorists certification every 6 months.	None	Revisit of alien terrorists certification every 6 months
Electronic tacking of foreign students	None	None	Authorized 36 millions for implementation of SEVIS.
Accountability: Inspection	None	None	Established Inspector General for Civil Liberties and Civil Rights inside the Department of Justice.
Accountability: Court liability	None	None	Provide for Federal tort relief for improper government release of wiretap information.

Source: Extracted form House floor debate, USAPA, October 23, 2001. Congressional Record: October 23, 2001 (House) Page H7159-H7207.

A Breach of Faith

On October 23rd 1001, the USAPA was debated in the House for one hour. The major objections concerned two key issues: i.e. legislative procedure and legal due process:

First the legislative process was considered highly unusual and irregular. The draft bill was reported out the House Judiciary Committee 36-0. But that bill was jettisoned in lieu of a new one that was negotiated by the Congressional leadership and behind closed door, without input from the Committee or House members. The Congressional members were informed of the change, *afterward*. Each Party was given two copies of the bill shortly before the floor debate on October 23, 2001. No amendments were entertained. The debate was held late at night and after working hours. As a result most members were ignorant of the content of the bill when asked to vote on it.[390] Representative Frank (D – Mass.) found the process totally unacceptable:

> "There is no reason why we could not have had this open to amendment tonight. This bill should not be debated now. Was it really necessary to debate one of the most profound pieces of legislation and its impact on our society that we have had, was it really necessary to debate

---

[390] Kelly Patricia O'Meara, "Police State," *Insight magazine* November 9, 2001 (Rep. Ron Paul of Texas, one of only three Republican lawmakers to vote against the USAPA, observed: "It's my understanding the bill wasn't printed before the vote — at least I couldn't get it. They played all kinds of games, kept the House in session all night, and it was a very complicated bill. Maybe a handful of staffers actually read it, but the bill definitely was not available to members before the vote").

it at night after all of the Members who have been working all day were told to go home? Why could this not have been a full-fledged debate with some amendments?"[391]

Representative John Conyers, Jr. (D - MI) likewise complained:

"The members of the Committee on the Judiciary had a free and open debate; and we came to a bill that even though imperfect, was unanimously agreed on. That was removed from us, and we are now debating at this hour of night, with only two copies of the bill that we are being asked to vote on available to Members on this side of the aisle. I am hoping on the other side of the aisle they at least have two copies...there is something wrong with that process....79 Members were not able to go along with the bill, is that a legislative body that does not debate is being railroaded whether they know it or not, whether they want to accede to it or not."[392]

Varieties of Objection

Some members also complained of the lack of due process for citizens subject to the USAPA and possibility of abuse of power by the government empowered (and emboldened) by the USAPA. For example, Representative Jackson – Lee (D – Texas) was heard to complain:

Mr. Speaker, I think Americans know very well that character is judged not so much on how a man or woman acts in the good times, but how we act in the face of adversity ...I do believe that in making our country safe against terrorism, that we do not necessarily need to do away with due process, and that we should not target innocent people unfairly because of their race, color, sexual orientation, creed, gender, or religion.[393]

Other criticism was more pointed and specific. For example, Mr. Scott (D-VA)[394] observed that:

First, the new wiretap power is not limited to intelligence gathering but broad enough to be used to investigate common crime and innocent citizens;

Second, there are very little protection against the abusive use of wire tape, e.g. no probable caused is required for issuance of a FSIA search warrant.

Third, pen register and track and trace search violates people's privacy right and Constitutional protection against government search and seizure powers;

Fourth, the government can conduct "sneak and peak" searches without informing the target.[395]

The Final Debate

Finally, on October 25th the final bill, HR 3162, the "USAPA" was debate in the Senate and passed.[396] The floor debate was a tightly managed one. Except for Senator Feingold, only

---

[391] USAPA, House floor debate, Congressional Record: October 23, 2001 (House) Page H7159-H7207.
[392] Id. H7206.
[393] *Id.* H7203.
[394] Congressional Record: October 23, 2001 (House), Page H7159-H7207, 7201.
[395] *Op Cit.* H7201.
[396] The ACT was passed in the Senate without a conference with the House, which passed a similar bill a day earlier.

those Senators who were involved in the drafting or negotiation process were allowed to participate in the debate.

In terms of actual floor procedure, "[t]he PRESIDENT pro tempore. The chairman and ranking member of the Judiciary Committee have 90 minutes each; the Senator from Michigan, Mr. Levin, has 10 minutes; the Senator from Minnesota, Mr. Wellstone, has 10 minutes; the Senator from Maryland, Mr. Sarbanes, has 20 minutes; the Senator from Wisconsin, Mr. Feingold, has 1 hour; the Senator from Florida, Mr. Graham, has 15 minutes; and the Senator from Pennsylvania, Mr. Specter, has 15 minutes."[397]

Senator Leahy opened the floor speech with an emphatic observation that the bill was the result of a hard earned compromise: "This was not the bill that I, or any of the sponsors, would have written if compromise was unnecessary. Nor was it the bill the Administration had initially proposed and the Attorney General delivered to us on September 19, at a meeting in the Capitol."[398]

He was also quick to point out that: First, the bill was a much improved legislation from the September 19, 2001 Administration proposal (ATA – MATA); Second, both Senate and Administration has made much concession; Third, important safeguards are put in place to limit government abuse of power and protect citizens' rights; Fourth, the USAPA would remain to be a work in progress, subject to supervision by court, monitoring by Senate, and revisions on sunset by the Congress and amendments along the way.

As to improvements, the Senator named ten areas that the USAPA has been improved from the Administrative proposal of September 19, 2001:[399]

First, improve security on the Northern Border; Second, added money laundering provisions; Third, enhance information sharing and coordination with State and local law enforcement, provide grants to State and local governments to respond to bioterrorism, and increased payments to families of fallen first responders; Fourth, add humanitarian relief to immigrant victims of the September 11 terrorist attacks; Fifth, hire more translators for the FBI; Sixth, add more comprehensive victims' assistance; Seventh, add measures to fight cybercrime; Eighth, add measures to fight terrorism against mass transportation systems; Ninth, use technology to make our borders more secure; Tenth, provide additional checks on the proposed expansion of government powers contained in the Attorney General's initial proposal.[400]

As to supervision and oversight, a key issue in the floor debate/speeches, Senate Leahy observed:

"I do believe that some of the provisions contained both in this bill and the original USA Act will face difficult tests in the courts, and that we in Congress may have to revisit these issues at some time in the future when the present crisis has passed, the sunset has expired or the courts find an infirmity in these provisions. I also intend as Chairman of the Judiciary Committee to exercise careful oversight of how the Department of Justice, the FBI and other executive branch agencies are using the newly-expanded powers that this bill will give them. I

---

[397] USAPA, Floor Debate, Congressional Record: October 25, 2001 (Senate), Page S10990-S11060; From the Congressional Record Online via GPO Access [wais.access.gpo.gov] [DOCID:cr25oc01-91]. (USAPA, Floor Debate).

[398] *Id.* Page S10991.

[399] S10091.

[400] *Id.* (verbatim quotes).

know that other members of the Judiciary Committee—including Senator Specter, Senator Grassley, and Senator Durbin--appreciate the importance of such oversight."[401]

The USAPA passed the Congress with an overwhelming majority, i.e. 356-66 in the House and 98-1 in the Senate and in record time (six weeks – 9/19 to 10/26/2001); with the nation laboring in a war time environment and Congress operating with a siege mentality.

The Lack of Public Feedback

As to the process, there were few opportunities made available and no time se aside for public consultation,[402] community feedbacks, professional study, special interests lobbying, and Congressional scrutiny.[403] Not only were there no consultation, the public has a difficult time in obtaining the necessary information to formulate an informed judgment on the issues involved.

The only public feedback on the USAPA and related drafts came in the form of personal letters to individual Congressman[404] or Editorial comments in the Newspapers. For example, on September 25, 2001 an editorial entitled "Why the rush?" appeared in the *St. Petersburg Times (Florida)*.[405] It observed that the House Judiciary Committee Chairman F. James Sensenbrenner Jr. (R-Wis.) was rushing the ATA of 2001 through Congress and the Justice Department was suspected of using 9/11 to get as many powers it has failed to obtain from the Congress in the past. The editorial concluded with the observation, since then repeated by many others: "Congress needs to slow down and get this right."

Another editorial - "An improved antiterrorism bill" – a week later (October 3, 2001) in the same page [406] observed that Congressional leaders of both parties were doing their best in crafting a compromised ATA that would give law enforcement more tools to combat terrorism while protecting civil liberties.

---

[401] S 10091 – 2.

[402] It is extremely difficult for UUA and other organization to obtain information on the USAPA, then being considered behind closed door. UUA Washington Office. http://www.witnessforcivilliberties.org/doc/ education/factsheetspatriotact.pdf.

See also "USAPA: A Summary of ALA activities," ALA Washington Office, January 19, 2002. (The ALA has to be kept informed about the progress and language of the ACT through informal channels, e.g. via leaks from Congressional staffers.) http://www.ala.org/Content/NavigationMenu/Our_Association/Offices/ALA_

Washington/Issues2/Civil_Liberties,_Intellectual_Freedom,_Privacy/The_USA_Patriot_Act_and_Libraries/backgro und.pdf

[403] For a contrary observation, see Orrin G. Hatch, *Square Peg: Confessions of a Citizen Senator* (Basic Books, 2002) (According to Hatch, there were much debate and full discussion behind close door by Congressional leadership and staff alike. See pp. 80-90). The Patriot Act did have hearings and discussion in the House, but the House anti-terrorism bill was virtually ignored in favor of the Senate version, by fiat. Similarly, there was time set aside for presentations of individual Senators on the USAPA in the Senate on October 25, 2001. The Congressional leadership has decided that the ACT would pass on October 25, 2001, notwithstanding many strong and vocal objections, remainng. See Congressional Record: October 25, 2001 (Senate), Page S10990-S11060. http://www.cdt.org/security/011025senate.txt

[404] Sonia Arrison is the director of the Center for Freedom and Technology at the San Francisco-based Pacific Research Institute, "OPINION, " New anti-terrorism law goes too far." *The San Diego Union-Tribune*, October 31, 2001, Wednesday, Pg. B-9, 791 words. (Defending the nation against terrorist acts can and should be done without eroding America's liberties).

[405] EDITORIAL: Why the rush?" *St. Petersburg Times (Florida)* September 25, 2001, Tuesday, South Pinellas Edition, Pg. 10A, 505.

[406] "EDITORIAL: An improved antiterrorism bill," *St. Petersburg Times (Florida)*, October 03, 2001, Wednesday, Pg. 14A, 650 words.

There were many others editorials during the legislative period, e.g. an editorial in *The Washington Post*: "Stampeded in the House," (October 16, 2001)[407] faulted the House Republican leadership in bypassing the legislative process and forcing a vote on a major anti-terrorism bill (USAPA) that was anonymously drafted in the middle of the night before without Judiciary Committee approval, in lieu of one that was unanimously approved of by the House Judiciary Committee.

On the day the USAPA was passed, October 26, 2001, the *Denver Post* published an editorial: "Proceed with caution."[408] It cautioned: "We hope that the executive branch and Congress will be especially vigilant to make sure that, in the rush to defeat terrorism, they don't turn a free country into a virtual prison."

Feedback from special interest groups, e.g. ACLU[409] or EFF,[410] came with many blow by blow analysis and point to point rebuttal to the USAPA when it was moving through the Congress. But none of these NGOs were invited to submit their comments, officially.[411] There is evidence that any of such "unofficial" submissions, which were widely circulated, received the attention or consideration they deserved,[412] from a zealous Attorney General and close minded Bush Administration.[413]

The Lone Dissenter

In the Senate, Senator Feingold cast the lone dissenter voted against the USAPA. Senator Russ Feingold, chairman of the Constitution Subcommittee of the Judiciary Committee, has consistently expressed his strong reservations about the USAPA (H.R. 3162). In his final floor speech, the Senator called upon the Nation, Congress and public to "continue to respect our Constitution and protect our civil liberties in the wake of the attacks" and cautioned against "the mistreatment of Arab Americans, Muslim Americans, South Asians, or others in this country."[414]

Senate Feingold reminded the Nation that "wartime has sometimes brought us the greatest tests of our Bill of Rights" such as the passage of "Alien and Sedition Acts [of 1798], the suspension of habeas corpus during the Civil War, the internment of Japanese-Americans, German-Americans, and Italian-Americans during World War II, the blacklisting of supposed communist sympathizers during the McCarthy era, and the surveillance and harassment of antiwar protesters, including Dr. Martin Luther King Jr., during the Vietnam War."

---

[407] "EDITORIAL: Stampeded in the House," *The Washington Post* October 16, 2001, Tuesday, Final Edition, Pg. A22, 541 words.

[408] "EDITORIAL Proceed with caution," *The Denver Post* October 26, 2001 Friday, Pg. B-06, 458 words.

[409] USAPA (11/14/2003) ACLU – Safe and Secure. http://www.aclu.org/safefree/resources/17343res20031114.html

[410] "EFF Analysis Of The Provisions Of The USAPA: That Relate To Online Activities" (October 31, 2001) *Last updated October 27, 2003*. Electronic Frontier Foundation (EFF) http://www.eff.org/Privacy/Surveillance/Terrorism/20011031_eff_usa_patriot_analysis.php

[411] On September 24, 2001, the House Judiciary Committee held a "briefing" for civil liberties groups regarding the ATA of 2001. See note 116, *supra*.

[412] For example, "EFF: Analysis of Anti-Terrorism Act (ATA) of 2001," Electronic Frontier Foundation (Sep. 27, 2001) (ATA expands FISA powers to cover non-terrorism cases and increase surveillance of U.S. citizens and non-citizens alike.) http://www.eff.org/Censorship/Terrorism_militias/20010927_eff_ata_analysis.html;
Chris Elliott, "Public Inexcusably Tolerant of Bush's Law-Breaking," *Seacoast Online* (New Hampshire) January 6, 2006 ("This arrogant administration is so assured of its own righteous providence that any kind of process associated with its self-appointed directives is regarded as a nuisance and optional at its own discretion.") http://www.commondreams.org/views06/0106-27.htm

[414] "Statement Of U.S. Senator Russ Feingold On The Anti-Terrorism Bill From The Senate Floor," October 25, 2001.

The Senator objected to the USAPA on philosophical, procedural and substantive grounds:

Philosophically, Feingold was against trading liberties for security:

> "Of course, there is no doubt that if we lived in a police state, it would be easier to catch terrorists...But that probably would not be a country in which we would want to live...Preserving our freedom is one of the main reasons that we are now engaged in this new war on terrorism. We will lose that war without firing a shot if we sacrifice the liberties of the American people."[415]

Procedurally, he was against rushing the USAPA through Congress:

> "You may remember that the Attorney General ...provided the text of the bill the following Wednesday, and urged Congress to enact it by the end of the week....the pressure to move on this bill quickly, without deliberation and debate, has been relentless ever since...It is one thing to shortcut the legislative process in order to get federal financial aid to the cities hit by terrorism...It is quite another to press for the enactment of sweeping new powers for law enforcement that directly affect the civil liberties of the American people without due deliberation by the peoples' elected representatives." [416]

Substantively, Feingold was of the opinion that the USAPA ("bill") failed to "strike the right balance between empowering law enforcement and protecting civil liberties." Particularly, he has the following objections:[417]

(1) The bill gives the law enforcement agencies new and expansive powers to investigate not only terrorism but other crimes, e.g. the "sneak and peak" warrant can be used to investigate all kinds of crime, e.g. official corruption and organized gambling.

(2) The bill gives law enforcement officials too much power to investigate crime. Law enforcement agents can now avoid the stricture and protection of the Fourth Amendment.

(3) The bill allows law enforcement officials to monitor a computer with the permission of its owner or operator, but without knowledge or consent of the user. The bill allows search and seizure of unauthorized use of company computer by employees or library computer by patrons. No warrant is required.

(4) The bill allows the use of FISA to conduct search and seizure without meeting the rigorous probable cause standard under the Fourth Amendment. Under the bill the government only needs to show that the intelligence gathering is *a* "significant purpose" of the investigation, even if the underling criminal investigation is *not* the primary purpose.

---

[415] *Id.*

[416] *Id.*

[417] Feingold was supportive of many provisions in the bill, including: FBI should be able to seize voice mail messages as well as being able to tape a phone; federal criminal law on the possession and use of biological weapons should be re-written; cable - communication should be treated the same way as phone lines communication; penalties of terrorist crimes should be increased; statues of limitations for terrorist offenses should be extended or eliminated.

(5) The bill allows the use of FISA to compel the production of business records regarding any person if that information is sought in connection with a terrorism or espionage investigation.

(6) The bill allows the Attorney General extraordinary powers to detain immigrants, including legal permanent residents, indefinitely, based on no more evidence than "mere suspicion" that the person is engaged in terrorism.

(7) The bill allows the Attorney General to charge a detained immigrant within seven days. It further allows the Attorney General or its deputy to continually hold a detained immigrant indefinitely, subject only to a review of detention decision every six months. Suspected or non-deportable aliens might be detained without trial based on *mere suspicion* for an *indefinite period* of time.

(8) The bill allows the detention and deportation of aliens for mere association with terrorists. For example innocent people can be arrested, detained and deported for rendering lawful assistance to terrorist groups, without their knowledge. They can be held accountable even when such groups were not designated by the Secretary of State as terrorist organizations, but instead have engaged in vaguely defined "terrorist activity" which happened sometime in the past. To avoid deportation, the immigrant is required to prove a negative, i.e., that he or she did not know, and should not have known, that the assistance rendered would further unknown terrorist activity.

(9) The broad definition of terrorism is so loose and imprecise that it might easily include philanthropic activities, such as Operation Rescue, Greenpeace.

Feingold was also not pleased to the intense pressure asserted and high handed tactics employed first by the Administration and later by his own party to speed up the legislative process and otherwise forced him to consent to the Act. In Feingold's own word:

> "When the original Ashcroft anti-terrorism bill came in, they wanted us to pass it two days later.... But then something happened in the Senate, and I think the Democratic leadership was complicit in this. Suddenly, the bottom fell out. I was told that a unanimous consent agreement was being offered with no amendments and no debate. They asked me to give unanimous consent. I refused. The Majority Leader came to the floor and spoke very sternly to me, in front of his staff and my staff, saying, you can't do this, the whole thing will fall apart. I said, what do you mean it'll fall apart, they want to pass this, too. I said, I refuse to consent. He was on the belligerent side for Tom Daschle. And everybody said they were surprised at his remarks. Reporters thought it was so unlike him. And it is unlike him.

> One of the interesting stories in this-and this is one that a lot of progressives don't want to hear, but it's the truth-is that John Ashcroft gave me a call and said, what are your concerns? And I told him my concerns about the computer stuff and sneak and peek searches. He said, you know, I think you might be right. The White House overruled him, which is a fundamental point here. Anyone who wants to focus their fire on Ashcroft is missing the point. This is the Bush Administration. Ashcroft is its instrument. What happened in the Senate was that even though the Attorney General was going to allow these changes to make it moderately better, the Administration insisted, and Daschle went along with pushing this through. I finally got to offer the amendments late at night, and I got up there and I made my arguments. And a lot of Senators came around to me, who, of course, voted for the bill, and said, you know, I think you're right. Then Daschle comes out and says, I want you to vote against this amendment and all the other Feingold amendments; don't even consider the

merits. This was one of the most fundamental pieces of legislation relating to the Bill of Rights in the history of our country! It was a low point for me in terms of being a Democrat and somebody who believes in civil liberties."[418]

The Final Passage

The USAPA was signed into law by President G.W. Bush on October 26, 2001.

III. CONCLUSION

This chapter addressed the question of how the USAPA was passed, leaving the issues of why to the next chapter. The chapter confirmed that the legislative process was hurried and flawed. The USAPA was passed with little Congressional scrutiny and still less public input. The USAPA became law without the citizens being fully aware of its impact and implication.[419] For example, an investigation into the media coverage of USAPA found that both ABC and NBC did not give the USAPA the coverage it was due. Only ABC has a short segment on 9/25/01 warning that that proposed anti-terrorism law: "give the government more power to spy on Americans here at home, monitor internet use with little oversight from a judge, lock up immigrants whom the government says might be a threat to national security without presenting evidence." [420]

The lack of public awareness and involvement in the drafting and passage of the USAPA caused grave consequences with our political system.

First to observe is that the USAPA has real impact on the public, especially on affected institutions (universities) and discriminated groups (Muslim). [421] For example, notwithstanding the fact that Section 215 of the USAPA has rarely been invoked, library patrons feared that their reading habits were constantly being monitored.[422] More tellingly, Senator Feinstein reported that her office has received 21,434 anti-Patriot Act letters, but less than half cited USAPA provisions as a basis of complain.[423] In essence, the citizens knew

---

[418]   Matthew   Rothschild,   "Russ   Feingold   interview,"   *The   Progressive   magazine*,   May   2002. http://www.thirdworldtraveler.com/Politicians/Russ_Feingold.html

[419] The public have a lot of misunderstanding about the USAPA. "Don't fault the misunderstood Patriot Act," "Letter to Editor" *Detroit Free Press*, July 26, 2003 (Jeffrey G. Collins, U.S. Attorney Eastern District of Michigan, pointed out that the public oftentimes misconstrued the USAPA. For example, they wrongly assumed that the investigative (surveillance) powers given to the government is a sharp departure from the past. Or, they erroneously blamed the USAPA for allowing "holding prisoners as "enemy combatants.") http://www.freep.com/voices/letters/ecoll26_20030726.htm

[420] The USAPA was not widely known, before, and in some quarters, long after it became law. The National news agencies and wire syndicates that inform citizens, define issues, provide perspective and establish frame of reference, did not see fit to report upon the USAPA See "Analysis of the Nightly News Glossing Over Anti-Terrorism Act" *8th Day Center for justice* http://www.8thdaycenter.org/092801.html

[421] Judging by public surveys, the public was hardly concerned much less alarmed with any loss of civil liberties, when the USAPA was passed. Majority of the citizen, until very recently, think that it is right and proper to allow the government to have more power to fight terrorism at the expense of civil liberties. But "ignorance" and "misunderstanding" do contribute to breeding concerns and cultivating alarms, especially when the fear of terrorism begin to subsides after 9/11.

[422] Nat Hentoff, "Big John wants your reading list," *The Village Voice*. Mar 5, 2002. Vol. 47 (9); p. 27 (1 page) (The public is not informed and aware of the extent of government powers.)

[423] Susan Schmidt, "Patriot Act Misunderstood, Senators Say Complaints About Civil Liberties Go Beyond Legislation's Reach, Some Insist," *Washington Post* Wednesday, October 22, 2003; Page A04. (At a Senate Judiciary Cmte. oversight hearing (Oct. 21, 2003) Senators expressed concerns that the public has been misinformed about the scope and reach, implementation and utility of the Act.). Watch, Sen. Orrin Hatch (R-

something was wrong with the government's draconian anti-terrorism measures but was not able to articulate the source, nature, prevalence or magnitude of the problem.

The pubic were further confused and aggrieved when the government, in order to "mollify" the public,[424] mischaracterized the intent and purpose,[425] reach and scope,[426] and impact and effect of the USAPA.

For example, U.S. Attorney for Alaska testified before a state Senate Committee: "[T]here is concern that under the PATRIOT Act, federal agents are now able to review library records and books checked out by U.S. Citizens... If you read the Act, that's absolutely not true... It can't be for U.S. citizens." *In fact*, Section 215 of the USA Patriot makes clear that "U.S. persons" – a term referring to citizens and some non-citizens alike -- can have their record seized by the FBI with a FISA order.

Mark Corallo, Justice Department Spokesperson, spoke to the *Bangor (ME) Daily News*: "For the FBI to check on a citizen's reading habits....it must convince a judge "there is probable cause that the person you are seeking the information for is a terrorist or a foreign spy." *In fact*, Section 215 of the USAPA allows the government to obtain materials like library records without probable cause.[427]

The government's failure to provide the public with timely, responsive and accurate information over USAPA enforcement policy (e.g., under what circumstances would Section

---

UT) chairs a Senate Judiciary Cmte. hearing on the adequacy of federal laws for responding to and preventing acts of terrorism at C-Span on Tuesday, Oct. 21, 2003)

[424] "Interested Persons Memo on Congressional oversight of the USAPA and Department of Justice anti-terrorism policies – DOJ's dismissive response on civil liberties," ACLU Memo, dated June 4, 2003. ("DOJ has been deceptive in describing the scope of the powers it has been granted, apparently to mollify widespread public concern") http://www.aclu.org/SafeandFree/SafeandFree.cfm?ID=12812andc=206

[425] "Rights and the New Reality; Telemarketer Terrorists?" *Los Angeles Times* California Metro; September 13, 2003. Part 2; Page 10 (476 words) (The USAPA was being used to investigate common criminals, e.g. telemarketers accused of swindling elderly consumers, a lawyer accused of stashing stolen funds in a Belize bank account and various drug dealers. This was contrary to the original purpose of the USAPA, and avowed promise of the Department of Justice.)

[426] Maine Civil Liberty Union Executive Director, Louise G. Roback, wrote a letter on April 16, 2003 to Senator Olympia Snowe complaining of FBI spokesperson's untruthful characterization of the USAPA when responding to a *Bangor Daily News* article: "Calais library fights Patriot Act" (April 1, 2003) about Calais Free Library's opposition to the USAPA. Deputy Director Corallo's misrepresentation was reported in "Official counters Patriot Act critics." On April 9, the *Bangor Daily News* printed an editorial criticizing DOJ's misstatements. See "MCLU Demands Truth From Justice Department," MCLU ("We are concerned that Deputy Director Corallo provided false information concerning the powers of the Justice Department under the USAPA to the public.") http://www.mclu.org/calais_letter_041603.htm See also Net Hentoff, "Op-ed: The state of our liberties," *Washington Post* Aug. 25, 2003. (The government put a spin of USAPA.) http://www.washtimes.com/op-ed/20030824-110950-4866r.htm

[427] See "Reports: Government Missteps After Sept. 11," Summer 2003.ACLU of Northern California. http://www.aclunc.org/aclunews/news0309/reports.html Both the government and ACLU have accused each other of misleading the public. For ACLU's allegations, see *Seeking Truth From Justice: PATRIOT Propaganda - The Justice Department's Campaign to Mislead The Public About the USAPA* (ACLU, July 2003) ("The Justice Department's repeated assertion that the USAPA's surveillance provisions cannot be used against U.S. citizens. In fact, the surveillance provisions are applicable to citizens and non-citizens alike.") http://www.aclu.org/Files/OpenFile.cfm?id=13098 The DOJ's answer to "Seeking Truth From Justice" is the DOJ's "Dispelling the Myths" on Life and Liberty web. ("Myth: The ACLU claims that the Patriot Act "expands terrorism laws to include 'domestic terrorism' which could subject political organizations to surveillance, wiretapping, harassment, and criminal action for political advocacy."...Reality: The Patriot Act limits domestic terrorism to conduct that breaks criminal laws, endangering human life. "Peaceful groups that dissent from government policy" without breaking laws cannot be targeted." (Emphasis in the original) http://www.lifeandliberty.gov/subs/u_myths.htm

215 powers be invoked?[428]) and practices (e.g., how often has Section 215 powers been invoked?[429]) generated wide spread anxiety and induced indeterminate fear,[430] leading to personal resentment, individual protests and collective resistance across the United States.[431] Even Representative Bob Barr, a keen supporter of Bush, has reason to be concerned: "The administration has not been at all forthcoming since then in explaining in a clear and open way how that act would be used and is being used. The lack of being forthcoming about discussing that has bothered me."[432]

Finally, the Attorney General Ashcroft's farcical justification[433] and inept defense of USAPA[434] infuriated USAPA hard opponents and alienated the core Bush supporters.[435] For example, Attorney General Ashcroft was openly contemptuous of the law makers who want to find out more about the of USAP: "To those who scare peace-loving people with phantoms of lost liberty, my message is this: Your tactics only aid terrorists, for they erode our national unity and diminish our resolve They give ammunition to America's enemies and pause to America's friends." [436]

Ashcroft was also publicly dismissive of librarians' legitimate concern with the erosive impact of USAPA on library privacy: "The charges of the hysterics are revealed for what they are: castles in the air built on misrepresentation, supported by unfounded fear, held aloft by hysteria." [437]

Last not least, Barbara Comstock, a spoke person the DOJ, was heard oudly belittling local grassroots communities' anti-Patriot sentiments:

---

[428] Eric Lichtblau, "Patriot Act's reach has gone beyond terrorism," *Seattle Times* September 28, 2003 (Government is using the USAPA to investigate all kinds of crimes: suspected drug traffickers, white-collar criminals, blackmailers, child pornographers, money launderers, spies and corrupt foreign leaders.)

[429] The DOJ chose to answer only 28 of the 50 questions posed by the House Judiciary Committee by letter of July 13, 2002. See letters to Congress on implementation of the USAPA, dated July 26, August 26, and September 20, 2002. http://www.fas.org/irp/news/2002/10/doj101702.html

[430] Eric Lichtblau (NYT), "Demand for library records? Zero," *Deseret Morning News* (Salt Lake City) Pg. A02, September 19, 2003, Friday (872 words) (Emily Sheketoff, executive director of the Washington office of the American Library Association observed: "If the Justice Department had been more forthcoming with the public ... this high level of suspicion wouldn't have developed. But they've been fighting for two years not to tell people what they were doing, and that left a lot of people wondering what they had to hide.")

[431] Eric Lichtblau, "Patriot Act debate needless, Ashcroft says," *New York Times* September 18, 2003. http://www.chron.com/cs/CDA/ssistory.mpl/nation/2108405. See Chapter 7: Grassroots resistance.

[432] Michael Tomasky, "Strange Bedfellows: Conservative civil libertarians join the fight," *The American Prospect* Vo. 14, no. 8, September 1, 2003. http://www.prospect.org/print/V14/8/tomasky-m.html

[433] "Civil libertarians criticize FBI rules; They fear the terrorism crisis is being used as a cover to erode personal freedoms," *The Associated Press. The Grand Rapids Press* May 31, 2002. p. A.3. (James X. Dempsey, deputy director of the Center for Democracy and Technology observed: "They are using the terrorism crisis as a cover for a wide range of changes, some of which have nothing to do with terrorism." Dempsey predicted that the power will be used for "every other type of investigation the FBI does").

[434] "Ashcroft's Endless Attacks Diminish Office," *Dayton Daily News* (Ohio), August 11, 2003, Monday, City Edition, Editorial; Pg. A6 (540 words) (The Attorney General was best remembered for his fear-mongering and vindictive antics.)

[435] Myriam Marquez, "Blame Game: The 9-11 Buck Should Stop With Ashcroft," *Sentinel Columnist. Orlando Sentinel*. Jun 4, 2002. p. A.9 ("To Ashcroft, it seems, the answer to fighting terrorism is cracking down on Americans' civil liberties and immigrants' basic human rights.") More recently, the Attorney General described librarian's concerns with the Patriot Act as "breathless reports and baseless hysteria." See Prepared Remarks of Attorney General John Ashcroft "The Proven Tactics in the Fight against Crime" Washington, D.C., September 15, 2003. See also ERIC LICHTBLAU, "Ashcroft Mocks Librarians and Others Who Oppose Parts of Counterterrorism Law," *New York Times*, September 16, 2003. http://www.nytimes.com/2003/09/16/politics/16LIBR.html

[436] See Testimony of Attorney General John Ashcroft Senate Committee on the Judiciary. December 6, 2001. http://www.usdoj.gov/ag/testimony/2001/1206transcriptsenatejudiciarycommittee.htm

[437] Ashcroft later explained to ALA that he was not directing his comments to the librarians, but the ACLU.

"Some of the different ordinances that have passed throughout the country, about 45 percent of them, almost half, are either in cities in Vermont, very small populations, or in sort of college towns in California. It's in a lot of the usual enclaves where you might see nuclear-free zones or, you know, they probably passed resolutions against the war in Iraq."

The statement drew predictable and angry response from Senator Leahy:

"It is unfortunate that the Justice Department felt it appropriate to ridicule these grass-roots efforts to participate in an important national dialogue. The opportunity to engage in public discourse is one of the essential rights of Americans, and I am proud that Vermont towns are among those dedicated to thinking about and acting on these important issues. More importantly, the concerns expressed in my home state are being echoed by Americans in all 50 states. These communities represent millions upon millions of Americans, not just a few liberty-and-privacy-conscious Vermonters, as the Justice Department has insinuated. Impugning Vermonters, dedicated librarians and United States Senators for asking questions and raising concerns does not advance the debate or instill public confidence in the Ashcroft Justice Department's use of the vast powers it wields. In fact, it achieves the opposite."[438]

As a result of above observed public confusion and anxiety, government zealotry and ineptitude, the USAPA continues to draw vociferous criticism[439] and fiery protests,[440] five years after its passage.[441] Many of the issues that should and could have been carefully investigated and seriously discussed,[442] such as the impact and implications of the USAPA on

---

[438] Statement of Senator Patrick Leahy, Ranking Member, "Senate Committee on the Judiciary Hearing on Protecting Our National Security from Terrorist Attacks: A Review of Criminal Terrorism Investigations and Prosecutions." October 21, 2003. http://www.senate.gov/~judiciary/member_statement.cfm?id=965andwit_id=2629

[439] By far the most vocal and prolific commentator is Nat Hentoff, a columnist with the Village voice. For his brief Bio. See "Nat Hentoff" *Washington Post.* (1998) http://www.washingtonpost.com/wp-srv/politics/opinions/hentoff.htm For a sample of his critique of the Patriot Act, see "Ashcroft Out of Control: Ominous Sequel to USAPA," *Village Voice* February 28th, 2003 and "Crossing Swords With General Ashcroft: Where Is Our Bill of Rights Defense Committee?" *truthout* December, 20., 2002 (Citing Thomas Jefferson: "The spirit of resistance to government is so valuable on certain occasions, that I wish it to be always kept alive." (letter to Abigail Adams, February 22, 1787), he called for active grassroots resistance to the USAPA.) There are to be many others across the United States and from the very beginning. See "Opinion: The Patriot Act is a threat," *Deseret Morning News* (Salt Lake City), OPINION; Pg. A15, August 27, 2003, Wednesday (479 words) (USAPA was compared with "general search warrants" used by British customs agents during American Revolution.)

[440] The Attorney General's 16 states and 18 cities road show to promote the USAPA was met with protesters everywhere. Diane Urbani, "Patriot Act undercuts King's dream, Utahn says," *Deseret Morning News* (Salt Lake City, August 29, 2003. Friday (762 words) (The Attorney General was met with 200 protesters.) [Another account put it at 150. See Angie Welling and Jennifer Dobner, "Act called vital tool in war on terror." *Deseret Morning News* (Salt Lake City), WIRE; Pg. A01, August 26, 2003.

[441] See Leonard Kniffel, "CPL head's comments provoke outrage," *American Libraries.* Jan 2002. Vol. 33, Iss. 1; p. 30 (Librarian should never surrender library information except by court order and with judicial process.) "EDITORIAL: Tempest in a teapot," *Las Vegas Review - Journal.* Jun 3, 2002. p. 6.B (It is necessary to trade liberty for security in time of crisis.)

[442] See GREG BLUESTEIN, "University professors: Country must not overreact," *redandblack.com* (University of Georgia student newspaper) September 12, 2001. (Notwithstanding the catastrophic nature and tragic consequences of 9/11 attack, the nation should not overact.). CATO analyst Timothy Lynch echoed many other others in saying that we should not react to 9/11 in a knee jerk fashion. Looking back in history, Lynch observed that all of the country's effort to fight terrorism was reactionary in nature and laboring under a crisis mentality. "Government officials typically respond to terrorist attacks by proposing and enacting "antiterrorism" legislation." The Feb. 26, 1993 bombing of the World Trade Center gave us the Terrorism prevention and Protection Act of 1993. The April 19, 1995 bombing of the Murrah Federal Building Bombing

civil liberties, are now only beginning to be seriously addressed by the lawmakers,[443] critically debated by the public, [444] and systematically analyzed by the Courts.[445]

The voices of dissents could be heard from interested citizens and concerned activists across the Nation, from California to New York, Wisconsin to Florida, on campaign trails[446] and in public forums. [447] The dissenters included republican and democrats, [448] civil libertarians and conservatives.[449]

Activists mobilized grassroots movements to establish "Civil Liberties Free Zone"[450] in open defiance of the Patriot Act.[451] The Congress worked with afflicted groups and aggrieved citizens to pass law to limit the actual harm and contain the potential fallout of the Patriot Act, including denying money for enforcement,[452] requiring oversight into implementation, [453] and

---

Oklahoma led to the passage of Comprehensive Terrorism Prevention Act of 1995. Lynch argued that "The cycle: Terrorist Attack and "Anti-Terrorism Legislation" must be stopped. Particularly, policy makers should refrain from legislation until they have time to study and deliberate upon four issues: (1) accountability; (2) history; (3) reality; (4) freedom. Timothy Lynch, "Breaking the Vicious Cycle: Preserving Our Liberties While Fighting Terrorism," *Cato Policy Analysis* No. 443, June 26, 2002. http://www.cato.org/pubs/pas/pa443.pdf

[443] See "Ron Paul Applauds Congressional Restrictions on Patriot Act," The Office of Rep. Ron Paul (R-TX), July 25, 2003. http://www.antiwar.com/paul/paul72.html (Reprint)

[444] See Editorial: "Privacy in time of crisis," *Orange County Register*. Oct 1, 2001. p. Edit; Chuck McGinness, "Librarian's Post-Attack Report to FBI Sparks Privacy Debate," *Palm Beach Post*, Dec 1, 2001, p. 1.B; Anonymous, "FBI spies on suspect at library," *American Libraries*. Dec 2001. Vol. 32, Iss. 11; p. 24 (2 pages); Pat Schneider, "New U.S. Law Aids Snooping on Readers; Local Bookstores, Libraries Worry," *Madison Capital Times*. Dec 25, 2001. p. 1.A; Nat Hentoff, "Big Brother in the library; Patriot Act turns librarians into FBI informants," *The Washington Times*. Feb 25, 2002. p. A.21; Nat Hentoff, "Big John wants your reading list," *The Village Voice*. Mar 5, 2002. Vol. 47, Iss. 9; p. 27 (1 page

[445] Carl Carlson, "Patriot Act Provision Challenged in Court," *e-Week* July 30, 2003 http://www.eweek.com/article2/0,4149,1208043,00.asp For the text of first ever legal complaint filed to challenged Section 215 of the USAPA, see *Muslim Community Ass'n of Ann Arbor, et al. v. Ashcroft* No. 03-72913 (E.D. Mich. July 30, 2003)., "Complaint for Declaratory and Injunctive Relief." The complaint alleged that Section 215 of the Patriot Act unconstitutional in violating First, Fourth, Fifth Amendments of the U.S. Constitution ("Preliminary Statement," para. 1, 2.) http://news.findlaw.com/cnn/docs/aclu/mcaa2ash73003 cmp.pdf

[446] BILL ADAIR, "Graham quiet about his role on Patriot Act: On the campaign trail, he isn't bringing up that he co-wrote the controversial bill in the Senate," *St. Petersburg Times*. June 14, 2003. (Senator Graham did not reveal his role in drafting part of the USAPA as former chairman of the Senate Intelligence Committee. Governor Dean publicized the fact that he opposed the USAPA as unconstitutional: "It can't be constitutional to hold an American citizen without access to a lawyer... Secondly, it can't be constitutional for the FBI to be able to go through your files at the library or the local video store, to see what you've taken out in the last week, without a warrant." http://www.sptimes.com/2003/06/14/Worldandnation/Graham_quiet_about_hi.shtml

[447] "Panelists Examine Consequences of Patriot Act." Virginia Law School. September 23, 2005. The panel was sponsored by the ACLU-UVA Law, the ACLU of Virginia, and the Charlottesville chapter of the ACLU. (Panelists included: Imad Damaj, president of the Virginia Muslim Coalition for Public Affairs, ACLU of Virginia executive director Kent Willis, and law professor Robert M. O'Neil, director of the Thomas Jefferson Center for the Protection of Free Expression.) http://www.law.virginia.edu/home2002/html/news/2005_fall/patriotact.htm

[448] On May 21, 2003, Alaska's Senate unanimously approved the country's second statewide anti-Patriot resolution entitled: "HJR 22: PATRIOT ACT and Defending Civil Liberties" as a bipartisan effort. It passed the State Senate unanimously and the House 32-1. http://www.akrepublicans.org/coghill/23/spst/ cogh_hjr023.php

[449] Nicholas Confessore, "In Bed with Bob Barr: How conservatives became the ACLU's best friends," *American Prospect*. Vol. 12 (19) Nov. 5, 2001 http://www.prospect.org/print/V12/19/confessore-n.html

[450] As of September 18, 2005, 394 Resolutions Upholding Civil Liberties and Rights have been passed in communities across the U.S. affecting 61,947,419 people: being Community resolutions: 387 and State resolutions: 7. http://www.bordc.org/index.php

[451] http://www.bordc.org/states.htm

[452] Republican Congressperson Butch Otter from Idaho introduced an amendment to a House Appropriations bill (HR 2799) to remove funding from the DOJ to conduct "sneak and peek" searches. The vote for Otter's amendment was 309-118 with widespread bi-partisan support. See also Congressman Bernie Sanders (I-VT)'s

limiting the applicability of the Patriot Act.[454] For example, on March 6, 2003, House Representative Sanders (I-Vermont) introduced the "Freedom to Read Protection Act of 2003" (HR 1157) in the House "To amend the Foreign Intelligence Surveillance Act to exempt bookstores and libraries from orders requiring the production of any tangible things for certain foreign intelligence investigations, and for other purposes.") HR1157 was cosponsored by 129 bipartisan cosponsors. It was support by 20 newspapers editorial boards, 40 library, book, publishing industry, and civil liberty groups.

On May 23, 2003, Sen. Barbara Boxer (D-CA) introduced that "Library and Bookseller Protection Act" (S. 1158) in the Senate "To exempt bookstores and libraries from orders requiring the production of tangible things for foreign intelligence investigations, and to exempt libraries from counterintelligence access to certain records, ensuring that libraries and bookstores are subjected to the regular system of court-ordered warrants."[455]

On July 31, 2003 Senator Russell D. Feingold (D-WI) introduced "The Library, Bookseller, and Personal Records Privacy Act" (S. 1507) introduced on July 31, 2003 "To protect privacy by limiting the access of the Government to library, bookseller, and other personal records for foreign intelligence and counterintelligence purposes"[456]

July 31, 2003 Sen. Lisa Murkowski (R-AK) introduced "Protecting the Rights of Individuals Act (S.1552) in the Senate "To amend title 18, United States Code, and the Foreign Intelligence Surveillance Act of 1978 to strengthen protections of civil liberties in the exercise of the foreign intelligence surveillance authorities under Federal law, and for other purposes."[457]

The unmaking of the USAPA has began!

---

effort in offering an amendment to the Commerce, Justice, State and Judiciary Appropriations Bill of 2004 to cut off Justice Department funding for searches of bookstore and library records under Section 215 of the USAPA. It is co-sponsored by John Conyers, Jr. (D-MI) and C.L. "Butch" Otter (R-ID).

[453] On February 25, 2003, Senators Leahy, Grassley and Specter introduced S. 436, the "Domestic Surveillance Oversight Act of 2003." http://www.aclu-or.org/issues/terrorism/FISA_oversightbill.htm On June 11, 2003, Representative Hoeffel and others introduced H.R. 2429, the "Surveillance Oversight and Disclosure Act of 2003. " The bills amend the Foreign Intelligence Surveillance Act of 1978 to improve the administration and oversight of foreign intelligence surveillance." http://www.fas.org/irp/congress/2003_cr/hr2429.html

[454] HR 1157 IH. 108th CONGRESS. 1st Session. HR 1157. http://www.fas.org/irp/congress/2003_cr/hr1157.html See "The Sanders-Otter-Conyers Amendment to the Commerce, Justice, State, and Judiciary Appropriations Bill of 2004" http://listproc.ucdavis.edu/archives/ncal-lib/ncal-lib.log0307/att-0017/01 talking_points_on_the_ Sanders-Otter-Conyers_C_J_S_amndt.doc

[455] http://www.fas.org/irp/congress/2003_cr/s1158.html

[456] http://www.theorator.com/bills108/s1507.html

[457] Specifically the Act provides: "Sec. 4 would....return the standards for the FBI to get orders from the FISA Court to the standards that applied pre-USA PATRIOT." "Sec. 4(b) would clarify that a library shall not be treated as a wire or electronic communication service provider for purposes of 18 U.S.C. 2709, so that a library cannot be required to turn over Internet usage records (including e-mail) about its patrons." "Sec. 6(c) would impose a specific limitation on what aspects of electronic communications could be captured with a pen/trap order" http://www.fas.org/irp/congress/2003_cr/s1552.html. For other legislative effort to scale back the scope and impact of the Patriot Act, see "Proposed Legislation" Bill of Rights Defense Committee, http://www.bordc.org/legislation.htm (Visited October 12, 2003)

Chapter 3

LEGISLATIVE CLIMATE

"The destruction of the World Trade Center on September 11,
2001 had all the hallmarks of a turning point in history."[458]

Ted Goertzel
The World Future Society (2002)

I. INTRODUCTION

The prior chapter established the fact that the USAPA was "rushed" through Congress by the Bush administration without following formal legislative process. To date, no serious attempt has been made to understand *why* the USAPA was able to rush through Congress without serious contest and effective challenge. This chapter is a first attempt to provide a systematic investigation into this most important and intriguing question. Important because there is a lot we can learn about legislative dynamics and process of emergency legislation. Intriguing because the passage of USAPA cannot easily be explained with existing legislation theory.

This article is organized into the following parts. After this brief "Introduction," Part II: "Public Sentiments" sets the stage by detailing how 9/11 impacted the psychological well being of the public, causing them to trade security for liberty and seeing government as trustworthy than menacing. PART III: "Legislative Climate" investigates into the legislative climate and behavior of the 9/11 Congress. It finds that the Congress members were as eager as the public to do anything and everything to secure the Nation, including deferring to an imperial President in time of war. PART IV: "Political Gamesmanship" analyzes Bush's post 9/11 rhetoric and actions. It finds that Bush has seized upon 9/11 as an opportunity to promote his political agenda, including ushering in a police state. Part V: "Media Patriotism" tells a story of how the media was changed from an independent democratic institution guarding our liberty into a propaganda machine promoting a national security state. PART IV summarizes the key findings in observing that the USAPA passed the Congress with the

---

[458] Ted Goertzel, "September 11, 2001: A Turning Point for America's Future?" The World Future Society. http://www.wfs.org/goertzel.htm ("But not all such traumas trigger a lasting shift in what the Germans call the *zeitgeist,* or the "spirit of the age")

approval of a traumatized people, acquiescent of a complaint Congress, manipulation of an endangered President and complicity of a patriotic media. In the end, the passage of USAPA, like any other war time legislation, was to be expected given the prevailing public sentiments, national ethos and political realities of the time.

II. PUBLIC SENTIMENTS

"I am becoming ever more enraged that a terrorist attack, however evil, brilliant, and devastating, has been used by the Bush administration to justify virtually every attempt to deprive Americans of long-held rights and values."
Anonymous (2001)[459]

For the American people 9/11 brought fear of terror as they discovered hope in self-help and trust in government.[460] For the Congress it faced challenges as a co-equal branch of government[461] as it found strength as a bi-partisan institution.[462] For the President it posed the first challenge to his leadership of a country at war but also offered a second chance to re-invent himself as a leader of the free world.[463] Overnight "Bush underwent a metamorphosis for many Americans from an inept usurper into a competent, strong, and eloquent president."[464] Finally, the media was asked to defend freedom and democracy, from illusive enemies without (terrorists) and an imperialistic President within (Bush), under the stricture of patriotic journalism, Dan Rather style. This was the social-political climate that gave birth to the USAPA.

Public Sentiments

9/11 was a traumatic event.[465] The public was hurt and angry, uncertain and anxious, and above all else scared and fearful.[466] Stress symptoms - recurrent and intrusive distressing

---

[459] *Understanding America after 9/11* (Corporation for Public Broadcasting). See "Is your life different today because of September 11?" *UnderstandingAmerica.org* http://understandingamerica.publicradio.org/form /index.shtml

[460] Michael Traugott; Ted Brader; Deborah Coral; Richard Curtin; David Featherman; Robert Groves; Martha Hill; James Jackson; Thomas Juster; Robert Kahn; Courtney Kennedy; Donald Kinder; Beth-Ellen Pennell; Matthew Shapiro; Mark Tessler; David Weir; Robert Willis, "How Americans Responded: A Study of Public Reactions to 9/11/01," *PS: Political Science and Politics* Vol. 35 (3): 511-516 (2002).

[461] James Lindsay, "Deference and Defiance: The Shifting Rhythms of Executive-Legislative Relations in Foreign Policy," *Presidential Studies Quarterly* Vol. 33 (3): 530-46 (2003). ("September 11 explains Congress's shift from defiance of Clinton to deference to Bush.")

[462] USAPA passed the Senate 98-1, and the House 357-66, with bi-partisan support.

[463] Denis M. Bostdorff, "George W. Bush's post-September 11 rhetoric of covenant renewal: Upholding the faith of the greatest generation," *Quarterly Journal of Speech* Vol. 89 (4): 293-319 (2003)

[464] *Id.* P. 313.

[465] Sarah Graham, "9/11: The Psychological Aftermath," *Scientific America.com* November 12, 2001 (9/11 changed many people's life. A lot of them suffered from PTSD.) Erina L. MacGeorge, *et al.* "Stress, Social Support, and Health Among College Students After September 11, 2001," *Journal of College Student Development* Volume 45 (6): 655-670 (2004) (In December 2001, A survey of 666 students from Eastern universities (N= 666; 482 women, 184 men; average age 19.5 yrs.) showed that "terrorism-related stress was associated with greater depression and illness symptoms (p < .05). Emotional and tangible support were associated with fewer symptoms (p < .05)." (Abstract).)

recollections of the event (i.e.,, flashbacks of the traumatic event), persistent avoidance of stimuli associated with the trauma (i.e.,, avoiding tall buildings), numbing of general responsiveness (i.e.,, diminished interest in others and/or participation in activities once considered enjoyable), and persistent symptoms of increased arousal (i.e.,, becoming startled upon hearing any loud noise) - were to be found everywhere.[467]

A survey was conducted of US national and cities' residents immediately after 9/11,[468] particularly: "What was the general psychological response of Americans both individually and collectively? Indicators include psychosomatic symptoms, psychological well-being, anomie, misanthropy, locus of control, anxiety and fear, and related dimensions." It finds that upon hearing the news of 9/11 attack people were by and large upset in what happened.[469] More specifically, they experienced stress symptoms, i.e., nervous (nationwide 50.6%, NYC 63%), cried (nationwide 60.0%, NYC 71%) and have trouble going to sleep (nationwide 52.2%, NYC 62.0%). (Table 1 below) They were also angry (nationwide 65%, NYC 73%) and to a lesser extent worried about own life/safety (nationwide 28.0%, NYC 40%).[470]

During national crisis, people yearned for Presidential leadership expected Congressional action. The public wanted retribution from the terrorists and a peace of mine from terrorism.[471] The public demanded immediate security. The President promised quick revenge[472] and a long war.[473] The FBI was committed to tracking down the terrorists and sealing the border.[474] The Congress was ready to do something, anything to improve upon homeland security preparedness. This was the mood of the Nation and mentality of the people immediately after 9/11.

The Nation was in great turmoil, but two things seemed to be certain. Stringent security measures were needed to protect the Nation from future terrorist attacks. The people desired and expected substantial curtailment of personal freedom and and civil liberties.

---

[466] It also appears that 9/11 was able to make American society come together as never before. People were more communitarian, public spirited and trusting of their government. Amitai Etzioni, "American Society in the Age of Terrorism," *The Communitarian Network* http://www2.gwu.edu/~ccps/news_american_society.html#n_1

[467] PTSD clinical criteria, according to the Diagnostic and Statistical Manual of Mental Disorders (DSM IV), the

[468] Tom Smith, Kenneth A. Rasinksi, Mariana Toce, "America Rebounds: A National Study of Public Response to the September 11th Terrorist Attacks – Preliminary Finding' NORC, University of Chicago, October 25, 2005. The study sample was drawn randomly from around the nation (1000) and in New York City; Washington, DC; and Chicago areas (500).

[469] Table 4 "Feelings When First Heard About Assassination/Terrorist Attacks: Percentage Reporting Selected.

[470] Table 5: Feelings Hen First Heard About Assassination/Terrorists Attacks: Percentage Reporting Selected Feelings Among "Very Deepest", *Id.* P. 16.

[471] See Rep. Tome Petri, "Congress after 9/11," Weekly Column, Nov. 21, 2001. http://www.house.gov/petri/weekly/nov21_01.htm ("The heightened security around the U.S. Capitol building serves to remind the Congress every day that we are at war. Of course, the real fight is half a world away. But we are doing our part.")

[472] President Bush, "Address to a Joint Session of Congress and the American People," White House, September 24, 2001. ("Whether we bring our enemies to justice, or bring justice to our enemies, justice will be done")

[473] James Gerstenzang and Greg Miller, "Bush Warns of Long War." LA Times September 16, 2001 (Bush: "They will try to hide, they will try to avoid the United States and our allies--but we're not going to let them...") See Bob Woodward, Bush at War (Simon and Schuster, 2002) (Bush: "They had declared war on us, and I made up my mind at that moment that we were going to war")

[474] "FBI targets Florida sites in terrorist search: Survivors may be still in Trade Center rubble," *CNN* September 11, 2001 Posted: 11:56 PM EDT (0356 GMT) (FBI reacted immediately on 9/11 to trace the terrorists. Relying on passenger lists, FBI searched Florida for suspects and evidence responsible for 9/11. Within 48 hours the FBI has identified all 19 suspected terrorists, with one at large; with photos displayed on TV and media.)

Table 1. Post – 9/11 vs. 1963 Kennedy Assassination - Physical/ Emotional symptoms

Symptoms	1963 Kennedy Assassination	2001 Nationwide	2001 New York City
Felt nervous and tense	68.0%	50.6%	63.0%
Felt sort of dazed and dumb	57.0%	45.9%	42.6%
Cried	53.0%	60.0%	71.0%
Had trouble going to sleep	48.0%	52.2%	62.0%
Didn't feel like eating	43.0%	29.3%	42.6%
Felt more tired and usual	42.0%	36.4%	48.0%
Kept forgetting things	34.0%	18.6%	24.2%
Smoked much more than usual	29.0%	21.4%	19.9%
Had rapid heartbeat	26.0%	15.8%	24.0%
Had headaches	25.0%	20.4%	25.4%
Had an upset stomach	22.0%	35.4%	25.1%
Lost temper more than usual	19.0%	20.0%	25.9%
Hand sweat felt clammy	17.0%	8.9%	13.2%
Dizzy at time	12.0%	8.4%	16.0%
Felt like getting drunk	4.0%	6.7%	12.4%
Felt none of these	11.0%	10.8%	4.1%

Source: Adapted from Table 7 "Comparison of Physical/ Emotional symptoms." Tom Smith, Kenneth A. Rasinksi, Mariana Toce, "America Rebounds: A National Study of Public Response to the September 11th Terrorist Attacks – Preliminary Finding' NORC, University of Chicago, October 25, 2005.

Table 2. Pre and Post 9/11 Public Opinion on the Necessity to Give Up Civil Liberties[475]

Date	Question	Necessary	Not necessary	Don't know
April 1995[a]	In order to curb terrorism in this country, do you think it will be necessary for the average person to give up some civil liberties, or not?	49	43	8
March 1996[b]	In order to curb terrorism in this country, do you think it will be necessary for the average person to give up some civil liberties, or not?	30	65	5
April 1997[c]	In order to curb terrorism in this country, do you think it will be necessary for the average person to give up some civil liberties, or not?	29	62	9
September 2001[d]	In order to curb terrorism in this country, do you think it will be necessary for the average person to give up some civil liberties, or not?	55	35	10

---

[475] See Amitai Etzioni and Deirdre Mead , "The State of Society - A Rush to Pre-9/11," The Communitarian Network (9/2002). http://www.gwu.edu/~ccps/The_State_of_Society.html

Date	Question	Necessary	Not necessary	Don't know
September 2001[e]	In order to curb terrorism in this country, do you think it will be necessary for the average person to give up some liberties, or not?	61	33	6
September 2001[f]	In order to curb terrorism, do you think it will be necessary for the average person to give up some liberties, or not?	63	32	5
October 2001[g]	Do you think Americans will have to give up some of their personal freedoms in order to make the country safe from terrorist attacks, or not?	79	17	4
November 2001[h]	In order to curb terrorism in this country do you think it will be necessary for the average person to give up some rights and liberties, or do you think we can curb terrorism without the average person giving up rights and liberties?	51*	46*	3
November 2001[h]	Do you think you will have to give up some of your OWN rights and liberties in order to curb terrorism, or not?	58**	39**	3
January 2002[i]	In order to curb terrorism, do you think it will be necessary for the average person to give up some liberties, or not?	55	39	6
June 2002[j]	In order to curb terrorism, do you think it will be necessary for the average person to give up some liberties, or not?	49	45	6
June 2002[k]	In order to curb terrorism, do you think it will be necessary for the average person to give up some liberties, or not?	46	44	8

Sources: a. Los Angeles Times Poll 26-27 April 1995. b. Pew Research Center for the People and Press News Interest Poll, 28-31 March 1996. c. Pew Research Center for the People and Press News Interest Poll, 3-6 April 1997. d. Los Angeles Times Poll, 13-14 September 2002. e. Pew Center for The People and Press, Poll, 13-17 September 2001. f. Princeton Survey Research Associates/Newsweek Poll, 20-21 September 2001.g. CBS News Poll, 8 October 2001. Responses included "will have to" (79 percent) and "will not" (17 percent) h. National Public Radio/Kaiser/Kennedy School Poll on Civil Liberties, 31 October -12 November 2001. i. Pew Research Center for the People and Press News Interest Index Poll, 9-13 January 2002. j. Pew Research Center for the People and Press News Interest Index Poll, 19-23 June 2002. k. Princeton Survey Research Associates/Newsweek Poll, 27-28 June 2002. Responses includes "yes" and "no" Notes: * Responses include "necessary for the average person to give up some rights and liberties" (51 percent) and "we can curb terrorism without the average person giving up rights and liberties" (46 percent).** Responses include "yes" (58 percent) and "no" (39 percent).

The public expressed ambivalent feelings about the impact of war on terror legislation. Thus, while the public expressed support the President in fighting terrorism (Table 2), they were also concerned with restriction on liberties and lack of strong terrorism law, *at the same time* (Table 3). Specifically, in September 2001, 39% of the public were concerned the government fail to enact strong anti-terror laws and 34% of Americans were concerned that such laws would too restrictive of civil liberties. The concern for more restrictive law grew by the month, i.e., September 2001 (34%) to November 2002 (44%). In essence, the public are quite confused about what they really want.

Table 3. Concerns about Restrictions of Civil Liberties

What concerns you more right now? That the government will fail to enact strong, new anti-terrorism laws, or that the government will enact new anti-terrorism laws which restrict the average person's civil liberties?

	Enact laws that restrict civil liberties	Fail to enact strong laws	Neither	Don't know/ refused
September 2001	34	39	10	17
January 2002	45	40	3	12
June 2002	49	35	3	13
November 2002*	44	40	3	11

Sources: Pew Research Center for the People and the Press Post-Terrorist Attack Poll, 13-17 September 2001; Pew Research Center for the People and the Press News Interest Index Poll, 9-13 January 2002; Pew Research Center for the People and the Press News Interest Index Poll, 19-23 June 2002; and CBS News/New York Times Poll, 20-24 November 2002.

Note: * The November 2002 poll asked "Which concerns you more right now?" instead of "What concerns you more right now?" It also offered the option both (3 percent).

One might be tempted to dismiss the public sentiments as uninformed, implying that if the public knew better they would feel, think and react to 9/11 differently. Two responses should suffice to lay this observation to rest. First, research has shown that 9/11 is one of the most watched events in world of all time.[476] Otherwise, the public was more knowledgeable about political matters after 9/11 than ever before.[477] Second, even if we concede that public sentiments were driven by ignorance, influenced by media,[478] or manipulated by politicians,[479] their impact on public policy and influence on political leaders are real, substantial and consequential.

---

[476] Scott L. Althaus, "American News Consumption during Times of National Crisis," *PS: Political Science and Politics* Vol. 35 (3): 517-521 (2002)

[477] See "Table 1: Knowledge of the "War on Terrorism" and Current Political Issues." In p. 529 Markus Prior, "Political Knowledge after September 11," *PS: Political Science and Politics* Vol. 35 (3): 523-529 (2002). (Knowledge of political issues ranged from low of 32% (name of Secretary of State) to 89% (anthrax most difficult to treat).

[478] Stephanie Craft and Wayne Wanta, "U. S. Public Concerns in the Aftermath of 9-11: A Test of Second Level Agenda-Setting," *International Journal of* Public Opinion *Research*, Vol. 16 (4): 456-463 (2004) (Public opinion correlated with media coverage.)

[479] Chaim Kaufmann, "Threat Inflation and the Failure of the Marketplace of Ideas: The Selling of the Iraq War," *International Security* Volume 29 (1): 5-48 (2004) ("Most important, the marketplace of ideas failed to correct the administration's misrepresentations or hinder its ability to persuade the American public." (p. 6).

The discussion above makes clear that overall post 9/11 public sentiments were anxious about terrorism. Repeated surveys immediately after 9/11 showed that the public were more afraid of the terrorists than concerned with their own civil liberties. In this regard, they expected their government to do the right thing to protect them (from "evil") and trusted the officials to be solicitous of their well being (to hold them harmless).[480] Both sentiments were unrealistic, if romantic and idealistic, notions of what democratic governance in all about, and both of these were also what the people expect of their government in time of crisis.

Observations

Viewed in the above context, it can hardly be said that the USAPA was not drafted in response to the public's needs. The public simply has chosen to defer to the political leadership and government experts to protect them. In this regard, the observation by public intellectuals and policy elite, a/k/a left of center thinkers the like of Noam Chomsky,[481] that the passage of USAPA was undemocratic in process[482] and violating of Constitutional norm in outcome was nothing but "barking up the wrong tree". The democracy was functioning as well as it could be under the circumstances, i.e., expressing the view and registering the voices of the people,[483] however emotional, irrational, ignorant or gullible. In the ultimate analysis, in a democracy, what public wants, public gets. The public vote according to their sentiments. Sentiments are neither right nor wrong; they do dictate and decide. To argue otherwise is to substitute "elite" rule for "popular" governance.

We can derive three observations from this short discussion on post 9/11 public sentiments: First, democracy is a messy business. It is "messy" because people do not necessary know what they want. It is "messy" because people do not decide rationally. Finally it is also messy because we cannot clearly decide who wins or loses. Second, democracy does not foster optimal and absolute black and white choices. The best one can hope for is sensible compromises. Everyone wins some. Everyone loses some. Third, democracy is judged as a long drawn process, not by a one time result. For example, it takes long time to right political wrongs.

Ultimately, there is an issue and how to measure success of a democratic form of government, e.g., public participation, constitutional safeguards and check and balance; here the USAPA. In the present case, the democratic process might not have failed as much as it is too early to tell. It took the Nation 50 years to right the wrong of the WWII unconstitutional

---

[480] Darren W. Davis; Brian D. Silver, "Civil Liberties vs. Security: Public Opinion in the Context of the Terrorist Attacks on America," *American Journal of Political Science* Vol. 48 (1): 28-46 (2004). (Political ideology, national pride and social trust has determinative impact on willingness to forgo civil liberties in the face of threats.(p. 43)

[481] "On 9-11: Noam Chomsky interviewed by Nicholas Holt," *Asheville Global Report*, March 8, 2002. (The way to undermine democracy is to privatize state power and keeping the citizens uninformed and distracted: "So yes, they used the Sept. 11 opportunity to get that through and if they can keep the public ignorant and frightened and involved in something else...) http://www.chomsky.info/interviews/20020308.htm

[482] Tony Platt, Cecilia O'Leary, "Patriot acts," *Social Justice*. Vol. 30 (1): 5 (The Bush administration and conservative Republican Party was about to subvert the democratic process through fear and intimidation after 9/11)

[483] Deborah Wilkins Newman, "September 11: A societal reaction perspective," *Crime, Law and Social Change*. Vol. 39 (3): 219 (2003)

internment of Japanese in the name of national security.[484] It might take as long to recognize that the waging of war of terror is wrong headed and ill executed, if it ever happened. If not the public has spoken by and through the democratic process.

The proper assessment of USAPA must take these lessons to heart.

III. LEGISLATIVE CLIMATE

"The heightened security around the U.S. Capitol building ....serves to remind the Congress every day that we are at war. Of course, the real fight is half a world away. But we are doing our part."

See Rep. Tome Petri (November 2001) [485]

On September 13, 2001, House Democratic Leader Richard A. Gephardt (D-Mo.) spoke forebodingly and ominously about the impending civil liberties great chill, i.e., the tilting of balance on the debate of security vs. liberty, in favor of the former: "We're in a new world where we have to rebalance freedom and security ... We can't take away people's civil liberties . . . but we're not going to have all the openness and freedom we have had."[486]

A Conservative Agenda

Even in normal time, not to speak of during national crisis, the Republicans were far more prone to want security over liberties.[487] The republican stance was well represented by Senate Minority Leader Trent Lott (R-Miss.): "when you're at war, civil liberties are treated differently ... We've been having an academic discussion and holding our breath in this area for several years .. We can't do that anymore."

The Democrats, while mindful of the urgency and dangerousness of a national crisis, called for a more reflective and in turn balanced response. Rep. Christopher Cox (R-Calif.), typical of the Democratic approach in observing:

"Frisking everyone on the planet to find the one person with the weapon is a high-cost, low-yield way to go ... That's a fair analogy to searching through everyone's e-mail. Not only

---

[484] "Righting an old wrong," Journal Sentinel Online Nov. 30, 2000 (The U.S. Government has recognized doing wrong to Japanese-American citizens who were interned 50 years ago for security grounds, but no such consolations have been offered to the 11,000 German-Americans in Wisconsin detained during WWII.) Leslie T. Hatamiya, *Righting a Wrong: Japanese Americans and the Passage of the Civil Rights Act of 1988.* (CA: Stanford University Press, 1993)

[485] See Rep. Tome Petri, "Congress after 9/11," Weekly Column, Nov. 21, 2001. http://www.house.gov/ petri/weekly/nov21_01.htm

[486] Eric Pianin and Thomas B. Edsall, "Terrorism Bills Revive Civil Liberties Debate," *Washington Post* Friday, September 14, 2001; Page A16 http://www.washingtonpost.com/ac2/wp-dyn/A28636-2001Sep14?language=printer

[487] *Fox Butterfield, "Bush's Law and Order Adds Up to Tough and Popular," New York Times August 18, 1999. http://partners.nytimes.com/library/politics/camp/081899wh-gop-bush.html*

do such schemes threaten civil liberties, they are such scattershot approaches that they are bound to fail." [488]

The USAPA reflected and reinforced the political agenda of Republican Party. In the end, the USAPA was used more by police officers to fight crime than relied upon to homeland security officials to secure the nation. [489]

A cursory inspection of the Congressional records revealed that there were a total of 374 U.S. Congressional actions - bills, resolutions, and amendments – introduced from September 11, 2001 through June 18, 2002 having to do with September 11 attacks (Table 4). Most of the legislative actions appeared in September, i.e., 33 in September, 26 in October, 16 in November, 11 in December, 0 in January and February, 2 in March, 3 in April. 72 legislative actions were acted upon by the House or Senate with some sort of floor action. Sixteen resolutions were passed. Seventeen bills and joint resolutions became law. There was a total of 11 "General Terrorism/ Security" bills or resolutions, including H.R. 3004: Financial Anti-terrorism Act of 2001; S. 1981: Enhanced Penalties for Enabling Terrorist Act of 2002; and S. AMDT. 1562 to H.R. 2500: To enhance the capability of the United States to deter, prevent, and thwart domestic and international acts of terrorism against United States nationals and interests ("2001 Combating Terrorism Amendment"). Only one, i.e., H.R. 3162: USAPA made it into law.

Table 4. The number of 9/11 legislative actions acted upon within six (6) months*

Bills/ Res.	1 D	2 D	1 W	2 W	3 W	4 W	1 M	2 M	3 M	4 M>	Total (%)
No.	41*	8	4	10	6	3	1	9	5	4	91 (100%)
%	45%	8.8%	4.4%	11%	6.6%	3.3%	1.1%	9.9%	5.5%	4.4%	
Total	45%	53.8%	58.2%	69.2%	75.3%	78.6%	79.7%	89.6%	95.1%	99.5%	

*Including 19 floor amendments.

Source: Extracted from Margaret F. Klemm and Albert C. Ringelstein, "Congressional Response to the September 11, 2001 Terrorist Attacks," *extensions. A Journal of Carl Albert Center* (Fall 2002).

As to the nature of post 9/11 legislative actions, they were sponsored by Republicans and Democrats in equal number. Most of them actually enjoyed bipartisan support, with many being co-sponsored. An analysis of 91 of such legislative acts reveals that most of them are symbolic in nature, e.g., H.J. Res. 71 designates September 11 as "Patriot Day" or compensatory in kind, e.g., H.R. 2884: Victims of Terrorism Relief Act 2001 sought financial relief for 9/11 victims (Table 5).

---

[488] Eric Pianin and Thomas B. Edsall, "Terrorism Bills Revive Civil Liberties Debate," *Washington Post* Friday, September 14, 2001; Page A16 http://www.washingtonpost.com/ac2/wp-dyn/A28636-2001Sep14?language=printer

[489] J.M. KALIL and STEVE TETREAULT, "PATRIOT ACT: Law's use causing concerns: Use of statute in corruption case unprecedented, attorneys contend," *Las Vegas Review-Journal*, November 05, 2003 (USAPA powers were used to investigate stripe clubs political corruption in Las Vegas, including Galardi, owner of Jaguars and Cheetah's topless clubs; Malone; former Commissioner Erin Kenny; County Commission Chairwoman Mary Kincaid-Chauncey; former County Commission Chairman Dario Herrera; and former Las Vegas City Councilman Michael McDonald.)

Of all the post 9/11 measures, only the USAPA substantially alters the balance of power between executive and judiciary and dilutes the constitutional rights of the citizens. [490] The most egregious constitutional right violations include: the use of "sneak and peek" to search premises without the presence or notice of the owner; the use of "roving wiretaps" to in a premise or area he/she a target can reasonably be found; the use of FISA wiretap to gather criminal evidence without traditional showing that foreign intelligence collection is "the" primary objective of the wiretap; the use of "pen register" to retrieve dialing, routing and signaling information, including content revealing URL or web "address"; and finally the use of Section 215 to access personal information, including medical records, student records, financial records, employment records, DNA samples, and drug testing records.[491]

Table 5. Post 9/11 (to April 25, 2002) Action on Legislation

Type of Legislation	Bills/Joint Resolutions Signed into Law	Non-Legally Binding (Other) Resolutions Approved	Bills/Joint Resolutions Floor Action	Non-Legally Binding Resolutions Floor Action	*Total*
Economic Relief – General	2		5		7
Economic Relief – Bonds			4		4
Economic Relief / Small Business			1		1
Victim Relief	2		10		12
Budget Acts	3		3		6
Aviation	2		5		7
General Terrorism / Security	1		10		11
Immigration	1				1
Foreign Affairs / Assistance / Military Affairs	3		1	1	5
Symbolic	2	15	6	10	33
Education	1		2		3
Total	15	15	47	11	91

Source: Margaret F. Klemm and Albert C. Ringelstein, "Congressional Response to the September 11, 2001 Terrorist Attacks," extensions. A Journal of Carl Albert Center (Fall 2002). http://www.ou.edu/special/albertctr/extensions/fall2002/Klemm.html.

More significantly for our purposes, most of the legislative action was acted upon quickly with great urgency and little scrutiny, just when contemplation, scrutiny and deliberation is most needed.[492] However, the observation that more time should or could have been spent

---

[490] Dan Eggen, "Key Part of Patriot Act Ruled Unconstitutional Internet Providers' *Washington Post*, Thursday, September 30, 2004; Page A16 (Federal District Judge Victor Marrero of Southern District in a lengthen decision (120 pages) ruled in favor of ACLU and against the Attorney General finding that the use of FBI administrative subpoena known as a national security letter as applied to Internet providers to be unconstitutional because it "effectively bars or substantially deters any judicial challenge" making it "an unlimited government warrant to conceal . . . has no place in our open society.") See Decision and Order to *Doe and ACLU v. Ashcroft et al.,* No. 04-CIV-2614, issued September 28, 2004. http://nccprivacy.org/handv/041001hero.htm

[491] "The Patriot Act: One Step Closer to a Police State?" *The NorthStar News*, April 22, 2003.(.)

[492] See also Margaret F. Klemm and Albert C. Ringelstein, "Congressional Response to the September 11, 2001 Terrorist Attacks," *extensions. A Journal of Carl Albert Center* (Fall 2002).

deliberating on the Anti-Terrorism Act of 2001 and later USAPA must take into account the frantic and pressing nature of the legislative environment immediately after 9/11. The Congressional members have to deal with many legislative actions right after 9/11. This precluded them from spending much time on each and every legislative action. This is not to suggest that Congress should not prioritize their time better, i.e., focus on more significant bills like those of Anti-Terrorism Act of 2001 or the administration could not have been more forthcoming with their cooperation and support, e.g., attending more Congressional hearings. It is to observe that it is humanly impossible for the Congressional members to read, much less debate, each and every pieces of bill or resolutions in detail. Something (bills, resolutions) have to give.

Observations

The speedy passage of a conservative USAPA is a victim of circumstances. Both houses of Congress were dominated by hawkish Republicans who preferred security over liberty. The crisis mentality prevailing in the Capital in time of "war" made the Congressional members less judicious and more receptive to 9/11 bills and resolutions. In the end the USAPA was "rushed" passed Congress by the Bush administration without following the formal legislative procedure, i.e., agency review, public hearings, mark up, floor debate, and conference report, in both chambers.

Judge by all indications, the USAPA was an imperfect legislation, in process and outcome. But given the dire circumstances afflicting the nation, it is a piece of legislation that everyone can live with, for the time being.

USAPA as proposed by the Bush administration was supported by the people and approved by the Congress. Any change to the content and language of the USAPA must wait for the Constitutional – political and/or judicial – process to run its natural, if contentious course; five years hence.[493] However once in place, USAPA starts to take roots, grow branches and bear fruits, getting harder and harder to remove. That is exactly what the Bush administration wants.

---

http://www.ou.edu/special/albertctr/extensions/fall2002/Klemm.html This line of research advises that balanced analysis and fruitful evaluation of the legislative process of USAPA cannot be conducted without an understanding of the context. See also "9-11 prompts orgy of federal "legislation" *Idaho Observer* Nov. 9, 2001. http://proliberty.com/observer/20011208.htm (USAPA is one of many legislative actions taken to address and redress 9/11 related problems and issues. There were 140 odd pieces of 9/11 related legislative actions, from legislation to resolution, as of November of 2001.)

[493] See Chapter 7: Grassroots resistance.

IV. POLITICAL GAMESMANSHIP

Just how elastic are the uses of fear in a democracy …?

Eric Alterman (2004)[494]

President in Search of a Vision and Mission

President Bush arrived at the White House in search of a personal image,[495] domestic agenda, [496] Party identity, [497] political legitimacy, [498] governing mandate, [499] and public support.[500] Bush was elected to office after losing the popular vote with a wide margin (330,000) and winning the highest office by a few electoral votes. Worse, there were persistent allegations and clear evidence of vote fraud.[501]

In the end, Bush's presidency was secured with the thinnest vote margins (by 537 votes in Florida, a state governed by his brother Jeff Bush) and only after the intervention of a

---

[494] Eric Alterman, "Fear: What Is It Good For?" *Social Research* Vol.: 71 (4): 997-1014 (2004).

[495] James Carney, "The Bush Team: Losing Control of the Spin," *Time Online Edition* July 1, 2001 (When first elected to office, the public did not have a positive image of Bush. He was seen as inexperience, not serious and beholden to special interests.) http://www.time.com/time/nation/article/0,8599,166000,00.html Matthew Yglesias, "The Brains Thing," *The American Prospect* September 1, 2004 (Liberals did not think he has enough smart to be a good President.) http://www.prospect.org/web/page.ww?section=rootandname=View PrintandarticleId=8343

[496] Jeffrey M. Jones, "Analysis: Americans' Support for Bush's 2002 Domestic and Foreign Policy Agenda (2 Part Analysis),"Gallup, 2-28-02. (After 9/11, according to CNN/USA Gallup Poll (1/25-27/02), 73% believe the country was moving in the right direction and only 19% think they the country is moving in the wrong direction.)

[497] David Brooks, "How to reinvent the G.O.P." *New York Times Magazine*, August 29, 2004. Late Edition - Final, Section 6, Page 32 , Column 1 (The Bush they nominated was not the same man after 9/11. The Republican Party now has an identity crisis on hand – Bush does not fit conventional Republican label!)

[498] U.S. Supreme Court has to intervene to decide that Bush was the winner. Per Curiam, GEORGE W. BUSH, et al., PETITIONERS v. ALBERT GORE, Jr., et al. ON WRIT OF CERTIORARI TO THE FLORIDA SUPREME COURT, SUPREME COURT OF THE UNITED STATES [December 12, 2000] See Norman Solomon, "Media Crucial As Bush Faces 'Legitimacy Gap'," *FAIR's Media Beat* December 14, 2000 ("Only pressure from the grassroots, fueled by tenacious memory and independent thought, can deny the incoming Bush administration the national sense of legitimacy that it craves.") http://www.commondreams.org/views/121400-107.htm Kevin Phillips, "His Fraudulency the Second? The illegitimacy of George W. Bush," *American Prospect* Vol. 12 (2): 22 – 5 (2001).

[499] "The accidental president," *The Economist* Dec 14th 2000 and "The Accidental President," *Newsweek* September 17th edition.

[500] John Roper "The Contemporary Presidency: George W. Bush and the Myth of Heroic Presidential Leadership," *Presidential Studies Quarterly* Vol. 34 (1):132-42 (2004) (President Bush has a public image problem of "doubtful intellectual abilities, a nodding acquaintance with the English language, and a semidetached attitude to international relations, indeed to the whole idea of governance.") Before 9/11 Bush has a job approval rating of less than 50%. After 9/11 his rating soured to 90%.

[501] Alastair Thompson, "Diebold Memos Disclose Florida 2000 E-Voting Fraud," *Scoop.* Friday, 24 October 2003, 11:18 am (An internal memo revealed that a possible computer error caused 16,000 of Gore votes to disappear in Florida.) http://www.scoop.co.nz/stories/HL0310/S00211.htm

"politicized"[502] Supreme Court stopping the recount of "butterfly" votes on "equal protect grounds."[503] Bush was accused of stealing an election.[504]

Bush was drifting along listlessly before 9/11 struck.[505] 9/11 supplied the President with a golden opportunity to galvanize a divided nation[506] to his ideological cause[507] with certitude and certainty for all.[508] It was also a transforming and defining moment of Bush's Presidency.
[509] 9/11 gave him a purpose, identity, and legitimacy. He seized the moment and quickly established himself as the quintessential war time President, avenging wrong and doing right; all in the name of freedom, democracy and the people[510]

> "After September 11, he struck Americans as just the right leader to express our collective sorrow, rage, and resolve to defeat a loathsome enemy…First, it was apparent that Bush had "the vision thing" — in abundance…Second, throughout the autumn of 2001, Bush showed the American people that he had an unclouded view of good and evil...Third, it helped that Bush surrounded himself with a first-rate team of advisers. ..Fourth, after 9/11 Bush seemed to be the right man for the job because of his ability to deal with crises. It helps that

---

[502] Professor William G. Ross, "*Bush v. Gore* and the Prestige of the Supreme Court: A "Self-inflicted Wound"? [Commentary] *Jurist* December 13, 2000 ("all five conservative members opposed Gore's plea for additional vote recounts, while all four liberal members took a contrary position. Each of the Justices moreover favored a position on federalism that is ostensibly contrary to his or her usual position").

[503] Alan M. Dershowitz, *Supreme Injustice: How the High Court Hijacked Election 2000* (New York, 2001). For a more balanced view, see Howard Gillman's *The Votes That Counted: How the Court Decided the 2000 Presidential Election* (Chicago, 2001). For a sympathetic treatment of Court's role in the 2000 election. Richard A. Posner, *Breaking the Deadlock: The 2000 Election, the Constitution, and the Courts* (Cambridge, Mass., 2001).

[504] Marc Morano, "Feminists Compare Bush's 2000 Election Victory to 'Savage Rape," *CNSNews.com* September 02, 2004 (Four years after Bush was elected to office, people still remember a stolen election. The feminist organization NOW depicted Bush 2000 election as a "savage rape".)

[505] Greenstein, Fred I., "The Contemporary Presidency:" The Changing Leadership of George W. Bush: A Pre- and Post-9/11 Comparison," *Presidential Studies Quarterly* Vol.32 (2): 387-96 (2002) (9/11 transformed George W. Bush. Before 9/11 Bush was decidedly unimpressive in his handling the office of the Presidency.)

[506] G. C. Jacobson, "The Bush Presidency and the American Electorate," *Presidential Studies Quarterly* Vol. 33 (4): 701-29 (2003) (President Bush inherited a divided nation. Of the 28 Gallup and CBS News/New York Times polls taken prior to September 11, Bush's approval ratings average 88 percent among self-identified Republicans but only 31 percent among Democrats.)

[507] David Westphal, "The Bush Administration: Year 1: Replacing doubt with dominance," http://www.sacbee.com/content/news/projects/attacks/story/1497485p-1574215c.html Published 5:30 am PST Sunday, January 20, 2002 (9/11 saved Bush's presidency. It allowed him to demonstrate his leadership in crisis as it tapped into the public's need for unity in time of a national crisis and external threats.) Jacobson, G.C. "The Bush Presidency and the American Electorate," *Presidential Studies Quarterly* Vol. 33 (4): 701-29 (2003).

[508] Shawn J. Parry-Giles and Trevor Parry-Giles, Trevor, "INTRODUCTION: CAMPAIGN 2004: LOOKING TO THE PAST FOR IDEOLOGICAL CERTAINTY IN A PERIOD OF NATIONAL ANXIETY," *Rhetoric and Public Affairs*, Vol. 8 (4): 543-548 (2005) (Bush 2004 campaign rhetoric favored "polarization and absolutism over ambiguity and contingency" (p. 544) He did so by appealing to nationalism and exceptionalism. (p. 545). Christian Spielvogel, "YOU KNOW WHERE I STAND": MORAL FRAMING OF THE WAR ON TERRORISM AND THE IRAQ WAR IN THE 2004 PRESIDENTIAL CAMPAIGN," *Rhetoric and Public Affairs*, Vol. 8 (4): 549-569 (2005). (Bush won the election by invoking conservative moral claim of good vs. evil.)

[509] "Attacks Mature, Transform Bush Presidency." *Fox News* Thursday, September 05, 2002 ("Bush has taken the historical opportunity to move from the image of a man who some said couldn't lead a horse to water to a wartime leader with popularity ratings that peaked at 91 percent shortly after Sept. 11.") http://www.foxnews.com/story/0,2933,62176,00.html

[510] John M. Murphy, "Our Mission and Our Moment": George W. Bush and September 11th," *Rhetoric and Public Affairs* Volume 6 (4): 607-632 (2003).

his disposition is action oriented... Whatever the decisions, we know this: 9/11 wholly recast the Bush presidency. Bush, through gutsy leadership, is recasting the post-9/11 world..."[511]

President Bush did not change. 9/11 provided the context and supplied the impetus for Bush to thrive and shine as a crisis leader.[512] 9/11 shattered the gridlock in Washington which in peaceful time is designed to hamstrung a sitting President's power.[513] For example, the passage of the USAPA and the establishment of the Homeland Security cannot usually be achieved except with prolong negotiation, extensive consultation and bouts of partisan free fight; things that Bush is not good at doing – has no knowledge of, experience with, and has very little patience for. In this regard, in spite of his pedidegree – being son of a President – he is very much an outsider. [514]

The ideas Bush used to lead the country were the "culture of fear,"[515] "nation at war,"[516] and "patriotism under fire".[517] The allegations that Bush ruled by a "culture of fear" has often been summarily alleged but rarely conclusively demonstrated:

"Moreover, since the September 11 strikes, the Bush administration has arguably used fear tactics to advance its political agenda, including tax breaks for the rich, curtailment of social programs, military buildup, the most draconian assaults on U.S. rights and freedoms in the contemporary era in the so called USAPA, and a highly controversial and divisive March 2003 war on Iraq."[518]

The problem with proof is *not* one of evidence, of which there are plenty to be had, e.g., from color coded warning system to calling for the use of "duck tape" to secure again WMD attack to sounding alarm of "October Surprise" in an election year. The problem is with interpretation of data and attributing of motive, without all the information on hand during war time. Was Bush and his administration being cautious and over-reacting in sound yet

---

[511] Gleaves Whitney, "9/11 and George W. Bush: The drama of the presidency," *National Review Online*, September 11, 2003. http://nationalreview.com/comment/comment-whitney091103.asp

[512] Michael Genovese, "Presidential Leadership and Crisis Management," *Presidential Studies Quarterly* (1986)

[513] Michael Genovese, "Democratic Theory and Emergency Power of the President," *Presidential Studies Quarterly* Vol. 9 (3) (1979).

[514] Fred I. Greenstein, "The Changing Leadership of George W. Bush: A Pre – Post 9/11 Comparison," *Presidential Studies Quarterly* (June 2002).

[515] Ruth Rosen, "Politics of Fear," *San Francisco Chronicle* Monday, December 30, 2002 (The Bush administration shameless used the politics of fear to achieve its political objectives, e.g., instead of dealing with the imminent threat of nuclear weapon in Korea, it chose to launch a pre-emptive attacked on Iraq, a nation broken by war and contained with sanctions.) "Three Years Later," 9/11 Families for Peaceful Tomorrows Statement," *truthout*, Saturday 11 September 2004 ("The terrorism of September 11th has been neither neutralized, nor ended, by the terrorism of war...When actions that are making the world less secure are carried out in the name of US security, we must reconsider the true sources of the security, freedom, and respect we once commanded around the globe.") http://www.truthout.org/docs_04/091204Z.shtml

[516] J. Roper, "The Contemporary Presidency": George W. Bush and the Myth of Heroic Presidential Leadership," *Presidential Studies Quarterly* Vol. 34 (1): 132-42 (2004) (18 months into his presidency, Bush was able to remake himself as the right man for the job as a steadfast heroic leader of a nation at war.)

[517] Norman Solomon, "The Media Politics of 9/11," Thursday, March 25, 2004, *CommonDreams.org* (Relying on mages and rhetoric about 9/11, Bush team silenced critics and consolidated base with frequent invocation of devastating impact of 9/11 and need for patriotism and unity.) http://www.commondreams.org/views04/0325-18.htm Video and DVD release, *Hijacking Catastrophe: 9/11, Fear, and the Selling of American Empire Media Education Foundation.*

[518] Douglas Kellner, "9/11, Spectacles of Terror, and Media Manipulation: A Critique of Jihadist and Bush Media Politics," Thematic Session. The Media and the Making of a War Culture, American Sociological Association Annual Meeting 2004. August 17, 2004. http://www.gseis.ucla.edu/courses/ed253a/911terrorwarmedia.htm

another alarm of terrorists' attack? Or, was Bush being aggressive and manipulative when he constantly reminded the American people that the Nation faced unrelenting and undiminished threats of terrorism?[519] However, it does appear to be more than co-incidental that terrorism alarms were raised when critical political events occurred,[520] and more generally, whenever it is convenient for President Bush to do so when there are political advantages to be had.[521]

Secrecy, Information Control and Image Management

Three of the more important vehicles Bush used to launch and maintain his imperial Presidency are secrecy,[522] information control[523] and image management.[524] The Bush White House communications team is most adept at limiting press access, plugging administration leaks, rationing important information, crafting sexy images and coordinating policy messages.

Bush is hostile to the news media acting as the "Fourth Estate". Consistent with Bush's personal style and political strategy, he has little use for the press and media.[525] He does not believe the public and the press has a right to know. He does not think the public is capable of retaining, interpreting and digesting complicated information. They need to be spoon fed with processed data; Hollywood style and in sound bites form. With regard to the press, Bush, while understanding of the journalists' traditional role and functions, instinctively does not

---

[519] Ruth Rosen, "Politics of Fear," *San Francisco Chronicle* Monday, December 30, 2002

[520] John Prados, "DEFCON Artists: How the Bush administration uses terrorist threats to its advantage," *The American Prospect* June 2002. ("There is ample reason to suspect that some of these recent warnings of terrorist threats have been made for political purposes.") http://www.prospect.org/print-friendly/webfeatures/2002/06/prados-j-06-12.html

[521] Derrick Z. Jackson, "Bush Shifting Terror Alarm Onto Iraq," *Boston Globe* May 28, 2004. ("Terrorist alerts about Al Qaeda may not be a lie. There is no question the alarming rhetoric on Iraq was.") http://www.commondreams.org/views04/0528-02.htm.
Bill Gallagher, "Delusional Bush Cynically Uses Fear as a Weapon in Sinking Re-election Bid," *Niagara Falls Reporter,* June 1, 2004. ("He is again trying to sell the nutty notion that Iraq represents the frontline in the war on terror, a feeble fabrication that more and more Americans are seeing right through.") http://www.commondreams.org/views04/0601-12.htm

[522] Ken Auletta, "Fortress Bush: How the White House keeps the press under control," *New Yorker,* Issue of 2004-01-19. (Bush sees the press as an elitist institution driven by its own values, interests and agenda, instead of serving the public objectively and selflessly in providing for fair and balance news) http://www.newyorker.com/printables/fact/040119fa_fact2

[523] . See also Nancy Snow, *Information War American Propaganda, Free Speech and Opinion Control since 9-11* (Seven Stories Press, 2003) (William Bennett claimed that those who spoke out against Afghanistan and Iraq are un-American if not even engaging in treasons) *Why We Fight: Moral Clarity and the War on Terrorism* (Henry Regency, 2003)

[524] Martha Joynt Kumar, Communications Operations in the White House of President George W. Bush: Making News on His Terms," *Presidential Studies Quarterly* Vol. 33(2): 366-93 (2003). See especially section on "Carrying Strategy into Messages and Appearances: The Operations Level".

[525] Howard Fineman, "The 'Media Party' is over: CBS' downfall is just the tip of the iceberg," *MSNBC,* Updated: 12:43 p.m. ET Jan. 13, 2005 (President Bush came to town intending on "dictating the terms of dealing with the AMMP (the American Mainstream Media Party) — or simply ignoring it altogether.") http://msnbc.msn.com/id/6813945.
Nicholas Confessore, "Beat the press," *American Prospect* Vol. 13 (5): 12-13 (2002). (The White House treats journalists, e.g., Bob Woodward vs. Dana Milbank (both from Washington Post), based on their support or criticism of the government).

trust the journalists to be interested in or capable of reporting facts in an objective and fair manner.[526]

However, if he must, Bush insists on a well managed press process with abundance of good media coverage, i.e., media coverage at a time, place, manner and content of the President's choosing. Dan Rather of CBS recalled his experience with the White House: "I recently did a story on a senior figure in the Bush White House and was told in advance, 'It better be good.' Jennings at ABC recalled: "There is a feeling among some members of the press corps that you are either favored by the Administration or not, and that will have something to do with your access."

Bush officials are also dismissive of news staff. Senior White House staff members, Card and Rove, usually do not return calls. Junior staffers take pride in not answering reporters' questions. Their view is that the press wants more from the White House – headlines, information, exclusives – than they are willing to give in return for favorable press account or good PR for the White House. For the later, the Bush White House chooses to do it itself, in corporate – Madison Avenue style.[527]

As to information warfare, the Bush administration learned from President Wilson who was successful in transforming a pacifistic and apathetic American public into a belligerent crowd willing to consider entering WWI. With the help of Creel, an American journalist and editor and, an F.O.W. (Friend of Woodrow), Wilson established a Committee on Censorship which was responsible for preparing the American public mentally for war. 90 years later, William Bennett, Ronald Reagan's education secretary and George Bush Sr.'s "drug czar, together with CIA director James Woolsey found the Americans for Victory over Terrorism (AVOT) in the Spring of 2002 to sell Bush's war on terrorism. As part of its strategy, AVOT aligned with the American Council of Trustees and Alumni (ACTA) to silence anti-war dissenters and pro-civil liberties elements. In the fall of 2001 ACTA issued the report "Defending Civilization: How Our Universities are Failing America" which claimed that American professors, some cited and quoted by names, were anti-America and against war on terror.[528]

Bush's information control philosophy was best explained by Rall, a reporter:

> "The Bushies have lifted their reelection strategy straight out of "1984," and not just by creating ominous-sounding agencies like the Office of Homeland Security, the supposedly-closed Office of Strategic Information, and a "Shadow Government." *As in "1984," the Bush regime tolerates zero dissent-a two-party system in name only has been distilled* to one in which only Republicans express acceptable opinions. And an absence of follow-up attacks has been met by endless alerts, advisors and empty hysterics in the name of security, most recently culminating with Tom Ridge's much-mocked color-code warning system."[529] (*Underline supplied*)

---

[526] Ken Auletta, "Fortress Bush: How the White House keeps the press under control.," *New Yorker,* Issue of 2004-01-19.

[527] That job fell on the shoulder of Bush's personal friend and close advisor Karen Hughes who was in charge of external communication form the President from day one. For Bush White House communication organization and style see, Martha Joynt Kumar, Communications Operations in the White House of President George W. Bush: Making News on His Terms," *Presidential Studies Quarterly* Vol. 33(2): 366-93 (2003).

[528] See also Nancy Snow, *Information War American Propaganda, Free Speech and Opinion Control since 9-11* (Seven Stories Press, 2003)

[529] Ted Rall, "From Little Boy to Big Brother in 180 Days: George W. Bush's Perpetual Warfare, " *Washington Post* March 19, 2002 http://www.uexpress.com/tedrall/?uc_full_date=20020319.

What is Bush goal in the strategic use of fear? Speculation runs from advancing neo-conservative political agenda, to imposing an imperial presidency, to bringing about a national security state.[530] Of the three the last is the most plausible explanation in light of the traumatic experience the Nation has just gone through. It is also the rationale most often used by the President and the Congressional leadership to change American value and way of life, from displaying good will to all to finding suspicion in every corner.

In a broader context, the use of fear as a political tool has a long history in the United States. In 1964 Lyndon B. Johnson launched the most famous "daisy girl" ad to "warn" people of a nuclear war if Barry M. Goldwater were to be elected.[531] In 1980 Jimmy Carter portrayed Ronald Reagan as a warmonger to get votes.[532]

The passage of the USAPA must be viewed in this political context; the remaking of President Bush's presidency.

A Textbook Case of Fear Management (Mongering)[533]

The Bush administration achieved their political objectives by inducing fear through disciplined image management, [534] refined rhetorical strategy [535] and finally planned propaganda campaign. "The Department of Defence said they needed to do this, and they were going to actually plant stories that were false in foreign countries -- as an effort to influence public opinion across the world.[536]

A comprehensive review of Bush administration's reaction to 9/11, particularly those of the Attorney General, showed deliberate and coordinate effort to use post 9/11 penned up

---

[530] See "Jennifer Hancock Responds to the Fear Mongering of Rev James Kennedy of the Coral Ridge Ministry," (n.d.) *The Humanists of Florida Association* http://www.floridahumanist.org/issues/revkennedy.htm "mobilizing through fear" is the twin brother to "mobilizing through resentment and hatred." "Fear" and "hatred" is the stock of trade of politicians. When they are joined as a strategic force, they promise to bring the voters home. Jean Hardisty, *Mobilizing Resentment : Conservative Resurgence from the John Birch Society to the Promise Keepers* (Beacon Press (September 15, 2000) (The right wing conservatives attained and retained power by attacking immigrants, public education, reproductive rights, welfare recipients, and religious pluralism.) The politics of hate and fear is not beholden to the right. David Horowitz, "Party of Fear, Politics of Hate," *FrontPageMagazine.com*, October 30, 2000 (The Democratic National Committee promoted fear and hate against President Bush.) Nor are fear and hate an exclusive past time of America. Aijaz Ahmad, "The politics of hate," *Frontline* (India's National Magazine) Vol. 16 (3), Jan. 30 - Feb. 12, 1999 (Hindus use the politics of hate to undermine the onslaught of secularism, democracy and socialism in India.) http://www.frontlineonnet.com/fl1603/16030160.htm

[531] Jack Beatty, "Politics and Prose: The Man Behind the Movement," *Atlantic Unbound*, August 8, 2001 http://www.theatlantic.com/doc/prem/200108u/pp2001-08-08

[532] Jim VandeHei and Howard Kurtz, "The Politics of Fear: Kerry Adopts Bush Strategy of Stressing Dangers," *Washington Post* Wednesday, September 29, 2004; Page A01

[533] Bill Van Auken, "Bush uses lies, fear-mongering to defend war in Iraq, police state measures at home," *World Socialist Web Site* 20 December 2005.

[534] Jeremy D. Mayer, "The Contemporary Presidency: The Presidency and Image Management: Discipline in Pursuit of Illusion," *Presidential Studies Quarterly* Vol. 34 (3): 620-31 (2004) (President Bush was adept at using image (or photo ops) to sell policy, e.g., thanks giving dinner with troops (December 4, 2003) and aircraft carrier landing declaring "major hostilities" were ended in Iraq (April 2003).

[535] David Zarefsky, "Presidential Rhetoric and the Power of Definition," *Presidential Studies Quarterly* 34 no3 607-19 S 2004. (After 9/11, President use "we are at war" rhetoric to consolidate his base and mobilize the nation to his side, giving him tremendous personal power as a war time President to impose restrictions and take away rights of the people.) Citing George C. Edwards III, "Presidential Rhetoric: What Difference Does It Make?" in *Beyond the Rhetorical Presidency*, edited by Martin J. Medhurst (College Station: Texas AandM University Press, 1996).

[536] Interview with Steve Adubato, *Fox News*, 26 December 2002.

emotion and deep seated fear of terrorism to achieve political objectives, e.g., redefining the role of the Presidency and advancement of political ideology.[537] The former made the President and executive first amongst equals of the three branches of government. The later sought expansive and unsupervised law enforcement powers. Both reflected and reinforced Bush's management philosophy and Republican Party's governing ideology.[538]

One of the more damning allegation of using 9/11 fear for President Bush 's personal – political gain, came from Dan Rather. Dan Rather accused the Bush administration (FBI) of issuing unfound and unsubstantiated terrorist alert in New York City to divert the public attention (or mount political damage control) from its ill handling of pre-9/11 intelligence, i.e., CBS reported that the White House was briefed about 9/11 but did not follow up as it should.[539]

It is also clear that the President would *stop at nothing* to exploit the nation's fear for political gain.[540] For example, during this second run for office, Bush ran on the platform of being a war time President. Karen Hughes, a Bush campaign adviser said on CBS "The Early Show."

> "September 11th was not just a distant tragedy. It's a defining event for the future of our country....Obviously, all of us mourn and grieve for the victims of that terrible day, but September 11 fundamentally changed our public policy in many important ways, and I think it's vital that the next president recognize that."[541]

On March 3, 2004 the Bush administration ran three nationwide 30 second ad with 9/11 ground zero as background and actor fire fighters as plot in order to promote President's 9/11 leadership. This attracted wide ranging complaints, at times outrage and outburst, especially from the liberals[542] and some 9/11 victims.[543] Tom Roger, surviving daughter of a flight

---

[537] The use of crisis, as justification to advance political ideology, objectives and agenda is nothing new, nor restricted to the Republican or Democratic Parties. This thesis is most eloquently argued in James Bovard, *Terrorism and Tyranny: Trampling Freedom, Justice, and Peace to Rid the World of Evil* (Palgrave Macmillan, 2003), especially Chapter 4: "Patriot Railroad" (Bush Administration used 9/11 to secure imperial presidency powers, with no oversights from the Congress, supervision by the courts, and accountability to the people.) See also William F. Jasper, "Battling Terrorism With Tyranny," *New American* Vol. 11, No. 11, May 29, 1995. http://www.aros.net/~hempower/drugwar/policestate/90s/950529.html (In 1968 President Lyndon Johnson "exploiting the assassinations of Martin Luther King and Senator Robert Kennedy" rode on a media-led campaign to pressure the Congress to pass the "Omnibus Crime Control and Safe Streets Act." In 1995, on the heel of Oklahoma City bombing, President Clinton sent to Congress for "immediate consideration and enactment," 111-page Omnibus Counter-terrorism Act (S. 390 in the Senate and H.R. 896 in the House).

[538] The fear tactic is attributable to Karl Rove, Bush chief political strategist. See James Moore and Wayne Slater, "Who is Bush's Brain? Karl Rove is, according to a New Book Chronicling the Political Life of the Machiavelli Behind the Throne of King George," A Buzzflash Interview June 2, 2003. http://www.alternet.org/story/16080/

[539] "Dan Rather: Bush Issued Fake Terror Alert To Cover 911 Bungle," May 24, 2002. http://www.rense.com/general25/ratherbush.htm

[540] Chaim Kaufmann, "Threat Inflation and the Failure of the Marketplace of Ideas: The Selling of the Iraq War," *International Security* - Volume 29 (1): 5-48 (The ability of Bush to manipulate 9/11 events (terrorism threats) in support of his political agenda (removing Saddam and controlling Iraq) speaks loudly of Bush's political skills and demonstrates clearly the limitations of market place of ideas in checking government powers.)

[541] "Bush campaign defends 9/11 images in ads," *USA Today* March 4, 2004. http://www.usatoday.com/news/politicselections/nation/president/2004-03-04-bush-ads-911_x.htm

[542] "4. CBS's Early Show Doesn't Move On, Leads Friday with Bush TV Ads," Cyber Alert, *Media Research Center* Monday March 8, 2004 (Vol. Nine; No. 40) (CBS showed no letting up on 9/11 ad controversy, reporting it negatively 2 days in a row.) http://www.mediaresearch.org/cyberalerts/2004/cyb20040308.asp

attendant on American Airlines Flight 11 was bitter and angry: "I would be less offended if he showed a picture of himself in front of the Statue of Liberty … But to show the horror of 9/11 in the background, that's just some advertising agency's attempt to grab people by the throat."[544] Firefighter Tommy, a 9/11 Rescue Squad 270 was appalled and sick. "It's as sick as people who stole things out of the place. The image of firefighters at Ground Zero should not be used for this stuff, for politics."[545]

Finally it was the Harold Schaitberger, The General President of the International Association of Fire Fighters, AFL-CIO (IAFF), who was able to put Bush's political use of 9/11 in perspective:

"I'm disappointed but not surprised that the President would try to trade on the heroism of those fire fighters in the September 11 attacks. The use of 9/11 images are hypocrisy at its worst. Here's a President that initially opposed the creation of the Department of Homeland Security and now uses its first anniversary as cause to promote his re-election. Here is a President that proposed two budgets with no funding for FIRE Act grants and still plays on the image of America's bravest. His advertisements are disgraceful. [546]

Some conservatives however supported Bush's use of such distasteful and manipulative ads. On NBC's "Meet the Press" with Tim Russert, Giuliani approved of Bush's 9/11 ad:

"Well, if you left out September 11, 2001, I think people would be asking, 'Why is he leaving it out?' That was probably the biggest challenge that he's faced…Those of us who support him think he did a terrific job in getting the country through it," Giuliani said. "You know, other people on the other side have taken shots at him for not doing as good a job. So it's kind of unrealistic to think you're not going to have that as part of the political debate." [547]

Observations

As observed, whether Bush used of 9/11 "fear" for personal[548] vs. Party gain,[549] private[550] vs. public goods, political vs. natural vs. moral reasons generated a lot of debates. They are

---

[543] The first new source to raise the issues was the *DAILY NEWS* in New York City. See MAGGIE HABERMAN and Thomas M. DeFrank, "Furor over Bush's 9/11 ad," *DAILY NEWS* March 4, 2004 http://www.nydailynews.com/front/story/170291p-148587c.html

[544] "Denying Bush's Leadership," *Blogs for Bush* March 4, 2004. (Bush blogers cited none other than NCY Mayor Rudy Giuliani to support the President decision to rely on 9/11 in running for reelection.) http://www.blogsforbush.com/mt/archives/000692.html Still others endorsed the use of 9/11 ad. For example, Jennie Farrell, who lost her brother, electrician James Cartier in 9/11 found the Bush ad "tastefully done": "It speaks to the truth of the times. Sept. 11 … was something beyond the realm of imagination, and George Bush … led us through one of the darkest moments in history." See Maggie Haberman and Thomas M. DeFrank, "Furor over Bush's 9/11 ad," *N.Y. DAILY NEWS* March 4, 2004 http://www.nydailynews.com /front/story/170291p-148587c.html

[545] Bill Berkowitz, "Bush Exploiting 9/11" *AlterNet* Posted March 4, 2004. http://www.alternet.org/story/18039

[546] International Association of Fire Fighters, "Fire Fighters - Bush 911 Ads Political Opportunism," *Scoop* Friday, 5 March 2004, 4:31 pm http://www.scoop.co.nz/stories/WO0403/S00083.htm

[547] "Giuliani Defends Bush on 9/11 Ad," *NewsMax.com* Monday, March 8, 2004 http://www.newsmax.com/ archives/articles/2004/3/7/153108.shtml

[548] To salvage a failed presidency. To get re-elected. To create diversions.

[549] To win election for Republicans. To marginalize Democrats influence. To advance ne-conservative causes.

[550] To use 9/11 to advance private causes, from avenging failed attempted on President senior to securing professional careers of New American Century Project ideologues.

unsettling, and unsettled issues, still. The ultimate questions are empirical and judgmental ones: empirically, is President Bush using scarce tactics to "mobilize" the public to fight terror or to achieve self-serving political "agenda"; from gaining more executive powers to avoiding necessary constitutional accountability? Or was Bush just following his "instinct" in doing the best for a Nation in crisis, i.e., using color coded alert system to better prepare the public for terrorist attacks? The more basic issue of judgment is: to what extent is the Nation's reaction driven by self-inflicted fear, not commensurate with objective risks or correspond to realistic dangers. Or, is the use of 9/11 driven by an inexperience and a paranoid White House and manufactured by a seasoned and self-serving news corps, foisted upon a gullible and excitable crowd. Lastly, as a perennial policy issue, how *should* government deals with subjective "fear" of terrorism vs. objective "reality" of terrorism. [551]

The use of fear tactic did not start with the Bush administration.[552] In 1968 President Lyndon Johnson "exploiting the assassinations of Martin Luther King and Senator Robert Kennedy" rode on a media-led campaign to pressure the Congress to pass "Omnibus Crime Control and Safe Streets Act." In 1995, on the heel of Oklahoma City bombing, President Clinton sent to Congress for "immediate consideration and enactment," 111-page Omnibus Counter- terrorism Act (S. 390 in the Senate and H.R. 896 in the House) and later the 18-page Anti-terrorism Amendments Act. The Omnibus Counter- terrorism Act federalized a number of state crimes. It allows the use of *posse commitatus* for law enforcement purpose. It grants the President unchecked authority to apply the "terrorist" label to organizations. It prosecutes "terrorist" group members for exercising first amendment rights. It permits law enforcement agencies greater access to personal financial and credit information. It allows a much broader use if wiretaps.[553]

The passage of USAPA could not have sailed through Congress without the help of Bush White House "political gamesmanship." How and how much such gamesmanship was involved and ultimately mattered is a rightful and ripe subject of debate. The single most important conclusion one can draw from the above discussion is that 9/11 provided an opportunity for the Bush to assert his leadership and manipulate public's sentiments – anxiety and fear, paranoia and hate, nationalism and xenophobia – to promote a war of terror abroad and usher in a police state at home; starting with the passage of the USAPA.

Public sentiments, recognized and catered to by legislators and exploited and amplified by political gamesmanship, need a fertile soil to grow and blossom. This job of tilting the soil

---

[551] Barry Glassner. *The Culture of Fear: Why Americans Are Afraid of the Wrong Things* (Basic Books, 1999). For a more focused discussion on how fear can be manipulated to achieve personal or political goals, see "Professor Barry Glassner, "The Man Who Knows About Fear in American Culture," *A Buzzflash Interview* April 10, 2003. (Fear-mongering is prevalent in America, from TV executives who try to sell programs to lawyers who want to sell services to politicians who want to win elections.) http://www.buzzflash.com/interviews/03/04/10_glassner.html For a discussion of how to deal with fear real or imagined after 9/11, see "Interview - Barry Glassner: Dealing with fear and rumor in the wake of terrorism," *CNN.com* September 25, 2001 (The best way to deal with "false fear" is through constant education and critical thinking. People should be aware of "false reasoning," i.e., to assume that just because something completely unexpected happed, like 9/11, other terrorist attacks are imminent and inevitable. This kind of fear projection is unwarranted.) http://www.cnn.com/2001/COMMUNITY/09/25/glassner/

[552] James Bovard, *Terrorism and Tyranny: Trampling Freedom, Justice, and Peace to Rid the World of Evil* (Palgrave Macmillan, 2003), especially Chapter 4: "Patriot Railroad" (Bush Administration used 9/11 to secure imperial presidency powers, with no oversights from the Congress, supervision by the Courts, and accountability to the people.)

[553] See also William F. Jasper, "Battling Terrorism With Tyranny," *New American* Vol. 11, No. 11, May 29, 1995. http://www.aros.net/~hempower/drugwar/policestate/90s/950529.html

of public opinion (hysteria?) is left with the journalists and media. To this last subject matter we now turn.

V. MEDIA PATRIOTISM?

"Wherever [Bush] wants me to line up, just tell me where."

Dan Rather (2002) [554]

After 9/11 news media and journalists in the US turned overwhelmingly, un-mistakenly and radically patriotic; some might add shamefully and regrettably so. "Patriotic journalism" can be heart felt as driven by a strong sense of civil responsibility, as in the case of Dan Rather, or it can be manufactured for unabashed commercial gains, as in the case FOX TV, or it can be just a case of marriage for convenience, government wants outlet, as in the case of CIA leak case,[555] and journalists want access, as in the case of Judith Miller (NYT).[556] The ultimate issue raised here is not whether the media can realistically separate itself from the society – public expectations, economic pressure, corporate influence, state cooptation; it cannot and it should. The question is whether and what moral principles, ethical guidelines, and professional codes exist to guide and restrict journalists (in a democratic society) in rendering news that is "of interest" to the public, to the journalists, either in the name of public goods or for the realization of personal gains. Issues abound. Is patriotic journalism in time of war, quite apart on how such patriotism was derived or manifested, *ipso facto* objectionable?[557] What is the impact of "patriotic journalism" on post 9/11 politics and policy? More pertinently, how did "patriotic journalism" affected the USAPA legislative process? These and other issues are explored in the following pages.

Media Impact Post 9/11

Media sets agenda, frames issues, and shapes perception of 9/11, and in turn influence our perception, reception of and reaction to it[558]: For example:

The editor of *Minneapolis Star Tribune* has opined on September 21, 2001

"Even if Congress subscribes to the 'whatever-it-takes' philosophy, it's not clear this [recently introduced] legislation should pass. The White House has made no case that existing

---

[554] Tamara Straus "The War for Public Opinion," *AlterNet.org.* http://www.stelling.nl/konfront/1e2002/13403.html

[555] Desiree N. Williams, "Plame says White House 'carelessly and recklessly' exposed CIA identity," Jurist. March 17, 2007. (White House "carelessly and recklessly" disclosed the name of CIA operative Valeria Phame in order to retaliate against her husband, Diploma Wilson, for publicly challenging Bush's pre-war WMD illegience on Iraq.)

[556] Oliver Boyd-Barrett, "Judith Miller, "The New York Times, and the Propaganda Model," *Journalism Studies*, Vol. 5 (4): 435-449, 435 - 6 (2004).

[557] G. Stuart Adam, Stephanie Craft and Elliot D. Cohen, "Three Essays on Journalism and Virtue," *Journal of Mass Media Ethics* Vol. 19 (¾): 247-275, (2004) (Dan Rather sacrificed his objectivity and independency when he surrendered his professional judgment in service of the Nation in a time of war (p. 270)

[558] Joseph M Wober, "A seismic start to the third millennium: learning about American responses to terrorist attack on the USA (Book)," *Information, Communication and Society* Vol. 7 (2): 293-304 (2004).

law enabled last week's attack or hindered the ensuing investigation. Nor has it established that squelching civil liberties is a wise response to the threat of terror. In truth, forsaking American freedom is precisely the wrong answer to the fear terrorists sow. It gives them the victory they seek. It flouts an article of American faith: that just as some sacrifices must be made in safety's name, others must never be made."[559]

The editor of *Baltimore Sun* opined on September 19, 2001:

"Yes, tough and pragmatic laws are needed to prevent terrorism and espionage. And that should include keeping closer tabs on visitors to our country. But terrorism will have won if those laws unnecessarily fetter the fundamental civil liberties that have distinguished the United States from the rest of the world."[560]

The editor of *Boston Globe* opined on September 20, 200:

"There is general acknowledgement that society's delicate balance between freedom and security will tip toward greater security at the expense of individual liberties... Vigilance will be needed to make sure that the precious freedoms central to the American idea are not eroded by equally necessary new safety precautions."[561]

These three editorials above written shortly after 9/11 clearly helped to set agenda, define issues and provide a framework for analysis of 9/11. While *Minneapolis Star Tribune* cautioned against over – reacting to 9/11 attack in adopting a "whatever it takes" attitude in fighting terrorism at home, *Baltimore Sun* kept the readers focused on what the Nation was fighting for, i.e., a free and democratic America. Finally, *Boston Globe* called for a measured response, seeking a balance between security and liberty, in a time of war.

After 9/11, the media played a key role in shaping public opinion.[562] There were ample evidences to suggest that the media, in the name of patriotism, abdicated its public-trust role

---

[559] http://www.startribune.com/stories/1519/703260.html

[560] http://www.baltimoresun.com/

[561] http://www.boston.com/globe/

[562] Three issues must be addressed before we start to investigate the impact and influence of patriotic journalism in post 9/11 America: *First,* as a matter of context and for purpose of reference, post-9/11 patriotic journalism in the US recalls nationalistic journalism in other countries, such as terrorists attack on India Parliament House in New Delhi in December 2001 or Akshardham Temple in Gandhinagar in September 2002. Sometimes the distinction between patriotic patriotism, which is applauded for showing a love of ones country, and nationalistic patriotism, which is detested as a result of blind rejection of other nations, can be fine indeed. In any case, when professional responsibility confronts national calling, the later prevails. *Second,* the analysis and assessment of media (patriotic) role and influence is affected by the emergence of Internet as a popular and populist information source. Internet allows for free sharing of (unstructured) information and do away with mediated exchange of (diverse) opinions. After 9/11, more and more people were going to the net for real time and interactive news coverage. During the week after 9/11, 11.7 million people used the net to gather information. This exceeded viewer-ship with all the major networks: ABC, NBC, CBS, CNN, FOX, combined. The internet traffic was double that of one week before. "Since September 11, The Internet has played a useful role as an alternate source of news and opinion." The importance of traditional media – TV and newspapers – was much diluted and circumvented. *Third,* this analysis of media patriotism and impact does not address Bush government's attempt to influence the news by putting journalists or columnists on media payroll to promote its position or programs. For example, it is revealed that conservative columnists Maggie Gallagher, whose writing was distributed by Universal Press Syndicate and Mike McManus, whose column appeared in over 50 newspapers, were on the payroll of the Department of Health and Human Services. Armstrong Williams, a conservative African-American broadcaster, was paid $240,000 to produce advertisements on the No Child Left Behind Act (NCLB). U.S. House Committee on Government Reform

in exploiting the nation's fear and fanning the people's anxiety in defense of Bush's war policy and to usher in a police state. Specifically, the media embraced Bush's war on terror in supporting draconian counter-terrorism measures and legislations (USAPA), including secret surveillance of citizens and open torture of terrorists.[563]

The press and media reactions to 9/11 are typical of those of a nation at war.[564] It voluntarily turned patriotic[565] and exercised self censorship.[566] Overall, the media has been soft on Bush and critical of liberals after 9/11.[567]

Manifestation of Media Patriotism

The most famous "sound bite" manifesting media patriotism is that uttered by Dan Rather, the anchor for CBS, immediately after 911: "Wherever he [Bush] wants me to line up, just tell me where."[568] The most blatant declaration for self censorship came from CNN Chairman Walter Isaacson who wrote a memo calling for self-censorship by his staff: [569]

"As we get good reports from Taliban-controlled Afghanistan, we must redouble our efforts to make sure we do not seem to be simply reporting from their vantage or perspective.

---

further found that under the Bush administration federal agencies spent more than $250 million on PR agencies between 2001 and 2004, nearly twice as much ($128 millions) as that of Clinton years (1997 and 2001).[562] The line between proper public relations campaign and illegal manufacturing of support all but disappeared within the Bush administration.

[563] Jennifer Harper, "Hysteria runs riot; networks fuel the fear," *Washington Times* 02/13/03. http://www.prisonplanet.com/news_alert_021303_general9.html

[564] John Pilger. "Here we are again: the same old footage of planes against the sunrise, the same military jargon used by reporters - media treatment of the war on terrorism - Brief Article - Statistical Data Included," *New Statement*, Oct. 1, 2001. (In time of war and national crisis – from attacking Falklands to invading Panama, news media sided with the government in under reporting civilian casualties.) http://www.findarticles.com/p/articles/mi_m0FQP/is_4557_130/ai_79029897

[565] Michael Scherer, "In Review: Framing the Flag," *Columbia Journalism Review* 40:10 March-April 2002. (Media Research Center found that after 9/11 U.S. media was engaging in home team sports reporting, i.e., non-critical reporting for some (CBS) and cheerleading by others (FOX). Between September 11 and December 31, MRC found that Bush government staff members were quoted eighty separate times by major news outlets. Not all media were as patriotic. ABC banned the wearing of American flag lapel.) See also MRC research showing that from October 7 to October 31, 2001, ABC spent more time reporting upon the casualties of war, by one study ABC spent 15.54 minutes on casualties over a number of weeks, nearly twice that of NBC and four times as much as CBS. "ABC's War: US Military vs. Afghan Civilians," *Media Research Center* November 5, 2001 http://www.mediaresearch.org/realitycheck/2001/pdf/fax1105.pdf

[566] Gloria Cooper, "New patterns in opinion control" *Columbia Journalism Review* Vol. 43 (2): 58 – 60 (July/Aug 2004). (On April 30, 2003, Sinclair Broadcast Group, ordered its eight ABC affiliates not to air the April 30 Nightline special "The Fallen," in which Ted Koppel read aloud the names of the 721 U.S. military members killed in action in Iraq, up to that point. On April 7, 2003, Roxanne Walker was fired for saying that Iraq war was not justified on Clear Channel's WMYI in Greenville, South Carolina. On April 8, Clear Channel permanently dropped Howard Stern's program for his anti-Bush view. In May of 2004, Disney refused to distribute Michael Moore's Fahrenheit 9/11 for its anti-Bush, anti-war content.) http://archives.cjr.org/year/02/2/Scherer.asp Since then PBS News Hour has make remembrance of fallen soldiers with on screen printing of names in silence a routine feature.

[567] Rachel Smolkin, "Are the News Media Soft on Bush?," *American Journalism Review* October/November 2003 (Bush has a relative clean professional background, straight forward personal history and well disciplined staff working for him. The media found little negative to report about him and his staff.) http://www.ajr.org/Article.asp?id=3406

[568] Tamara Straus "The War for Public Opinion," *AlterNet.org.* http://www.stelling.nl/konfront/1e2002/13403.html

[569] "The memo was written as a result of CNN's reporting of war casualties. Remember: They're Deliberate," December 15, 2001 *the rational radical* http://www.therationalradical.com/dsep/1201/self-censorship.htm

We must talk about how the Taliban are using civilian shields and how the Taliban have harbored the terrorists responsible for killing close to 5,000 innocent people."[570]

When being interviewed over CNN's approach to war reporting, Walter further elaborated:[571]

> "I want to make sure we're not used as a propaganda platform…We're entering a period in which there's a lot more reporting and video from Taliban-controlled Afghanistan …You want to make sure people understand that when they see civilian suffering there, it's in the context of a terrorist attack that caused enormous suffering in the United States.".[572]

Not all major networks were in agreement on how to report on the Iraq war, especially on civilian casualties. ABC and CBS were more circumspect. Jim Murphy, executive producer of the "CBS Evening News," reacting to the CNN Isaacson instructions (above): "I wouldn't order anybody to do anything like that. Our reporters are smart enough to know it always has to be put in context." NBC News Vice President Bill Wheatley responded in like manner: "I'd give the American public more credit, frankly. I'm not sure it makes sense to say every single time you see any pictures from Afghanistan, 'This is as a result of September 11th.' No one's made any secret of that." Fox News Vice President John Moody endorsed CNN's approach: "not at all a bad thing" because "Americans need to remember what started this. . . . I think people need a certain amount of context or they obsess on the last 15 minutes of history. A lot of Americans did die."[573]

Meantime, the government actively managed the information available to the public, i.e., restricting freedom of the press,[574] censoring content of the media,[575] and finally planting and fabricating news[576] in the name of security.[577]

---

[570] "CNN Says Focus on Civilian Casualties Would Be "Perverse" *FAIR* November 1, 2001 http://www.fair.org/activism/cnn-casualties.html

[571] Howard Kurtz, "CNN chief orders "balance" in war news: Reporters Are Told To Remind Viewers Why U.S. Is Bombing," *Washington Post* Wednesday, October 31, 2001; Page C01 http://www.newhumanist.com/cnn.html

[572] *Id.*

[573] *Id.*

[574] The Pentagon has taken aggressively steps to manage the news on the war. It bought up all accessible commercial satellite photos of the war zone. It actively engaged in disinformation campaign. It placed restriction on press coverage of the war, except on terms favorable to the military, e.g.,, single press pool and embedded journalists. Violet Jones, "Mainstream Media is Pentagon's Propaganda Arm," *Infowar.com* Dec. 14, 20004. (After 9/11 Pentagon routinely used and aggressively co-opted the media in order to promote war effort, e.g., misled the public or deceive the enemy. All the time, Pentagon was conducting war time psychological operation or "psy-op") http://www.infowars.com/articles/military/psy-ops_meets_pr.htm According to John Walcott from Knight Ridder, Bush's "management of information is far greater than that of any administration" in two ways (1) positively--"rewarding sympathetic reporters with leaks, background interviews and seats on official flights" and (2) negatively--"freezing out reporters who didn't play along." Michael Massing, *Now They Tell Us: The American Press and Iraq* (New York Review Books: May, 2004)

[575] *How the War on Terrorism Affects Access to Information and the Public's Right to Know*, *FIFTH EDITION* The Reporters Committee for Freedom of the Press, White Paper (September 2004). http://www.rcfp.org/homefrontconfidential/; http://www.rcfp.org/homefrontconfidential/Homefront_Confidential_5th.pdf

[576] The New York Times reported that the Pentagon was setting up the Office of Strategic (OSI) Influence on February 19, 2002. Douglas Feith, the official in charge of OSI, admitted that: "We are going to preserve our ability to undertake operations that may, for tactical purposes, mislead an enemy." OSI was staffed by U.S. Army's Psychological Operations Command (PSYOPS), specifically the 4th PSYOPS Group. The OSI was closed down within one week (Feb. 26, 2001) as a result of negative publicity. Rachel Cohen, "Behind the Pentagon's Propaganda Plan," Extra! Update, April 2002 FAIR http://www.fair.org/extra/0204/osi.html "The Office of Strategic Influence Is Gone, But Are Its Programs In Place?" Press Release (11/27/02) *FAIR*

It was Senator Hiram W Johnson (1866-1945) who first declared in 1917 "The first casualty of War is Truth"[578] This is validated once again in the reporting of 9/11.[579]

Patriotic Journalism in Action [580]

Patriotic journalism is defined as:

> "Patriotic journalism is used to describe a form of journalism that especially seems to occur in some countries when they are in a state of war or other major distress. Patriotic journalism aims at giving the home public an image of the current event that are in accordance to the views of the government, and in accordance with what is regarded as "best for the country".[581]

After 9/11, patriotic journalism has been in vogue. Three operating principles informed patriotic journalism, then as now:

1. After 9/11 the media was ready and willing to do and say everything to promote the war effort. This is the principle of political propaganda.
2. After 9/11, the media is no longer neutral and objective in reporting the war on terror. This is the principle of personal loyalty.

(Rumsfeld has not given up ideas of OSI. He tried to redesign the U.S. military to make "information warfare" central to its functions. In so doing Rumsfeld blurred the boundaries between government information distribution and private news reporting, on the one hand, and turned public relations campaign and psychological warfare, on the other). http://www.fair.org/index.php?page=1859

[577] Neil Hickey, "Access denied: Pentagon's war reporting rules are toughest ever," *Columbia Journalism Review*, Jan/Feb 2002. (Interviews (Oct. – Dec. 2002 with foreign editors, Pentagon correspondents, Washington bureau chiefs, top news executives, media critics showed that news reporters were routine and unreasonably denied access to the war zone in ways unimaginable in Vietnam, and even more so that the first Gulf war.) http://www.findarticles.com/p/articles/mi_qa3613/is_200201/ai_n9073215

[578] Original quote: "The first casualty when war comes is truth." Originally, it was Aeschylus the Greek tragic dramatist (525 BC - 456 BC) who claimed that in war truth is the first casualty. More recently, Samuel Johnson has uttered the words: 'Among the calamities of war may be jointly numbered the diminution of the love of truth, by the falsehoods which interest dictates and credulity encourages.' (from The Idler, 1758). "Who coined the phrase, "The first casualty of War is Truth"? http://www.guardian.co.uk/notesandqueries/query/0,5753,-21510,00.html

[579] Depending on your political persuasion, liberal vs. conservative, the press and media has never been true to its creed, i.e., independent, objective, fair and balance. The most common criticism is that journalists and media exhibit liberal bias, from pundits like Ann Coulter (*How to Talk to a Liberal (If You Must): The World According to Ann Coulter* (Crown Forum, 2004) For a more balanced and nuanced account, see veteran CBS reporter Bernard Goldberg, *Bias: A CBS Insider Exposes How the Media Distort the News* (Regnery Publishing, 2001) (CBS were sympathetic to black, homeless and gay in its reporting.) For a counter-point, by Eric Alterman, *What Liberal Media? The Truth About Bias and the News* (Basic Books, 2003) (Alterman, while acknowledging that vast majority of journalists are: "pro-choice, pro-gun control, pro-separation of church and state, pro-feminism, pro-affirmative action, and supportive of gay rights" (p. 21), but the So-Call Liberal Media (SCLM) is still a myth created by the far right.) For a comprehensive treatment of "Media Bias Basics" see *Media Research Center* http://www.mediaresearch.org/biasbasics/welcome.asp

[580] For a general discussion, see Barbie Zelizer and Stuart Allen (eda.) *Journalism After September 11'* (London and New York: Routledge, 2002). Joan Konner, "Media's Patriotism Provides a Shield for Bush," *Newsday* January 9, 2002. (Media cowed by Bush and lured by revenue to promote patriotism in news reporting in support of a war time President without criticism.) http://www.commondreams.org/views02/0109-01.htm

[581] http://www.answers.com/topic/patriotic-journalism

3. After 9/11, the media do not want to embolden the terrorists or enemies of state.[582] This is the principle of not giving aid and support to the enemy.

"Patriotic terrorism" turned "professional journalism" on its head. According to Journalism.org, "The central purpose of journalism is to provide citizens with accurate and reliable information they need to function in a free society." It further listed 9 core principles of journalism in a democracy: 1. Journalism's first obligation is to the truth; 2. Its first loyalty is to citizens; 3. Its essence is a discipline of verification; 4. Its practitioners must maintain an independence from those they cover; 5. It must serve as an independent monitor of power; 6. It must provide a forum for public criticism and compromise; 7. It must strive to make the significant interesting and relevant.; 8. It must keep the news comprehensive and proportional. 9. Its practitioners must be allowed to exercise their personal conscience.[583]

After 9/11, the media instinctively and collectively turned decidedly patriotic.[584] Is a commercial enterprise, media learned that personal patriotism sells and professional neutrality is often equated with disloyalty, in time of war.[585] Alternatively, media learned that patriotism, appropriately displayed, was professionally rewarding for the journalists and institutionally lucrative for the media.[586]

---

[582] Jasna Bastic, "Responsibility of Media in War Time" http://www.russfound.org/Launch/bastic.htm

[583] See "A Statement of Shared Purpose" *Journalism.org* http://www.journalism.org/resources/guidelines/principles/purpose.asp

[584] In this regard, the media was just following national trend and reflecting public public sentiments. Louay M. Safi, "Confounding Patriotism and Bigotry in Post 9/11 America," (In the aftermath of 9/11 the nation was turning patriotism into bigotry. For example, Lt. Gen. William G. Boykin, the deputy undersecretary of defense for intelligence, told church members: "I knew that my God was bigger than his [Muslim leader]; I knew that my God was a real God, and his was an idol" and John Ashcroft, US attorney General, saying "Islam is a religion in which God requires you to send your son to die for him," while "Christianity is a faith in which God sends his son to die for you.") *Media Monitor Network.* Saturday 29 January 2005.http://usa.mediamonitors.net/headlines/confounding_patriotism_and_bigotry_in_post_911_america

[585] Erin Mclaughlin, "Television Coverage of the Vietnam War and the Vietnam Veteran," December 31, 2001. http://www.warbirdforum.com/media.htm

[586] Media in America is controlled by big military and industrial complex which have a vested interest in the political future of Bush and the successful prosecution of the war. Anthony Arnove, "Pro-war Propaganda Machine: Media Becomes Branch of War Effort," *Socialist Worker*, March 19, 2003 http://www.thirdworldtraveler.com/Propaganda/ProWar_Propaganda_Machine.html "The television commercial is not at all about the character of products to be consumed. It is about the character of the consumers of products. ...What the advertiser needs to know is not what is right about the product but what is wrong about the buyer." Neil Postman, *Amusing Ourselves to Death Public Discourse in the Age of Show Business* (Penguin Books, 1985), p. 127.

Table 6. Professional journalism principles vs. patriotic journalism principles

Professional journalism principles	Patriotic journalism principles
First obligation is to the truth.[587]	First obligation is to the national – state - security.[588]
First loyalty is to citizens[589]	First loyalty is to the state or government [590]
A discipline of verification[591]	An enterprise of received information[592] and bestowed authority.[593]
Maintain an independence from those they cover[594]	Embedded to see things in the government's perspective[595]

---

[587] Deborah Potter, "Flagging the Problem," American Journalism review, June 2002 (Immediately after September 11, News Director Stacey Woelfel of KOMU-TV (owned by the University of Missouri and was staffed largely by faculty and students in Columbia) issued a memo banning the wearing of red-white-and-blue ribbons and flag pins on the air: "Our news broadcasts are not the place for personal statements of support for any cause … no matter how deserving the cause seems to be." Within days, the memo got out and the criticism poured in.") http://www.ajr.org/Article.asp?id=2541

[588] *How the War on Terrorism Affects Access to Information and the Public's Right to Know, FIFTH EDITION* The Reporters Committee for Freedom of the Press, White Paper (September 2004). http://www.rcfp.org/homefrontconfidential/; http://www.rcfp.org/homefrontconfidential/Homefront_Confidential_5th.pdf

[589] The observation here is that journalists work for an enlightened citizenry, not a country, a place, a people, or a set of ideology. The journalists help the people to see clearer, broader, further and deeper. Robert Jensen, "What's Wrong With Patriotic Journalism?" *Global Media Journal* (Journalists should work for what Socialist Eugene Debs called "a citizen of the world" (1915): "I have no country to fight for; my country is the earth, and I am a citizen of the world." http://www.progressivetrail.org/articles/031119Jensen.shtml

[590] CBS *60 Minutes II* agreed not to publish the ABU Grab torture story and photos at the request of General Richard Myers, chairman of the Joint Chiefs of Staff on national security grounds. "Abuse Of Iraqi POWs By GIs Probed" *CBS.com* April 28, 2004. http://www.cbsnews.com/stories/2004/04/27/60II/main614063.shtml Raphael F. Perl, "Terrorism, the Media, and the Government: Perspectives, Trends, and Options For Policymakers." Pamala L. Griset and Sue Mahan (Ed.) *Terrorism in Perspective* (SAGE 2002) (Oftentimes, terrorists, governments, and the media see the function, roles and responsibilities of the media in differ and often competing perspectives. "The media and the government have common interests in seeing that the media are not manipulated into promoting the cause of terrorism or its methods.") http://www.au.af.mil/au/awc/awcgate/state/crs-terror-media.htm

[591] The failure to validate government information took many forms. For example, the military would not provide security for the journalists except for those whowere embedded. Robert Fisk, "The US Press in Iraq Hotel Room Journalism," January 17, 2005 *The Independent* http://www.counterpunch.org/fisk01172005.html see Michael Massing, *Now They Tell Us: The American Press and Iraq* (New York Review Books: May, 2004). (For the most part the press corp. in Iraq has to rely on the government for information. They have no ability to independently verify basic information, e.g., civilian deaths.)

[592] Orville Schel said it best when he observed: "Until the war effort began to unravel in spring 2004, the upper-tier -- a relatively small number of major broadcast outlets, newspapers, and magazines -- had a far more limited bandwidth of critical views, regularly deferring to the Bush Administration's vision of the world." "Preface" to Michael Massing, *Now They Tell Us: The American Press and Iraq* (New York Review Books: May, 2004).

[593] ABC's Cokie Roberts proclaimed her faith in military war reporting at the Letterman show (10/10/01): "Look, I am, I will just confess to you, a total sucker for the guys who stand up with all the ribbons on and stuff and they say it's true and I'm ready to believe it." "Jennings Mad at Pentagon; U.S. and Taliban Kill "Innocents"; Rather Urged Perseverance; More Skeptical of bin Laden Than Bush?" *Media Research Center*, Tuesday October 9, 2001 (Vol. Six; No. 159) http://secure.mediaresearch.org/news/cyberalert/2001/cyb20011011.asp#8 Judith miller actively cultivated government sources to develop her, now famous, WMD as a new kind of unconventional (terrorist) warfare thesis. Franklin Foer, "The Source of the Trouble," *New Yorker* June 7, 2002. (Miller's sin was in not following journalistic protocol, e.g., double checking her source and over reliance on a few Bush insiders. In time, Miller became a White House policy tool and Pentagon's mouth piece.) Ray Suretta, *Media, Crime, and Criminal Justice* (West/Westworth 1998) p. 62.

[594] On October 7, 2001, the five national news organizations, ABC News, CBS News, NBC News (and MSNBC), the Cable News Network and the Fox News Channel all carried an unedited taped message from Mr. bin Laden. Again on Tuesday (October 9, 2001), CNN, Fox News and MSNBC carried the complete speech of a

Table 6. (Continued)

Professional journalism principles	Patriotic journalism principles
Serve as an independent monitor of power[596]	Promote and consolidate government power
Provide a forum for public criticism and compromise.[597]	Discourage debate[598] and reduce dissent[599]
Strive to make the significant interesting and relevant.	Strive to excite and mobilize.[600]
Keep the news comprehensive and proportional.	Keep the message simple and focused.[601]
Practitioners allowed to exercise their personal conscience	Practitioners expected to follow organizational lines[602]

spokesman for Al Qaeda. On October 10, 2001, National Security Adviser Rice implored the press and media to restrict and censor inflammatory news and broadcast from bin Laden. Ari Fleischer was blunt in warning that Americans "need to watch what they say. BILL CARTER and FELICITY BARRINGER, "At U.S. Request, Networks Agree to Edit Future bin Laden Tapes," *New York Times*, October 11, 2001.

[595] The embedding of reporters allowed the journalists to see things from the military's perspective alone. This raises serious issues of dependency and intimacy which affected journalists' independence and objectivity. Sherry Ricchiardi, "Close to the Action," *American Journalism Review* May 2003. http://www.ajr.org/Article.asp?id=2991

[596] In an opening segment of the October 10, 2001 World News Tonight, Jennings was questioning John McWethy, a Pentagon reporter after military activities: "We've been three days now, we've had three photographs of bomb damage. Is the Pentagon unable to assess what it has done or just doesn't want to share it with the public?" McWethy replied: "It appears, Peter, that the Pentagon does not want to share the details of what is going on. They keep saying that it is a different kind of war, and so far it has been a war with very little information." See "Jennings Mad at Pentagon," The 1,159th CyberAlert. Tracking Media Bias Since 1996, *Media Research Center*, Thursday October 11, 2001 (Vol. Six; No. 161). http://secure.mediaresearch.org/news/cyberalert/2001/cyb20011011.asp#1 See Networks Accept Government "Guidance" Press Release (10/12/01), *Fair and Accuracy in Reporting* http://www.fair.org/index.php?page=1849

[597] "Politically Incorrect' loses FedEx, Sears ads," *The Daily Journal* (09-20-01) (Bill Maher called 9/11 terrorists heroes and American launching cruise missiles cowardice. In dense of Maher, ABC issued the followings statement: "While we remain sensitive to the current climate following last week's tragedy, and continue to do our part to help viewers cope with unfolding events, there needs to remain a forum for the expression of our nation's diverse opinions.") http://www.smdailyjournal.org/article.cfm?storyID=7298

[598] Andrew Card, Bush's chief of staff, said of the press, "They don't represent the public any more than other people do. In our democracy, the people who represent the public stood for election. . . . I don't believe you have a check-and-balance function."

[599] Dan Duthrie wrote a column critical of President Bush's handling of 9/11. "Dogwatch column," *Grants Pass Daily Courier*, September 15, 2001. (The President was a coward for hiding in Nebraska and not returning to the Capital to direct the national crisis.) Editor Dennis Roler fired Dan Duthrie "Criticism of our chief executive and those around him needs to be responsible and appropriate. Labeling him and the nation's other top leaders as cowards as the United States tries to unite after its bloodiest terrorist attack ever isn't responsible or appropriate." Adair Lara, "Odd, isn't it? But of course, there's more to the story. This is No Time to Keep Your Mouth Shut," *San Francisco Chronicle*, October 4, 2001 (Silencing dissents and leveling free speech is against what Walter Lippmann preached for a free country: 'The theory of a free press is that truth will emerge from free discussion, not that it will be presented perfectly and instantly in any one account')

[600] On Monday (October 8, 2001) at the end of CBS Evening News, Dan Rather signed off with this exhortation: " On a day when President Bush swore-in the first Director of Homeland Security in our history, thoughts turn to the words of the late newsman Elmer Davis: 'This will remain the land of the free only so long as it is the home of the brave.'" See *Media Research Center* "CyberAlert. Tracking Media Bias Since 1996, " Tuesday October 9, 2001 (Vol. Six; No. 159) http://www2.mediaresearch.org/cyberalerts/2001/cyb20011009.asp#2

[601] Dan Rather has this to observe about the government's approach to an informed public, post 9/11: "The belief weren't so strong in both the political and military leadership of the current war effort, that those who control the images will control public opinion..."Hey, we had the Hollywoodisation of the news, we've had the Hollywoodisation of almost everything else in society, why not the Hollywoodisation of the war?" Transcript of Madeleine Holt's item : Is Truth the Victim? *BBC* Thursday, 6 June, 2002, 14:03 GMT 15:03 UK.

[602] "The Source of the Trouble" New York June 17, 2004 http://news.bbc.co.uk/1/hi/programmes/newsnight/archive

Immediately after 9/11 the press and media openly displayed patriotism. [603] The propensity to display patriotism, while afflicting the press and media, was not uniform between medium and across segments. Liberal presses (NYT) were more circumspect while conservative stations (FOX) were all unabashedly zealous.

There were many instances where the media was accused of "cheerleading" for the war on terror or grandstanding for the administration instead of just reporting of facts.

Right after 9/11 there was tremendous pressure to defend America and be a patriot. Jingoism stood for critical analysis and cheerleading replaced serious reporting.[604] CNN logo was draped in Old Glory. TV anchors wore red, white and blue. "Fox News anchors all quickly adopted red, white and blue lapel ribbons as official on-air dress." [605] Dan Rather (CBS) was outwardly angry and joined the President calling for a war. Tom Brokaw (NBC) was struck with emotion.

Table 7. Public Opinion on the Press: 1985 – 2001

	July 1985	February 1999	Early Sept 2001	November 2001
Usually get facts straight	55	37	35	46
Usually report inaccurately	34	58	57	45
Don't know	11	5	8	9
	100	100	100	100
Stand up for America	52	41	43	69
Too critical for America	30	42	36	17
Neither/Don't know	18	17	21	14
	100	100	100	100
Protect democracy	54	45	46	50
Hurt democracy	23	38	32	19
Neither/Don't know	23	17	22	21
	100	100	100	100

Source: See Table on "Opinion of the Press" in "Terror Coverage Boost News Media's Images: But Military Censorship Backed" The PEW Research Center for the People and the Press, November 28, 2001.[606]

Pew Research Center survey of 1,500 adults in the aftermath of 9/11 reveals that the press is playing a more responsible role in standing up for America and defending democracy, i.e., being pro-American. Whereas in February of 1999 sizable minority of the public – 42%

/2029634.stm

[603] A. Eisman, "The media of manipulation: patriotism and propaganda – mainstream news in the United States in the weeks following September 11," *Critical Quarterly* Volume 45 (1-2): 55 – 72 (2003).

[604] "Grading The Media's Post-9/11 Performance: An Interview With Journalism Professor Ted Gup," ("I think that they did succumb to some degree to jingoism, a kind of identification with the cause, the campaign. They somewhat surrendered their objectivity and allowed themselves to be compromised. ") Tompain.com Oct 15 2002 http://www.tompaine.com/feature.cfm/ID/6538

[605] Michael I. Niman, "Up From the Rubble: Salvaging Journalism in Post 9-11 America," *ArtVoice* 10/17/02, esp. "News Anchors Wrapped in the Flag" http://mediastudy.com/articles/av10-17-02.html

[606] The nation wide random telephone survey was conducted on 1,500 adults under the direction of Princeton Survey Research Associates during the period November 13-19, 2001. It has an error of +/- 4%.http://people-press.org/reports/display.php3?PageID=13

thinks that the press is too critical of America, in November of 2001, only 17% still feels that way. On the other hand, in February of 1999 a minority (45%) perceives that the press protects democracy, after 9/11, 50% do. The improvement in standing shows up more with whether the press hurts democracy, only 17% believe so after 9/11 and 38% do in 1999.

Confession of Patriotism and Self-Censorship

Much of the post 9/11 censorship is self imposed by the journalists and news agencies themselves. Dan Rather, CBS anchor, provided a good case study of how even a well established and very respected journalist has to come to terms with being a war time reporter, i.e., having to cater to multiply expectations (public vs. government vs. profession) and balancing of conflicting demands (loyalty vs. truth, free speech vs. state security).

In May of 2002, Dan Rather was asked by BBC about appropriate media rules to follow during 9/11 and after. He admitted to being compelled by existing circumstances to display patriotism as the whole country did after 9/11:

> "What we are talking about here--whether one wants to recognize it or not, or call it by its proper name or not--is a form of self-censorship. It starts with a feeling of patriotism within oneself. It carries through with a certain knowledge that the country as a whole felt and continues to feel this surge of patriotism within themselves. And one finds oneself saying: 'I know the right question, but you know what? This is not exactly the right time to ask it.'"[607]

It turned out that the lofty "feeling of patriotism" arising from within and instinctively, actually reflected post 9/11 nation ethos. It has a simple and down to earth explanation: fear of being ridiculed by the public, sanctioned by the organization, or rejected by peers. For example, veteran NPR reporter Nina Totenberg admitted feeling pressure to get along in Washington: "It's crossed my mind from time to time that you don't want people to think you're unpatriotic ... But lots of things cross my mind. It's not necessarily a bad thing, you just sort of have to live with it."[608] She even told Supreme Court Justice Lewis Powell *"the only thing I hate about my job is that some people hate my guts."*[609] (Underline supplied).

For Dan Rather it was fear of external consequences (lynching) not giving vent to internal compulsion (patriotism) that eventually cowed him to display patriotism and exercise self censorship:

> "It's an obscene comparison but there was a time in South Africa when people would put flaming tyres around people's necks if they dissented. In some ways, the fear is that you will

---

[607] "Rather Says US Patriotism Causes Journalism Self-Censorship," *News-Journal Wire Services*, May 19, 2002. http://www.rense.com/general25/as.htm

[608] The pressure was in part self induced (Dan Rather, wanting to be part of loyal and patriotic American). It was also partly externally imposed (the whole country is getting inflamed). There were concerns in the heartland of America that the press and media, particularly the anchors at the major networks, were too liberal and elitist, or just being full of themselves and out of touch with reality. Online News Hour: Media Credibility Gap -- January 13, 2005.

[609] Ted Gup, "Working in a Wartime Capital," *Columbia Journalism Review* Posted September 12, 2002 (The self doubt and internal questioning is more understanding when one realizes that the whole Washington has changed after 9/11. Everyone in the Capital was conscious of the fact that it might be the main target of next terrorists attack) http://www.alternet.org/story/14100

be neck-laced here, you will have a flaming tyre of lack of patriotism put around your neck. *It's that fear that keeps journalists from asking the toughest of the tough questions* and to continue to bore-in on the tough questions so often. Again, I'm humbled to say I do not except myself from this criticism....*I know the right question but you know what, this is not exactly the right time to ask it?*[610](Emphasis provided)

Always honest and controversial, Dan Rather is the only major network anchors who openly and honestly dealt with the issue of what it was like to be a major network host in time of war. In so doing so Rather confronted the often conflicting and at time irreconcilable demands of patriotism (personal, institutional) and professionalism (objectivity, independence, integrity) associated with doing war time journalism. He ended up endorsing patriotic journalism unabashedly.[611]

Characteristic of Rather's style and true to the journalism creed, he was frank and direct, if at times apologetic and self-serving. Listening to Rather, it is both refreshing and informative to find out what was going on behind closed doors at CBS (one of the major media) and in the head of Rather (easily one of the most prominent TV journalist of our time though never match up to the bench mark set by Cronkite). In the end, notwithstanding Rather's thoughtfulness and forthrightness, or perhaps because of it, he did not clear up all that was to be cleared up, if only he was sometimes confused, e.g., what does patriotism mean and entail, and in critical spots contradictory, e.g., can journalist be loyal and critical at the same time, or unclear, e.g., loyalty to whom – government or the people.

Rather was much more unreservedly patriotic at home (interviewed by Letterman, September 17, 2001). When asked about his role as a journalist in times of war, Rather made it clear that choice between loyalty to country (patriotism) comes before devotion to profession (professionalism): "George Bush is the president. He makes the decisions, and, you know, it's just one American, wherever he wants me to line up, just tell me where, and he'll make the call."

In a more elaborate and nuanced response to the same line of inquiry, he said

> "I want to fulfill my role as a decent human member of the community and a decent and patriotic American. And therefore, I am willing to give the government, the president and the military the benefit of any doubt here in the beginning. I'm going to fulfill my role as a journalist, and that is ask the questions, when necessary ask the tough questions. ...I want to be a patriotic American without apology."[612]

Rather's rendition of "patriotic journalism" in the face of 9/11 was as clear as it was foreboding; ones devotion to country comes before ones devotion to ones profession. From the perspective of Rather, yet to be fully explained in his own words, the context (complexity of issues) and circumstances (urgency of the situation) of a national emergency precludes a meaningful role for the journalist, or for that matter any citizen; to second guess the President,

---

[610] Transcript of Madeleine Holt's item : Is Truth the Victim" *BBC* Thursday, 6 June, 2002, 14:03 GMT 15:03 UK
[610] "The Source of the Trouble" *New York* June 17, 2004.
[611] Robert Jensen, "Dan Rather and the problem with patriotism: Steps toward the redemption of American journalism and democracy," *Global Media Journal*, 2:3 (Fall 2003). ("Rather, anchor of the CBS Evening News and the dean of American television journalism, spoke more openly after 9/11 than any other mainstream commercial journalist.")
[612] L. Brent Bozell, "Media coverage at its best," *Washington Times*, September 25, 2001, p. A-18.

his motive, intent, judgment. Rather was quick to add that the deference ("benefit of doubt") is not without limit. What counts for an emergency? How far would the "benefit of doubt" go? Many of the real, concrete and important questions and issue were not resolved, perhaps unsolvable. View in this light, and contrary to his originally intent, Rather's remarks were not only unhelpful, they were distorting and confusing. It muddled up the water, more.

Rather's comments were distorting because they implied that journalists have no meaning role to play once an emergency is declared, much like the court in time of war. In time of war, the court, and now the media, is there to support the military defense of the U.S. against the enemy.

Rather's comments were confusing because, allowing "benefit of doubt" suggested constant evaluation of and passing judgment on the President's position and performance on war and related issues, e.g., is he using war fear for political purposes (e.g., the "wag the tail" thesis in Clinton's Lewinski affair) or is the President correct in his factual analysis and value choice for the country? What a war time journalist is suspending is not doubt, but the right to air it.

More significantly, doubt is second nature to a journalist. The suspension of doubt is not possible. So when Rather said: "George Bush is the president. He makes the decisions, and, you know, it's just one American, wherever he wants me to line up, just tell me where, and he'll make the call" he was not about giving the President any benefit of doubt. He was saying, instead: "America right or wrong, here I come." Rather became a soldier taking orders, not a journalist probing policies. Rather could not have it both ways, theoretically, practically, realistically. Rather wanted to inform us that as a journalist he could find a balance sitting on the fence, being an obedience solider one day and an independent journalist another. This is illusory, if disingenuous, argument.

One last issue on Rather's confession. What Rather did not explain is why, he as a seasoned journalist, did not or could not arrest such "feeling" of "patriotism" sufficient to give himself some space between him and the event, distance between him and the public, and barrier between himself as Dan the American and himself as Rather the journalist. He was clearly giving into his natural instinct, i.e., emotions and impulses. The best test here is to ask whether, if invited, Rather would have gone to protest in the street, or join the military to fight in Iraq. If the answer is no, which I suspect to be the case, the journalist Rather (collective, public, formal, professional) could be and should be distanced from the private citizen Dan (individual, private, informal, personal).

Rather offered a slightly different rendition of the reason for and meaning of being a "patriotic journalist" in his London – BBC interview vs. US – Letterman show. To start off, Rather was much more apologetic of being patriotic and defensive of the profession's right to speak out. Gone is the bravado. Gone is the certitude. Gone is the clarity. Instead, Rather returned to be Rather; contemplative, profound, nuanced; to do doublespeak. But at home and with Letterman, he gave off the impression that he would do battle at moments notice with the President in the helm: "Mine is not to ask the reason why." No question asked ("just tell me where"). No question need to be asked ("benefit of doubt").

At BBC he started to talk more like Rather than Bush. He started with observing that after 9/11, he found himself possessive of and in time struggling with: "a feeling of patriotism within oneself," naturally and inevitably, just liked so many other Americans on that eventful day. After all there was a war going on and Rather is one of the guys. There is little evidence to show that he got carried along or carried away, to act rashly or react unreasonably. This sets Rather up for the claim that he aced naturally and reasonably throughout 9/11 reporting. Of course, here there is a slippage in argument, being natural, is not the same as being reasonable, especially when reasonableness calls for different evaluative standard, that of a seasoned journalists and not hot blooded American.

In England, Rather was much more defensive on the issue of patriotism. Rather's strategy, in speaking to a skeptical audience, was to convince his U.K. audience that he had done nothing wrong in acting as a patriotic journalist; pro-war and in support of Bush.[613] By focusing on the realities of post 9/11 – "flaming tyre of lack of patriotism," Rather made it clear that he, as the "Dean of journalism" knew what the right thing to do, but did not "speak his mind" (truth) because of pragmatic reasons, i.e., it was the wrong time to do it. In do doing, he was appealing to the good sense and pragmatic nature of the British people. He seemed to be saying: "Walk in my shoe and you will understand." He tried to redefine the role of journalist in time of war. Thus "speak truth to power" in emergency setting means that you wait for the right moment to speak your mind, lest the message gets lost and the messenger is blamed.

Free Speech and Political, Social and Economic Fallouts

ABC was perceived by the public to be an anti-war news network. Peter Jennings was one of the most independent minded anchor during and after 9/11. Jennings received more than 10,000 (hate) emails calling for his resignation after made the following remarks on air: "The country looks to the president on occasions like this to be reassuring to the nation. Some presidents do it well, some presidents don't."[614]

Rightwing talk show host, Rush Limbaugh, alerted his listeners, suggesting that Jennings had questioned the president's character and an email campaign against Jennings was launched.[615] A look at some of the e-mails over Jennings' "indiscretion" showed why Jennings was rightfully distressed and explained why Rather was justifiably cowed in the face of strong and overwhelming public pressure.[616] For example, the public want respect for the President in time of crisis:[617]

---

[613] U.K., our staunchest ally is overwhelmingly against the war and completely against Bush.

[614] Howard Kurtz, "Peter Jennings, in the News for What He Didn't Say," *Washington Post* Staff Writer, Monday, September 24, 2001; Page C01 http://www.washingtonpost.com/ac2/wp-dyn?pagename=articleandnode= andcontentId=A14272-2001Sep23andnotFound=true

[615] Rush Limbaugh, "Jennings and ILK Proven Dead Wrong," EIB ^ | Posted on 09/12/2001 6:48:57 PM PDT by VinnyTex http://209.157.64.200/focus/f-news/521549/posts "Patriots attack media amid cries of treason," *The Guardian*, London, 10/3/01 http://www.refuseandresist.org/resist_this/100401patriots.html

[616] Attention Peter Jennings http://www.rushonline.com/war/peterjennings.htm

[617] Phil Donahue was calling for tolerance of others at a commencement speech at North Carolina State and was booed. "Take a liberal to lunch…Take a Dixie Chick to lunch." "Donahue Gets Crowd Riled Up At N.C. State Graduation: Some In Crowd Walk Out During Commencement Address" WRL.com POSTED: 7:39 p.m. EDT May 17, 2003 Updated: 7:11 a.m. EDT May 19, 2003 http://www.wral.com/news/2211223/detail.html Carrie Watters, "Speaker disrupts RC graduation: A New York Times reporter delivers an antiwar speech that offended many," *Rockford Register Star* May 20, 2003. (Hedges delivered an 18-minute anti-war speech comparing U.S.'s policy in Iraq to pariahs and a tyranny over the weak. Students and audience protested by unplugging the mike, blowing foghorns, turning their backs, rushing up the aisle, and one student tossed his cap and gown to the stage and left.) http://www.rrstar.com/localnews/your_community/rockford/ 20030520-4814.shtml

"Text of the Rockford College graduation speech by Chris Hedges," *Wednesday, May 21, 2003 Rockford Register Star (Illinois)* ("Killing, or at least the worst of it, is over in Iraq. Although blood will continue to spill

"Jennings Should Apologize! … It was with utter sadness and disgust that I listened to Peter Jennings make negative comments about the whereabouts of our President Bush, critical of him for not being in Washington. Our country was hurting in more ways than can be imagined and he was trying to drive a wedge in the solidarity that was happening."

On September 17, 2001, in the first episode of his "Politically Incorrect" after 9/11, Bill Maher the comedian political commentator was discussing with his guests as to how best to prevent future terrorists attacks.[618] Part of the exchange involved Bill Maher comparing the bravery of American politicians (or lack thereof) with that of al-Qaida terrorists: "We have been the cowards, lobbing cruise missiles from 2,000 miles away. That's cowardly …Staying in the airplane when it hits the building, say what you want about it, it's not cowardly."[619]

The actual exchange between liberal Maher and conservative writer/ commentator Dinesh D'Souza was as follows:

Dinesh: Bill, there's another piece of political correctness I want to mention. And, although I think Bush has been doing a great job, one of the themes we hear constantly is that the people who did this are cowards.

Bill: Not true.

Dinesh: Not true. Look at what they did. First of all, you have a whole bunch of guys who are willing to give their life. None of 'em backed out. All of them slammed themselves into pieces of concrete.

Bill: Exactly.

Dinesh: These are warriors. And we have to realize that the principles of our way of life are in conflict with people in the world. And so -- I mean, I'm all for understanding the sociological causes of this, but we should not blame the victim. Americans shouldn't blame themselves because other people want to bomb them.

Bill: But also, we should -- we have been the cowards lobbing cruise missiles from 2,000 miles away. That's cowardly. Staying in the airplane when it hits the building, say what you want about it, it's not cowardly. You're right.

-- theirs and ours -- be prepared for this. For we are embarking on an occupation that, if history is any guide, will be as damaging to our souls as it will be to our prestige, power, and security. But this will come later as our empire expands and in all this we become pariahs, tyrants to others weaker than ourselves. Isolation always impairs judgment and we are very isolated now.") http://www.commondreams.org/headlines03/0520-13.htm

[618] "What Happened: The Very Quick Version," http://www.millionflagmarch.com/bill/quick.htm

[619] Some context is important. During the week after 9/11, not one TV host raised a dissenting voice, except for Bill Maher. Leno and Letterman played it safe, telling mostly politically correct and safe jokes, against Taliban and Osama bin Laden. Jon Stewart even cried. Robert Thompson, director of Syracuse University's Center for the Study of Popular Television, observed that Maher paid a heavy price for speaking out: "He was the only dissenting voice out there that week," Chris Raphael, "Politically Incorrect: A Eulogy Maher was one of the few with enough guts to dissent," *The Big Story*, June 3, 2002. http://thebigstory.org/ov/ov-politicallyincorrect.html

Maher's remark stirred up a storm in a nation still recovering from 9/11. Gregg Easterbrookm, editor of TNR, wrote an article faulting Maher for bad logic, poor taste: "Cruise missiles are designed to be launched from far away, thus "doesn't make sense to judge their use as cowardly or courageous; it is instead of matter of right or wrong." Terrorists attacking civilians are cowardice." [620]

Chris Ulbrich coming to the rescue:[621]

"When Maher and D'Souza argued against describing the terrorists as cowards, they were arguing that the terrorists were persistent, determined, and unafraid to die -- an enemy we underestimate at our peril ...The second charge, ... Maher said, "We've been the cowards"... He was contrasting America's reluctance to take casualties "...

The White House got into the fray with Mr. Fleischer, the White House spokesman issuing a strong statement:

"I'm aware of the press reports about what he said. I have not seen the actual transcript of the show itself. But assuming the press reports are right, it's a terrible thing to say, and is unfortunate. And that's why -- there was an earlier question about has the President said anything to people in his own party -- they're reminders to all Americans that they need to watch what they say, watch what they do. This is not a time for remarks like that; there never is.'[622]

As a result, Washington, D.C.'s WJLA (channel 7) pulled the show for the second time.[623]

Under pressure, Maher was forced to issue a public clarification and apologized two days later:

"In no way was I intending to say, nor have I ever thought, that the men and women who defend our nation in uniform are anything but courageous and valiant, and I offer my apologies to anyone who took it wrong. My criticism was meant for politicians who, fearing public reaction, have not allowed our military to do the job they are obviously ready, willing and able to do, and who now will, I'm certain, as they always have, get it done."

Still this did not appease the critics. Finally, when several sponsors – Fedex, Sears - pulled their advertising,[624] [625] ABC cancelled the show.[626] Six months later, on June 22, 2002,

---

[620] Gregg Easterbrookm, editor of TNR, provided one of the most sophisticated indictment against Bill Maher. "DAILY EXPRESS - Profiles in Courage," *TNR Online* Post date October 2, 2001 http://www.tnr.com/express/easterbrook100201.html

[621] For a defense of Maher, see Chris Ulbrich, "Politically Intolerable - Takes Bill Maher to the Woodshed," *The New Republic* - October 10, 2001

[622] See "18. Bill Maher's comments," Press Briefing by Ari Fleischer, White House Press Office, September 26, 2001.   http://www.whitehouse.gov/news/releases/2001/09/20010926-5.html#BillMaher-Comments Washington, D.C.'s WJLA (channel 7) has been the most important of such stations; last Wednesday, the station pulled the show for the second time, not because Maher had done something offensive, but in apparent reaction to statements by White House spokesman Ari Fleischer

[623] *The Daily Howler*, Oct. 1, 2001. http://www.dailyhowler.com/h100101_1.shtml

[624] "Sears took this action after reviewing a transcript of the September 17 conversation among Maher and his guests in which the U.S. military was described as cowardly."

Maher was awarded the L.A. Press Club's President's Award, its highest honor, for "championing free speech." Subsequently, Maher became the host of HBO's *Real Time with Bill Maher*, a show very similar to *Politically Incorrect*.

ABC Chairman Lloyd Braun denied that Maher was fired for his controversial comments: "We made a decision to go with straight entertainment programming in late night ... That's just basically a scheduling opportunity that we felt over the long term had more potential."

More Cases of "Imposed" Self- Censorship

On 10 October 2001, National Security Adviser Rice implored the press and media to restrict and censor inflammatory news and broadcast from bin Laden: based on the fact that he "was a charismatic speaker who could arouse anti-American sentiment getting 20 minutes of air time to spew hatred and urge his followers to kill Americans." Initially the rationale for self-censorship was to prevent coded messages. Later, the White House spokesman Ari Fleischer became blunter in warning that Americans "need to watch what they say".

On October 12, 2001, Fleischer requested major newspapers not to print to bin Laden's messages in full. "The request is to report the news to the American people...But if you report it in its entirety, that could raise concerns that he's getting his prepackaged, pretaped message out" Rupert Murdoch, News Corp executive, agreed to do so enthusiastically: "We'll do whatever is our patriotic duty"(Reuters, 10/11/01). CNN also agreed to comply: "In deciding what to air, CNN will consider guidance from appropriate authorities".[627]

The third TV host penalized for being politically incorrect after 9/11 was Ted Koppel. On April 30, 2003, the host of ABC Nightline.[628] Ted Koppel was to read out aloud the name, military branch, rank and age of each of "The Fallen" (721) soldiers in the Iraq war. "The Fallen" was not well received in some quarters as an anti-war ploy.[629] The Sinclair Broadcast Group ordered all of its eight ABC affiliates in Columbus, Ohio and St. Louis, Missouri not to carry the show because it "appears to be motivated by a political agenda designed to undermine the efforts of the United States in Iraq." not to carry the show."[630]

The first large scale of self-censorship happened right after the 9/11 event. Clear Channel Communications[631] requested 1,170 radio stations nationwide not to broadcast 150 songs

---

[625] Maher remarked went unnoticed until a Houston conservative talk show host Dan Patrick urged listeners to complain to two of the show's advertisers, Sears and Federal Express, pressuring them to drop the ad.

[626] "Maher canceled, Kimmel lands slot at ABC," *CNN* May 14, 2002 Posted: 2:25 PM EDT (1825 GMT) (ABC Chairman Lloyd Braun denied that Maher was fired for his controversial comments: "We made a decision to go with straight entertainment programming in late night ... That's just basically a scheduling opportunity that we felt over the long term had more potential." http://archives.cnn.com/2002/SHOWBIZ/TV/05/14/television.kimmel/index.html

[627] Bill Carter and Felicity Barringer, "At U.S. Request, Networks Agree to Edit Future bin Laden Tapes," *New York Times*, October 11, 2001.

[628] ABC said: broadcast "simply seeks to honor those who have laid down their lives for this country. Frazier Moore, `Nightline' reads toll of war dead - tribute or propaganda?" *AP Television*, Thursday, April 29, 2004. http://www.sfgate.com/cgi-bin/article.cgi?file=/news/archive/2004/04/29/entertainment1414EDT0172. DTLandtype=tvradio

[629] Frazier Moore, `Nightline' reads toll of war dead _ tribute or propaganda?" *AP Television*, Thursday, April 29, 2004.

[630] Frazier Moore, "`Nightline' reads toll of war dead _ tribute or propaganda?" AP Television. Thursday, April 29, 2004

[631] Clear Channel, a Texas-based company, made substantial contributors to George W. Bush before he became president. Tom Hicks then vice chairman of Clear Channel purchased the Texas Ranger from Bush, making

because it might upset the traumatized public, including Gap Band's "You Dropped a Bomb on Me" and Soundgarden's "Blow Up the Outside World". Some the songs have no connection to 9/11, e.g., "Ticket to Ride" (Beatles), "On Broadway" (Drifters) and "Bennie and the Jets" (Elton John).[632]

Another high profile "imposed" self-censorship happened on March, 2003 when lead singer Natalie Maines (of Dixie Chick fame) said in a concert in London that she was "ashamed the president of the United States is from Texas" in planning to invade of Iraq. Cumulus Media, owner of 262 radio stations around the country, stops all of its forty-two country outlets from playing Dixie Chicks music. It asked its listeners to drop off their Dixie Chicks CD ton be demolished in Shreveport, Louisiana. Many of the 1,225 radio stations owned by Clear Channel Communications also ban the Dixie Chicks. Station managers said their decisions were prompted by calls from irate listeners who thought that the singers were being unpatriotic and disrespectful to criticize the commander in chief in war. In May, country music station KKCS, in Colorado, suspended two disc jockeys for playing songs by the Dixie Chicks in violation of a ban imposed by the station manager.[633]

Observations

The above discussion shows clearly and conclusively that the pressure to do the right thing for journalists – free speech for the right cause – after 9/11, was immerse, some say overwhelming. It affected established TV anchors like Rather and Jennings, personally and professionally, not withstanding their individual stance on issue of "patriotic journalism" – Rather (carries away by patriotism) vs. Jennings (standing firm for independence).

"Patriotic journalism" affected 9/11 reporting focus, issues, content and style. For example, anti-terrorism measures such as USAPA was not adequate covered and analyzed. Except for a few in-depth coverage by public interest media, e.g., PBS, the news media did not show great interest in covering the MATA, ATA, and Patriot Act. When media reported on 9/11 legislation, the focus was on need to protect the nation against another attack. During the first round of public debate (i.e., September 17, 2001 (ATA public release) to September 24, 2001(ATA Congressional hearing) over the ATA, the three major networks – NBC, CBS, ABC failed to report upon the ant-terrorism measures in depth. On September 21, 2001 NBC Nightly News stated as a matter of fact that after 9/11 security concerns should trump civil liberties considerations. As of September 27, 2001, there was no reporting of the ATA or USAPA. On September 25, 2001, CBS Evening News reported that George Bush was asking the Congress for more power "to conduct wiretaps and detain suspects," and that some in the Congress "aren't so sure" the proposal won't violate civil liberties. No further details on the legislation were provided. On September 25, 2001, ABC's World News Tonight aired one segment on the proposed ATA, reporting that ATA "give the government more power to spy on Americans here at home, monitor Internet use with little oversight from a judge, lock up

---

him a millionaire. Hicks and Clear Channel was pro-war as well as pro Bush. See "FCC and Clear Channel. Clear Channel Is A Subsidiary Of Bush, Inc," *Rense* June 15, 2003. http://www.rense.com/general38/clkear.htm

[632] Neil Strauss, "After the Horror, Radio Stations Pull Some Songs," *New York Times* September 19, 2001.

[633] "Dixie Chicks Boycotted on Country Radio," *about.com* March 17, 2003.

immigrants who the government says might be a threat to national security without presenting evidence."[634]

VI. CONCLUSION

A Changed America

9/11 was a defining moment for America and turning point for the Nation. As President Bush observed, 9/11 has changed the world we lived in, once and for all:

> "I realized I was in a unique setting to receive a message that somebody attacked us, and I was looking at these little children and all of the sudden we were at war…And it became evident that we were, you know, that the world had changed."[635]

More forebodingly Ted Goertzel observed a change of spirit of the age for all time:

> The destruction of the World Trade Center on September 11, 2001 had all the hallmarks of a turning point in history. Suddenly everything seemed different and nothing would ever be the same. People felt a similar shock after the bombing of Pearl Harbor in 1941, the stock market crash in 1929, the murder of John F. Kennedy in 1963 and, perhaps, even the stock market crash of 1987. But not all such traumas trigger a lasting shift in what the Germans call the *zeitgeist,* or the "spirit of the age."[636]

In substantive terms, 9/11 gave us the war on terror; which slowly evolved into a religious crusade (Islam vs. Christianity)[637] and in time a cultural war.[638] It tipped the balance between security vs. liberty and changed our view about role of government.

The main thesis of this article is that if Bush were to be believed and Goertzel taken seriously, we cannot begin to understanding the Nation's reaction to 9/11 in general and the passage of USAPA in particular without first discerning and documenting how 9/11 changed

---

[634] Extra! magazine (FAIR), December 2001. http://www.thirdworldtraveler.com/Terrorism/Are_You_Terrorist.html

[635] "60 Minutes II: The President's Story," *CBS News* September 10, 2003. http://www.cbsnews.com/stories/2002/09/11/60II/main521718.shtml Much like the assassination of President Kennedy, everyone in America and most people around the world remember the moment, and everyone has his/her story to tell. Steven Brill, *After: How American Confronted the September 12 Era* (N.Y.: Simon and Shuster, 2003).

[636] Ted Goertzel, "September 11, 2001: A Turning Point for America's Future?" The World Future Society. http://www.wfs.org/goertzel.htm

[637] Richard T. Cooper, "General Casts War in Religious Terms: The top soldier assigned to track down Bin Laden and Hussein is an evangelical Christian who speaks publicly of 'the army of God.'" *Los Angeles Times* October 16, 2003. (Lt. Gen. William G. "Jerry" Boykin, the deputy undersecretary of Defense for intelligence, described reason for the war on terror as: "'because we're a Christian nation, because our foundation and our roots are Judeo-Christian ... and the enemy is a guy named Satan.")

[638] Howard F. Stein, "Days of Awe: September 11, 2001 and its Cultural Psychodynamics," *Journal for the Psychoanalysis of Culture and Society* Volume 8 (2): 187-199 (2003). ("Three popular cultural texts articulated much of the national discourse: Samuel Huntington's *The Clash of Civilizations and the Remaking of World Order* (1998), Bernard Lewis's *What Went Wrong: Western Impact and Middle Eastern Response* (2001), and Benjamin Barber's *Jihad vs. McWorld: How Globalism and Tribalism are Reshaping the World* (1996).

America people's ways and means, psyche and ethos; specifically how Americans as citizens, law makers, President and journalists reacted to 9/11.

9/11 changed America radically, precipitously, in fundamental and irrevocable ways:[639] socially, [640] psychologically, [641] spiritually, [642] morally, [643] politically, [644] economically, [645] culturally,[646] and legally.[647] Its view of self and the world changed drastically overnight and forever.[648] Specifically, between August 26th, 2002 and September 15, 2002 the Corporation for Public Broadcasting launched a write in program with the question: "As you look at your

---

[639] For contrary observations, see Dean, Wally, Brady, and Lee Ann, "After 9/11, has anything changed?" *Columbia Journalism Review* Nov/Dec 2002 (9/11 did not change the reporting pattern of local news station.); Garrick Utley, "Did 9/11 change everything? Americans have always adapted to new challenges," *CNN* September 6, 2002 Posted: 6:48 PM EDT (2248 GMT) (USA has always been for and in the process of change. 9/11 did not change America in any discernible ways.) See "After Sept. 11 Archive" Social Science Research Council. http://www.ssrc.org/sept11/essays/

[640] Nancy Foner (editor), *Wounded City: The Social Impact of 9/11* (Russell Sage Foundation, 2005)

[641] "American Psyche Reeling From Terror Attacks," (September 19, 2001) PEW Research Center, especially "Emotional Aftershocks" (A national survey between September 13 – 17, 2001 showed that 9/11 has immediate, but disparate, emotional impact on most American. For example, female, parents, urban, Eastern region people were affected more.) http://people-press.org/reports/display.php3?PageID=30 Michael Jonathan Grinfeld, "Achieving Balance in 9/11 Media Coverage," *Psychiatric Times*, September 2002, Vol. XIX, Issue 9 (Media reporting of 9/11 with graphic re-enactment might have triggered 9/11 posttraumatic stress disorder (PTSD) in people who were directly affected.) http://www.psychiatrictimes.com/p020901a.html

[642] "Post-911 attitudes: RELIGIOUS MORE PROMINET, MUSLIM AMERICAN MORE ACCPETED," (December 6, 2001) PEW Research Center (Religion became more important in people's life. In November of 2001, a nation wide PEW survey showed that 78.8% of the respondents were of the opinion that the influence of religion was increasing. Similar survey conducted between 1997 and March 2001 was 37%.) http://pewforum.org/publications/surveys/post911poll.pdf

[643] "American Virtue After 9/11," *Belienet* (9/11 and terrorism has been used by Bush to embrace the medieval notion of crusade.) http://www.beliefnet.com/story/152/story_15246.html

[644] Joe Drymala, "9/11 Changed Everything (The End Of The Beginning)," (9/11 gives us a one party fascist state with no institutional check and balance and political or legal accountability.) http://www.notgeniuses.com/archives/002050.html (last visited march 23, 2005)

[645] For a comprehensive review of direct and indirect economic impact of 9/11 on NYC, see "Review of Studies of the Economic Impact of the September 11, 2001, Attacks on the World Trade Center," GAO Report: GAO 02 7003 (May 29, 2002). http://www.gao.gov/new.items/d02700r.pdf

[646] 9/11 and Bush's handling of it, generated a culture of hate, domestically against Islam, and internationally against the U.S. Mohamed Elmasry, "In the Shadow of 9/11: Hate of Culture, or Culture of Hate," *Media Monitor Network* (Monday 08 September 2003) http://usa.mediamonitors.net/content/view/full/548/ For impact on American culture generally, see B. J. Sigesmund, "September 11's Cultural Impact," *MSNBC* 9/5/2002. (Dwight Blocker Bowers of Smithsonian Institution observed that except for pop culture, the cultural impact of 9/11 is yet to be felt.) http://www.msnbc.msn.com/id/3068110/site/newsweek/
For impact on TV culture, see also Lynn Spigel, "Entertainment Wars: Television Culture after 9/11," *American Quarterly*, Vol. 56, No. 2. (Jun., 2004), pp. 235-270. (Notwithstanding initial fear that 9/11 would change TV culture as we know it, the market driven "narrowcasting and taste cultures" promises to return TV programming and to making things as usual after 9/11.)

[647] Dempsey, James X. *Terrorism and the Constitution; Sacrificing Civil Liberties in the Name of National Security* (Washington, DC: First Amendment Foundation, 2002). (9/11 and war on terror diluted the Constitution and eroded Americans' rights.)

[648] "One Year Later: America's Agenda." Remarks by Samuel R. Berger, Chairman, Stonebridge International. "9/11 a Year On: America's Challenges in a Changed World," United States Institute of Peace Conference, September 5, 2002. (Domestically, U.S. was changed from a "threat based" to a "vulnerability-based" approach in dealing with domestic security. Internationally, it taught the U.S. lessons about the importance of interdependence and cooperation.) http://www.usip.org/events/2002/america/berger.html Gara LaMarche, "Another Way in Which 9-11 "Changed Everything" The Impact of Counterterrorism and Security Legislation on the Work of Human Rights Defenders," at the Human Rights House Foundation Conference in Oslo, Norway, on October 13, 2004. The conference was titled "Activists under Attack: Defending the Right to Be a Human Rights Defender." (U.S. foreign policy after 9/11 has emboldened dictatorships to suppress dissents and violate human rights of people in the name of fighting terrorism.) http://www.soros.org/resources/articles_publications/articles/garaspeech_20041013.

life today, is it different because of September 11?"[649] The survey elicited incredibly rich, diverse and soul searching responses, as one might expert of Americans,[650] known for being individualistic as a culture[651] and diverse as a nation.[652] Most of the respondents observed that 9/11 changed their life, definitively and irrevocably, either in terms of how one look at values,[653] habits,[654] work,[655] relationship,[656] life, culture,[657] society,[658] nation,[659] Politics.[660]

In terms of culture and values, the biggest discernable change after 9/11 was the nation's dismissive attitude towards human, civil and constitutional rights in the face of terrorist threat. After 911, it is considered acceptable, if not even necessary, to torture suspected terrorists for information,[661] to imprison terrorists - Taliban and al-Qaeda members - without due process,[662] to compromise citizens' privacy rights in the name of security,[663] and to deny information to journalists to facilitate the prosecute of a war on terror.[664]

---

[649] Part of *Understanding America after 9/11* project funded by Corporation for Public Broadcasting. See "Is your life different today because of September 11?" *UnderstandingAmerica.org* http://understandingamerica. publicradio.org/form/index.shtml

[650] "The events of September 11th made me stop and reexamine my perspective of life, values, goals, and relationships" and "It made me reassess my goals...".

[651] For a high school teachers' reaction, see Michael W Apple, "Patriotism, Pedagogy, and Freedom: On the Educational Meanings of September 11th." *Teachers College Record*, Vol. 104(8), Nov 2002. pp. 1760-1772 (2002)

[652] Female responded differently than male, see Sandra P. Thomas;" *Health Care for Women International*, Vol. 24(10), Dec 2003. pp. 853-867 (2003); white different than black, see Roxanna Harlow and Lauren Dundes; 'United' We Stand: Responses to the September 11 Attacks in Black and White," *Sociological Perspectives*, Vol. 47(4): 439-464 (2004) (White and black interpret and react to 9/11 differently and based on racial paradigm.); adolescent different from teachers, see Illene C Noppe, Lloyd D. Noppe and Denise Bartell, "Terrorism and resilience: Adolescents' and teachers' responses to September 11, 2001," *Death Studies*, Vol. 30(1): 41-60 (2006) (A survey in January 2002 of 973 Upper Midwest adolescents and teachers showed that they reacted different to 9/11, e.g., "adolescents (especially girls) were frightened and upset but also used many coping strategies.' They were also angry and tired of the event. "Teachers discussed the attack's historical significance, student safety, and a desire to resume "normalcy.")

[653] "That said, the awful events of that day reinforced something I have always believed: evil exists...", Op. cit. note 190, *supra*.

[654] "I do not put things off anymore." "I do everything exactly the same as I did on September 10...", *Id.*

[655] "My job certainly feels less meaningful after 9/11..." *Id.*

[656] "Yep; this attack has made me stronger at persisting to 'love away'..." *Id.*

[657] "The terrorists don't really scare me. What really scares me is the blindness, the ignorance and lack of concern about what goes on here every minute of everyday, not just on 9/11." *Id.*

[658] "I suspect the whole idea that everything has changed is mostly media hype designed to win support for militarism." *Id.*

[659] "My life is different as I am now convinced beyond any doubt that America is caught in an inevitable downward slide caused by its own ignorance and arrogance." *Id.*

[660] "I am becoming ever more enraged that a terrorist attack, however evil, brilliant, and devastating, has been used by the Bush administration to justify virtually every attempt to deprive Americans of long-held rights and values." *Id.*

[661] Dana Priest, "Justice Dept. Memo Says Torture 'May Be Justified," *Washington Post.* Sunday, June 13, 2004; 6:30 PM. See U.S. Dept. of Justice Memo To Alberto R. Gonzales, White House Counsel (August 1, 2002). http://news.findlaw.com/hdocs/docs/doj/bybee80102ltr.html

[662] Michael Byers, **"Ignore the Geneva Convention and put our own citizens at risk,"** (Civil Liberties Watch). *The Humanist* March-April 2002, Vol. 62 (2): 33 (The 1949 Geneva Convention on the treatment of prisoners of war stipulates that PoWs are to be afforded "the same courts according to the same procedure as in the case of members of the armed forces of the detaining power." In treating Taliban and al-Qaeda fighters, as not entitling to POWs status, the U.S. violated the fundamental principles of international law and war conventions, and in time putting our soldiers at risks and the US's international human right leadership under attack.) Inspector General Report, **"The September 11 Detainees: A Review of the Treatment of Aliens Held on Immigration Charges in Connection with the Investigation of the September 11 Attacks,"** (June 2003), Office of the Inspector General, DOJ (The report examined 762 aliens under Immigration and Naturalization Service (INS) custody as a result of post 9/11 PENTTBOM investigation. The detainees were subject to

Finally and most controversially, 9/11 have transformed U.S.A. from an open – democratic society to a closed – garrison state.[665]

In light of the above, it is fair to observe that 9/11 was a rude awakening for America. It changed American people's psyche radically and the Nation's ethos permanently. For the first time in its history, a terrorist group has declared war on America with an attack on its soil. The devastation to people, property and economy revealed US vulnerability and demonstrated the terrorists' strength. As expected the people became anxious and disoriented and the nation turned defensive and militant. The best anecdote to anxiety is certainty. The best cure for disorientation is focus. Both of these remedies to post 9/11 traumatic syndrome found a convenient home in war on terror. War provides certainty in defining people in starch black and white terms and separate people into good vs. evil categories. War also makes us focus on winning and losing. Finally, war brings people together, in uniform and unison. Uniform makes people feel secure and unison allows people to find strength in number and gain solidarity in agreement. In order to successfully prosecute a war, the country needs to change from an open society to a garrison state.[666] This is what USAPA is all about, i.e., laying the necessary foundation of a garrison state.

The USAPA was introduced and passed Congress under a set of most unique circumstances: U.S. mainland was attacked by a fundamentalist and resourceful enemy and the Nation declared a war on terror under an evangelical and crafty President. 9/11 shocked the awed the Nation.[667] The people were despondent and disoriented in the face of fear and uncertainly. President Bush's war on terror divided the world but united a people.[668] Patriotism helps people to close ranks in the face of danger.[669] Nationalism causes people to

---

[663] lengthy detention without notice, representation and hearing. They were subjected to personal humiliation and physical abuse without recourse.) http://www.usdoj.gov/oig/special/0306/chapter1.htm#I

[663] C. William Michaels, *No Greater Threat: America After September 11 And The Rise Of A National Security State* (Algora Publishing 2002). ("Indeed there is no greater threat to the security of this country than a systematic dismantling of civil liberties and the rule of law with a dramatic shift of political will and resources to investigate, surveillance, and prosecution, coupled with the almost uncanny ability of the American public to place too much faith in government at the precise time when just the opposite approach is required." (Italic is in the original).

[664] Danny Schechter, "How Did 9/11 Change Big Media?" *Intervention Magazine* (From Murdock to Rather, 9/11 has changed the media substantially. After 9/11, "patriotic correctness" has become in vogue. The media put concern with fear before commitment to facts. Overall journalists were more respectful of the authority and deferential to officials, and more trusting of government and less critical of the officials.) www.interventionmag.com/cms/modules.php?op=modloadandname=Newsandfile=articleandsid=495 - 62k – (last visited March 23, 2005).

[665] "The Ratings: A National Security State "Scorecard," C. William Michaels, *No Greater Threat: America After September 11 And The Rise Of A National Security State* (Algora Publishing 2002), pp. 299-300. For a review, see Mark S. Zaid, "Was September 11, 2001 Actually A Prelude To 1984?" *A Review of A New Book* (2004). "Forecasting The Possible Rise Of A National Security State," *FindLaw's Writ*, Jan. 24, 2003. http://writ.news.findlaw.com/books/reviews/20030124_zaid.html

[666] Ron Paul, "Trading Freedom for Security: Drifting Toward a Police State," *Mediterranean Quarterly* Volume 14 (1): 6-24 (2003).

[667] Lisa Anderson, "Shock and Awe: Interpretations of the Events of September 11," *World Politics* - Volume 56 (2): 303-325 (2004).

[668] Jon M. Murphy, "Our Mission and Our Moment": George W. Bush and September 11th," *Rhetoric and Public Affairs* Volume 6 (4): 607-632 (2004)

[669] Linda J. Skitka, "Patriotism or nationalism? Understanding post-September 11, 2001, flag-display behavior.," *Journal of Applied Social Psychology*, Vol. 35(10): 1995-2011 (2005) (Survey (N=605) showed that "post-9/11 flag-display behavior motivated by patriotism (love of country and in-group solidarity) and not nationalism (uncritical acceptance of national, state, and political authorities and out-group antipathy)

avoid introspection.[670] Patriotism and nationalism combined to allow America to overlook here problems at home in search of solutions abroad.

For example, America blame age old Middle East problem for a new found America's imperialistic global ambitions.[671] Instead of working on our corrupted foreign policies,[672] we declared war on terrorism. 9/11 and America's response, foreign and domestic, reflected and reaffirmed who Americans are as a nation and people,[673] from how they embrace adversities, by demonization of others, to how they react to challenges, with the use of violence and technology.[674]

---

[670] Keeton, Patricia, "Reevaluating the "Old" Cold War: A Dialectical Reading of Two 9/11 Narratives," *Cinema Journal* Vol. 43 (4): 114-121 (2004) (Citing Susan Sontag: "Where is the acknowledgement that this was not a 'cowardly' attack on 'civilization' or 'liberty' or 'humanity' or 'the free world' but an attack on the world's self-proclaimed super-power, undertaken as a consequence of specific American alliances and actions?) http://www.newyorker.com/printable/?talk/010924ta_talk_wtc

[671] George Steinmetz, "The State of Emergency and the Revival of American Imperialism: Toward an Authoritarian Post-Fordism," *Public Culture* Volume 15 (2):323-345 (2003)

[672] Eland, Ivan, "Bush's War and the State of Civil Liberties," *Mediterranean Quarterly* - Volume 14 (4): 158-175 (2003) (Osama bin Laden in declaring war against the U.S. was not seeking to promote Islamic beliefs or railed against decadent Western culture. Instead, he found corruption and abuse in U.S. foreign policy, e.g., support of Israel and presence in Saudi Arabia.) See also Peter Bergen, *Holy War, Inc.: Inside the Secret World of Osama bin Laden* (New York: Free Press, 2001), 222-3.

[673] George Steinmetz, "The State of Emergency and the Revival of American Imperialism: Toward an Authoritarian Post-Fordism," *Public Culture* Volume 15 (2):323-345 (2003) 9/11 is not successful in altering U.S. foreign policy (militarism in aid of capitalism), still less its self imposed world role (policeman of the world) and historical destiny (remaining super-power). But it does awaken U.S. to the stark reality of her vulnerability in a dangerous world (p. 325).

[674] Howard F. Stein, "Days of Awe: September 11, 2001 and its Cultural Psychodynamics," *Journal for the Psychoanalysis of Culture and Society* - Volume 8 (2): 187-199 (2003).

Chapter 4

IMPLEMENTATION OF USAPA

"I must say in all candor that we wish we could have been spared the SEVIS experience ..." [675]

Marlene M. Johnson
Exec. Dir. and CEO, NAFSA (2004)

I. INTRODUCTION

After the September 11 attacks, it was discovered that two of the terrorist pilots, Mohamed Atta and Marwan Alshehhi, were trained to fly at Huffman Aviation International in Venice, Florida, in September of 2000.[676] Both of these men entered the country on a visitor's visa. Their applications for a change of visa status from "visitor" to that of "vocational student" were processed by the Immigration and Naturalization Service (INS).[677] Another September 11 terrorist pilot, Hani Hanjour entered the United States on October 9, 2000 on an F-1 student visa to study English at an English as a Second Language (ESL) Center in Oakland, California. Hanjour never attended and was not reported missing by the school.[678] Consequently, legitimate questions were raised as to whether the tragedy could

---

[675] Letter from Marlene M. Johnson, Exec. Dir. and CEO, NAFSA, to The Honorable Tom Ridge, Secretary of Homeland Security. NAFSA Response to Department of Homeland (DHS) Security SEVIS Updates [P 1] (2004) (available at http://www.nafsa.org/public policy.sec/international student 1/iss archive/nafsa response to department 2).

[676] The most detail account of what happened on 9/11 iks *The National Commission on Terrorists Attack on the United States.* (July 22, 2004).

[677] "The Immigration and Naturalization Service's Contacts with Two September 11 Terrorists: A Review of the INS's Admissions of Mohamed Atta and Marwan Alshehhi, its Processing of Their Change of Status Applications, and its Efforts to Track Foreign Students in the United States," Off. of the Inspector Gen. Special Rept. 1 (DOJ May 20, 2002) (available at http://justice.gov/oig/special/0205/fullreport.pdf) [hereinafter Immigration and Naturalization Service's Contacts].

[678] Natl. Rev. Online, Nonimmigrant Visa Application: Hani Hanjour, 2000(b), http://www.nationalreview.com/document/document100902c.asp (accessed Nov. 20, 2006); Chitra Ragavan, "Coming to America: An Already Overburdened Immigration System Faces the New Demands of a Post-9/11 World," *U.S. News and World Report* [P 11] (Feb. 18, 2002), http://www.usnews.com/usnews/news/articles/020218/archive 020243.htm (other terrorists have also been found to have overstayed their business visas, for example, Nawaf Alhazmi and Satam Al Suqami each overstayed their B-1/B-2 visas).

have been prevented if the visas obtained by Atta, Alshehhi, and Hanjour had been properly screened and monitored.

September 11 precipitated a renewed call for stricter monitoring of foreign visitors.[679] On this subject, Senator Dianne Feinstein called for a complete overhaul of the foreign student tracking system. In particular, she proposed a six-month moratorium on the issuance of foreign student visas, giving the INS "time to remedy the many problems in the system."[680] Specifically, Senator Feinstein wanted to fund, develop, and deploy an electronic foreign students tracking system.[681]

Although Feingold's proposal was not enacted, Congress subsequently passed the Uniting and Strengthening America by Providing Appropriate Tools Required to Intercept and Obstruct Terrorism Act (USA PATRIOT Act, hereinafter "USAPA") on October 26, 2001[682] mandating the establishment of the Student and Exchange Visitor Information System (SEVIS)[683] by January 30, 2003.[684] SEVIS was designed to electronically track and monitor international students in the United States.

The idea of an electronic student tracking system within an open-university community in a democratic society has long generated heated debates and passionate protests. SEVIS only renewed the controversy.[685] While schools generally agree that SEVIS is necessary after 9/11, schools are not in agreement with the government as to its initial feasibility and ultimate utility.[686]

To its proponents, SEVIS is a much needed and long overdue tool for keeping the U.S. borders secure from illegal immigrants and its domestic front safe from terrorists. SEVIS allows the government to track foreign students and international visitors for educational, as well as security reasons, in a real-time, paperless, cost-effective, error-free environment.[687]

To its opponents, the implementation of SEVIS is fraught with many unresolved and (some say) un-resolvable, financial, legal, and technical problems. School associations for educators and administrators have expressed major misgivings and grave reservations with the unrealistic implementation of deadlines, unavailable administrative regulations, unreliable agency guidance, unreasonable workload, unfunded legislative mandate, uncertified vocational schools, untested software programs, untrained INS staff, uninformed Help Desk,

---

[679] Alison Siskin, Monitoring Foreign Students in the United States. CSR. Updated October 20, 2004. RL32188.

[680] Dianne Feinstein, "Senator Feinstein Urges Major Changes in U.S. Student Visa Program" [P 4], http://feinstein.senate.gov/releases01/stvisas1.htm (Sept. 27, 2001).

[681] Id.

[682] Pub. L. No. 107-56, 115 Stat. 272 (2001).

[683] Patty Croom and Jim Ellis, A Glossary of SEVIS-Related Terminology 2, http://www.educause.edu/ir/library/pdf/EDU0212.pdf (Sept. 30, 2002).

[684] Higher Educ. and Natl. Affairs 17 (Sept. 23, 2002) [hereinafter Congress Learns]; Patty Croom and Kathy Bellows, "Understanding the Student and Exchange Visitor Information System (SEVIS)," 25 *EDUCAUSE Q.* 14. (No. 3 2002) (available at http://www.educause.edu/ir/library/pdf/EQM0232.pdf).

[685] Mary Clarke-Pearson, "Federal Agents Tracking Foreign Students in U.S.: Hundreds of Colleges Have Faced Inquiries from the FBI and INS," *The Daily Pennsylvanian* [PP 11, 17] (Nov. 13, 2001) (available at http://www.dailypennsylvanian.com/media/storage/paper882/news/2001/11/13/News/Federal.Agents.Tracking .Foreign.Students.In.U.s-2159316.shtml) (Professor Jacques deLisle observed that international law does not require foreign visitors be given the same rights as American citizens. Professor Robert Vitalis considered such targeted investigations of foreigners as discriminatory.).

[686] Terry W. Hartle and James R. Burns, "Interconnecting Worlds," 37 *EDUCAUSE Rev.* 88, 88-89 (Sept./Oct. 2002).

[687] Bd. of Regents of the U. of Sys. of Ga. Off. of Intl. Educ., SEVIS Presentation to GACRAO 5-8, http://www.georgiaqualityteachers.org/oie/news/archive/SEVIS 102803.pdf (Oct. 28, 2003) (stating that SEVIS allows for centralized, real-time, and up-to-date maintenance of information by university and INS).

and unresponsive Department of Homeland Security (DHS) officials, particularly at the Immigration and Customs Enforcement (ICE).[688]

A cursory review of literature reveals that there are very few comprehensive and systematic studies of SEVIS-related implementation problems and issues,[689] particularly from the university administration perspective.[690] This chapter is a first attempt to fill this inexplicable, yet critical gap. The research discussed in this chapter seeks to answer the question: What were the implementation problems and resulting impact of SEVIS on university administration, particularly at international offices of higher learning, all over the nation?

The purpose of the study, which is the foundation of this chapter, is to allow a better understanding of SEVIS' impact on university administration.[691] Furthermore, this research also provides data and a context for critical analysis and objective assessment of the desirability of the USAPA. In order to accomplish this task, Section II will discuss the context for this study, including a brief excursion into the history and design of SEVIS. Section III anchors the discussion by providing an overview of the implementation issues and problems that will be critically examined and extensively discussed in Sections IV through VI. These three sections describe in detail and illustrate, different kinds of internal (Section IV) and external (Section V) SEVIS implementation problems (Section VI) experienced by universities and schools across the nation. Section VII summarizes the findings and discusses the implications of SEVIS on the American higher education system.

---

[688] See NAFSA: Assn. of Intl. Educators, Summary of SEVIS Conference Call, NGLU 2004-h (July 14, 2004) (copy on file with Author); "Follow-up Review on the Immigration and Naturalization Service's Efforts to Track Foreign Students in the United States through the Student and Exchange Visitor Information System," DOJ Evaluation and Inspections Rpt., I-2003-003 11 (Mar. 2003) (available at http://www.usdoj.gov/oig/reports/INS/e0303/final.pdf) [hereinafter Follow-up Review]. For a summary of the problems associated with SEVIS, see "Academe, International Access to American Higher Education," 89 *Academe* 47 (Sept./Oct. 2003) (reporting testimony of Shirley M. Tilghman, President of Princeton University, on March 26, 2003 before the Committee on Science of the U.S. House of Representatives, summarizing problems with SEVIS).

[689] See "Homeland Security: Performance of Information System to Monitor Foreign Students and Exchange Visitors Has Improved, but Issues Remain," GAO Rpt. to Cong. Comms., GAO-04-690 (June 2004) (available at http://www.gao.gov/new.items/d04690.pdf) (this is the only comprehensive study of SEVIS, which was performed by the General Accounting Office); see also "Homeland Security: Performance of Foreign Student and Exchange Visitor Information System Continues to Improve, but Issues Remain," GAO Testimony Before Cong. Subcomms., GAO-05-440T, 9, 13, tbls. 4, 6 (Mar. 17, 2005) (available at http://www.gao.gov/new.items/d05440t.pdf) (Table 3: Examples of Performance Requirements and Table 5: SEVIS Problems Identified by Organizations.)

[690] Vicky J. Rosser, et al., "How SEVIS Has Changed Our Worklives 4-9," http://www.nafsa.org/ /File/ /sevis study for ie - final.pdf (accessed Nov. 20, 2006). A survey of International Students and Scholars Advisors (ISSA) by NAFSA in the spring of 2005 showed ninety-one percent have an increased workload; eighty-six percent reported changes of decision making authority; seventy percent reported cleanup of databases and better maintenance of records; eighty-six percent spent more time on regulatory duties than advising; sixty-two percent experienced conflicts between SEVIS mandates and administrative practices; and fifty-six percent were satisfied with SEVIS troubleshooting support. The survey consisted of 1,226 responses from a sample of 2706 (forty-five percent response) with 1168 usable responses. Id.

[691] Jim Bloedel, "Academic Impact of September 11: New Infrastructure Demands and Policies," http://www.nasulgc.org/AM2002/presentations/AM2002 Bloedel.pdf (accessed Nov. 20, 2006).

II. Understanding SEVIS

A. The Legislative Context[692]

Section 641 of the Illegal Immigration Reform and Immigrant Responsibility Act (IIRIRA) was signed into law on September 30, 1996.[693] IIRIRA required the Attorney General, in consultation with the Department of State and Department of Education, to set up a program to collect current information from schools and exchange programs relating to nonimmigrant foreign students and exchange visitors during the course of their stay in the United States.[694] This law serves as the foundation of the Student and Exchange Visitors Program (SEVP).

In response to the terrorist attacks, on October 26, 2001, the USAPA amended Section 641 of the IIRIRA. The amendment required the development and implementation of SEVIS before January 30, 2003. The Enhanced Border Security and Visa Entry Reform Act of 2002 added to and clarified the information to be collected by SEVIS.

B. The Historical Context

Historically, the State Department, the INS, the Department of Justice (DOJ), and colleges and universities have long struggled with the problem of how to track the status and location of tens of thousands of international students and exchange scholars in the United States.[695] In 1983, in an attempt to solve this problem, the INS implemented a foreign students monitoring system entitled the Student and School System (STSC). The STSC contained basic information on foreign students and foreign academic visitors enrolled in certified schools in the United States. Under STSC, the INS required universities and institutes of higher education to document and keep track of foreign students and scholars in the United States. Through the use of I-17 and I-20 forms, the universities were to collect the necessary information under the Act, such as application and admission data, arrival and departure dates, academic disciplinary and termination actions, continuation of study, and changes of status of foreign students and scholars.[696]

Procedurally, the INS sent a computer printout containing information on all the F-1 students believed to be currently enrolled in a school. The school would then be required to

---

[692] H.R. Subcomm. on Immig., Border Sec. and Claims of the Jud. Comm., Nonimmigrant Student Tracking: Implementation and Proposed Modifications, 108th Cong. 28 (Apr. 2, 2003) (available at http://commdocs.house.gov/committees/judiciary/hju86265.000/hju86265 0f.htm) (testimony of Thomas P. Fischer, former INS District Director, Atlanta District, of the student monitoring system in the United States from WWII to the present submitted).

[693] The information to be collected under 641(a) includes the identity and current address of the alien, the nonimmigrant classification of the alien and any subsequent changes as approved by the attorney general, the current academic status of the alien; and any disciplinary action taken by the institution against the alien as a result of the alien's being convicted of a crime. Illegal Immigration Reform and Immigrant Responsibility Act of 1996 (IIRAIRA), 8 U.S.C. 372(c)(1)(A)-(D) (2002). The 641 information "shall be collected electronically, where practicable." 8 U.S.C. 372(c)(3).

[694] Id.

[695] Inst. of Intl. Educ., Open Doors 2005 Data Tables, http://opendoors.iienetwork.org/?p=69688 (Nov. 14, 2005) (In fiscal year 2004, 362,400 F-1 students and 312,400 J-1 exchange visitors were expected to enter the United States.).

[696] See Follow-up Review, supra n. 14.

verify the information and return the printout to the INS, which the INS would then use to update the Student/School (ST/SC) data-base.[697] By 1988, the INS determined that the ST/SC paper tracking system was inefficient, inaccurate, and unreliable.[698] At one point, INS officials openly acknowledged to Congress that they had no idea how many schools were certified to issue I-20s or how many foreign students were enrolled, obtained their visas by fraud, were out of status, or were overstaying their visas. In effect, once in the United States, foreign students and visitors were free to do whatever they wanted, with minimal hindrance or monitoring.[699]

The university community shared this bleak assessment. As recently as 2001, a self study by the e-Berkley Steering Committee conceded that all that was needed to register at University of California, Berkeley as a foreign student was a claim stating that the applicant was a foreign student.[700] Foreign student applications were not subjected to close inspection of documents or any independent verification of status:

Students, both UGs and Grads, self-report their intended (at the time of enrollment) immigration status on the application for admissions ... There is no visual confirmation of immigration status by checking the I-94 card at the Office of the Registrar, although there was one required up until about five years ago. The Residence Office does require a visual inspection of documents to support immigration status claims related to claims of California residency. This feeds into the Reg system ... The result is that there are few confirmed immigration statuses for international (nonimmigrant) students at Berkeley, and there are a number (as high as 30%) whose immigration status as recorded in the campus Registrar system is erroneous.[701]

After the 1993 terrorist bombing of the World Trade Center[702] there were renewed calls for immigration reform[703] especially when it was found that many of the acts of terrorism in the United States before and after 1993 were conducted by individuals who had entered the country on student visas or were non-immigrants. For example, Eyad Ismoil, the driver of the van that blew up the World Trade Center in 1993, was a Jordanian who entered the United States as a Wichita State University foreign student in 1989 and subsequently dropped out.[704]

---

[697]   Boston   U.,   Intl.   Students   and   Scholars   Off.,   Chronology   of   Significant   Events, http://www.bu.edu/isso/sevis/background/chronology/ (Feb. 28, 2005).

[698] See Follow-up Review, *supra* n. 14.

[699] H.R. Subcomm. on Immig. and Claims of the Jud. Comm., INS's March 2002 Notification of Approval of Change of Status for Pilot Training for Terrorist Hijackers Mohammed Atta and Marwan Al-Shehhi, 107th Cong. (Mar. 19, 2002) (available at http://commdocs.house.gov/committees/judiciary/hju78298.000/hju78298 0.htm).

[700] See SEVIS @ Berkeley, Focus on students, Working Paper #1: What We've Been Learning (unpublished paper Nov. 6, 2001, rev. May 2002) (available from SEVIS Project Manager, 3-8305, dwalker@uclink) (briefing paper summarized these types of errors and concerns).

[701] *Id.*

[702]   Federation   for   American   Immigration   Reform,   Terrorism   Chronology,   http://www.sullivan-county.com/id3/fair.htm (accessed Nov. 20, 2006) (gives a chronology of terrorism in the United States).

[703] 139 Cong. Rec. 26794, 26795 (May 27, 1993). The 1993 incident led to the formation of a multi-jurisdiction task force in June of 1995 to study the problems and issues with monitoring of foreign students and exchange visitors in the United States.

[704] Steven A. Camarota, "The Open Door: How Militant Islamic Terrorists Entered and Remained in the United States, 1993-2001" 19 (Ctr. for Immig. Stud. 2002) (available at http://www.cis.org/articles/2002/ theopendoor.pdf) (Analyzing the immigration status of forty-eight suspected terrorists since 1993, Camarota concludes that the nation would be more secure against terrorists with improved visa screening, tighter border control, and tracking of foreign students in the United States. Most of the policy recommendations were eventually adopted by the Bush administration and pressed into legislation.).

In 1995, the INS formed the Task Force on Foreign Students Control to investigate how best to reform the foreign students tracking system. The final report, "Control Governing Foreign Students and Schools That Admit Them," became a blueprint for a new kind of INS student tracking reform, with many of its recommendations adopted by the Clinton Administration and incorporated into IIRIRA in 1996.[705]

IIRIRA's passage in 1996 amended the Immigration and Nationality Act (INA) to require universities to report information on nonimmigrant students and exchange scholars from selected countries by 1998.[706] Higher education institutions were required to collect fees and report information for all nonimmigrant foreign students with F, M, or J visas from five countries that were designated by the Attorney General.[707] Beginning no later than January 1, 1998, the universities were required to collect the following information on foreign students and visitors: identity and address in the United States, visa classification, dates of visa issuance and/or extension/change, current academic status, whether exchange scholars for the exchange visitor program (J scholar/student) satisfied the terms and conditions of the program, and whether the alien was convicted of and disciplined for a crime.[708]

In June of 1997, the INS started a pilot project called the Coordinated Interagency Partnership Regulating International Students (CIPRIS), later called the Student and Exchange Visitor Program (SEVP),[709] to test the feasibility of the electronic tracking and monitoring of foreign students in the United States. The project was the creation of the INS and the Department of State Bureau of Consular Affairs, the Department of State Bureau of Educational and Cultural Affairs (formerly the U.S. Information Agency (USIA)), the Department of Education, and members of the educational and exchange program communities.[710]

The pilot project involved twenty-one institutions of higher education in Georgia, Alabama, North Carolina, and South Carolina.[711] However, the foreign student tracking system did not materialize due to lack of resources as well as vocal and persistent objections by universities.[712] CIPRIS was officially terminated in October 1999 by INS Deputy

---

[705] Jennifer Bell, *Georgetown Initial CIPRIS Implementation Study* (unpublished ms. Fall 1998) (copy on file with Author).

[706] Deborah Hebert, "Illegal Immigration Act Update," *Assn. for Student Jud. Affairs Newsletter* (Spring 1997) (available at http://www.uiowa.edu/asjaleg/IIRIRA96analysis.html).

[707] 8 U.S.C. 372 (a), (b) (2002) (Section 641 of IIRAIRA (a) and (b)).

[708] *Id.*

[709] Memo. from Michael Cronin, Acting Exec. Assoc. Commr., Off. Of Programs, U.S. Dept. of Just., Immig. and Naturalization Serv., to Paul Arthur, et al., Memorandum for Management Team (July 20, 2001) (available at http://www.uscis.gov/files/pressrelease/SEVPmemo.pdf).

[710] *Id.*

[711] For a list of test schools and programs, see Auburn U. Off. Of Intl. Educ., CIPRIS Pilot School Document Background, http://web.archive.org/web/20031127163727/http://web6.duc.auburn.edu/academic/other/international education/sevp/letters/AU cipris92402.pdf (Sept. 24, 2002).

[712] Ltr. from Stanley O. Ikenberry, Pres., Am. Council on Educ., to Richard Sloan, Dir., INS Policy Directives and Instrs. Branch, Eye on Washington: Letter to INS Expressing Opposition to CIPRIS Draft Regulations (Feb. 22, 2000) (copy on file with Author) (expressing strong opposition to the draft regulations issued by the INS on 21 December 1999, "Authorizing Collection of the Fee Levied on F, J, and M Nonimmigrant Classifications Under Public Law 104-208;" the collection of fees was a federal unfunded mandate and a costly burden to the university administrators); Natl. Assn. of St. Us. and Land-Grant Colleges, NASULGC Criticizes Proposal for College to Collect INS Fees, 9 NASULGC Newsline 2 (Feb. 2000) (available at http://www.nasulgc.org/Whatsnew/Newsline/2000/NewsFeb00.pdf) (stating that it is inappropriate, inefficient, and costly for colleges and universities to collect fees and remit them to the INS for implementation of an electronic tracking system). For a rejoinder, see the opinion of twenty-one pilot schools at Am. Assn. of

Commissioner Mary Ann Wyrsch [713]. Since then, CIPRIS has been shelved, awaiting federal funding and national deployment.

September 11 provided the necessary national will, [714] political impetus, [715] financial resources, [716] and institutional commitment[717] to revisit the electronic tracking idea, called SEVIS, [718] as of July 2001. [719] Following 9/11, Congress held a number of high profile hearings on the problems with foreign students and visitors and the need for tracking them.

In December 2001, beta testing of SEVIS formally launched at ten schools in the Boston area. In May 2002, the Enhanced Border Security and Visa Entry Reform Act of 2002 was enacted. [720] This act required that additional information be captured by the electronic system, including issuance of I-20s and visas and enrollment of students. On May 16, 2003, the INS published a proposed rule for the implementation of SEVIS to solicit public comments. [721] On June 13, 2002, the INS released the final interface control document for third-party vendors to

---

Collegiate Registrars and Admis. Officers, Pilot Program Participants Oppose CIPRIS Repeal, http://www.aacrao.org/federal relations/cipris/cipris repeal.cfm (accessed Apr. 12, 2006) (stating that the CIPRIS project group members objected to the repeal of CIPRIS arguing that electronic tracking was the future and collection of fees is necessary, that with or without CIPRIS schools were required by law to report data manually and charge fees for processing student applications, that the introduction of CIPRIS did not mean ceding control to the federal government and perhaps enhanced the authority of the school in granting Optional Practical Training (OPT), and that the INS would not be mining the schools for information more than they are doing now). For related comments for or against CIPRIS, see Auburn U., Comments Received in Response to the CIPRIS Pilot School Statements (as of 11/13/2000), (Nov. 13, 2000) (copy on file with Author).

[713] For an official account of the origin and development of CIPRIS, see Memo., *supra* n. 31.

[714] On September 18, 2002, the Immigration, Border Security, and Claims Subcommittee of the House Judiciary Committee held a hearing entitled the Implementation of the Foreign Student Tracking Program by the Immigration and Naturalization Service. H.R. Subcomm. on Immig., Border Sec. and Claims of the Jud. Comm., Implementation of the Foreign Student Tracking Program by the Immigration and Naturalization Service, 107th Cong. 1 (Sept. 18, 2002) [hereinafter Implementation of Foreign Student Tracking]. On September 24, 2002, there was a hearing before the House Subcommittees on Twenty-First Century Competitiveness and Select Education held a hearing entitled Homeland Security: Tracking International Students in Higher Education - Progress and Issues Since 9-11. H.R. Subcomms. on 21st Cent. Competitiveness and Select Educ. Of the Jud. Comm., Homeland Security: Tracking International Students in Higher Education - Progress and Issues Since 9-11, 107th Cong. 1 (Sept. 24, 2002).

[715] Fedn. for Am. Immig. Reform, *An Invitation to Terror: How Our Immigration System Still Leaves America At Ris*k 9-10 (FAIR Horizon 2002) (available at http://www.fairus.org/site/DocServer/ACF2C5B.pdf?docID =361).

[716] Ltr. from David Ward, Pres., Am. Assn. of Collegiate Registrars and Adm. Officers, to George W. Bush, Pres., U.S., Regarding the Student and Exchange Visitor Information System (SEVIS) (Oct. 12, 2001) (available at http://www.aacrao.org/federal relations/cipris/bushletter.cfm) ("I write to urge you to designate $ 36.8 million of the Emergency Supplemental appropriations package (P.L. 107-38) to the Immigration and Naturalization Service (INS). These funds would be used to implement the Student and Exchange Visitor Information System (SEVIS), as proposed by Sen. Dianne Feinstein.")

[717] H.R. Subcomms. on 21st Cent. Competitiveness and Select Educ. of the Comm. on Educ. and the Workforce, Tracking International Students in Higher Education: A Progress Report, 109th Cong. 9 (Mar. 17, 2005) (available at http://edworkforce.house.gov/hearings/109th/21st/jointhea031705/cerda.htm) (testimony of Mr. Victor X. Cerda).

[718] See Memo., *supra* n. 35.

[719] Philip Martin and Susan Martin, "Immigration and Terrorism: Policy Reform Challenges," http://migration.ucdavis.edu/ceme/more.php?id=21 0 5 0 (Oct. 18, 2001).

[720] Pub. L. No. 107-173, 116 Stat. 543 (2002). For a summary of key provisions of the Enhanced Border Security and Visa Entry Reform Act, see U.S. Sen. Republican Policy Comm., Legislative Notice: H.R. 3525 - Enhanced Border Security and Visa Entry Reform Act, http://rpc.senate.gov/ files/L37IMMIGRATIONjj041102.pdf (Apr. 11, 2002) (analyzing H.R. 3525, 107th Cong. (Dec. 19, 2001)).

[721] Retention and Reporting of Information for F, J, and M Nonimmigrants; Student and Exchange Visitor Information System (SEVIS), 67 Fed. Reg. 34862 (May 16, 2002).

facilitate the development of software supporting SEVIS.[722] On July 1, 2002, the INS invited voluntary participation in SEVIS. The final regulation was published on December 11, 2002.[723]

C. SEVIS's Design

SEVIS provides one-stop shopping for the processing of international students and exchange scholars entering the United States.[724] ICE described SEVIS as "an automated process to collect, maintain and manage information about international foreign students and exchange scholars during their stay in the United States."[725] SEVIS tracks international students and scholars while they are in the United States throughout the entire process, including visa application, Port of Entry (POE) documentation, attending school, changing of status, and leaving the country. In doing so, SEVIS provides an electronic information exchange system between the DHS (ICS), ports of entry, the State Department (Office of Exchange Coordination and Designation and the Bureau of Educational and Cultural Affairs), U.S. embassies and consulates, and every institution of higher education that sponsors international students.[726]

SEVIS collects the following data on students/scholars: student registration; local address; full-time student status; leave of absence information; disciplinary action; termination of studies; dependents information; change in major or research specialty; change in title date of departure; change in funding or salary; change of name; program extension, school transfer, change in level of study, employment authorization, and reinstatement; failure to maintain status or complete program; prior approval to work or do research outside of the university or to transfer to a different U.S. institution.[727] In addition to collecting the above information, SEVIS also adopts a twenty-four-hour reporting window, which is "data-centric" as opposed to "document-centric."[728] The system is initiated by the students and scholars as opposed to the system itself (student driven), requires continuous updating (just-in-time reporting), uses forms generated and controlled by the INS (centrally controlled), provides a real-time, interactive interface, and provides for real-time web-based input and batch input.[729]

---

[722] PeopleSoft, PeopleSoft Student Administration and SEVIS: Statement of Direction - Update, http://cms.calstate.edu/T6 Documents/NewsAndPublications/General/SEVIS%20Direction%207 26 02.pdf (July 2002).

[723] 67 Fed. Reg. 7656 (Dec. 11, 2002); U.S. Immig. and Customs Serv., Student and Exchange Visitor Information System (SEVIS), Final Rule Implementing SEVIS: Tightening and Improving Procedures for Foreign Students Visiting the United States, http://www.ice.gov/pi/news/factsheets/0212FINALRU FS.htm (Dec. 11, 2002).

[724] See Immigration and Naturalization Service's Contacts, *supra* n. 6, at 3.

[725] U.S. Dept. of Homeland Sec., ICE Prepares U.S. Schools and Foreign Students for August 1, 2003 SEVIS Deadline 3, (July 29, 2003) (available at http://www.immigration.com/newsletter1/icepressreleasesevis.pdf).

[726] For step-by-step processing of foreign student visa with SEVIS, see Lawrence Martin, S.E.V.I.S. and International   Student   Admissions, http://web.archive.org/web/20041029165047/http://cgsnet.org/pdf/Martin.pdf (accessed Jan. 21, 2006).

[727] Data required to be sent to SEVIS includes data specified in the following: 8 C.F.R. 214.3(g) (2006); 22 C.F.R. 62.70 (2002); 8 U.S.C. 2372; Pub. L. No. 107-56 at 416; Pub. L. No. 107-173 at 501.

[728] Newfront Software, Roadmap to SEVIS 3, http://www.newfrontsoftware.com/sevis/docs/fsaATLAS6RoadMap SEVIS.pdf (Apr. 24, 2002).

[729] *Id.*

D. How SEVIS Works [730]

After admitting an international student or research scholar, the university notifies DHS via SEVIS. If DHS approves, it will issue either a bar-coded I-20 or DS-2019 to the student or scholar to confirm that he/she is accepted by an authorized university to pursue study or conduct research in the United States. The student or research scholar can then apply for a visa at the nearest U.S. consulate abroad. The consulate will confirm the student's I-20 or DS-2019 with the university and DHS via SEVIS. If everything is in order, the student or scholar will be issued a visa. When the student/scholar arrives in the United States, the DHS at the immigration desk will check the student/scholar's visa against SEVIS and confirm that the student/scholar has arrived in the United States. The student/scholar must report within 15 days to the university. Failing to timely appear at the university will result in automatic termination of student/scholar status, requiring voluntary departure or forced deportation. If the student/scholar arrives on time, the school promptly confirms the enrollment of the student/scholar at the school with SEVIS. The university must provide regular and timely updates via SEVIS on the status and progress of the student/scholar at the university via SEVIS for the duration of his/her academic career in the United States. [731]

III. IMPLEMENTATION DIFFICULTIES WITH SEVIS

A. Introduction

It is evident that given the highly-charged political environment against nonimmigrants and foreign students after 9/11, SEVIS was a fait accompli. After 9/11, it was no longer tenable to debate about the necessity, utility, or effectiveness of SEVIS, as had been done with CIPRIS. Instead, the focus of the debate shifted from policy to execution problems. Specifically, who should be responsible for the funding, operation and control of SEVIS? The problems and difficulties with SEVIS must be viewed in this larger context (i.e. implementation issues were used as a pretext to debate the propriety and utility of SEVIS).

The implementation problems that attracted the most attention and repeated complaints involved the feasibility, functionality, and effectiveness of SEVIS in monitoring thousands of schools, tracking hundreds of thousands of students, and documenting millions of "events" each year. The schools were obsessed with operational issues such as economic, legal, technical and managerial issues. They wanted to fulfill the SEVIS mandate with least disruption and minimal resource outlay possible. The INS was pre-occupied with compliance and enforcement concerns. Ultimately, the INS wanted SEVIS to be technically "available" in accordance with the USAPA by January 30, 2003. [732] Although, the INS and the schools had

---

[730] The substantive requirements and procedures for SEVIS have been promulgated in separate rule-making proceedings. See 67 Fed. Reg. 34862 (May 16, 2002) (proposed rule implementing SEVIS); 67 Fed. Reg. 44344 (July 1, 2002) (interim rule for schools to apply for preliminary enrollment in SEVIS); 67 Fed. Reg. 60107 (Sept. 25, 2002) (interim rule for certification of schools applying for enrollment in SEVIS); 67 Fed. Reg. 76256 (Dec. 11, 2002) (DHS's final rule implementing SEVIS); 67 Fed. Reg. 76307 (Dec. 12, 2002) (DOS interim rule implementing SEVIS).

[731] See Implementation of Foreign Student Tracking, *supra* n. 42.

[732] Michael McCarry, "Hill Questions INS Capacity to Use SEVIS Data," http://www.aacrao.org/transcript/index.cfm?fuseaction=show viewanddoc id=673 (Mar. 8, 2002) (stating that at a hearing on March 7, 2002,

their own expectations about SEVIS, however, both were less interested in making the system serve the educational objectives and personal needs of the students. The welfare and interests of the consumers of international education were never seriously taken into account. This is the sub-text of the SEVIS high drama waiting to be explored, and should be deplored.

B. The Implementation Process

The implementation of SEVIS, which consists of development,[733] deployment,[734] employment,[735] was and still is a huge undertaking in terms of resources and manpower, for both the government and universities. The USAPA required the creation of an entirely new[736] electronic monitoring and tracking system, with the ability to monitor and track every international students/scholar coming into the United States, for programs admitting international students/scholars by January 30, 2003.[737] This implementation was to be followed by a full accounting of all existing students in the United States by August 1, 2003.[738] All of this was to be achieved within a tight time frame established by Congress: last minute regulations imposed by INS/DHS,[739] and unilateral rule making concocted by administrators,[740] all within a chaotic and uncertain regulatory regime and a complex and intricate technical environment.[741]

In the USAPA, the U.S. Government set forth a January 30, 2003 deadline for the full implementation of SEVIS without consulting universities and other agencies. On May 16, 2002, the INS published the proposed rule[742] to implement the electronic collection and reporting process mandated under Section 641 of the IIRIRA Act of 1996 (IIRIRA). On June 13, 2002, the INS first released the final interface control document to facilitate SEVIS

Rep. Harold Rogers of Kentucky, former chairman of the Commerce, Justice, State appropriations subcommittee, expressed concern with INS's ability to use SEVIS to track and prosecute offending foreign students and exchange visitors holding F, J, and M visas).

[733] Development is the conceptualization, planning, and preparation stage, including CIPRIS (1997) and Operational Prototype (1999).

[734] Deployment is the first step of implementation, i.e. making SEVIS available for use. With the DHS it meant "technical availability" and with the schools it meant "functional availability."

[735] Employment is the actual use of SEVIS for processing foreign students.

[736] As shall observed below, the idea of an international student tracking system was not new and has been experimented with since 1996. See Fedn. For Am. Immig. Reform, *supra* n. 44.

[737] The date was extended to Feb. 15, 2003 for technological reasons. Natl. Assn. for Student Fin. Aid Adminstrs., SEVIS Grace Period Extended Until February 15, 2003, http://www.nasfaa.org/publications/2003/rsevisextend013103.html (Jan. 29, 2003).

[738] Elizabeth B. Guerard, New SEVIS Rules Extend Deadline for Entering Student Information to August 1; Compliance Date of January 30 Remains, http://www.nasfaa.org/publications/2002/rsevisdeadlines 121802.html (Dec. 18, 2002).

[739] In the last six months to launch date, May 2002-Jan. 2003, DHS/DOS promulgated no less than five sets of regulations to implement the SEVIS. See *supra* n. 58. For a more detailed discussion, see infra sec. VI(B)(3).

[740] Hartle and Burns, supra n. 12. (The progress in the implementation of SEVIS to date resulted from a unilateral imposition of the regulators, hoping that the schools would comply and could adjust.).

[741] Ltr. from NAFSA: Assn. of Intl. Educators, to Immig. Naturalization Serv., U.S. Dept. of Homeland Sec., Letter of Comment to INS on the Service's Proposed Rule, Published on May 16, 2002, Entitled "Retention and Reporting of Information for F, J, and M Nonimmigrants; Student and Exchange Visitor Information System (SEVIS)" (June 12, 2002) (at http://www.nafsa.org/content/publicpolicy/NAFSAontheIssues/NAFSAcomment letterfinal.htm) ("Given that the Service does not realistically know at this time when the system will be fully available to schools, the reporting deadline should be set through a separate rulemaking once the system is fully tested and complete").

[742] 8 C.F.R. pts. 103, 214 (2002).

software development by third-party vendors.[743] On July 1, 2002, the INS invited voluntary participation in SEVIS. The final regulations, "Retention and Reporting of Information for F, J, and M nonimmigrants; Student and Exchange Visitor Information System (SEVIS); Final Rule," was published on December 11, 2002, just fifty days before "D-Day."[744]

C. A Fundamentally Flawed Process

From the very beginning of the program, school administrators and educator associations, not to mention foreign students and exchange scholars, have expressed grave reservations and major misgivings about the design, planning, funding, and operability of SEVIS.[745] The President of the University of Maryland, C.D. Mote Jr., testified before the House Subcommittee on the Twenty-first Century Competitiveness and Select Education that after initial difficulties in implementation, SEVIS was functioning relatively well. However, some enduring problems existed which included the following: schools unable to fix data entry problems, limited university resources devoted to maintaining SEVIS and not to servicing student education, SEVIS fees ($ 100) absorbed by the University ($ 50,000) to avoid brain drain, lack of feedback from SEVIS on institutional performance, visa application fees prohibitive to new students, and a complicated process disruptive for continuing students. [746]

D. The SEVIS Challenge

1. Enormity of Challenge

The task of implementing SEVIS was a daunting challenge and stressful experience from the perspective of the schools and programs. Ms. Danley, Executive Director of Enrollment Services from Washington State University, observed:

The January 30, 2003, implementation deadline seemed unrealistic and impossible. Further, the enormity of this unfunded mandate created serious concerns at institutions. Those with moderate to large international student and scholar populations, such as Washington State University, seemed particularly vulnerable. Washington State University enrolls 22,166 students, of whom 1255 are international students. Additionally, the University employs approximately 150 scholars at any given time.[747]

The enormity of the implementation task can be gauged by looking at the total number of schools the government (DHS) inspected and certified between July 1, 2002 and January 30, 2003 - the final months before the SEVIS program was supposed to be operational.

---

[743] PeopleSoft, *supra* n. 50, at 6.

[744] 8 C.F.R. pts. 103, 214, 248, 274a (2002).

[745] *Id.*; See Melissa Flagg et al., Visa and Visiting Scientists, Students, and Trainees 15, http://thefdp.org/Present 2 May2003.pdf (accessed Jan. 16, 2006) (panel discussion focusing on student recruitment problems, student/mentor relations and implementation and maintenance issues)

[746] H.R. Subcomms. on 21st Cent. Competitiveness and Select Educ. of the Comm. on Educ. and the Workforce, Tracking International Students in Higher Education: A Progress Report, 109 Cong. 61 (Mar. 17, 2005) (available at http://www.house.gov/ed workforce/hearings/109th/21st/jointhea031705/mote.htm) (testimony of C.D. Mote Jr., President, University of Maryland, College Park).

[747] Janet V. Danley, SEVIS: One Institution's Tale of Implementation, http://www.pacrao.org/docs/resources/writers team/SEVIS.doc (accessed Nov. 21, 2006).

Table 1. SEVIS Certification Workload Statistics as of January 31, 2003[748]

Application dates	Applications	Approved	Denied	Pending
July 1 to Sept. 24, 2002	1,779	1,418	361	0
Sept. 25 to Nov. 15, 2002	2,856	1,927	36	893
Nov. 16, to Jan. 30, 2003	1,305	0	0	1,305
Total	5,940	3,345	397	2,199

According to DHS data, as of December 10, 2003, DHS had successfully certified 8,795 schools and 1,383 exchange programs for the SEVIS system. Depending on sources consulted, there were between 8,000 to 74,000 SEVIS schools and programs in the United States at that time, many of them yet to be certified.

As SEVIS end-users, international departments and exchange programs were responsible for the input, update, and maintenance of all incoming and continuing students/scholars found in the United States by January 30, 2003. In 2003, the total number of J-1 students and J-1 scholars (excluding dependents) that needed to be tracked was 869,118, of which 353,342 were new students and 515,776 were continuing students. [749] This was an impossibly enormous task. DOJ inspector general Glenn A. Fine testified before the Subcommittee on Immigration, Border Security, and Claims on September 18, 2002 and observed that "full implementation of SEVIS is unlikely by January 30, 2003, based on the amount of work that remains to be accomplished."[750]

Furthermore, SEVIS required schools to keep track of students and scholars in 150 data element areas (for example, address, department, etc.). Any change in one of the 150 data elements was to be reported within twenty-four hours. Since historically foreign student/scholar data was not routinely collected and centrally organized, and there was little communication between different databases and no reporting relationship between university departments, international offices found themselves delayed. These offices had to find ways to create a centralized and integrated foreign student information administration system capable of meeting SEVIS data recording and reporting requirements, which was not an easy task.[751]

2. Lack of Support

In the months before the SEVIS launch, many school administrators and international educators pled with the federal government to provide clearer and better guidance, accessible and competent help, available and helpful training, and reasonable and adequate lead time before the implementation of SEVIS. Most requests were ignored and many cautions were brushed aside. This frustrated many people involved in SEVIS, even private software

---

[748] Follow-up Review, *supra* n. 12., at 13 tbl. 1 ("SEVIS Certification Workload Statistics as of January 30, 2003").

[749] See NAFSA: Assn. of Intl. Educators, Summary of SEVIS Conference Call, NGLU 2003-12-a (Dec. 3, 10, and 17, 2003) (available at http://web.archive.org/web/20040407163840/http://www.nafsa.org/content/ProfessionalandEducationalResources/ImmigrationAdvisingResources/nglu200312a.pdf) [hereinafter NGLU 2003-12-a].

[750] See Congress Learns, *supra* n. 8, at 17 (Fine's observation was echoed by Terry W. Hartle, senior vice president of the American Council on Education (ACE) who represented more than 75 education and exchange visitor organizations before the same hearing).

[751] See Newfront Software, *supra* n. 52, at 7-10.

developers. For example, in April of 2002, Newfront, one of the largest international student administration software developers responsible for developing a SEVIS interface for the schools, cautioned against rushing towards implementation of the SEVIS program and disregarding technology readiness issues.[752]

No one had expected SEVIS would impose such drastic requirements on international offices. Specifically two aspects of SEVIS, the 24-hour reporting window and the extensive data element, will have a huge impact on the international offices. Added this to the frustrating lack of information on the SEVP from the INS over the last two years. I persistently urged SEVP officials to deliver technical specification as early as possible so that Newfront would have adequate time to design and test fsaATLAS and SEVIS, and so that school could reevaluate their business processes, workload, data systems, and make financial arrangements. [753]

3. Signs of Frustration

The friendly reminders and bitter objections fell on deaf ears. The INS (later DHS) decided to impose SEVIS on the education community on its own terms and according to its own timetable. This led frustrated administrators and anxious educators to vent their individual anger and collective grievances privately at conferences and at public hearings.[754] A satiric song prepared at a NAFSA conference reflected the level of frustration and provide insights into its cause:[755]

SEVIS Caused Psychosis[756]

Chorus

I've been diagnosed today with SEVIS caused psychosis
Even just the sound of it is something quite atrocious
If you have it long enough you just might need hypnosis
I've been diagnosed today with SEVIS caused psychosis.

Verse 1:

We thought that we'd be really smart and get on SEVIS early
Even though the program seemed to be a little squirrelly
We put all the I-20s in we thought that we could handle
Then last week we learned all those I-20s had been cancelled.
Repeat Chorus
Verse 2:

---

[752] Id.

[753] Id.

[754] For a day by day account of how a University of California administrator was frustrated by the INS and SEVIS, see Sheldon Zola, Request for Moratorium on BCIS Requirement for Electronically-produced I-20 Forms and for Reversion of SEVIS to "Test and Development' Status, http://web.archive.org/web/20040108150914/http://www.ias.berkeley.edu/siss/hurricane/sissworkingpapers/moratorium.doc (Mar. 25 and 26, 2003) (working paper #18 for UC-wide SEVIS meeting, U. Cal. Irvine, proposing a moratorium on SEVIS).

[755] See NAFSA New Orleans Conference, SEVIS Songs Song at C (Oct. 27-Nov. 1, 2003) (copy on file with Author).

[756] Julie Sinclair, SEVIS Watch: News About the INS SEVIS Program, from a Technology Perspective, http://radio.weblogs.com/0103492/categories/sevis/2003/04/09.html (accessed Nov. 21, 2006) (song entitled "SEVIS Caused Psychosis," sung to the tune of "Supercalifragelisticexpealidocious.").

Last week I had a problem that was totally confusing
The stress I felt from SEVIS then was truly not amusing
The manual was clear as mud, I needed help much faster
So I called the Help Desk and I got 4 different answers.

Repeat Chorus

Verse 3:

Whenever SEVIS kicks you off and doesn't seem to work right
When data entry's piled so high that it gives you a big fright
Remember this advice next time you find yourself in this plight
SEVIS works the best if you log on just after midnight

Repeat Chorus

4. Call for Help

As early as June of 2002, the American Council on Education (ACE), one of the largest and most prestigious higher education associations in the United States, called for delayed compliance with SEVIS:

In lieu of picking a January 30, 2003 deadline at this point, we recommend that a compliance date be set at 180 days after the Inspector General certifies that, based on benchmarks similar to those outlined above, SEVIS is fully operational. Colleges and universities will work to meet the deadline INS ultimately sets for compliance. It is impossible, however, to make an estimate as to how long it will take institutions to comply with a system that does not yet exist. Certification by the Inspector General should follow expeditiously once that office ascertains that the steps outlined above have been completed.[757]

Even the DOJ's Inspector General, Glenn A. Fine, concluded that the compliance date was an unrealistic one by asserting, "full implementation of SEVIS is unlikely by January 30, 2003, based on the amount of work that remains to be accomplished."[758]

IV. INTERNAL IMPLEMENTATION DIFFICULTIES

A. Legal-Technical Requirements

In order to meet SEVIS statutory requirements, technological specifications, and student administration needs, a university SEVIS information data system should preferably have the

---

[757] Ltr. from David Ward, Pres., Am. Council on Educ., to Dir., Regulations and Forms Servs. Div. Immig. and Naturalization Serv., Re: Comments on Proposed Rule: "Retention and Reporting of Information for F, J, and M Nonimmigrants: Student and Exchange Visitor Information System (SEVIS)" INS No. 2185-02 (RIN 115-AG55) (June 14, 2002) (available at http://web.archive.org/web/20040625030727/http://www.acenet.edu/washington/letters/2002/06june/ins.sevis.cfm) (ACE recommended that SEVIS compliance deadline be set at 180 days after "Inspector General certifies that SEVIS is fully operational and software is available for purchase").

[758] See Congress Learns, supra n. 10, at 17 (Fine's observation was echoed by Terry W. Hartle, Senior Vice President of the American Council on Education (ACE) who represented more than seventy-five education and exchange visitor organizations before the same hearing.).

following features. In terms of operating system and platform, it should be a web-based system that is accessible worldwide via the Internet and capable of interfacing with other university IT systems, such as registrar, human resources, student information, payroll, and tax systems. For schools which have a large foreign student/visitor contingent, batch data export/import capabilities connected to the INS are a necessity.[759]

In terms of functional capacity, the schools must perform many functions. The school's SEVIS system should be able to store and generate authorized forms, such as Form I-20, Form IAP-66, Form I-538, Form I-539, Form I-129, Form I-140, Form I-485, and Form I-765.[760] The system must also keep track of critical events in a student's course of study, like program enrollment, performance and extensions, adjustment and change of status petitions, reinstatement petitions, and applications for Optional Practical Training (OPT) for students in F-1 visa classification.[761] Further the system needs to generate a variety of standard reports for auditing purposes, "alert" users to major expiration dates (e.g. expiration of an international's employment authorization) and should have drop-down lists as required by law.[762] Also, the system must meet legislative and regulatory requirements, protect the privacy of the information collected, be stored with multi-level security access, and be highly integrated with other databases in the university so that there is no duplication of effort or waste of resources.[763]

Additionally, the university has to take many steps to successfully deploy and effectively employ SEVIS with batch technology.[764] The first step is to review SEVIS-related law, such as Section 641 of the IIRIRA, and related regulations, such as the final regulations for F, J, and M nonimmigrants, and technical documents such as the final interface control document.[765] These documents set forth the basic legal-technical-functional specifications/ requirements of the SEVIS system. The second step is to conduct a detailed analysis of current data elements and processing routines in the university to determine what foreign student data is being collected and how and where the data is stored and processed.[766] This exploratory data mapping exercise provides critical information on current data structures and information processes in the university necessary for the SEVIS interface.

The next step is to conduct a detailed analysis of the university's overall IT infrastructure, architecture, and strategy to determine how to gather and electronically transmit SEVIS data via the batch interface mode.[767] This helps to ascertain existing capacity and readiness of the university to implement SEVIS. The following step is to compile a formal and comprehensive report, which describes in detail the current data management process to ascertain and

---

[759] As designed, the SEVIS system allowed for both interactive and batch mode input. The INS, however, did not make batch mode input of data one of its "available" technology features. Schools had to and still have to develop and deploy batch mode at their own expense. Who was to provide for and fund the development of batch technology was an area of heated dispute.

[760] David Clubb, SEVIS COMPLIANCE: Project Scope Definition Document, Database Development Project, http://web.archive.org/web/20050522032219/http://www.auburn.edu/academic/other/international education/sevp/regs/SEVIS+Project+Scope+Definition+Document NAFSA generic.doc (June 5, 2002).

[761] Id.

[762] Id.

[763] Id.

[764] For a look at a typical month-by-month/activity-by-activity SEVIS implementation plan at the University of Wisconsin-Milwaukee, see U. of Wis. -Milwaukee, UWM Ensures SEVIS Compliance, http://www.uwm.edu/IMT/Info/IOTOnline/FocusOctNov03/ensures.html (accessed Nov. 21, 2006).

[765] Id.

[766] Id.

[767] Id.

identify any deficiencies or inadequacies in meeting SEVIS legislative and technological requirements.[768] During this process there is a need to outline, in checklist form, what needs to be done to make SEVIS operational and functional.

Next, based upon the above legal, systematic, and process assessment, the university has to make a critical decision whether to develop its own SEVIS compatible system or purchase an off-the-self SEVIS application kit from the market.[769] This decision requires the involvement of university senior administrators with input from mid level IT executive and front-line computing staff.[770] It also requires balancing costs and benefits of using internal resources versus external resources in the implementation process. If the school decides to purchase an off-the-shelf kit, the purchase decision must be coordinated with the university's purchasing office in compliance with university policies and guidelines and may involve product research and comparison testing.[771]

Finally, the school must install the hardware and implement the software, which entails extensive, complex, and time consuming technical and managerial tasks.[772] The entire SEVIS implementation process involves working with many people such as a financial controller, legal counsel, and IT staff and involves integrating a large number of academic and business departments, such as an international student office and graduate schools. Implementation also involves interfacing with a variety of different information systems within the university.[773] These steps take time and coordination and cannot be imposed by fiat. In addition, fully and successfully integrating SEVIS with an existing university IT system is a trial and error process.

Determining the scope of the cost and benefit analysis of an electronic tracking system it is very difficult because there are many factors involved.[774] Costs include initial migration, ongoing system costs, and costs for specialized and dedicated international service personnel.[775] Some cost savings result from improving the processing of international students. The benefits include reducing data duplication, increasing reliability, improving efficiency, and timely fulfillment of international student services.[776] These cost/benefit considerations do not include indirect costs or benefits such as impacts on the mission of the international student office, the role of foreign student advisors, the relationship between international students and the university, staff morale, and foreign student/visitors welfare.[777]

In the following sections, this chapter will document and discuss the variety of in-house problems and difficulties, legal and technical, encountered by school administrators in developing and deploying SEVIS. The issues covered include legislative administrative burden, implementation problems, technical difficulties, and capitalization and maintenance costs.

---

[768] Id.

[769] Id.

[770] Id.

[771] Since no final SEVIS regulation was available by October 2002, vendors were delayed in offering software meeting legal and technical specifications before January 2003.

[772] U. of Wis. -Milwaukee, supra n. 88.

[773] Id.

[774] The Georgetown CIPRIS implementation report concluded by observing that it was too early to tell the net cost versus the benefits to the CIPRIS system.

[775] U. of Wis. -Milwaukee, supra n. 88.

[776] Id.

[777] Id.

B. The SEVIS System and Institutional Barriers

The building of a centralized, comprehensive, and integrated foreign student and visitor IT system with tracking capabilities sufficient to meet the SEVIS legislative mandate as well as following existing university protocols is a daunting, transformational task. There are many reasons for this. First, the introduction of SEVIS into an existing IT system implicates the school's own IT vision and strategy. An IT initiative, such as SEVIS, is not a one-time investment or stand-alone program. The initiative is tied into the schools' core values,[778] institutional mission,[779] strategic planning,[780] governance structure,[781] and communication networks.[782] In essence, SEVIS (as an IT initiative) must be aligned with the school's values, structure, process, and culture. In this regard, understanding a school's education and IT vision, mission, values, environment, and culture is critical for the successful implementation of SEVIS. These factors were ignored in the current SEVIS implementation process. The DHS has approached this as a purely legal, administrative, and enforcement exercise. This approach reflected a large degree of ignorance and a certain amount of arrogance inside the beltway Washington D.C. mindset.

Second, the introduction of new SEVIS technology upset long established institutional arrangements, threatened deeply ingrained organizational culture and challenged broad personal interests.[783]

---

[778] For example, the core values of Bowling Green University include: "respect for one another; cooperation; intellectual and spiritual growth; creative imaginings; [and p]ride in a job well done." Bowling Green U., University Values, Vision and Goals, http://www.bgsu.edu/colleges/gradcol/catalog03-04/University/univ9.htm (accessed Nov. 20, 2006). These values are not compatible with a draconian police state upon which SEVIS is built.

[779] A university's primary mission is to educate rather than monitor, and foster free exchange of ideas rather than restrict offensive ideas. Jonathan Laurence, Ramadan's US Ban is Ill-Conceived, The Daily Star (Beirut, Lebanon) 10 (Sept. 4, 2004) (available at http://www.jonathanlaurence.net/downloads/tarek oped.pdf) (Swiss theologian Tariq Ramadan was not allowed to accept a visiting professor position at Notre Dame University after State Department denied a visa at the behest of the Department of Homeland Security due to an unarticulated security risk.)

[780] The imposed SEVIS system has the effect of disturbing a university's strategic plan. For example, in 2002-2003 the University of Pennsylvania (U. Penn.) had 3,856 foreign students, of which 24% (937) were undergraduate, 25% (969) were Ph.D.s, 33% (1259) were in Masters programs, 4% (160) were in English language programs, and 14% (531) were in practical training. The stringent visa process affected the university's strategic plan in maintaining UPenn as the premier leader in international education. Robert Barchi, Council State of the University, 50 U. Pa. Almanac 3, 4 at "International Students" (Nov. 11, 2003) (available at http://www.upenn.edu/almanac/v50/n12/council.html).

[781] In university governance, academic matters are in the hands of the professors, chairs, deans and provost. With SEVIS, university academic governance has to accept non-negotiable instruction and zero-tolerance enforcement from the Department of Homeland Security in the name of national security. V. Lane Rawlins, President's Updates for the Faculty and Staff of Washington State University Number 16, http://www.wsu.edu/president/update16.html (Mar. 7, 2003) (WSU will cooperate with the government on national security matters but will be vigilant in carrying out its function and responsibility as a free and just educational institution).

[782] The university has many networks, usually not centralized. "Thomas Jefferson University faced the challenge of SEVIS compliance on many different levels. The university comprises an upper-division undergraduate heath professions college, a graduate school, a medical college, and a teaching hospital. The information required for reporting to SEVIS was stored in different systems." John Martines and Kenneth Oeffler, EDUCAUSE Mid-Atlantic Regional Conference 2004 Archives, Poster Sessions, "SEVIS Implementation Challenges," http://www.educause.edu/Poster%20Sessions/1436?MODE=SESSIONSandHeading=Poster%20SessionsandP roduct Code=marc04/PS%25andMeeting=marc04 (Jan. 14, 2004).

[783] Shirley Gregor et al., Web Information Systems Development: Some Neglected Aspects, http://cq-pan.cqu.edu.au/david-jones/Publications/Papers and Books/wis99/ (Jan. 28, 1999) ("It is suggested that when developing WIS, particular attention should be paid to the social and political aspects of interorganizational

Vermeer and Veth (1998) consider the problems of inter-organizational data integration and the development of a common data model across many interdependent network participants. After a study of over 10 different central database initiatives they found that almost all of them suffered from lack of support. They concluded there were two important reasons for the lack of success; first, political reasons such as hidden agendas and disruption of the balance of power and second, the large number of data fields resulting in large data administration costs and lack of flexibility at a local level." [784]

Theoretically speaking, SEVIS is an Inter-Organization System (IOS), within and without the university.[785] As such, it raises traditional IOS problems in the design and implementation phases.[786] Developing and implementing an IOS requires the cooperation and coordination of two or more information trading partners. This includes the adoption of standards for the external trading environment and educating trading partners about new technologies and procedures. The need to synchronize development efforts among the trading partners, especially in shared standards and required updates, requires lengthy negotiation and flexible compromise.[787] The need to reevaluate business practices to improve efficiency of operation among the organizations, for the betterment of a collective whole (the U.S. as a nation), is difficult given vested interests, entrenched values, and fortified connections. Most importantly, discovering relationship issues that are often more complex than technical issues requires reevaluation and readjustment of past practices by the trading partners.

Any successful organizational change process must start with incorporating other university community members and integrating other academic/business units within the university. This requires educating the university community as to the needs for and benefits of having such a system on campus. Conversely, it entails pointing out the inadequacies and dysfunctional aspects of the existing foreign student information system in addressing emerging security and administrative needs.[788]

This can be achieved by keeping the university community members (executives, administrators, business managers, and faculty) and other academic units (law school, business school, and medical school) informed and abreast about latest SEVIS developments and requirements.[789]

---

systems, to human-computer-interaction issues and usability guidelines, and to issues associated with the development of hypermedia systems").

[784] *Id.* (citing B. H. P. J. Vermeer and T. F. L. Veth, *Presentation, Interorganizational Data Integration: Theory and Practice* (11th Intl. Bled Elec. Commerce Conf., Bled, Slovenia, 1998).

[785] R.H. Sprague and B.C. McNurlin, *Information Systems Management Practice passim* (3d ed., Prentice Hall 1993).

[786] Id.

[787] Id.

[788] Id.

[789] One of the very few universities which has studied the implications of a student electronic monitoring system is Georgetown University. In the summer of 1998, the English as a Foreign Language program and the International Students and Scholars Services conducted a study to assess the implications of introduction of CIPRIS for Georgetown University. As part of the study, the researcher interviewed Duke University, one of the first CIPRIS (21 university testers) pilot project groups. Duke was picked because it was considered similar to Georgetown in terms of mission, size, structure, and international student environment. The report concluded that it was too early to determine the net cost versus benefits of the CIPRIS system, but certain observations could be safely made. The report further observed that the successful implementation of electronic tracking entailed complicated tasking, complex coordination and delicate negotiation within (and without) the university. It required a committed reformer, dedicated administrator, seasoned manager, and shrewd politician, willing to invest untold hours of efforts and tens of thousands of resources.). See Bell, *supra* 29.

Having enlisted other university community units and members in the cause of change, the next step is to mobilize their resources and coordinate their efforts to achieve a common goal. This includes centralizing foreign student admission functions and processes in one physical location to reduce redundancy, assure uniformity, and achieve efficiency; purchasing hardware and software to produce I-20s from one central office; upgrading existing hardware to facilitate software program adaptation and reduce application errors; negotiating with the registrar to include J visitors on student information systems; appointing and training specialized and dedicated Designated School Officials (DSOs) to handle data input and forms production; building up organization expertise in SEVIS system maintenance and operations; standardizing the policies and processes for foreign students between DSO from different schools, e.g. law versus business versus medicine; integrating and reconciling different foreign student databases within the university IT systems, e.g. registrar's office (enrollment, degree pursued, course taken, drop/add) with housing office (arrival date, on campus address); providing for real-time interoperability between university student information systems and the international student data-base; and finally, providing for interoperability between the university student information system and DHS SEVIS without disrupting existing university information processing protocol and computer system design.[790]

The business end of the technology conversion requires elaborate planning and precision execution. First, one must determine the institutional ownership of SEVIS, particularly its organizational structure and reporting line.[791] Without ownership the change process will not materialize. Lacking reporting protocol, there would be no control. Second, one must decide whether to buy or upgrade computer hardware and software and seek the necessary approval for this decision.[792] Third, one must identify a vendor and purchase, install, and test the software and hardware.[793] Fourth, the interface with other related databases must be implemented.[794] Next, university staff from departments such as admissions, international services, registrar, payroll, human services, IT, and others must be trained on SEVIS functions and use. These staff members must speak the same language and function at the same level and operation. Fifth, the academic advising process must be realigned by

---

[790] See Newfront Software, SEVIS Readiness Workshop, http://www.newfrontsoftware.com/sevis/docs/SRW-SanAntonio.ppt (2002). For an actual implementation plan, see Greg Leonard, Planning and Implementation Design Student and Exchange Visitor Program, http://www.newfrontsoftware.com/sevis/docs/Planning%20 and%20Implementation%20Design.pdf (Feb. 22, 2002).

[791] Ltr. from Mark Olson, Senior Vice Pres., Natl. Assn. of College and U. Bus., to Dir., Regs. and Forms Servs. Div., Immig. and Naturalization Serv., To INS Re: SEVIS (June 17, 2002) (available at http://www.nacubo.org/x576.xml).

[792] Ib.

[793] One of the very few universities which has studied the implications of a student electronic monitoring system is Georgetown University. In the summer of 1998, the English as a Foreign Language program and the International Students and Scholars Services conducted a study to assess the implications of introduction of CIPRIS for Georgetown University. As part of the study, the researcher interviewed Duke University, one of the first CIPRIS (21 university testers) pilot project groups. Duke was picked because it was considered similar to Georgetown in terms of mission, size, structure, and international student environment. The report concluded that it was too early to determine the net cost versus benefits of the CIPRIS system, but certain observations could be safely made. The report further observed that the successful implementation of electronic tracking entailed complicated tasking, complex coordination and delicate negotiation within (and without) the university. It required a committed reformer, dedicated administrator, seasoned manager, and shrewd politician, willing to invest untold hours of efforts and tens of thousands of resources.). See Bell, supra 31.

[794] Id.

designing internal forms and training academic deans and staff on SEVIS requirements.[795] Sixth and finally, SEVIS data collection forms must be designed and initial data conversion must be performed.[796]

C. SEVIS Is Costly to Install

As SEVIS end users, international departments and exchange programs are responsible for the input, update and maintenance of all incoming students and scholars found in the United States by January 30, 2003. In 2003, the total number of J-1 students and J-1 scholars (excluding dependents) to be tracked was 869,118, of which 353,342 were new students and 515,776 were continuing students.[797] According to some schools, it usually takes thirty to sixty minutes to input one student record.[798] At that rate it would require 434, 559 man hours or 54,319 man days (assuming an eight hour shift), excluding computer downtime and staff human error, to input all the student records into the SEVIS system. Take the example of the University of Southern California (USC) in the year 2003. In that year USC had 6,270 international students and 1,214 visiting scholars in attendance.[799] This made for 7,484 international students/scholars to be processed and monitored.[800] In order for USC to be in compliance with the USAPA, it had to spend 3,717 DOS hours (assuming thirty minutes per record) to input 7,487 student/scholar records into SEVIS by August 2003.[801] This amounted to 92.9 students per five DOS working days (assuming an eight hour day).[802] This also assumed that the DOS had no other assignment to do for the international office he/she attached (e.g. processing applications and counseling students), an unrealistic scenario, especially during enrollment season when all foreign students and visitors were required to be entered into the system. The estimate also did not take into account SEVIS shutoff or computer downtime.[803]

The estimated extra workload for the nation's universities to come into compliance with the SEVIS program is summarized in the following two tables.

---

[795] Id.

[796] Id.

[797] See NGLU 2003-12-a, supra n. 75, at 17. "Update on SEVIS Statistics

[798] The time it took to process SEVIS records and papers differed from institution to institution. The difference depended as much on sophistication and maturity of technology, as it did on the experience and competence of the input staff. The INS cost estimate was based on thirty-one minutes for each student record. The University of Georgia reported thirty minutes in processing one document. Kate Carter, "Implementing Tracking System Frustrating: UGA's Foreign Exchange Students," http://www.onlineathens.com/stories/040903/uga 20030409041.shtml (Apr. 8, 2003).

[799] IIENetwork, Open Doors 2003: Institutions with 1,000 or More International Students, 2002/03 Ranked by International Student Totals, http://opendoors.iienetwork.org/?p=35937 (Nov. 2003) (reporting foreign student enrollment data extracted from IIE Open Doors) [hereinafter IIE Network, Open Doors 2003]; IIE Network, Table 40: Institutions Hosting the Most International Scholars, 2001/02 and 2002/03, http://opendoors.iienetwork.org/?p=37195 (Nov. 2003) (reporting foreign student enrollment data extracted from IIE Open Doors) [hereinafter IIE Network, Table 40].

[800] Id.

[801] Id.

[802] Id.

[803] Id.

Table 2. Estimated SEVIS Data Input Time for International Students: Top Forty Research Institutions, 2002/2003[804]

Rank	Institution	City	State	Total: Int'l Students*	Total: SEVIS DSO Hours (Days)**
1	U. Southern California	Los Angeles	CA	6,270	3,135 (78.4)
2	New York University	New York	NY	5,454	2,727 (68.2)
3	Columbia University	New York	NY	5,148	2,574 (64.3)
4	Purdue U. - Main Campus	West Lafayette	IN	5,105	2,554 (63.8)
5	U. Texas at Austin	Austin	TX	4,926	2,464 (61.6)
6	U. of Michigan - Ann Arbor	Ann Arbor	MI	4,601	2,300 (57.5)
7	U. of Illinois at Urbana-Champaign	Champaign	IL	4,555	2,277 (56.9)
8	Boston U.	Boston	MA	4,518	2,258 (56.4)
9	U. of Wisconsin - Madison	Madison	WI	4,396	2,198 (54.95)
10	The Ohio State U. - Main Campus	Columbus	OH	4,334	2,167 (54.2)
11	U. of California - Los Angeles	Los Angeles	CA	3,927	1,963 (79.1)
12	U. of Pennsylvania	Philadelphia	PA	3,856	2,928 (73.2)
13	U. of Maryland College Park	College Park	MD	3,734	1,867 (46.7)
14	Texas AandM U.	College Station	TX	3,702	1,851 (46.27)
15	Penn State U. Park	University Park	PA	3,681	1,840 (46.0)
16	SUNY at Buffalo	Buffalo	NY	3,628	1,814 (43.3)
17	University of Florida	Gainesville	FL	3,547	1,773 (44.3)

---

[804] IIE Network, Open Doors 2003, supra n. 125 (reporting foreign student enrollment data extracted from IIE Open Doors).

Table 2. (Continued)

Rank	Institution	City	State	Total:	Total: SEVIS DSO
18	Indiana U. at Bloomington	Bloomington	IN	3,495	1,747 (43.7)
19	Harvard U.	Cambridge	MA	3,459	1,729 (43.2)
20	U. of Houston	Houston	TX	3,358	1,679 (42.0)
21	U. of Minnesota - Twin Cities	Minneapolis	MN	3,351	1,675 (41.9)
22	Arizona State U. Main	Tempe	AZ	3,268	1,634 (40.8)
23	Wayne State U.	Detroit	MI	3,224	1,612 (40.3)
24	Michigan State U.	East Lansing	MI	3,202	1,601 (40.0)
25	Cornell U.	Ithaca	NY	3,096	1,548 (38.7)
26	U. of Arizona	Tucson	AZ	3,011	1,505 (37.6)
27	Stanford U.	Stanford	CA	2,991	1,495 (37.4)
28	U. of Illinois at Chicago	Chicago	IL	2,950	1,475 (36.9)
29	U. of Washington	Seattle	WA	2,908	1,454 (36.3)
30	Rutgers U. - New Brunswick	New Brunswick	NJ	2,906	1,453 (36.3)
31	M.I.T.	Cambridge	MA	2,819	1,409 (35.2)
32	Georgia Institute of Tech	Atlanta	GA	2,798	1,354 (33.9)
33	U. of California - Berkeley	Berkeley	CA	2,739	1,369 (34.2)
34	U. of Chicago	Chicago	IL	2,554	1,277 (31.9)
35	Carnegie Mellon U.	Pittsburgh	PA	2,534	1,267 (31.7)
36	Iowa State U.	Ames	IA	2,387	1,193 (29.8)
37	Oklahoma State U. Main Campus	Stillwater	OK	2,321	1,160 (29.0)
38	Northeastern U.	Boston	MA	2,282	1,141 (28.5)
39	SUNY at Stony Brook	Stony Brook	NY	2,233	1,116 (27.9)
40	U. of South Florida	Tampa	FL	2,197	1,098 (27.4)

* Does not include exchange visitors/scholars.

** DOS Day = 8 hrs. x 5 DS0 = 40 DSO day.

**Table 3. Estimated SEVIS Data Input Time for International Scholars:
Institutions Hosting the Most International Scholars,* 2002/2003**[805]

Rank	Institution	City	State	2002/03	DSO	DOS Days
					Hours	**
1	Harvard U.	Cambridge	MA	2,403	1,201	30.0
2	U. of California - Berkeley	Berkeley	CA	2,365	1,182	29.6
3	U. of California - Los Angeles	Los Angeles	CA	2,098	1,049	16.22
4	U. of Pennsylvania	Philadelphia	PA	2,082	1,041	26.0
5	Columbia U.	New York	NY	1,890	945	23.6
6	U. of California - San Diego	La Jolla	CA	1,817	908	22.7
7	U. of Illinois at Urbana-Champaign	Champaign	IL	1,694	847	21.2
8	Yale U.	New Haven	CT	1,637	818	20.5
9	U. of California - San Francisco	San Francisco	CA	1,600	800	20
10	Massachusetts Institute of Tech.	Cambridge	MA	1,573	786	19.7
11	U. of Washington	Seattle	WA	1,556	778	19.4
12	The Ohio State U. Main Campus	Columbus	OH	1,423	711	17.8
13	U. of Michigan - Ann Arbor	Ann Arbor	MI	1,342	671	16.77
14	U. of Florida	Gainesville	FL	1,335	667	16.7
15	U. of Minnesota - Twin Cities	Minneapolis	MN	1,252	626	15.6
16	Washington U.	St. Louis	MO	1,246	623	15.6
17	Cornell U.	Ithaca	NY	1,236	618	15.4
18	U. of Southern California	Los Angeles	CA	1,214	607	15.2
19	U. of Wisconsin - Madison	Madison	WI	1,131	565	14.1
20	Duke U., Med. Center, and Health System	Durham	NC	1,117	558	14.0
21	U. of California - Davis	Davis	CA	1,109	554	13.9
22	Penn State U. Park	University Park	PA	1,080	540	13.5
23	U. of North Carolina at Chapel Hill	Chapel Hill	NC	1,024	512	12.8
24	U. of Texas at Austin	Austin	TX	1,013	506	12.6

[805] IIE Network, Table 40, supra n. 125 (reporting foreign student enrollment data extracted from IIE Open Doors).

Table 3. (Continued)

Rank	Institution	City	State	2002/03	DSO	DOS Days
25	Boston U.	Boston	MA	975	487	12.2
26	Michigan State U.	East Lansing	MI	910	455	11.4
27	U. of Illinois at Chicago	Chicago	IL	900	450	11.2
28	Emory U.	Atlanta	GA	868	434	10.8
29	U. of Iowa	Iowa City	IA	865	432	10.8
30	U. of Maryland College Park	College Park	MD	861	430	10.7

* Does not include international students.

** DOS Day = 8 hrs. x 5 DS0 = 40 DSO day.

After public consultation, it has been estimated the one-time SEVIS compliance cost to be $ 4,680,000 computed as follows:

Table 3.1. Continuing Student Reporting Burden[806]

Number of Continuing Students	625,000
Number of Continuing Exchange Visitors	275,000
Number of Responses per Respondent	1
Hours per Response	0.52*
Total One-Time Reporting Burden	468,000
Total Public Cost	$ 4,680,000**

(a)* Time for Processing SEVIS Records[807]

Activity	Time (Minutes)
Learning about the Law and the Program	1
Data Collection and Input	30
Total per Response	31 (0.52 hours)

The INS estimations did not come close to the actual time spent by universities in setting up the SEVIS system.[808] The estimations failed for a number of reasons. First and foremost, the estimations were based on a "time and motion" kind of analytical exercise, which failed to take into account real life conditions in the field. [809] Universities are not all alike in

---

[806] . 67 Fed. Reg. at 76268 (Dec. 11, 2002) ("estimate based upon the amount of time it would take to complete a Form I-20 in order to enter a continuing student in SEVIS").

[807] *Id.* ("estimate is based upon the amount of time it would take to complete a SEVIS Form I-20").

[808] Carter, *supra* n. 122

[809] *Id.*

experiences, resources, and capacities in dealing with SEVIS. Each student recording process is different.[810]

The INS estimates did not make explicit the types of schools for which the estimation was meant to apply.[811] As an aggregate and average, the estimation "appeared" to have some face validity. The validity and usefulness of the estimates (i.e. thirty minutes per record and $ 4.68 millions for all schools) depended on variations amongst schools, for instance, big versus small, differences between records (old versus recent records), and disparity in all sort of situations, such as summer versus fall terms.[812]

The estimation had little predictive value and was not useful for the schools in planning their activities. First of all, as a methodological proposition, the INS failed to specify the range and differences between each student entry.[813] If the range was great, for example, from five minutes to sixty minutes, and was contingent on specific school or particular student or even a unique situation and set of circumstances, the average was of very little use, except perhaps for aggregate level policy analysis, i.e. how much it cost to move from a paper based system to an electronic one.

Second, the INS has failed to articulate its underlying assumptions in estimating the time and cost per student record processed.[814] Specifically, it failed to make clear what the average school or average record looked like.[815] Without this key information, the estimation was of little use for planning purpose, individually or collectively. For example, if an average time of thirty minutes is allotted for each record entry in a major university with three thousand foreign students/visitors, the smaller schools with few foreign students have little reason to use the estimate as their own. The thirty-minute research school estimate also should not be used as a base to calculate the total time for all schools involved.[816]

The time it takes to process a student record hinges on a number of factors including: (1) existence of paper records; (2) completeness of paper records; (3) accessibility of paper records; (4) familiarity with university databases; (5) familiarity with university IT technology; (6) familiarity with INS-SEVIS technology; (7) familiarity with INS laws and regulations; (8) stability university SEVIS technology; (9) reliability of SEVIS technology at INS; (10) availability of SEVIS work station; and (11) competency of SEVIS staff.[817] If one or more of these factors is not met, substantial delay might occur, and in fact did occur![818]

D. SEVIS Is Costly to Operate

The SEVIS system was not only burdensome to set up, it is also costly to operate and maintain. Congress allotted a one-time funding of $ 36.8 million for setting up the SEVIS system. The seed funding, however, did not include support for ongoing maintenance and routine operational costs at the universities. The USAPA called for students and visitors to

---

[810] See *supra* nn. 128-130 and accompanying text.
[811] *Id.*
[812] *Id.*
[813] *Id.*
[814] *Id.*
[815] *Id.*
[816] *Id.*
[817] *Id.*
[818] See Ltr., *supra* n. 115.

pay a SEVIS fee before they were ever granted a visa. SEVIS community users are responsible for its upkeep and administration. In order to be certified, SEVIS schools have to pay $ 580 comprising $ 230 for I-17 petition of approval and $ 350 for on-site review before a school can accept F-1 students.[819] In order to set up SEVIS, each school is required to pay out $ 30,000 to $ 50,000 for software and hardware.[820]

The cost of implementing and operating SEVIS differs according to the type of school and program. Factors include whether the school is a university or a vocational college, whether distance learning is involved, and the size of the school's student body. The basic implementation costs include software, hardware, dedicated SEVIS IT staff and DSOs. As illustrated in Table 4 below, the costs of implementing SEVIS differed from institution to institution and depended on the size of the foreign student population.[821] With campuses of one hundred students or less, the estimated cost of implementing SEVIS is between $ 5,000 and $ 100,000 for 73 percent of the participating schools.[822] However, when there are more than 2,500 foreign students, the majority (56.2 percent) estimate that they will have to spend between $ 100,000 and $ 249,999 to make SEVIS operational on campus.[823] Only six percent reported that they will spend less than $ 5,000 in meeting implementation needs.[824]

Ultimately both the campus with few foreign students (e.g. small research universities, large teaching colleges, ESL and vocational programs) and those with many research students and exchange scholars (research universities), had a critical decision to make: could they afford to accept foreign students or sponsor exchange scholars anymore given the SEVIS "surcharge"? The SEVIS costs hit profit-driven vocational schools particularly hard. It is more difficult to justify the initial capital outlay and continued maintenance costs when foreign student enrollment is less than ten students. Since foreign students are not a major income stream for these schools, they might choose to opt out of international education altogether. This is particularly the case when the price of non-compliance is potential criminal liability.

Different universities dealt with the funding of SEVIS differently. The University of Chicago proposed to charge all foreign students $ 25 per quarter to enroll.[825] The University of Georgia charged $ 50 to offset $ 150,000 of SEVIS costs as of April 2002.[826] The University of Wisconsin-Madison first imposed a SEVIS fee on foreign students and backed down when confronted with student protests and a city council objection.[827] Iowa State University decided to absorb the SEVIS costs itself.[828]

---

[819] 66 Fed. Reg. 65811, 65814. (Dec. 21, 2001). Federal guidelines require that the full cost of providing immigration and naturalization services must be recovered through fees and therefore cannot be supported by tax dollars. *Id.* at 65811-65813.

[820] Patty Croom, Comments on SEVIS Compliance Dates and Costs, http://web.archive.org/web/20030815140430/ http://ias.berkeley.edu/siss/hurricane/sissworkingpapers/workingpapersixbycroom5-23-02.pdf (May 20, 2002).

[821] See Ltr., *supra* n. 117.

[822] *Id.*

[823] *Id.*

[824] *Id.*

[825] U. of Chi., No Surveillance Fee at the University of Chicago, http://www.math.uchicago.edu/johann/fee/ (accessed Apr. 14, 2006).

[826] Kimberly Bowers, "New SEVIS Fees Anger Intl. Students," Redandblack.com (U. of Ga. student newspaper) (Nov. 26, 2002), http://www.redandblack.com/vnews/display.v/ART/2002/11/26/3de3a5b5e0779?in archive=1.

[827] U. of Wis.-Madison, Chancellor's Statement Regarding SEVIS Funding, http://www.chancellor.wisc.edu/ sevis.html (last updated Nov. 20, 2006).

The cost of implementing the SEVIS system at universities is often a heavy burden on universities. For example, the cost for putting SEVIS into operation at Iowa State was $ 24,000, including $ 10,800 for software and $ 7,000 for a computer server that holds the information plus a $ 5,000 fee for the use of a commercial software database and Administrative Technology Services hired four SEVIS technicians.[829]

Table 4. Estimated cost of SEVIS implementation as a function of size of campus foreign student population[830]

Estimated cost of SEVISImplementation	Campus foreign students population				
	Less than 100	100 - 499	500 - 999	1,000 - 2,499	More than 2,500
Less than $ 5000	73%	30%	8.7%	3.8%	6.0%
$ 5000 - $ 24,000	23.4%	50%	17.3%	19.2%	
$ 24,000 - $ 99,999	3.1%	16.6%	56.5%	57.7%	18.7%
$ 100,000 - $ 249,999	NA	3.3%	17.4%	15.4%	56.2%
$ 250,000 - $ 499,999	NA	NA	NA	3.8%	6.0%
More than $ 499,999	NA	NA	NA	NA	12.5%

The INS has estimated the annual SEVIS operational costs to be:

Table 5. INS Estimated SEVIS Reporting Cost Burden[831]

Activities	Time (Minutes)
Learning about the Law and the Program	10
Data collection and Updates	5
Adjudication, notification, reports	5
Total minutes per Response	20
Total Public Cost.	$ 14,985,000

Charging students was met with protests, resistance, and legal action nationwide, such as at the University of Wisconsin - Madison. On April 1, 2003 the university proposed to charge international students a $ 100 to $ 125 SEVIS fee ($ 50 per semester and $ 25 for the

---

In April, the University of Wisconsin-Madison announced a plan to charge foreign students $ 50 a semester ($ 25 summer) to support the SEVIS operational cost, projected to be $ 330,000 per year. The decision was based on the fact the university could not fund the $ 330,000 and that considered best for end-users of SEVIS to pay. *Id.*

[828] Eric Rowley, "ISU Ahead of Game - No SEVIS Fees for International Students, Looming Budget Cuts Could Prompt Tracking Fee," *Iowa St. Daily* 5 (Oct. 28, 2003), http://www.iowastatedaily.com/media/storage/paper818/news/2003/10/28/News/Isu-Ahead.Of.Game.No.Sevis.Fees.For.International.Students-1097374.shtml.

[829] *Id.*

[830] *Id.*

[831] 7 Fed. Reg. at 76268 ("estimate is based upon the amount of time it would take to complete a SEVIS Form I-20").

summer).[832] The students protested.[833] The Teaching Assistants' Association at the University of Wisconsin-Madison worked with the students, faculty, administrative staff, and departments to challenge the appropriateness of the fees on equity grounds. They argued that foreign students should not be singled out.[834] On May 7, 2003, the administration decided to temporarily suspend the $ 125 SEVIS fee to further study the issue. On May 16, 2003, the Madison, Wisconsin, City Council passed a resolution objecting to a SEVIS fee for international students.[835] The chancellor's SEVIS Fee Advisory Committee recommended against charging the foreign students:

The committee therefore respectfully recommends to the chancellor that the administrative costs of SEVIS be absorbed as part of the necessary institutional costs of fulfilling our academic mission, and as such, should therefore ideally be covered by the usual sources of funding for administrative costs, namely [general public revenue] and tuition.[836]

On September 9, 2003, UW-M chancellor Wiley decided to adopt the recommendation of the Advisory Committee and absorb the SEVIS costs as a general administration charge.[837]

At Binghamton University in New York, the Graduate Student Organization decided to file suit against the University for charging SEVIS fees, arguing that the fees discriminated against foreign students.[838] The Graduate Student Organization filed a lawsuit against Binghamton University because they believe a fee imposed only on international students is discriminatory.[839] Thus, universities have encountered numerous obstacles in determining how to pay SEVIS fees while not appearing discriminatory against foreign students.

E. SEVIS Fee Disputes

The IIRIRA of 1996 authorized schools to collect fees of not more than $ 100 to implement the IIRIRA mandate.[840] In February of 2000, the INS proposed to set the fees at $ 95,[841] but experienced strong oppositions from universities[842] and lawmakers alike.[843]

---

[832] U. of Wis. -Madison, *supra* n. 155.

[833] Rachek Alkon, "Students Oppose SEVIS Cost," *Badger Herald* (U. of Wis.-Madison student newspaper) (Apr. 30, 2003), http://badgerherald.com/news/2003/04/30/students oppose sevi.php. The Teaching Assistants Association at the University of Wisconsin-Madison organized a protest against the University charging $ 100 to $ 125 SEVIS fees. The fees were considered to be discriminatory. *Id.*

[834] See Am. Fedn. Of Teachers, TAA Persuades UW-Madison To Withdraw SEVIS Fee, http://www.aft.org/higher ed/news/2003/taa withdraw.htm (accessed Apr. 17, 2006).

[835] Nikki Woodworth, "Council takes stand against SEVIS," *Badger Herald* (U. of Wis.-Madison student newspaper) (May 7, 2003), http://badgerherald.com/news/2003/05/07/council takes stand .php (stating that the Madison City Council voted on May 6, 2003 to "defend the equal protection of international students" and denounced the proposed imposition of SEVIS fees on international students.)

[836] Matthew Dolbey, "Chancellor Rules on SEVIS Fee," *Badger Herald* (U. of Wis.-Madison student newspaper) (Aug. 29, 2003), http://badgerherald.com/news/2003/08/29/chancellor rules on .php

[837] U. of Wis. -Madison, "University to Cover Future Sevis Costs," http://www.news.wisc.edu/8886.html (Sept. 9, 2003).

[838] Liza Schwartz, "Administration is Sued for Foreign-Student Fee," *LXV Pipe Dream* (Binghamton U. student newspaper) 10, P 1 (Oct. 17, 2003), http://www.bupipedream.com/101703/news/n2.htm.

[839] *Id.*

[840] Authorizing Collection of the Fee Levied on F, J, and M Nonimmigrant Classifications Under Public Law 104-208, 64 Fed. Reg. 71323, 71325 (Dec. 21, 1999) (proposed rule stating that a fee of $ 95 was proposed to support SEVIS implementation, maintenance and operations).

[841] *Id.* at 71324-71325.

On October 31, 2000, the President signed H.R. 3767, the Visa Waiver Permanent Program Act. Section 404 of this law amended sections 641(d)-(h) of the IIRIRA, by requiring the Attorney General (rather than the colleges and universities) to collect a CIPRIS fee from students in the F, J, or M visa categories. The Attorney General has since set the fees at $ 100.[844] This proposed fee was earmarked for CIPRIS related personnel, operations, maintenance, training, and other program costs. It would also support sixty-one SEVIS liaison officers and 182 other ICE officers in the field.[845] The collection of SEVIS student fees raised two concerns with higher education administrators and educators:[846] the reasonableness of the fee amount[847] and the appropriateness of the fee collection process.[848]

1. Legislative Mandate

On December 21, 1999, INS published proposed rule "Authorizing Collection of the Fee Levied on F, J, and M Nonimmigrant Classifications under Public Law 104-208" seeking public consultation.[849] The proposed rule called for the collection and remission of $ 95 visa applications fees for F-1,[850] J-1,[851] or M-1[852] nonimmigrants who first register or enroll in school or first commence an exchange program in the United States. The proposed rule implemented the mandate set forth in Section 641 of the IIRIRA of 1996.[853]

---

[842] Ltr., *supra* n. 38 (opposing fees collection procedure under then under the Coordinated Interagency Partnership Regulating International Students (CIPRIS) program as being "substantial and costly workload burden on all colleges and universities and exchange visitor programs").

[843] In a letter from Attorney General, John Ashcroft, then a senator, and twenty other senators, including Edward M. Kennedy (D-Mass.), Trent Lott (R-Miss.) and Patrick J. Leahy (D-Vt.), objected, stating that "requiring U.S. institutions to collect fees to fund a federal program is an inappropriate role for higher education institutions." Dan Eggen and Cheryl W. Thompson, INS to Monitor Foreign Students Ashcroft Reverses Stance on System, Wash. Post A10 (May 11, 2002).

[844] See 68 Fed. Reg. 61148 (Oct. 27, 2003).

[845] See 68 Fed. Reg. at 61151.

[846] See Ltr. from Betty McCollum, Rep. 4th Dist. Minn., et al., to Tom Ridge, Sec. of Homeland Sec., and Colin Powell, Sec. of St. (Dec. 19, 2003) (available at http://www.nafsa.org/ /Document/ /rep.pdf) (expressing concerns with the SEVIS fee amount and process; the $ 100 fees and collection process would have an adverse impact on student enrollment).

[847] 68 Fed. Reg. at 61151 (reporting that 4,617 comments were received regarding the 1999 proposed Section 641 SEVIS fees collection rule and that many suggested that the fee of $ 95 was excessive, especially for short term visitors and third world students).

[848] Ltr. from David Ward, Pres., Am. Council on Educ., to Asa Hutchinson, Off. of the Under Sec., Dept. of Homeland Sec., Letter to the Department of Homeland Security Regarding SEVIS Fees (Sep. 2, 2003) (available   at http://www.acenet.edu/AM/PrinterTemplate.cfm?Section=HomeandTEMPLATE=/CM/ContentDisplay.cfman dCONTENTID=4024 (letter on behalf of American Council on Education and six other higher education associations stating that SEVIS fees should be collected just like any other visa fees which would make the SEVIS a truly paperless "integrated, all-electronic system")

[849] 64 Fed. Reg. at 71323-71331.

[850] "F-1 nonimmigrants are foreign nationals enrolled as students in service-approved colleges, universities, seminaries, conservatories, academic high schools, private elementary schools, other academic institutions, and in language training programs in the United States. An F-2 nonimmigrant is a foreign national who is the spouse or qualifying child of an F-1 student." *Id.* at 71324.

[851] "J-1 nonimmigrants are foreign nationals who have been selected by a U.S. Information Agency (USIA) designated sponsor to participate in an exchange visitor program in the United States. A J-2 nonimmigrant is a foreign national who is the spouse or qualifying child of a J-1 exchange visitor. " *Id.* at 71324.

[852] "M-1 nonimmigrants are foreign nationals enrolled as students in Service-approved vocational or other recognized nonacademic institutions, other than in language training programs in the United States. An M-2 nonimmigrant is a foreign national who is the spouse or qualifying child of an M-1 nonimmigrant. " *Id.* at 71324.

[853] The IIRIRA, Pub. L. 104-208 (Sept. 30, 1996), was codified as 8 U.S.C. ?372 (2002). Section 641(a)(1) of the IIRIRA, in particular, directed the Attorney General, in consultation with the Secretary of State and the

Section 641(a)(1) of the IIRIRA directed the Attorney General, in consultation with the Secretaries of State and Education, to develop and conduct a program to collect information on nonimmigrant foreign students and exchange visitors. Section 641(e) of the IIRIRA authorized the INS to collect a fee of no more than $ 100 from each F-1, M-1 and J-1 visa applicant to fund the information collection process. The proposed rule was also authorized by Congress under 31 U.S.C. 9701 (2000), which required all federal agencies to recover costs and benefits conferred by federal actions (in this case, the execution of Sections 103 and 214 of the Immigration and Naturalization Act).[854] Under Section 9701, the fees and charges were to be calculated based on "the costs to the Government" or "the value of the service or thing to the recipient" or "public policy or interest served." As applied:

The proposed fee was calculated based on the program and system costs and the estimated population base of covered fee payers. The calculated costs include those expenses incurred by the Government to develop, produce, deploy, operate, and maintain the program and system. In addition, the proposed fee will cover the costs associated with the creation and population of new positions required to support this program. The revenue from the proposed fee will also cover the costs of technical and program support that the Government needs to administer benefits and to monitor schools, program sponsors, students, and exchange visitors solely for the purpose of this reporting program. In addition, a portion of the revenue from the proposed fee will be used for the direct support of Service operations relating to student and exchange visitor-related activities.[855]

2. SEVIS Fees and Charges

The fees and charges under the proposed rule include both "nonrecurring costs" and "recurring costs."[856] "Nonrecurring Costs" were assessed at $ 12.3 million.[857] This covered development and deployment costs for SEVIS implementation. Development costs included those associated with the design and development of an Internet-based, electronic information data collection system, including system design, development, integration, testing, verification and validation.[858] Deployment costs included installation of the new electronic system in the INS and DOS HQ and field offices.[859]

"Recurring Costs" were estimated to be $ 31 million from October 1, 1999 through September 30, 2001.[860] These costs were designated to pay for the personnel costs of supportive staff at the INS and DOS, such as service field offices, and Help Desk staff.[861] These costs were also set aside to pay for system operations and maintenance (OandM) costs,

---

Secretary of Education, to develop and conduct a program to collect information on nonimmigrant foreign students and exchange visitors from approved institutions of higher education and designated exchange visitor programs. Pub. L. 104-208, at ?41(a)(1).

[854] 31 U.S.C. ?701(b) (2000) ("Fees and charges for Government services and things of value" provides in pertinent part: "The head of each agency ... may prescribe regulations establishing the charge for a service or thing of value provided by the agency." The fees and charges are to be calculated based on "the costs to the Government"; "the value of the service or thing to the recipient"; or public policy or interest served").

[855] 64 Fed. Reg. at 71325.

[856] Id.

[857] Id.

[858] Id. at 71325-71326..

[859] Id. at 71326.

[860] Id.

[861] Id.

such as server maintenance and beta testing.[862] Finally, these costs were to pay for management and administrative (MandA) costs such as planning and administration. The user base for cost and fees calculation was estimated at 251,000 in both fiscal year 2000 and fiscal year 2001.[863] The total projected population for this two-year period was estimated at 501,000 paying students and exchange visitors.[864]

3. Universities and Schools' Objections

The proposal was strongly objected to by university administrators. The comments received were universally negative ones. There were a total of 4,617 comments received. Three types of comments were the most prominent: the fee should not be charged at all, the fee was too excessive, and the fee should not be collected by the schools. For example, the National Association of State Universities and Land-Grant Colleges (NASULGC) strongly opposed the fee collection process as proposed by the INS for two reasons.[865] First, the fee collection system imposed extra legal responsibilities on the schools.[866] It rendered school administrators de facto designated federal regulators, enforcers and collection agents. Such a fee collection system was inefficient and at odds with the spirit of the Paperwork Reduction Act. Second, the electronic information collection system was also an unfunded mandate contrary to Unfunded Mandates Reform Act of 1995 and an illegal infringement of state laws and regulations.[867]

The American Association of Collegiate Registrars and Admissions Officers (AACRAO), while supportive of the goals of the CIPRIS project, nevertheless objected to the proposed federal regulation on substantive and technical grounds.[868] Substantively the proposed rule set a bad precedent in allowing federal agencies to shift regulatory duties and responsibilities onto universities and colleges by effectively making them a collection agent for the federal government.[869] Second, the proposed regulation compromised the role of international educational advisors by making them hated federal law enforcers, instead of trusted educational counselors.[870] Third, a decentralized college-based fee collection system was not the most efficient way to collect fees.[871] Fourth, the operational cost and compliance burden associated with fee collections on behalf of the INS was an unfunded federal mandate prohibited by law, which also compromised university's major mission and function.[872] Finally, the proposed fee collection process would create significant financial and legal

---

[862] Id.

[863] Id.

[864] Id.

[865] Ltr. from Peter Magrath, Pres. Nat. Assoc. of St. U. and Land-Grant Colleges, to Dir., Policy Directives and Instrs. Branch, Immig. and Naturalization Serv., Re: Proposed Rule (INS No. 1991-99), Authorizing Collection of the Fee Levied on F, J, and M Nonimmigrant Classifications Under Public Law 104-208 (Jan. 24, 2000) (available at http://www.nasulgc.org/Washington Watch/Letters2000/FR Coord. Interagency Partnership regulat. Int'l.Stud.htm).

[866] Id.

[867] Id.

[868] Ltr. from Jerome Sullivan, Exec. Dir., Am. Assn. of Collegiate Registrars and Collegiate Officers, to Dir., Policy Directives and Instrs. Branch, Immig. and Naturalization Serv., Re: Proposed Rule (INS No. 1991-99) Authorizing Collection of the Fee Levied on F, J, and M Nonimmigrant Classifications Under Public Law 104-208 (Feb. 22, 2000) (available at http://www.aacrao.org/federal relations/cipris/comments.cfm).

[869] Id.

[870] Id.

[871] Id.

[872] Id.

liabilities for institutions in the form of law suits based on mistakes in the handling of student fees.[873]

Technically, the INS violated the SEVIS enabling legislation, Section 641 of the IIRIRA in a number of ways. First, Section 641(e)(1)(A) of the IIRIRA clearly requires F-1 and M-1 students to pay a fee "when the alien first registers with the institution or program after entering the United States." [874] The proposed regulatory amendments to 8 CFR ?14.2(f)(17)(iv) and (m)(18)(iv) however imposed a fee on F-1 and M-1 nonimmigrants who began a new program at the same institution.[875] This was illegal and was not intended by the law or within the contemplation of the legislators.

Second, section 641(e)(4)(A) of the IIRIRA requires the Attorney General to set the fee on the basis of estimated cost for collecting information.[876] Inasmuch as the INS proposed the fee amount of $ 95 based on erroneous computations which included foreign student transfering within the same institution, the fee estimation was erroneous.[877]

Third, section 641(e)(4)(B) of the IIRIRA limits the use of the fees for international student and exchange visitor tracking system activities.[878] It does not allow INS to charge fees for "operations relating to student and exchange visitor-related activities" in general.[879]

Fourth, the proposed regulation requires F-1, J-1 and M-1 nonimmigrants to pay a fee for entering a program of study "on or after August 1, 1999." [880]This retroactive collection of fees is not allowed by section 641 of the IIRIRA.[881]

Fifth, the proposed regulation provided that "failure by the school to impose, collect and remit the fee is conduct that does not comply with Service regulations." [882] Section 641 of the IIRIRA required the school to impose and collect fees.[883] It did not require the schools to remit the fees when international students failed to do so. The university administrators and educators associations should not have been made responsible for the students/visitors mistakes.

Public comments and political pressure resulted in substantial modification to the original proposal, particularly with respect to the fee collection and remittance process. The American Council on Education (ACE) was also supportive of SEVIS but objected to its implementations.[884]

On October 27, 2003, the DHS published a new proposed rule, "Authorizing Collection of the Fee Levied on F, J, and M Nonimmigrant Classifications Under Public Law 104-208" for public comment.[885] The new proposed rule was required as a result of the establishment of

---

[873] Id.

[874] Pub. L. 104-208 at ?41(e)(1)(A).

[875] 64 Fed. Reg. at 71329-71330.

[876] Pub. L. 104-208 at ?41(e)(4)(A).

[877] 64 Fed. Reg. at 71325.

[878] Pub. L. 104-208 at ?41(e)(4)(B).

[879] 64 Fed. Reg. at 71325.

[880] 64 Fed. Reg. at 71326.

[881] Pub. L. 104-208 at ?41.

[882] 64 Fed. Reg. at 71329.

[883] Pub. L. 104-208 at ?41(e).

[884] Ltr. from David Ward, Pres., Am. Council on Educ., to Dir., Regs. and Forms Serv. Div., Dept. of Homeland Sec., RE: Comments on Proposed Rule: "Authorizing Collection of the Fee Levied on F, J, and M Nonimmigrant Classifications Under Public Law 104-208" ICE No. 2297-03 (RIN 1653-AA23) (Dec. 10, 2003) (available at http://www.acenet.edu/AM/Template.cfm?Section=Searchandtemplate=/CM/HTML Display.cfmandContentID=6301).

[885] 68 Fed. Reg. 61148 (2003).

the DHS and the merging of the INS functions into the Border Coordination Initiative (BCI) and ICE. The new proposed regulations addressed many of the concerns raised by the comments to the original INS regulations. There were significant differences between the INS Proposed Rule (1999) and the DHS Proposed Rule (2003): (1) DHS proposed to charge $ 100[886] instead of $ 95 for operating and maintaining SEVIS, except for au pairs, camp counselors, or participants in a summer work/travel program for whom the fee would be $ 35; (2) DHS would be charge the fees directly, instead of requiring schools to handle the fees; (3) DHS exempted from fee payment those aliens who initially paid a SEVIS fee and applied for an F-1, F-3, J-1, M-1, or M-3 visa, but were denied by the DOS overseas.[887] These applicants could apply within nine months without paying a new SEVIS fee.[888]

The new DHS proposal was not without controversies. The American Immigration Lawyers Association objected to the new fee regulations on a number of grounds.[889] First, the fee was set higher than permitted by enabling statues. Section 641 of the IIRIRA of 1996 (Public Law 104-208), the Visa Waiver Permanent Program Act of 2000 (Public Law 106-396), or the USAPA (Public Law 107-56) only provided authority for charging fees for the collection of student/visitor information.[890] DHS was charging the visa applications 60% for cost of enforcement and monitoring of foreign students and visiting scholars. Second, the fee was set higher than necessary.[891] The initial 1999 CIPRIS (predecessor of SEVIS) fee study set the fee at $ 95.[892] This included all direct and indirect program costs. In 2002, an INS sponsored KPMG fee study recommended a $ 54 SEVIS fee. One year later, the DHS proposed a fee of $ 100 and the hiring of 240 staff. Third, secondary (high school) students should not have to be charged a SEVIS fee. Neither the IIRIRA nor the USAPA required such a fee.[893] Fourth, short term students, e.g. English language students, should not be charged $ 100 SEVIS fees. They would not come to the United States for a short course if the fees are high. Fifth, the SEVIS fee should be paid together with the visa application fees, at the US Embassy, not separately.[894] Sixth, the fees should only be paid once per alien student per program, not when the students transferred to another program.[895] Seventh, CDHS should clarify when duplicate fees are required (e.g. "when an individual begins a new course of

---

[886] *Id.* at 61149. DHS undertook to retain KPMG to conduct a new fee review for full compliance with federal law and fee guideline. The fee review was based on the recovery of costs over the FY 2003/2004 time period, having regard to the USA PATRIOT Act SEVIS appropriation of $ 36.8 million. It included costs incurred for increase DHS staffing and training dedicated to SEVIS related functions in DHS HQ, field offices and Help Desks. *Id.* at 61151.

[887] *Id.* at 61150-61152.

[888] *Id.* at 61151.

[889] Ltr. from Am. Immig. Laws. Assn. to Dir., Regs. and Forms Servs. Div., Dept. of Homeland Sec., AILA's Comments on DHS Proposed Regulation on SEVIS Fees: Re: Comments to Proposed Rule "Authorizing Collection of the Fee Levied on F, J, and M Nonimmigrant Classifications Under Public Law 104-208," ICE No. 2297-03; RIN 1653-AA23; 68 Fed. Reg. 61148, October 27, 2003 (Dec. 29, 2003) (available at http://www.aila.org/content/default.aspx?docid=9821).

[890] *Id.*

[891] *Id.*

[892] *Id.*

[893] *Id.*

[894] *Id.*

[895] *Id.*

study or new program").[896] Eighth, SEVIS fee collection should be as simple as possible to promote and facilitate international educational exchange.[897]

V. External Implementation Difficulties with SEVIS

A. Introduction

For purposes of organization and analysis, external implementation problems and operational difficulties with SEVIS can be classified into those before and after the legal deadline of January 31, 2003 (including the extensions of February 15 and August of 2003). Each deadline raised a new set of problems and concerns. For example, the concern with January 30, 2003 was whether SEVIS would be operational by August 2003, (i.e. able to handle thousands of records and millions of transactions at the same time). The second category of problems, those after February 15, 2003, included concern with getting SEVIS to work properly by making POEs notify the schools of I-20 landings. After August 2003, the concern was in fine tuning the SEVIS process in the most effective and efficient manner.

Alternatively and for analytical purposes, SEVIS implementation problems can be classified as technical, managerial and legal ones. Technical problems were those that related to SEVIS software and hardware malfunctioning, commonly reported as "glitches", such as bleeding or lock out. Managerial problems were those that related to organizing, coordinating, accounting, monitoring of the system, such as funding and technical support. Lastly, legal problems dealt with interpretation and application of SEVIS laws, rules and regulations issues, for example, how law and regulations should be interpreted and applied in a given case or context.

B. Problems before January 31, 2003 versus Problems after January 31, 2003

In Table 6 below, the number of SEVIS implementation issues raised between June 5, 2002 and February 14, 2002, as well as after February 14, 2003 (February 15, 2003 to August 6, 2003) were close in proximity (i.e. eighty-five before that date and ninety-one after).[898] However, the nature of the cases before and after February was quite different.

---

[896] *Id.* (questioning whether this included a change in major at the same sponsoring institution or a change in degree level at the same sponsoring institution or a change in category at the same sponsoring institution).

[897] *Id.*

[898] The data in Table 6 has been reconstructed from the following NAFSA Government Liaison Updates (NGLUs): NAFSA: Assn. of Intl. Educators, Summary of NAFSA's conference call with DHS and DOS regarding SEVIS, NGLU 2003-08-a (Aug. 6, 2003) (copy on file with Author); NAFSA: Assn. of Intl. Educators, NGLU 2003-07-d (July 28, 2003) (copy on file with Author); NAFSA: Assn. of Intl. Educators, NGLU 2003-07-c (July 23, 2003) (copy on file with Author); NAFSA: Assn. of Intl. Educators, July 18, 2003 Update from DHS, NGLU 2003-07-b (July 16, 2003) (copy on file with Author); NAFSA: Assn. of Intl. Educators, NGLU 2003-07-a (June 18, June 25, July 2, and July 9, 2003) (copy on file with Author); NAFSA: Assn. of Intl. Educators, SEVIS Conference Calls: June 4 and June 11, 2003, NGLU 2003-06-a (June 11, 2003) (available at http://web.archive.org/web/20030707192109/http://nafsa.org/content/ProfessionalandEducationalResources/I mmigrationAdvisingResources/nglu200306a.pdf) [hereinafter NGLU 2003-06-a]; NAFSA: Assn. of Intl. Educators, SLC SEVIS Session Summary (May 2003) (copy on file with Author); NAFSA: Assn. of Intl. Educators, NGLU 2003-04-c (Apr. 30 and May 5, 2003) (copy on file with Author); NAFSA: Assn. of Intl.

First, before February 14, approximately forty-three percent of the issues concerned general management policy issues.[899] Twenty percent concerned applied legal issues.[900] This was an outcome of a one-time NAFSA conference held in anticipation of the upcoming January 30, 2003 deadline.[901] These statistics were influenced by the INS' involvement in planning activities, such as setting directions and putting out policies. Second, after February 15, 2003 most of the issues (approximately thirty-four percent) were applied legal and thirty-three percent were concrete technical issues.[902] At this stage, the SEVIS system was up and running and most of the regulations were promulgated.[903] The schools, with the help of DHS, were left to work through the legal ambiguities and technical glitches.

Third, while most of the issues dealt with before February 15, 2003 were general in nature. General management (37), general law (16) and general technical (9) issues made up of seventy-two percent of the cases.[904] A majority of those after the implementation date (February 15, 2003) were applied ones - applied management (11), applied law (31), and applied technical (30), i.e. seventy-eight percent of the cases.[905]

Educators, NGLU 2003-04-b (Apr. 16 and 23, 2003) (copy on file with Author); NAFSA: Assn. of Intl. Educators, Summary of NAFSA Discussions with DHS, DOS, and EDS April 2, 9 and 10, 2003, NGLU 2003-04-a (Apr. 10, 2003) (available at http://web.archive.org/web/20040612141620/http://www.nafsa.org/content/ProfessionalandEducationalResources/ImmigrationAdvisingResources/NGLU200304a.pdf) [hereinafter NGLU 2003-04-a]; NAFSA: Assn. of Intl. Educators, SEVIS Conference Call: NAFSA, DHS, EDS, DOS Wednesday, March 26, 2003, NGLU 2003-03-26 (Mar. 26, 2003) (copy on file with Author) [hereinafter NGLU 2003-03-26]; NAFSA: Assn. of Intl. Educators, NGLU 2003-03-20 (Mar. 20, 2003) (copy on file with Author); NAFSA: Assn. of Intl. Educators, NAFSA-INS February 14, 2003 Q and A, http://web.archive.org/web/20050309214529/http://www.nafsa.org/content/ProfessionalandEducationalResources/ImmigrationAdvisingResources/sevisQA20030214.htm (Feb. 14, 2003) (INS response to a series of SEVIS questions posed by NAFSA) [hereinafter NAFSA-INS Q and A]; NAFSA: Assn. of Intl. Educators, Summary of NAFSA-INS SEVIS Conference Call, NGLU 2002-12-19 (Dec. 19, 2002) (available at http://web.archive.org/web/20041015002933/http://www.nafsa.org/content/ProfessionalandEducationalResources/ImmigrationAdvisingResources/nglu20021219.htm) [hereinafter NGLU 2002-12-19]; NAFSA: Assn. of Intl. Educators, SEVIS Resource 2002-f (Dec. 16, 2002) (copy on file with Author); NAFSA: Assn. of Intl. Educators, NGLU 2002-10-22 (Oct. 22, 2002) (copy on file with Author); NAFSA: Assn. of Intl. Educators, NGLU 2002-10-09 (Oct. 9, 2002) (copy on file with Author); NAFSA: Assn. of Intl. Educators, NGLU 2002-06-20 (June 20, 2002) (copy on file with Author); NAFSA: Assn. of Intl. Educators, NGLU 2002-06-13 (June 13, 2002) (copy on file with Author); NAFSA: Assn. of Intl. Educators, Summary of June 5, 2002 NAFSA Conference Call with INS, NGLU 2002-0605 (June 5, 2002) (available at http://web.archive.org/web/20040616004126/http://www.nafsa.org/content/ProfessionalandEducationalResources/ImmigrationAdvisingResources/NGLU20020605.htm) [hereinafter NGLU 2002-0605]. Hereinafter, all citations will be collectively known as Conference Call Summaries.

[899] Conference Call Summaries, *supra* n. 224.
[900] *Id.*
[901] *Id.*
[902] *Id.*
[903] *Id.*
[904] *Id.*
[905] *Id.*

Table 6. Break down of SEVIS implementation - management, legal, technical - issues from June 6, 2002 to August 6, 2003[906]

Week	Issues	Man. Policy	Man. Applied	Legal Rule	Legal Applied	Tech. General	Tech. Applied	Total
6/5/02	9	5	0	4	0	0	0	18
6/27/02	14	8	0	0	0	6	0	14
6/20/02	2	2	0	0	0	0	0	2
10/9/02	19	9	0	8	0	2	0	19
10/22/02	5	4	0	0	0	1	0	5
12/16/02	5	5	0	0	0	0	0	5
12/19/02	21	2	0	2	17	0	0	21
1/30/03	USAPA Implementation Date							
2/15/03	INS Implementation Grace Period							
2/14/03	7	2	2	2	0	1	3	7
3/20/03	6	0	0	0	0	6	0	6
3/26/03	9	0	4	0	0	5	0	9
4/2,9 and 10/03	12	1	1	0	6	0	10	12
6/18,25/03 and 7/2,9/03	25	0	2	0	14	0	9	25
7/16/03	7	0	1	1	1	3	1	7
7/18/03	5	5	0	0	0	0	0	5
7/23/03	6	0	1	0	4	0	1	6
7/28/03	3	0	1	0	2	0	0	3
8/6/03	12	1	1	0	4	0	6	12
Total	176	44	13	17	48	24	30	176

C. Problems at Planning Versus Launch Versus Operational Stage

Next, the study investigated the types of problems and issues that confronted the schools in the preliminary/planning stage (Table 7) compared with the before operational launch stage (Table 8) compared with the full operational stage (Table 9).

1. Planning Problems and Issues

In the preliminary/planning stage and with a fast-approaching January 30, 2003 deadline, the schools were trying to seek clarification from INS about the implementation process.[907]

---

[906] *Id.*. Note the following terminology - Management Policy: General direction of a non-legal and non-technical nature, e.g. training provided; Management Applied: Specific direction of a non-legal and non-technical nature bearing on a specific issue, e.g. better coordination between DHS and DOS; Legal rule: General discussion of certain legal rule or policy, e.g. discussion of Transitional procedures mandated by the Border Security Act; Legal applied: Specific analysis of conflicting interpretation of rules; Technical general: General discussion of technical issues, e.g. new version of SEVIS; Technical applied: Specific analysis of technical problems, e.g. data bleeding.

There were concerns with (1) lack of final implementation regulations, (2) inadequate and unclear implementation regulations, (3) certification requirements and enrollment process, (4) lack of training for INS officers, and (5) lack of contingency planning.[908] Inessence, SEVIS schools were laboring under great uncertainty and suffered from grave anxiety as a result of INS's lack of a well conceived plan to implement SEVIS.[909]

Table 7. SEVIS Implementations problems at the preliminary/planning stage – six months before launch (June 2002)[910]

Date	Technical	Legal	Managerial	Summary
June 2002	NAFSA inquired about contingency Planning for SEVIS failure.[911]	INS informed NAFSA on status of SEVIS regulations. [912]	NAFSA requested permission to Pose electronic forms on the web[913]	The schools were seeking clarifications(inquiry) on Procedure matters, technical, legal, and managerial
	None	NAFSA informed INS of the inadequacy with I-20 rules.[914]	NAFSA provided feedback on the kind of training to be provided to INS officers.[915]	The attention of the schools Were focused on providing feedback(consultation) on procedure matters; technical, legal and managerial.
	INS provided general information on discovery procedure.[916] \	N/A	INS clarified enrollment and [917] registration plan.[918]	The exchanges between schools and DHS were concerned with general rules, not applied rule or specific case information.

---

[907] The INS did have a plan for step-by-step SEVIS implementation, but the plan was abruptly cut short by 9/11. See Student and Exchange Visitor Program Development Plan - Past, Present and Future, U.S. Immig. and Naturalization Serv. Rpt. 23-25 (Feb. 26. 2002) (copy on file with Author) (stating that deployment started with small colleges in Boston in 2001 before reaching out to other major foreign student educational institutions nation wide, including big cities of Chicago, Denver, and Dallas).

[908] *Id.*

[909] *Id.*

[910] All references in Table 7 come from NGLU 2002-0605, *supra* n. 224.

[911] *Id.* at "Issue: Transitional Procedures Mandated by the Border Security Act" (stating that "Section 501(c)(1)(B) of the Border Security Act requires the Department of State (DOS) to transmit to INS notification that an F or M visa has been issued. INS said that they are working with DOS on this data sharing requirement").

[912] *Id.* at "Issue: SEVIS Back-Up Systems" (NAFSA request for information on contingency planning - backed up, redundancy - in case SEVIS fails. For example, existence of "mirror site" and losing "batch" data transmitted.).

[913] *Id.* at "Issue: Sample SEVIS Screens and Forms" ("NAFSA requested electronic copies of SEVIS screens and forms to post on the NAFSA Web site.").

[914] *Id.* at "Issue: I-20's for F-2 Dependents" (I-20 issuance regulations do not make reference to dependents)

[915] *Id.*

[916] *Id.* at "Issue: I-17s, SEVIS, and Recertification Issues" (INS informed NAFSA on stages of enrollment in SEVIS and where to look for "regular" and "preliminary" enrollment rules and regulations.).

[917] *Id.*

[918] *Id.* at "Issue: SEVIS Back-Up Systems" ("If a school using the "batch" option lost data kept on-campus in a batch solution software, INS would be open to downloading (data dumping) files to the schools").

Table 7. (Continued)

Date	Technical	Legal	Managerial	Summary
	INS provided basic information on data loss in Batch Transfer.[919]	INS informed NAFSA on the need for and timing of compliance review of J and M schools.[920]	INS reported it was currently gathering information on how to collect SEVIS fees.[921]	Inquiry and feedback concerns mostly preliminary, fundamental, basic, threshold and tentative matters.[922]

2. Launch Problems and Issues

In the middle stage, the schools were directly confronted with SEVIS. The schools legally dealt with ill-defined regulations and operational difficulties dealing with untested INS software.[923] The questions raised were more pointed and practical than theoretical and overarching.[924] For example, the schools were concerned with how to communicate with the SEVIS system users in situations when the system is inaccessible.

Table 8. SEVIS Implementation problems before operational launch date (December 19, 2002 and February 14, 2003)

Date	Technical	Legal	Managerial	Summary
Feb.14 2003[925]	INS: "request users register. For batch from The server they intend to Use to post And get files from batch so their server will have both	DHS provided step by step: "Guidance from INS on STUDENT ENTRIES AT INS POE - SEVIS I-20 PROCESSING"[926]	"Q: SEVIS System inaccessibility.	At this stage, the problems and issues raised were mainly practical in nature and operational in kind.

---

[919] Id.

[920] Id. at "Issue: I-17s, SEVIS, and Recertification Issues" (Border Security Act ?02 (BSA) requires INS to conduct regular compliance review of F and M schools every two years, beginning no later than May 2004, two years after promulgation of BSA).

[921] Id at "Issue: SEVIS Fee." (INS was studying ways of making SEVIS payment and to clearly define the role of the DOS in the process.).

[922] Id.

[923] See infra nn. 251-261 and accompanying text.

[924] Id.

[925] NAFSA-INS Q and A, supra n. 224. INS responded to a series of SEVIS questions posed by NAFSA. Issues addressed included: effective date of restrictions on duration of reduced course load authorizations, SEVIS training for INS personnel, SEVIS system inaccessibility; processing of SEVIS I-20s at ports of entry, vendor certification, and customer agreements for use of Batch functionality. Id.

[926] NAFSA-INS Q and A, supra n. 224, at "Q: Questions about Language in the Customer Agreement for Using the SEVIS Batch-File Transfer Process."

Date	Technical	Legal	Managerial	Summary
Dec. 19, 2002[927]	The SEVIS site certificate in their certificate store and their ".pem' client certificate in a location where their automated application		How does the Service plan to communicate information to System users when the System is inaccessible?"[928]	
	Can use their certificate to establish an SSL connection."[929]	However, in The case . . . The system isInaccessible or abnormally slow for a Period that May impact the Business process of schools, the Service is developing a Contingency plan to allow schools to despite system problems. . . carry out their normal Processes		
		The Service would contact each school in Such circumstances And advise them of any temporary processes.		
		This contact would most Likely be via e-mail."[930]		
		"Service Personnel . . . are unfamiliar with SEVIS Documents and procedures.		
		What steps is The Service Taking to educate its Personnel about SEVIS?" (2/14/03)[931] vs. "What is the scope, nature, And intent of INS' plans to train its field officers in SEVIS systems, procedures, And forms?" (6/5/2002)[932]		The questions asked were more confrontational and demanding.
		"The Service Has already carried out a number of Extensive Training sessions . .		
		As with any. New program . . . it will take some time		The answers given are more defensive

---

[927] NGLU 2002-12-19, *supra* n. 224.

[928] *Id.* at "Q: SEVIS Related Guidance/Training for INS personnel."

[929] *Id.* at "Q: SEVIS System Inaccessibility."

[930] *Id.*

[931] *Id.* at "SEVIS Related Guidance/Training for INS Personnel."

[932] NGLU 2002-0605, *supra n.* 224, at "Issue: SEVIS Training for INS Officials."

Table 8. (Continued)

Date	Technical	Legal	Managerial
		For every Individual involved to be fully trained. . . Service is working with schools that make inadvertent mistakes in The system, we will work with schools that Are experiencing problems due To unfamiliarity on the part of Service entities . . ." (2/14/03)[933] vs. "INS assured NAFSA that service center personnel are And will continue to receive training and guidance." (6/5/2002)[934] "How does the Service plan to communicate information to system users when the system is inaccessible?"[935]	The three kinds of questions most often asked are: access, corrections, and communication/ help

3. Operational Problems and Issues

Finally, when SEVIS was fully operational, the schools and programs confronted case-specific operational issues or application problems. These problems ranged from ambiguous SEVIS regulations to unresolved legal issues to a mismatch between SEVIS regulations and SEVIS technology. The defining characteristics of the issues and problems posed during this period were increasingly concrete and sophisticated.

Table 9. SEVIS Implementation problems at the full-operational stage, during six months after launch to January 2004

Date	Technical	Legal	Managerial	Summary
Jan. 2004[936]	The SEVIS program did not have extension of stay for more than 12 Months. DHS did not promise to Change it, but instead was "open to discussion" if the year limit Was insufficient.[937]	J-1 was departing from the country, leaving his/ her J-2 dependent behind with his spouse who was how to complete this information in SEVIS.[938]	Some students did not have POE data, and DHS requested for "school and program officials [to] fax examples of those who have entered the US and for whom there is no POE data."[940]	At the full - operational stage the problems and issues were all operational ones and driven by particular and specific case based concerns.

---

[933] NAFSA-INS Q and A, *supra* n. 224, at "SEVIS Related Guidance/Training for INS Personnel."

[934] NGLU 2002-0605, supra n. 224, at "Issue: SEVIS Training for INS Officials."

[935] NAFSA-INS Q and A, supra n. 224, at "Q: SEVIS System Inaccessibility."

[936] NAFSA: Assn. of Intl. Educators, SEVIS Conference Call Summary: January 10 and 17, 2004 Calls, NGLU 2004-01-a (Jan. 17, 2004) (copy on file with Author) [hereinafter NGLU 2004-01-a].

[937] NAFSA: Assn. of Intl. Educators, SEVIS Conference Call: Wednesday, November 19, 2003, NGLU 2003-11-b, "3. When Will F SEVIS Allow Extensions of Stay Over 12 Months?" (copy on file with Author) [hereinafter NGLU 2003-11-b].

Schools had been trying to enter OPT data	The DOS did not know the answer and needed to determine the answer.[939]		
Beyond the day the program is scheduled to end, but were prevented from doing so by The software.[941] The problem arose because of an incorrect interpretation, which listed the program end date as""date student's program will be completed. Full program includes Optional Practical Training the student will undertake after coursework.'(sic)"[942]	Question raised was whether an OPT student was Considered to be engaging in another level of education if they took Courses"incidental to their OPT employment."[943] Legal counsel at DHS - CIS advised that OPT I-765 must be received on or before Program End Date.[944]	DSO reportedly made a mistake of authorizing OPT for student 1 in the name of student 2, who has a identical name and a SEVIS ID number that had a one digit difference in the middle of the number.	Inquiries and concerns are directed at solving/ Correcting Specific problems on hands.
SEVIS 4.9.2, Release planned for Feb. 6, 2004 "will allow Batch users to Submit"create' requests for F, M or J's who will be beginning new programs and who have had a SEVIS record in the same Visa Classification in the past."[945]		The Texas Service center a SEVIS ID number that had a one digit difference in the middle of the number.	
		Meanwhile student 2 wanted to apply for OPT but could not receive a recommendation because the mistake left an OPT recommendation in his file already.[946]	The discussion of and solution to problems and issues at this stage were engaged at a legal-Technical level, with Correct answers.

[938] NAFSA: Assn. of Intl. Educators, SEVIS Conference Call: NAFSA, DHS, DOS Wednesday, September 10, 2003, NGLU 2003-09-b, "4. How should an A/OR switch the dependents of J-1 parents?" (copy on file with Author) [hereinafter NGLU 2003-09-b].

[939] NAFSA: Assn. of Intl. Educators, SEVIS Conference Call: NAFSA, DHS, DOS Wednesday, September 10, 2003, NGLU 2003-09-b, "4. How should an A/OR switch the dependents of J-1 parents?" (copy on file with Author) [hereinafter NGLU 2003-09-b].

[940] NGLU 2004-01-a, supra n. 262, at "3. Records of Students and Exchange Visitors without POE Data."

[941] NAFSA: Assn. of Intl. Educators, SEVIS Conference Call: NAFSA, DHS, DOS, Friday, September 5, 2003, NGLU 2003-09-a, "5. Banner Software and Recommending OPT," (September 5, 2003) (copy on file with Author) [hereinafter NGLU 2003-09-a].

[942] NGLU 2003-09-a at "2. OPT and Incidental Study."

[943] NGLU 2003-09-a at "2. OPT and Incidental Study."

[944] Id. at "5. CIS Says OPT I-765 Must be Received on or Before Program End Date."

[945] NGLU 2004-01-a, supra n. 262, at "4. SEVIS 4.9.2 Implementation."

[946] NAFSA: Assn. of Intl. Educators, SEVIS Conference Call: NAFSA, DHS (SEVIS, Service Center and Adjudications) BCIS, BICE, EDS, CA, CIEE, Wednesday, October 1, 2003, NGLU 2003-10-a, "7. OPT Errors" (Oct. 1, 2003) (available at http://web.archive.org/web/20031212021850/www.nafsa.org/content/

Table 9. (Continued)

| | | The SEVIS Required students who take up to 18 hrs. a week of school work to apply for a student visa, subject to SEVIS fees and Lengthy interviews.[947] Consulates have been giving B-1 visa when students asked for F-1 to study for Short intensive Courses. DHS said that F-1(student status) was the proper way to go if that was the category they belonged to. |
| | | DHS and DOS did not finish This conversation during this call.[948] |

VI. VARIETIES OF IMPLEMENTATION PROBLEMS: SUMMARY AND DISCUSSION

A. Varieties of Managerial Problems

Most of the difficulties throughout the SEVIS implementation process resulted from poor project planning and management. The successful implementation of SEVIS requires good management, adequate resources, sound technology and clear legal guidelines. However, it seems none of these issues have been attended to.

1. Problems with Planning

The implementation of SEVIS suffered from a lack of overall detail and long-term planning. The objectives, role and responsibilities, steps, activities, timelines and deadlines were not well thought-out and articulated in advance. Many universities were unaware of what changes they would have to make in order to accommodate SEVIS.[949] This approach

---

ProfessionalandEducationalResources/ImmigrationAdvisingResources/nglu200310a.pdf) [hereinafter NGLU 2003-10-a].

[947] NAFSA: Assn. of Intl. Educators, SEVIS Conference Call: NAFSA, DHS, EDS, DOS, Wednesday, October 8, 2003, NGLU 2003-10-b, "7. Short Academic Programs" (Oct. 2003) (available at http://web.archive.org/web/20040407143433/http://www.nafsa.org/content/ProfessionalandEducationalResources/ImmigrationAdvisingResources/nglu200310b.pdf) [hereinafter NGLU 2003-10-b].

[948] NGLU 2004-01-a, supra n. 262, at "4. SEVIS 4.9.2 Implementation."

[949] "Gaston Lacombe, SEVIS Implementation," *European Advisers Newsletter* 3 (Summer 2002), http://www.bibl.u-szeged.hu/oseas/newsletter/02summer lacombe.html.

resulted in schools having to adopt a "wait and see" or "play it by ear" approach to program management.[950] This generated substantial amounts of uncertainty, frustration, anxiety, animosity, complaints, and antagonism. For example, Stanford's Bechtel International Center noted:

As of April 2002 much is still unclear. The Immigration Service is currently developing regulations that will clarify the system to both monitor and collect data on foreign students and scholars. We have no clear date as to when these regulations will be published.[951]

As a result, some universities were not able to comply with SEVIS in time, such as the University of Nevada, Las Vegas (UNLV).[952] UNLV planned to comply with SEVIS, but because they did not have the computer specifications they missed the deadline set to implement the program.[953]

Others expressed similar concerns about the deadlines and timetables that INS was putting in place:

First, we should jointly establish a timetable for the implementation of SEVIS with interim deadlines for specific activities. It is, for example, important for campuses to know the precise date by which EDS will have written all the programming for [real-time] and batch entry, and the date by which a test file will be available on a web site to permit schools to practice with the system. Having such a timetable will provide a framework for implementation, allow all parties to measure progress against a clear benchmark, and enable campus officials to better plan the changes that will be necessary at their institution. If delays occur, resources can be shifted and the schedule can be adjusted appropriately by both federal and campus officials. [954]

2. Problems with Training

INS/DHS has not offered formal SEVIS implementation training for its own agency employees, as shown below, and SEVIS training and certification was not required of DSO and other school officials who were the front line operatives responsible for complying, operating and maintaining SEVIS. For example, it was unclear to school officials what was

---

[950] Id.

[951] Bechtel Intl. Ctr. at Stanford U., SEVIS, Tracking Systems and other Recent Legislation and Regulations, http://www.stanford.edu/dept/icenter/new/sevis/sevis 1.html (April 2002).

[952] Jennifer Knight , "Nevada Sees Deadline Pass for Student Database," Las Vegas Sun (Feb. 27, 2003), http://www.lasvegassun.com/sunbin/stories/text/2003/feb/27/514723089.html (detailing how UNLV failed to meet SEVIS compliance because INS has failed to organize the implementation of SEVIS in a comprehensive and systematic manner).

[953] Id.

[954] Ltr. from David Ward, Pres., American Council on Education, to James W. Ziglar, Commr., Immig. and Naturalization Serv, U.S. Dept. of Just., (Jan. 24, 2002) (available at http://www.nasulgc.org/Washington Watch/Letters2002/Ziglar 0124.pdf); H.R. Subcomm. on Immig., Border Sec. and Claims of the Jud. Comm., Nonimmigrant Student Tracking: Implementation and Proposed Modifications, 108th Cong. 58 (Apr. 2, 2003) (available at http://commdocs.house.gov/committees/judiciary/hju86265.000/hju86265 0f.htm) (testimony of David Ward that "the INS has not provided adequate training to anyone") (emphasis in the original); see also H.R. Subcomms. on 21st Cent. Competitiveness and Select Educ. of the Comm. on Educ. and the Workforce, Homeland Security: Tracking International Students in Higher Education - Progress and Issues Since 9-11, 107th Cong. 61 (Sept. 24, 2002) (available at http://edworkforce.house.gov/hearings/107th/21st/studvisa92402 /fine.htm) (statement of Glenn A. Fine, making recommendations about how to improve the effectiveness of SEVIS and the uncertainty in the field in regards to standards to certify schools).

required by SEVIS.[955] School officials learned through trial and error and through sharing SEVIS experiences with others.

Originally, INS intended to offer face-to-face training to schools officials.[956] Later, all scheduled training sessions for the use of the SEVIS data-base were cancelled due to the elimination of the INS implementation team.[957] INS offered to send training videos, to organize informational seminars at higher educational conferences, and to give access to 800 Help Desk assistants to assist with the implementation and use of SEVIS.[958] In retrospect, this approach to launching SEVIS accounted for many of the problems confronted by DHS and schools in the SEVIS implementation and operation stages.

University officials have relied on school associations, in-house trainers or third party vendors[959] to provide for the missing SEVIS training. As a result, many school employees were inexperienced and uneducated about INS and SEVIS requirements.[960] This was particularly a problem with small schools or vocational institutions with few resources and few connections. Likewise, INS officials were untrained to approve and monitor schools, and the Help Desk staff was not properly briefed. As a result, the staff was uncertain as to the exact legal requirements and detailed operation procedures.[961]

3. Problems with Coordination

The success of SEVIS required the cooperation and coordination of different government agencies, such as DOS, DHS-Custom, DHS-Immigration, DEA, and the Help Desk, as well as participating schools. The agencies were often in disagreement as to policy, rule interpretation, technical sophistication, and SEVIS integration. Schools were frustrated when government agencies in sometimes not in accordance with the law. For example, in order for schools to monitor the arrival time of F-1 and J-1 students, the schools must be informed by the POEs of their arrival in the United States. In September 17, 2003, schools reported that relatively few EV and students appeared on the POE list.[962] The DHS explained that the problem was due in part to different POE codes adopted by INS and customs agencies.[963] In

---

[955] See Nonimmigrant Student Tracking: Implementation and Proposed Modifications, 108th Cong. at 58 (claiming INS has given inadequate training).

[956] See e.g. U.S. Dept. of Just., Immigration and Naturalization Service Student and Exchange Visitor Information System Seminar, http://nafsa3.okstate.edu/oknafsa/Docs/sevis-training.doc (June 7, 2002). The seminar prepared DSO, RO, ARO for the summer release of SEVIS. It addressed issues of "system functionality, program history, and user access." Id. There was no "technical discussion or presentation on the batch file transfer functionality." Id.

[957] Id.

[958] Id.

[959] See e.g. Amy Rogers, EDS Among Solution Providers Seizing Opportunity in Foreign-Student Tracking, P 5, http://certivo.net/document/crneds.pdf (Jan. 14, 2003) (EDS and Drake Certivo developed the SEVIS interactive training course based on comments gathered from 2000 school officials); see also e.g. EDS, Homeland Security Goes to School, http://www.prnewswire.com/cgi-bin/stories.pl?ACCT=104andSTORY=/www/story/02-03-2003/0001883761 (Feb. 03, 2003) (describing course for SEVIS training).

[960] See Nonimmigrant Student Tracking: Implementation and Proposed Modifications, 108th Cong. at 58 (claiming INS has given inadequate training).

[961] Homeland Security: Tracking International Students in Higher Education - Progress and Issues Since 9-11, 107th Cong. at 61.

[962] Id.

[963] Id.

order to not reject all files, the mismatch of codes forced the transfer of data to an "unknown" category.[964]

Table 10. Implementation difficulties confronted by users as a result of poor SEVIS project management[965]

Management functions	Implementation problems	Manifestations of problems at the operational level
Planning	There was no or inadequate planning for the effective implementation of SEVIS. Procedurally, university administrators and educator associations were not involved with the formulation of the implementation plan. Substantively, the INS SEVIS implementation plan failed to take into account the shortage of time, limitations of resources, volume of work, complexity of tasks, degree of difficulties, multiplicity of parties and uniqueness of universities.	Schools were not consulted on implementation deadlines. INS and SEVIS imposed deadlines at odds with the university calendar. INS and SEVIS imposed mandates, requirements and processes at odds with university philosophies, missions, cultures and routines. INS provided competing opinions and wrong information, e.g. regulations and guidelines, and missed critical path deadlines for meeting compliance. INS did not provide for the timely and adequate training of change agents, INS agents and school officials alike. Many school applications were still not processed days before January 30, 2003. SEVIS program was not fully debugged before launched. SEVIS lacked capacity to handle sudden surge of workloads. SEVIS software program and attending INS guidelines and procedures did not reflect university operational realities, interests or needs.
Organizing	There was a gross lack of integration and coordination of functions and efforts between and within DHS and DOS charged with implementing SEVIS. Particularly: DHS and DOS did not share in the same organizational mission, structure process or culture. DHS and EDS have yet to develop a smooth working relationship. DHS has not fully integrated INS and Customs into a coherent organizational framework, creating unresolved jurisdiction, identity, role and functions problems.	DOS did not have access to SEVIS data real-time. There were problems of lost and delayed data transmission. DHS and DOS interpreted SEVIS differently. In some cases, DOS worked at odds with DHS. There was a lack of coordination between EDS (private contractor) and DHS.

---

[964] Id.
[965] Id.

Table 10. (Continued)

Management functions	Implementation problems	Manifestations of problems at the operational level
Staffing	There was inadequate staff placement, insufficient staff training, and poor staff support to meet SEVIS implementation needs	DHS did not have sufficient staff to service SEVIS. There was not enough staff to provide for research. There was not enough staff to man Help Desk. There was not enough training for DHS SEVIS officials and inspector.
Directing	There was a gross lack of leadership, motivation, communication in achieving SEVIS goals and objectives.	The INS was not forthcoming on the readiness and availability of SEVIS. This affected the confidence of schools in DHS judgment. The DHS has failed to work with schools as equal partners, failed to inform the schools of problems and issues afflicting SEVIS, failed to consider SEVIS' impact on schools, and has failed to listen to schools. The DHS has not been solicitous of schools welfare by anticipating their needs and protective of their welfare.
Controlling	There was a total lack of process and outcome evaluative measures pointing to success.	INS/DHS define successful implementation, differently than universities and schools. Except for limited SEVIS functions, e.g. Help Desk response time, there was no attempt to measure the performance of SEVIS as a system or process. No one knew whether the SEVIS was functioning as designed. DHS testified that it was successful. Schools complained of shortcomings and students were not coming to the United States to study.

B. Types of Legal Problems

1. Problems with Clear Legislative Mandate

Successful implementation of SEVIS required a clear understanding of the roles and responsibilities of all parties involved. From the very beginning, there was a debate as to who was legally responsible for the development, funding, and deployment of SEVIS.

According to Section 641(a) of the IIRIRA of 1996 the Attorney General is legally responsible to "develop and conduct a program to collect from approved institutions of higher education, other approved educational institutions, and designated exchange visitor programs in the United States" certain specified information.[966] Furthermore, "the Attorney General ...

---

[966] 8 U.S.C. ?372(a)(1) (2000).

shall establish an electronic means to monitor and verify "certain enumerated events pertaining to foreign individuals that require visas."[967]

The central issue when dividing SEVIS responsibilities between the government (as provider) and universities (as end users) during the implementation phase of the SEVIS project was how to adequately "develop and conduct a program to collect from approved institutions of higher education, other approved educational institutions, and designated exchange visitor programs" necessary data and adequate information for efficient and effective electronic tracking of students and scholars.[968] More specifically, who is responsible for implementing the SEVIS program, and when is the SEVIS program deemed fully implemented? Does this mean that the government, specifically INS/DHS, is only required to make SEVIS "technically available" via interactive mode to some users by January 30, 2003? Or does it mean that the INS/DHS is also responsible for making SEVIS "functionally available" via batch transmission to all users?

The government argued for a restrictive definition of "full implementation."[969] SEVIS is "fully implemented" when it is technically available for service, such as an INS-SEVIS web site that is ready for interactive input and output on a case by case basis.[970] Whereas, the schools argued for a broad definition of "full implementation:"

Full implementation of the monitoring program necessarily includes the process by which schools develop or acquire the technology necessary to accomplish the reporting required under the program in accordance with technical specifications provided by the Service. It is inherently impossible for schools to meet the program's reporting requirements without this stage of the implementation of the process having taken place.[971]

More fundamentally, "full implementation" should include fully beta tested SEVIS technology as operated and supported by well trained DSOs and competent and supportive INS officials.

The DOJ-IGO adopted a still broader definition of "full implementation."

Full deployment requires that all elements of the program be functional to ensure the integrity of SEVIS. Our finding that SEVIS was not fully implemented as of January 1, 2003, was not based solely on the INS's deployment of a phased-in schedule. Instead, as stated in our testimony in September 2002 and in this report, we believe full implementation includes not only the technical availability of SEVIS, but also ensuring that sufficient resources are devoted to the foreign student program, ensuring that only bona fide schools are provided access to SEVIS, adequately training DHS employees and school representatives, ensuring that schools are completely and accurately entering information on their foreign students into SEVIS in a timely manner, and establishing procedures for using SEVIS data to identify noncompliant and fraudulent operations as well as following up when SEVIS data indicates fraud in a school's program.[972]

Based on the above criteria, DOJ-OIG found that the SEVIS implementation was not complete. Specifically, the INS did not complete certification reviews of all school

---

[967] *Id.* at ?372(a)(3).
[968] *Id.* at ?372(a)(1)
[969] Follow-up Review, *supra* n. 14, at app. III
[970] *Id.*
[971] *Id.*
[972] *Id.* (emphasis in original).

applications at the time originally promised.[973] Also, the INS did not sufficiently monitor the internal controls of schools that would detect and prevent fraud.[974] Further, INS adjudicators and INS port of entry inspectors had not been given adequate training and guidance,[975] and the INS had not provided sufficient resources for investigating potential fraud.[976]

Table 11. Interpretations of "full implementation" of SEVIS[977]

School/Agency	Interpretation	Ready by January 30, 2003?
Universities	(1) SEVIS system meeting legislative requirements?	No tracking for J - 1 visitors
		No tracking for J - 1 dependents (J-2)
	(2) SEVIS system technically available?	Too slow
		Too many flaws
	(3) Batch system technically available?	Final regulations for F visa not timely issued
		Final regulations for J visa not Issued
		Technical specifications not timely released to vendor
		No beta testing for batch system
	(4) SEVIS system functionally available?	Lack of timely school certifications
		Lack of training for DSOs
		Lack of training for INS
		Officials
		Lack of coordination with DOS
		Lack of timely and competent help-support
		Unfunded mandates
	SEVIS full implementation? (1) + (2) + (3) + (4)	No

---

[973] *Id.* See also H.R. Subcomm. on Immig., Border Sec., and Claims of the Jud. Comm., Implementation of the Student and Exchange Visitor Information System (SEVIS), 107th Cong. 16, 19 (Apr. 2, 2003) (available at http://judiciary.house.gov/media/pdfs/printers/108th/86265.PDF) (statement of Glenn A. Fine detailing problems with school certifications and procedures).

[974] Follow-up Review, *supra* n. 14, at 22

[975] *Id.* at 23-25.

[976] *Id.*

[977] Follow-up Review, supra n. 14, at app. III.

School/Agency	Interpretation	Ready by January 30, 2003?
DOJ - IGO[978]	(1) SEVIS system meeting legislative requirements?	No comment.
	(2) SEVIS system technically available?	No comment.
	(3) Batch system technically available?	No comment
	(4) SEVIS system functionally available?	Schools not approved for timely Access Compliance audits not properly Performed Need additional training and guidance for adjudicators and Inspectors Need sufficient resources needed for enforcement procedures
	SEVIS full implementation?	No.
INS - DHS	(1) SEVIS system meeting legislative requirements?	Yes. SEVIS Technically available as of January 30, 2003.
	(2) SEVIS system technically available?	Yes.
	(3) Batch system technically available?	Yes.
	(4) SEVIS system functionally available?	Yes.
	SEVIS full implementation?	Yes.

2. Problems with Lack of Timely Regulations

The implementation of SEVIS suffered from a lack of timely, comprehensive and clear regulations. In the last six months prior to the launch date, May 2002 to January 2003, there had been no less than five sets of regulations to implement SEVIS.[979] It is clear that these administrative regulations were promulgated to meet the SEVIS deadline of January 30, 2003. Very little thought was expended on whether such rules could or would be complied with given the shortage of time, complexity of rules, and difficulties of compliance.

As early as January 28, 2002, AARAO raised an alarm: Since no formal regulations regarding implementation of SEVIS have been issued by the INS, many higher education advocates are concerned that colleges and universities will have inadequate time to test and

---

[978] Id.

[979] See 67 Fed. Reg. at 34862 (proposed rule implementing SEVIS); 67 Fed. Reg. at 44344 (interim rule for schools to apply for preliminary enrollment in SEVIS); 67 Fed. Reg. at 60107 (interim rule for certification of schools applying for enrollment in SEVIS); 67 Fed. Reg. at 76256 (DHS's final rule implementing SEVIS); 67 Fed. Reg. at 76307 (DOS interim rule implementing SEVIS).

implement the SEVIS system on their campus and comply with the January 2003 implementation date.[980]

By March 20, 2002, the INS and DOS were openly discussing the possibility of issuing more SEVIS-related implementations and regulations. These included (1) regulations for a shorter default period for visitor's visa, including students,[981] (2) regulations preventing students from taking classes before visa approval,[982] (3) regulations governing recertification of schools authorized to issue I-20 forms,[983] (4) regulations governing implementation of SEVIS for F and M visas,[984] (5) regulations governing implementation of SEVIS for J visa,[985] and (6) regulations governing the collection of SEVIS fees.[986]

Such regulations, however, were not forthcoming until the final compliance date of January 30, 2003. Throughout the implementation period, from October 26, 2001 to January 2003, the INS and the DHS had failed to provide the schools, administrators, students, visitors and vendors with necessary and timely regulations and guidelines to put SEVIS into place before January 30, 2003.

The USAPA set a January 30, 2001, deadline for compliance. On May 16, 2002, the Service published a proposed rule[987] to implement the foreign student data electronic collection, reporting, and tracking process as mandated under Section 641 of the IIRIRA of 1996. On June 13, 2002, the INS released the final Interface Control Document to third-party vendors to facilitate SEVIS software development.[988] On July 1, 2002, INS invited voluntary participation in SEVIS. The final regulations, entitled "Retention and Reporting of Information for F, J, and M Nonimmigrants; Student and Exchange Visitor Information System (SEVIS)" was finally published on December 11, 2002.[989]

By September 24, 2002, approximately 125 days before the final compliance day, a number of key regulations were yet to be finalized and published.[990] These included SEVIS regulations governing international student visas (F and M) to be issued by DHS,[991] exchange visitor visas (J) to be issued by the State Department,[992] and recertification of schools authorized to issue I-20s.[993]

---

[980] Shelley Rodgers, Colleges, Universities Consider SEVIS Implementation, http://www.aacrao.org/transcript/index.cfm?fuseaction=show printanddoc id=610 (Jan. 28, 2002)..

[981] Shelley Rodgers, Possibly Six SEVIS Regulations Outstanding, http://www.aacrao.org/transcript index.cfm?fuseaction=show printanddoc id=684 (Mar. 20, 2002).

[982] Id.

[983] Id.

[984] Id.

[985] Id.

[986] Id.

[987] 67 Fed. Reg. at 34862.

[988] PeopleSoft, supra n. 48.

[989] 67 Fed. Reg. at 76256.

[990] H.R. Subcomms. on 21st Cent. Competitiveness and Select Educ. of the Comm. on Educ. and the Workforce, Homeland Security: Tracking International Students in Higher Education - Progress and Issues Since 9-11, 107th Cong. 107 (Sept. 24, 2002) (available at http://edworkforce.house.gov/hearings/107th/21st/studvisa 92402/ward.htm) (testimony of Dr. David Ward).

[991] Id. ("They must still be reviewed and cleared by both the Justice Department and the Office of Management and Budget (OMB).").

[992] Id. ("The draft regulations have been under review at OMB for more than 100 days... . Again, without regulations, we do not know what is expected of us.")

[993] Id.

3. Problems with Inadequate Regulations

Not only was there a lack of implementation regulations to put SEVIS into practice, the regulations that were promulgated were often incomplete and imprecise. This caused much anxiety when the deadline for SEVIS approached. For example, no one at the schools or the DHS knew how to deal with the following scenario: Both parents of a J-2 dependent have J-1 status, and one of those parents was graduating from school.[994] The question was whether the J-2 dependent record should be amended to shift the dependency status to the non-graduating J-1 parent and reference the ID in the remarks, whether the J-2 student "graduated" with the graduating J-1, or whether a new and independent J-2 file should be created for the child.[995] The DHS representative asserted that they should change the record according to the first option listed above.[996]

Similarly, the INS was not ready to deal with OPT issues without a clear guideline. Schools were complaining about the "absence of post-completion OPT language in the proposed F regulation."[997] NAFSA pointed out that there was an ambiguity in the regulations because paragraphs three and four of 8 CFR 214.2(f)(10)(2)(A), dealing with "optional practical training (OPT) after completion of studies," was absent from the INS proposed rule, but post-completion OPT was alluded to in other INS literature.[998] INS agreed to look into the problem.[999]

In the proposed regulations for implementing SEVIS, information regarding issuing I-20's for F-2 dependents was absent, although it was contained in the supplementing language to the proposed rule.[1000] INS promised to investigate.[1001]

4. Problems with Conflicting Regulations

There were often conflicts between the INS rule and the DOS rule. For example, in December 2003, language in the supplementary text of the J SEVIS rule, indicated that J-2s must change status in order to pursue a course of study "other than vocational or recreational." However, there was no corresponding language in the Federal Regulatory Rule text. The F SEVIS rule, at 248.3(e)(2) suggested that dependents of a J-1 may attend school, provided the principal maintains status.[1002]

DOS confirmed that full-time students were not permitted in J-2 status, except for J-2 dependents enrolling in K-12 programs.[1003] However, the intention of this rule was expressed only in the preamble to the J regulations and not in the language of the SEVIS rule itself.[1004]

---

[994] NGLU 2003-11-b, supra n. 263, at "1. J-2 and F-2 Dependents Moving from One Parent Record to Other."

[995] Id.

[996] Id.

[997] NGLU 2002-0605, supra n. 224, at "Issue: Absence of Post-Completion OPT Language from in the Proposed Regulation."

[998] Id.

[999] Id.

[1000] Id. at "Issue: I-20's for F-2 dependents."

[1001] Id.

[1002] See Memo. from Jim Ellis, Dir, Auburn U. and Derek Yu, Asst. Dir., Auburn U., to all international students and scholars enrolled at Auburn U., INS and Department of State F, M, and J SEVIS Rule Changes, 10. Dependents (Dec. 16, 2002) (available at http://www.auburn.edu/academic/other/international education/office/advisories/newregs121602.htm) ("At this time there is conflicting information in the regulations on whether J-2 dependents may study full time - to be safe assume that J-2's are NOT allowed to pursue full time study.").

[1003] Id

[1004] Id.

In order to legally prohibit J-2 dependents from studying, the SEVIS regulations would have to be changed. DOS stated that they intended to change the language in their final SEVIS regulations.[1005] Such a correction would also have to be coordinated, however, with a corresponding change to INS regulations, which on their face permitted full-time study by J-2 dependents.[1006] Until these corrections to the regulations are made, there is no restriction on study for J-2 dependents.

5. Problems with Unclear Regulations

Many of the regulations were ambiguous and unclear. A case on point involved the reporting of timely participation of exchange visitors in designated programs. As NAFSA understood it, J program sponsors were required to report an exchange visitor's participation within thirty days of the program start date. However, what should be done if the exchange visitor enters the country late, for example two months after the program start date? NAFSA requested the DOS to clarify in writing that "sponsors are required to report exchange visitor's participation within thirty days of the start date on the DS-2019; or, if the exchange visitor enters after the DS-2019 start date, the sponsor is required to report participation within thirty days of inspection at the POE."[1007] The INS responded by stating that if the EV arrives after the start date on the DS-2019, INS would most likely be given an I-515 upon admission. When an EVP knew or has reason to suspect that an exchange visitor would not arrive by the start date on the DS-2019, the EVP could go into SEVIS and amend the program start before the EV's initial entry. Ideally a new DS-2019 should be sent to the EV. This complicated response was confusing and confounding to the EV participating programs. Any good faith misunderstanding of such an unclear provision might result in the EV being declared out of status and rejected by DHS-INS officials at the POE.

6. Problems with and Application of Regulations

Schools were very much concerned with inconsistent interpretation and differential application of SEVIS regulations. It became clear that different schools and government agencies interpreted SEVIS legal requirements differently. Furthermore, different officials within the same agency also had a different understanding of the rules and applied them differently. This resulted in conflicting guidance and contradictory instructions. The following examples illustrate the nature and magnitude of the problem.

(a) DHS v. DOS

Conflicts sometimes arose between federal regulations, SEVIS rules, and DOS policy. A relevant example is the conversion of status between professors and researchers. Federal regulations provided that change of status between professor and research scholars did not require approval of DOS.[1008] But the SEVIS rules did not allow for such a change of status without a formal request for change of category.[1009] DHS has taken the position that whether it was a change in category requiring approval was to be taken on a case by case basis that

---

[1005] Id.
[1006] 8 C.F.R. ?48.3 (2006).
[1007] NGLU 2003-04-a, supra n. 224, at "12. OPT Adjudication and Status."
[1008] NGLU 2003-11-b, supra n. 263, at "10. Changing from J Professor to J Research Scholar."
[1009] Id.

"may require an official request for change in category."[1010] The schools who relied on federal regulations might find their visitors rejected by the SEVIS.

(b) DHS v. Help Desk

What happens if a J-1 student came to the United States with a J-2 listed as a dependent, but the J-2 did not enter at the same time?[1011] However, upon the J-1's entry, the J-2's record was also automatically validated.[1012] The Help Desk said that canceling the J-2's record pending his application for a visa, or if he already had a visa, his entry to the United States would suffice. Then re-adding them to the J-1's record and re-issuing a DS-2019 when either of those situations occurred was acceptable.[1013] The DHS disagreed and wanted the J-2 visa kept current until the J-2 was ready to travel with the original DS 2019.[1014]

Help Desk told schools that "if a pending OPT student's case is not adjudicated within 60 days of program completion, the student would have to return home."[1015] However, DHS suggested that the student's status would not be automatically terminated even if OPT was not approved within 60 days, but instead he or she would be placed on an "alert" list.[1016]

(c) DHS v. Schools

A school raised the issue of whether an approved OPT student was considered to be engaging in another level of education when he took a supplementary course during his OPT employment.[1017] The rule was that students could take courses during their OPT employment provided that the classes were not in furtherance of a different educational aspiration, but were instead ""incidental"" to the students' employment.[1018] DHS was of the opinion that the student could take an OPT related course if it was required by OPT employment.[1019] However, NAFSA wanted reassurance that the DHS interpretation was given to other administrators, such as the "DHS Service Centers, district offices, enforcement units, and ports of entry, to ensure consistency of interpretation."[1020]

Regulations for F SEVIS required that schools request OPT training before the student finished their studies.[1021] Some Service Centers denied paperwork received after the students completed their studies, but NAFSA contended that the regulation could be interpreted to provide that the important date is the one on which DSO approval is given for an OPT training request in SEVIS instead of when the Service Center received I-765 forms.[1022] However, the DHS insisted that the correct date was "before the student's program end date."[1023]

[1010] Id.
[1011] NGLU 2003-10-a, supra n. 270, at "9. J-2 Visas and Validations."
[1012] Id.
[1013] Id.
[1014] Id.
[1015] NGLU 2003-10-a, supra n. 270, at "9. J-2 Visas and Validations."
[1016] Id.
[1017] NGLU 2003-09-a, supra n. 267, at "2. OPT and incidental study."
[1018] Id.
[1019] Id.
[1020] Id.
[1021] NGLU 2004-01-a, supra n. 262, at "5. CIS says OPT I-765 must be received on or before Program End Date."
[1022] Id.
[1023] Id.

(d) School (DOS) v. Help Desk

One typical problem was that the Help Desk would give out erroneous information based on SEVIS requirements or Help Desk working practices not conforming to the law. In one case, the Help Desk informed the schools that they must register F-1 students within thirty days of when the program started. In another case the Help Desk advised the school to change the program start day to correspond with registration day.

Additionally, many times DHS did not have a ready answer for questions and various situations. For example, a J-1 student was leaving the country and leaving a J-2 dependent behind with his spouse who was also a J-1. The DHS pled ignorance and stated that it would need to research the issue.[1024]

7. Problems of Lack of Fit between SEVIS Regulations and Technology

In many instances the SEVIS regulations did not match the technology operating requirements, or SEVIS technology did not otherwise support SEVIS laws and regulations. For instance, J-1 regulations called for the schools to "update the Exchange Visitor's SEVIS record to reflect details of such [on campus] employment."[1025] However, the SEVIS software program has no such entry function.[1026] Another problem occurred when SEVIS was originally programmed. The law provided for designations in length of one, two, or five years.[1027] However, new regulations published just before SEVIS went into service only provided for a two-year re-designation period for the sponsored program.[1028] The disparity created confusion and was never satisfactorily resolved.

Thirdly, NAFSA informed DHS on August 13, 2003 that the states of Serbia and Montenegro were not listed in the SEVIS country codes. DHS said they would update the list that day.[1029] But as of November, the country codes had not been included.[1030] Consequently, students from this country had a difficult time getting their applications processed.

Another problem occurred when the SEVIS program did not have an extension of stay for more than twelve months. Schools brought the issue up and expected changes to the SEVIS 4.8 version. DHS promised they would be open to discussion. However, they did not accept the proposed change or commit to a firm date.[1031]

C. Varieties of Technical Problems

At the implementation stage, the schools faced a number of technical problems, some of which were unanticipated, but most of which could have been avoided through detailed planning and testing.

[1024] NGLU 2003-09-b, *supra* n. 264, at "4. How should an A/RO switch the dependents of J-1 parents?"

[1025] NAFSA: Assn. of Intl. Educators, Summary: August 20, 2003. SEVIS Conference Call NAFSA, DHS, DOS, NGLU 2003-08-c, "2. Authorizing On-Campus Employment for Exchange Visitors," (Aug. 20, 2003) (copy on file with Author) (alterations in original).

[1026] *Id.*

[1027] NGLU 2003-09-b, *supra* n. 264, at "7. Redesignation alert for J exchange programs."

[1028] *Id.*

[1029] NGLU 2003-11-b, *supra* n. 263, at "2. Serbia and Montenegro Still Not Listed in SEVIS Country Codes."

[1030] *Id.*

[1031] Id. at "3. When Will F SEVIS Allow Extensions of Stay Over 12 Months?"

1. Problems with Lack of Technical Specifications

David Ward, President of the American Council on Education, on behalf of thirty-three higher education associations, urged the federal government to push for SEVIS implementation only when the technology was fully developed, tested, functional and reliable:

First, the specifications and the interface for batch processing must be finalized ... . Second, the operating software for SEVIS must be made available for purchase, installation, and testing by all institutions in advance of the compliance deadline, including the technical assistance and training in the use of the software that vendors will provide ... . Third, adequate technical training and infrastructure at INS is necessary to ensure that the SEVIS web site is fully interactive for campuses before SEVIS can be said to have gone "live."[1032]

Many problems and issues confronted by the schools, especially in the early SEVIS implementation stages, resulted from the schools inadequate technological capacity (hardware, software, or human resources) to interface with SEVIS. INS promised, but never released technical specifications for SEVIS until it was too late for them to be implemented. Therefore, schools wishing to develop their own software were not able to do so. A school wanting to buy software in the market discovered that such software was not available because software vendors were not provided with technical details to develop SEVIS compatible software.[1033]

2. Problems with Incompatibility between Systems

Many of the interface problems were caused by the INS imposing standards and requirements that deviated from common accepted industrial standards. In so doing, the universities were forced to adjust their industrial standards to SEVIS protocol at substantial cost and delay to the universities.[1034] The challenge was to create different proprietary and independent data systems that had common data models, ("consolidated business logic")[1035] and separate functional processes that communicated with one another. The question that remained was how the federal SEVIS system could interact freely and securely with local university systems, particularly when the universities and the federal government refused to give up their own authority to define and control the information protocol and process.

3. Problems with Structural Difficulties and System Deficiencies

Structural difficulties that stood in the way of successful interfacing between universities and SEVIS could be categorized as system deficiencies, (2) information deficiencies, and (3) policy deficiencies. These deficiencies are not exhaustive but represent some of the more egregious, recurring, and structural technological lapses to the existing information gathering system and process which promised to hamper the successful launch and effective operations of SEVIS.

[1032] Ltr., *supra* n. 83. "The proposed compliance deadline of January 30, 2003 is unlikely to prove workable, a view shared by the Department of Justice's Office of the Inspector General (OIG). We believe a compliance deadline should be set 180 days after the Inspector General certifies that SEVIS is fully operational and software is available for purchase." Id. ACE recommended that SEVIS compliance deadline be set at 180 days after "Inspector General certifies that SEVIS is fully operational and software is available for purchase." *Id.*

[1033] *Id.*

[1034] *Id.*

[1035] *Id.*

(a) System Deficiencies

The existing university information technology (IT) structure and data collection processes were not designed to serve SEVIS needs. Foreign student information collection has not traditionally been clearly defined on paper, well organized within a department, seamlessly coordinated between business units, or tightly centralized within a university. Many universities have a lack of connectivity between international student offices and other academic departments and administrative offices. For example, if a student is put on academic hold for poor performance or criminal misconduct, such information would usually not be shared with other academic departments and business units. Therefore, the international student office would be excluded. Failure to share information stems from privacy concerns and jurisdictional habits. Thus, if the student chooses not to challenge the academic hold and instead ratifies the problem the international student office will generally not be informed. Even if the international student office received these types of reports, it would be incredibly difficult and time consuming to verify the validity of each of the events to determine whether the information is sufficient to justify reporting it to SEVIS.

(b) Information Deficiencies

In addition to system deficiencies stemming from common practices and operations of a university are informational deficiencies concerning the data that universities presently collect and whether that information is sufficient for SEVIS compliance. Although the final list of SEVIS data elements required by the university's submission remains unknown, existing information systems and databases in most international student offices across the nation are not able to capture all required data elements to fully comply with SEVIS. In order to capture all the information required, the university may come into conflict with various federal, state, and local government's laws, rules, and regulations.

(c) Policy Deficiencies

There was no uniform and university-wide policy governing the collection and processing of SEVIS-related information. As a result, many international student offices and other universities and business units were left to their own devices. Correlating information between the departments was often difficult, and one department may not comply with SEVIS as well as another. In addition, there was no policy or procedure governing when or how to perform compliance audits and data integrity audits sufficient to assure that the data collected was valid and reliable.

4. Problems with Lack of Technical Assistance

Throughout the SEVIS implementation period from 2001 to 2003, NAFSA members repeatedly complained of lengthy hold-times when seeking assistance from the Help Desks. For the month of March 2003, Help Desks nation wide were working on eight hundred calls per day.[1036]

Discrepancies between the various company and administrative records for hold-times varied. For the month of August in 2003, the Help Desk's record showed that the average hold-time was just under two minutes, but that some calls held for as long as twelve

---

[1036] NGLU 2003-09-b, supra n. 264, at "2. Help Desk hold times and statistics.

minutes.[1037] EDS showed that the hold time was about five minutes while NAFSA had reports of a much longer holding pattern.[1038]

As for the data fixes, DHS reported that a total of 3,700 data fix tickets were received over a three month interval.[1039] The data fixes may have included fixes for complex problems and issues involving multiple students.[1040] DHS promised to assist the Help Desk in reducing the workload by "correlating all of the necessary work-arounds," while asking that NAFSA members take more care so there would be fewer requests for data fixes.[1041]

The NAFSA members reported negative encounters in trying to communicate with DHS.[1042] They found that DHS district level student/school officers were often not well-trained to deal with SEVIS technical details nor adequately informed as to the latest developments in procedures and practices.[1043] They also received confusing and conflicting opinions from different agencies and officials.[1044] As a result, many school officials had little faith in DHS in helping with their inquiry or addressing their concerns.[1045]

5. Problems with System (Zero) Tolerance

SEVIS is designed to have zero tolerance for mistakes, which means that once a mistake is made the schools cannot correct it, but instead must ask the Service Center or Help Desks for a data fix ticket. DHS and schools resorted to creative ways to "work around" the problem, which was frequently and routinely done. However, a "work around" might cause unintended and larger problems down the road.[1046] For example, in dealing with erroneous transfer entries, the Help Desk recommended two ways to bypass the system and avoid data fix.[1047] The transfer-out school may either write a letter requesting a transfer or the transfer-in school can create a record for a student and then transfer it back.[1048] DHS did not have a problem with either of these options.[1049] However, SEVIS was not designed for multiple records and files pertaining to an individual student enrolled in the United States.

6. Problems with Program Inflexibility

SEVIS would not make allowance even when there was a mistake on the part of the system administration, and schools were not allowed to make exceptions to SEVIS rules. This included cases when the system was found to be dysfunctional and the process was flawed. In many cases, a student who intended to enter a new program after he finished an old one would not be able to do so until he obtained an I-20. This sometimes did not allow the transfer school enough time to complete the I-20 form and send it back to the transfer student.

[1037] Id.

[1038] NGLU 2003-03-26, supra n. 224, at "Help Desk Statistics."

[1039] NGLU 2003-09-b, supra n. 264, at "2. Help Desk hold times and statistics."

[1040] Id.

[1041] Id.

[1042] See e.g. NGLU 2003-12-a, supra n. 75, at "11. SEVIS ICE Communication with CIS Student/School Officers" (discussing problems with communication).

[1043] See id. (questioning the current practices regarding information and "timely updates").

[1044] See supra □I(B)(6) (detailing an example of conflicting instructions).

[1045] See NGLU 2003-12-a, supra n. 75, at "11. SEVIS ICE communication with CIS Student/School Officers" (discussing communication issues).

[1046] NGLU 2003-09-c, supra n. 269, at "6. SEVIS Work Arounds" (e.g. SEVIS does not allow for extension of more than one year or 5 years and no data entry from POE).

[1047] NGLU 2003-10-a, supra n. 270, at "8. Transfers and Data Fixes for Transfers."

[1048] Id.

[1049] Id.

There were other cases of inflexibility which negatively impacted the schools and frustrated the students. For example, SEVIS did not allow for "reverse matriculation,"[1050] SEVIS instead only allowed matriculation for ascending degrees, such as Bachelors to Masters, etc., which would not allow for a student initially beginning a Ph.D. to receive a Masters degree at the end of their program.[1051] The response was that DOS did not anticipate this type of scenario.[1052]

7. Problems with Delay in Fixing Problems

There was often a substantial delay in fixing problems due to enormous work loads and limited resources.[1053] For instance, a DSO reported that he made a mistake of authorizing an OPT for student one in the name of student two, with a name identical to student two's name but with a different SEVIS number.[1054] The Texas Service Center corrected the record and student one was afforded a correct OPT.[1055] Student two, however, could not get an OPT recommendation because there was already an OPT recommendation on the record from the earlier mistake.[1056] The Help Desk was called and they promised a fix within twenty-four hours, but failed to do so.[1057]

8. Problems with Lack of Accommodation for Unconventional Programs

SEVIS was not designed to accommodate unconventional programs such as distant learning with occasional onsite visits, short intensive English training courses, or intensive weekend MBA courses. SEVIS required students who took more than eighteen hours a week of instruction to apply for an F-1 visa subject to repeated, steep SEVIS fees and lengthy interviews.[1058] Consulates have been giving B-1 visa when students asked for F-1 as a "work around" to avoid the problem.[1059] DHS insisted that giving the correct visa for the circumstances was the proper course of action.[1060]

9. Problems with Less than Appreciation for Educational Practices

SEVIS was also ill-suited to accommodate educational mishaps and disciplinary actions. NAFSA raised a question about how to process student suspension, termination and reinstatement cases,[1061] which adversely affected students' visa status. The DHS recommended that disciplinary actions should not be recorded until an appeal from the action

---

[1050] NAFSA: Assn. of Intl. Educators, SEVIS Conference Call: NAFSA, DHS, ICE, DOS, EDS, CA, ASSET, CSIET, AASCU, NGLU 2003-10-d, "1. DOS to review "Reverse Matriculation' Scenario" (Oct. 29, 2003) (copy on file with author).

[1051] Id.

[1052] Id.

[1053] NGLU 2003-06-a, *supra* n. 224, at "3.Resoultion of User Problems" (NAFSA was concerned with substantial delay before a problem was fixed and the impacts on schools and students); see also NGLU 2003-11-b, supra n. 263, at "4. Help Desk Statistics on Data Fixes and Help Desk Calls" (the Help Desk usually receives over 11,000 calls a month); NGLU 2003-10-a, supra n. 270, at "7. OPT Errors" (delay in fix because of the quantity of tickets the Help Desk receives).

[1054] NGLU 2003-10-a, *supra* n. 270, at "7. OPT Errors."

[1055] Id.

[1056] Id.

[1057] Id.

[1058] NGLU 2003-10-b, *supra* n. 273, at "7. Short Academic Programs."

[1059] Id.

[1060] Id.

[1061] Id. at "6. Suspensions, Terminations, and Reversals of Academic Decisions."

is final.[1062] If the discipline is recorded, however, the DSO should get a data fix for the record.[1063]

10. Problems with Breach of Confidentiality

There were a few reports of "breaches of confidentiality."[1064] However, the likelihood that these breaches would occur was 1 in 40,000 system transactions.[1065] DHS realized this was not permissible, and a system solution to this problem has been implemented.[1066] Since that time there have been no data crossover problems.[1067]

11. Problems with Trial and Error

The SEVIS system was very much a work-in-progress project for the schools as well as DHS. As end users, the school officers often had to confront problems and deal with issues that were not anticipated or provided for. In such cases, the school officials consulted the Help Desk on a case by case basis while NAFSA met in conferences with DHS to resolve the difficulties. However, the Help Desk usually could not solve the problems and had to refer them to DHS, which would then have to conduct an investigation and research before an answer was available. This often resulted in long delays and great anxiety for the students and visitors.

VII. CONCLUSION: TAKING STOCK

"When the plan meets reality, reality always wins"[1068]

A. Introduction

Everyday SEVIS grows stronger, and more mature. Many predicted that it would fail to materialize, but it miraculously survived. Whatever has transpired, SEVIS will be recorded as the first ever electronic foreign students and visitor tracking system in United States history. Now that it is in place, it is time to take stock.

B. What Has Been Achieved?

While SEVIS has been declared a total success by the Bush administration and its utilities demonstrated in many instances with end users, its process of implementation is an

---

[1062] Id.

[1063] Id.

[1064] Asa Hutchinson, Under Sec., Border and Transp. Sec., Dept. of Homeland Sec., The Conflict Between Science and Security in Visa Policy: Status and Next Steps: Hearing Before the Science Committee House of Representatives, http://www.house.gov/science/hearings/full04/feb25/hutchin.htm (Feb. 25, 2004). ???

[1065] Id.

[1066] Id.

[1067] Id.

[1068] U. Cal.Berkeley, SEVIS @ Berkeley Home Page, http://web.archive.org/web/20031221213424/www.ias. berkeley.edu/siss/hurricane/ (accessed Dec. 21, 2003).

unmitigated failure, reflecting poorly on the Bush administration in leading, planning and executing nation-wide security programs.

The DHS-ICE reported the following achievements.[1069] SEVIS, administered by two agencies, the Immigration and Customs Enforcement (ICE) and U.S. Customs and Border Protection (CBP), has kept the United States safe by tracking foreign exchange students and others who wanted to study in the country.[1070] Two agencies, the ICE and CBP administer the program.[1071] As of July 2004, it reported certifying 8,737 schools and exchange visitor programs, approving 770,000 students and exchange visitors (F-1, M-1, and J-1 visa categories), and maintaining data on more than 100,000 visitors' and students' dependents.[1072] In terms of enforcement, SEVIS referred 36,600 potential student violators to the ICE Compliance Enforcement Unit (CEU) for investigation, of which 2,900 were "no-shows," and "expulsion, suspension, and failure to maintain a full course of study."[1073] As a result 1,591 were referred for more investigation, resulting in 155 arrests.[1074] Under "Enforcement Successes" it reported three sets of cases.[1075] The first case involved a student and an exchange visitor who were investigated for fraudulently applying for "SEVIS certification for schools that were already SEVIS-certified."[1076] There were also several cases of corrupt school officials who sold fraudulent I-20 forms and fake transcripts.[1077] The last case involved a complaint in which a student, supposedly from Nigeria, tried to get duplicate approval of a school, which would give access to not only a user ID and password, but also the ability to create fake Forms I-20.[1078]

C. What Have We Learned?

SEVIS, as designed and now implemented, is far from perfect and leaves much to be desired. As it relates to policy, SEVIS has centralized the control of foreign students and visitors in the hands of DHS, putting security considerations over and above university administrative concerns and international students educational needs. At an operational level, it was found that SEVIS was a learn-as-you-go, trial-and-error project, with many managerial, technical and legal problems that remain unresolved and more problems that are waiting to be discovered.

The DHS forged ahead with the implementation of SEVIS, against arbitrary "imposed" deadlines and without due considerations for the problems it might pose for the schools and the hardships it certainly would inflict on the students. It failed to be successful on at least two counts: universities were frustrated and students were anxious. With days to go before final implementation, schools were not certified, regulations were not promulgated, training

---

[1069] U.S.   Immig.   and   Cust.   Enforcement,   Fact   Sheet,   SEVIS: One   Year   of   Success, http://www.ice.gov/graphics/news/factsheets/sevis 1year success.htm (Aug. 3, 2004).
[1070] *Id.*
[1071] *Id.*
[1072] *Id.*
[1073] *Id.*
[1074] *Id.*
[1075] *Id.* at "Enforcement Successes."
[1076] *Id.*
[1077] *Id.*
[1078] *Id.*

was not provided, and program codes were not released. During implementation, SEVIS was not accessible, files were misplaced, Help Desks were unhelpful, inquiries were not responded to, data fixes were long delayed, and more.

The high-handed manner in which the SEVIS system was imposed on the universities - from lack of consultation to unfunded mandate - spoiled the delicate working relationship between the universities and the government, making future cooperation difficult, if not impossible.

Finally, the rush to put SEVIS in place without due consideration of the universities' educational philosophy and foreign students' welfare has eroded the hard-earned status and leadership of United States higher education systems throughout the world. Increasingly, foreign students are staying away instead of yearning to come to United States to study, to learn, and to exchange experiences and ideas.

Chapter 5

IMPACT ON MUSLIMS

And we must be mindful that as we seek to win the war that we treat Arab Americans and
Muslims with the respect they deserve.
- Statement from President Bush (September 13th, 2001)[1079]

The act, written in response to the September 11 attacks, in theory applies to all citizens,
but it was written with Muslims in mind and in practice denies them their civil liberties by
empowering law enforcement authorities to raid their homes, offices, and mosques in the
name of the war on terrorism.
- Geneive Abdo (2005)[1080]

INTRODUCTION

This Chapter is a case study of how USAPA and related anti-terrorism measures impact upon on the Muslim community.[1081] Muslims, individually and as a group, have been singled out for special (mis)treatment since 9/11.[1082] They were treated to domestic registration,

---

[1079] Press Release, White House Office of the Press Sec'y, President Pledges Assistance for New York in Phone Call with Pataki, Giuliani: Remarks by the President in Telephone Conversation with New York Mayor Giuliani and New York Governor Pataki (Sept. 13, 2001), http://www.whitehouse.gov/news/releases/2001/09/20010 913-4.html.

[1080] Geneive Abdo, "Islam in America: Separate but Unequal," *Wash. Q.* 7, 12(2005); see also Chrystie Flournoy Swiney, "Racial Profiling of Arabs and Muslims," in the **US: *Historical, Empirical, and Legal Analysis Applied to the War on Terrorism, 3 Muslim World Journal of Human Rights* 1 (2006) (Post-9/11 profiling of Muslims is not a cost-effective deterrent to terrorists and threats. The government needs to re-evaluate post-9/11 anti-Muslim policies and practices in place) available at http://www.bepress. com/mwjhr/vol3/iss1/art3.

[1081] For another case study, see Sally Howell, "Cracking Down on Diaspora: Arab Detroit and America's "War on Terror" *Anthropological Quarterly* Volume 76 (3): 443-462 (2003)

[1082] Muslims were not the only group of people who were subject to indiscriminate application of post-9/11 counter-terrorism measures. See e.g. David Morton, "Detained," *Cleveland Free Times*, Dec. 17, 2001, http://alternet.org/story/12092 (describing an incident in which eleven Israelis were rounded up and questioned after being picked up for visa violations. They were detained in local jails with no legal justification, rights or due process); see also Eric Lichtblau, "New Details on F.B.I. Aid for Saudis after 9/11," *N.Y. Times*, Mar. 27, 2005, at 8 (describing how some Arabs and Muslims were luckier than others. The Bush administration helped hundreds of prominent Arabs escape the frontal attack of the 9/11 aftermath) available at http://www.nytimes.come/2005/03/27/ politics/27exodus.html.

airport profiling, and immigration detention.[1083] The USAPA enables the government to monitor, investigate, detain, and deport Muslims legally in the name of security, without rudimentary due process of the law and in gross violation of their rights.[1084] All in all "U. S. government "anti-terrorism" policies and initiatives launched since the September 11 attacks have had a profoundly negative impact on Arabs and Muslims in the U. S., largely because they have targeted members of these communities indiscriminately. Of the roughly twenty policies and initiatives implemented in the first twelve months after 9/11, fifteen explicitly targeted Arabs and Muslims."[1085]

This case study also supplies evidence for the assessment of the impact and implications of the USAPA. The USAPA is now five years old and little is known about the implementation, and in turn the impact, of the Act. While the Bus administration, as supported by a Republican Congress,[1086] was able to renew the USAPA in 2006,[1087] there is very little information on the law's impact and virtually no assessment of its effectiveness.[1088] The Bush administration has routinely resorted to national security,[1089] executive privilege,[1090] operational secrecy,[1091] or Presidential fiat[1092] to keep the specifics of the USAPA secret from the public. As time passes, the unintended consequences of the Act and

---

[1083] See Louise Cainkar, "Post 9/11 Domestic Policies Affecting U. S. Arabs and Muslims: A Brief Review," 24 *Comp. Stud. S. Asia, Afr. and Middle E.* 247 (2004).

[1084] See, e.g., Office of the Inspector Gen., U.S. Dep't of Justice, 107th Cong., Report to Congress on Implementation of Section 1001 of the USA PATRIOT Act: (as required by Section 1001(3) of Public Law 107-56) (2002); Philip Shenon, "Report on U.S. Antiterrorism Law Alleges Violations of Civil Rights," *N.Y. Times*, July 21, 2003 at A1.

[1085] Louise Cainkar, "Post 9/11 Domestic Policies Affecting U. S. Arabs and Muslims: A Brief Review," *Comparative Studies of South Asia, Africa and the Middle East* - Volume 24 (1): 245-248 (2004)

[1086] CNN, "House Approves Renewal of Patriot Act: Critics Voice Concern Over Civil Liberties," *CNN.com*, July 22, 2005, http://www.cnn.com/2005/POLITICS/07/21/ patriot.act ("The final vote was 257-171. The bill makes permanent 14 of 16 provisions in the act set to expire next year and extends two others for another 10 years ... In the final tally, 14 Republicans bucked Bush and the party leadership to vote against the Patriot Act renewal. Among Democrats, 43 supported it, while 156 voted no"); see also CNN, "Patriot Act Renewal Fails in Senate: GOP Fights to Save Provisions Before End-of-Year Deadline," *CNN.com*, Dec. 16, 2005, http://www.cnn.com/2005/POLITICS/12/16/patriot.act (discussing the defeat of the renewal of USAPA bill by filibuster in the Senate).

[1087] See Associated Press, "President urges renewal of Patriot Act," *USA Today*, Apr. 17, 2004, available at http://www.usatoday.com/news/washington/2004-04-17-bush-terroris m_x.htm ("To abandon the Patriot Act would deprive law enforcement and intelligence officers of needed tools in the war on terror, and demonstrate willful blindness to a continuing threat"); see also R. Jeffrey Smith, "Attorney General Urges Renewal of Patriot Act: Gonzales Gives First Policy Speech," *Wash. Post*, Mar. 1, 2005, at A2 (USAPA "has helped prevent additional terrorist attacks ... Giving law enforcement the tools they need to keep America safe while honoring our values").

[1088] Nancy Kranich, "Commentary: The Impact of the USA PATRIOT Act: An Update," The Free Expression Policy Project (FEPP), Brennan Center for Justice at NYU School of Law, Aug. 27, 2003, http://www.fepproject.org/commentaries/ patriotactupdate.html.

[1089] See DOJ Oversight: Terrorism and other Topics Before the H. Comm. On the Judiciary, 108th Cong. 16 (2004) (When Senator Grassley asked why the Attorney General classified information about whistleblower Edmonds, a translator who was fired from the FBI, the Attorney General said, "If I am not mistaken, in the matter to which you make reference, the national interests of the United States would be seriously impaired if information provided in one briefing to the Congress were to be generally available").

[1090] See *id.* at 98. (When questioned by Senator Durbin on a memo defining permissible torture by Assistant Attorney General Jay Bybee, the Attorney General refused to answer on executive privilege grounds).

[1091] Seth Rosenfeld, "9-11-01: Looking Back, Looking Ahead: A Nation Remembers: Patriot Act's Scope, Secrecy Ensnare Innocent, Critics Say," *S.F. Chron.*, Sept. 8, 2002, at A1, ("So far, the full impact of the Patriot Act remains unknown, partly because the Bush administration has insisted on secrecy that some courts and members of Congress have called excessive").

[1092] See Edward Epstein, "Bush to Face Tough Questions Over Patriot Act, Spy Orders," *S.F. Chronicle*, Dec. 24, 2005, at A11. (The President ordered electronic surveillance on US soil without consulting Congress).

related anti-terrorism measures have mushroomed. The adverse impacts of the USAPA are increasingly felt throughout American society. Foreign students have been deterred from coming to the United States.[1093] Librarians have started to concern themselves with government monitoring activities.[1094] Neither of these examples, however, compare to the impact felt by Muslims in the U.S., the group most affected by the Act.[1095]

The purpose is to put a public face on many private grievances[1096] and place public policy debate in a community context.[1097] In essence, the chapter contributes to our understanding of the USAPA by providing private voices and grassroots perspectives; something that is missing in post 9/11 – USAPA narratives and dialogues.[1098]

This chapter provides a brief overview of how Muslims were treated after 9/11. It documents how the USAPA and related measures have been used to monitor, investigate, detain, and deport Muslim U.S. citizens in violation of their civil rights.[1099] Of particular importance, is how the life circumstances of the Muslims in America have changed for the worse as a result of zealous enforcement and discriminatory application of the USAPA.[1100] Ultimately, this Chapter seeks to provide detail facts and a rich context to ascertain the implications of 9/11 on American society; a major objective of this book.[1101] This chapter points to the need for systematic and comprehensive investigation into the impact of the USAPA on the Muslim community in the U.S., and in turn analyzes the implications of 9/11 on American society.[1102]

This Chapter is organized into the following sections. Section I is a "Literature Review" of popular and scholarly readings, which notes that while there were many discussions over the impact of the USAPA, many of them were produced by interested parties, and more than a few of them are tainted by motives ranging from patriotism to political gamesmanship.[1103]

[1093] See Adrian Arroyo, "Comments: The USA PATRIOT Act and the Enhanced Border Security and Visa Entry Reform Act: Negatively Impacting Academic Institutions by Deterring Foreign Students from Studying in the United States," 16 *Transnat'l Lawy*. 411 (2003), available at http://www.iienetwork.org/index.v3page?d_v=rmandd_mid= 50357andp=33311.

[1094] See American Library Association, "The USA Patriot Act in the Library," http://www.ala.org/ala/oif/ifissues/usapatriotactlibrary.htm (last visited Nov. 6, 2006) ("[The USA PATRIOT Act's]... enhanced surveillance procedures pose the greatest challenge to privacy and confidentiality in the library").

[1095] See infra Section II: "Literature Review."

[1096] Many of the aggrieved people are powerless (foreigners with no representation), marginalized (minority under majority rule) and demonized (terrorists as sub-human), their grievances were justified in careless and callous bureaucratic terms, e.g., casualties of war.

[1097] See Chapter Seven: "Grassroots resistance".

[1098] There are many 9/11 stories, the official version – war on terror – is but one that is rehearsed and imposed, ultimately debated and dominated. "Narratives of 9/11" http://www.georgetown.edu/users/tarverws/number2.htm

[1099] See Cato Institute, Cato Handbook for Congress: Policy Recommendations for the 108th Congress 117-24 (Edward H. Crane and David Boaz eds., 2003); AsiaSource, Interview by Nevmeen Shaikh with Dalia Hashad, Advocate, ACLU (Apr. 10, 2003), http://www.asiasource.org/news/special_reports/hashad.cfm.

[1100] See Steven Salaita, "Ethnic Identity and Imperative Patriotism: Arab Americans Before and After 9/11,' 32 C. *Literature* 146 (2005) (examining "the effects of 9/11 on Arab Americans and other minorities").

[1101] Anthony Petrosino (American Academy of Arts and Sciences and Harvard University), Robert F. Boruch (University of Pennsylvania), David Farrington (University of Cambridge), Lawrence Sherman (University of Pennsylvania) and David Weisburd (Hebrew University and University of Maryland, "Toward Evidence-Based Criminology and Criminal Justice: The Campbell Collaboration." (Criminal justice policy must be informed by empirical research and with the use of meta-analysis.) http://www.jrsa.org/pubs/forum/archives/Apr01.html

[1102] Chapter Eight: "Conclusion."

[1103] Chapter Three: "Legislative Climate".

Section II details the "Research Questions and Model of Analysis." Section III provides an overview of "Post 9/11 Counter-Terrorism Strategy", such as total information control. Section IV discusses "Post 9/11 Counter-Terrorism Operations" including FBI dragnet and INS preventive detention. The Conclusion provides a detailed account and in-depth analysis of the "Impact Upon the Muslim Community and Implications for America."

I. LITERATURE REVIEW

A cursory review of news accounts,[1104] investigative reports,[1105] popular readings,[1106] commissioned studies,[1107] Congressional testimonies,[1108] forum presentations,[1109] learned treatises,[1110] and journal articles[1111] makes it clear that 9/11 has had a grave impact on

---

[1104] "Rosenfeld," *supra*, not 13.

[1105] "Caught in the Crossfire: Arab Americans in Wartime" (PBS television broadcast Sept. 4, 2002) (following the lives of three Arab American New Yorkers after the September 11th terrorist attacks).

[1106] William Fisher, "Govt Targets Arab, Muslim Americans Again," *Antiwar.com*, Oct. 5, 2004, http://www.antiwar.com/ips/fisher.php?articleid=3707 (FBI agents are again contacting Arab and Muslim Americans for "voluntary interviews" before Nov. 2, 2004 election to intimidate electorate or impress would-be voters of war on terror); see also Abdus Sattar Ghazali, "Muslims American Muslims Four Years After 9/11," *American Muslim Perspective*, Sept. 11, 2005, http://www.amperspective.com/html/four_years_after_9-11.html ("Stereotyping and scapegoating Muslims and Islam remain a popular past time for the US media ... ").

[1107] Arab Am. Inst., "Healing the Nation: The Arab American Experience After September 11" (2002), http://www.arabvoices.net/healing_the_nation.pdf.

[1108] See, e.g., Detainees: Hearing Before the Sen. Comm. on the Judiciary, 109th Cong. (2005) (statement of Glenn A. Fine, Inspector Gen. U.S. Dep't of Justice) (summarizing findings and recommendations to OIG's June 2003 report entitled "The September 11 Detainees: A Review of the Treatment of Aliens Held on Immigration Charges in Connection with the Investigation of the September 11 Attacks" and December 2003 report, entitled "Supplemental Report on September 11 Detainees' Allegations of Abuse at the Metropolitan Detention Center in Brooklyn, New York"); America after 9/11: Freedom Preserved or Freedom Lost?: Hearing Before U.S. Sen. Judiciary Comm., 108th Cong. (2003) (testimony of Dr. James Zogby, President of Arab Am. Inst.); Implementation of the USA Patriot Act: Prohibition of Material Support Under Sections 805 of the USA Patriot Act and 6603 of the Intelligence Reform and Terrorism Prevention Act of 2004: Hearing Before the Subcomm. On Crime, Terrorism, and Homeland Security of the H. Comm. on the Judiciary, 109th Cong. (2005).

[1109] See Virginia Law, Panelists Examine Consequences of Patriot Act, Oct. 3, 2005, http://www.law.virginia.edu/home2002/html/news/2005_fall/patriotact.htm (Panelists included: Imad Damaj, President, Va. Muslim Coal. For Pub. Affairs; Ken Willis, Executive Dir., ACLU of Va.; Robert M. O'Neil, Law Prof. and Dir. of the Thomas Jefferson Ctr.).

[1110] See, e.g., Nat Hentoff, *The War on the Bill of Rights - and the Gathering Resistance* (2003); *Lost Liberties: Ashcroft and the Assault on Personal Freedom* (Cynthia Brown ed., 2003) [with an introduction by Aryeh Neier]; *The War on Our Freedoms: Civil Liberties in an Age of Terrorism* (Richard C. Leone and Greg Anrig, Jr. eds., 2003); David Lyon, *Surveillance After September 11* (2003); Barbara Olshansky and the Ctr for Constitutional Rights, *Secret Trials and Executions: Military Tribunals and the Threat to Democracy* (2002); Christian Parenti, *The Soft Cage: Surveillance in America from Slavery to the War on Terror* (2003).

[1111] Abdo, Geneive, "Islam in America: Separate but Unequal," *The Washington Quarterly* - Volume 28 (4): 7-17 (2005) (Greatest challenge at home is to deal with Muslim culture and identity), Bill Ong Hing, "Misusing Immigration Policies in the Name of Homeland Security," *CR: The New Centennial Review*, Volume 6 (1): 195 – 224 (2006) (Evidence points to misuse of immigration law to exclude undesirable aliens), Sally Howell, "Cracking Down on Diaspora: Arab Detroit and America's "War on Terror" *Anthropological Quarterly* Volume 76 (3): 443-462 (2003) (Bush "war on terror" destroy decades of Muslim social integration and international connectedness in Detroit), Sunaina Maira, "Youth Culture, Citizenship and Globalization: South Asian Muslim Youth in the United States After September 11th," 24 Comparative Studies of South Asia, Africa and the Middle East 219-231 (2004); Muqtedar Khan, "American Muslims and the Rediscovery of America's Sacred Ground," in *Taking Religious Pluralism Seriously: Spiritual Politics on America's Sacred Ground* 137 (Barbara A. McGraw and Renee Formicola eds., 2005), available at

American society. The USAPA, for better or worse, has come to be associated with the war on terror. Harmful impacts of the USAPA on America are evident everywhere. No one was spared, even Senator Kennedy was stopped from boarding a plane five times because his name appeared on the "no fly" list.[1112] All matters have been impacted, including travel and banking.[1113] A systematic and comprehensive analysis of related literature shows that Muslims in America suffered the most as a result of Bush's war on terror.[1114]

One of the most critical and damning reports of post 9/11 anti-terrorism performance and its impact on Muslims and aliens, came from the Office of the Inspector General (OIG) of the Department of Justice (DOJ). The OIG testified before the Congress as to the plight of 9/11 detainees:

> Our review determined that 762 aliens were detained on immigration charges in connection with the PENTTBOM[1115] investigation in the first 11 months after the terrorist attacks ... Our review found that many September 11 detainees did not receive notice of the charges against them in a timely manner ... More than a quarter of the 762 detainees' clearance investigations took longer than 3 months ... Our review found serious problems in the treatment of the September 11 detainees housed at the MDC ... the BOP[1116] imposed a total communications blackout for several weeks on the September 11 detainees held at the MDC[1117] ... Most of the September 11 detainees did not have legal representation prior to their detention at the MDC ... detainees were placed in full restraints whenever they were moved, including handcuffs, leg irons, and heavy chains ... The detainees also were subjected to having two lights illuminated in their cells 24 hours a day ... We concluded that on occasion staff members used strip searches to intimidate and punish detainees.[1118]

The government's high handed counter-terrorism measures and tactics were egregious enough to attract the intervention of the court. The judge in United States v. Awadallah, 202 F. Supp.2d 55, (S.D.N.Y. 2002) opined:

---

http://www.brookings.edu/views/articles/ fellows/khanchapter.pdf (prior to Sept. 11th, the external influence and cultural identity of Muslims was strong. But, after 9/11 the Muslim community was put on the defensive, and that identity was shaken. The USAPA in particular was a rude awaking for the Muslim community).

[1112] Sarah Kehaulani Goo, "Terror no-fly list singled out Kennedy. Senator was stopped 5 times at airports," *S.F. Chronicle,* Aug. 20, 2004, at A3, available at http:// www.sfgate.com/cgi-bin/article.cgi?file=/c/a/2004/08/20/MNGQ28BM1O1.DTL.

[1113] See, e.g., Harvey M. Silets and Carol R. Van Cleef, "Compliance Issues in the Wake of the USA PATRIOT Act," 10 *Journal of Financial Crime* 392 (2003) (compliance with USAPA is costly and non-compliance is devastating); James Fisher, James Gilsinan, Ellen Harshman, Muhammed Islam and Fred Yeager, "Assessing the Impact of the USA PATRIOT Act on the Financial Services Industry," 8 *Journal of Money Laundering Control* 243 (2005) (a cost-benefit analysis of the Act in not possible since the deterrent effect of the Act cannot be ascertained. Experience with the Act to date, however, confirms that there are substantial financial costs and a whole host of privacy concerns).

[1114] Information available on the impact of 9/11 in general and as a result of the USAPA was limited by the pre-9/11 information-communication structure in the Nation and within the immigrants' communities. The reporting on the impact and effect of 9/11 might also be biased against reporting positive news. For a discussion of the information flow within immigrant network pre-and post-9/11, see Suzette B. Masters and Ted Perlmutter, "Reactions of the Immigration Community to the Events of September 11th" (2002), http://www.newschool.edu/icmec/reaction.html (last visited Oct. 18, 2006).

[1115] "PENTTBOM" is the FBI code name for the investigation into the September 11, 2001 "Pentagon/Twin Towers Bombing." It is the largest FBI investigation in U.S. history.

[1116] Acronym stands for "Bureau of Prison."

[1117] Acronym stands for "Metropolitan Detention Center."

[1118] Hearings, *supra* note 30 (statement of Glenn A. Fine).

"Having committed no crime - indeed, without any claim that there was probable cause to believe he had violated any law - [the witness] bore the full weight of the prison system designed to punish convicted criminals as well as incapacitate individuals arrested or indicted for criminal conduct ... [He was] repeatedly strip-searched, shackled whenever he [was] moved, denied food that complies with his religious needs ... prohibited from seeing or even calling his family over the course of 20 days and then [pressured into] testifying while handcuffed to a chair."

The observations of the government and opinions of the court also found their way into the press, as newsworthy human stories. For example, The Times of London in May 2003 received this letter from Tony Willoughby of Willoughby and Partners, a firm of solicitors:

"The head of IT at our law firm is a Muslim. He is a gentleman in every sense of the word. His fanaticism, if he has any, is restricted to cricket. Sunday he went on a business trip to California. On arrival at Los Angeles he was detained and interrogated on suspicion of being a terrorist ... . "For the first 12 hours he was refused access to a telephone. After 16 hours, not having been given any food, he asked if he could have some. He was given ham sandwiches and, when he explained that he could not eat pork, was told: "You eat what you are given.' He did not eat. He was eventually escorted back to the airport in handcuffs and deported."[1119]

The San Francisco Chronicle has documented many instances of the USAPA being used in abusive ways.[1120] For example, a Pakistani scientist and permanent U.S. resident was asked by the FBI why he ordered certain technical books via E-bay.[1121] E-Bay was suspected of providing the information to the FBI.[1122] A group of Middle East students from San Francisco State University turned over to the FBI a fax pointing to an Arabic terrorist warning. Instead of investigating the looming threat, the FBI investigated the student group as suspected terrorists. [1123] A Muslim woman, with a traditional face covering, went to the Bank of America branch near Tarzana (Los Angeles County) where she had been a customer for 10 years, but the bank refused to cash her check or open her account because she looked suspicious.[1124] Randy Hamud, a Muslim lawyer in San Diego who has represented several men detained since September 11, had his phone tapped and computer searched.[1125] Barry Reingold, 61, a retired Pacific Bell employee, was visited and questioned by FBI agents for being critical of US foreign policy when working out in a San Francisco gym.[1126] His name was supplied to the FBI as a result of Operation TIPS (Terrorism Information and Prevention System).[1127] Soon after the September 11 attacks, FBI agents went to the San Francisco home of Kamal Hakim, who came to the United States from Yemen and became a permanent

---

[1119] A Tale of Two Brits, Posting of David Cohen, http://www.brothersjudd.com/ blog/archives/009541.html (Dec. 9, 2003).

[1120] Rosenfeld, *supra* note 13.

[1121] *Id.*

[1122] *Id.*

[1123] *Id.*

[1124] *Id.*

[1125] *Id.*

[1126] *Id.*

[1127] *Id.*

resident in 1995. Hakim, 34, said he voluntarily spoke twice with agents, who asked about his associates, his travels and his views on the attacks.[1128]

Similar observations were made by other individual state government[1129] and university studies.[1130] For instance, the California Senate Office of Research investigated the personal experience and human costs of the war on terror as well as the tactics used by the federal government to prosecute the war on terror. It found that many Muslim, South Asians, and Arab immigrants in California have faced humiliation, embarrassment and intrusions of privacy.[1131] To blame for this problem, is the "sometimes overzealous enforcement of the Patriot Act, including indefinite detentions, secret searches and surveillance and the monitoring of computer traffic." [1132]

The implementation of the Act and related measures has affected Muslims in America individually and collectively, in psychological, social, economic and political terms. Imand Damaj, president of the Virginia Muslim Coalition for Public Affairs, best summed up the Muslim experience post 9/11 by noting:

> After 9/11, I learned that free speech is not an equal right to all of us ... National origin, skin color, accent, religion do make a difference ... It's a sad reality, but that's the reality ... It is hard to quantify the impact of the Patriot Act itself, because it's not only the Patriot Act ... A lot of people feel they are being treated as guilty by association. We know we are under supervision in our mosque and worship centers. We have regular visits from the FBI in Richmond ... We certainly feel that our citizenship is becoming less and less meaningful ... [1133]

As might be expected, popular writings on the Act, like everything in America post 9/11, have been heavily influenced by an acute concern with security and tempered with a visceral reaction of patriotism. Dispassionate impact studies and policy analyses of the Act have been influenced by fierce and fiery partisanship and blind and blinding advocacy, as driven by entrenched fundamental values and established vested interests.[1134] Intellectual debates have been determined more by accepted assumptions and received perspectives than by enlightened theory, discovered evidence and informed discussion. In practical terms, there was a lot more rhetoric and propaganda than painstaking investigation and in-depth analysis. As a result there is more fire than heat, smoke than light.

[1128] Id.

[1129] Max Vanzi, Sen. Office of Research, "The Patriot Act: Other Post-9/11 Enforcement Powers and the Impact on California's Muslim Communities: From a California Perspective: An Analysis of the Fallout from Investigations, Interrogations, Arrests, Detentions, and Deportations," 62 (2004) http://www.sen.ca.gov/sor/reports/REPORTS_BY_SUBJ/PUBLIC_SAFETYanduscore ;JUDICIARY/PATRIOTACT.PDF.

[1130] Stephen Wessler, Ctr. for the Prevention of Hate Violence, Univ. of Southern Me., "After 9-11: Understanding the Impact on Muslim Communities Maine: The Responding to September 11th Project 6-9," 11 (2002) http://www.cphv.usm.maine. edu/911%20Report.pdf (Commissioned study of 2000 to 2500 Muslims living in Maine immediately after 9/11 showed that they were made targets of bias and hate crimes perpetrated by civilians as well as harassment, surveillance and profiling by officials on the other. Muslims were made to feel alienation, anxiety and fear, notwithstanding the many gestures of compassion and good will).

[1131] Vanzi, supra note 51.

[1132] Id.

[1133] Virginia Law, supra note 31.

[1134] David Horowitz, "Unholy Alliance: How the Left Supports the Terrorists at Home," FrontPage Magazine, Sept. 24, 2004, http://www.frontpagemag.com/articles/ Printable.asp?ID=15221.

II. RESEARCH QUESTIONS AND MODEL OF ANALYSIS

This Chapter investigates two major issues: (1) How has the implementation of the USAPA impacted the Muslim community in the U.S.?; and (2) What are some of the more salient and lasting implications of 9/11, including the USAPA, on American society?

For the purpose of this research, the following definition or understanding of Muslim community is adopted:

"Muslim community' denotes a type of a grouping of people, where Islam is the decisive common denominator not only in the religious practice but also in the behavior of the community in general. Secularizing tendencies are often inhibited or reverted by activities of internal fundamentalist movements that advocate obedience to religious prescriptions in everyday life. As for decision-making, a kind of communalism is prevalent, based usually on broader kinship structures.[1135]

There are many ways to observe, measure, document and evaluate the impact and implications of the USAPA on society. As with most other policy analysis research, the observed impact and implications of the USAPA depends as much on where you look as with whom you ask. For example,

What kinds of activities, rights or interests were being affected? The USAPA affected many activities, (e.g. research vs. teaching),[1136] rights, (e.g. academic freedom [1137] vs. right to free speech[1138]), and interests, (e.g. legal vs. economic).[1139]

Who is being affected?[1140] Many people are differently affected by the USAPA, e.g. South Asian Americans, Arab Americans, Muslim Americans, and look alike "Muslims."[1141]

How is the impact being felt? Impact can be felt individually as well as collectively, psychologically and physically, and socially as well as politically.

Finally, and perhaps more significantly, policy and program impact analysis ultimately depends on the perspective adopted and the frame of reference used by the evaluator.

[1135] Jannaidauf, "Major Security Implications of Muslim Communities' Presence in Western-Type Societies," Association for International Affairs, Prague Security Studies Institute (May 23, 2003) http://www.js.amo.cz/archive/me_islam/PP-MuslimCommun.html.

[1136] David Lombard Harrison, "Higher Education Issues After The USA Patriot Act," University of North Carolina, Office of the President available at http://www.nacua.org/ documents/PatriotAct_Outline.pdf (last visited Oct. 18, 2007).

[1137] Beshara Doumani, *Academic Freedom after September 11* (MIT Press, 2006) (Kathleen J. Frydl discussed issues surround on the loyalty-oath and free-speech controversies at the University of California. Amy Newhall described the contentious relationship between universities and the government regarding language acquisition programs. Joel Beinin raised issues with policing of thought in the academy on Middle East subject matters.)

[1138] Resolution On The USA Patriot Act and Related Measures that Infringe on the Rights of Library Users, 2002-2003 CD # 20.1 2003 ALA Midwinter Meeting. http://www.ala.org/ala/washoff/WOissues/civilliberties/theusapatriotact/alaresolution. htm.

[1139] SR 03-17 Bank Secrecy Act Examination Procedures to the USA PATRIOT Act (PDF) (Section 313 of USAPA limits banks' economic activity by prohibiting banks from setting up corresponding accounts for off shore "cell" banks, Section 341 requires banks to share client information with other banks and law enforcement agencies, this affects the propriety rights of banks and privacy rights of banking customers) http://www.ffiec.gov/ffiecinfobase/resources/retail/frb-sr03-17_new_exam_proced_patriot_act.pdf#search='USA%20PATRIO T%20ACT%20and%20Banking'.

[1140] Robert Hefner, "Remarks on Muslim Politics and U.S. Policies: Prospects for Pluralism and Democracy in the Muslim World," The Pew Forum on Religion and Public Life and the Institute on Religion and World Affairs (Sept. 17, 2003).

[1141] Maira, *supra* note 33.

From whose perspective is the impact being evaluated? (E.g. from the perspective of the administration or of society generally).

With what frame of reference is the impact evaluated? (E.g. from a security or liberty perspective)

What is the time frame in evaluating impact? The impact can be measured in long or short-term.

In this study, I will be looking at the impact of the USAPA from the Muslim perspective, as representing their personal experience and group reaction to post 9/11 anti-terrorism measures, specifically those dragnet anti-terrorism operations, such as operation PENTTBOM and "Special Registration" programs.

III. POST 9/11 COUNTER-TERRORISM STRATEGY: TOTAL INFORMATION CONTROL

A. Post 9/11 Strategy and Tactics

On September 11, 2001, immediately after the attack, the President of the United States promised that "the United States will hunt down and punish those responsible for these cowardly acts."[1142] A day later, on September 12, 2001, the President declared war on terrorism, pledging, "[the] United States of America will use all our sources to conquer this enemy."[1143] On September 14, 2001, the President, pursuant to the National Emergencies Act,[1144] declared that the nation was in a state of emergency.[1145] The Attorney General was charged by President Bush with the responsibility of tracking down the terrorists and protecting the nation from another terrorist attack. President Bush instructed Attorney General Ashcroft immediately after the 9/11 attacks, "John, make sure this [9/11 - terrorism] can't happen again."[1146] The Attorney General took the charge serious and issued this warning:

> Let the terrorists among us be warned ... If you overstay your visa, even by one day, we will arrest you. If you violate a local law, you will be put in jail and kept in custody as long as possible. We will use every available statute. We will seek every prosecutorial advantage. We will use all our weapons within the law and under the Constitution to protect life and enhance security for America.[1147]

Immediately after 9/11, the Attorney General acted to empower government officials and restrict the rights of the people, in the name of promoting national security and fighting

---

[1142] Remarks by the President Upon Arrival at Barksdale Air Force Base (Sept. 11, 2001) available at http://www.whitehouse.gov/news/releases/2001/09/20010911-1.html.

[1143] Remarks by the President in Photo Opportunity with the National Security Team (Sept. 12, 2001) available at http://www.whitehouse.gov/news/releases/2001/ 09/20010912-4.html.

[1144] 50 U.S.C. 1601 (2006)

[1145] Declaration of National Emergency by Reason of Certain Terrorist Attacks (Sept. 14, 2001) available at http://www.whitehouse.gov/news/releases/2001/09/ 20010914-4.html.

[1146] Steven Brill, *After: How America Confronted the September 12 Era, 15* (Simon and Schuster) (2003).

[1147] Newsmax.com Wires, "Ashcroft Eager to Expand Police Powers," http:// www.newsmax.com/archives/articles/ 2001/10/25/160238.shtml (last visited Oct. 18, 2006).

terrorism.[1148] According to the Attorney General the key to winning the war on terror is information control, total awareness of the enemy's position, and complete cover-up of the government's activities. The Attorney General sought and achieved complete information blackout of DOJ enforcement operations. On October 12, 2001, Ashcroft issued new Administration policy on the Freedom of Information Act (FOIA), which superseded the Department of Justice FOIA policy memorandum released in October 1993. The old FOIA policy was in favor of liberal information release; there was a "presumption of disclosure" to achieve "maximum possible disclosure." [1149] Contrary to the former presumption, the new policy favors withholding information until justified.[1150] The Ashcroft policy implored the agencies to release information only after careful consideration of national security, law enforcement and personal privacy needs. Under the new policy, the DOJ stands ready to defend against any FOIA request on "sound legal basis."[1151] Research has shown that since 9/11, the Bush administration has consistently denied public access to government information based on the First Amendment or through the FOIA. As observed by Public Citizen, a national, non-profit consumer advocacy organization:

> From the first days of his administration, President Bush has taken steps to tighten the government's hold on information and limit public scrutiny of its activities. Expansive assertions of executive privilege, restrictive views of the Freedom of Information Act, increasing use of national security classification, stonewalling in response to congressional requests for information - all these were evident even before the September 11 attacks. Since then, the clamps on information have only tightened. [1152]

The Bush administration's stance has been supported by sympathetic courts with an inhospitable attitude toward free access to government information when national security is at stake, as well as a willingness to defer to the President in time of war.[1153]

With the new FOIA policy, the Bush administration is able to keep much of its anti-terrorism polices and decision-making secret, thus insulating the administration from public accountability and political consequences. For example, the DOJ successfully withheld "sensitive" USAPA implementation information from being released, such as the number, names and whereabouts of people being held by the government, as well as the frequency,

---

[1148] "Insatiable Appetite: The Government's Demand for New and Unnecessary Powers After September 11," Am. Civ. Liberties Union Rep. (ACLU Washington National Office), Oct. 15 2002, at 2.

[1149] U.S. Gen. Accounting Office, "Freedom of Information Act: Agency Views on Changes Resulting from New Administration Policy," G.A.O Doc. No. 03-981, at 2,4 and 8 (Sept. 2003).

[1150] See John Ashcroft, U.S. Attorney General, Memorandum from Attorney General John Ashcroft to Heads of All Federal Departments and Agencies on The Freedom of Information Act (Oct. 12, 2001) available at http://www.usdoj.gov/oip/foiapost/ 2001foiapost19.htm. (This memo was buttressed by another memo calling for reclassification of "Previously Unclassified or Declassified Information" and more restrictive release of "Sensitive But Unclassified Information." Memorandum from Andrew H. Card, Jr., Assistant to the President and Chief of Staff to Heads of Executive Departments and Agencies on Action to Safeguard Information Regarding Weapons of Mass Destruction and Other Sensitive Documents Related to Homeland Security (Mar. 19, 2002) available at http://www.usdoj.gov/oip/foiapost/2002foiapost10.htm).

[1151] *Id.* ("When you carefully consider FOIA requests and decide to withhold records, in whole or in part, you can be assured that the Department of Justice will defend your decisions unless they lack a sound legal basis or present an unwarranted risk of adverse impact on the ability of other agencies to protect other important records").

[1152] "Public Citizen," Bush Secrecy.org, available at http://www.bushsecrecy.org/ (last visited Nov. 15, 2006).

[1153] See Mary-Rose Papandrea, "Under Attack: The Public's Right to Know and the War on Terror 25 B.C.," *Third World L.J.* 34-81, 36 (2005) (discussing President Bush's attitude and policy toward information control).

manners and targets for which Section 215 USAPA powers have been used. [1154] The DOJ justified withholding of information from public disclosure on the grounds of "mosaic theory," which supposes that innocuous pieces of information can be used by terrorists to discover anti-terrorism strategies or tactics. [1155]

Consistent with Attorney General John Ashcroft's strategy of secrecy, he refused to release information to the Congress on anti-terrorism operations and measures. [1156] This led Senator Leahy to call for more cooperation between the legislative and executive branches in fighting the war on terror:

Attorney General Ashcroft has repeatedly declined to appear before the Judiciary Committee to answer questions, and his Department is painfully slow to respond to written requests for information. To quote my friend Senator Grassley, "getting information from the Justice Department under Ashcroft is like pulling teeth." By ignoring oversight requests until answers are moot or outdated, and responding in only vague and conclusory fashion, if at all, the Justice Department frustrates our constitutional system of checks and balances, and sows the sort of public distrust that now accompanies the USAPA. [1157]

Along the same vein, the Attorney General resisted public request and court order for information. In 2002, the Attorney General successfully had state and local governments refuse to release names of people detained since September 11, with the use of the preemption doctrine, which states that federal law supersedes any state or local claims to the information.[1158] In January 2002, the ACLU of New Jersey sued for the release of ghost detainee's name under the New Jersey right-to-know law.[1159] A New Jersey court granted the relief on April 22, 2002. [1160] Ashcroft declined to follow state court order.[1161]

On September 21, 2001, 10 days after 9/11, Chief Immigration Judge Michael Creppy issued a memo [1162] closing all deportation proceedings to the public and press,[1163] if and when

---

[1154] See, e.g., Ctr. for Nat'l Sec. Studies v. Dep't of Justice, 215 F. Supp. 2d 94 (D.C.C. 2002); Am. Civil Liberties Union v. Dep't of Justice, 321 F. Supp. 2d 24 (D.D.C. 2004); Am. Civil Liberties Union and Elec. Privacy Info. Ctr. v. Dep't of Justice, Civil Action No. 05-845 (D.D.C. April 2005) ("EPIC, joined by the American Civil Liberties Union and library and booksellers' organizations, filed suit on October 24, 2002 under the FOIA in seeking the disclosure of information concerning implementation of the controversial USA PATRIOT Act"); Elec. Privacy Info. Ctr. v. Dep't of Justice, No. 05-845 (D. D.C. Nov. 16, 2005) (EPIC files a federal complaint forcing the FBI to disclose information about its use of USAPA investigative powers under the sunset provisions).

[1155] David E. Pozen, Note, "The Mosaic Theory, National Security, and the Freedom of Information Act," 115 *Yale L.J.* 628 (Dec. 2005) (this Note traces the evolution of the "mosaic theory" in the Freedom of Information Act (FOIA) national security jurisprudence. It observes that after 9/11 the "mosaic theory" was heavily borrowed to justify executive secrecy and elicit judicial deference).

[1156] See generally People for the American Way, "Two Years After 9/11: Ashcroft's Assault on the Constitution," Sept. 9, 2003 available at http://www.pfaw.org/pfaw/ dfiles/file_232.pdf.

[1157] Statements on Introduced Bills and Joint Resolutions Congressional Record Oct. 1, 2003, P. S12278-S12299 available at http://www.fas.org/irp/congress/2003_cr/ s1695.html.

[1158] Release of Information Regarding Immigration and Naturalization Service Detainees in Non-Federal Facilities, 67 Fed. Reg. 19, 508 (Proposed Apr. 22, 2002) (to be codified at 8 C.F.R. pts. 236 and 241).

[1159] N.J. high court won't hear appeal on releasing detainees' names Associated Press, July 10, 2002. (The N.J. Supreme refused to hear appeal of state appellate court decision to allow the federal government to withhold name of 9/11 detainees held in N.J. state prison).

[1160] Am. Civil Liberties Union of New Jersey v. County of Hudson, 352 N.J. Super. 44 (2002).

[1161] 67 Fed. Reg. 19, 508 *supra* note 80.

[1162] Memorandum from Michael Creppy, Chief Immigration Judge on Cases Requiring Special Procedures and with Instructions for Cases Requiring Additional Security to All Immigration Judges (Sept. 21, 2001) available at http://files.findlaw.com/ news.findlaw.com/cnn/docs/aclu/creppy092101memo.pdf. The Chief Immigration Judge's authority in this case is derived from 8 U.S.C. S 1103(a) (1994) (Under the Immigration and Nationality Act the Attorney General has the responsibility for "administration and enforcement" of "all laws

it is deemed appropriate to do so and as directed by DOJ in "special interest cases."[1164] The designation of "special interest"[1165] is summarily made with no input from the detainees and cannot be appealed. The need for a special Creppy Memo procedural hearing is based on two justifications: 1)Avoiding setback to the terrorism investigation, e.g. disclosure might reveal focus, direction or progress of the investigation and 2) Protecting detainees from harm or stigma, e.g. disclosure might subject detainee to harm or intimidation and prevent him/her from cooperating.

The Creppy Memo was challenged by the ACLU in Detroit Free Press, v. Ashcroft,[1166] filed in U.S. District Court in the Eastern District of Michigan, Southern Division.[1167] "The primary issue on appeal in this case, is whether the First Amendment to the United States Constitution confers a public right of access to deportation hearings. If it does, then the Government must make a showing to overcome that right."[1168]

B. Total Information Awareness

As the Attorney General John Ashcroft was restricting access to the federal government anti-terrorism effort, he was seeking more and more information on the terrorists, through Total Information Awareness (TIA)[1169] and the Terrorism Information and Prevention System (TIPS).[1170] Even the established attorney-client privilege or Constitutional privacy was considered no obstacle to the Attorney General's hunt for information. Thus, on October 31, 2001, the Department of Justice published a new regulation, 28 C.F.R. ?501.3(d), authorizing the Bureau of Prisons (BOP) to monitor communications between prisoner detainees and their lawyers without obtaining a court order. This rule applied to all detainees, irrespective of the alleged crime and stage of legal proceeding. The rule grants the Attorney

---

relating to the immigration and naturalization of aliens." The Act authorizes the Attorney General to prescribe "such regulations ... as he deems necessary for carrying out his authority").

[1163] *Id.* (In designated "special interest" cases there is supposed to be complete blackout of information. The immigration judge is authorized "to close the hearings to the public, and to avoid discussing the cases or otherwise disclosing any information about the cases to anyone outside the Immigration Court ... the courtroom must be closed for these cases - no visitors, no family, and no press ... [this] includes confirming or denying whether such a case is on the docket or scheduled for a hearing").

[1164] Heidi Kitrosser, "Secrecy in the Immigration Courts and Beyond: Considering the Right To Know in the Administrative State," 39 *Harv. C.R.-C.L. L. Rev.* 95 (2004).

[1165] North Jersey Media Group v. Ashcroft, 308 F.3d 198 (3d Cir. 2002), (According to Dale L. Watson, the FBI's Executive Assistant Director for Counterterrorism and Counterintelligence, "special interest" cases involved aliens who "might have connections with, or possess information pertaining to, terrorist activities against the United States").

[1166] Detroit Free Press v. Ashcroft, 195 F. Supp. 2d 937, 946 (E.D. Mich. 2002).

[1167] Detroit Free Press v. Ashcroft, 303 F.3d 681, 682 (6th Cir. 2002); see also Amy E. Hooper, "Investigation Terrorism: The Role of the First Amendment," 2004 *Duke L. and Tech. Rev.* 0002 (providing a historical context of the case) http://www.law.duke.edu/journals/ dltr/articles/PDF/2004DLTR0002.pdf.

[1168] Detroit Free Press, *supra* note 88, at 945.

[1169] American Civil Liberties Union, QandA on the Pentagon's "Total Information Awareness" Program, (Apr. 20, 003) available at http://www.aclu.org/privacy/spying/ 15578res20030420.html (TIA is run by the Defense Advanced Research Projects Agency (DARPA) at the Department of Defense. TIA collects as much information as possible about as many people as possible and compiles it into an "ultra-large-scale" database in order to identify terrorists by discerning patterns of activities and discovering linkages in relationships).

[1170] Nat Hentoff, "Ashcroft's Master Plan to Spy on Us," *The Village Voice*, Aug. 2, 2002, http://www.villagevoice.com/news/0232,hentoff,37174,6.html (The Terrorism Information and Prevention System sought to recruit a million letter carriers, meter readers, cable technicians, and other workers with access to private homes as informants to report to the Justice Department any activities they think suspicious).

General the authority to listen in on attorney-client communication if there is "reasonable suspicion" that a person in custody "may" use communications with attorneys or their agents "to further or facilitate acts of terrorism." [1171] The Justice Department "shall ... provide appropriate procedures for the monitoring or review of communications between that inmate and attorneys or attorneys' agents who are traditionally covered by the attorney-client privilege." [1172] Except in court ordered cases, the BOP "shall provide written notice to the inmate and to the attorneys involved, prior to the initiation of any monitoring or review," that "all communications between the inmate and attorneys may be monitored, to the extent determined to be reasonably necessary for the purpose of deterring future acts of violence or terrorism." [1173]This rule was a radical departure from an established Constitutional rule.[1174] The rule undermined existing legal professional ethical norms [1175] and attracted scorn from civil rights advocates, [1176] legislators, [1177] lawyers, [1178] and a variety of public interest groups.[1179]

After 9/11 the Attorney General, DOJ, FBI, and NSA mounted the largest surveillance program in the nation to track down terrorists and prevent another attack. [1180] Most of the effort has been directed towards the Muslim community and has been spurred by ethnic considerations.

In 2002, building upon the community policing framework and National Neighborhood Watch Program,[1181] Attorney General John Ashcroft announced the creation of the Terrorism

---

[1171] 28 C.F.R. Ë 500-501; see National Security; Prevention of Acts of Violence and Terrorism, 66 Fed. Reg. 55062 (October 31, 2001); see also Eavesdropping on Attorney-Client Communications, Friends Committee on National Legislation, Dec. 20, 2001, http://www.fcnl.org/issues/item_print.php?item_id=265andissue_id=69.

[1172] 28 C.F.R. 501.3(d) (October 31, 2001).

[1173] 28 C.F.R. 501.3(d)(3) (October 31, 2001) (discussing that limited privilege is allowed. The Department "shall employ appropriate procedures to ensure that all attorney-client communications are reviewed for privilege claims and that any properly privileged materials ... are not retained during the course of the monitoring." Review is conducted by a "privilege team." "Except in cases where the person in charge of the privilege team determines that acts of violence or terrorism are imminent, the privilege team shall not disclose any information unless and until such disclosure has been approved by a federal judge").

[1174] Coplon v. U. S., 191 F.2d 749 (D.C. Cir. 1951) (monitoring of conversations between detainees and their attorneys denies the accused of their constitutional right to effective assistance of counsel); Hoffa v. U. S., 385 U.S. 293, 306 (1966) (affirming holding in Coplon); Shillinger v. Hayworth, 70 F.3d 1132, 1141 (10th Cir. 1995) (Sixth Amendment protects against intentional intrusion into attorney-client relationship).

[1175] See generally DR 1-103 [1200.4] Disclosure of Information to Authorities, New York Lawyer's Code of Professional Responsibility, http://www.law.cornell.edu/ ethics/ny/code/NY_CODE.HTM.

[1176] See National Lawyers Guild, Written Comment by the Mass Chapter to a Final Rule of the AG Authorizing the Monitoring of Communication Between Detainees and their Attorneys Without a Warrant (Dec. 22, 2001) http://nlgmass.org/events/ news0202.html#eavesdrop.

[1177] See Patrick Leahy, U.S. Senator, Letter to Attorney General John Ashcroft, "Deeply Troubled' About Monitoring Of Conversations Between Detainees And Their Attorneys; Asks Answers From Attorney General Ashcroft, Office of U.S. Senator Patrick Leahy (November 9, 2001) available at http://leahy.senate.gov/press/200111/ 110901.html.

[1178] See Robert J. Anello, "Justice Under Attack: The Federal Government's Assault on the Attorney-Client Privilege," Cardozo Pub. L. Pol'y Ethics J. 1 (2003) (Anello was Chairman of the Committee on Professional Responsibility of the Association of the Bar of the City of New York).

[1179] American Civil Liberties Union, Coalition Comments Regarding Eavesdropping on Confidential Attorney-Client Communications (Dec. 20, 2001) available at http://www.aclu.org/crimjustice/gen/10088leg20011 220.html.

[1180] Lowell Bergman, "Post-9/11 Tips to FBI Often Led to Dead Ends: NSA Forwarded Flood of Eavesdropping Data," San Diego Union Tribune, Jan. 17, 2006, http://www. signonsandiego.com/uniontrib/ 20060117/news_1n17nsa.html.

[1181] ATTORNEY GENERAL ASHCROFT ANNOUNCES NEIGHBORHOOD WATCH CAMPAIGN, Press Release, Department of Justice, March 6, 2002 ("The Attorney General announced a grant of $ 1.9 million ... to double the number of National Neighborhood Watch programs over the next two years ... to enhance local

Information and Prevention System (TIPS). [1182] The program asked citizens and recruited informants to spy on their neighbors, report on their friends and look over the shoulder of everyone. [1183] Those who were recruited include: letter carriers, utility employees, truck drivers and train conductors, i.e. those who have routine contact, unimpeded access and privileged information to homes, businesses, transport systems, and databases. The pilot program as announced on the government website, www.citizencorps.gov, [1184] was to be started in August 2002 with the government recruiting 1 million informants in ten cities. This amounted to one in twenty-four people in those cities turning into government spies. As described on the website, TIPS is "a nationwide program giving millions of American truckers, letter carriers, train conductors, ship captains, utility employees, and others a formal way to report suspicious terrorist activity." [1185] As designed the TIPS program involved a million workers, who, "in the daily course of their work, are in a unique position to serve as extra eyes and ears for law enforcement." TIPS volunteers will receive "training ... in how to look out for suspicious and potentially terrorist-related activity ... [and] a formal way to report [that activity] through a single and coordinated toll-free number." [1186] The TIPS program was also linked to the FOX television program "America's Most Wanted." [1187]

Tom Ridge, the Secretary of Homeland Security, defended the TIPS program, noting that the civilians "might pick up a break in the certain rhythm or pattern of a community. They may pick up in the course of their daily business something that's very unusual." [1188] It was not intended for "Americans spying on Americans." [1189]

The TIPS program received mixed review from the public; some deemed it essential to fight terror, [1190] others thought it reminiscent of the state of government in 1984, [1191] still others considered it incompatible with their professional status and responsibilities. If our experience with the immediate aftermath of 9/11 is any guide, TIPS would have resulted in selective attention, discriminatory reporting, if not even racial bias. What is "unfamiliar" "suspicious" or "not normal" is quite often a mere figment of one's imagination.

---

homeland security efforts and make preparedness a part of our daily lives") available at http://www.usdoj.gov/opa/pr/2002/March/02_ag_125.htm.

[1182] See American Library Association, Terrorism Information and Prevention System (TIPS), (providing a documentary archive of TIPS) http://www.ala.org/ala/oif/ ifissues/terrorisminformationprevention.htm (last visited Oct. 18, 2006).

[1183] Ritt Goldstein, "US planning to recruit one in 24 Americans as citizen spies," *SMH.com.au*, July 15, 2002, http://www.smh.com.au/articles/2002/07/14/ 1026185141232.html. \

[1184] See Citizen Corps, Neighborhood Watch Program, http://www.citizencorps.gov/ programs/watch.shtm (last visited Oct. 18, 2006) (The site no longer contains information on TIPS, but references the importance of the Neighborhood Watch program after 9/11).

[1185] See American Library Association, *supra* note 104.

[1186] Dave Lindorff, "Analysis: When Neighbors Attack!' *Salon,* Aug. 6, 2002, http://www.why-war.com/news/2002/08/06/whenneig.html#terrorism_information_prevention_system.

[1187] Why-war.com, "What Is Operation TIPS?," *Washington Post,* July 14, 2002, available at http://www.why-war.com/news/2002/07/14/whatisop.html.

[1188] DOJgov.net, Justice Department Prepares Citizen Watch. USDOJ registered postal workers, plumbers, police and painters ... spying on you in your home, July 19, 2002, http:// www.dojgov.net/TIPS-01.htm.

[1189] *Id.*

[1190] Liza Porteus, "Labor Union Supports Bush TIPS Plan," *Fox News,* Aug. 7, 2002, http://www.why-war.com/news/2002/08/07/laboruni.html.

[1191] Daniel Kurtzman, "Bush Channels Orwell," *S.F. Chronicle,* July 28, 2002, http:// www.why-war.com/news/2002/07/28/bushchan.html. See also George Orwell, 1984 (Penguin Books 1961) (1949) (1984 depicts in vivid detail how totalitarian government and national security state operates).

While the TIPS program never materialized, the intent of the Administration was made clear, and its rhetoric became reality: Big Brother is around the corner and here to stay. Government spokesman repeatedly warned people to: "watch what you say."[1192]

In order to be able to predict and prevent terrorism, the Bush administration, from the DOJ to NSA, has resorted to "data mining" techniques and programs to keep track of terrorist activities.[1193] Data mining, the ability to use computer programs and statistical modeling to uncover hidden patterns and subtle relationships, has long existed and was widely used in the commercial world to discern consumer taste or market trends. It has since been adopted by the government for a variety of purposes. A survey of 28 government agencies (with 12 responding) in 2004, revealed that the government has engaged in 199 data mining operations, of which 122 involve personal information. The top six purposes for which data mining of personal information is used are: increasing tax compliance (7 data mining efforts), to collecting terrorist intelligence (10), managing human resources (15), detecting criminals (15), uncovering fraud, waste and abuse (24), and improving services (33).[1194]

One such counter-terrorism data mining program is the Total Information Awareness Program (TIA), operated under the Information Awareness Office (IAO) at the Defense Advance Research Agency (DARPA).[1195] The first director of IOA was Adm. John Poindexter, former United States National Security Advisor to President Ronald Reagan.[1196] In fiscal year 2003, IOA started to fund research and development of the Total Information Awareness (TIA) Program. The TIA's function and capabilities have been described in the following manner:

> The TIA program sought to develop information technology in three areas. Those areas are language translation, data search with pattern recognition and privacy protection, and advanced collaborative and decision support tools. Language translation technology would enable the rapid analysis of foreign languages, both spoken and written, and allow analysts to quickly search the translated materials for clues about emerging threats. The data search, pattern recognition, and privacy protection technologies would permit analysts to search vast quantities of data for patterns that suggest terrorist activity while at the same time controlling access to the data, enforcing laws and policies, and ensuring detection of misuse of the information obtained. The collaborative reasoning and decision support technologies would allow analysts from different agencies to share data.[1197]

[1192] Reacting to Bill Maher's comments that terrorists are not cowards, but members of the U.S. Armed Forces are, the White House Press Secretary, Mr. Fleischer warned that these remarks are "reminders to all Americans that they need to watch what they say, watch what they do. This is not a time for remarks like that; there never is." WhiteHouse.gov, Press Briefing by Ari Fleischer, Sept. 26, 2001, http://www.whitehouse.gov/news/releases/2001/09/20010926-5.html#BillMaher-Comments.

[1193] Eavesdropping 101: What Can The NSA Do? NSA Watch - ACLU (n.d.) http://www.nsawatch.org/eaves101.html.

[1194] United States General Accounting Office, Data Mining: Federal Efforts Cover a Wide Range of Uses (2004), http://www.gao.gov/new.items/d04548.pdf.

[1195] The IAO seeks to devise innovative and technologically sophisticated ways to analyze data. John Poindexter, Overview of the Information Awareness Office, DARPATech 2002 Conference, Anaheim, Calif., Aug. 2, 2002, http://www.fas.org/irp/ agency/dod/poindexter.html ("I think the solution [to asymmetric warfare, including terrorism] is largely associated with information technology. We must become much more efficient and more clever in the ways we find new sources of data, mine information from the new and old, generate information, make it available for analysis, convert it to knowledge, and create actionable options").

[1196] John Markoff, "Chief Takes Over at Agency to Thwart Attacks on U.S.," *N.Y. Times*, Feb. 13, 2002, at A27.

[1197] GlobalSecurity.org, Total Information Awareness (TIA): Terrorism Information Awareness (TIA), http://www.globalsecurity.org/security/systems/tia.htm (last visited Oct. 18, 2006).

In May 2003, the TIA program was renamed the Terrorism Information Awareness Program for political reasons.[1198] The ultimate objective is to predict, preempt and interdict terrorist activities. Very rapidly TIA came to represent the problems with President Bush's Big Brother approach to counter-terrorism. Congress stopped funding the project, and Poindexter resigned in August of 2003.[1199] While the TIA program never got beyond the laboratory stage, the ideas behind it were sufficient to rattle a nation skeptical of the intent, and frightened about the prospect, of a government bent on keeping anything and everyone under electronic surveillance.[1200]

C. Government as "Big Brother" - FBI Intelligence Gathering Operations

On May 30, 2002, the Attorney General's Guidelines on General Crimes, Racketeering and Terrorism ("Guidelines")[1201] were released to the public.[1202] The Guidelines revised pre-existing guidelines by former Attorney Generals. The 2002 version was a sharp departure from the Guidelines of the 1970s (Levi Guidelines)[1203] and the 1980s (Reno Guidelines).[1204] The new Guidelines allow the FBI to monitor political groups without suspicion of any criminal or terrorist activities. As a result, the FBI may go on a fishing expedition and listen in to intimate conversation or watch over the private conduct of lawful citizens. Worse yet, the Guidelines allows the FBI to monitor political dissidents and advocacy groups, at will.

The Guidelines also allow for "full investigation" to gather criminal intelligence "concerning the nature and structure of the enterprise - including information relating to the group's membership, finances, geographical dimensions, past and future activities, and goals - with a view toward detecting, preventing, and prosecuting the enterprise's criminal activities."[1205]

A terrorism enterprise investigation may be initiated when facts or circumstances reasonably indicate[1206] that two or more persons are engaged in an enterprise for the purpose of: (i)furthering political or social goals wholly or in part through activities that involve force

[1198] Report to Congress regarding the Terrorism Information Awareness Program, May 20, 2003, http://www.information-retrieval.info/docs/tia-exec-summ_20may2 003.pdf.

[1199] Bradley Graham, "Poindexter Resigns but Defends Programs; Anti-Terrorism, Data Scanning Efforts at Pentagon Called Victims of Ignorance," *The Washington Post*, Aug. 13, 2003, A02, http://www.washingtonpost.com/ac2/wp-dyn/A51578-2003Aug12.

[1200] Scott Berinato, "The Short Life, Public Execution and (Secret) Resurrection of Total Information Awareness," *CSO online*, August 10, 2004, http://www.csoonline.com/ read/080104/poindexter.html. ("Was it an Orwellian nightmare or an intelligence savior? John Poindexter says TIA was sucked into a vortex of politics and knee-jerk foolishness before anyone could answer that question").

[1201] The Attorney General's Guidelines on General Crimes, Racketeering Enterprise and Terrorism Enterprise Investigations, May 30, 2002, http://www.usdoj.gov/olp/ generalcrimes2.pdf.

[1202] David Johnson and Don Van Natta Jr., "Ashcroft Weighs Erasing FBI Limits for Surveillance. Seeking to Free FBI to Spy on Groups," *The N.Y. Times*, Dec. 1, 2001 at A2.

[1203] Guidelines by Attorney General Edward Levi on Domestic Intelligence, March 1976, available at Statutory Charter: Hearings Before the Senate Committee on the Judiciary, 95th Cong. pt. 1, 20-26 (1978) (hereafter "1978 Senate Hearings on FBI Statutory Charter Part I") and in FBI Oversight: Hearings Before the Subcommittee on Civil and Constitutional Rights of the House Judiciary Committee on the Judiciary, 95th Cong. 181-87 (1978).

[1204] Electronic Privacy Information Center, The Attorney General's Guidelines, http://www.epic.org/privacy/fbi/ (last visited Oct. 18, 2006).

[1205] The Attorney General's Guidelines, *supra* note 123.

[1206] The "reasonable indication" threshold for undertaking such an investigation is substantially lower than probable cause.

or violence and a violation of federal criminal law, (ii)engaging in terrorism as defined in 18 U.S.C. 2331(1) or (5) that involves a violation of federal criminal law or (iii) committing any offense described in 18 U.S.C. 2332b(g)(5)(B).[1207]

In practical terms, the "reasonable indication" standard for opening a criminal intelligence investigation of an enterprise in the terrorism context could be satisfied in a number of ways. While no particular factor or combination of factors is required, considerations that will generally be relevant to the determination of whether the threshold standard for a terrorism enterprise investigation is satisfied are a group's statements, its activities, and the nature of potential federal criminal law violations suggested by its statements or activities, including:

(1) Threats or advocacy of violence or other covered criminal acts ...
(2) Apparent ability or intent to carry out violence or other covered activities ...

> (i) By acquiring, or taking steps towards acquiring, biological agents or toxins, toxic chemicals ... or other destructive or dangerous materials (or plans or formulas for such materials), or weapons, under circumstances where, by reason of the quantity or character of the items, the lawful purpose of the acquisition is not apparent;
> (ii) By the creation, maintenance, or support of an armed paramilitary organization;
> (iii) By paramilitary training; or
> (iv) By other conduct demonstrating an apparent ability or intent to injure or intimidate individuals, or to interfere with the exercise of their constitutional or statutory rights.[1208]

The Guidelines allow the FBI to look into any individual or organization that the FBI considers to be subversive or dangerous, or professes ideas different from the administration, such as anti-war protestors who advocate civil disobedience.

Under the Guidelines, FBI agents can attend public meetings, visit houses of worship, listen in on chats, download information from message boards, and purchase commercial data mining information. Specifically, the Introduction to the Guidelines enumerates:

> (i) Visiting places and events which are open to the public for the purpose or detecting or preventing terrorist activities (VI.A(2));
> (ii) Carrying out general topical research, such as searching online under terms like "anthrax" or "smallpox" to obtain publicly available information about agents that may be used in bioterrorism attacks (VI.B(1));
> (iii) Surfing the Internet as any member of the public might do to identify, e.g., public websites, bulletin boards, and chat rooms in which bomb making instructions, child pornography, or stolen credit card information is openly

---

[1207] III. Criminal Intelligence Investigation (B)(1)(a) General Authority, The Attorney General's Guidelines on General Crimes, Racketeering Enterprise and Terrorism Enterprise Investigations, 15, May 30, 2002, http://www.usdoj.gov/olp/ generalcrimes2.pdf.
[1208] *Id.*

traded or disseminated, and observing information open to public view in such forums to detect terrorist activities and other criminal activities (VI.B(2)). [1209]

The FBI's unlimited surveillance and monitoring of political speech has also been abused. For example, The FBI Interviewed San Franciscan Barry Feingold after he made remarks in his local gym that "Bush has nothing to be proud of. He is a servant of the big oil companies and his only interest in the Middle East is oil." [1210] Subsequently, two agents showed up at his home. [1211] After the agents assured him he was entitled to freedom of speech, Reingold said "Thank you. That ends our conversation." [1212] When Reingold closed his door, he heard one of the agents say, "But we still need to do a report."[1213]

IV. POST 9/11 COUNTER-TERRORISM OPERATIONS DRAGNET AND PREVENTIVE DETENTION

A. FBI "Special Interest" Dragnet [1214]

The campaign against domestic terrorism started immediately after 9/11. [1215] The FBI launched the PENTTBOM or "Pentagon/Twin Towers Bombing" to investigate the September 11, 2001 attacks on New York and Washington, D.C. In time, PENTTBOM would become the largest criminal investigation in U.S. history.[1216]

[1209] Id.

[1210] Kris Axtman, "Political Dissent Can Bring Federal Agents to Door," *Christian Sci. Monitor*, Jan. 8, 2002, http://www.csmonitor.com/2002/0108/p1s4-usju.html.

[1211] *Id.*

[1212] *Id.*

[1213] *Id.*

[1214] Laura W. Murphy and Timothy H. Edgar, ACLU Testimony on "Immigration Enforcement Since September 11, 2001" before the House Judiciary Subcommittee on Immigration, Border Security and Claims, ACLU, May 8, 2003, http://www.aclu.org/ safefree/general/17298leg20030508.html (shortly after 9/11 the DOJ, as instructed by Attorney General Ashcroft, launched a "massive preventive detention" campaign with the use of immigrant charges as a pretext and afforded few legal rights, process, resource and relief to investigative subjects. "Under new Department of Justice policies, immigrants today can be arrested and held in secret for a lengthy period without charge, denied release on bond without effective recourse, and have their appeals dismissed following cursory or no review. They can be subjected to special, discriminatory registration procedures involving fingerprinting and lengthy questioning concerning their religious and political views. An immigrant spouse who is abused by her husband must fear deportation if she calls the local police. Asylum-seekers fleeing repressive regimes like those of the Taliban or Saddam Hussein may face mandatory detention, without any consideration of their individual circumstances").

[1215] As of September 14, 2001 the FBI had assigned 4,000 special agents and 3,000 support staff to the 9/11 investigation, and had processed 36,000 leads; of which more than 30,000 were received via the Internet, 3,800 were called in, and 2,400 were generated by field offices. The Avalon Project at Yale Law School, September 11, 2001: Attack on America Attorney General and FBI Director News Conference; Sept. 14, 2001, http://www.yale.edu/lawweb/avalon/sept_11/ashcroft_briefing04.ht m.

[1216] Dan Eggen, "FBI's 9/11 Team Still Hard at Work: Dwindling Group Wants to See Probe Through to the End," *Washington Post*, June 14, 2004, at A01. ("Originally numbering more than 70 people, the team chased more than a quarter-million leads in the months after the attacks, dispatching thousands of FBI agents worldwide") (the PENTTBOM interviewed 180,000 people and reviewed millions of pages of documents); see The "PENTTBOM" Investigation, http://www.washingtonpost.com/ wp-srv/nation/daily/graphics/penttbom_061404.html (summarizing PENTTBOM investigative activities; see also Criminal Complaints and Indictments, FoxNews.com, http://www.foxnews.com/projects/pdf/112801_complaints.pdf (listing PENTTBOM and related detentions, criminal complaints and indictments).

In 2003, after an extensive internal investigation, the Office of the Inspector General (OIG) of the Department of Justice (DOJ) released its audit report on the FBI's post 9/11 investigation effort and its impact on civil rights. The report was entitled, "The September 11 Detainees: A Review of the Treatment of Aliens Held on Immigration Charges in Connection with the Investigation of the September 11 Attacks." [1217] This is one of the most comprehensive reports conducted by the DOJ on problems with the implementation of post 9/11 anti-terrorism measures. The investigation benefited from Congressional authority and internal access to sources and information. The report was based on systematic and extensive examination of government records and interview of government officials at different levels, e.g. FBI field office supervisors and street FBI agents, and at many enforcement agencies, e.g. BOP, FBI, INS.

The report made the following findings about the PENTTBOM investigation:

(1) In the aftermath of the September 11 attacks, the FBI launched the PENTTBOM investigation. Many people (of Middle East extraction) were detained as material witnesses or persons of interests based on no more than their ethnicity, association with terrorists or just anonymous clues, e.g. reports of suspicious Arab and Muslim neighbors who kept odd schedules. [1218]

(2) If the arrested persons were of interest, they would be placed on the INS Custody list as September 11 detainees. They would remain in that status until being cleared by the FBI, under the "hold until clear policy." They were not allowed to be on bond. They were not allowed to be removed by the INS or depart voluntarily. [1219]

(3) "September 11 detainees did not receive notice of the charges against them in a timely manner ... We found that the INS served only 60 percent of the September 11 detainees with NTAs within its goal of 72 hours. Many detainees did not receive their charging documents for weeks, and some for more than a month, after being arrested." [1220]

(4) The FBI was under-resourced. The FBI only cleared less than 3 percent of the 762 September 11 detainees within 3 weeks of their arrest, the average "hold until clear" lasted 80 days, and 25% took 3 months or more. [1221]

(5) The September 11 detainees were treated harshly, inhumanely and abusively while in detention at the NYC Metropolitan Detention Center (MDC). [1222] First, the BOP imposed a total communications blackout at MDC for weeks. [1223] Second, BOP used "Witness Security" classification to restrict access to information about them, including their identity, location, and status - No one knew of their existence and

---

[1217] U.S. Dep't of Justice, Office of the Inspector Gen., The September 11 Detainees: A Review of the Treatment of Aliens Held on Immigration Charges in Connection with the Investigation of the September 11 Attacks (2003) available at http://www.usdoj.gov/oig/ special/0306/full.pdf (hereinafter Office of the Inspector Gen. I); see also U.S. Dep't of Justice, Office of the Inspector Gen., "Supplemental Report on September 11 Detainees' Allegations of Abuse at the Metropolitan Detention Center in Brooklyn, New York" (2003)available at http://www.usdoj.gov/oig/special/0312/index.htm.

[1218] Office of the Inspector Gen. I, at 16-17.

[1219] Id. at 18, 25, 37-71.

[1220] Id. at 29.

[1221] Id. at 52-3.

[1222] Id. at 141.

[1223] Id. at 112-115.

whereabouts.[1224] Third, detainees were placed in total isolation and subjected to cells lighted for 24 hours a day.[1225] Fourth, "the evidence showed a pattern of physical and verbal abuse by some correctional officers at the MDC against some September 11 detainees, particularly during the first months after the attacks and during intake and movement of prisoners."[1226]

(6) Most of the September 11 detainees did not have timely and competent legal representation before and during their MDC stay.[1227] MDC misled the detainees in their effort to obtain representation.[1228] Further complicating the detainees' efforts to obtain counsel, the lists of pro bono attorney provided to the September 11 detainees contained inaccurate and outdated information.[1229] As a result, detainees often used their sole legal call during the week to try to contact one of the legal representatives on the pro bono list, only to find that the attorney either had changed their telephone number or did not handle the particular type of immigration situation faced by the detainees[1230].

Subsequently, the DOJ, FBI and INS launched four successive waves of investigative/enforcement operations, all of which targeted the Muslim communities as possible threats to U.S. security. Many innocent and law abiding Muslims were caught up in the "dragnet" by happenstance, mistakes, incompetence, neglect, zealotry, and discrimination. For example, on December 17, 2001, Abdallah Higazy, an Egyptian engineer graduate student, was arrested for having information to or being involved in the 9/11 attack by the FBI.[1231] The FBI arrested him as a result of having a pilot's radio in his hotel room, which was left there by the prior resident. Though Abdallah volunteered and passed the lie detection test, the FBI continued to interrogate him coercively and without the presence of a lawyer.[1232] A second example involves three Middle Eastern men stopped by the New York Police Department for a traffic violation on September 15, 2001.[1233] They were found with construction plans to a public school. Later, it was confirmed that they worked at the school and had authority and reason to be carrying the plans. Nevertheless, the men were subjected to a prolonged detention under the auspices of September 11.[1234]

[1224] *Id.*

[1225] *Id.* at 123.

[1226] *Id.* at 142.

[1227] *Id.* at 132.

[1228] *Id.* at 134.

[1229] *Id.* at 145.

[1230] *Id.*

[1231] In re Material Witness Warrant, 214 F. Supp. 2d 356, 358 (S.D.N.Y. 2002).

[1232] Human Rts. Watch, "Presumption of Guilt: Human Rights Abuses of Post-September 11 Detainees," 37 n. 133 (2002), available at http://www.hrw.org/reports/ ,2002/us911/USA0802.pdf.

[1233] Regarding Overseeing Impact of Antiterrorism Initiatives on Immigrant Communities: Hearing Before the N.Y. City Council Comm. On Immigration (2004) (testimony of Udi Ofer, Attorney, N.Y. Civil Liberties Union) available at http://www.nyclu.org/antiterror_initiatives_testimony_021 704.html.

[1234] *Id.*

B. Attorney General "Special Registration" Program[1235]

Shortly after 9/11 and until December 2003, the DOJ and INS launched a nation-wide program, The National Security Entry and Exit Registry System (NSEERS), [1236] in order to screen and track non-immigrants [1237] who posed increased national security risks. The INS sought new special registration rules on June 1, 2002. [1238] The strategic aim of the Bush administration and the DOJ was to utilize every resources at their disposal, in this case immigration law, to weed out suspect terrorists, through preventive detention and deportation. [1239] As Ashcroft made clear in a post 9/11 anti-terrorism policy speech:

> We have modeled our tactics after a previous Justice Department fighting a different threat in this same nation. The Justice Department of Robert F. Kennedy, it was said, would arrest a mobster for spitting on the sidewalk if it would help in the fight against organized crime. In the war on terror, it is the policy of this Department of Justice to be equally aggressive in protecting Americans. We will arrest and detain any suspected terrorist who has violated our laws. Suspects without links to terrorism or who are not guilty of violations of the law will not be detained. But terrorists who are in violation of the law will be convicted; in some cases they'll be deported; in all cases they'll be prevented from doing further harm to Americans. [1240]

The purported reasons for a new registration system are as follows:

> Deploy a pilot entry-exit program as quickly as possible, focusing on aliens who present the highest risk of involvement in terrorist organizations.
> Disrupt the activities of terrorists residing in the United States under false pretenses.
> Notify the FBI and other law enforcement agencies when aliens purporting to visit the United States for legitimate reasons deviate from their stated plans.
> Notify the FBI and other law enforcement agencies when aliens overstay the terms of their non-immigrant visas.
> Match the fingerprints of high-risk aliens entering against the fingerprints of known or suspected terrorists at the port of entry.
> Obtain fingerprint and photograph data on aliens from high-risk countries for law enforcement use.
> Obtain current address, telephone, and email information on aliens from high-risk countries.

[1235] Nora V. Demleitner, "Misguided prevention: The War on Terrorism as a War on Immigrant Offenders and Immigration Violators," 40 No. 6 *Crim. L. Bull.* 2 (2004).

[1236] Louise Cainkar, "Targeting Muslims, at Ashcroft's Discretion," *Middle East Report Online*, Mar. 14, 2003, http://www.merip.org/mero/mero031403.html.

[1237] *Id.* (NSEERS requirements applied only to certain non-immigrant aliens. It did not apply to U.S. citizens, lawful permanent residents, refugees, asylum applicants (Who filed before November 22, 2002), asylum grantees, and diplomats or others admitted under A or G visas).

[1238] U.S. Dep't of Justice, Immigration and Naturalization Serv., Department of Justice Proposes New Rule for Nonimmigrant Aliens (2002), available at http://www.state.gov/s/ct/ rls/fs/2002/11409.htm.

[1239] David Cole, "The Priority of Morality: The Emergency Constitution's Blind Spot," 113 *Yale L.J.* 1753, 1755 (2004) (arguing against emergency regulations and suspension of constitution); see also Bruce Ackerman, The Emergency Constitution, 113 Yale L.J. 1029 (2004) (arguing against emergency regulations at the expense of constitutional protection).

[1240] Attorney Gen. Ashcroft, Announcement of Reorganization of the Nation's Justice and Law Enforcement Resources (Nov. 8, 2001) available at http://www.fas.org/ irp/news/2001/11/ag-110801.html.

Enforce the law requiring aliens to notify the Attorney General when they change address.[1241]

The program collected detailed information about the background and purpose of an individual's visit to the United States, periodic verification of their location and activities, and departure confirmation. The Department of Homeland Security has justified the NSEERS on the following grounds:

> NSEERS allows the United States to run the fingerprints of aliens who may present elevated national security concerns against a database of wanted criminals and known terrorists;[1242] (2) NSEERS enables DHS to determine instantly when such an alien has overstayed his visa, which was the case with three of the 9/11 hijackers);[1243] (3) NSEERS enables DHS to verify that an alien in the United States on a temporary visa is doing what he said he would be doing, and living where he said he would live.[1244]

In 1996, Congress mandated the development of a comprehensive entry-exit program by 2005. Before 9/11, a registration system existed in name only. Under the Immigration and Nationality Act, it is the duty of any alien over 14 years old who remains in the United States more than 30 days to be registered and fingerprinted (INA section 262). Under current law (INA section 263), the Attorney General can require the registration and fingerprinting of any class of aliens, other than those admitted for permanent residence. In most cases, the regulations have waived the fingerprinting requirements. Current regulations have limited registration to aliens from Iraq, Iran, Sudan and Libya. [1245]

Under NSEERS, aliens were first registered and fingerprinted at the port-of-entry. They were then required to re-register after 30 days, and annually thereafter. On December 1, 2003, the Department of Homeland Security suspended [1246] the NSEERS automatic re-registration requirement that mandated aliens to re-register after 30 days and after one year.[1247] Instead, the DHS has the discretion to ask for continuing registration in specific cases. Foreign students and visiting scholars who change address or educational institution through Student and Exchange Visitor Information System (SEVIS) constitute a notification for the purposes of NSEERS registration.

[1241] U.S. Dep't of State, National Security Entry-Exit Registration System: System designed to protect U.S. citizens from terrorism, (2002) available at http://usinfo.state.gov/is/ Archive_Index/EntryExit_Registration_System.html.

[1242] Department of Homeland Security, Fact Sheet: Changes to National Security Entry/Exit Registration System (NSEERS), (Dec. 1, 2003), http://www.dhs.gov/dhspublic/ display?theme=43andcontent=3020.

[1243] Id.

[1244] Id.

[1245] "Section 262(a) of the Immigration and Nationality Act ("INA') (8 U.S.C. 1302(a)) provides that all aliens who are age 14 or older and who have not previously been registered and fingerprinted at a consular office abroad, pursuant to section 221(b) of the INA (8 U.S.C. 1201(b)) or sections 30 or 31 of the Alien Registration Act, 1940, have a duty to apply for registration and to be fingerprinted if they remain in the United States for 30 days or longer." Registration and Monitoring of Certain Nonimmigrants from Designated Countries, 67 Fed. Reg. 57, 032 (Sept. 6, 2002).

[1246] The DHS never gave a reason for the suspension. The most common reasons for suspension were: First, NSEERS was inconsistently applied; Second, it was discriminatorily applied; Third, it was indiscriminately applied; Fourth, it was not cost-effective to apply. Jane Black, "At Justice, NSEERS Spells Data Chaos," *Business Week*, May 2, 2003 http://www.businessweek.com/technology/content/may2003/tc2003052_6532_tc073.htm.

[1247] See Agency Information Collection Activities: Proposed Collection, 68 Fed. Reg. 67, 464 (Dec. 2, 2003).

As operated, the NSEERS program [1248] targeted citizens and nationals from Afghanistan, Algeria, Bahrain, Bangladesh, Egypt, Eritrea, Indonesia, Iran, Iraq, Jordan, Kuwait, Libya, Lebanon, Morocco, North Korea, Oman, Pakistan, Qatar, Somalia, Saudi Arabia, Sudan, Syria, Tunisia, the United Arab Emirates, and Yemen, though others have been involved.

Between November 5, 2002 and September 30, 2003 the NSEERS conducted a total of 290,526 registrations and registered a total of 177,260 people, i.e. 207,007 registrations (93,741 individuals) at the points of entry, and 83,519 individuals at the former INS offices. The total number of notices to appear issued was 13,799, of which 1 in 5 (20.79%) or 2,870 were detained and 23 placed in custody. Registration with the NSEERS was conducted in waves: Groups 1, 2, 3 and 4. Group 1 was comprised of nonimmigrant males from Iran, Iraq, Libya, Sudan and Syria. Group 2 was nonimmigrant males from Afghanistan, Algeria, Bahrain, Eritrea, Lebanon, Morocco, North Korea, Oman, Qatar, Somalia, Tunisia, the United Arab Emirates and Yemen. Pakistan and Saudi Arabia comprised Group 3, according to the INS. Nonimmigrant Pakistani and Saudi Arabian males born before January 13, 1987, make up Call-In Group 3 of the National Security Entry-Exit Registration System (NSEERS) and are required to report to the INS to be interviewed and fingerprinted. Group 4, with a deadline of March 28, consisted of nonimmigrant males from Bangladesh, Egypt, Indonesia, Jordan and Kuwait.[1249]

A number of studies by Muslim self-help, immigration reform and civil rights groups conducted studies on the impact of the "Special Registration" program. Newspapers [1250] as well as investigative reporters covered the story with intense interest. [1251] There were also many personal accounts. Yashar Haider described what happened to him on February 2, 2003, when he reported to the San Jose INS offices for special registration and was arrested and detained at the Yuba County Jail for allegedly overstaying his visa for 20 days:

By 9:30 pm we reached Yuba County Jail and the shackles were removed; we were all thoroughly checked and huddled into another hall, the so-called "Booking Area." By 11:00 pm we were getting booked. Tags were issued and my criminal number 103957 was given to me. For the first time in my life I realized that my identity was lost and I became a number in the criminal justice system. My crime was going to the San Jose INS offices on February 2, 2003, for special registration.[1252]

[1248] Cainkar, *supra* note 158.

[1249] Rachel L. Swarns and Christopher Drew, "Aftereffects: Immigrants; Fearful, Angry or Confused, Muslim Immigrants Register," `N.Y. Times*, Apr. 25, 2003, at A1.

[1250] See, e.g., Lillian Thomas, "Muslim Men Register Warily Under U.S. Requirement as Terror Precaution," *Post-Gazette,* (Pittsburgh), Mar. 16, 2003, at A3 ("If you were called down - you, a European-American who's a citizen - if you got a call to come down to some government office, you'd be a little bit nervous." "There is a threat to the U.S. I think it's a threat to humanity. If there is reason to interview someone because of suspicious behavior, that's fine. But I don't think it's right, I don't think it's fair, to interview everyone"); see also Chaleampon Ritthichai, "The Special Registration Program," *Gotham Gazette*, Feb. 2003, http://www.gothamgazette.com/article/20030203/11/270 (Donna Lieberman, Executive Director at New York Civil Liberty Union: "This definitely bred fear, intimidation and confusion on the part of many affected ... There are so many who just don't understand: why them?").

[1251] "Targets of Suspicion: The Impact of Post-9/11 Policies on Muslims, Arabs and South Asians in the United States," *Immigr. Pol'y in Focus* Vol. 3(2), (Immigration Policy Center, a division of the American Immigration Law Foundation, Washington, D.C.) (2004).

[1252] Press Release, ACLU, Immigrants Targeted for Deportation After Participating in INS Special Registration Program Speak Out, http://www.aclu.org/safefree/general/ 16830prs20030701.html (last visited Oct. 17, 2006).

"This program has created a culture of anxiety, humiliation, and despair in communities throughout this country," said Samina Faheem, Executive Director of the American Muslim Voice and Pakistan American Alliance. [1253]. "It has made people feel like common criminals, to register and re-register every time they leave the country. We are wasting precious resources on this program." [1254]

CONCLUSION: IMPACT UPON THE MUSLIM COMMUNITY AND IMPLICATIONS FOR AMERICA

Muslims in America are not the same after 9/11 attacks which changed America for ever and this change has profoundly affected the seven million-strong American Muslim community.

Abdus Sattar Ghazali, "Portrait of a Post 9/11 American Muslim," Al-Jazeerah, September 8, 2005[1255]

A. Immediate Impact

Never before has an international terrorist act had such a devastating impact on Muslim life in the U.S. The USAPA created fear that gripped Muslim communities.[1256] The Muslims in America found themselves living in a "virtual internment camp"[1257] where everything they said or did was being closely inspected and negatively construed. [1258]

Muslim Population Estimates of Virtual Internment Camp.

Government Actions	Government Admissions	Conservative Estimates
FBI: interviewed/interrogated investigated/questioned/raided	27,000	90,000
Detained or arrested	6,483	15,000
Deported	3,208	3,208
In process of deportation	13,434	13,434
Undergoing voluntary deportation	n/a	unknown
Fled the country in fear	n/a	50,000
Subpoenas/search warrants	18,000	18,000
NSEERS: special registration/interviewed/ fingerprinted/photographed	144,513	144,513
Under surveillance through libraries	n/a	unknown

[1253] "Immigrants Targeted for Deportation After Participating in INS Special Registration Program Speak Out, American Muslim Perspective," July 1, 2003, http://www.civilrights.ghazali. net/html/body_aclu-amv_presser.html (last visited Oct. 17, 2006).

[1254] *Id.*

[1255] Abdus Sattar Ghazali, "Portrait of a Post 9/11 American Muslim," *Al-Jazeerah*, Sept. 8, 2005, http://www.aljazeerah.info (follow Opinion Editorials hyperlink; then follow September 2005 Opinion Editorial Links; then see September 8, 2005).

[1256] Abdul Malik Mujahid, "In a Virtual Internment Camp: Muslim Americans since 9/11," *Soundvision*, (2003-2004), http://www.soundvision.com/info/muslims/internment.asp.

[1257] *Id.*

[1258] *Id.*

Electronic surveillance	n/a	100,000
Gone underground	n/a	unknown
Total	212,638	434,155
Source: Abdul Malik Mujahid. In a Virtual Internment Camp: Muslim		
Americans since 9/11. http://www.soundvision.com/info/muslims/ Internment.asp.		

There were many documented instances of cruel and illegal treatment of Muslims by federal officials, only some of which were acknowledged by the DOJ Inspector General. For example, people were arrested without notice, detained and held incommunicado, deported for the slightest infraction, and subjected to hearings based on secret evidence without a charge or evidence of terrorism brought. [1259]

Of all the post-9/11 policies, "the National Security Entry-Exit Registration System (NSEERS), commonly referred to as "Special Registration," has had the most serious impact on the targeted communities.[1260] Interviews conducted with attorneys, community groups and registrants themselves indicate that the deportations and heightened immigration scrutiny resulting from NSEERS and other post-9/11 policies have created widespread fear, stress and alienation in the nation's Muslim, Arab and South Asian communities."[1261]

NSEERS and other post-9/11 policies have had a devastating impact on Muslim and South Asia immigrant communities. These communities bore the brunt of post-9/11 restrictive polices and became targets of suspicion resulting from heightened security.[1262] Particularly:

Fear, stress and alienation: 9/11 policies generated fear, stress and alienation in Muslims, Arabs and South Asians. This led "many hard-working, law-abiding new Americans to question their future in this country."[1263]

Confusion and misinformation: Enforcement of NSEERS suffered from inadequate publicity by the government, misinformation by the officials, misreporting by the press and erroneous understanding by the affected public. This led to unintentional violation and unjust application of the laws.

Selective and discriminatory enforcement: Muslims, Arabs and South Asians felt that they were targets, and NSEERS enforcement and immigration laws were selectively and discriminatorily applied.[1264]

Economic and social impact: Arrest, detention and deportation of husbands and fathers affected their households economically. Deportation placed long time resident and school-age children in foreign lands. Children 16 years of age and under were afforded even less legal rights under NSEERS deportation policies.[1265]

Fear and uncertainty: Selected enforcement of minor immigration regulations in large scale on Muslims, Arabs, and South Asians generated fear within the ranks of lawful residents

---

[1259] Office of the Inspector Gen. I, *supra* note 139, at 134.
[1260] Bill Ong Hing, "Misusing Immigration Policies in the Name of Homeland Security," 6 *The New Centennial* 195 (2006).
[1261] Immigration Policy Center, *supra* note 173, at 1.
[1262] *Id.* at 2.
[1263] *Id.*
[1264] *Id.* at 8-9.
[1265] *Id.* at 7-8.

and students. [1266] This caused them to turn away from the government in providing information [1267] or seeking help. [1268]

Unmet legal needs: The afflicted populations, Muslims, Arabs, and South Asians, were not properly represented and protected legally. NSEERS alone generated 14,000 removal cases mostly in four areas of the nation: New York, Los Angeles, Houston, and Florida. [1269]

B. Long Term Implications

September 11 brought a lot of changes to America. First and foremost were attitudinal changes, e.g. more trust in the government, increased faith in religion, increased family unity, and more compassion for strangers. It also caused the public to become more involved and engaged as citizens in a variety of ways, thus revitalizing American democracy. It motivated people to become more informed about politics, sacrifice personal rights to the government, get involved in the war on terror, and feel proud to be American, embracing "patriotism" over "individualism." [1270]

C. War of Identity [1271]

But the 9/11 induced changes may also have resulted in misdirected impact, unintended consequences and other undesirable effects over time. That is exactly what happened to the Muslim community. [1272]

In the very beginning, the Muslim communities were at a loss as to what to do. 9/11 stirred up mixed emotions in U.S. Muslims and other immigrants. Condemnation of the attack raised emotions of guilt for being Muslim. Criticism of the Bush administration raised feelings of shame for not being as patriotic as an American should. Nothing they can do will right the wrong of 9/11 by their "people." In supporting the war against Osama Bin Laden, they feel lied to by the administration. Finally, it appears that no matter what they do, Muslims are not judged on their acts as individuals, but held accountable based on their ethnicity and the color of their skin. These are no doubt very frustrating and anxious experiences. In order to alleviate these doubts, tensions, and anxieties, the Muslim community came together and forged a plan to fight for their own stake in America.

The motivation to re-invent the Muslim community also has deeper roots in a concern for justice. Most Islamic scholars agree that jihad is nothing more than a call for personal struggle, i.e. exerting one's utmost toward the true path of Islam. It is an effort to purify

---

[1266] *Id.* at 15.

[1267] *Id.* at 10.

[1268] *Id.* at 16-18.

[1269] *Id.* at 11-14.

[1270] Markus Prior, "Political Knowledge after September 11," 35 *PS: Pol. Sci. and Politics* 523 (2002).

[1271] Federico V. Magdalena, "Islam and the Politics of Identity: Lessons from the Philippines and Southeast Asia," http://www.hawaii.edu/cps/identity.html (last visited Oct. 17, 2006)

[1272] Muneer Ahmad, "Homeland Insecurities: Racial Violence the Day After September 11, "20 *Soc. Text* 101 (2002)(arguing that 9/11 is a rude awakening for Muslims and that America has never been a place of the free and land of equality; Muslims, like other minorities, need to learn their place in America - not as free willing masters but as indentured slaves).

oneself and get rid of the evil from within through prayers (salat), giving of alms, helping the needy (zakat), and fasting during the month of Ramadan. In another sense, there is a global struggle waged against injustice and oppression. Hence the Islamic response of jihad is meant to cleanse the world. Of these two, the first concept of jihad is the most favored. It is the greater jihad, involving a life-long activity among Muslims. Muslims are pursuing this by coming together, setting political goals (gaining election), and more importantly, establishing a socio-political identity in the America polity.[1273]

D. Consolidating Opposition

Before 9/11, the Muslims and South Asian communities were splintered and disorganized.[1274] The first wave of East Asian immigrants who came in the 1960s and 1970s were technology immigrants. They were comfortably middle class and contributed more to American life than they took. The second wave came in the 1980s. They came to the United States for purposes of family reunion.[1275] Soon they became welfare immigrants. They took more than they gave from society. They are dependent on the main culture for welfare and support, and they did not attempt to integrate.[1276] Unlike the Chinese immigrants of old, both of these groups failed to work with each other. They also lacked a defined identity to rally around, until, the events of September 11. There is also the younger generation, who refuses the old identity, and seeks to be accepted into the mainstream.[1277]

9/11 and the USAPA helped the Muslim and South Asian community to come together as a cohesive group for a common cause; that is the common cause of protecting themselves against an external threat of post-9/11 Muslim phobia.[1278] For example, before 9/11, about eighty percent of the American public thought it was wrong for law enforcement to use racial profiling, popularly used to refer to the disproportionate targeting of African American drivers by police for the offense of "driving while black."[1279] However, after the shock of the 9/11 attacks, sixty percent favored racial profiling, "at least as long as it was directed at Arabs and Muslims."[1280]. This shift in attitude is a wake up call for Muslims. They must do something, anything to defend their interests and restore "justice." In the context of the USAPA this means taking the initiative to proclaim their loyalty to the flag and condemn the

---

[1273] Mona Eltahawy, "9/11 was Good for the Muslim World," *Christian Science Monitor*, Oct. 18, 2005, http://www.csmonitor.com/2005/1018/p09s01-coop.html.

[1274] DawaNet Report 2: "Charlotte Muslim Community Overview," Council of American Muslim Professionals - Charlotte Chapter (March 19, 2005, at 6. (Muslim communities are disorganized due to a lack of leadership and interests) available at http://www.campnet. net/charlotte-nc/report2final.pdf.

[1275] Maira, *supra* note 33.

[1276] *Id.*

[1277] *Id.*

[1278] Kemal Argon, "Islam in America: A brief overview and some prospects for resurgence," http://scholar.google.com/scholar?hl=enandlr=andq=cache:ritSUygA4qoJ:w   ww.ips.org.pk/ publications/Perspectives/Chapter%25206.pdf+Islam+in+America:+A+brief+over view+and+some+prospects+for+resurgence.

[1279] Wikipedia, "Driving While Black," http://en.wikipedia.org/wiki/Driving_ While_Black (last visited Oct. 17, 2006) ("Driving While Black" is a parody of the real crime driving while intoxicated; it refers to the idea that a motorist can be pulled over by a police officer simply because he or she is black and then charged with a trivial or perhaps non-existent offense).

[1280] David Cole and James Dempsey, *Terrorism and the Constitution: Sacrificing Civil Liberties in the Name of National Security*, 168 The New Press (2002).

attack in no uncertain terms. This also means that when they find that their overture is rejected and they are hated no matter what they do, they must start to turn inward, gaining emotional support from their own group.

E. Implications for America

For better or worse, 9/11 was a transformational event, for the people, for the nation. 9/11 changed the nation's ethos.[1281] This event has transformed people's lives. It has made them self conscious of what they can say or do, what they can read and with whom they can associate. It has also prepared them for war with a heightened sense of patriotism and a willingness to stand behind America, "right or wrong." Most significantly for this project, it has made some people hate foreigners while others feel ashamed of their identity.

In terms of culture and values, the biggest discernable change after 9/11 was the nation's dismissive attitude towards human, civil and constitutional rights in the face of terrorist threats. After 9/11, it came to be considered acceptable, if not even necessary, to torture suspected terrorists for information,[1282] to imprison terrorists (Taliban and al-Qaeda members) without due process,[1283] to compromise citizens' privacy rights in the name of security,[1284] and to deny information to journalists to facilitate the fighting of a war on terror.[1285]

[1281] n203. Amitai Etzioni, "American Society in the Age of Terrorism," http://www.gwu.edu/ccps/ news_american_society.html (last visited Nov. 15, 2006) (As reported by Etzioni: "A year before the attack, in September 2000, Muslim Americans were viewed favorably by 50 percent of Americans, and unfavorably by 21 percent. Six months later, in March 2001, 45 percent viewed Muslim Americans favorably and 24 percent viewed them unfavorably. Two months after the attack (and the first time the data on this topic was provided after September 11), the proportion of those who viewed Muslim Americans favorably increased to 59 percent and the proportion who viewed them unfavorably decreased to 17 percent. A few months later, in February and March 2002, the percentages changes only slightly - 54 percent of Americans viewed Muslim Americans favorably and 22 percent viewed them unfavorably).

[1282] Dana Priest, "Justice Dept. Memo Says Torture "May Be Justified," *Washington Post*, June 13, 2004, http://www.washingtonpost.com/ac2/wp-dyn/A38894-2004Jun13? language-printer. See also Memorandum from the U.S. Dep't of Justice to Alberto R. Gonzales, Counsel to the President (Aug. 1, 2002), available at http://news.findlaw.com/hdocs/ docs/doj/bybee80102ltr.html.

[1283] Michael Byers, "Ignore the Geneva Convention and Put Our Own Citizens at Risk," 62 *The Humanist* 33, (2002) (The 1949 Geneva Convention on the treatment of prisoners of war (P.O.W.s) stipulates that they are to be afforded "the same courts according to the same procedure as in the case of members of the armed forces of the detaining power." Article 102. Geneva Convention relative to the Treatment of Prisoners of War. Adopted on 12 August 1949 by the Diplomatic Conference for the Establishment of International Conventions for the Protection of Victims of War, held in Geneva from 21 April to 12 August, 1949 entry into force 21 October 1950. By not treating Taliban and al-Qaeda fighters as entitled to P.O.W. status, the U.S. violated fundamental principles of international law as well as war conventions, and in time these actions will put our soldiers at risk and the United States' international human rights leadership under attack); see U.S. Dep't of Justice, Office of the Inspector Gen., The September 11 Detainees: A Review of the Treatment of Aliens Held on Immigration Changes in Connection with the Investigation of the September 11 Attacks (2003)(The report examined 762 aliens under Immigration and Naturalization Service (INS) custody as a result of post 9/11 PENTTBOM investigation. The detainees were subject to lengthy detention without notice, representation and hearing. They were subjected to personal humiliation and physical abuse without recourse).

[1284] C. William Michaels, *No Greater Threat: America After September 11 And The Rise Of A National Security State* (Algora Publishing 2002) ("Indeed there is no greater threat to the security of this country than a systematic dismantling of civil liberties and the rule of law with a dramatic shift of political will and resources to investigate, surveillance, and prosecution, coupled with the almost uncanny ability of the American public to place too much faith in government at the precise time when just the opposite approach is required").

[1285] Danny Schechter, "How Did 9/11 Change Big Media?" *Intervention Magazine*, Sept. 11, 2003," www.interventionmag.com/cms/modules.php?op=modloadandname= Newsandfile=articleandsid=495 (9/11 has changed the media substantially. After 9/11, "patriotic correctness" has become in vogue. The media put

Finally and most controversially, 9/11 has transformed the United States from an open, democratic society, to a closed, garrison state. Michaels outlines twelve defining characteristics, with ratings, of a national security state.[1286] They are:

(1) Visible increase in uniform security (100%), e.g. increased private security and military jets patrolling the sky.

(2) Lack of accountability in law enforcement (75%), e.g. indiscriminate arrests and unconstitutional detention of immigrants.

(3) Reduced judiciary supervision and enhanced executive mistreatment of suspects (30%), e.g. as evidence of reduced judiciary supervision, the establishment of the military tribunals and expansion of the FISA secretive courts in the processing of terrorism cases. As to executive mistreatment of suspects, the government's discriminatory and abusive treatment of Muslims, abusive use of FISA process (12,179 cases since 1979 with 1 denied),and the oppressive nature of the Military Tribunal.

(4) Secrecy of ruling authority and momentum of threat (60%), e.g. the "Secrecy Surrounding the Rationale for Afghanistan War and Further Military Actions" and "Secret Surveillance Orders by Expanded FISA Court."

(5) Media in the service of the State (55%), e.g. concentration of media ownership and lack of criticism of government activities.

(6) National resources devoted to security threat (85%), e.g. $ 40 billion in Congressional emergency appropriations after 9/11 ear-marked for anti-terrorism activities.

(7) Patriotism moving to nationalism (60%),e.g. American flag waving, increased enrollment in ROTC and application to the FBI and CIA and increased blind trust in the government.

(8) Lack of critical response by religions (30%), e.g. Bush enlisting the church to support his war on terror.

(9) Wartime mentality and permanent war economy (100%), e.g. the establishment of the Department of the Homeland Security with 170,000 employees and $ 37.7 billion of budget for the first year.

(10) Targeted individuals and groups (60%), e.g. dragnet kind of interviewing and interrogation of foreign nationals and students, especially those of Middle East origin or Muslim persuasion.

(11) Direct attack on dissent (10%, e.g. local (e.g. Denver) police keeping files on peace activists and organizations and conservative public interest groups reporting and criticizing views of liberal and anti-war faculty.

(12) Increased surveillance (35%), e.g. increased surveillance in public places and government involvement with cyberspace defense.

---

concern with fear before commitment to facts. Overall, journalists were more respectful of the authority, more deferential to officials, more trusting of government, and less critical of the administration).

[1286] Michaels, *supra* note 206 at 299-300 ("The Ratings: A National Security State "Scorecard,'"); see also Mark S. Zaid, "Was September 11 Actually a Prelude to 1984?: A Review of a New Book Forecasting the Possible Rise of a National Security State," Findlaw, Jan. 24, 2003, http://writ.news.findlaw.com/books/reviews/20030124_zaid.html.

(13) The impact of the USAPA on Muslims bears witness to such a transformation process. The impact of 9/11, including the USAPA, and its implications for America are not yet understood by scholars, nor are they fully appreciated by the people.

F. Final Thoughts

Senator Feingold reminded the Nation that "wartime has sometimes brought us the greatest tests of our Bill of Rights."[1287] Looking back in history, there is ample evidence of backlash against minorities during national crisis, e.g. the internment of Japanese-Americans, German-Americans, and Italian-Americans during World War II, the blacklisting of supposed communist sympathizers during the McCarthy era, and the surveillance and harassment of antiwar protesters, including Dr. Martin Luther King Jr., during the Vietnam War. The pattern seems to repeat itself. With 9/11, we have adopted a policy of large scale preventive detention of Muslims and wholesale deportation of South Asians. It does not appear that we, as a nation, have learned from our past mistakes; we keep on violating Constitutionally-protected rights during national crisis, only to have to make amends later. The ill treatment of Muslims in America will likely meet with the same fate. The only question is when will the apology come? By then, it might be too late.

> "Oh, When will you ever learn?
> Oh, When will you ever learn?"
>
> - Pete Seeger (1961)[1288] Where Have All the Flowers Gone.

[1287] Electronic Privacy Information Center, Statement Of U.S. Senator Russ Feingold On The Anti-Terrorism Bill, Oct. 25, 2001 http://www.epic.org/privacy/terrorism/ usapatriot/feingold.html.

[1288] Pete Seeger, Where Have All the Flowers Gone? On Pete Seeger's Greatest Hits (Sony 2002).

Chapter 6

THE IMPACT ON LIBRARIES

"The data from the public library survey suggest that overall there has been limited impact on public libraries as a result of law enforcement activities since October 2001."

Dr. Velma Rogers Graham (2005)[1289]

"It used to be a librarian would be pictured with a book ... Now it is a librarian with a shredder."

Ms. Snider, a library manager (2005).[1290]

I. INTRODUCTION

In the weeks and months immediately following 911, teams of federal FBI agents[1291] visited the libraries to track down suspected terrorists.[1292] Such visits raised a host of philosophical, administrative, ethical and legal issues for the library.[1293] This chapter investigates the impact and discusses the implications of the USAPA on the nation's libraries,[1294] operationally and institutionally.[1295]

[1289]"Impact and Analysis of Law Enforcement Activity in Academic and Public Libraries." (August 25, 2005) (ALA impact study of 2005). http://www.ala.org/ala/washoff/contactwo/oitp/LawRptFinal.pdf

[1290] Dean Murphy, "Librarians Use Shredder to Show Opposition to New F.B.I. Powers," *New York Times*, April 7, 2003. http://www.commondreams.org/headlines03/0407-03.htm

[1291] Section VII "Implementation of USAPA Section 215: Newspaper Accounts," *infra.* (FBI mounted a man hunt for 9/11 suspects immediately after the WTC attack, in many instances with eager (unsolicited) cooperation of patriotic librarians and help from local police.)

[1292] As to be expected, according to library survey, local police has more contacts with the libraries than federal agents, before and after 9/11. Dahlia Lithwick and Julia Turner, "A Guide to the Patriot Act, Part 1: Should you be scared of the Patriot Act?" *Slate* http://slate.msn.com/id/2087984/Posted Monday, September 8, 2003, at 8:06 AM PT (According to a University of Illinois survey only 10% of the nation's libraries have been visited by law enforcement officials "seeking Sept. 11-related information about patron reading habits." It was 13.8% before.)

[1293] "9/11 and Patron Privacy in the Public Library." ("The Michigan Library Privacy Act, Section 3(2), MCL 397.603(2), clearly forbids the disclosure of a patron's library record without a court order. ") http://www.michigan.gov/hal/0,1607,7-160-17451_18668_18689-54951--,00.html

[1294] "The USAPA and Library Privacy." (Librarians in the State of Michigan must be prepared to adapt to change after the passage of USAPA.) http://www.michigan.gov/hal/0,1607,7-160-17451_18668_18689-54486--

To anchor this study and sharpen the focus of this inquiry it is best to discuss a real case. Within days after 9/11, Kathleen Hensman, a Delray Beach (FL) librarian, reported the sighting of 9/11 suspects using library facilities. In so doing she violated Florida's state library confidential law and ALA professional ethics.[1296]

The Hensman incident raised a number of issues pertaining to law enforcement and counter-terrorism activities in library: Do librarians have a duty to monitor patron activities? Conversely, what can patrons expect when visiting a library? More specifically, should a librarian call the police to report suspected terrorists vs. criminal activities?[1297] Is the case for reporting make stronger if terrorism leads are supplied or demanded by library patrons?[1298] Should a librarian cooperate with FBI investigation without first seeking administrative approval or consultation with a lawyer? Should a library cooperate with FBI terrorism investigation which violates state privacy law or library confidential policy? Can librarians properly identify suspected terrorists? Is the use of ethnic profiling in library appropriate? Should the library ignore professional confidentiality rule or patrons' privacy expectations, in time of national crisis? How to deal with FBI fishing operations vs. targeted investigation in a library? How should libraries and librarians respond to government's requests/edicts to censor non-classified but sensitive information? How might such censorship affect citizenry's right and ability to be informed?[1299]

This chapter is divided into the following sections. After this brief "Introduction", Section II surveys existing literature on USAPA and library. Section III describes in brief the purpose and objective of this research. Section IV contextualizes the research with a brief historical account of the FBI Library Awareness Program (LAP) (1987), its origin, development and demise. Section V is a brief legal analysis of USAPA - Section 215, the legal authority being studied. Section VI outlines how much we (do not) know about the implementation of USAPA as a result of Bush's personal/political preference for information control and counter-terrorism's need for secrecy. Section VII and VIII investigates the implementation of USAPA from newspaper reports (VII) and through library survey (VIII). Section IX investigates into library's reception and reaction to USAPA nationally and at the

---

,00.html For a survey study of the impact of USAPA on libraries, see ALA impact study 2005, *supra*, note 1. For a collection of primary and secondary sources on the subject of "FBI in Your Library" by ALA, http://www.ala.org/ala/oif/ifissues/fbiyourlibrary.htm#news For a legal discussion, see Robert A. Pikowsky, "An overview of the law of. electronic surveillance post-September 11, 2001," *Law Library Journal* 94(4): 602 – 620, 617 - 620 (2001) http://www.aallnet.org/products/pub_llj_v94n04/2002-37.pdf

[1295] S.N. Mart, "Protecting the Lady from Toledo: Post-USAPA Electronic Surveillance at the Library," *Law Library Journal* Vol. 96(3):449 -473 (2004) (USAPA tips the balance in favor of the government in our right to be left along, i.e., having privacy. (Section 59, p. 473) http://www.aallnet.org/products/pub_llj_v96n03/2004-27.pdf; Cristine S Martins, "The Impact of the USAPA on Records Management"*Information Management Journal*, Vol. 39 (3) (2005). (The impact of the USAPA on information management must be evaluated sector by sector. In the case of Section 215 and 216, the impact on library is minimal.) http://www.findarticles.com/p/articles/mi_qa3937/is_200505/ai_n13638967

[1296] David E. Rosenbaum, "A Nation Challenged: Questions of Confidentiality; Competing Principles Leave Some Professionals Debating Responsibility to Government," *New York Times*, (23 November, 2001).

[1297] The issue came ahead when the library staff at UCLA called (city) police when a foreign student refused to show his ID, and was later tasered repeatedly. Darque Wing "An assault on civil disobedience," Monday, 20 November 2006. http://www.shadowmonkey.net/articles/general/assault-on-civil-disobedience.html

[1298] Swartz, Nikki, "ALA: Government Asks About Patrons," *Information Management Journal*, Sep/Oct 2005 (In June of 2004, a patron to Whatcom County, Washington, checked out a book on *Bin Laden: The Man Who Declared War on America* and noticed a handwritten note in the margin: "Hostility toward America is a religious duty and we hope to be rewarded by God." The user reported it to the FBI), which sought cooperation from libraries to identify the borrowers. The library's lawyer declined.)

[1299] William Z. Nasri (ed.), *Legal Issues for Library and Information Managers* (Haworth Press, 1987)

grassroots. Section X discusses the impact and implications of USAPA on library and society. It tells the story of how the nation's librarians feel that they are under siege with the passage of the USAPA, and their determination to fight back. It comes to the conclusion that USAPA and war on terror has changed America, drastically and irrevocable, starting with the changing of libraries ways, means and image.

II. LITERATURE REVIEW

A cursory review of legal literature shows that the issues raised by policing library have long been debated and thoroughly investigated in the past, especially by civil libertarians[1300] and legal scholars.[1301] Most people strongly objected to the monitoring of library and patrons, unless serious criminality is afoot, and only as a last resort.[1302]

In terms of legal literature, Carolyn M. Hinz's work exemplifies this gem of scholarly.[1303] The COMMENT captured the essence of the library security vs. liberty debate as it analyzed the issues involved with a case from Iowa: *Brown v. Johnston* (328 NW.2d 510 (Iowa 1983). The case is about a library patron's First Amendment rights to free speech, i.e., right to read and acquire knowledge, and privacy, i.e., right to protect reading habits, without undue government interference.

The Brown case arose as a result of an Iowa Division of Criminal Investigation (DCI) agent seeking library circulation records from the Des Moines Public Library in November of 1979, as a result of a series of cattle mutilations. The demand for records was made with a subpoena *duces tecum* issued pursuant to rule 5(6) of the Iowa Rules of Criminal Procedure.[1304]

[1300] ACLU Sues Texas City for Public Library Censorship (7/16/1999) (ACLU filed federal law suit to challenge city resolution calling for removal of two books from child to adult section.) http://www.aclu.org/lgbt/speech/12018prs19990716.html?s_src=RSS; David Hudson, "libertarians blast Internet pornography proposals," *First Amendment Center*, March 13, 1998 (The American Civil Liberties Union, the People for the American Way and the American Library Association also strongly disapproved of Sen. John McCain's Internet School Filtering Act.) http://www.freedomforum.org/templates/document.asp?documentID=9392

[1301] E.A. Ulrika, "The FBI's library awareness program: Is big brother reading over your shoulder?" *New York University Law Review* 65: 1532 (1990); C.M. Hinz, "The unexamined issue of privacy in public library circulation records in Iowa," *Iowa Law Review*, 69(2): 535-550 (1984); M.K. Wilson, "Surveillance of individual reading habits: Constitutional limitations on disclosure of library borrower lists," *American University Law Review*, 30(1): 275-321 (1984); J. McClellan, "Library records: Provide for confidentiality and non-disclosure," *Georgia State University Law Review*, 3(2): 443-445 (1987); B.M. Kennedy, "Confidentiality of library records: A survey of problems, policies, and laws," *Law Library Journal*, 81(4), 733-767 (1989); B.S. Johnson. "A more cooperative clerk": The confidentiality of library records" *Law Library Journal,* 81(4), 769-804 (1989).

[1302] Louise S Robbins, "Champions of a cause: American librarians and the Library Bill of Rights in the 1950s.(The Library Bill of Rights)," *Library Trends* 6/22/1996 (Bernard Berelson (1938) reminded librarians that "the library, as an institution, is not impartial between, let us say, education and non-education, or knowledge and ignorance" (p.88) and should choose between "between democracy and dictatorship, or between intelligence and stupidity or prejudice, or between the general public welfare and special interests" (p. 88). http://www.encyclopedia.com/doc/1G1-18616658.html

[1303] Carolyn M. Hinz, "COMMENT: *Brown v. Johnston:* The Unexamined Issue of Privacy in Public Library Circulation Records in Iowa," 69 *Iowa L. Rev.* 535 (1984).

[1304] IOWA R. CRIM. P. 5(6) provides in pertinent part: "Investigation by prosecuting attorney. The clerk of the district court, on written application of the prosecuting attorney and the approval of the court, shall issue subpoenas, including subpoenas duces tecum for such witnesses as the prosecuting attorney may require in

The petitioner in the case, Brown, was a library patron. He complained that the State of Iowa, under the U.S. Constitution has no right to force the Des Moines Public Library to produce the requisite library records to the police. Specifically, it violated his First Amendment right to be left alone at the library and chilled patrons' right to read and acquire information.

The commentator criticized the Iowa Supreme Court for failing to decide the case within the analytical framework laid down by the U.S. Supreme Court in well established free speech and privacy cases. The U.S. Supreme Court asked the following questions before allowing the policing of libraries:

- First, it there a privacy right in library circulation records;[1305]
- Second, is privacy right infringed upon by the forced disclose of library circulation records;[1306]
- Third, it individual privacy rights outweighed by the need to exercise police power?
- Fourth, are there less intrusive means in achieving the state's investigation needs?

The Iowa Supreme Court decided in favor of the State DCI without first deciding whether there were privacy interests at stake, legally and factually. It also did not apply a "strict scrutiny test" in balancing state investigation needs vs. library patron's privacy right. The Court chose instead to apply an unarticulated and unspecified "weighing of interests" standard.

Most of the recent articles take an unsavory view of the USAPA. They uniformly condemned Section 215 of the USAPA as bordering on being unconstitutional. For example, in a note written by Kathryn Martin, the author analyzed how the USAPA, especially Section 215, has infringed the privacy rights of library patron, protected by the Fourth Amendment. In a broad stroke the USAPA has do away with probable cause, dispense with evidentiary proof and reduce judicial supervision.[1307] The author observed that: "These searches cause patrons to censor themselves, harming their First Amendment rights, but have not revealed any intelligence information."[1308] The author also observed that neither the Congress's oversight, e.g., reporting by DOJ, or ALA self-help measures, e.g., destruction of library records, are effective in checking on the USAPA powers. The Note concluded by arguing for a higher legal standard for searching into library patron records, e.g. by making library records privileged, as in the case of British Anti-Terrorism Act.[1309]

---

investigating an offense, and in such subpoenas shall direct the appearance of said witnesses before the prosecuting attorney at a specified time and place."

[1305] See e.g.,, Carey v. Population Servs. Int'l, 431 U.S. 678, 684 (1977) (fourteenth amendment due process clause protects right of personal privacy); Katz v. United States, 389 U.S. 347, 351-53 (1967) (recognizing that fourth amendment protects individual right to be free from unreasonable government surveillance);

[1306] See e.g., Buckley v. Valeo, 424 U.S. 1, 64-82 (1976) (per curiam) (Federal Election Campaign Act which provides for disclosure of independent contributors and expenditures, infringes upon first amendment right to associate, but found constitutional); Savola v. Webster, 644 F.2d 743, 746-47 (8th Cir. 1981) (per curiam) (FBI interrogatories seeking disclosure of names of Communist Party members and sympathizers violate first amendment right to privacy in one's associations);

[1307] Kathryn Martin, "NOTE: THE USAPA'S APPLICATION TO LIBRARY PATRON RECORDS," 29 *J. Legis.* 283 (2003), Pp, 296-3001.

[1308] "Government investigations of library records have never shown a librarian guilty of treason or provided other intelligence information." See note 52, 53 and attending text, p. 292.

[1309] See notes 128 to 129 and text.

Beyond legal analysis, library articles are mostly devoted to educating the library community on how to adjust to the new post 9/11 environment, e.g., how to react to USAPA requests at the door step.[1310] Geraldine Collins, a University of North Florida librarian, provides a "check-list" approach and offers a "how to do it" manual in formulating post USAPA policy. The libraries should adopt a well thought out privacy policy and a clear cut set of USAPA procedures in dealing with law enforcement inquiry. Such policy and procedures should at a minimum comply with ALA confidentiality policy, state's privacy law and librarian ethical rules.

The key elements to be considered in preparing for a USAPA request for information policy are: (1) consult with legal counsel before acting; (2) report to the management; (3) designate a responsible person to handle USAPA requests; (4) train staff to follow established policies and procedures; (5) prepare a contingency plan to address service interruptions if equipment or materials are removed from the library upon a court order; (6) post privacy policy electronically and conspicuously; (7) limit the amount of records being kept to the minimum.

Still another kind of USAPA scholarship details the impact of the Act on the library.[1311] But most of these studies are based on anecdotal evidence, such as case studies, and not based on empirical data. Finally, there are a few articles commenting upon the implications of USAPA on libraries.[1312]

The above review informs that there is a dearth of research literature on the implementation, impact and implications of the USAPA on America society.[1313] While there are many journalistic accounts, a few commissioned reports, and a handful of Congressional hearing records describing how the Act has affected various segments, many people and diverse activities of American society, there is as yet no *scholarly* study of the *overall* impact and *long term* implications of USAPA on libraries in America. This study is a first attempt to fill such a literature gap.

III. RESEARCH FOCUS

The research focus of this paper is on the impact and implications of USAPA on libraries, operationally and institutionally. By "operationally" I mean how a library conducts its business, from keeping records to loaning books. By "institutionally" I mean how library is perceived and perceived, cognitively and affectively, over time and in point of time, as an enduring social organization.

[1310] Herbert N Foerstel, Refuge of a scoundrel: the Patriot Act in libraries (Westport, 2004).

[1311] Tracy Mitrano, "Taking The Mystique Out of The USA-USAPA: Information, Process And Protocol," Cornell University - Information Technologies Policy Office. http://www.cit.cornell.edu/oit/PatriotAct/article.html (Last modified: October 14, 2003). See also Nicole Rivard, "USAPA: How to be Response Ready," University Business, May 2002. http://www.universitybusiness.com/page.cfm?id=89

[1312] Judy Matthews and Richard Wiggins, "Libraries, the Internet and September 11," First Monday, Volume 6 (12) (December 2001) http://firstmonday.org/issues/issue6_12/matthews/index.html

[1313] See Section II, supra.

Library is chosen as a research site because it is inviting to terrorists as a sanctuary [1314] and vulnerable to police surveillance.[1315] Library is also chosen because of its privileged standing in the hearts and mind of the public.[1316] It is a purveyor of civilized culture:[1317] a symbol of intellectual freedom, [1318] a bastion of personal privacy,[1319] and a foundation of democracy.[1320] Library is a special place reserved for the actualization of self, enrichment of family, and empowerment of the public.[1321] Most significantly, all share in the belief that the library is a place we least expects a "big brother" to be looking over our shoulder and plying into our business.[1322] The attack on library is a personal attack on each and every one of us. In this regard, it has been said that:

"Libraries in the United States of America have long cultivated democratic environments. The foundation of our public library system is built on the assumption that access to information should be free and open to all. Indeed, libraries ... offer materials representing all points of view on a given topic, freedom of expression, and freedom of access are all principles of library philosophy. It follows that libraries, microcosms of democracy, are integral to a truly democratic society." [1323]

[1314] Paul Walfield, "The ALA Library: Terrorist Sanctuary," *FrontPageMagazine.com*, May 8, 2003. (Terrorists like to use library computers to communicate and do research.) http://frontpagemag.com/articles/ReadArticle. asp?ID=7704

[1315] Kyleen Kenney and Edward J. Valauskas, "Libraries and national security: An historical review by Joan Starr," *First Monday,* Volume 9 (12) (Historically, librarians have been called upon to serve national security needs, e.g., during WWI, library board endorsed the removal of German books. In WWII, the War Department ordered libraries to remove materials on munitions and cryptology. In both instances, libraries readily complied.) URL: http://firstmonday.org/issues/issue9_12/starr/index.html

[1316] Michael Baldwin, "Can libraries save our democracy?" *Library Journal.* October 15, 2002. ("No nation can remain ignorance and free.") http://www.libraryjournal.com/index.asp?layout=articleandarticleid=CA250022

[1317] Alexis McCrossen, "One Cathedral More" or "Mere Lounging Places for Bummers"? The Cultural Politics of Leisure and the Public Library in Gilded Age America," *Libraries and Culture* Vol. 41 (2): 169-188 (2006) (Public libraries serve civilizing function in creating an informed and responsible citizenry (pp. 172-3)

[1318] "9. ...Provision should be made for as wide a range of publications and as varied a representation of viewpoints as is consistent with the policies of the library and with the funds available." 1939 Code of Ethics for Librarians, ALA. See "Article II: We uphold the principles of intellectual freedom and resist all efforts to censor library resources." Code of Ethics of the American Library Association (Adopted June 28, 1995, by the ALA Council)

[1319] "11. The librarian should try to protect library property and to inculcate in users a sense of their responsibility for its preservation." 1939 Code of Ethics for Librarians, ALA. See also "Article III: We protect each library user's right to privacy and confidentiality with respect to information sought or received and resources consulted, borrowed, acquired or transmitted." Code of Ethics of the American Library Association (Adopted June 28, 1995, by the ALA Council)

[1320] ALA impact study 2005, *supra*, note 1(Librarian informant: "And the libraries I think - whether academic or public or even special for that matter - are among the ranking democratic institutions because they are free and open to the public for reasons that are specified in the Constitution and the Declaration of Independence."(p. 31)

[1321] "IV. Education, Democracy and the Public Good." In Ed D'Angelo, *Barbarians at the Gates of the Public Library: How Postmodern Consumer Capitalism Threatens Democracy, Civil Education and the Public Good* (Library Juice Press, 2006) (Library exists to educate the public for the public good, e.g., inculcate reasoning and civil responsibility.) http://www.blackcrow.us/Section%204%20-%20Education,%20Democracy%20and%20the%20Public%20Good.htm

[1322] Alistair Black, "The Library as Clinic: A Foucauldian Interpretation of British Public Library Attitudes to Social and Physical Disease, ca. 1850–1950," *Libraries and Culture* Vol. 40 (3): 416-434 (2005) (As an institution, public libraries are not as liberating and progressive as they appear. They are devoted to the control of ideas, disciplining of the mind and molding of culture, e.g., libraries were designed to alleviate social diseases that threatened the social order and political economy, with structured surveillance and inculcation of scientific rationalism.)

[1323] Laura A. Pinhey, "Libraries and Democracy" (2003). http://www.michaellorenzen.com/eric/democracy.html

The main focus of the investigation is on how the original design and later implementation of the USAPA affected the role and functions, administration and operations, stature and status of libraries in the community.

This "impact study" calls for two kinds of investigations. One kind of investigation looks into the impact of USAPA on the libraries' daily activities, e.g., what is the impact of Section 215 on record keeping in the library.[1324] The other kind of investigation examines the implications of USAPA library in the society as a whole, e.g., how has the high profile fight by the library and DOJ affected the image and standing of library in our society.

This study is important for two reasons. First, it is one of the few handful publications to investigate into the impact of USAPA and related anti-terrorists activities on the nation's library. The chapter compels us to reflect upon the library's institutional role, professional ethics, social responsibility, legal duty and public expectation after 9/11.[1325] The challenge is difficult because we have to balance different requirements and divergent expectations, e.g., professional ethics vs. public expectation, USAPA vs. state privacy law, citizens' librarians' role as citizens and professionals, amidst a changed political landscape (neo-conservative rule) and changing national ethos (siege mentality). Second, it promises to be the first research to offer a systematic and comprehensive investigation into how USAPA affects library, operationally and institutionally.

IV. NATIONAL SECURITY, LIBRARY PRIVACY, PERSONAL FREEDOM

The struggle between national security and personal privacy is a perennial, ebb and flow, affair in the annals of library history in America.[1326] FBI snooping in libraries based on national security reasons is not new.[1327] In 1987 the National Security Archive and People For the American Way Foundation discovered the existence of FBI's Library Awareness Program (LAP) through a Freedom of Information Act (FOIA) lawsuit. The LAP is a classic example of how government put national security concerns over library's duty of confidentiality and patrons' rights to privacy, in time of war.

The LAP was designed to prevent Soviet spies from learning about American secrets from open sources in the library stacks. In the late 1980s, FBI was on the look out for tens of thousands of foreigners considered to be a "hostile presence" in America. There were over 23,000 students from communist countries, 70,000 foreign visitors and more than 4,500 communist diplomatic and commercial representatives. FBI feared that about one-third of those 4,500 were involved active spies. The FBI could not keep track of all the (suspected)

[1324] Patriot Act and Library records, Vermont Library Association March 20, 2007. University of Vermont (Before 9/11 about 8000 NSL were issues, after 9/11 there are 40,000 NSK yearly. 170,000 thousand people were gagged after receiving NSL)

[1325] Judy Matthews and Richard W. Wiggins, "Libraries, the Internet, and September 11," *First Monday*, Volume 6 (12) (December 2001) (Library has a duty to help the public to understand 9/11.) http://firstmonday.org/issues/issue6_12/matthews/index.html

[1326] "Libraries and National Security: An Historical Review," *First Monday*, (December 30, 2004. http://firstmonday.org/issues/issue9_12/starr/

[1327] Herbert Foerstel, "A Chilling Intrusion," *Baltimore Sun* April 29, 2002 http://www.commondreams.org/views02/0429-02.htm Foerstal, Herbert N. *Surveillance in the Stacks: The FBI's Library Awareness Program.* (New York: Greenwood Press, 1991).

foreigners with only 9,500 agents. They recruited the librarians as informants; to "see things" and report "suspicious activity."[1328] For example, University of Maryland librarians were questioned about the reading habits of people with "East European or Russian-sounding names" and a librarian at the Brooklyn Public Library was urged to "look out for suspicious looking people who wanted to overthrow the government."

The FBI even recruited Robert Colburn, a librarian from Columbia, as an asset to investigate into Russian spies in America, including Igor N. Mischenko the third secretary of Ukrainian Mission to the U.N. who made a habit of visiting with the Documentary Depository at Columbia University's Engineering Library and purchased unclassified technical reports.[1329]

For years, the FBI revealed little about the LAP. It was first disclosed in 1987. Director Webster acknowledged that FBI agents have visited libraries around the country, including Columbia University, New York University, New York Public Library, Brooklyn Public Library, State University of New York-Albany, University of Maryland, University of Cincinnati, University of California-Los Angeles, University of Houston, University of Utah, University of Michigan, University of Wisconsin, Pennsylvania State University and Broward County Public Library in Florida to monitor spies.[1330] In time, the American Library Association listed a total of 18 libraries being approached by the FBI, including:

- At the University of Maryland, FBI agents asked for information on the reading habits of people with foreign-sounding names.
- At the Broward County Library in Fort Lauderdale, Fla., agents sought access to computer records of ``agitators'' in the area.
- At the University of Houston, agents examined reading habits of Americans.[1331]

The revelation caused an uproar. LAP was terminated in 1988. The FBI responded with an investigation of the protesters. According to an FBI memo (2/6/89), the agency responded (retaliated) by investigating 266 people "to determine whether a Soviet active measures campaign had been initiated to discredit the Library Awareness Program."[1332]

Not all librarians were cooperative. Zoia Horn was a librarian at Bucknell University in Lewisburg, Pa. who refused to testify against Rev. Philip Berrigan and other anti-Vietnam War activists in the Harrisburg Seven case: ``The library is a sacrosanct place, and the FBI has no business there ... `It undermines the very thing that the government is supposed to support, which is freedom of thought and speech and public debate. Librarians cannot accept the role of informants.".[1333]

The discovery of the LAP precipitated a national debate.[1334] C. James Schmidt, then chairman of the American Library Association's Intellectual Freedom Committee, called for abolishing the LAP, for philosophical as well as practical reasons. Philosophically, LAP intruded into library patrons' privacy. It violated state privacy law and created a chilling

---

[1328] Columbia had over 2,000 international students enrolled in each year through the mid-1980s.

[1329] "I Spy: Spying on a Spy for the People Who Spy on Spies," *Washington Post Magazine*, March 2, 1986, p. 8.

[1330] Dan Carmichael, "FBI'S Monitoring of Library Use Called Widespread," *Seattle Times.* Jun 21, 1988. p. A.2.

[1331] "The Debate: FBI and SPIES; Don't ask librarians to be spy catchers." *USA TODAY* May 24, 1988. p. 10.A

[1332] John Broder, "FBI Checked on Critics of Its Library Probes," *Los Angeles Times* Los Angeles, Nov 5, 1989. p. 1.

[1333] Amy Linn, "FBI program has librarians keep eyes open for spies," *Houston Chronicle* Feb 28, 1988. p. 8.

[1334] "The Debate: FBI and SPIES; Don't ask librarians to be spy catchers," *USA TODAY* May 24, 1988. p. 10.A.

effect on intellectual freedom. Practically, FBI should not ask librarians to violate state privacy law. Libraries contained no classified data or information that might endanger national security. LAP was too small a program to be effective. Librarians were not trained to identify or recruit foreign spies. Finally and most importantly, if FBI were serious about gaining "information mosaic", they could only do so by monitoring all libraries and tracking every patron, i.e., turning America into a police state.

V. USAPA AND THE LIBRARY: A LEGAL ANALYSIS

The Language of the USAPA

The USAPA[1335] does not target the Nation's library system.[1336] There is no specific provision directed at the libraries. However, a few of the USAPA provisions implicated patron's constitutional rights and librarians' professional obligations. For example, Section 215 authorizes the FBI to obtain library records during a counter-intelligence operation.[1337]

Section 215 of USAPA amends 50 USC 1862 in allowing the FBI to apply for a FISA (Foreign Intelligence Surveillance Act) court order to compel the production of any "tangible things" in the investigation of international terrorism or clandestine intelligence activities.[1338] Specifically, it amends Section 501 of the FSIA in authorizing:

> "The Director of the Federal Bureau of Investigation or a designee of the Director (whose rank shall be no lower than Assistant Special Agent in Charge) may make an application for an order requiring the production of any tangible things (including books, records, papers, documents, and other items) for an investigation to protect against international terrorism or clandestine intelligence activities, provided that such investigation of a United States person is not conducted solely upon the basis of activities protected by the first amendment to the Constitution." (Section 215 (a)(1).

Furthermore, Section 215 prohibits the disclosure of any execution of a Section 215 order:

> "No person shall disclose to any other person (other than those persons necessary to produce the tangible things under this section) that the Federal Bureau of Investigation has sought or obtained tangible things under this section."

[1335] For full text of the law, see "USAPA of 2001 - Sections 213-220 ," http://www.ratical.org/ratville/CAH/Section213.html#215

[1336] For legal analysis of the USAPA, see Center for Democracy and Technology, www.cdt.org/security/usapatriot/analysis.shtml; Congressional Research Service, April 15, 2002, www.fas.org/irp/crs/RL31377.pdf For a brief overview of the impact of USAPA on the library, see Charles Doyle, "CRS Analysis: Libraries and the USAPA"

[1337] Section 215 of USAPA "Access to Records and Other Items Under the Foreign Intelligence SURVEILLANCE AcT." Feb. 26, 2003.

[1338] For a brief analysis of Section 215, see "Frequently Asked Questions about Section 215," see CLU of Florida http://www.aclufl.org/section215q_a.html

Legal Analysis of Section 215

Section 215 allows the FBI to obtain an FSIA order to compel any person or entity to turn over "any tangible things" provided that the investigation is "for an authorized investigation", i.e., "to protect against international terrorism or clandestine intelligence activities." Section 215 empowers the FBI to conduct domestic intelligence operations on *every person* living in the United States. In order to do so:

(1) The FBI does not need to show probable cause, as required by the Fourth Amendment;

(2) The FBI needs not demonstrate that the investigation target is a foreign power or agent of a foreign power, as required by prior FSIA;

(3) The FBI can investigate non-United States persons based solely on their exercise of First Amendment rights;

(4) The FBI can investigate United States citizens based in part upon their exercise of First Amendment rights;

(5) Section 215 investigation are kept secrete. Those who are served with Section 215 order are not allowed to tell anyone. Those who are subjected to Section 215 surveillance are never notified.

VI. IMPLEMENTATION OF USAPA SECTION 215: HOW LITTLE DO WE KNOW?

Introduction

USAPA researchers are hampered in their research due to the lack of research data. Specifically, there is a lack of transparency on the employment of USAPA and related counter-terrorism measures. USAPA enforcement patterns cannot be readily discernible from examining reports and records of law enforcement agencies (FBI, DOJ),[1339] government auditing offices (GAO),[1340] Congressional research agencies (CRS)[1341], Congressional

---

[1339] "DOJ Says It Has Never Used Key PATRIOT Provision," CDT Analysis, Center for Democracy and Technology. September 23, 2003. (On September 18, 2003, DOJ announced that FBI has not once used Section 215 powers to obtain business records from library or business establishments.) However, at a May 20, 2003 hearing before the Congress, Assistant Attorney General Viet Dinh said, in response to a question about the USAPA, "And I think the result from this informal survey is that libraries have been contacted approximately 50 times based upon articulable suspicion or calls -- voluntary calls from librarians regarding suspicious activity.) The discrepancy can be explained. Library contacts by law enforcement officials need not be based on expressed USAPA authorities.) http://www.cdt.org/security/usapatriot/030923cdt.shtml On Sep 18, 2003 Ashcroft informed the president of the American Library Association, Carla Hayden, that Section 215 had never been invoked. "FBI library data to be made public / Ashcroft OKs disclosure of number of records requests under Patriot Act," *Houston Chronicle*. Sep 18, 2003. p. 5.

[1340] There is no GAO report on Section 215 of USAPA. There are GAO reports on other aspects of USAPA enforcement. GAO: 05-412 "USAPA: Additional Guidance Could Improve Implementation of Regulations Related to Customer Identification and Information Sharing Procedures."

[1341] "Libraries and the USA PATRIOT Act," Congressional Research Services, updated July 6, 2005 (The extent to which Section 215 authorities have been invoked is not clear. The librarians and public usually do not discriminate between grand jury vs. National Security Letter vs. 4th Amendment search and seizure authorities.)

oversight committees,[1342] media (press, TV) investigative reporting[1343] or public interest groups inquiry (ACLU, EPIC),[1344] and in rare instances, personal accounts.[1345]

A Secretive Bush Administration[1346]

The Bush administrative is one of the more secretive administrations in US Presidential history. Bush, under the tutorage of Karl Rove and with the support of Vice President Cheney, established an imperial Presidency at the expense of open and accountable government.[1347] 9/11 and war on terror provided a justifiable reason and convenient excuses to allow Bush to keep government business under seal and beyond reach of the public.

A Non-Responsive DOJ

After 9/11 DOJ has consistently refused to disclose information on how the USAPA was implemented and enforced. In spite of repeated requests by Congressional oversight committees[1348] and human rights organizations,[1349] the government (Department Justice, FBI) has steadfastly refused to release any data on the use of Section 215 and related powers on national security [1350] and executive privileges grounds.

Specifically, on June 13, 2002 the House Judiciary Committee sent a letter requesting information on 50 questions from Attorney General Ashcroft and FBI Director Robert F. Mueller "concerning the Department of Justice's use of these new [USAPA enforcement] tools and their effectiveness." On July 26, 2002, the Justice Department belatedly responded to the House Judiciary Committee questionnaire, answering only 34 of the 50 questions posed. Of those six answers were classified[1351] and five were answered in a perfunctory (and

---

[1342] Statement of Alberto R. Gonzales Attorney General of the United States Before the United States Senate Committee on the Judiciary, April 5, 2005. (Failed to discuss circumstances of USAPA being used, or adduced any evidence of its effectiveness.) http://www.fas.org/irp/congress/2005_hr/040505gonzales.html

[1343] See APPENDIX I: "Journalistic accounts of FBI visiting local libraries 9/11/01 to 9/10/02".

[1344] FOIA request to DOJ and FBI, August 21, 2002. http://www.aclu.org/patriot_foia/FOIA/FOIAreq.PDF ACLU and EPIC v. Department of Justice, Civil Action No. 03-2522 (D.D.C. ESH) (On October 23, 2003, EPIC, the ACLU and library and booksellers' organizations submitted a FOIA request to the FBI seeking information about Section 215 of the USAPA. FBI refused to expedite the request. On May 10, 2004, U.S. District Judge Ellen Huvelle ordered the FBI to expeditiously process the request.)

[1345] Patriot Act and Library records, Vermont Library Association March 20, 2007. University of Vermont (Librarians at Vermont and Connecticut recounted their successful effort in challenging USAPA gag order.) "John Doe challenges Patriot Act gag order," *Vermont Guardian* September 28, 2005. http://www.infowars.com/articles/ps/patriot_act_doe_challenge_gag_order.htm

[1346] See Chapter 1.

[1347] See Chapter 2, especially "IV Political Gamesmanship"

[1348] See June 13, 2002 letter sent by Committee Chairman Rep. James Sensenbrenner Jr. and Ranking Member John Conyers Jr. of House Judiciary Committee, seeking answers from Attorney General Ashcroft and FBI Director Robert F. Mueller to 50 questions on "concerning the Department of Justice's use of these new tools and their effectiveness." http://www.house.gov/judiciary/ashcroft061302.htm

[1349] See "Freedom of Information Request" to Office of Information and Privacy, Department of Justice and FBI, Letter dated September 24, 2002. Center for Cognitive Liberty and Ethics. http://www.cognitiveliberty. org/pdf/FOIA1.pdf

[1350] Adam Clymer, "Justice Dept. Balks At Effort to Study Antiterror Powers," *New York Times.* Aug. 14, 2002.(The Justice Department has refused House Judiciary Committee requests for information about "roving surveillance"; calls to and from telephone numbers; bookstore, library and newspaper records; and subpoenas served on Americans or permanent US residents.) Reprinted http://www.nytimes.com/2002/08/15/politics/ 15PATR.html?ex=1064376000anden=cfeff6942d197054andei=5070

[1351] Answers to 8 (on implementation of Section 206 – "roving order"),10 (on implementation of Section 214 – "pen registers and trap and trace", 11 (on implementation of Section 215), 12 (on implementation of Section 215),

non-responsive) manner, such as the Justice Department could not answer because it failed to keep records or statistics needed.[1352]

A Misinformation Campaign [1353]

Not only was the Attorney General and DOJ not forthcoming with information about the USAPA, the DOJ was actively engaging in "disinformation" campaign to misled[1354] or at least to confuse the public.[1355] The prime example is the systematic abusive use of National Security Letters by the FBI from 2002 to 2006, covered up by inaccurate recording in the FBI and under reporting to the Congress.[1356]

The following analysis USAPA used is based on a systematic examination of statements made by US DOJ official, from the Attorney General to the FBI agents to the US Attorneys, in a three months period (9/1/03 to 11/30/03).

The three months is chosen because it is at the height of the anti-Patriot movement.[1357] It is also chosen because during this time the Attorney General has decided to take on the anti-USAPA forces, i.e., the librarians, ACLU, head on.

A note on analytical methodology used. By now it is clear that the Bush Administration has no intention of sharing with the public USAPA enforcement data. This restrictive – secretive information policy is based on a sound anti-terrorism strategy, i.e., operational secrecy is necessary to keep terrorists at bay. This secretive policy also conforms to the Bush-Cheney's governance philosophy, i.e., government knows best, and Bush-Rove's politics, i.e., political control is best exercised by means of information manipulation and distortion. In the end, counter-terrorism strategy and Bush governance philosophy requires the Bush Administrative to stay on top of the (information) "game": who gets[1358] (or not get) what[1359] kind of government information and at what time is never left to chance.

---

15 (on FSIA surveillance order), 27 (on implementation of Section 206 – "roving order") will be sent to the House Permanent Select Committee on Intelligence or appropriate channels) under separate cover.

[1352] See Justice Department's reply to the June 13, 20002 letter from House Judiciary Chairman F. James Sensenbrenner, Jr. and Ranking Minority Member John Conyers, Jr. of July 26, 2002.

[1353] Since 2003 and for 2.5 years, the Bush administration spent 1.6 billion in advertisement and PR to promote his programs and polish his image. Media Contracts: Activities and Financial Obligations for Seven Federal Departments, GAO-06-305, January 13, 2006. The report investigated advertisement, media, and PR contracts awarded by seven federal agencies: DOC, DOI, DOD, VA, HHS, DHS, and Treasury from 2003 to May of 2005. http://www.gao.gov/new.items/d06305.pdf

[1354] Setting the Record Straight: An Analysis of the Justice Department's PATRIOT Act Website." Center for Democracy and Technology. October 27, 2003 (The Department of Justice has launched a website, http://www.lifeandliberty.gov, to defend the PATRIOT Act, but the assertions were dubious.)

[1355] Paul M. Holt, "Hallmark of Bush presidency: control over information flow," *Christian Science Monitor*, September 01, 2005. From "Mission Accomplished photo opt. to WMD intelligence doctoring, Bush left nothing to chance when it comes to information control. http://www.csmonitor.com/2005/0901/p09s01-coop.html

[1356] "A Review of the Federal Bureau of Investigation's Use of National Security Letters, DoJ Office of Inspector General, March 2007. (The Patriot Reauthorization act requires the DOJ – Inspector General's Office to report to the Congress the use and misuse of National Security Letter. The DOJ – IG uncovered systemic abuses by the FBI and gross under reporting of NSL authorities to the Congress. For example, FBI has no established guidelines and systematic tracking system for the issuance of NSL. The IG found incomplete, inaccurate and delayed recording/reporting on NSL application, issuance and execution.) http://www.fas.org/irp/agency/doj/oig/natsec.pdf

[1357] See Chapter 7

[1358] Columnist Novak, NYT report Judith Miller or NBC Washington Chief Political Correspondent Tim Russet and Associate Editor to Washington Post are all foot soldiers to and mouth pieces to Bush information campaign, in different ways.

To the Bush administration, there is little distinction, and still less incentive, to draw a distinction between selective information withholding, creative information manufacturing, and crafty information manipulation. They are all tools to control public opinion.

View in this light, information release by the government on USAPA should not be viewed as factual, still less truthful. Rather, information to the Bush Administration, much like cloth to a designer, is there to be cut and sewed together to appeal to the public. Thus, when US Justice Department spokesman Mark Corallo informed the public that there was "zero, none" search by federal agents under USAPA, he *did not* mean "no" (counter-terrorism) search ever took place. He only meant (perhaps) that 'technically" no USAPA warrant was used. We know now that FBI agents are able to obtain information from libraries in many ways, from appealing to patriotism to threatening with legal action: "We will return with a warrant".

A researcher should not look at Bush's announcements on USAPA for the substantive "information" imported but rather the symbolic "message" sent. This requires reading into the mind of the speaker more so than analyzing the text of the document, understanding the text in context (what it meant in the totality of circumstances). This also requires the researcher to look at what is NOT being said (and still technically correct) as much as what is being suggested (and still technically not lying). In the end, the research should stay focus on what the Administration was trying to achieve with the kind, amount, mode and timing of information released, starting with an understanding the rules of Bush's "language game".[1360]

Textual Analysis[1361]

A systematic analysis of the content of the DOJ announcements and statements on the use of Section 215 USAPA and related anti-terrorism measures,[1362] uncovers the following messages and themes:

(1) DOJ has been trying very hard to kept the public informed

(1.1)   DOJ spokesman Mark Corallo informed the public that DOJ briefed the intelligence committee on the application of USAPA routinely twice a year.[1363]

(1.2)   Ashcroft informed the president of the American Library Association, Carla Hayden, that he would disclose how many times Section 215 had been invoked.[1364]

(2) The DOJ is very interested in facts and truth

(2.1)   In a memo to FBI Director Robert Mueller, Ashcroft explain the need for declassifing of USAPA information: "I know you share my concern that the public not be misled regarding the manner in which the U.S. Department of

---

[1359] The declassification of national security by the President and VP for political purposes is now all but acknowledged. The use of CIA information to attack political enemies led to the public disclosure of a CIA officer.

[1360] Lois Shawver, "On Wittgenstein's Concept of Language game" http://users.california.com/~rathbone/word.htm

[1361] By textual analysis, I mean what is being said or not said, on face value, to an intended audience.

[1362] FBI and US Attorney's Public Announcement on the Use of Section 215: September 1, 2003 to November 2003.

[1363] "Patriot Act's critics tap hysteria, Ashcroft says," *Washington Post. Journal - Gazette*. Ft. Wayne, Ind.: Sep 19, 2003. p. 3.A

[1364] "FBI library data to be made public / Ashcroft OKs disclosure of number of records requests under Patriot Act," *Houston Chronicle*. Houston, Tex.: Sep 18, 2003. p. 5

Justice, and the FBI in particular, have been utilizing the authorities provided...." [1365]

(2.2)   The Attorney General decided to release Section 215 application information[1366] because "the troubling amount of public distortion and misinformation" about section 215 and "that it is in the public interest and the best interest of law enforcement to declassify this information." (9/21/03) [1367]

(2.3)   President of the American Library Association, Carla Hayden reacted to was informed Attorney General Ashcroft disclose of Section 215 pattern of use: "He didn't apologize, but he said he was concerned that he'd been misunderstood. He wanted to allay public fears that he wasn't concerned about civil liberties." [1368]

(3) USAPA is necessary to secure liberty

(3.1)   In Omaha, Neb., the US Attorney General remarked: "These are things that secure liberties, and I think it's important that people know that" (9/21/03) [1369]

(3.2)   The fact that Section 215 has never been used does not mean that it is necessary.[1370] COJ spokesman Corallo observed: "You don't ever know when you may need it ...You could have a career FBI agent or a career police officer who has never fired his gun. Does that mean you take it away from him?" [1371]

(3.3)   Attorney General Ashcroft said that the act has helped root out terrorist cells in America and win 515 deportations and 132 convictions for terrorism-related crimes. [1372]

(4) USAPA – Section 215 has not been abused

(4.1)   In a memo to FBI Director Robert Mueller Ashcroft stated: "The number of times section 215 has been used to date is zero." [1373]

(4.2)   Ashcroft speaking to the Federalist Society's National Lawyers Convention: "Despite all the hoopla to the contrary ... the Patriot Act, which allows for court-

---

[1365] Curt Anderson, "Ashcroft says FBI hasn't sought any reading records," *Advocate*. Baton Rouge, La.: Sep 18, 2003. p. 2.A

[1366] Audrey Hudson, "Librarians dispute Justice's claim on use of Patriot Act," *Washington Times*. Washington, D.C.: Sep 19, 2003. p. A.10. See also "Sensenbrenner Statement on DOJ's Disclosure of Number of Times Library, Business Records Have Been Sought Under Section 215 of USA- PATRIOT Act," *U.S. Newswire* Sep 18, 2003. p. 1 ("I have long supported disclosing this information as helpful to the public without compromising our anti-terrorism efforts and applaud this decision by the Justice Department...For too long, inflamed rhetoric, erroneous conspiracy theories, and misinformation has characterized much of the discussion about Section 215...Regardless of today's disclosure, the House Judiciary Committee will continue aggressive oversight of the Justice Department and how it implements the USA-PATRIOT Act.")

[1367] "Mr. Ashcroft's Tantrum," *The Washington Post*. Sep 21, 2003. p. B.06

[1368] Mike Bowler, "Report on accessing library records to be open ; Ashcroft, under pressure over privacy rights, offers to declassify some data," *The Sun*. Sep 18, 2003. p. 5.A.

[1369] Curt Anderson, "In Defense of Anti-terror Campaign Ashcroft Crusade Headed Here," *Pittsburgh Post - Gazette*. Sep 21, 2003. p. A.13.

[1370] Emily Sheketoff, head of ALA Washington office argued that USAPA has proven to be not necessary: "If there's been any time when law enforcement has been aggressively pursuing anti-terrorism, it's been in the past two years ... So obviously the laws that are on the books other than the Patriot Act are wholly adequate for what they need."

[1371] Michelle Mittelstadt, "Justice Department aggressively defending the Patriot Act," *Knight Ridder Tribune News Service*. Sep 26, 2003. p. 1

[1372] "Ashcroft Faces Law, Disorder," *Boston Herald* Sep 10, 2003. p. 007.

[1373] Curt Anderson, "Ashcroft says FBI hasn't sought any reading records," *Advocate*. Baton Rouge, La.: Sep 18, 2003. p. 2.A

approved requests for business records, including library records, has never been used to obtain records from a library…" [1374]

(5) USAPA powers are nothing new or unusual.

(5.1) USAPA kinds of powers existed prior to 9/11. At a USAPA panel discussion at Dar-Ul-Islam mosque in west St. Louis County Assistant U.S. Attorney Mike Fagan observed that many of the USAPA provisions have long been available to law enforcement officials. The USAPA only set forth uniform standards for application. [1375]

(5.2) The U.S. attorney for Massachusetts Mr. Sullivan observed that before 9/11 grand juries could subpoena library records. (9/23/03) [1376]

(5.3) Idaho U.S. Attorney Tom Moss observed that USAPA powers are nothing new. Before 9/11, the DOJ has a number of administrative subpoenas powers to investigate all types of criminal cases, including health care fraud and against doctors. USAPA is an extension of such conventional investigative powers. "I would suggest that if it's good enough for doctors, it ought to be good enough for terrorists." [1377]

(5.4) U.S. attorney for the Northern District of California noted in a column that USAPA: "ensured that investigators could use the same tools in terrorism cases that have been available for many years in drug, fraud and racketeering cases…brought the law up to current technology, so we no longer have to fight a digital-age battle with antique weapons from an era of rotary telephones…allows information-sharing and cooperation among government agencies so that they can better 'connect the dots' … The fact is, business records, including library records, have been available to law enforcement for decades through grand jury investigations." [1378]

(6) *USAPA is not directed at library.* FBI has no interest, time or resource to investigate libraries. Attorney General John Ashcroft observed in a speech to police and prosecutors in Memphis: "charges of abuse of power are ghosts unsupported by fact or example…The fact is, with just 11,000 FBI agents and over a billion visitors to America's libraries each year, the Department of Justice has neither the staffing, the time nor the inclination to monitor the reading habits of Americans…No offense to the American Library Association, but we just don't care." [1379]

(7) *USAPA is for investigating terrorists.* Law abiding citizens have nothing to fear. Attorney General Ashcroft made clear that the purpose of the USAPA is aimed solely at terrorists. "Allow me to take a moment to clarify who should, and who

---

[1374] David Reinhard, "The gripes against the USAPA -- They just don't add up," *The Grand Rapids Press* Nov 30, 2003. p. G.2

[1375] Phillip O'Connor, "Muslims Here Air Their Fears About Patriot Act," *St. Louis Post - Dispatch.* St. Louis, Mo.: Oct 7, 2003. p. C.3

[1376] Shaun Sutner, "Librarians erase records to skiurt Patriot Act; ACLU honors McGovern, Oliver at Statehouse ceremony," *Telegram and Gazette.* Worcester, Mass.: Sep 23, 2003. p. A.1

[1377] Betsy Z. Russell, "Experts argue for freedom, security; National speakers at Boise symposium address; 450 people attending all-day event," *Spokesman Review.* Spokane, Wash.: Oct 3, 2003. p. B.1

[1378] M.D. Harmon, "Is USAPA a threat to Americans - or are its critics? So far, so good - both with the law, and with the lack of loud noises it has helped to achieve," *Portland Press Herald.* Sep 15, 2003. p. 9.A.

[1379] "Patriot Act's critics tap hysteria, Ashcroft says," *Washington Post. Journal - Gazette.* Sep 19, 2003. p. 3.A.

should not, be worried about these tools in the hands of law enforcement. If you are spending a lot of time surveilling nuclear power plants with your al Qaeda pals, you might be a target of the Patriot Act. If your idea of a vacation is two weeks in a terrorist training camp, you might be a target of the Patriot Act. If you have cave-side dinners with a certain terrorist thug named bin Laden . . . if you enjoy swapping recipes for chemical weapons from your 'Joy of Jihad' cookbook . . . you might be a target of the Patriot Act." [1380]

(8) FBI used USAPA is targeted specific crime and identifiable suspect.

(8.1)   Craig Buthod, Director of Louisville library confirmed that FBI agents have asked for library information on two occasions. Their requests were not based on the USAPA and no subpoena presented. FBI was attempting to find a man who was suspected of buying merchandise over the Internet with a stolen identity. [1381]

(8.2)   U.S. attorney for the Northern District of California wrote in a USAPA column: "The Patriot Act does not allow federal law enforcement free and unchecked access to libraries, bookstores or other businesses. The act only allows a high-ranking FBI official to ask a federal court to grant an order in specific investigations" directly related to anti-terrorism investigations, not "fishing expeditions." Illegal detention is not part of USAPA. Portions of USAPA would sunset. [1382]

(9) Most of the people are not concern with the abusive use of USAPA Speaking at Kentucky Library Association's annual convention FBI Agent Byer observed: "The only vocal concerns I've ever heard" about the Patriot Act "are from the librarians."[1383]

(10) Fear of USAPA is distorted

(10.1)   The US Attorney General conducted a 16-city tour to defend the USAPA, starting Aug. 2003. On his third stop – Minneapolis, he defended the USAPA by observing: "On this and every other tool provided in the Patriot Act, charges of abuse of power are ghosts, unsupported by fact or example." [1384]

(10.2)   The U.S. attorney for Massachusetts Mr. Sullivan charged that many librarians have a "distorted" view of the USAPA Act, e.g., before 9/11 grand juries could subpoena library records. [1385]

[1380] "Mr. Ashcroft's Tantrum," *The Washington Post*. Washington, D.C.: Sep 21, 2003. p. B.06.

[1381] June Kronholz, "Patriot Act Irks U.S. Librarians; Terrorism Fears Clash With Concerns About Patrons' Privacy," *Wall Street Journal (Europe)*. Oct 29, 2003. p. A.10.

[1382] M.D. Harmon, "Is USAPA a threat to Americans - or are its critics? So far, so good - both with the law, and with the lack of loud noises it has helped to achieve," *Portland Press Herald*. Portland, Me.: Sep 15, 2003. p. 9.A

[1383] David Reinhard, "The gripes against the USAPA -- They just don't add up," *The Grand Rapids Press* Nov 30, 2003. p. G.2.

[1384] Curt Anderson, "N Defense of Anti-Terror Campaign Ashcroft Crusade Headed Here," *Pittsburgh Post - Gazette*. Pittsburgh, Pa.: Sep 21, 2003. p. A.13.

[1385] Shaun Sutner, "Librarians erase records to skiurt Patriot Act ; ACLU honors McGovern, Oliver at Statehouse ceremony," *Telegram and Gazette*. Worcester, Mass.: Sep 23, 2003. p. A.1

(10.3)   David E. Nahmias, Deputy Assistant Attorney General (counterterrorism) called public concern with government monitoring of library libraries "one of the biggest red herrings out there."

(10.4)   In an opinion "Facts Don't Support Criticism Of Patriot Act" Kevin J. O'Connor, U.S. attorney for Connecticut observed that the USAPA does not mention libraries. Second, he stated that "public libraries have been used to carry out criminal conduct"[1386]

(11)Ignorance of USAPA leads to unfound fear

(11.1)   In defense of the USAPA, the Attorney General made the following remark: "The charges of the hysterics are revealed for what they are: castles in the air ... Built on misrepresentation. Supported by unfounded fear."[1387]

(11.2)   DOJ spokesman Mark Corallo observed that lawmakers (especially ones on intelligence committee) who attacked the government for being abusive are not being responsibility: "There are members of Congress who ought to be held accountable for their statements, because they had access to this information but continually charged that abuses were taking place ... They knew better. . . . We hope that the release of this information will bring some rationality back to the debate."[1388]

(12)*Lawmakers were misleading the public on the USAPA.* DOJ spokesman Mark Corallo informed the public that DOJ briefs the intelligence committee on the application of USAPA routinely twice a year: "There are members of Congress who ought to be held accountable for their statements, because they had access to this information but continually charged that abuses were taking place," Justice said. "They knew better. . . . We hope that the release of this information will bring some rationality back to the debate."[1389]

(13)*The media is misleading the public.* At a USAPA panel discussion at Dar-Ul-Islam mosque in west St. Louis County Assistant U.S. Attorney Mike Fagan said: "The media has ginned people up to believe there's something wrong with the Patriot Act, and there's not ..." (10/7/07)[1390]

(14)USAPA is subject to stringent control

(14.1)   Mark Corallo, a U.S. Justice Department spokesman, said that in order to obtain a USAPA search warrant, the FBI must:

[1386] "Patriot Act Can Have Chilling Effect on Library Use," *Hartford Courant.* Sep 20, 2003. p. A.8. (Other Opinion, Sept. 11, 2001).

[1387] "Mr. Ashcroft's Tantrum," *The Washington Post.* Washington, D.C.: Sep 21, 2003. p. B.06.

[1388] "Patriot Act's critics tap hysteria, Ashcroft says," *Washington Post. Journal - Gazette.* Sep 19, 2003. p. 3.A (In a debate in Baltimore last week, Sen. John Edwards, D-N.C., warned of turning over "our constitutional rights to John Ashcroft" and decried "the notion that they are going to libraries to find out what books people are checking out, going to bookstores to find out what books are being purchased." Edwards was on the Senate Intelligence Committee had access to the reports on the use of the USAPA.)

[1389] "Patriot Act's critics tap hysteria, Ashcroft says," *Washington Post. Journal - Gazette.* Sep 19, 2003. p. 3.A.

[1390] Phillip O'Connor, "Muslims Here Air Their Fears About Patriot Act," *St. Louis Post - Dispatch.* Oct 7, 2003. p. C.3

(a) show that the records sought involve international terrorism or clandestine intelligence activities;

(b) "The FBI is prohibited from conducting investigations of U.S. citizens solely on the basis of activities based on the First Amendment."

(c) Libraries were not breaking any federal law by destroying their circulation records "under the misguided notion that the FBI is monitoring what people are reading." [1391]

(14.2)   U.S. attorney for Southern West Virginia, Kasey Warne, letter to the editor:

(a) "The Patriot Act actually adds additional safeguards: To get production of records, we must first satisfy independent judges that law enforcement is attempting "to obtain foreign intelligence information not concerning a United States person" or "to protect against international terrorism or clandestine intelligence activities."

(b) Further, the act specifically prohibits investigations of "a United States person solely on the basis of activities protected by the First Amendment of the Constitution.

(c) Finally, close congressional oversight is provided, with the attorney general required to "fully inform" Congress every six months of how these provisions have been implemented. [1392]

(15) *USAPA provide for civil damages for abusive use of Section 215 cases.* Ashcroft speaking to the Federalist Society's National Lawyers Convention (lat month): "The Patriot Act includes yet another layer of judicial scrutiny by providing a civil remedy in the event of abuse. Section 223 ... allows citizens to seek monetary damages for willful violations of the Patriot Act."

Contextual Analysis

DOJ public announcements are not spontaneous statements. They are carefully prepared and meticulously orchestrated announcements to promote the Administration's policy positions in advancing a Bush political agenda. Perusing the above news items, it is clear that the Administration – DOJ is trying to change the public's perception of USAPA in general and Section 215 in particular, both in terms of what it entails and how it has been implemented in the libraries. The ultimate objective is to change public's way of thinking, and with it the national discourse, about post 9/11 security vs. liberty issues. Particularly, the whole DOJ whole public information campaign was to shift the public discourse since the passage of USAPA from a civil liberty focus to a national security direction, i.e., from how civil liberties of library patrons' should be protected to why national security of the nation need to be secured. A shift in analytical framework, discourse focus and evaluation paradigm would change the issues raised and questions asked, e.g., from the impact of USAPA on library to the effectiveness of USAPA in fighting terrorism, from the need for control over

---

[1391] June Kronholz, "Patriot Act Irks U.S. Librarians; Terrorism Fears Clash With Concerns About Patrons' Privacy," *Wall Street Journal (Europe)*. Oct 29, 2003. p. A.10

[1392] "Letters to the Editor," *Charleston Daily Mail*. Charleston, W.V.: Sep 9, 2003. p. 4.A.

(Section 215) police powers to need for (library) information in tracing suspected criminals, from promoting library patrons' privacy to empowering police officers job. In a still larger context, from fostering a liberal democratic state to defending a national security one.

First of all, in order to make a case for the USAPA, DOJ pointed to the need of powers to track down terrorists and prevent terrorism after 9/11. It also tried to make that case that FBI needed and was able to use the USAPA powers to track down *both* criminals and terrorists.

In order to make the public more aware of the USAPA content, process and application, DOJ undertook an orchestrated a publicity campaign, ending with the Attorney General touring the nation.

In order to ally fear that USAPA gives DOJ more and more intrusive powers, DOJ kept reminding the public that powers granted under USAPA and Section 215 are nothing new. Specially, FBI has used USAPA type of powers to investigate organized crimes and grand jury has powers to look into libraries records.

In order to allay the fear that USAPA – Section 215 powers have been misused extensively and abusively, DOJ released a FBI memo saying that Section 215 powers have never been used. DOJ also pointed out that USAPA powers were only used to target terrorists and were never used to intimate law abiding citizens. In fact, the Attorney General made repeated claims that the FBI has no interest whatsoever in investigating libraries lending records and their patrons' reading habits. FBI is just too small and too busy to be concerned with plying into citizens personal secrets.

In order to allay the feat that USAPA – Sections are not being properly supervised, DOJ pointed to the fact that USAPA is subjected to stringent and effective legislative, judicial and civil monitor.

The other strategy of the DOJ was to shift the debate from substantive issues to political ones. The DOJ tried to laid the blame of USAPA misinformation squarely at the feet of Bush's political opponents, e.g., John Edwards (a vice presidential candidate), ideological groups, e.g., ACLU, interested parties, e.g., librarians, and media; blaming them for creating a problem when none existed.

In the end, the messages the DOJ wanted to transmit were as clear as they were troublesome: In times of war on terror the DOJ knows best how to protect America. The public should feel safe and secure. Ultimately and in real terms the public knows very little and care still less. The government can be trusted to do what is best for the nation. The unspoken message is also clear. America is governed best, in war (as well as in peace?) by an all knowing, all caring, all powerful paternalistic government, with a strong executive branch and an imperial presidency to watch. To what extent this vision of government is required by the situation (war on terror) or reflective of Bush personality (insecure of self) or conservative governing philosophy (elite rule) is an area crying out for more research.

VII. IMPLEMENTATION OF USAPA SECTION 215: NEWSPAPER ACCOUNTS

This section used news stories or journalistic reports as research data to discern the nature and issues of post 9/11 FBI – USAPA investigative contacts - with local libraries. This research strategy posed a number of problems.

The first and foremost concern is one of reliability of news accounts. A case in point is with the column: "The FBI has Bugged Our Public Libraries" (Nov. 3, 2001)[1393] by Bill Olds, an ex-ACLU member. He observed that the FBI has "bugged the computers at the Hartford Public Library. And it's probable that other libraries around the state have also been bugged."[1394] It turned out that that Mr. Olds' information was grossly inaccurate. Mr. Olds has since retracted his opinion.[1395] Nevertheless such "misinformation" has been quoted and referenced as facts,[1396] and used as a rally point[1397] against the FBI or USAPA.[1398]

The other concern is with a total lack of context and background information. This gross lack of contextual - methodological related and background specific - information affects our interpretation of the facts reported. For example, Peter Maller of the *Milwaukee Journal Sentinel* reported on July 8, 2001 that: "Last year, agents sought and received 234 court warrants nationwide to review library records, Caldwell-Stone said. However, some of those warrants were issued under a different law, with a higher standard, before President Bush signed the Patriot Act in October."[1399] It is not apparent from the report: (1) what kinds of warrants or legal authority were used, i.e., FISA vs. Fourth Amendment vs. NSL; (2) what was the period under investigation; (3) what was the purpose and content scope of the 234 warrants; (4) when and how were the 234 warrants executed. Without such critical content and process type of background information, it is difficult, if not even impossible, to answer the question as to the nature and extent of FBI - USAPA library activities after 911.

A keyword search on September 28, 2003 of ProQuest Newstands[1400] with key words "FBI" W/DOC library"[1401] recovered 539 news items since 9/11/2002.[1402] There are many

---

[1393] *Hartford Courant* November 3, 2002. http://www.mail-archive.com/cryptography@wasabisystems.com/msg 03044.html (Reprint)

[1394] *Id.*

[1395] "Claim Made In Sunday Courant Was Wrong, Columnist Says FBI Searched Library Computer, Didn't Install Monitoring Program," *The Hartford Courant*, November 7 2002. (The FBI denied the news report as ``outrageously fallacious column." FBI denied the charge of bugging libraries but acknowledged that they have used a search warrant to seize evidence (download data) from a specific library computer used for criminal ``hack" into a business computer system in California. Mr. Olds acknowledged that he made a mistake. The newspaper apologized.) http://the_phoenix_news.tripod.com/ib100017.html (Reprint)

[1396] See Kurt Nimmo, "Snoops at library," *CounterPunch,* Nov. 8, 2001. http://www.counterpunch.org/ nimmo1108.html; "Our Libraries are Bugged," Nov. 12, 2002 ("The Hartford Courant, discovered the Feds have bugged the computers at the Hartford Public Library…") (The article came out after the retraction and is still on the web with no update or clarification!) http://www.unknowncountry.com/news/?id=2133

[1397] Connecticut librarians were up in arms over the reported incident. Martin Kasindorf, "FBI's reading list worries librarians," *USA TODAY*12/16/2002

[1398] "Re: FBI Not Massively Violating Privacy and Free Expression Rights" Anonymous on Thursday, November 07 @ 17:51:24 EST (Even if the FBI did not do it this time, they can legally and technologically conduct such e-search.) http://research.yale.edu/lawmeme/modules.php?name=Newsandfile=articleandsid=500

[1399] Deborah Caldwell-Stone was an attorney and the deputy director of the Office of Intellectual Freedom of the Chicago-based American Library Association.

[1400] ProQuest is an electronic research data base. ProQuest Newsstand offers access to 554 newspaper/media sources around the world. According to its own literature, it provides: "Full text of 300+ U.S. and international news sources. Includes coverage of 150+ major U.S. and international newspapers such as The New York Times and the Times of London, plus hundreds of other news sources and news wires"

[1401] The search phrase "USAPA" W/DOC library" gives me access to articles with USAPA and library anywhere in the document. I have limited my search to articles after 9/11/2001. I settled on this keyword because it gives me the broadest data base connecting FBI and library after 9/11/2003. The search is likely to return many articles not associated with the exercise of USAPA powers but it will include all cases the FBI contact the libraries for whatever reasons.

[1402] I also searched under "USAPA" W/DOC library" and "Section 215" W/DOC library". I recovered 144 items under the former (earliest being Nat Hentoff, "Big John wants your reading list," *The Village Voice.* New

items that are not relevant on the subject of FBI investigation of libraries, e.g., "November 26-December 1, 2001."[1403] There are also many duplicated items, e.g., Karen Rase three identical reports of "PANEL DISCUSSES EMERGENCY PREPAREDNESS, PUBLIC SAFETY" in *Dayton Daily News*[1404] The electronic search uncovered many duplicate entries, especially from the same source and by the same author. For example, as a syndicated columnist, Maureen Dowd wrote two different column, i.e., "BRING ON THAT YANKEE INGENUITY"[1405] and "Wake-up call still sounding"[1406] in two different papers with identical points of views.[1407]

Analysis[1408]

Systematic examination of newspapers accounts after 9/11 painted a complicated, rich and nuanced picture of USAPA enforcement pattern and process, than first meet the eyes. Research have shown that newspapers set agenda, define issues, and otherwise provide an analytical frame. Journalists report as they create social reality.

Immediately after 9/11 the FBI was interviewing everyone and anyone who were remotely connected to 9/11. A massive manhunt was launched to reconstruct the 9/11 terrorism plot, uncover terrorists hiding places, track down terrorists, and prevent future attacks. Throughout this time, local law enforcement officials played a key role in assisting the FB1 in their investigation. It is impossible to understand the scope and reach of 9/11 law enforcement contacts with librarians without first considering federal, state and local police working relationship, e.g. a local sheriff can get information from the library, the FBI cannot get with a warrant. Oftentimes this obscures and underestimates the role of FBI in obtaining information from local libraries.

There were many law enforcement visits, before and after 9/11. Many of them were initiated by the libraries voluntarily, to seek help, to report crime, and to identify wanted persons. To many librarians, such visits are deemed not problematic. Post 9/11 law enforcement visits must be viewed in this larger perspective. Illinois library survey shows that pre-9/11 police visits to libraries exceeds that of post-9/11.

Within hours of 9/11 attack, the FBI has concluded that 9/11 terrorists have been using libraries as a focal communication center.[1409] As a result, most FBI investigations into the libraries at this time are all targeted searches, not fishing expeditions.

Right after the 9/11 attack, the nation was in shock. No one knew the likeliness of another attack. FBI expedited the investigative process in order to catch 9/11 terrorists and prevent future attacks. To do so effectively, FBI agents combed the nation for leads. They asked citizens to surrender information and implored librarians to part with records; on patrons, on

---

York: Mar 5, 2002. Vol. 47, Iss. 9; p. 27) and 61 items with the later (earliest being Herbert Foerstel, "A chilling intrusion," *The Sun* Baltimore, Md.: Apr 29, 2002. p. 11.A).

[1403] "November 26-December 1, 2001," *The Washington Post.* D.C.: Nov 25, 2001. p. T.14.

[1404] Karen Rase, "Panel Discusses Emergency Preparedness, Public Safety," *Dayton Daily News*, Ohio: Nov 15, 2001. p. Z.4.11; Karen Rase, "Panel Discusses Emergency Preparedness, Public Safety," *Dayton Daily News*, Ohio: Nov 15, 2001. p. Z.7.9; " Town Hall Meeting Panel Discusses Emergency Preparedness, Public Safety," *Dayton Daily News*, Nov 22, 2001. p. Z.5.9.

[1405] Maureen Dowd, "Bring on that Yankee Ingenuity," *Seattle Post – Intelligencer*, Wash.: Nov 6, 2001. p. B.5.

[1406] Maureen Dowd, "Wake-up call still sounding," *Milwaukee Journal Sentinel. Milwaukee*, Nov 6, 2001. p. 13.A

[1407] For original data, see APPENDIX I.

[1408] I have summarize my observations without quoting the news sources.

[1409] Michael Seamark, "Hijackers lived the American dream Neighbour tell how evil plotters passed themselves off as law- abiding members of their communities," *Daily Mail.* Sep 17, 2001, p. 8.

library, on computer, voluntarily and without following cumbersome legal process. The strategy worked. Many libraries, and still more librarians, cooperated with the FBI, out of personal patriotism or for the nation's security, notwithstanding ALA guidelines, professional ethics, library policy and state law.

In order to keep the investigation secret from terrorists, the FBI has requested for non-disclose of their visits. This was usually agreed to, again voluntarily. This meant two things. First, immediately after 9/11 FBI investigations were conducted without formal legal process and with maximum secrecy. Second, the nature and extent of FBI investigations were not revealed. It is clear that there is no reliable way to ascertain the scope and extent one of the biggest FBI investigations in the nation's history. However, even at this time, there is evidence suggesting that the FBI has tried to follow the law, if possible and when needed. For example, in Broward Country, Florida, a federal grand jury ordered two libraries, where hijackers were believed to have used the Internet, to turn over their electronic computers files.[1410]

The FBI manhunt was conducted both to bring the 9/11 terrorists to justice or prevent future attacks. At this juncture, there were few concerns for the legality or propriety, and still less the necessity or efficacy, of FBI investigation. Simply, the FBI was trusted to exercise good judgment and do whatever it takes to secure the nation. A nation in crisis demands no less.

At this time, the nation and the public take for granted that: First, the FBI has a duty to investigate terrorism. Second, the FBI has the capacity to investigate. Third, the FBI has powers to investigate. Fourth, citizens have a duty to cooperate. Working under this set of assumptions, many of the libraries, a majority of the librarians and all the public were eager to help, in identifying wanted terrorists or reporting of suspected terrorism.[1411]

Laboring under one of a kind post 9/11 climate, librarians cooperated with law enforcement. Whether the librarians were cooperating willingly or not, the librarians has taken up a new role, i.e., acting as "thought police" for the state. This creates an irreconcilable role conflicts for the librarians, i.e. guardianship of state secrets or patrons' confidentiality. It also raises incidental practical problems, how to identify suspected terrorists and activities.

The problem of profiling and discrimination of ethnic minorities has long troubled law enforcement officials, e. g., war on drug. It is only now being confronted by the library community, which shuns it as a matter of first principle.

It is clear from news reports that 9/11 caught the librarians and ALA by surprise. Neither the ALA nor local libraries under FBI investigation has a contingency plan in dealing with 9/11 kind of national emergency. This is not surprising. While a terrorist attack on American soil was anticipated by many independent commission reports and think thank studies, the actual occurrence and magnitude of a 9/11 was still shocking. For example, many libraries, especially smaller ones, have no library search policy. On top of that, libraries have to comply with many laws and protect many rights. For many libraries caught in the 9/11 frenzy, the easy way out was to do noting, i.e., taking a wait and see attitude. That is exactly what happened. For the library community, leadership, operatives, it is much easier to argue from

---

[1410] Tom Mooney, "Attack on America - Scope of investigation poses logistical challenge," *Providence Journal*, R.I.: Sep 21, 2001. p. A.01.

[1411] Shay Wessol, "Suspicious Package Discovered at Tech," *Roanoke Times and World News*. Oct 12, 2001. p. B; Chuck Ayers, "Bethlehem tightens security at City Hall on FBI's advice," *The Morning Call*. Sept. 19, 2001. p. B.5.

position of strength as buttressed by tradition, i.e., maintaining the status quo, rather than to seek change. That means arguing for intellectual freedom and personal privacy.

From journalistic reports, there were clear evidence that USAPA powers were abused; due to over zealousness on the part of enforcement agents or as a result of heightened sensitivity of concerned citizens. However, the extent and magnitude of such abuses cannot be properly ascertained from the media. People fall back on anecdotal accounts to back up their own accounts. To many, one of the most representative and egregious abusive use of USAPA is the arrest by police and interrogation by Secret Service agents of a lawyer, O'Connor, using the St. John's College library computer to chat. O'Connor was arrested and interrogated for 5 hours because he condemned Bush's decision to go to war in Iraq and opined that Bush was "out of control.[1412] This kind of reporting has been used by opponents of USAPA to mobilize support and promote its cause, quiet effectively.

The most contentious issue being raised during this time was (re)defining the role of the librarians in time of war. Even the ALA leadership was not in complete agreement as to the library's role in fighting terror. This ambivalence was clearly evident with two conflicting conceptions of the role of libraries after 9/11.

One ALA statement - "Library Community Statement on Freedom of Speech and Access to Information" states:

> "By maintaining, on a daily basis, the balance between access to information for all, the privacy rights of our users, and the responsibility to cooperate with law enforcement agencies, libraries continue to be cultural and living symbols for the freedoms that we enjoy …America's libraries support President Bush and Congressional leaders"

The other ALA statement - "In Defense of Freedom" states:

> "We affirm the right of peaceful dissent… now, when it is most at risk … We must have faith in our democratic system and our Constitution, and in our ability to protect at the same time both the freedom and security of all Americans."

The first ALA statement called for the uniform support of the President and Congress in time of war, the later called for uncompromising support of the "right of peaceful dissent."

The case that brought the issue into sharp focus is that of Kathleen Hensman, a Reference Librarian who worked at the Delray Beach Public Library, Florida.

> "On Saturday September 15, 2001, Kathleen Hensman, a Reference Librarian at the Delray Beach Public Library read a news report that listed the names of those identified as the perpetrators of the events of September 11, 2001. Ms. Hensman believed she recognized one of the hijacker's names as a person with whom she had interacted at the reference desk. Ms. Hensman contacted the Library Director, John Callahan, to determine what action, if any, should be taken. With the full support of the Library Director, Ms. Hensman contacted the local police who then forwarded her report to the FBI. The question as to whether the Library violated the Florida laws concerning confidentiality of library records has been raised. Florida law is specific in protecting patron records. In this case the initial contact with law enforcement was based on the Librarian's recollection and not on library records. Subsequent release of library records was undertaken only after receipt of a properly drawn subpoena.

[1412]Bill of Rights Defense Committee (citing American Libraries) http://www.bordc.org/freedomtoread.htm#current

Since Ms. Hensman acted with full support of the Library's administration, she has not been subject to disciplinary action nor was any such action ever considered. All legal opinions obtained since September 15, 2001 indicate that the Library did not violate Florida law." [1413]

The Hensman case was hotly debated in Bill O'Riley FOX TV show entitled: "Controversial talk show with Mary Dempsey," INSIDE on Dec. 4, 2001. [1414] The case raised the central issue in post 9/11 USAPA vs. library debate: role and responsibilities of a librarian in time of national crisis. [1415]

To many librarians because Ms. Hensman has violated his long established professional ethics and state law in informing on a library patron. [1416] In taking upon herself to report patrons as "suspicious" terrorists, she effectively denounced library s' institutionalized mission, i.e., to provide a privacy free zone for people to read and think.

Librarians are most solicitous of intellectual freedom and protective of privacy right because of professional ethics and by din of personal temperament. At first, the librarian's reaction to USAPA is one of anxiety and uncertainty. In the end, librarians become defenders of free speech and privacy.

The trenchant debate was succinctly captured a New York Times columnist:

[1413] "News Digest" January 2002. Florida Library Association http://216.109.117.135/search/cache?p=Delray+Beach+library+board,+Kathleen+Hensman+andsub=Searchandei=UTF-8andurl=SLUGoRHKYacJ:www.flalib.org/library/fla/libnews/ndjan2002.htm

[1414] Sub title: "Partial transcript of interview with Chicago Public Library Commissioner Mary Dempsey from Bill O'Reilly of "The O'Reilly Factor," Dec. 4," http://www.insideonline.com/site/epage/3483_162.htm

[1415] Michael Rogers and Norman Oder, "Privacy Questions Raised in Aftermath of Terror Attacks," *Library Journal.* October 15, 2001 (http://www.libraryjournal.com/article/CA170438.html

[1416] All states except Hawaii, Kentucky, and Oregon have legislation that protects library record privacy. See, Ala. Code § 41-88-10 (2002); Alaska Stat. § 40.25.140 (Michie 2002); Ariz. Rev. Stat. § 41-1354 (2002); Ark. Code Ann. § 13-2-701 (Michie 2002); Cal. Gov't Code § 6267 (West 2002); Colo. Rev. Stat. § 24-72-204 (2002); Conn. Gen. Stat. § 11-25 (2001); Del. Code Ann. tit. 29 § 10002 (2002); D.C. Code Ann. § 39-108 (2002); Fla. Stat. ch. 257.261 (2002); Ga. Code Ann. § 24-9-46 (2002); Idaho Code § 9340E (Michie 2002); 75 Ill. Comp. Stat. 70/1 (2002); Ind. Code Ann. § 5-14-3-4 (Michie 2002); Iowa Code § 22.7 (2002); Kan. Stat. Ann. § 45-221 (2002); La. Rev. Stat. Ann. § 44:13 (West 2002); Me. Rev. Stat. Ann. tit. 27 § 121 (West 2001); Md. Code Ann., State Gov't § 10-616 (2002); Mass. Gen. Laws ch. 78, § 7 (2001); Mich. Comp. Laws § 397.601-603 (2002); Minn. Stat. § 13.40 (2001); Miss. Code Ann. § 39-3-305 (2002); Mo. Rev. Stat. § 182.817 (2001); Mont. Code Ann. § 22-1-1101-03 (2002); Neb. Rev. Stat. § 84712.05 (2002); Nev. Rev. Stat. Ann. 239.013 (Michie 2000); N.H. Rev. Stat. Ann. § 91-A:15 (2002); N.J. Stat. Ann. § 18A:73-43.2 (West 2002); N.M. Stat. Ann. § 18-9 (Michie 2002); N.Y. C.P.L.R. Law § 4509 (Consol. 2002); N.C. Gen. Stat. § 125-19 (2001); N.D. Cent. Code § 40-38-12 (2002); Ohio Rev. Code Ann. § 149.432 (West 2002); Okla. Stat. tit. 65, § 1-105 (2003); Or. Rev. Stat. § 192.502 (2001); Pa. Stat. Ann. tit. 24, § 4428 (West 2002); R.I. Gen. Laws § 38-2 (2002); S.C. Code Ann. § 60-4-10 (Law. Co-op. 2001); S.D. Codified Laws § 1-27-3, 14-2-51 (Michie 2002); Tenn. Code Ann. § 10-8-101-03 (2002); Tex. Gov't Code Ann. § 552.124 (Vernon 2003); Utah Code Ann. § 63-2-302 (2002); Vt. Stat. Ann. tit. 1 § 317 (2001); Va. Code Ann. § 2.2-3705 (Michie 2002); Wash. Rev. Code Ann. § 42.17.310 (West 2002); W. Va. Code § 10-1-22 (2002); Wis. Stat. § 43.30 (2001); Wyo. Stat. Ann. § 16-4-203 (Michie 2002). These state statutes either specifically provide for library record confidentiality or privacy, or create an exemption from a public record disclosure statute when library records identify the patron and/or their use of the library. Some of these statutes penalize prohibited disclosure, while others offer no remedy for improper disclosure. Almost all statutes require librarians to release the records when presented with a court order. Even Hawaii and Kentucky have provided Opinions of the Attorney Generals stating that library patron records should be kept private because the individual's right to privacy outweighs the public's interest in disclosure of the information. 90 Op. Att'y Gen. 30 (Hi. 1990); 81 Op. Att'y Gen. 159 (Ky. 2002). For a discussion of the motivation of some states in passing the library record privacy laws, and the variety of the laws, see Foerstel, supra note 1, at 133-50. Contra Paul D. Healey, "Chicken Little at the Reference Desk: The Myth of Librarian Liability," 87 *Law Libr. J.* 515, 527 (1995) ("Any obligation to protect exchanges at the reference desk derives from ethics, not law.").

"Ms. Hensman's decision to call the police has been the topic of considerable debate in professional library circles, especially in Florida." There were two schools of thoughts. The "absolute" school would not release library information under any circumstances, except by court order. For example, Judith Krug, director of the American Library Association's office of intellectual freedom, said, "I would have felt better if she had followed the Florida law." The "relative" school would argued for release of library information under extreme circumstances, such as 9/11. For example, Mary Wegner, Iowa's chief librarian, was of the opinion that: "our duty to our fellow humans trumps everything else."[1417]

There were however widespread support in some quarters for Ms. Hensman's action in the community.[1418] For example, a letter to editor to the local newspaper (Palm Beach Post) has this to say:

"About last Saturday's article on the librarian's post-attack report to the FBI: No one has any more gratitude and respect for our public library system (and therefore librarians also) than I, but when librarians start envisioning themselves as having the same plight as priests, as far as confidentiality goes, their self- possession has taken them a bit over the top."[1419]

Even those who disagree with her, e.g., ACLU, they understand her motive and accept her action.[1420]

USAPA impact different kind of libraries, differently. Functionally, there are many kinds of libraries, e.g., research vs. public, academic vs. vocational, general vs. specialized. Organizationally, libraries are managed differently, e.g., central administration (university library) vs. locally run (community library). Libraries, as a function driven and community based organization, have different mission orientation, organization structure and community culture. For example, university's mission is to promote intellectual curiosity and to encourage the students to explore different areas of interests. FBI investigation into students' reading habits is likely to chill students' free speech and retard intellectual curiosity. It also inhibits free exchange of ideas in class and contaminate relationship between faculty and students. FBI checking into library is not likely to yield any meaningful information or operational intelligence. Specifically, FBI cannot tell whether a student is a terrorist by looking into his/her reading habits; political science major and literature students are as likely to read Communist Manifesto as leftists or terrorists. As a screening device, the FBI net is cast too wide (netting those unsuspecting and innocent) and not wide enough (letting away those who are more conniving).

USAPA were received differently in different states and communities. States might have different understanding and expectation of what police officers should do when investigating into library records. Local communities are all different in terms of history (Idaho has a

---

[1417] David E. Rosenbaum, "Confidentiality: Breaking Law or Principles to Give Information to U.S." *New York Times*, November 23, 2001. The ethical dilemma – to release or not to release life saving information in trust - faced by the librarians as a profession, is not unique. Other professionals faced same kind of dilemma, e.g., clergy, journalists, lawyers, doctors. http://www.nytimes.com/2001/11/23/national/23LIBR.html?ex= 1064808000anden=d92c19e32152c244andei=5070.

[1418] "Put Zealous Librarian, ACLU on the Front Line," *Palm Beach Post* Dec 7, 2001. p. 13.

[1419] "Defenders of Secrecy at Libraries Over the Top," *Palm Beach Post*, Dec 7, 2001. p. 13.A

[1420] Chuck McGinness,"Librarian's Post-Attack Report to FBI Sparks Privacy Debate," *Palm Beach Post*, Dec 1, 2001. p. 1.B

history of fostering rugged individualism), culture (university town fosters diversity) and political orientation (Boston is much more liberal than Sam Houston.).

USAPA and FBI investigation into library has real and substantial consequences on library operation, from violating existing library information release policy to by passing established library board rule on consultation with lawyers before cooperating with police.

Not all post 9/11 investigation into the library raises the same kinds of issues. Police officials have known to carry out uncover investigation inside libraries. For example, post 9/11 FBI investigation guidelines allows agents to monitor library use. The issue is raised as to whether the police/FBI is allowed to monitor library activities, surreptitiously? I

There is also an interesting issue as to whether and how to make librarians change its privacy stance. There is evidence that in the face of an immediate threat, e.g., anthrax attack, and imminent danger, e.g., known terrorists searching for sensitive information, the librarians are more inclined to cooperate?[1421] ALA and local librarians have been quite willing to cooperate with police when their own interests are at stake. In taking this beggar thy neighbors approach is ALA adopting a double standards.

In the aftermath of 9/11, libraries across the nation took different positions and adopted a variety of approaches in working with police. In Las Vegas-Clark County Library District, the library administration encouraged employees to cooperate with law enforcement officials, including supplying them with library's confidential records and patrons' private data. There were also many instances of front line librarians cooperating with the police out of ignorance of their rights, unclear of their responsibilities, deference to state authority or just following their own conscience.

The willingness of the library to cooperate with the FBI must be viewed in a larger context of post-9/11 political climate in the country. The library is not a stand alone social institution. It is there to serve the best interests of the community. When the community political culture changes, as in the case of 9/11, so must the library guiding principles and operational procedures. The library, as a dependent institution and service organization, must subsist on the good will and with the support of the community, of which it is an integral part. How Chicago's Regenstein Library handled the students' objections to the Hezbollah poster at the library is a good example.[1422] By yielding to the students in removing the Hezbollah poster, the library makes clear that it is willing to abandon clear institutional guidelines, if only temporarily, to appease collective political furor, which, if allow to repeat and persist will one day change core values of the university.

VIII. IMPACT OF USAPA: LIBRARY SURVEYS

The most reliable and accessible data on the nature and extent, impact and reaction to law enforcement activities on the nation's libraries come from scientific surveys conducted by

---

[1421] Chad Brooks, "Events reinforce decision to review library security," *Daily Herald* Oct 16, 2001. p. 4. (After an anthrax scare, the Schaumburg Township District Library started to review its security procedures, including negating some tradition freedom enjoyed by the patrons.)

[1422] Susan Dodge, "Hezbollah poster stripped off wall; U. of C.'s Mideast center takes it down after students object," *Chicago Sun - Times*. Oct 23, 2001. p. 9 (The students at University of Chicago objected to the display of a Hezbollah poster in a Middle Eastern studies room at the University of Chicago's Regenstein Library.)

library associations and independent researchers. [1423] These studies dealt with four kinds of issues. First, frequency and nature of (federal and local) law enforcement contacts with the libraries, formally or informally, invited or uninvited, with or without legal authority. Second, reactions of librarians to the USAPA, administratively, operationally, professionally, and politically. Third, changed the library as a social institution, post 9/11 and in light of USAPA?

(1) In the summer of 2003, Sacramental Bee and California Library Association conducted a survey into impact of USAPA on California libraries, since 9/11. The survey was conducted by Karen G. Schneider, chair of CLA's Intellectual Freedom Committee. The study surveyed all CLA 2,000 members. 344 libraries - 260 are public, 47 academic, and 27 special libraries - responded with usable data. Respondents reported a total of 16 FBI informal information-seeking contacts since 9/11 with 6 libraries compiling. 41% of respondents established new patron-confidentiality policies because of USAPA.[1424] Local community members were very concerned with the impact of USAPA, including library staff (71%), library administer (57%), library board (35%), library users (42%), local reporters (25%), and local officials (21%).[1425]

(2) Professor Leigh Estabrook from University of Illinois Library Research Center conducted two national surveys on the impact of the USAPA on the nation's libraries. The first survey, entitled *The Responses of Public Libraries to the Event of September 11, 2001*[1426] was conducted in summer of 2002. The second, entitled *Public Libraries and Civil Liberties: A Profession Divide*[1427] was conducted in June of 2002 and again on January 2003. The 2002 survey showed that 85 libraries have been asked by the federal or local law enforcement officers to provide patron information. The 2003 survey shows that: "In the year after the World Trade Center and Pentagon attacks …federal and local law enforcement officials visited at least

---

[1423] Leigh Estabrook, *Public Libraries and Civil Liberties: A Profession Divided.* (Urbana, IL: U. of Illinois Library Research Center, January 2003), www.lis.uiuc.edu/gslis/research/civil_liberties.html (narrative) and www.lis.uiuc.edu/gslis/research/finalresults.pdf (questionnaire with summary of responses); and *Public Libraries' Response to the Events of 9/11.* (Urbana, IL: U. of Illinois Library Research Center, Summer 2002), www.lis.uiuc.edu/gslis/research/national.pdf. See also, Leigh Estabrook, "Response Disappointing," *American Libraries*, September 2002, pps. 37-38.

[1424] "Liberty in the Balance: Librarians step up" The Sacramento Bee http://www.modbee.com/ local/story/7517313p-8431668c.html Sam Stanton and Emily Bazar, "Librarians step up: They prepare for 'knock on the door," Published 2:15 am PDT Monday, September 22, 2003, http://dwb.sacbee.com/content/news/projects/liberty/story/7463163p-8405751c.html
For a power point presentation, see http://frl.bluehighways.com/talks/Patriot%20Games.ppt#263,13,Tech-Oriented Responses

[1425] http://frl.bluehighways.com/talks/Patriot%20Games.ppt#263,13,Tech-Oriented Responses

[1426] "The Responses of Public Libraries to the Event of September 11,2001 " *Illinois Libraries*, Vol. 84(1), pp. 1-8 (Winter 2001) http://www.cyberdriveillinois.com/publications/pdf_publications/illibrary_v84_n1.pdf
Public Libraries' Response to the Events of 9/11 (Urbana, IL: U. of Illinois Library Research Center, Summer 2002), www.lis.uiuc.edu/gslis/research/national.pdf.

[1427] *Public Libraries and Civil Liberties: A Profession Divided.* (Urbana, IL: U. of Illinois Library Research Center, January 2003) www.lis.uiuc.edu/gslis/research/civil_liberties.html (narrative) and www.lis.uiuc.edu/gslis/ research/finalresults.pdf (questionnaire with summary of responses); and See also, Leigh Estabrook, "Response Disappointing," *American Libraries*, September 2002, pp. 37-38.

545 libraries (10.7 percent) to ask for these records. Of these, 178 libraries received visits from the FBI itself."[1428]

State Survey Findings

In the summer of 2003, the Library Research Center of University of Illinois conducted a state wide survey of librarians. The study randomly surveyed 531 public and 148 academic library directors by e-mail, out of a total population of 795 public and 189 academic libraries statewide.[1429] The response rate was exceptionally high, being: 465 (87.6%) of public and 120 (81.1%) of academic libraries. The findings of the survey are as follows:

First, libraries were better prepared to deal with law enforcement visits than appeared or expected. For example, two years after 9/11 about 33.4% of the libraries have issued memo/guidelines on the content and analysis of USAPA[1430] and a full 83% have provided specialize training to librarians on state privacy law and USAPA legal requirements.[1431] However, only a minority (16%) of the libraries has provided dedicated USAPA law enforcement visit policy [1432] or made special arrangements to secure the library, e.g., only 18.3% has consulted security experts over library security.[1433] This finding is disturbing. The librarians seem to be more concerned with talking about security issues, than actually providing for them.

As to taking affirmative steps in reaction to USAPA, the libraries, again, have done surprising little: only 2.5% (3 libraries) have placed notice sign about USAPA[1434] and only 12.6% (15) have amended their policies in light of USAPA challenges.[1435]

As to concerns with USAPA - FBI/police visits on the libraries, only a minority of the citizens (83 (18.1%) at the public libraries and 17 (14.3%) at the academic libraries have expressed concerns.[1436]

As to the nature and extent of post 911/law enforcement activities in the library, the survey finds that only about 6% of public libraries and 5% of academic libraries were visited

---

[1428] "Libraries fear loss of privacy as FBI searches for terrorists," *toledoblade.com* Feb. 23, 2003. (While a survey of some libraries in northwest Ohio and southeast Michigan indicates that hasn't happened here, library officials said there is concern that it could.) http://www.toledoblade.com/apps/pbcs.dll/article?Site=TOand Date=20030223andCategory=NEWS15andArtNo=102230078andRef=AR

[1429] The Library Research Center surveyed all public and academic libraries in Illinois for which it had valid email addresses. The web-based survey was delivered by an email invitation sent on September 3rd, with a follow-up email reminder on September 15th. Additionally, the LRC sent a paper mail follow up on November 3rd, 2003.

[1430] Q1: "Issued any memoranda/guidelines to staff regarding provisions of the USAPA?"

[1431] Q2: "Reviewed with staff Illinois library law that states, The registration and circulation records of a library are confidential information. Except pursuant to a court order, no person shall publish or make any information contained in such records available to the public?"

[1432] Q4: 'Does the library have a formal (written) policy or set of guidelines on how to handle a search warrant or subpoena from law enforcement?(If "NO" please skip to question 5)"

[1433] Q3: "Consulted with any outside experts (e.g., police, security consultants) regarding the security of your library building(s) and premises?"

[1434] Q5: "Does your library post any public notice to users about provisions of the USAPA?"

[1435] Q6: "Has your library adopted or changed any library policies as a consequence of/or to address concerns related to the passage of the USAPA?(If "NO," please skip to question 7)"

[1436] Q7: "Are you aware of any concern of patrons about their privacy rights under the USAPA?"

by law enforcement authorities.[1437] This amounted to a total of 31 requests since 9/11. Most of these requests, 30/32 or 2/3[1438] were for circulation records and patrons' identity. Another revealing finding is that most of the requests or contacts were make by local law enforcement officials, rather than the Feds., i.e., 21 (police) vs. 8 (7 FBI 1 others)[1439] Another surprising discovery is that most of the requests were NOT for national security, i.e., 18 (crime) vs. 11 (security).[1440] None of those requests were supported by legal warrants or subpoena (10).[1441] Most information was supplied by voluntary help.[1442]

National Survey Findings

In 2004, the ALA commissioned a national survey on post 9/11 law enforcement activities on the nations' libraries. The report is entitled: "Impact and Analysis of Law Enforcement Activity in Academic and Public Libraries" (2005)[1443]

The study investigated the impact and implication of post 9/11 law enforcement activities on library administration policy, librarians' and patrons' attitude and behavior. The study sought to answer two descriptive questions: (1) The nature and extent of law enforcement activities afflicting academic and public libraries after 9/11. (2) The impact of such activities on the administration and operations of the library.[1444]

The study was conducted between January and April 2005[1445] based on a random sample of 1,536 public libraries (from a study population of 8,974) and (all) 4200 academic libraries.[1446] There were a total of 1,354 responses, representing 33% of public libraries and 23% of academic librarians. The research team also interviewed 50 librarians (25% of population) all over the nation. Regrettably, the response rate of the study is too small to provide for valid general observations from findings.[1447]

The study concluded by observing: "Overall, the study finds that there have been limited impacts on public and academic libraries in terms of law enforcement activity since the September 11, 2001 terrorist attacks in the United States."[1448]

On Issue of Preparedness

The survey shows that most public libraries [1449] have established polices (298 or 63.8%) [1450] and provided for formal training (289, 62%) [1451] in dealing with of law

---

[1437] Q8: "Have authorities (e.g.,, FBI, INS, police officers) requested any kind of information about any of your patrons since Sept. 11, 2001? (if "NO" please skip to Q9)"

[1438] Q8a. "Since 9/11/01 how many requests for information about patrons or circulation records have you received from any type of law enforcement official?"

[1439] Q8b: "Who requested information? (Circle all that apply)"

[1440] Q8C: "How many of these requests were in reference to national security? (if "NONE" please skip to Q9)"

[1441] Q8d: "How many national security related requests were accompanied by a subpoena or search warrant?"

[1442] Q8f: "How many of the national security related requests for patron information were for voluntary release of information?"

[1443] ALA impact study 2005, *supra*, note 3.

[1444] *Id.* P. 1.

[1445] *Id.* P. 2.

[1446] *Id.* P. 3.

[1447] *Id.* P. 5

[1448] *Id.* P. 1

[1449] Unless otherwise referenced, only public library responses will be reported and analyzed. Other academic libraries responses are not sufficiently different to warrant special treatment.

enforcement request for information. This is less so with academic libraries which stands at 47.9%[1452] and 45.8%,[1453] respectively.

On Issue of Change of Policy

How has USAPA changed library's administrative and operational policies: on patron information retention, on books borrowing limits and on library collection administration? The common impression, as suggested by the librarians and reported in the media, is that USAPA has changed the nation's library policy and service level drastically. The survey findings fail to support this impression.

Overall, a majority of the public libraries have not changed its patron information collection policy (64.5%),[1454] patron-use policy (87.5%),[1455] and government information availability (92.5%).[1456] In real terms usage of library services has not affected.[1457] The patrons did not feel that there was any noticeable change to the libraries' service level.[1458] Specifically there were no discernible efforts to remove materials from library – books (88.1%),[1459] newspaper (95.8%),[1460] magazines (93.8%), online databases (98.7%) and government documents (98.6%). If removals were done, they were done voluntarily and as a result of library budge and funding, rather than 9/11 reasons.[1461]

On Issue of Changes to Professional Conduct

Contrary to media reports, the survey shows the USAPA has little impact on librarians' professional conduct, from keeping patrons' borrowing records to maintaining computer log,[1462] e.g., 94.7% of the respondents indicted that "library staff have not altered their professional activities in reaction to the USA PATRIOT Act."[1463] A sizable minority (34.8%) of the librarians did "attempts to make patrons aware of the existence of the USA PATRIOT Act."[1464] If changes were made, they were mandated by the library board, and some at the behest of ALA. Very few resulted from 9/11.

[1450] *Id.* "Figure 4: Public Library Established Policies or Procedures for Requests for Information", p. 8

[1451] *Id.* "Figure 6: Public Library Librarian Training for Requests for Information", p. 8.

[1452] *Id.* "Figure 22. Academic Library Established Policies or Procedures for Requests for Information", p. 18.

[1453] *Id.* "Figure 24. Academic Library Librarian Training for Handling Requests for Information", p.19.

[1454] *Id.* Figure 7: "Public Library Changes to Policies Regarding the Collection and Retention of Patron Information Since Passage of the USAPA"

[1455] *Id.* Figure 8: "Public Library Changes to Patron-Use Policies for Materials as a Result of the USAPA"

[1456] *Id.* Figure 9: "Public Library Reduction of the Availability of Government Information as a Result of the USAPA"

[1457] *Id.* Figure 10: "Public Library Change in Usage of Library Services Since the Passage of the USAPA.

[1458] *Id.* Figure 11: "Public Library Number of Patrons that Indicated to Library Staff that the USAPA is Causing Changes in Usage of Selected Services."

[1459] *Id.* Figure 12, "Figure 12. Public Library Percentage of Removal of Selected Library Collection Aspects Since October 2001"

[1460] .*Id.*

[1461] Figure 13, and P. 10. Figure 13: "Public Library Reasons for Removal of Selected Library Materials Change in Usage of Library Services Since October 2001"

[1462] See "Sample Changes in Behavior" to Figure 15t.

[1463] Figure 15. Public Library Staff Alterations in Professional Behavior in Reaction to the USAPA.

[1464] Figure 14: "Figure 14. Public Library Patron Awareness of the Existence of the USAPA"

Contacts with Law Enforcement Agencies

One of the most contentious issues about the impact of USAPA on library is the extent of law enforcement contacts with the libraries. DOJ claimed there were few contacts. ALA claimed that law enforcements contacts were many.

The survey shows there were limited contacts by law enforcement officials, at the federal (informal requests for patron information: 1.7% or 8 times) and state (3.5% or 16 times) government level.[1465] There were fewer library initiated contacts to provide information on patrons to federal officials (1.3% or 6 times), than with state police authority (4.4% or 20 times).

In terms of legal contacts for library, the federal agencies have served the library with legal order in 26 cases whereas the state has done so in 47 times, of which 7 federal order is for electronic/computer data and 10 state order is for electronic/computer data.[1466]

IX. REACTION TO SECTION 215

Introduction

The reaction of the library community to Section 215 is influenced by a number of factors: institutional mission, political climate, historical experience, community expectation, organization culture, professional ethics, and public demand.

From its inception, Section 215 of the USAPA was not well received, at the national as well as at the local level:

> "Almost 60 percent (59.9%) of librarians responding to the Library Research Center Poll stated they thought the secrecy provision is an abridgement of First Amendment rights. One in five (21.7%) librarians feels strongly enough that they state they probably or definitely would challenge a court order regarding information about a patron by disclosing a request that ordered non-disclosure."[1467]

In fact Section 215 has come to stand for what all is wrong with the USAPA as a whole – lack of public consultation, failure of legislative process, infringement of human rights, denial of civil liberties, and violation of Constitutional protection. For example, a news reporter has characterized the problems of USAPA in the following way:

> "The searches of some records kept by libraries and bookstores were authorized in an obscure provision of the USAPA, quietly approved by Congress six weeks after Sept. 11. The act, passed virtually without hearings or debate, allowed a variety of new federal surveillance

---

[1465] Figure 17: "Public Library Number of Instances of Voluntarily Providing Information about the Activities of Patrons"

[1466] Figure 18: "Public Library Number of Instances of Requests for Records and Other Items by Law Enforcement Agencies"

[1467] The survey was mailed in October 2002 to directors of 1,505 of the 5,094 U.S. public libraries serving populations of over 5,000. This report provides estimates of the situation in those 5,094 libraries, based on the 906 responses (60.2% of those sampled). Leigh S. Estabrook, "Public Libraries and Civil Liberties:A Profession Divided," The Library Research Center, University of Illinois at Urbana-Champaign. http://www.lis.uiuc.edu/gslis/research/civil_liberties.html

measures, including clandestine searches of homes and expanded monitoring of telephones and the Internet.,"[1468]

The concern with Section 215, more so than any other USAPA provisions, has been used as a rally cry for the repeal of the USAPA.

ALA Efforts in Defense of Intellectual Freedom and Privacy

In 1876 the American Library Association (ALA) was founded in Philadelphia by Justin Winsor, William Frederick Poole and Melvil Dewey. Since 1909, the ALA is headquarters in Chicago, Illinois. ALA has 50,000 members representing all types of libraries and librarians.

ALA was originally formed to promote high-quality information services. It is founded for "the purpose of promoting the library interests of the country by exchanging views, reaching conclusions, and inducing cooperation in all departments of bibliothecal science and economy: by disposing the public mind to the founding and improving libraries and by cultivating good will amend its own members." (1897) According to ALA Constitution, ALA is to promote library service and librarianship. [1469]

In line with its Charter, ALA has long been a champion of intellectual freedom and guardian of personal privacy. The Cold War (1945 – 1991) saw increased censorship of "subversive" and "un-American" publications of all kinds by government and citizens alike. In reaction, the ALA adopted a strengthened Library Bill of Rights to intellectual freedom[1470] on June 18, 1948.[1471] The "Library Bill of Rights" affirms that "all libraries are forums for information and ideas" and libraries should following certain fundamental principles and policies in rendering their services, including: libraries should promote enlightenment, [1472] seek diversity, [1473] challenge censorship, [1474] advance intellectual freedom, [1475] prohibits discrimination,[1476] and facilitate open/equal accessibility.[1477]

[1468] Bob Egelko, "FBI checking out Americans' reading habits Bookstores, libraries can't do much to fend off search warrants," *San Francisco Chronicle*, June 23, 2002.

[1469] Taken from the American Library Association *Fact Sheet*.

[1470] Louise S. Robbins, "The Overseas Libraries Controversy and the Freedom to Read: U.S. Librarians and Publishers Confront Joseph McCarthy," *Libraries and Culture* Volume 36 (1): 27-39 (Winter 2001).

[1471] Adopted June 18, 1948. Amended February 2, 1961, and January 23, 1980,inclusion of "age" reaffirmed January 23, 1996, by the ALA Council. http://www.ala.org/Content/NavigationMenu/Our_Association /Offices/Intellectual_Freedom3/Statements_and_Policies/Intellectual_Freedom2/librarybillofrights.pdf

[1472] "Books and other library resources should be provided for the interest, information, and enlightenment of all people of the community the library serves. Materials should not be excluded because of the origin, background, or views of those contributing to their creation." See Article I, "Library Bill of Rights."

[1473] "Libraries should provide materials and information presenting all points of view on current and historical issues. Materials should not be proscribed or removed because of partisan or doctrinal disapproval." See Article II, "Library Bill of Rights."

[1474] "Libraries should challenge censorship in the fulfillment of their responsibility to provide information and enlightenment." See Article III, "Library Bill of Rights."

[1475] "Libraries should cooperate with all persons and groups concerned with resisting abridgment of free expression and free access to ideas." See Article IV, "Library Bill of Rights."

[1476] "A person's right to use a library should not be denied or abridged because of origin, age, background, or views." See Article IV, "Library Bill of Rights."

[1477] "Libraries which make exhibit spaces and meeting rooms available to the public they serve should make such facilities available on an equitable basis, regardless of the beliefs or affiliations of individuals or groups requesting their use." See Article IV, "Library Bill of Rights."

The McCarthy era (1950 - 1954) led to the adoption of *The Freedom to Read*, a strong public statement rejecting censorship of all kinds and in favor of unlimited intellectual freedom. It enunciated seven basic propositions in defense of the freedom:

- "First, publishers and librarians have a responsibility to "make available the widest diversity of views and expressions," including "unorthodox or unpopular" ones.
- Second, they need not "endorse every idea or presentation contained in the books they make available," nor should they "establish their own political, moral, or aesthetic views as the sole standard for publication or selection."
- Third, it is "contrary to the public interest" for them to "determine the acceptability of a book solely on the basis of the personal history or political affiliations of the author."
- Fourth, while obscenity laws "should be vigorously enforced," extralegal activities "to coerce the taste of others, to confine adults to the reading matter deemed suitable for adolescents, or to inhibit the efforts of writers to achieve artistic expression" have no place in our society.
- Fifth, labeling books or authors as "subversive or dangerous" is not in the public interest.
- Sixth, publishers and librarians have a responsibility "to contest encroachments" upon the freedom to read by those "seeking to impose their own standards or tastes upon the community at large."

And finally, publishers and librarians should "give full meaning to the freedom to read by providing books that enrich the quality of thought and expression." In doing so, they can demonstrate "that the answer to a bad book is a good one, the answer to a bad idea is a good one." They concluded: "We do not state these propositions in the comfortable belief that what people read is unimportant. We believe, rather, that what people read is deeply important; that ideas can be dangerous but that the suppression of ideas is fatal to a democratic society. Freedom itself is a dangerous way of life, but it is ours." [1478]

From 1967 to 1974, the ALA spearheaded the social responsibilities movement. During this time, intellectual freedom was progressively institutionalized and increasingly bureaucratized within ALA with the creation of the Library Bill of Rights (1938), the Intellectual Freedom Committee (1940), the Office for Intellectual Freedom (1967), and the Freedom to Read Foundation (1969). [1479] Finally, in 1970 ALS developed its "Policy on Confidentiality of Library Records" in reaction to growing attempts by U.S. law enforcement agencies to examine patron's library records as part of their investigations. [1480]

Since its inception, the ALA has encountered many challenges and fought numerous battles to promote intellectual freedom and protect patrons' privacy, from shielding

---

[1478] Louise S. Robbins, "The Overseas Libraries Controversy and the Freedom to Read: U.S. Librarians and Publishers Confront Joseph McCarthy," *Libraries and Culture* Volume 36, Number 1, Winter 2001, pp. 27-39.

[1479] Toni Samek Intellectual Freedom and Social Responsibility in American Librarianship, 1967-1974 (Jefferson, NC: McFarland, 2001).

[1480] Kenneth A. Winter, "Privacy and the Rights and Responsibilities of Librarians," The Katharine Sharp Review No. 4, Winter 1997, paragraph 16. http://edfu.lis.uiuc.edu/review/winter1997/winter.html

"objectionable" library materials from community censorship [1481] to defending against patrons' privacy against state encroachment. By far the most controversial of ALA's stances is its staunch support for free library access to pornographic sites. This set the ALA on a collision course with the church and family, and by extension the community. The confrontation led to a resounding defeat for the ALA. It also resulted in the passage of the Children's Internet Protection Act (CIPA). The result of the confrontation suggested that ALA has taken a philosophical stance on free speech and intellectual freedom that is out of touch with the general public sentiment. [1482]

The ALA's stance against FBI's LAP is another prime example of ALA's commitment to and activism in protecting intellectual freedom and personal privacy. [1483] During the cold war years, the FBI, as part of its counter-intelligence initiative, wanted to find out what East European spies were reading in the nation's premiere science and technology libraries, including the libraries Columbia University Mathematics and Science Library, the New York Public Library, the Lockwood Memorial Library at Buffalo, NY, the Courant Institute of Mathematical Sciences Library, the University of Maryland at College Park Engineering and Physical Sciences Library, the University of Houston Library, and the UCLA Engineering and Mathematical Sciences Library. As a result they launched the Library Awareness Program, a secret surveillance program within America's unclassified scientific libraries. The program has two goals: (1) to detect and prevent foreign (Soviet and East European) access to unclassified but sensitive scientific information; (2) to recruit librarians to inform upon suspected "foreigners" using America's unclassified scientific libraries.

The ALA was in the forefront defending libraries from FBI plying in the stacks and otherwise recruiting librarians as informants. [1484] As of November 1989, The FBI had investigated 266 persons, most of whom were librarians, under the auspices of the LAP. [1485]

From a historical perspective, USAPA is nothing more than a continue struggle to protect library patrons' First Amendment rights to intellectual freedom, freedom of speech and personal privacy.

[1481] "Coping with Challenges: Strategies and Tips for Dealing with Challenges to Library Materials," ALA http://www.ala.org/Content/NavigationMenu/Our_Association/Offices/Intellectual_Freedom3/Challenge_Sup port/Dealing_with_Challenges/coping.pdf

[1482] See "Battle against liberal library policies having positive effect: Report from American Library Association national convention," Family Association Journal Volume 23 Issue 09 (September 1999) http://www.afajournal.org/archives/23090000094.asp

[1483] For the only authoritative account of the origin, development and demise of the Library Awareness Program, see Herbert N. Forestel, *Surveillance in the Stacks* (N.Y.: Greenwood Press, 1991) pp. 54-69. For an abbreviated account, see also Ulrika Ekman Ault. "Reading Over Your Shoulder? 65 N.Y.U. L. Rev. 1532, 1535 (1990). (FBI enlisting librarians to monitor the reading habits of 'suspicious individuals.') Id. at 1534. For a negative assessment of the Library Awareness Program, see Ronald Kessler, The Bureau: The Secret History of the F.B.I. (2002) p. 225 (The FBI was insensitive to the symbolic significance of the library as defending for the nation's First Amendment right.) For Congressional oversight hearing, see "F.B.I. Counterintelligence Visits to Libraries," Hearings Before the Subcomm. on Civil and Constitutional Rights of the Comm. on the Judiciary, 100th Cong. 121 (1989).

[1484] "Remarks by Herbert Foerstel, former Head of Branch Libraries at University of Maryland and board member of the National Security Archive," Speech Delivered at MIT, Cambridge, MA, March 29, 1999. http://www.aaas.org/spp/secrecy/Presents/foerstel.htm

[1485] Johnston, "Documents Disclose FBI Investigations of Some Librarians" *N.Y. Times*, Nov. 7, 1989, at A1.

National – ALA Challenging to USAPA

ALA was much concerned about the impact of the USAPA and related anti-terrorism activities on the nation's libraries, especially its implication for privacy, confidentiality and civil liberties.[1486] ALA's activities focused on the impact of the legislation of library community and our library user." [1487]

From the very beginning, ALA and sister library associations, e.g., American Association of Law Libraries (AALL) and the Association of Research Libraries (ARL), have joined hand with other civil liberties NGOs, e.g., Center for Democracy and Technology (CDT) and ACLU, to monitor the development of the USAPA, from the Administration's Anti-Terrorism Act to the Senate's USA Act, to the House's USAPA, and finally the USAPA. ALA and other activist groups formed the "In Defense of Freedom Coalition" (IDOFC) to monitor 9/11 anti-terrorism legislation and measures. IDOF includes Free Congress Foundation, Friends Committee on National Legislation, Gun Owners of America, The Eagle Forum, the American Muslim Council, Americans for Tax Reform, and many other diverse groups.[1488] The IDOF was most concerned with the following issues: expansion of Internet surveillance (e.g., pen register and trap and trace); expansion of access to business records (e.g., NSL); expansion of access to educational records (e.g., student academic reports); and expansion of the definition of terrorism (e.g., Green Peace)

As early as September 19, 2001 and within days after the administration released it proposed the Anti-Terrorism Act of 2001 (ATA), ALA together with other library associations[1489] issued a public statement affirming the need for a balanced national security vs. intellectual freedom policy in times of crisis: "By maintaining, on a daily basis, the balance between access to information for all, the privacy rights of our users, and the responsibility to cooperate with law enforcement agencies, libraries continue to be cultural and living symbols for the freedoms that we enjoy."[1490] The statement did not once mention the ATA, but it is clear that the ALA was much concerned about the impact of ATA on the nation's library.

During the entire legislative process – September 19, 2001 to October 25, 2001, the ALA was heavily engaged with monitoring the legislative process, organizing lobbying efforts, working with Congressional staffers and mobilizing of grassroots. As soon as ALA got wind

---

[1486] ALA was also concerned with access to government information, e.g., sanitizing of library information of sensitive but not classified information. USAPA: A Summary of ALA activities," ALA Washington Office, January 19, 2002. http://www.ala.org/Content/NavigationMenu/Our_Association/Offices/ALA_ Washington/Issues2/Civil_Liberties,_Intellectual_Freedom,_Privacy/The_USA_Patriot_Act_and_Libraries/ba ckground.pdf

[1487] ALA was also concerned with access to government information, e.g., sanitizing of library information of sensitive but not classified information. USAPA: A Summary of ALA activities," ALA Washington Office, January 19, 2002. http://www.ala.org/Content/NavigationMenu/Our_Association/Offices/ALA_Washington/ Issues2/Civil_Liberties,_Intellectual_Freedom,_Privacy/The_USA_Patriot_Act_and_Libraries/background.pdf

[1488] See "USAPA: A summary of ALA activities," (Jan. 19, 2002. http://www.ala.org/Content/NavigationMenu/ Our_Association/Offices/ALA_Washington/Issues2/Civil_Liberties,_Intellectual_Freedom,_Privacy/The_USA_Pat riot_Act_and_Libraries/background.pdf

[1489] The statement was countersigned by Mary Alice Baish of American Association of Law Libraries, Lynne Bradley of American Library Association, Prue Adler of Association of Research Libraries and Mary Langman of Medical Library Association.

[1490] "Library Community Statement on Freedom of Speech and Access to Information," September 19, 2001. http://www.arl.org/info/frn/other/statement.html

of the specifics of the administration's proposed ATA, it started to develop a strategy to counter the administration's initiative.

In point of time, the ALA's Office of Information Technology and Policy (OITP) organized a meeting with American Association of Law Librarians (AALL), Association of Research Librarians (ARL), chairs of ALA Committee on Legislation, OITP Advisory Committee and technology experts and legal advisors to analyze the content and impact of the Act. The discussion focused on three main issues: (1) broad definition of domestic terrorism in the ATA to include cyber crime; (2) expansive power to access library records; (3) using library systems for surveillance and wiretapping. Throughout the process, the ALA was in close consultation with CDC and IDOFC.[1491]

October 2, 2001, the ALA sent an open letter to Congressional members outlining its concerns, cautioning against rash judgment,[1492] and specifically calling for balancing "the impact of any legislative and regulatory proposals on the privacy and First Amendment rights of library users." The ALA listed five objections to the ATA: the expansion of pen register and trap and trace devices to the Internet; the expansion of access to business records; the expansion of access to educational institution records; the expansion of the definition of terrorism; and new mandates for installing technology at libraries.[1493]

In the House, ALA lobbying efforts focused on the persuading the more enlightened members in the House Judiciary Committee, including Congresspersons Sanders (D-VT), Walters (D-CA), Jackson-Lee (D-TX), and Conyers (D-MI). Many of the library communities suggested amendments did not make it pass the October 3, 2001 unanimous House Judiciary Committee vote approving HR2975 (PATRIOT ACT). Although there were a few amendments made during the markup, none were related to two of ALA's chief concerns: business records (including library and student records) and computer trespassing.

On October 11, the Senate passed S. 1510. The next morning the Senate bill language was substituted for the original House bill in a procedural move by the House Rules Committee. With no opportunity to add amendments, the House passed the "new" (basically the Senate bill) H.R. 3108 in a vote of 357 to 66 on October 12. Many members complained about the unusual process. Changes in the final language included a sunset provision on electronic surveillance authority and a provision for judicial oversight on the use of the FBI's Carnivore system. Some observers are now speculating whether the lack of hearings or any other kind of public record will subject the law to legal challenges because of lack of a legislative history.

During the Senate proceedings, the library associations focused on amendments proposed by Senator Russ Feingold (D-Wisconsin), subsequently offered during the floor debate. Unfortunately, these amendments were defeated in a procedural move. The Senate passed S. 1510 in a 98 to 1 vote late on October 11. During the floor debate on the business records and computer trespass amendments, key senators referenced the library issues in particular. In a procedural vote on the business records amendment, 11 senators voted with Feingold, including Senator Arlen Specter (R-Pennsylvania).

[1491] See Appendix I.

[1492] "Library Community Statement on Proposed Anti-Terrorism Measures," http://www.arl.org/info/frn/other/antiter2.html

[1493] Id.

During next week, a conference committee met to negotiate the differences between the Senate and House versions of the USAPA. President Bush signed the bill on October 26, 2001.

Immediately after the passage of the USAPA, the ALA's Office for Intellectual Freedom issued a statement informing its members of the passage of the USAPA, the scope of Section 213, and rights of the libraries and librarians under the Constitution:

"The new legislation amends the laws governing the Federal Bureau of Investigation's access to business records. One provision orders any person or institution served with a search warrant not to disclose that such a warrant has been served or that records have been produced pursuant to the warrant. The existence of this provision does not mean that libraries and librarians served with such a search warrant cannot ask to consult with their legal counsel concerning the warrant. A library and its employees can still seek legal advice concerning the warrant and request that the library's legal counsel be present during the actual search and execution of the warrant.

If you or your library are served with a warrant issued under this law, and wish the advice of legal counsel but do not have an attorney, you can still obtain assistance from Jenner and Block, the Freedom to Read Foundation's legal counsel. Simply call the Office for Intellectual Freedom (800-545-2433, ext. 1 + 4223) and inform the staff that you need legal advice without disclosing the reason you need legal assistance. OIF staff will assure that an attorney from Jenner and Block returns your call. You do not have to and should not inform OIF staff of the existence of the warrant."[1494]

ALA is now working with outside legal advisors to provide a systematic analysis of the law. For example, it was noted that the section on business records raises complicated questions relative to state and other privacy laws. New privacy provisions do not automatically preempt existing state confidentiality laws regarding library records unless an investigation is related to foreign intelligence and anti-terrorism investigations. In a related matter, we are also addressing the "take-down" of government information from Web sites and the depository library programs. Watch for additional reports; there is much more to come.

Since then ALA has counseled its members to take a number of measures, offensively, e.g., seeking repeal of the law, and defensively, e.g., offering legal advises to librarians, against the ACT, to effective neutralize the adverse impact of law on the book (through repeal) and in the street (through self-help).[1495]

Three of ALA's more effective measures to impede the application of Section 215 and alleviate its impact are: having the libraries maintain the minimum of patrons' records for the shortest period of time (e.g., by destroying borrowing records daily),[1496] resist voluntary compliance with government's request for information by referring all inquires to ALA

[1494] www.ala.org/alaorg/oif/alertusapatriotact.html

[1495] "Confidentiality and Coping with Law Enforcement Inquiries: Guidelines for the Library and its Staff," Offices of Intellectual Freedom, ALA. http://80-vnweb.hwwilsonweb.com.www.remote.uwosh.edu: 2048/hww/shared/shared_main.jhtml;jsessionid=4UHQIMKWWUAJ3QA3DILSFFQ?_requestid=27490.

[1496] Dean Murphy, "Librarians Use Shredder to Show Opposition to New F.B.I. Powers," *New York Times* April 7, 2003. http://www.commondreams.org/headlines03/0407-03.htm (Anne M. Turner, director of the Santa Cruz library system: "The basic strategy now is to keep as little historical information as possible.") Al Winslow, "Library Bristles At USAPA," *Berkeley Daily Planet,* April 25-03. http://www.berkeleydaily.org/text/article.cfm?issue=04-25-03andstoryID=16539#links (Berkeley public libraries destroyed its records every night.)

attorneys, and informing the public of the intrusiveness and stealthiest of the ACT by public display of warnings.

The ALA also wants to enlist the public to help in the cause. [1497] It started a nation wide ad campaign. In a chilling public service announcement, a young man approaches a librarian with a request for books. The librarian announces the books are no longer available and asks the patron's name. When the patron turns to leave, two men in suits stop him. The Ad Council created this ad as part of their "Campaign for Freedom" aimed at highlighting the dangers of outside forces present to our freedoms. This spot struck a chord with a library community coping with the anxieties presented by the expanded access provisions of the USAPA (ALA, 2002, American Library). It sent a clear message: when "they" (the government) know what "you" are reading, self-censorship is sure to ensue.

Following up with the ad campaign, the ALA Council, in January 2002, passed a "Resolution Reaffirming the Principles of Intellectual Freedom in the Aftermath of Terrorist Attacks" that includes a provision reaffirming the fundamental principles of the library profession encouraging "libraries and their staff to protect the privacy and confidentiality of the people's lawful use of the library, its equipment, and its resources."

On January 29, 2003 the ALA Council adopted a resolution - "Resolution on the USA Patriot Act and Related Measures That Infringe on the Rights of Library Users"[1498] (ALA Resolution) - voicing its objections to aspects of the USAPA and calling for concerted effort to deal with the Act. The ALA Resolution was initiated by Committee on Legislation and Cosponsored by Committee on Legislation and Intellectual Freedom Committee. It was endorsed by OITP Advisory Committee and LITA and endorsed in principle by: ACRL, ALTA Executive Board, ALSC, ASCLA, AASL Legislation Committee, Intellectual Freedom Round Table.[1499].

The Resolution declared that the ALA finds sections of the USAPA to be a clear and present danger to the constitutional rights and privacy rights of library patrons and urges the Congress to provide for active oversight and otherwise amend provisions of the Act that poses threats to right of inquiry and free expression. The ALA Resolution has since been endorsed and adopted by a majority of the state's library association.

Grassroots Library Reaction to USAPA

Grassroots library reaction to USAPA took the form of self help, e.g., posting warning sign that patrons' activities are being monitored, passively, or campaigning for resolutions resisting USAPA, assertively.

On March 3, 2003, Santa Cruz Library Joint Powers Board Resolution passed[1500] "A Resolution on the USAPA and Related Measures that Infringe on the Rights of Library

---

[1497] Bob Garfield, "Of propaganda, ad triumphs and advertrocities," *Advertising Age* 73 no51 14-15 D 30 2002. "The Freedom Campaign" (an Ad Council effort) reminded Americans of the importance of freedom and democracy, lest people take it for granted. http://80-vnweb.hwwilsonweb.com.www.remote.uwosh.edu:2048/ hww/shared/shared_main.jhtml;jsessionid=HJOOMHTQHPVP5QA3DILCFFI?_requestid=42861

[1498] http://www.ala.org/Template.cfm?Section=IF_ResolutionsandTemplate=/ContentManagement/ ContentDisplay.cfmandContentID=11891

[1499] Prior History: CD#19.1 January 2002, CD#20.5 January 2002, CD#20.3 January 2002

[1500] Jondi Gums, "Privacy piracy: Warning signs to be posted at libraries," *Santa Cruz Sentinel* March 5, 2003. http://www.santacruzsentinel.com/archive/2003/March/05/local/stories/01local.htm

Users." (Resolution)[1501] Santa Cruz, known for its progressive politics,[1502] was one the first library systems in the nation to take a stance and warn patrons about the ramifications of the federal law.[1503] The Santa Cruz Resolution, while not the only library anti- Section 215 resolution, gain prominence nationally and internationally.[1504]

The Resolution holds that "suppression of ideas undermines a democratic society" and "privacy is essential to the exercise of free speech, free thought, and free association." It finds that the USAPA increased the power of the government to obtain library records, secretly monitor electronic communication, and prohibit libraries from informing users of such monitoring or information requests. It asserts that such and other federal " laws, regulations, and guidelines increase the likelihood that the activities of library users … may be under government surveillance without their knowledge or consent." It affirms that "libraries are a critical force for promoting the free flow and unimpeded distribution of knowledge and information for individuals." It thus resolved to take a number of steps to neutralize the pernicious effects of Section 215, including: opposing government suppression of free exchange of ideas and intimidation of free inquiry; supporting amending obnoxious and unconstitutional sections of USAPA; taking steps to systematically protect users' privacy rights; referring all law enforcement requests to Director of Libraries Office; asking California Congressional delegation to "support legislation that would exempt libraries and booksellers from those parts of the Act that infringe on constitutional rights, and increase Congressional oversight of the Act"; posing warning signs that the library is under government surveillance without notice to the patrons; and raising the awareness of the public on USAPA issues.[1505]

On May 20, the Door County Library Board,[1506] after a brief discussion (20 minutes), voted unanimously to instruct Becca Berger, the library director to send letters to Congressional legislators to exempt libraries and private bookstores from Section 215 of the USAPA. The Board did not pass a resolution. The Board was spurred into action by resolutions and actions of other library boards across the name, e.g., Santa Cruz.

Board members thought that Section 215 is unconstitutional as well as unnecessary. [1507] Library board member, Jack Jordan, who made the motion, found Section 215 to be "repugnant" on moral and constitutional grounds:

> "The burden on our library staff to act as secret informants is wrong. I move that we as a board, send a letter to our … representatives to recommend them to take another look at

---

[1501] For text of the Resolution, see http://www.santacruzpl.org/libraryadmin/ljpb/patres.shtml

[1502] Santa Cruz is a community well known for its leftward leanings and progressive politics. Last fall, city officials allowed marijuana for medicinal purposes to be distributed from the steps of City Hall. The City Council also passed a resolution condemning the USAPA.

[1503] Bob Egelko, Maria Alicia Gaura, "Libraries post USAPA warnings Santa Cruz branches tell patrons that FBI may spy on them," *San Francisco Chronicle* March 10, 2003. http://www.sfgate.com/cgi-bin/article.cgi?file=/chronicle/archive/2003/03/10/MN14634.DTL

[1504] Lawrence Donegan, "Anger as CIA Homes in on New Target: Library Users," Observer/UK, March 16, 2003. http://www.commondreams.org/headlines03/0316-04.htm

[1505] For a discussion of how the impact of USAPA on Palo Alton, see "Palo Alto City Council Resolution In Support of Civil Liberties: Impact of the USAPA and Other Measures on the City of Palo Alto," May 2003. http://www.peaceandjustice.org/patriot/impact-report.pdf

[1506] By law, the Door County Library Board not Door County Board of Supervisor has the power and responsibility to protect the rights of library.

[1507] Carl Mickelson, "Local library objects to USAPA," News-Chronicle Green Bay, WI). May 20, 2003

section 215 and whether or not it might be unfair, and infringing on privacy rights. And whether that's an unfair burden on library staff." [1508]

Library board member Sharon Virlee, a high school librarian and member of the board considered Section 215 as unnecessary. Investigators can go to court for warrants to conduct necessary investigations. She was particularly concerned about the impact of the law on the 39,000 local residents, like amount of tourists and foreign workers who used the library for a variety of reasons, e.g., e-mail link with home. [1509]

On May 22, 2003, five-member Livermore library board in California voted unanimously to ask the City council to support the California and American Library Associations' resolutions denouncing Section 215 and to endorse the Freedom to Read Protection Act. [1510] The vote was supported by grassroots organizations, such as Save Our Rights Coalition of the Tri-Valley, or SAVOR which work to "protect our constitutional liberties, repeal new laws that threaten our freedom, resist Big Brother invasion into our lives." [1511]

The library board letter endorsing the Freedom to Read Protection Act seeking a waiver for Section for the libraries reads: "The USAPA expands the authority of the federal government to investigate citizens and non citizens in a manner which will increase the likelihood that the activities of library users, including the borrowing of library materials and their use of computers to browse the Internet, may be under government surveillance without their knowledge," the letter says." [1512]

On May 23, 2003 Sen. Barbara Boxer (D-Calif.) introduced the Library and Bookseller Protection Act, which would exempt libraries and bookstores from turning over personally identifiable information on patrons' reading choices for foreign-intelligence investigations.

From the very beginning local libraries have taken individual actions in protest against the scope and reach of Section 215, e.g., within days of the passage of the USAPA thousands of libraries around the Nation have started destroying their library records. [1513]

X. CONCLUSION:
IMPACT OF USAPA ON LIBRARY

9/11 is a transformational event for the United States, especially for the libraries, librarians and patrons. USAPA is successful in recalibrating the delicate balance between national security vs. civil liberties in America. [1514] "Some of our fundamental professional

---

[1508] Carl Mickelson, "Local library objects to USAPA," News-Chronicle Green Bay, WI). May 20, 2003

[1509] Carl Mickelson, "Local library objects to USAPA" News-Chronicle Green Bay, WI). May 20, 2003

[1510] "Wisconsin, California Trustees Seek USAPA Exemptions," ALA Libraries.com June 2, 2003. http://www.ala.org/al_onlineTemplate.cfm?Section=American_Librariesandtemplate=/ContentManagement/ContentDisplay.cfmandContentID=33327

[1511] SAVORS is a coalition of Livermore, Pleasanton, Dublin. Its main objective is "to rescind the "USAPA" and to keep the "USAPA II" from being enacted.." http://nowwatchthis.hypermart.net/savor/pdf/brochure4.pdf

[1512] Sam Richards, "Library seeks support for USAPA revise," *CONTRA COSTA TIMES.com* May 24, 2003. http://www.bayarea.com/mld/cctimes/news/5936766.htm

[1513] Dean Murphy, "Librarians Use Shredder to Show Opposition to New F.B.I. Powers," *New York Times* April 7, 2003. http://www.commondreams.org/headlines03/0407-03.htm

[1514] "Life with the Use USAPA: At the Crossroads of Privacy and Protection." In Fred Reenstjerna; Anna Grzeskiewicz, "Librarians in the Crisis. 9/11 One Year Later," *Oregon Library Association Quarterly* 8 no4 1-24 (Winter 2002)

concepts as librarians--freedom of information, access, and privacy--likewise have pre- and post-September 11 contexts."

One year after 9/11, Robert Truman, Head of Electronic Information Services, Paul L. Boley Law Library Lewis and Clark Law School observed:[1515]

> "The increased surveillance powers are forcing librarians to come to a new understanding of the relationship between privacy rights and patron information. The new laws make it easier for authorities to follow the path of individuals up to and through the library doors."
> [1516]

There are different phrases to post 9/11 library adjustments. Right after 9/11, the nation was worried about any attack. There was a rush to track down the terrorists, for retribution, as well as for prevention.

When survival is at stake and security is the main concern, there is little consideration of constitutional norm or civil liberties. The FBI was given a free hand. Everyone was expected to cooperate. This process lasted no more than the first year. After things calmed down, rationality returns. People started to question the constitutional authority of USAPA and over-zealousness of the FBI.

The next stage is a consolidation stage. The government and civil libertarians amassed their forces and coordinated their resources to fight a classical battle between security vs. liberties, with librarians (ALA) and libertarians (ACLU) in the lead. The battle has less to do with 9/11, library, security and liberties as it is about the clash of two ideologies and cultures, i.e., right vs. left, conservatism vs. progressivism. The cultural and ideological war of words is being fought over the necessity and effectiveness of USAPA.

In the post 9/11 era and with a patriotic crowd and inflammatory press, librarians are hard pressed to find support for their position. In the heat of battle, the higher purpose and longer vision of securing the nation's liberties and privacy in the midst of war finds no support.

Library has some power to resist cooperation with visiting law enforcement officials. However, such powers, .e.g., destroying of records, pale in comparison to government's censorship power, e.g., removal of sensitive but not secret materials. After 9/11 the government can by fiat declare a piece of information as off limits to the public, summarily and without recourse, on grounds of secrecy, security or sensitivity. It can government can deny the public's right to read altogether, i.e., restricting the distribution of government publications,[1517] with an administrative order from Washington.

Judging by past history, USAPA reflected a consistent pattern of government knee-jerk reactions during national crisis and emergencies, in trading liberty for security. Time after times, government wanted more and more powers to investigate suspected spies, communists,

---

[1515] *Id.*

[1516] Since Jan. 1, .2002, law enforcement authorities has approached 24 libraries in Oregon seeking information on 46 different patrons. *Id.*

[1517] Ariana Eunjung Cha, "Government Tells Libraries to Restrict Information," *The Washington Post. Pittsburgh Post - Gazette.* Feb 24, 2002. p. A.7 (The government librarians were instructed to destroyed all CD-ROM of the nation's water supply data, e.g., Source-Area Characteristics of Large Public Surface-Water Supplies in the Conterminous United States. FBI agents have visited several libraries to make sure that the documents were removed.

and now terrorists, at the expense of civil liberties and personal privacy.[1518] In the case of USAPA, the Bush Administration has jettisoned old privacy safeguards established since the Ford Administration[1519] and forgotten the lessons on McCarthy era.

The promulgation and implementation of USAPA has come to affect the libraries and their patrons in multiple ways:

First, the libraries are caught in the middle of a looming security vs. liberties war/debate, a dispute they did not ask for and have very little control over, but was most affected by it. As a perspective writer observed:

> "Like the government's war on Internet pornography, librarians and the information community are again in the middle of a battle in which both sides' positions arguably have merit. While practically no librarian would advocate unfettered access to obscene material in a library, to many the censorship cost associated with efforts to restrict access to obscene content, as well as the inevitable restriction of access to protected content, is too great."[1520]

About the only thing the librarians could do, and did, was to launch an all out, do or die, offensive against the USAPA, for a mixture of private interest and collective goods.

Second, as intimated above, there are substantial costs associated with the enforcement of USAPA. The USAPA created a chilling effect in the patrons' mind. Ironically, the heightened vigilance and increased effort of the librarians to protect patrons' rights might have the opposite effect of encouraging the patrons to avoid the library altogether or to part take in self protection – censorship when using the library. In the worse case, patrons avoid the library altogether. At a minimum, patrons use the library with apprehension. The librarians are in a no win situation. The Bush government has forced the hand of the librarians, and won decisively by default. From now on terrorists and citizens alike are made aware that "big brother" is in the library and here to stay. Caveat emptor, people are to use library at ones own risk.

Third, there is a question of whether USAPA is too heavy a price to pay. As observed by Senator Russ Feingold in voting against the USAPA:

> "There is no doubt that if we lived in a police state, it would be easier to catch terrorists. If we lived in a country where the police were allowed to search your home at any time for any reason; if we lived in a country where the government is entitled to open your mail, eavesdrop on your phone conversations, or intercept your e-mail communications; if we lived in a country where people could be held indefinitely based...on mere suspicion that they are up to no good, the government would probably discover and arrest more terrorists, or would-be terrorists ....But that wouldn't be a country in which we would want to live."[1521]

[1518] Herbert Foerstel who wrote *Surveillance In the Stacks* (Greenwood Press, 1991), a book about FBI's notorious "Library Awareness Program" in the 1980s, feared that the government is at it all over again in passing the USAPS. He recalled FBI agents visiting the Engineering and Physical Sciences Library at the University of Maryland, College Park, in April 1986 and asked library staff to report on the reading habits of "anyone with a foreign-sounding name or foreign-sounding accent."

[1519] Joyce Howard Price, "Scrapping domestic-spying restrictions 'goes too far' ; GOP representative speaks against new Bush administration policy," *Washington Times*. Jun 2, 2002. p. A.04.

[1520] Pike, G.H., "History Repeated with the USAPA," *Information Today* Vol. 19 (11): 19-21 (December 2002).

[1521] Hentoff, N. "The Tag of Capitulation," *The Progressive* Vol. 66 (12): 18 (December 2002).

Feingold warned about the true costs of security in terms of loss liberties, a rational argument. But war on terror is a hardly a rational choice exercise. In as much as the kinds and degree of terrorists' risks are unknown and unknowable, the nature and extent of our nation's vulnerabilities are many and unfathomable, it is not possible to make rational choice, which requires a balancing of costs vs. benefits. Until and unless we know the unknowable and unfathomable, it is fool hearted, and indeed impossible, to engage in rational calculus. The defense of USAPA remains to be an act of "blind" faith.

By the same token, the value of liberties and freedom cannot be easily ascertained; "priceless" is what comes to mind for the librarians. ALA's defense of intellectual freedom and personal privacy remains to be an ideological commitment. When "blind faith" confronts "zealous ideology", there is little ground for compromise that is based on rational analysis and utility balance. The dispute can only be settled in the political arena. That is exactly what happened after 9/11.

Fourth, after 9/11, there is a renewed sense (anxiety) of vulnerability and increased concern (obsession) with security. This has led to monitoring at the libraries by the librarians, e.g., checking of ID before authorizing computer use. In an unexpected, counter-intuitive and perverted way, 9/11 is successful in domesticating the librarians, in the name of security. "Or we may find ourselves spying on our patrons, not because we want to or are even forced to, but because the act makes us so conscious of a fractional minority of patrons' actions that we can't help but keep our eyes and electronic ears focused." In order to keep law enforcers at bay, the librarians now act as censors of ideas and policing of thoughts, through removing of materials and registering of patrons. This represents a radical and fundamental change in professional role for librarians and institutional values for libraries.

In the end, the passage of USAPA provides us with a rate opportunity to debate anew our democratic principles in time of war and crisis, [1522] including the following the issues:

(1) Whether USAPA will compromise libraries traditional role and mission, and with it its institutional authority, social identity and professional responsibility in the long run. [1523]
(2) Whether the USAPA will come to affect the library's institutional integrity and operational practices. [1524] For example, Section 215 requires librarians to act as thought police of the federal government, in break of public trust and patrons' confidentiality. Section 215 further provided that libraries were to keep the investigation a secret? More generally, how USAPA might come to affect the country's library's organization culture and librarians' professional ethics. [1525]

Thus far, robust debate of the above issues has been deterred and deferred as a result of successful DOJ effort in keeping the USAPA – Section 215 enforcement secret,

---

[1522] Pike, G.H., "History Repeated with the USAPA," *Information Today* Vol. 19 (11): 19-21. (December 2002)

[1523] *Id.* ("At the act's 1-year anniversary, information professionals and the public are increasingly concerned that the "proper balance between freedom and order" may have shifted too far.")

[1524] Albanese, A., et. al., "2002: Victories Muted by Money Worries," *Library Journal* Vol. 127(20): 70-2 (December 2002).

[1525] 50 USCA 1861(d), 1990 and Supp. 2002.

notwithstanding Congressional oversights and court litigations, [1526] e.g., by claiming executive privileges.[1527] The Courts have refused to order the DOJ to release any information. This created uncertainty to the library administrators, front line workers, as well as library patrons, creating unnecessary anxiety and fear for all concerns.

In the ultimate analysis, the impact of the USAPA on patrons and libraries alike depends very much on how librarians confront the thorny issues raised by the USAPA. As it stands, the library has a decisive vote on how Section 215 is enforced, if at all. Thus, as library law consultant Minow observed:

> "the library's individual policies and procedures will become increasingly important. Does the library require sign-ups? If there are no sign-up lists, the inquiry essentially halts. Does the library allow first names only, or made-up names? Does it require identification? Library cards with addresses? Does it keep sign-up records, and if so, for how long? Does it use an automated system that ties library card numbers (tied to registration information) to Internet use? Is such information electronically disengaged after use and electronically shredded? Is it backed up on computer tapes? How long are backup tapes kept?"

Currently, the USAPA has not required the libraries to keep record.[1528] If the library does not keep records, e.g., records deleted at the end of the day, or the records are of a kind that cannot be used to identify the patrons, e.g., allowing the use of alias for sign up purposes, there is no record or "thing" for the FBI to get its hand on.[1529]

Self-help might well be the best hope for the libraries in resisting USAPA encroachment on library autonomy and patrons privacy.

APPENDIX I.
JOURNALISTIC ACCOUNTS OF FBI VISITING LOCAL LIBRARIES 9/11/01 TO 9/10/02

Date	News
9/15/01	Richard A. Serrano, Carol J. Williams, "America Attacked; the Investigation" *Los Angeles Times*. Sep 15, 2001. p. A.23 During the massive investigation after 9/11 the FBI discovered that the terrorists have anonymous access to the Internet through public libraries.
9/16/01	John Holland, Jennifer Peltz and Robin Benedick, "Library links Investigated Computer Use by Suspects Reported to FBI," *South Florida Sun - Sentinel*. Sep 16, 2001. p. 8.A The newspaper first broke the story that Kathleen Hensman, a research librarian at Delray Beach Public library, called the police on September 15, 2001 to report the sighting of a 9/11

[1526] The American Library Association's (ALA) Freedom to Read Foundation and civil liberties groups recently filed suit seeking release of the number of times the federal government has sought records from libraries, bookstores or Internet service providers under the USAPA (Madigan, 2002).

[1527] Bryant D. J., 2002. Letter from Daniel J. Bryant, Assistant Attorney General, U.S. Department of Justice, to F. James Sensenbrenner, Jr., Chairman, House Committee on the Judiciary (September 22, 2002). Retrieved October 26, 2002, from http://www.house.gov/judiciary/patriotresponses101702.pdf

[1528] Once s record exists, the FBI has a S215 rights to the record, after the order for document is served on the library.

[1529] Mary Minow, "The USAPA and Patron Privacy on Library Internet Terminals," (Feb. 15, 2002) librarylaw.com http://www.llrx.com/features/usapatriotact.htm

suspect using a library computer. She was able to associate a library patron, Mohlad Alshehri's name on the computer sign up sheet with the names of 9/11 suspect on the FBI wanted web site. Hensman also volunteered to search the library records for any further match between known FBI suspects and the library's computer sign-in data sheets.

The newspaper reported that Mohamed Atta was sighed in other libraries, i.e., Hollywood (Florida) libraries. However, unlike Hensman, Assistant Broward County library director, Betty Dejean refused to disclose whether any of the 9/11 suspects have used the library, e.g., whether suspected terrorists possessed a library card or have access to a computer.

On 9/12/01, Dejean issued an internal memo to 37 Broward County libraries reminding them not to disclose library information – books checked out and computer use - without a court order. She later circulated a second memo after consulting with the Florida Secretary of State's Office and the county attorney. They advised that state law requires that all library records be kept confidential. The memo reiterated that it is first and foremost the duties of librarians to follow the Florida state law, notwithstanding 9/11.

9/17/01	"Second Man Arrested in Terrorist Probe," *Virginian - Pilot*. Sep 17, 2001. p. A.3. Liz Promen, Manager, Sherwood Regional Library in Fairfax County, Virginia reported that FBI agents have requested (9/14/01) the computer lab sign-in lists of the library from July 1 to Sept. 13 (50 pages) to assist with 9/11 investigation.
9/17/01	Sue Anne Pressley and Justin Blum, "Hijackers May Have Accessed Computers at Public Libraries," *Washington Post*, September 17, 2001. A04. Library officials at Sherwood Regional Library, Fairfax County, VA, reported that FBI agents have requested for computer logs from July 1 to Sept. 13.
9/17/ 01	Michael Seamark, "Hijackers lived the American dream Neighbour tell how evil plotters passed themselves off as law- abiding members of their communities," *Daily Mail*. Sep 17, 2001. p. 8. FBI come to believe that 9/11 terrorists used libraries and their Internet services as communication center.
918/01	Peter Slevin and Mary Beth Sheridan, "Suspects Entered U.S. on Legal Visas; Men Blended In; Officials Say 49 Have Been Detained on Immigration Violations," *The Washington Post*, Sep 18, 2001. p. A.06 Sam Morrison, director of Broward County libraries, reported that on September 17, 2001 FBI applied for subpoenas to search for electronic and paper records of library transactions in two Hollywood, Fla. libraries.
9/19/01	Jenni Bergal and Christine Winter," Library Computers Shed Light FBI Seeks Clues in Hollywood, Coral Springs," *South Florida Sun – Sentinel*, Sep 19, 2001. p. 6.A. On Monday, September 17, 2001, the FBI seized computers from two libraries in Hollywood, Fla. On Tuesday, September 18, 2001, FBI agents spent the day examining computers to trace the terrorists' communication patterns and conspiratorial links. The FBI looked into computer records of Coral Springs library branch, not far from where one of the suspects, Mohamed Atta, lived in the summer. The FBI also scrutinized the main servers for the entire Broward County library system of 600 computers at 37 branches.
9/19/01	Chuck Ayers, "Bethlehem tightens security at City Hall on FBI's advice," *The Morning Call*. Sept. 19, 2001. p. B.5. A custodian at the Bethlehem Public Library, PA discovered a flight instruction manual for an American Airlines plane in the wastebasket. Library officials determined that it did not belong to the library and notified the police. The Police Commissioner Francis Donches then turned it over to the FBI.

Appendix I. (Continued)

Date	News
9/20/01	Sanjay Bhatt, Clay Lambert, Alice Gregory, "FBI Seizes Delray Library Computers Suspects May Have Used Them to Buy Tickets, Communicate," *Palm Beach Post*, Sep 20, 2001. p. 14.A. On September 20, 2001 (Wed), the FBI seized 2 of the 14 computers from the Delray Beach public library. This resulted from a report made to the police by reference librarian Kathleen Hensman who claimed to recognize one of the suspect a Marwan Al- Shehhi, who had used computer in the library.[1530] The library's computers were off-limits to the public since Saturday (9/16/2001). The computer search failed to uncover anything from the computer seized. Library Director John Callahan thought that the search failed because the computer usage records were not stored after two months. Investigators believed 9/11 suspects used computers in local public libraries to communicate and to buy airplane tickets in the weeks before the deadly assaults.
9/21/01	Tom Mooney, "Attack on America - Scope of investigation poses logistical challenge," *Providence Journal*, R.I.: Sep 21, 2001. p. A.01. In Broward Country, Florida, a federal grand jury ordered two libraries, where hijackers were believed to have used the Internet, to turn over their electronic computers files.
9/23/01	Christine Evans, "Uncomfortably Close," *Palm Beach Post*. Sep 23, 2001. p. 1.A A human interest story about how people at Palm Beach County come to know 12 of the 19 terrorists living there. "Library a site of intrigue" interviewed librarian, Kathleen Hensman, 41, who just moved to the area from Sarasota in January 2001.
10/1/01	Editorial: "Privacy in time of crisis," *Orange County Register*. Oct 1, 2001. p. Edit. The editorial is one of the first in the nation to raise issue with the civil liberties implications of the then proposed USAPA, particularly how "roving wiretap" authority can be used to monitor all electronic communications at the library, without the patrons ever knowing about it.
10/1/01	Lisa Guernsey, "E-surveillance would be broad Technology allows detailed snooping," *Denver Post* Oct 1, 2001. p. E.05. In this Op-ed essay, the author is much concerned about the e-digital surveillance capabilities of the government to ply into everything we say or do, from credit-card purchases to automated toll booths records to library books checked out to videos surveillance images. There is a question whether the public will tolerate this infringement of privacy in the post 9/11 climate. But history has shown that the government is ready and willing to use the powers to check on people's secrets.
10/2/01	"Overreaching/ Don't let our rights become collateral damage in the war on terrorism," *The Gazette*, Oct 2, 2001. p. METRO.4. The editorial is concerned with the expansive powers given to the FBI after 9/11. For example, the "roving wiretap" would allow the government to tap into whatever communications device a target uses, including targeting and monitoring all communications from "library or cybercafé." This is a grave intrusion of privacy.

[1530] This account is slightly different from earlier accounts. The original report has Ms. Kathleen Hensman recognizing one of the 9/11 suspects by name. See John Holland, Jennifer Peltz and Robin Benedick, "Library links Investigated Computer Use by Suspects Reported to FBI," *South Florida Sun - Sentinel*. Sep 16, 2001. p. 8.A.

Appendix I. (Continued)

Date	News
Oct 6, 2001	Walter V. Robinson, "Some Recall Sightings," *Boston Globe*. Boston, Oct 6, 2001. p. A.13 .
	The library staff of Portland Public Library (Massachusetts) reported seeing the 9/11 suspect, Mohamed Atta, at the library using its computer a year before 9/11. On 9/13/01, the library employee, including Spruce White the security director, positively identified Atta's wanted photograph. Kaye immediately notified the police. The Portland Police detective did not investigate into the matter until two weeks afterward as a result of too 9/11 many tips.
Oct 10, 2001	Glenn Puit, "Terror Trail: Las Vegas library another hijacker haunt, employees say," *Las Vegas Review - Journal*. Oct 10, 2001. p. 7.A.
	According to investigation 5 of the 19 hijackers - Mohamed Atta, Ziad Jarrah, Marwan Al-Shehhi, Nawaf Alhazmi and Hani Hanjour - visited Las Vegas six times between May and August. Those five have been identified by employees of the West Charleston Library. The policy of Las Vegas-Clark County Library District is to cooperate with FBI and police investigation. The Director of Las Vegas-Clark County Library District Daniel Walters confirmed: "We encouraged those employees to contact the FBI directly, and they have." Walter refused to disclose what kind of information was provided to the police and FBI. The Las Vegas office of the FBI provided no comment on the investigation but computers at any of the West Charleston Library were not seized. State law requires a showing of probable cause that targeted person is involved in the commission of a crime before authorities can release library records to law enforcement. Director Walters was of the opinion that state law might have prevented the FBI from gathering library patron data, since the law enforcements officials did not have sufficient probable cause to seize any library records or information. Earlier, the FBI did confiscated computer records from other Las Vegas public computer outlets. It has copied the hard drives of 10 Cyber Zone computers to establish the time and place of terrorists' presence in Las Vegas. The Las Vegas- Clark County Library District Board of Trustees has since then adopted a new security policy requiring people to show identification before using Internet computers.
Oct. 11, 2001	Shay Wessol, "Suspicious Package Discovered at Tech," *Roanoke Times and World News*. Oct 12, 2001. p. B.3.
	The administers of Virginia Tech reported to the local police and FBI about the discovery of a suspicious package found Thursday afternoon at Newman Library. They requested for protection and investigation.
Oct 16, 2001	Chad Brooks, "Events reinforce decision to review library security," *Daily Herald* Oct 16, 2001. p. 4.
	After an anthrax scare, the Schaumburg Township District Library started to review its security procedures, including negating some tradition freedom enjoyed by the patrons.
Oct 23, 2001	Susan Dodge, "Hezbollah poster stripped off wall ; U. of C.'s Mideast center takes it down after students object," *Chicago Sun - Times*. Oct 23, 2001. p. 9
	The students at University of Chicago objected to the display of a Hezbollah poster in a Middle Eastern studies room at the University of Chicago's Regenstein Library.

Appendix I. (Continued)

Date	News
Oct 25, 2001	John Branton, "Police: Arrest Stuns Suspect, Patrons at Library," *Columbian*. Oct 25, 2001. p. C.3.
	On Oct. 22 (Wed.), the police investigated Dennis Henry Hudson, 42, for suspected identity fraud, after a tip off. The police followed Hudson into the Fort Vancouver Regional Library and watched him (over his shoulder). When Hudson tried to obtain a bogus credit card, he was arrested. Detectives photographed the computer screen as evidence and seized the computer for investigation.
Nov 6, 2001	Brooke A. Masters, "Not Guilty Plea in Espionage Case; Retired Air Force Sergeant Accused of Trying to Sell Secrets," *The Washington Post* Nov 6, 2001. p. B.05.
	The arrest of retired Air Force Master Sergeant, Brian P. Regan, for attempted espionage, showed how FBI was keeping track of spying activities by monitoring library computer. Regan was sending Libya classified information by way of a free email account "Steve Jacobs." FBI tracked the account and found that it was accessed from public libraries in Crofton, Falls Church and Prince George's County. The two Maryland libraries are within five miles from Regan.
	In June 2001, FBI watched Regan use public-access computer terminals in the Crofton library to look up the addresses of the Iraqi and Libyan embassies in France, Germany and Switzerland.
Nov 15, 2001	Michael Rogers and Norman Oder, "LC closes for Anthrax tests, scares around the country," *Library Journal*. Nov 15, 2001. Vol. 126 (19) p. 14 (1 page)
	Libraries around the country were forced to close and police was alerted when suspicious substances were found on returned items, e.g., the Richland County Public Library, Columbia, SC, was closed on October 16, 2001 after a book was returned with powder inside it. However when the police sought information from the library to investigate the crime, they were denied access.
Dec 1, 2001	Chuck McGinness, "Librarian's Post-Attack Report to FBI Sparks Privacy Debate," *Palm Beach Post*, Dec 1, 2001. p. 1.B.
	The case of Delray Beach Public Library librarian Kathleen Hensman reporting on three of the 9/11 suspects using the library's computer to the police has sparked a controversial and heated debate as to the proper role and responsibilities of librarians.
	Hensman's boss, Delray Beach library Director John Callahan, felt that Hensman has done the right thing by reporting a crime to the police. The 1978 Florida state law only protects the confidentiality of registration and circulation records at public libraries, not ones personal observation and knowledge. Hensman did not provide the police with any library records. What she observed on the job was not confidential. She has a duty to report under the circumstances, as most people would.
	However, American Library Association disagrees. Callahan and his staff librarian should not have volunteered information to the FBI. Libraries are the cornerstones of democracy. 48 states have law against release library record and information.
	Palm Beach County library officials would not have turned over information without a subpoena. Kathy Boyes, the library's community relations manager, observed: "People don't really want others to know what they're reading, regardless of what the reason may be."
	There is also the question of the applicability of the old state law (since 1978) in light of technology change and in the face of 9/11. The new ALA policy (4/21) concludes: "There has been no showing of a plausible probability that national security will be compromised by any use made of unclassified information available in libraries. Thus,

Appendix I. (Continued)

Date	News
	the right of access to this information by individuals, including foreign nationals, must be recognized as part of the librarian's legal and ethical responsibility to protect the confidentiality of the library user." Civil libertarians are much concerned about gradual erosion of library privacies in the name of fighting terror.
Dec 2001	Anonymous, "FBI spies on suspect at library," *American Libraries*. Dec 2001. Vol. 32, Iss. 11; p. 24 (2 pages). FBI monitored public-access Internet terminals at Anne Arundel County (Md.) Public Library's Crofton branch for two months before arresting Brian P. Regan for spying. The indictment said Regan used the Crofton computer in June to look up the addresses of the Iraqi and Libyan embassies in France, Germany, and Switzerland. Regan asked Libyan officials to contact a free e-mail account issued to "Steve Jacobs." The FBI learned the Jacobs account was being accessed from the Crofton library as well as branches of Prince George's County (Md.) Public Library and Falls Church (Va.) Public Library.
Dec 25, 2001	Pat Schneider, "New U.S. Law Aids Snooping on Readers; Local Bookstores, Libraries Worry," *Madison Capital Times*. Dec 25, 2001. p. 1.A Director of the Madison Public Library, Barbara Dimick's concern with the USAPA, particularly Section 215. Section provides no judicial supervision in open court. The power of search and seize is completely in the hand of the FBI agents. Librarians can no longer assure patrons of the sanctity and privacy of the library. FBI single handedly compromised the autonomy and authority of library. Dimick could not imagine how public information in libraries can provide a cause for concern or sued as evidence of a terrorist ink. Pete Hamon, director of the South Central Library System has the following concerns: USAPA places a gag order on librarians over public disclosure of record held in trust. Librarian is not allowed to consult Board appointed lawyers, since attorney fees must be authorized by the governing board. FBI seizure of the library system computers might result in shutting down of business between 50 libraries. Hamon recalled how in 1950s Nebraska, the John Birch Society wanted to use library records to identify anyone who had taken out "The FBI Nobody Knows," a book critical of the bureau. Many careers were ruined. Ken Frazier, director of the University of Wisconsin Libraries, have the following concerns: "We haven't seen any request for wholesale review of circulation records. The university's collection is not a legitimate site for investigation. It holds no information or evidence to a terrorism investigation." Nancy Lynch, associate Wisconsin University legal counsel, said a federal law protecting the privacy of educational records might protect library and Internet use records. And the state's public records law protects the privacy of records on employees.

Appendix I. (Continued)

Date	News
Jan 2002	Leonard Kniffel, "CPL head's comments provoke outrage," *American Libraries*. Jan 2002. Vol. 33, Iss. 1; p. 30 (1 page). On December 4, 2001, Chicago Public Library Commissioner Mary Dempsey appeared on Fox News Network's O'Reilly Factor show over Delray Beach, Florida, librarian Kathleen Hensman incident in 9/2001. She was asked whether she would report to the FBI if she had seen terrorists in her library. She insisted on defending the confidentiality of the library patrons. She would not report to the police. Her response sparked letters of protest directed at CPL and the American Library Association. [1531]
Feb 24, 2002	Ariana Eunjung Cha, "Government Tells Libraries to Restrict Information," *The Washington Post. Pittsburgh Post - Gazette*. Feb 24, 2002. p. A.7 The government librarians were instructed to destroyed all CD-ROM of the nation's water supply data, e.g., Source-Area Characteristics of Large Public Surface-Water Supplies in the Conterminous United States. FBI agents have visited several libraries to make sure that the documents were removed.
Feb 25, 2002	Nat Hentoff, "Big Brother in the library ; Patriot Act turns librarians into FBI informants," *The Washington Times*. Feb 25, 2002. p. A.21. Section 215 of the USAPA allows FBI to apply for an FSIA court order for "any tangible things (including books, records, papers, documents, and other items) for an investigation to protect against" terrorists. "Domestic terrorism" is defined as violent "acts [that] appear to be intended to ... influence the policy of government by intimidation." Libraries are prohibited to disclose "to any other person ... that the Federal Bureau of Investigation has sought or obtained tangible things under this section." The law allows FBI to monitor what one reads, if it is related to terrorism, i.e., not "solely upon the basis of activities protected by the First Amendment to the Constitution."
March 2002	Anonymous, "Child predator pleads guilty," *American Libraries*. Mar 2002. Vol. 33, Iss. 3; p. 27 (1 page). East Providence (R.I.) Public Library employees called authorities last June (2001) after finding discarded sexually explicit printouts of teenage girls near a workstation. The undercover investigation by FBI on the web led to the arrest and prosecution of Norman K. Foster, a Seekonk (MA) Public Library patron, for sex offense. An undercover FBI agent met Foster in a chat room. Foster was arrested Jun 22, 2001.
Mar 5, 2002	Nat Hentoff, "Big John wants your reading list," *The Village Voice*. Mar 5, 2002. Vol. 47, Iss. 9; p. 27 (1 page). The USAPA allows FBI to obtain court order ex parte and in secret. The public is not informed and aware of the extent of government powers. The government was able to pass the law according to Krug, director of the Office for Intellectual Freedom of the American Library Association, because the public is supporting the government's initiative to suppress liberties in the name of security.

[1531] Sub title: "Partial transcript of interview with Chicago Public Library Commissioner Mary Dempsey from Bill O'Reilly of "The O'Reilly Factor," Dec. 4," "Controversial talk show with Mary Dempsey," INSIDE http://www.insideonline.com/site/epage/3483_162.htm

Appendix I. (Continued)

Date	News
Mar 11, 2002	"How Sept. 11 Changed the U.S. --- Airlines, Pipelines, Stadiums and Theme Parks Have All Bolstered Security Since the Attacks --- Much Remains to Be Done," *Asian Wall Street Journal*. Mar 11, 2002. p. A.8. The USAPS gives FBI sweeping authority to subpoena data to investigate terrorism or clandestine intelligence activities. James X. Dempsey with the Center for Democracy and Technology observed that the USAPA allows the FBI "to go into a public library and ask for the records on everybody who ever used the library, or who used it on a certain day, or who checked out certain kinds of books."
Apr 1, 2002	Nat Hentoff, "Ultimate gag rule," *Editor and Publisher*. Apr 1, 2002. Vol. 135, Iss. 13; p. 30 (1 page). "John Ashcroft's war on terrorism includes the most far-reaching gag order in First Amendment history." Under the omnibus USAPA, the FBI can obtain a FISA Court order in secret to search for any tangible things (including books, records, papers, documents, and other items) as part of an investigation to protect against international terrorism or clandestine intelligence activities. Since it is an ex parte secret order it cannot be challenged in open court, except when it is too late. The public will never know about it because librarians are not allowed to disclose the details of investigation. According to the author, three Section 215 investigations have been conducted, to his knowledge. "My information is that there have been, as of this writing, at least three FBI searches of the reading preferences of people under suspicion. That is all the information I have, and I cannot reveal my sources lest they be subject to penalties for breaking the gag order."
Apr 14, 2002	Robyn E. Blumner, "Bookstores and libraries not safe from First Amendment pillaging," *St. Petersburg Times*. Apr 14, 2002. p. 6.D. "A government's extreme interest in the reading choices of its citizens has never been a historical positive. Nearly all Confucian books were destroyed by the Chinese Prime Minister Li Si in 208 B.C. because they encouraged political and philosophical thought. "Alien" ideas were purged by Nazi propagandist Joseph Goebbels in a massive book burning at the Wilhelm Humboldt University in 1933. And in the 1980s the FBI tried to implement the "Library Awareness Program," in which librarians were told to report to the FBI whenever a patron was interested in "suspicious" material. But the librarians wouldn't have it, and the program never got off the ground." Emily Sheketoff, executive director of the Washington D.C. office of the American Library Association calls it "scary." Librarians across the country, she says, have been approached by FBI agents demanding information on their patrons and under new rules established by the USAPA they have no recourse but to comply.
Apr 22, 2002	"On gag rules, spy tools and freedom of speech," *The Sun*. Apr 22, 2002. p. 10.A. One of the strongest denunciations of the Patriot Act came from the *Baltimore Sun* on April 22, 2002. The opinion denounced the Bush administration for using terrorist fear and patriotism to systematically undermine Americans' First amendment right. America will neither be safe nor strong if the elected officials hide their activities and the citizens are not well informed to debate the issues of the day.

Appendix. (Continued)

Date	News
Apr 29, 2002	Herbert Foerstel, "A chilling intrusion," *The Sun*. Apr 29, 2002. p. 11.A. Herbert Foerstel who wrote Surveillance *In the Stacks* (Greenwood Press, 1991), a book about FBI's notorious "Library Awareness Program" in the 1980s, feared that the government is at it all over again in passing the USAPS. He recalled FBI agents visiting the Engineering and Physical Sciences Library at the University of Maryland, College Park, in April 1986 and asked library staff to report on the reading habits of "anyone with a foreign-sounding name or foreign-sounding accent." The FBI's gross abuse of rights led to 48 of the 50 states plus DC passing state privacy legislation to law protect patrons' library record. Patron's privacy is once against at risk with the far reaching USAPA.
May 30, 2002	"New Guidelines Give FBI Agents Greater Latitude in Investigations," *Virginian – Pilot* May 30, 2002. p. A.12. The DOJ issued new guidelines allowing FBI agents great latitude to monitor Internet Web sites, libraries and religious institutions without first having to offer evidence of potential criminal activity or seeking FBI HQ permission. Rep. John Conyers of Michigan, the top Democrat on the House Judiciary Committee, denounced the Justice Department's action as an "embarrassing step backward for civil liberties in this country." Michael Ratner, president of the Center for Constitutional Rights, said it's just a question of time before the FBI abuses its new mandate. He pointed to the FBI's much-criticized conduct during the 1980s in an investigation of the Committee in Solidarity with the People of El Salvador, or CISPES, a liberal group that opposed Reagan administration policy in Central America.
May 31, 2002	Nancy Benac, "Who's watching you?; Uneasiness meets FBI's new rules for monitoring," *The Patriot – News* May 31, 2002. p. A.01. Reactions to the DOD new investigative guideline were swift and negative. Emily Sheketoff of the American Library Association warned of FBI looking over people's shoulder at the library and use those information to build a case against them. "What I'm afraid of as an American citizen is that they're going to look at the kinds of magazines I subscribe to and the kinds of things I'm interested in and use that as probable cause" to investigate further."
May 31, 2002	"Civil libertarians criticize FBI rules; They fear the terrorism crisis is being used as a cover to erode personal freedoms," *The Associated Press. The Grand Rapids Press* May 31, 2002. p. A.3. The new FBI guidelines were drawing criticism from civil libertarians. Libertarians feared that Ashcroft might be using 9/11 power to enhance its law enforcement powers. James X. Dempsey, deputy director of the Center for Democracy and Technology observed: "They are using the terrorism crisis as a cover for a wide range of changes, some of which have nothing to do with terrorism." Dempsey predicted that the power will be used for "every other type of investigation the FBI does."

Appendix. (Continued)

Date	News
June 5, 2002	"Blame game: The 9-11 buck should stop with Ashcroft," *Myriam Marquez. Knight Ridder Tribune News Service.* Jun 5, 2002. p. 1 Since the attacks, Ashcroft has used the 9-11 tragedy to attack the U.S. Constitution every which way. To Ashcroft, fighting terrorism means cracking down on fundamental civil liberties and basic human rights. Ashcroft has just relaxes FBI rules to allow agents to monitor libraries, political rallies, mosques or Internet sites in search of potential terrorists. See also PHILIP GAILEY, "Ashcroft owes us some answers," *The Record.* Jun 6, 2002. p. L.09; "Big Brother is looking over our shoulders' ** Some minority religious, political leaders wary of new FBI monitoring rules," *Mario F. Cattabiani Of The Morning Call.* Jun 6, 2002. p. A.1; Myriam Marquez, "BLAME GAME: THE 9-11 BUCK SHOULD STOP WITH ASHCROFT," *Sentinel Columnist. Orlando Sentinel.* Jun 4, 2002. p. A.9.
June 3, 2002	"Editorial: Tempest in a teapot," *Las Vegas Review - Journal.* Jun 3, 2002. p. 6.B. "FBI's first problem is its culture of cover-up," *The Grand Rapids Press* Jun 4, 2002. p. A.6. The problem with 9/11 is not they do not have sufficient power. It is that they have a protective culture.
Jun 3, 2002	Tom Breckenridge, "Librarians see searches getting little information Agents will find few records, they say," *The Plain Dealer.* Jun 26, 2002. p. 04. Librarians in Greater Cleveland were unaware of any FBI or other agencies requesting for information or patron records. John Lonsak, executive director of the Cuyahoga County Public Library, informed the public that long term library records would not be kept anymore. Medina County Library District, Interim Director Christine Gramm, informed that there is computer log listing users for the day. But they are destroyed at the end of the day. Joan Clark, head of Cleveland Public Library's Main Building. "We keep only information that's related to providing efficient service." Libraries have championed the ideals of free thought without censorship. The confidentiality of patrons' borrowing has been sacrosanct.
Jun 2, 2002	Joyce Howard Price, "Scrapping domestic-spying restrictions 'goes too far' ; GOP representative speaks against new Bush administration policy," *Washington Times.* Jun 2, 2002. p. A.04. Representative James F. Sensenbrenner Jr. (R-WI), Chairman of House Judiciary Committee (which has oversight responsibility of DOJ and FBI), appeared in CNN's "Novak, Hunt and Shields" and questioned the necessity and utility of DOJ-FBI new guideline (allowing surveillance of church, libraries, bookstore) in fighting terrorism. He pointed out the current "Levi surveillance guidelines" (Attorney General under Ford) originally promulgated by a Republican administration since 1976 have "worked so well." The guidelines required the FBI to show evidence of a crime before engaging in domestic spying. The restrictions grew out of the FBI's civil rights abuses under Director J. Eager Hoover.

Appendix. (Continued)

Date	News
Jun 26, 2002	Rick Bella, "Libraries Dismayed at FBI'S New Power," *The Oregonian. Portland*, Jun 26, 2002. p. E.01.

Librarians are uniformly disturbed by the FBI's new power and distressed over practice of monitoring patrons' reading habits. However, they do not want to challenge FBI's authority or the federal law. Candace Morgan, associate director of Fort Vancouver Regional Library system, said she would only "very reluctantly" comply USAPA. "All of us are concerned about terrorism, and all of us are concerned about the government's ability to respond to it ...But we're also concerned that we'll be asked to relinquish records that patrons thought would be held private."

| Jun 26, 2002 | Patricia Swanson, "Libraries Say They Will Give FBI Records," *Evansville Courier and Press*. Jun 26, 2002. p. B.1. |

Local libraries at Evansville, Indiana, said that they will comply with USAPA, as limited by policy. A study by the University of Illinois found that at least 85 libraries reported FBI agents had sought records. None of the libraries was in the immediate Evansville area.

According to Leslie Simmons, associate librarian for development, Evansville-Vanderburgh Public Library kept circulation information until the book is next borrowed. In the other libraries in the area, e.g., University of Southern Indiana and the University of Evansville, the record is eliminated once a book is returned. There is just not enough computer space to store all patrons' records forever.

Steve Thomas, director of the Ohio Township Library System, observed: "I personally do not believe a person is defined by what they read... If I read a book on terrorism, it does not make me a terrorist. If I read a book on bomb-making, it doesn't make me a bomb-maker." Ruth Miller of USI: "We want things to read because we want to understand things. We need the freedom for intellectual discussion.... In an academic setting people may be taking out books so they can understand something better so they can marshal arguments against it."

University of Evansville would accept a search warrant but immediately notify the university's attorney.

All libraries would "absolutely provide a record with a court order. We will comply with the law."

| Jun 26, 2002 | Beverly Beckham, "Op-Ed; Public safety must trump privacy," *Boston Herald*. Jun 26, 2002. p. 025. |

There are very few who supported the USAPA and the government expansive powers. The few who are in support argued that our life is an open book: "Barnes and Noble knows what books I read. Amazon.com knows what music I like. E-Bay knows what I collect. Sprint and ATandT know to whom I talk. The video store knows which movies I watch. The grocery store knows what food I buy. Visa has a record of everything I charge. At Costco last month, a salesman suggested I become an executive member, because according to a record of my purchases, I would save more money that way." It is necessary to give up some privacy to ensure security.

Appendix. (Continued)

Date	News
June 27, 02	Marlene NaaNes, "Patriot Act touches nerve at BR libraries," *Advocate*. Jun 27, 2002. p. 1.B.2.B. In the context of university library records, Jennifer Cargill, dean of LSU libraries, observed: "My feeling is that circulation records should be personal ... Depending on what you're studying as a student, you could be checking out books on numerous subjects. I'm not sure what a circulation record could tell you except what certain course you are taking or what you are researching." In May 2001, Louisiana Library Association Executive Director Beverly Laughlin testified in the Senate against a bill that would have allowed police access to reading records without a warrant or probable cause. State law now allows police access to library records only if a crime was committed on library property and was witnessed and reported by someone on the property, and with a warrant issued on probable cause.
Jun 28, 2002.	"Library Cops," *The Salt Lake Tribune*. Jun 28, 2002. p. A.20. The USAPA cannot be justified. The FBI has more information than it needs.
Jun 29, 2002	Mike Pearson, "How You Use Library Could Get You Booked," *Rocky Mountain News*. Jun 29, 2002. p. 2.E. "When I was younger, getting that first library card was a badge of honor. It didn't mean you were an adult, but it meant you could hold a literate conversation; that the world of ideas was just as important to you as the world of action. I wanted to tell him libraries aren't just about books; they're about though In April, the Colorado Supreme Court denied local law enforcement access to such records without a compelling reason; the Patriot Act trumps that ruling. While the act forbids the government from launching an investigation based on those records alone, it lets the government go fishing if it deems you the least bit suspicious."
June 30, 2002.	Karen Rivedal, "UW Libraries Wait For Warrants ; No Policies Developed For FBI Demands," *Wisconsin State Journal* Jun 30, 2002. p. E.1. Nine months after federal law opened the public library reading records of suspected terrorists to police scrutiny, UW-Madison officials have yet to develop new policies to handle USAPA inquiry. Library Director Ken Frazier said the university was taking a wait-and-see approach. With FBI contacts so far, the library is relying on its current practice, which under state law holds library records confidential. Federal law also protects student records. Frazier observed: "We are obliged to follow the law, but there's more than one law involved here.
July 2, 2002	"Library scrutiny risky," *The Herald. Herald*. Jul 2, 2002. p. 5.A. A poll shows that Forty-nine percent of the 1,000 people polled agreed with the statement: "We are living in dangerous times. If we need to relinquish some of our personal freedoms and privacy to protect our country, we should all be prepared to do that." The question is whether people would really give up liberty in specific instance and concrete situations.
Jul 4, 2002.	Greg Freeman, "On this 4TH of JULY, Celebrate, Protect Our Nation's Freedoms," *St. Louis Post - Dispatch*. Jul 4, 2002. p. B.1. On July 4, people should think about how 9/11 and USAPA affected our nation's freedom.

Appendix. (Continued)

Date	News
Jul 5, 2002	Brad Smith, "FBI Can Check Out Reading Habits," *Tampa Tribune*.Jul 5, 2002. p 1. Library director Mary Gaines disclosed that soon after USAPA was passed, the FBI subpoenaed the St. Petersburg Public Library about a suspicious e-mail sent from a library computer last year. The library complied but doesn't know what happened subsequently. A records clerk at the U.S. District Court in Tampa could find no affidavit, subpoena or search warrant with more detail. If the case was sealed by a judge, no public record would be available.
July 5, 2002.	John Accola, "State Isn't Seeing Much Impact From Patriot Act, Libraries Say ; Group Not Aware of FBI Snooping in Colorado," *Rocky Mountain News*. Jul 5, 2002. p. 29.A. Colorado librarians confirmed that USAPA has been used in the state's largest city: "We have not had a single inquiry from the FBI since the Patriot Act was instituted." While the general maxim is; "Librarians promote and believe in intellectual freedom, but we also believe in supporting the laws of the country and there has to be a meshing of those," Douglas Public Library District Director Jamie LaRue "fears that the new federal surveillance measures, which include clandestine monitoring of library patrons' Internet use, open the door for abuse, such as government "fishing expeditions." He finds the implications of the Patriot Act worrisome for a profession that long has held the confidentiality of patrons' reading habits sacrosanct." USAPA also runs counter to a recent Colorado Supreme Court ruling that gives booksellers and librarians a right to a court hearing before complying with a search warrant for customer records. Jeffco Librarian Bill Knotts confirmed that he has cooperated with an FBI inquiry for a patron's Hinckley's library record. The FBI was "careful and thoughtful about the legal process, unlike some representatives of the press."

Chapter 7

GRASSROOTS RESISTANCE

*Liberty lies in the hearts of men and women; when it dies there,
no constitution, no law, no court can save it.*

Judge Learned Hand (1944)[1532]

*Never doubt that a small group of thoughtful, committed citizens can change the world.
Indeed, it is the only thing that ever has.*[1533]

Margaret Mead (1901 – 1978)

I. INTRODUCTION

As observed in prior chapters, the USAPA did not get a proper hearing with the Congress, courts or public (Chapter 2). The ultra-secretive implementation process arouses skepticism. The blatant abuse of powers attracts resentment. The total lack of accountability undermines legitimacy. For example, the egregious treatment of "special interest" persons by the FBI and discriminatory profiling of ethnic minorities by the INS (Chapter 5) alienated vulnerable segments of our society.[1534] The ill-prepared launch of the USAPA - SEVIS program by the Department of Homeland Security poisoned federal-state relationships (Chapter 4). The refusal of Attorney General to provide information on how and how often USAPA - Section 215 was used in the library aggravated librarians and helped mobilized oppositions.[1535] All of the above results in immediate impact on the lives of many people and portents long term implications for our constitutional democracy (Chapter 8).

[1532] Judge Learned Hand, speech delivered on "I Am an American Day," New York City, May 21, 1944.

[1533] Hope Marston, organizer from Lane County Bill of Rights Defense Committee (BORDC) quoted Mead for being the inspirational leader behind BORDC in "Surveillance, Infiltration, and Harassment of Environmental Organizations, Part I," *t r u t h o u t* | Transcript. Friday 10 March 2006.

[1534] More generally, see Nancy Kranich, "The Impact of the USAPA: An Update." The Free Expression Policy Project. http://www.fepproject.org/commentaries/patriotactupdate.html

[1535] Chapter 6.

Ever since the passage of the USAPA, the constitutionality, [1536] necessity, [1537] effectiveness,[1538] utility,[1539] and wisdom of the Act[1540] has been assiduously examined[1541] and critically questioned.[1542] For example, in one of its earliest critique of the USAPA in draft, ACLU observed that: "This legislation does not meet the basic test of maximizing our

---

[1536] "Ensuring Liberty And Security Through Checks And Balances: A Fresh Start For The Senate Judiciary Committee In The New 110th Congress." By Senator Patrick Leahy (D-Vt.). Incoming Chairman, Senate Judiciary Committee, United States Senate. (As Prepared). Georgetown University Law Center. December 13, 2006. ("This Administration has rolled back open government laws and systematically eroded Americans' privacy rights"). See John W. Whitehead and Steven H. Aden, "Forfeiting "Enduring Freedom" for "Homeland Security": A Constitutional Analysis of the USAPA and the Justice Department's Anti-Terrorism Initiatives," 51 *American University Law Review* 1081-1133 (2002) (The USAPA variously raised First (free speech and association), Fourth (unreasonable search and seizure), Fifth (right to grand jury and right to due process), Sixth (right to counsel (pp. 1114 – 1117) and right to jury trial) Amendments issues. http://www.wcl.american.edu/journal/lawrev/51/51-6.cfm

For First Amendment issues, see Michael Cooper, "Dying Behind a Closed Door: Is There a First Amendment Right of Access to Deportation Hearings in the Wake of 9/11," American Immigration Law Foundation (2003); for Fourth Amendment issues, see Susan N. Herman, "USAPA and the Submajoritarian Fourth Amendment," 41 *Harvard Civil Rights Civil Liberties Law Review* 67 – 113 (Winter 2006); for Fifth Amendment (due process) issues, see Shirin Sinnar, "Note, Patriotic or Unconstitutional? The Mandatory Detention of Aliens Under the USAPA," 55 *Stan. L. Rev.* 1419 (2003); Daniel J. Steinbock, "DATA Matching, Data Mining, and Due Process," 40 *Ga. L. Rev. 1* (Fall, 2005); for Sixth Amendment issues, see Chris Ford, "Fear of a Blackened Planet: Pressured by the War on Terror, Courts Ignore the Erosion of the Attorney-Client Privilege and Effective Assistance of Counsel in 28 C.F.R § 501.3(d) Cases," 12 *Wash. and Lee J. Civil Rts. and Soc. Just.* 51 (2006); For privacy issues, see Kim Lane Scheppele, "Symposium: A New Constitutional Order? Panel II: The Emergency Constitution in the Post-September 11 World Order: We are all Post-9/11 Now," 75 *Fordham L. Rev.* 607 (2006). For a book length treatments, see Dave Cole and James X. Dempsey, *Terrorism and the Constitution; Sacrificing Civil Liberties in the Name of National Security* (W. W. Norton and Co., 2nd Ed., 2002), C. William Michaels, *No Greater Threat: America Since September 11 and the Rise of the National Security State* (Algora Publishing, 2002) and Jennifer Van Bergen, *The Twilight of Democracy: The Bush Plan for America* (Common Courage Press, 2004)

[1537] Christopher P. Raab, "Fighting Terrorism in an Electronic Age: Does the Patriot Act Unduly Compromise Our Civil Liberties?" 2006 *Duke L. and Tech. Rev.* 0003 (2006) (Section 210: Subpoenas for Communications Records and Section 505: National Security Letter authority of the USAPA *compromises civil liberties to a greater degree than is necessary to combat terrorism.*)
http://www.law.duke.edu/journals/dltr/articles/PDF/2006DLTR0003.pdf

[1538] 2005 *USAPA: A Review for the Purpose of Reauthorization.* Hearing Before the Committee on the Judiciary House of Representatives, One Hundred Ninth Congress, First Session. April 6, 2005. Serial No. 109–12. (Testimony of Alberto R. Gonzales, Attorney General, U.S. Department of Justice: USAPA has been effective in fighting terrorism, e.g., the Act facilitates the sharing of information between federal agencies: CIA vs. FBI.) http://commdocs.house.gov/committees/judiciary/hju20390.000/hju20390_0.HTM

The USAPA in Practice: Shedding Light on the FISA Process. Hearing before Committee on the Judiciary, U.S. Senate, 107th Congress, Second Session, September 10, 2002, Serial Number, J-107-102, p. 44 (Senator Devin (R-Ohio): "we don't have any really good indication of its effectiveness. ...)

[1539] Chapter 8.

[1540] Dick Thornburgh, "Tribute: Balancing Civil Liberties and Homeland Security: Does the USAPA Avoid Justice Robert H. Jackson's "Suicide Pact"?" 68 *Alb. L. Rev.* 801 (2005) ("If Justice Jackson were alive today, he would …take decisive steps to prevent our Constitution from becoming the "suicide pact" .. But he would do so with a sense of fairness and recognition of the importance of the presumption of innocence.")

[1541] The ACLU has appointed itself as the lead organization to monitor the legislation, application and impact of the USAPA. "Safe and Free : USAPA" ACLU http://www.aclu.org/safefree/patriot/index.html For a more reflective constitutional analysis, see John W. Whitehead and Steven H. Aden, "Forfeiting "Enduring Freedom" for "Homeland Security": A Constitutional Analysis of the USAPA and the Justice Department's Anti-Terrorism Initiatives," 51 *American University Law Review* 1081-1133 (2002). For a legal analysis of the Act and internet, see "EFF Analysis of The Provisions of The USAPA: That Relate to Online Activities (October 31, 2001). http://www.eff.org/Privacy/Surveillance/Terrorism/20011031_eff_usa_patriot_nalysis.php

[1542] ACLU Letter to Congress Strongly Urging A "No" Vote On Final Passage of the Conference Report Agreement Reauthorizing the USAPA (2/15/2006) http://www.aclu.org/safefree/general/24170leg20060215.html

security with minimizing the impact on our civil liberties."[1543] ACLU concluded that Administration bill permits unilateral and indefinite administrative detention of any non-citizen by order of the Attorney General based on vague and unspecified predictions of threats to the national security, with no judicial review. The bill allows for retroactive deportation of residents for associating with terrorist organization. The bill allows wiretapping base on FBI certification of "needs" for terrorist investigation. The bill allows FBI to get a pen register or trap and trace order by certifying that the information to be obtained is "relevant to an ongoing criminal investigation." The bill allows the use of Carnivore Internet surveillance system. The bill allows "roving" wiretap authority to gather unspecified intelligence. The bill allows for secret search and seizure without notification to the target of investigation.

Of late, the USAPA has been legally challenged[1544] and legislatively revisited.[1545] Legislative challenges included the following bills: *Civil Liberties Restoration Act, S. 2528* (Kennedy) -- amends Section 215 to ensure appropriate checks and balances; ensures access to evidence; requires accurate criminal databases; mandates data mining reports; ends secret hearings and special registration; ensures due process for detainees; *Security and Freedom Ensured Act, H.R. 3352* (Otter) -- amends sneak and peek, Section 215, John Doe roving tap authority, and the definition of domestic terrorism to include appropriate checks and balances; also sunsets additional provisions of the PATRIOT Act in 2005; *Protecting the Rights of Individuals Act, S. 1552* (Murkowski, Wyden) -- amends sneak and peek, definition of domestic terrorism, Section 215, John Doe roving taps, pen/traps for the Internet, access to education records, "significant" purpose test and use of FISA evidence at trial to include appropriate checks and balances; also imposes moratorium on data mining and requires additional public reporting on the FBI's use of FISA; *Security and Freedom Ensured Act, S. 1709* (Craig, Durbin) -- amends sneak and peek, Section 215 and John Doe roving tap authority to include appropriate checks and balances; also sunsets additional provisions of the PATRIOT Act in 2005; *PATRIOT Oversight Restoration Act, S. 1695* (Leahy, Craig) -- sunsets additional provisions of the PATRIOT Act in 2005; *Reasonable Notice and Search Act, S. 1701* (Feingold) -- amends sneak and peek provision to add stronger judicial and congressional oversight; *Library, Bookseller, and Personal Records Privacy Act, S. 1507* (Feingold) -- amends Section 215 to add stronger judicial and congressional oversight; *Library and Bookseller Protection Act, S. 1158* (Boxer) -- ensures that the FBI cannot obtain library and bookstore records with only a secret rubber-stamp court order; *Domestic Surveillance Oversight Act, S. 436* (Leahy, Grassley, Specter) -- requires additional public

---

[1543] "ACLU Says Congress Should Treat Administration Proposal Carefully; Says Many Provisions Go Far Beyond Anti-Terrorism Needs ACLU," Center for Democracy and Technology (Thursday, September 20, 2001)

[1544] Center for National Security Studies v. Department of Justice, 215 F. Supp 2d 94 (D.D.C. 2002) (Issue: Whether DOJ can legally withhold names of post-911 round of terrorist suspects and interested persons in the face of FOIA request? D.C. District Court ordered the Justice Department to release names, location, dates of arrest information on August 2, 2002. The Circuit Court of Appeals reversed that decision and dismissed the case.) (for legal proceedings and papers, http://www.cnss.org/cnssvdoj.htm; Detroit Free Press v. Ashcroft, U.S. App. LEXIS 17646 (6th Cir. 2002) and North Jersey Media Group, Inc. v. Ashcroft, 205 F.Supp. 2d 288, 300 (May 28, 2002). (Issue: Is there a First Amendment rights to deportation hearings of "special interests" hearings closed by virtual Creepy memo?: In the Detroit case, the Sixth Circuit voted affirmed the District Court order for opening. In the New Jersey case, the Third Circuit denied the right of media access); Padilla ex rel. Newman v. Bush, 233 F.Supp.2d 564, 576 (S.D.N.Y.2002) (Whether a U.S. citizen on American soil can be detained as "enemy combatant" and be denied the right to counsel and hearing? 2nd U.S. Circuit Court of Appeals voted 2-1 that the U.S. government must release Jose Padilla from military custody within 30 days);

[1545] For Congressional Attempts to Thwart the Impact of the USAPA, see Kranich, "The Impact of the USAPA: An Update." The Free Expression Policy Project. http://www.fepproject.org/commentaries/patriotactupdate.html

reporting on the FBI's use of FISA; *Freedom to Read Protection Act, H.R. 1157* (Sanders) -- ensures that the FBI cannot obtain library and bookstore records with only a secret rubber-stamp court order; *Surveillance Oversight and Disclosure Act, H.R. 2429* (Hoeffel) -- requires additional public reporting on the FBI's use of FISA; *Benjamin Franklin True Patriot Act, H.R. 3171*(Kucinich) -- repeals sections of the PATRIOT Act as well as other guidelines and regulations."[1546] There are also moves to shore up the USAPA. For example, in 2004, Senator Kyle introduced S. 2476 to amend the USAPA to repeal the sunsets to the Committee on the Judiciary.[1547]

Increasingly, there is a growing feeling of great disconnect and discontentment in and around the country (within the ranks of conservatives[1548] and liberals[1549] alike) between National aspiration, Bush's political agenda[1550] and USAPA policy and practices.[1551] Overall, the Bush government's anti-terrorism policy and rhetoric alienates,[1552] as it demoralizes, its supporters,[1553] and aggravates, as it emboldens, its oppositions.[1554]

Ultimately Bush policy and politics disillusioned and frustrated all who cared about the current state and future prospect of democracy and constitutional government in America. Overall, there is a keen realization in the country that democracy as practiced in

---

[1546] See "Legislative Proposals to Fix the PATRIOT Act" The Center for Democracy and Technology (CDT) (Verbatim) http://www.cdt.org/security/usapatriot/fix.shtml

[1547] STATEMENTS ON INTRODUCED BILLS AND JOINT RESOLUTIONS. Congressional Record: May 21, 2004 (Senate) Page S6096-S6099 (Senator Kyle cited President Bush in support of USAPA Act: "'to abandon the Patriot Act would deprive law enforcement and intelligence officers of needed tools in the war on terror, and demonstrate willful blindness to a continuing threat.") http://www.fas.org/irp/congress/2004_cr/s 2476.html

[1548] Abby Scher, "When Adversaries Become Allies: The Fight Against the Patriot Act and the Surveillance State," *The Public Eye Magazine* Vol. 20(1) (Spring, 2001). http://www.publiceye.org/magazine/v20n1/ scher_allies.html ("Gun Owners of America is not convinced that the FBI doesn't need to be watched.")

[1549] *Id.* Democrats who treasured Constitutional rights of liberty and privacy signed on to trump liberty with security. Only one Senator – Feingold – cast the lone dissenter vote on the USAPA.

[1550] Walter Brasch, "Compromising Americans' Civil Liberties," *OpEdNews* March 7, 2006. (Bush use fear to passed USAPA to advance conservative agenda.) http://www.opednews.com/articles/opedne_walter_b_ 060307_compromising_america.htm

[1551] Richard Allen Greene, "Bush's language angers US Muslims," *BBC* August 12, 2006. (Bush tried on many instances to disassociate the Muslim faith from terrorism and make a distinction between Muslim and terrorists, but acted otherwise.) http://adbusters.org/the_magazine/62/Creeping_Fascism.html

[1552] "Rhetoric has been defined as: "(from Greek ῥήτωρ, rhêtôr, orator, teacher) is the art or technique of persuasion through the use of oral or written language." *wikipedia* http://en.wikipedia.org/wiki/Rhetoric "Creeping Fascism" (After Bush brewed and exploited a culture of fear through rhetoric in turning the country into a fascist state. By the same token, "Bush's manipulation of his citizenry's national security concerns has proven enormously politically expedient." http://adbusters.org/the_magazine/62/Creeping_Fascism.html

[1553] Support for Bush's policy, during his entire tenure, is divided along partisan lines. Dan Balz and Claudia Deane, "Differing Views on Terrorism," Americans Divided on Eavesdropping Program, Poll Finds," *Washington Post* Wednesday, January 11, 2006; Page A04. While more people are still supportive of the President than not, ("Among Republicans, 75 percent said the Bush program is acceptable, while 61 percent of Democrats said it is unacceptable." *Id.*) Increasingly core Republicans and base supporters are backing away. (on issue of security vs. liberty: " some Democrats willing to support tough anti-terrorism policies at the expense of personal privacy and some Republicans fearful that individual rights may be compromised." *Id.*). See Washington Post-ABC News Poll. *The Washington Post.* Wednesday, Jan. 11, 2006. http://www.washingtonpost.com/wp-srv/politics/polls/postpoll_alito_010906.htm

[1554] California's Partisan Divide (PPIC (Public Policy Institute California survey – "Partisan Divide by Issues" – shows that approval for the President has dropped in the eyes of registered democrats vs. republicans: D approval: 47% (6/2002) to 13% (7/2006) vs. R: 90% to 71%. To the question of whether anti-terrorism policy ahs gone too far in infringing on citizens' liberty: D agreeing: 43% (8/2005) to 57% (1/2006) vs. R: 19% to 20%.) http://www.ppic.org/content/pubs/jtf/JTF_CaDivideJTF.pdf

Washington[1555] is not working; it is neither compatible with the nation's core values[1556] nor reflective of the people's basic sentiments, [1557] e.g., there is a gross lack of government accountable after 9/11.[1558] More generally, the country as a whole is dissatisfied with the direction of the country[1559] and performance of the Bush administration[1560] as a whole.

A sampling of dissenting voices even from conservative quarters shows that distrust and divisiveness runs wide and deep. They show that the Bush administration's anti-terrorism policy, or at least politics, is in disarray:[1561] Local politician Todd Lakey, Canyon County Republican Chairman "We want to support our president, and we want to fight terrorism throughout the world, but we also want to be careful of our personal liberties."[1562]; Lobbyists Harry Schneider, Legislative Chairman, Pennsylvania Sportsman's Association: "Most gun owners are not very enthusiastic and they're very apprehensive about aspects of the Patriot Act, specifically about search-and-seizure rules"[1563] and Larry Pratt, Executive Director, Gun Owners of America "Anytime the government is in a conflict, they see it as an opportunity to

---

[1555] PAUL CRAIG ROBERTS, "When Opposing Voices Do Not Oppose: American Rot," *CounterPunch*. April 4, 2005. (The America political system is in total disarray: special interest dominants, commercial media speaks for advertisers and nationalism, egoistical intellectuals are dismissive of different ideas, opposing parties are either too week or incompetent to make a difference.) http://www.counterpunch.org/roberts04042005.html

[1556] Dan Eggen, "Bush Authorized Domestic Spying Post-9/11 Order Bypassed Special Court," *Washington Post*. Friday, December 16, 2005; Page A01. (President Bush acknowledged authorizing the National Security Agency in 2002 to eavesdrop on U.S. in violation of the law. This attracted widespread condemnation of political activities and lawmakers, e.g., John D. Rockefeller IV (W.Va.), the ranking Democrat on the intelligence committee. http://www.washingtonpost.com/wp-dyn/content/article/2005/12/16/AR2005121 600021.html Aziz Huq, "A Spying Policy Still Without Warrant," *TomPaign* January 22, 2007. ("As Adam Litpak observed … The government invokes an extreme position on executive power to underwrite broad coercive or surveillance powers, but then ducks when it looks like those legal claims may be subject to any judicial scrutiny.") http://www.tompaine.com/articles/2007/01/22 /a_spying_policy_still_without_warrant.php Adam Litpak, "THREATS AND RESPONSES: NEWS ANALYSIS; The White House as a Moving Legal Target," *New York Times*. January 19, 2007, Friday. Late Edition - Final, Section A, Page 1, Column 2, 941 words (Bush administrative adopted illegal government policies/actions just when such policies/actions have to be reviewed by the courts. This raises an issue of government's respect for our constitutional check and balance system.)

[1557] "CONGRESS – Job Rating in recent national polls." PollingReport.com (Every survey polls on the issue of trust in and performance of the Congress in 2005 and 2005 shows that there is a deficit between approval and disapproval. The most recent AP-IPSOS poll (1/16-18/07) shows that the approval vs. disapproval rate is 60% vs. 34% http://www.pollingreport.com/CongJob.htm When asked in a Harris poll (Nov. 17-21, 2006. N=1,001 adults nationwide. MoE ± 3): "How do you rate the job Republicans in Congress are doing: excellent, pretty good, only fair, or poor?" 24% say Excellent/Pretty Good while 72 say Only Fair/Poor. http://www.pollingreport.com/cong_rep.htm

[1558] Abby Scher, "When Adversaries Become Allies: The Fight Against the Patriot Act and the Surveillance State," *The Public Eye Magazine* Vol. 20(1) (Spring, 2001). (People are taking matter in the own hand, e.g., liberals and conservatives are getting together to form coalitions to fight the USAPA, e.g., American Conservative Union and Gun Owners of America are working with ACLU and Libertarian Party to defeat the Act.)

[1559] Polling Interlude: Bush 's Popularity, Direction and NSA, January 2006. http://thenexthurrah.typepad.com/ the_next_hurrah/2006/01/polling_interlu.html

[1560] *Joseph Carroll* "Government Dissatisfaction as the Nation's Most Important Problem"Tuesday, January 10, 2006 ("Every month, Gallup asks Americans, without prompting, to name "the most important problem facing this country today." The latest poll, conducted Dec. 5-8, finds that dissatisfaction with government is the second most frequently mentioned problem, at 12%. The war in Iraq is the nation's top problem, with 22% of Americans mentioning it. Cited next-most frequently are the general state of the economy (8%), ethics and moral decline (7%), terrorism (6%), unemployment or jobs (6%), immigration (5%), poverty, hunger, or homelessness (5%), and healthcare (5%).") http://www.galluppoll.com/content/?ci=14338

[1561] Extracted from See Conservative Voices Against the USAPA (4/15/2004) http://www.aclu.org/safefree/general/ 17244res20040415.html.

[1562] "Idaho GOP for limits on the Patriot Act," *The Spokesman-Review*, 6/15/2004.

[1563] "Administration policies prompt some gun owners to recoil," *Associated Press*, 4/14/04.

aggrandize themselves and run roughshod over the Constitution"[1564]; Congressional leader Rep. James Sensenbrenner (R-WI), Chair of the House Judiciary Committee: "over my dead body" will the act be reauthorized without undergoing thorough re-examination in hearings held by the House"[1565]; Presidential hopeful Newt Gingrich, the former speaker of the House: "I strongly believe Congress must act now to rein in the Patriot Act, limit its use to national security concerns and prevent it from developing "mission creep" into areas outside of national security"[1566]; Grassroots political activist David Keene, Chairman of the American Conservative Union: " While the government should have all the power it needs to protect us, it shouldn't have all the power it'd like to have"[1567]; Advocate of public interest, Grover Norquist, president of Americans for Tax Reform, board member, National Rifle Association and American Conservative Union: "It's been two years since 9-11, and for the administration to still answer the public's questions about how these powers are being used with 'Just trust us' is insulting"[1568]; Senate leader Sen. Arlen Specter (R-PA), member of the Senate Judiciary Committee [On section 215 of the USAPA]:"I don't think that's any of the government's business. I don't think what people read is subject to inquiry"[1569]; Christopher Pyle, former U.S. Army intelligence officer who served on the Church Committee: "I don't think the Fourth Amendment exists anymore. I think it's been buried by the Patriot Act and some of the court rulings that have been handed down"[1570]

The convergence of general political factors, from mismanagement of Katrina disaster (administrative incompetence) to deliberate revel of CIA identity (ethical lapse), and coalescing of specific anti-terrorism policy concerns, from NSA spying (privacy breach) to Abu Grab torture (human rights violations) [1571] further galvanizes social activists and consolidates political oppositions to the anti-USAPA cause.[1572]

Such and other anti-Patriot oppositions took many forms, involved all kinds of people,[1573] implicated diversity of interest groups [1574] and adopted different strategies. The ultimate

---

[1564] "Coalition for Constitutional Liberties," Weekly Update, *Free Congress Foundations*, 2/27/2004
[1565] "Inside Politics," *Washington Times*, 1/23/2004.
[1566] "The Policies of War: Refocus the mission," *San Francisco Chronicle*, 11/11/03.
[1567] "Civil liberties advocates laud Sununu for stand on Patriot Act reform," *Manchester Union Leader*, 10/16/2003.
[1568] "Hatch alarms right over anti-terror act," *Salt Lake Tribune*, 9/15/2003
[1569] "Specter blasts part of anti-terrorism act," *Associated Press*, 8/2/2003
[1570] "Conservative Backlash Provisions of 'Patriot II' Draft Worry Those on Right," *ABCNews.com*, 3/12/2003.
[1571] Such factors and concerns are by no mean randomly distributed. Rather they bear witness to a revolutionary transformation in governing philosophy (neo-conservatism) and administrative style (secretive, manipulative). Henry A. Giroux, "Dirty Democracy and State Terrorism: The Politics of the New Authoritarianism in the United States," *Comparative Studies of South Asia, Africa and the Middle East* Vol. 26 (2) 163-177(2006).
[1572] See coalition building in Dallas, Idaho and D.C. beltway. "DAVE LINDORFF, "A Model for Political Organizing When There's No Party of Opposition: The Grassroots Resistance to the Patriot Act," *Counterpunch*. April 5, 2005. http://www.counterpunch.org/lindorff04052005.html
[1573] See objections of Professor Susan Herman, "THE USAPA AND THE US DEPARTMENT OF JUSTICE: LOSING OUR BALANCES?," Brooklyn Law School, JURIST Guest Columnist (The USAPA also increases the authority of the President - Attorney General little or no judicial review of legislative oversight.) http://jurist.law.pitt.edu/forum/forumnew40.htm and judicial officials in "Center for National Security Studies v. Department of Justice 215 F. Supp 2d 94 (D.D.C. 2002) (Issue: Whether DOJ is allowed to withhold names of post-911 round of terrorist suspects and interested persons in the face of FOIA request? Memorandum Opinion and Order filed August 2, 2002 by Judge Gladys Kessler -- D.C. District Court's order to Justice Department to release names, location, date of arrest information.) For legal proceedings and papers, http://www.cnss.org/cnssvdoj.htm. See also Michael Traynor (President, The American Law), "ADDRESS: CITIZENSHIP IN A TIME OF REPRESSION," 2005 *Wis. L. Rev. 1* (2005) (The Sixteenth Thomas E. Fairchild Lecture University of Wisconsin Law School April 23, 2004).
[1574] For example, *Free Congress Foundation* is concerned with erosion of privacy. Stephen M. Lilienthal (*Director of the Center for Privacy and Technology Policy at the Free Congress Foundation*), "Reauthorization the

objective of the opposition from the beginning is to repeal the USAPA or revise its content; at the very least restricts its application and dilutes its impact.

One of the most successful anti-Patriot political action groups, which distinguished itself in terms of early organization efforts and later mobilization success, is the Bill of Rights Defense Committee (BORDC). Soon after USAPA passage, the BORDC launched a grassroots anti USAPA ("anti-Patriot" for short) to defeat the law, one community at a time. The movement caught on and spread like wild fire. Vermont, one of the early success stories of the movement, is typical of such grassroots political activism.

On May 28, 2003, Vermont became the third states after Hawaii (April 25, 2003) and Alaska (May 21, 2003)[1575] to adopt a resolution seeking to repeal the USAPA.[1576] It is fitting that Vermont should take the lead. Vermont is one of the most progressive and liberal state in the Union.[1577] The Vermont state motto is: "Freedom and unity." Vermont's Congressman, Bernard Sanders boasted 100% liberal voting from ACLU.[1578] Vermont's Senator, Patrick Leahy, has one of the highest civil liberties voting record in Congress.[1579] As Karen Lane, President of the Vermont Library Association and Representative Sanders observed at an anti-Patriot meeting:

"It is a point of pride with Vermonters to stand tall for our principles. Movements for abolition, temperance, woman's suffrage, civil liberties and peace have all found strong proponents in this state. Runaway slaves found refuge here on the Underground Railroad. McCarthyism was first questioned in the halls of Congress in 1954 by Sen. Ralph Flanders of Vermont. In 1966, U.S. Senator George D Aiken demonstrated with quintessential Vermont wisdom and wit how the nation could end its involvement in Vietnam by "declaring victory and getting out!"[1580]

Vermonters also like to read and love its libraries:

USAPA: The Battle Moves to Conference," September 2, 2005 ("That is exactly why privacy advocates must insist upon anti-terrorism legislation that would protect privacy rights and civil liberties."); *The American Conservative Union*, the nation's oldest and largest grassroots conservative lobbying organization objects to USAPA on grounds that it give the government too much unchecked and un-checkable powers. W. Stephen Thayer, III, ACU Executive Director. American Conservative Union Public Memorandum to Conservative Leaders and Activists. February 26, 2003. RE: ACU Analysis of the Domestic Security Enhancement ACT (DSEA) of 2003, also known as "Patriot Act II". (ACU finds "Patriot Act II" to be objectionable, e.g., it expands the jurisdiction of the Foreign Intelligence Surveillance Act (FISA) to cover individuals who have *no ties to foreign governments* or terrorist organizations (Section 101) http://www.conservative.org/pressroom/030226.asp

[1575] For a list of the states which has adopted anti-Patriot Act resolutions, see "Progress on Statewide Civil Liberties Resolutions," Bill of Rights Defense Committee http://www.bordc.org/states.htm (Visited Feb. 1, 2007). For a critical analysis of how anti-Patriot groups are connected in ideology and with strategy., see David Horowitz and John Perazzo, "The Unholy Alliance of American Radicals and Islamic Terrorists Against the Patriot Act," Frontpage.com Tuesday, June 07, 2005 (Liberal left and radical Muslim is working together to disrupt and destroy America) *Frontpage.com* http://www.frontpagemag.com/Articles/ReadArticle.asp?ID=17702
See also Unholy Alliance: The "Peace Left" and the Islamic Jihad Against America," *Frontpage.com* Wednesday, April 13, 2005. http://www.frontpagemag.com/Articles/ReadArticle.asp?ID=18322

[1576] "Vermont Continues the Trend: Becomes Third State to Speak Out Against Federal Abuses Under USAPA," ACLU May 29, 2003. http://www.aclu.org/SafeandFree/SafeandFree.cfm?ID=12735andc=206

[1577] "The Sensible, Liberal Green Mountain State," ACLU, Nov. 13, 1996.

[1578] In 2005, American Conservative Union rated Sanders as 6/100 on conservatism (lifetime) and 8/100 for year 2004-5. http://www.acuratings.org/

[1579] In 2005, American Conservative Union rated Sanders as 6/100 on conservatism (lifetime) and 0/100 for year 2004-5. http://www.acuratings.org/

[1580] "Statement of Karen Lane on the Patriot Act's Effects on Vermont Libraries" (December 12, 2002). http://bernie.house.gov/documents/releases/20021220175727.asp

"The freedom to read is one of the cornerstones of democracy and Vermonters are readers. Vermont ranks first in the nation in the number of libraries per capita AND per square mile. 97% of all Vermonters have public library service available in their town or nearby. The average Vermonter borrows 6 ½ books each year from his/her public library. As librarians, we consider ourselves responsible for ensuring that all our library patrons have free access to information."[1581]

The "Vermont Legislature Resolution"[1582] was co-sponsored by Vermont Congressman Bernard Sanders.[1583] He is an independent who has long opposed the USAPA. [1584] In fact, he led the charge against the USAPA.[1585] As early as December of 2002 Congressman Sanders has talked about the need to introduce legislation to undo the USAPA. [1586] Sanders, was prompted to take action after receiving a letter from the Vermont Library Association. The Executive Board of Vermont Library Association in "Open Letter to Vermont's Congressional Delegation" (October 21, 2002): wrote: "We, the undersigned librarians and booksellers, implore Senators Leahy and Jeffords and Congressman Sanders to introduce legislation to eliminate provisions in the USAPA that undermine Americans' Constitutionally guaranteed right to read and access information without governmental intrusion or interference."[1587]

On May 6, 2003, Sanders, together with 24 other Congressmen,[1588] including Republican Ron Paul of Texas, and Congressman John Conyers, the Ranking Member of the House Judiciary Committee, offered HR 1157: Freedom to Read Protection Act of 2003. [1589] The Bill gathered a wellspring of populist support and enthusiastic Congressional endorsement. By March 12, 2003, the Bill attracted 28 co-sponsors and was endorsed by the American Library Association, the American Booksellers Association and newspapers throughout the country, including Los Angeles Times, the Detroit Free Press, the Honolulu Observer, the Providence Journal-Bulletin, the Caledonia Record, and the Valley News.[1590]

The Vermont Senate adopted the anti-Patriot resolution unanimously (29-0) on May 25, 2003. The Vermont House of Representatives approved the resolution by a vote of 101 to 23.

[1581] Statement of Karen Lane on the Patriot Act's Effects on Vermont Libraries" (December 12, 2002). http://bernie.house.gov/documents/releases/20021220175727.asp

[1582] See http://www.aclu.org/SafeandFree/SafeandFree.cfm?ID=12734andc=207

[1583] For Sanders' view on Section 215 of the USAPA, see Rep. Bernie Sanders, "Pulling FBI's Nose Out of Your Books," Los Angeles Times, May 8, 2003. (PATRIOT ACT gave the government too much power to invade citizens' privacy without proper check and balance. The government cannot be trusted. Such powers have been abused in the past and must be limited.) http://bernie.house.gov/documents/opeds/20030508100516.asp

[1584] For Sanders' view on "Anti-Terrorism Legislation and Civil Liberties" (10/15/2001), see http://www.fcnl.org/issues/item.php?item_id=244andissue_id=68 Surprisingly, Section 215 was not on Sanders' objection list.

[1585] See "Freedom to Read Protection Act: Talking Points by Rep Bernard Sanders" (Prepared by the Office of Representative Bernard Sanders (VT)) (5/15/2003) http://www.fcnl.org/issues/item.php?item_id=234andissue_id=68

[1586] Patrick Armstrong, "Sanders Works to Repeal Provisions of Patriot Act," Brattleboro Reformer, December 21, 2002. See http://www.commondreams.org/headlines02/1221-10.htm

[1587] http://www.vermontlibraries.org/patriot.html

[1588] Mr. Sanders (for himself, Mr. Paul, Mr. Defazio, Mr. Blumenauer, Mr. Owens, Ms. Lee, Mr. Farr, Mr. Towns, Mr. Grijalva, Mr. Conyers, Mr. MCDermott, Ms. Jackson-Lee of Texas, Mr. Hinchey, Mr. Olver, Ms. Woolsey, Mr. Frank of Massachusetts, Mr. Jackson of Illinois, Mr. MCGovern, Ms. Baldwin, Ms. Waters, Mr. Ford, Mr. Lipinski, Mr. Stark, and Mr. Udall of Colorado). See http://www.fas.org/irp/congress/2003_cr/hr1157.html

[1589] For a copy of the Bill and sponsorship, see http://www.fas.org/irp/congress/2003_cr/hr1157.html

[1590] "Hon. Bernard Sanders of Vermont in the House of Representatives, March 12, 2003. Congressional Record: March 12, 2003 (Extensions) Page E441-E442. http://www.fas.org/irp/congress/2003_cr/h031203.html

The resolution earned bi-partisan support; the Senate was controlled by Democrats[1591] and House was controlled by Republicans.[1592]

The story of Vermont is the story of each and every anti-Patriot resolution nation wide, and grass roots political resistant efforts everywhere:[1593] community culture (liberalism),[1594] political/intellectual leadership (commitment), [1595] public awareness (discontent or aspiration) [1596], interest group politics (synergy) [1597] and precipitating events (attack on liberty) [1598] provided the soil (culture), seed (event), nutrients (awareness), and care (leadership) for the resolutions to take roots, grow and blossom.

A cursory review of legal and political science literature informs that in spite of the huge success of the BORDC in opposing the USAPA, its mobilizing effort and political success has escaped serious scholarly investigation.[1599] An electronic search of legal data base Lexis-Nexis with the key word Bill of Rights Defense Committee uncovered 20 articles, not one of them discuss the BORDC effort or movement directly, systematically or comprehensively. Most of the legal scholars have focused federalism issues, and related cases and doctrines of preemption and commandeering. [1600] A keyword search of JSTOR Political Science Journals

---

[1591] See The Vermont Legislature Legislative Directory Senators 2003-2004 Legislative Session. http://www.leg.state.vt.us/legdir/alpha.cfm?Body=S

[1592] See the Vermont Legislature Legislative Directory Representatives 2003-2004 Legislative Session. http://www.leg.state.vt.us/legdir/alpha.cfm?Body=H

[1593] Ben Salt, "Institutional Responses to Grassroots Organizing: An Autobiography of an Attempt to Form a Graduate Union," *The Journal of the Midwest Modern Language Association*, Vol. 33 (1): 32-43 (2002); Evelyn Zellerer, "Women's Grassroots Struggles for Empowerment in the Repulblic of Kazakhstan," *Social Politics: International Studies in Gender, State and Society* - Volume 11 (3): 439-464 (2004).

[1594] Jeffrey W. Rubin, "Meanings and Mobilizations: A Cultural Politics Approach to Social Movements and States," *Latin American Research Review* 29.3 (2004) 106-142. (Social movement, its creation and evolution – can best be understood in historical and culture terms, less so on precipitating events, availability of resources or existing of leadership.)

[1595] Eileen Boris, "On Grassroots Organizing, Poor Women's Movements, and the Intellectual as Activist," *Journal of Women's History* 14.2 (2002) 140-142 (For 40 years Frances Fox Piven and her husband (Richard A. Cloward) provided a theoretical basis for the welfare rights organization of the 1960s.)

[1596] Nathanson, Constance A. "The Skeptic's Guide to a Movement for Universal Health Insurance," *Journal of Health Politics, Policy and Law* Volume 28 (2-3): 443-471 (2003) (Successful social movement – are usually ideologically and/or grievance-motivated.)

[1597] Scott, Kurashige, "Pan-ethnicity and Community Organizing: Asian Americans United's Campaign against Anti-Asian Violence," *Journal of Asian American Studies* Volume 3 (2): 163-190 (2000) (A new generation "Asian American" - Japanese, Chinese, Filipino, and Korean Americans – join hand to resist Western imperialism abroad and American racism at home, following a "reactive solidarity" path); Nadine C. Naber, "So Our History Doesn't Become Your Future:The Local and Global Politics of Coalition Building Post September 11th," *Journal of Asian American Studies* 5.3 (2002) 217-242 ("coalition building also necessitates consistency in the willingness to forge political unity with a variety of struggles against racism, classism, sexism, homophobia, colonialism, and imperialism, despite differences in the benefits or repercussions of supporting one struggle as opposed to another.")

[1598] Jennifer Brier "Save Our Kids, Keep Aids Out:" Anti-Aids Activism and the Legacy of Community Control in Queens, New York," *Journal of Social History* Vol. 39 (4): 965-987 (2006) (In NYC black and white parents unprecedentedly joined hands to fight to Board of Education's AIDS admission policy.)

[1599] There are however many newspaper accounts of the anti-Patriot movement. See Elain Scarry, "Resolving to Resist" *Boston Review* http://www.bostonreview.net/BR29.1/scarry.html For a collection of newspaper accounts, see Nat Hentoff, *The War on the Bill of Rights and Gathering Reistance* (Seven Stories Press, 2003).

[1600] Susan N. Herman, "David G. Trager Public Policy Symposium: Our New Federalism? National Authority and Local Autonomy in the War on Terror: Introduction," 69 *Brooklyn L. Rev.* 1201 (2004) (Study the impact of USAPA on state and local government, e.g., can local police be asked to help with federal law enforcement or what is the effect of anti-Patriot resolutions calling for non-collaboration with USAPA enforcement). For more point and representative treatment of role and functions, problems and issues with BORDC, see Susan N. Herman, "Laboratories of Democracy: Federalism and State Law Independency: Article: Collapsing Spheres: Joint Terrorism Task Forces, Federalism, and the War on Terror," 41 *Willamette L. Rev.* 941 (2005)

and Project Muse Political Science Journals (February 6, 2007), using key terms of "USAPA" and "Bill of Rights Defense Committee" recovers no item of interest.[1601]

This is a first attempt to fill this literature gap.

This chapter is devoted to studying the BORDC; its origination and development, charter and strategy, philosophy and typology, and finally reasons for success, with archived data at the BORDC web site, newspaper accounts all over the nation, and learned treatises from law to political science. From such an inquiry, it is discovered that "civil liberties safe zone" (anti-Patriot) efforts exemplifies the best of America democratic spirit, i.e., grassroots activism,[1602] and people's constitutionalism at work.[1603]

This chapter is divided into the following sections. After this brief introduction, section II states the "Research Focus and Method" of the chapter. Section III provides a brief overview of the theory and concepts to social movement. Section IV, "The Bill of Rights Defense Committee" details the origin and history, vision and mission, goals and objective, strategies and tactics of BORDC. Section V details the BORDC analyze and describe the varieties of resolutions being adopted – 408 in all – from May 2002 to December 30, 2006, in nature and kind, content and process. Section VI presents two successful "civil liberties free zone" initiatives, one at Madison, Wisconsin and the other at An Arbor Michigan. These two in-depth case studies provides rich and animated accounts of how anti-Patriot partisans teamed up in Madison to support the resolution and what kinds of opposition lied in wait in Ann Arbor to obstruct the effort. Finally, section VII summarizes the research in discussing the findings discovered and lessons learned, i.e., why the anti-Patriot movement is successful. This review of investigation into anti-Patriot movement shows that the resolutions are hardly uniform in content and approach, allowing observant researchers and discerning observers to questions some of the claims made by BORDC, i.e., "civil liberties free zone" initiatives demonstrated that there are a groundswell objection to the USAPA, universally. The study also validates the assertion that constitutional principles need to be upheld in the court as well as defended in the street.

("Portland's experiences with the Joint Terrorism Task Force, like other federal/state skirmishes over the allocation of decision-making authority, also reveal that the war on terror can disrupt a locality's internal system of governance by forcing a shift of the center of policy-making gravity away from legislative bodies and toward the executive branches, where accountability and transparency are minimized"); Anne Klinefelter, "The Role of Librarians in Challenges to the USAPA" 5 *N.C. J.L. and Tech.* 219 (2004) (Due to commitment to patrons' privacy and organizational strength, librarians was active in mustering opposition to the USAPA. "By early 2004, community resolutions against the Act totaled over 250, and many of the resolutions specifically mentioned libraries or library use (n. 9)"); Michael Traynor (President, The American Law), "Address: Citizenship in a Time of Repression," 2005 *Wis. L. Rev.* 1 (2005) (Citizens have a duty to defend the Constitution and protect their own rights, as with the BORDC grassroots movement); Sayaka Kawakami and Sarah C. MCcarty, "2004 Privacy Year in Review Annual Update: Government Information Collection: Privacy Year in Review: Privacy Impact Assessments, Airline Passenger Pre-Screening, and Government Data Mining," 1 *ISJLP* 219)(2005) (BORDC used as a source at n. 203: "Sharon R. Anderson, *Total Information Awareness and Beyond: The Dangers of Using Data Mining Technology to Prevent Terrorism,* Bill of Rights Defense Committee, *available at* http://www.bordc.org/data-mining.pdf; Taipale, *supra* note 152, at 11.").

[1601] One journal article is discovered in the web when BORDC keyword is used. http://www.economyandsociety.org/publications/Strang,etal_Civil_Liberty_in_America_JAN07.pdf

[1602] Tarrow, Sidney. 1994. *Power in Movement: Social Movements, Collective Action, and Politics.* Cambridge: Cambridge University Press.

[1603] Larry D. Kramer, *The People Themselves. Popular Constitutionalism and Judicial. Review* (New York : Oxford University Press, 2004) http://www.law.northwestern.edu/colloquium/legalhistory/Larry%20 Kramer.pdf

II. RESEARCH FOCUS AND METHOD

To date, judging by objective measures, the BORDC is one of the more successful grassroots social movements in history.[1604] All told, from October 2001 to December 30 2006, there were 406 anti-Patriot resolutions nationwide, make up of 8 State Resolutions and 398 Community Resolutions, covering a total of 84,617,547 people in America.[1605]

This is a first attempt to study the anti-Patriot movement. What is the origin and philosophy of BORDC? Why is the original BORDC resolution drafted the way it is? What strategies were employed by the BORDC to defeat the USAPA? What kind of process was involved in getting the resolutions adopted? Finally, why was BORDC successful in mobilizing a nation wide revolt against the USAPA?

The resolutions provided primary data for this study. The resolutions are first classified by nature and kind. Further investigation into and analysis of the resolutions are contextualized with national ethos, local history and individual case circumstances. Interpretation of the resolutions and understanding of the cases is achieved by drawing upon legal doctrines on federalism and political science theories on social movement. The case studies were picked for their realism and dynamism. They are used as representative cases, to provide evidence for propositions made, to demonstrate ideas presented, to raise issues for discussion and exploration. Finally, the anti-Patriot resolutions and movement will be assessed in terms of espoused objectives – upholding the Constitution and protecting rights.

III. CONCEPT AND THEORIES OF SOCIAL MOVEMENT: AN OVERVIEW

BORDC – anti-Patriotism is a classical case of a successful grassroots social movement. Social movements are about people seeking change to the status quo through collective action: "Social movements are a type of group action. They are large informal groupings of individuals and/or organizations focused on specific political or social issues, in other words, on carrying out a social change."[1606]

Professors Luther P. Gerlach and Virginia H. Hine have further elaborated upon the necessary conditions for the formation of "true" social movement.[1607]

[1604] There are to be others: Mothers Against Drunk Driving, or MADD, is a single-issue non-profit grassroots victims' rights organization established by Ms. Candy Lightner in the U.S. after his daughter was killed by a drunken driver in 1980. MADD campaigns to eliminate drunk driving. Wendy J Hamilton, "Mothers Against Drunk Driving—MADD in the USA," *BMJ* Injury Prevention 6:90-91 (2000) http://ip.bmj.com/cgi/content/extract/6/2/90

[1605] http://www.bordc.org/ For an interactive map, see http://www.aclu.org/projects/patriotmap/continentalmap/ The resolutions are not evening distributed, more resolutions were passed in the East and West coasts and few are in between. For a map display (2003), see "Local governments rejecting Patriot Act" http://www.sacbee.com/static/live/news/images/0924liberty.html

[1606] "Free Movement" From Wikipedia, the free encyclopedia. http://en.wikipedia.org/wiki/Social_movement For "Select Definitions of Social Movements" (Compiled by Benita Roth), see http://womhist.binghamton.edu/socm/definitions.htm

[1607] Luther P. Gerlach and Virginia H. Hine. *People, Power, Change: Movements of Social Transformation* (Indianapolis: Bobbs-Merrill, 1970) pp. xvi-xvii.

"A segmented, usually polycephalous, cellular organization composed of units reticulated by various personal, structural, and ideological ties.

Face-to-face recruitment by committed individuals using their own pre-existing, significant social relationships.

Personal commitment generated by an actor or an experience which separates a convert in some significant way from the established order (or his previous place in it), identifies him with a new set of values, and commits him to changed patterns of behavior.

An ideology which codifies values and goals, provides a conceptual framework by which all experiences or events relative to these goals may be interpreted, motivates and provides rationale for envisioned changes, defines the opposition, and forms the basis for conceptual unification of a segmented network of groups.

Real or perceived opposition from a society at large or from that segment of the established order within which the movement has arisen."[1608]

In terms of typologies, according to David Aberle,[1609] there are four types of social movements: transformative, reformative, redemptive, and alterative movements:

(1) Transformative movements are movements that seek radical change in social structure or culture, most often violent in nature, revolutionary in process and transformational in outcome. It seeks nothing short of challenge to the legitimacy and hegemony of the state in ideology and culture,[1610] e.g., cultural revolution in Mao's China.[1611]

(2) Reformative movements are movements that seek to change aspects of society that the movement found to be objectionable. They are usually pursued to improve (social, political) conditions or meet with (people, elite) expectations, e.g., anti-Vietnam war movement in the US.[1612]

(3) Redemptive movements are movements that seek to save the people from evil, e.g., anti-corruption movement in Hong Kong.[1613]

(4) Alterative movements are movements that seek to change people's individual way and mean, e.g., MADD in the United States.[1614]

[1608] *Id.*

[1609] David F. Aberle, *The Peyote Religion among the Navaho* (Chicago: Aldine, 1966).

[1610] Darrell Gene Moe, "Analysis of Social Transformative Movements in Advanced Capitalism: A Neo-Gramscian Approach." *Journal of Policy and Culture*: Vol. 3. March 1998. http://www.tsujiru.net/moen/essays/essay_4.html

[1611] "The Truth About the Cultural Revolution," Revolutionary Worker #1251, August 29, 2004 (Cultural revolution changed state ideology, social relationship and political status of all those who were involved. posted at http://rwor.org

[1612] Michael D. Coomes, *The Vietnam War on Campus: Other Voices, More Distant Drums.* (Westport, CT: Praeger, 2000/

[1613] Rance P. L. Lee, "The Folklore of Corruption in Hong Kong Asian Survey Vol. 21 (3): 355-368 (1981) (ICAC set up to deal with age old corruption problem; an evil in Hong Kong.)

[1614] Craig Reinarman, "The Social Construction of an Alcohol Problem: The Case of Mothers against Drunk Drivers and Social Control in the 1980s," *Theory and Society* Vol. 17 (1): 91-120 (1988) (MADD was able to change people's perception and conduct about drinking and driving.)

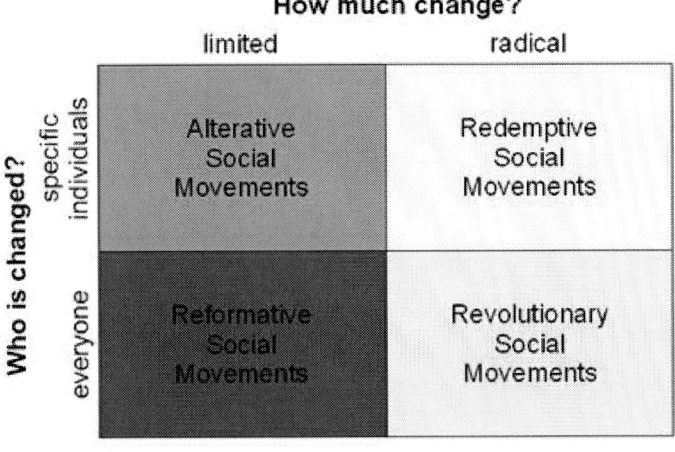

Figure 1.

In terms of casual explanation, traditional structure strain theory seeks to explain collective movement in terms of anomie, i.e., lack of fit between culturally promoted ends and socially approved means. "A disjuncture within the cultural system between the Goals (values) which define our lives and the culturally determined, institutionalized, legitimate Means for achieving them." For example, in an advance capitalistic society, it matters not how hard people work, in the ultimate analysis the rich get richer and poor get poorer. Quintessentially, it was Marx who called out for: "Workers of the World Unite!" to rise against the capitalistic class.

The New Social Movement theory suggested that the strain theory is dated. Social movement results not because people want to conform to existing social order, and failing that, seeking to reform the political power structure. They want to liberate from state hegemony and convention culture, to find their own independence and destiny. In essence, they deny the power of the state to define and determine what the meaning of life is and how should conduct oneself.

"A postmodern politics began to take shape during the 1960s with the appearance of numerous new political groups and struggles. The development of a postmodern politics is strongly informed by the vicissitudes of social movements in France, the United States, and elsewhere, as well as by emerging postmodern theories…The modern emphasis on collective struggle, solidarity, and alliance politics gave way to extreme fragmentation, as the "movement" of the 1960s splintered into various competing struggles for rights and liberties. The previous emphasis on transforming the public sphere and institutions of domination gave way to new emphases on culture, personal identity, and everyday life, as macropolitics were replaced by the micropolitics of local transformation and changes in subjectivity."[1615]

[1615] Steven Best and Douglas Kellner, "Dawns, Twilights, and Transitions: Postmodern Theories, Politics, and Challenges," *Democracy and Nature* Volume 7, Number 1 / March 1, 2001.

Both theories agree that in order to be successful a movement must be able to mobilize the people, obtain necessary resources and finally seek out political opportunity.

Stages of Social Movements

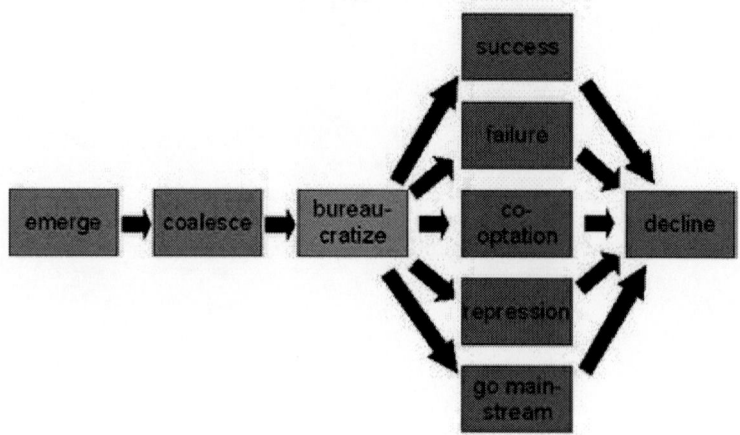

Adapted from Blumer (1969), Mauss (1975), and Tilly (1978)

Figure 2.

In terms of formation and development, Smelser[1616] identified six factors leading to formation of social movement, i.e., structural conduciveness; structural strains; growth of a generalized belief system; precipitating events; mobilization of participants; operation of social control. View in this light all social movement starts with a grievance, e.g., social strain and personal stress. However, having grievance alone is not enough. In order to build a successful social movement, SMO needs effective mobilization and organization, of resource, of people, of publicity.

In terms of mobilization, SMO must be effective in creating support, forming recruitment networks, framing and packaging of issues, building internal cohesion and cultivating external identity.[1617] In order to prevail, the SMO must also be able to obtain and retain powers: social, economical, and cultural.

Finally SMO has life cycle of its own from emergence to coalesce, bureaucratize and demise.[1618]

[1616] Neil J. Smelser, *Theory of Collective Behavior* (New York: Free Press, 1962)
[1617] *Id.* "Resource-Mobilization Theory".
[1618] Charles Tilly, *From Mobilization to Revolution. Reading* (Massachusetts: Addison-Wesley, 1978)

IV. THE BILL OF RIGHTS DEFENSE COMMITTEE

A Brief History

The BORDC (formerly the Northampton BORDC) was formed in November 2001[1619] to educate the local community about the threats posed by the USAPA to civil liberties and democratic institutions. It was also formed to organize "civil liberties safe zones" nation wide. "Civil liberties safe zones" are "a locale whose local government has passed a resolution declaring its commitment to protect the civil liberties of its residents."[1620]

Originally BORDC was made up of 300 teachers, lawyers, doctors, retirees, students and nurses in Northampton, Massachusetts area.[1621] One of the group's co-founders, Nancy Talanian, has substantial personal experience with organizing political action and social movement worldwide, including spearheading apartheid movements in South Africa and leading democratization actions in Nigeria. In her own words:

> I had worked to help end apartheid, and I had done work to help bring democracy to Nigeria, and when I heard terms like "military tribunals" it was reminiscent of what happened to Ken Saro-Wiwa and the Agoni activists who were hanged by the Nigerian military dictatorship, and when I heard about detentions without charges, without trial, it was reminiscent of how the apartheid government of South Africa treated the African people who were fighting for their freedom and felt this was not my country if this was the direction that we were going in, and I had to take action.[1622]

Nancy Talanian's personal experience made her highly critical of the USAPA. It also earned her a leadership role in the fight against the USAPA.[1623] Nancy Talania stated that her observation and objections to the USAPA in clear and un-compromising terms:

First, "[I]n the United States, the more the public learns about U.S. government antiterrorism policies and practices such as the USAPA, the more it fears a loss of privacy, a chilling of dissent and other First Amendment rights, and the targeting and mistreatment of people on the basis of their race, religion, or ethnic background."[1624] This is to observe that the more the public know about the truth with USAPA[1625] - broad impact, diverse effects,

---

[1619] There are different versions of when the BORDC originated. Many pointed to February 2002 as the start day. Nat Hentoff, "The New American Freedom Fighters Organizing Against General Ashcroft," *VillageVoice.com,* February 29, 2002. ("This grassroots network of freedom fighters actually began independently, with a meeting of the Bill of Rights Defense Committee in Northampton, Massachusetts, in February of this year.")

[1620] Nat Hentoff, "Hawaii, Alaska, Philadelphia Newest 'Civil Liberties Safe Zones' *Village Voice* May 30, 2003. http://www.villagevoice.com/news/0249,hentoff,40279,6.html

[1621] Nat Hentoff, "Ashcroft vs. civil liberties," Published 12/9/2002. http://www.villagevoice.com/news/0249, hentoff,40279,6.html

[1622] Interview with Nancy Talanian, "Civil Liberties Safe Zones", *On the Media,* April 29, 2003, WNYC (for a full transcript, go to http://www.wnyc.org/onthemedia/transcripts/transcripts_042903_civil.html)

[1623] Charles Dobson, "Social Movements: A summary of what works." (Movement leadership capacity a function of past social or political activism.) http://www.vcn.bc.ca/citizens-handbook/movements.pdf

[1624] Nancy Talanian, "License to Criticize the Patriot Act," *Common Dreams* April 02, 2004. http://www.commondreams.org/views04/0402-03.htm.

[1625] "Setting the Record Straight: An Analysis of the Justice Department's PATRIOT Act Website" (October 27, 2003) The Center for Democracy and Technology (CDT) ("the [DOJ] website does address controversial aspects of the law, it provides misleading, incomplete and, in some cases, incorrect information.") http://www.cdt.org/security/usapatriot/031027cdt.shtml "Washington Post's Response to DOJ Patriot Act

multifaceted consequences and long terms implications of the USAPA, the more likely the public will take action against the law.

Second, the USAPA subjects Muslims, Arabs and South Asians, and 33 other nationals, to extreme and discriminatory measures. The Act has the effect of turning citizens and residents into enemies of the state. For example; 'People of Arab and Muslim descent who live in the United States would be justified in staying silent about people they suspect out of fear that they themselves might be detained."[1626] However, in order to protect the United States from terrorism we need domestic support at home, e.g., information,[1627] and international cooperation abroad, e.g., extradition. This is to observe that the USAPA and related measures are counter-productive and self defeating in our fight with terrorism. Counter-productive because it aliens Arabs and Muslim who can help with defeating terrorism. Self-defeating because in fighting terror with discriminatory measures we have played into the hands of the terrorists in destroying the foundation of democracy.

Third, the USAPA has been used to subject thousands of people to humiliation and economic loss, as it exposes hundreds of innocent people to abusive legal process. "Approximately 5,000 men were rounded up after September 11th and detained for periods ranging from days to more than a year. Nearly all have been either released or deported, and not one has been charged with a connection to al Qaeda."[1628] This is to observe that USAPA and related measures have the potential of being discriminatory applied and systematically abused.

Fourth, the implementation of USAPA and related measures are very costly in economic and personal terms. The Special Registration (NSEERS) program was used to round up "87,000 men from North Korea and 19 primarily Muslim countries have submitted voluntarily to photographing, fingerprinting, and questioning. Not a single terrorism suspect has been found through this program, which cost U.S. taxpayers approximately $362 million last year alone."[1629] This is to observe that the USAPA and related measures are very costly to implement, and with dubious utility, at least unproven cost-effectiveness, in fighting error. Of record, the BORDC was established to pursue the following goals and objectives: (1) Opposes the USAPA; (2) Deems anti-terrorism legislation an assault on civil liberties; (3) Sees war on terror as a pretext for American empire-building[1630]

The BORDC was modeled[1631] after Committees of Correspondence[1632] started by the Sons of Liberty in Boston in 1756[1633] to share information with each of the colonies about

---

Letter," *Washington Post.* Monday, December 5, 2005; 7:00 AM (In a letter dated November 23, 2005 to Senator Specter, Chair, Committee on Judiciary, the FBI complained that a Washington Post article (November 6, 200) – "The FBI's Secret Scrutiny" - contained errors of facts and misinterpretation of the law.) For FBI letter, see http://www.washingtonpost.com/wp-srv/nation/documents/dojletter112305.pdf

[1626] Nancy Talanian, "License to Criticize the Patriot Act," *Common Dreams* April 02, 2004. http://www.commondreams.org/views04/0402-03.htm.

[1627] Department Of Justice, Federal Bureau of Investigation Reinforce Commitment to working with leaders of Muslim, Sikh and Arab-American Communities," Washington D.C., FBI National Press Office, July 9, 2004. ("As part of that effort, we are again reaching out to our partners in the Muslim and Arab-American communities for any information they may have. Their assistance has proven valuable in the past ...")

[1628] Nancy Talanian, "License to Criticize the Patriot Act," *Common Dreams* April 02, 2004. http://www.commondreams.org/views04/0402-03.htm.

[1629] *Id.*

[1630] Discoverthenetwork.Com http://www.google.com/firefox?client=firefox-aandrls=org.mozilla: en-US:official

[1631] Mary Jo McConahay, "It's Time for a New Sanctuary Movement," *Pacific News Service.* December 23, 2002. (The public has taken up grassroots social movements in the past to protect the oppressed or against the increasingly oppressive tactics of the British colonizer in levying British custom and controlling American currency.[1634] The first of such resolution was passed by Northampton City Council, which in time will become the prototype of such "civil liberties safe zones" resolutions. The petition was supported by over 1000 signatures.[1635]

The Northhampton BORDC experience soon becomes the model of resistance against the USAPA through the setting up of civil liberties safe zones nation wide with the help of "tips and tools" from BORDC:

> "See and use tips and tools from a committee in Northampton, MA, that worked with city officials to obtain the City Council's UNANIMOUS approval of a strongly worded Resolution in Defense of the Bill of Rights. Tools include an outline of the steps we took and downloadable documents we developed that can help you streamline a similar effort in your city or town.[1636]

The success of Northhampton was widely reported and enthusiastically embraced as on of the most effective ways to fight back at an administration which is bent on expanding police powers and taking away people's rights after 9/11.[1637]

The Resolution

The original Northhampton, MA City Council Civil Rights Protection Resolution as approved [1638] read as follows:[1639]

> *Whereas*, the City of Northampton has a long and distinguished history of protecting and expanding civil rights and civil liberties, often being a beacon for our country's citizens when liberties are threatened; and

---

authority. For example, the Sanctuary Movement in 1980 was started by the church to protect refugee fleeing from civil war in Central America from arrest and deportation by the INS) http://www.alternet.org/story/14857 James Walsh, "Sanctuary Cities and States -- Undermining the American Republic," *The Social Contract* 192 – 198 (Spring 2005). The sanctuary movement is alive and well today and feeding off each other with the anti-Patriot movement, see Catherine Elton, "Cities rethink sanctuary status: Cambridge studies 1985 resolution on immigration," *Globe Correspondent* April 21, 2006

[1632] Nat Hentoff, "Citizens Resist War on the Bill of Rights," *Free Inquiry magazine, Volume 22, Number 4. (Fall 2002). http://www.secularhumanism.org/index.php?section=libraryandpage=hentoff_22_4*

[1633] In 1805, Mercy Otis Warren in her book, *History of the Rise and Progress and Termination of the American Revolutions*, emphasized: "Perhaps no single step contributed so much to cement the union of the colonies, and the final acquisition of independence, as the establishment of the Committees of Correspondence . . . that produced unanimity and energy throughout the continent." http://www.samizdat.com/warren/rev4.html

[1634] Brian D. McKnight , "The Committee of Correspondence: Moving Towards Independence," *The Early American Review* Vol. II No. 4 (1998) http://www.earlyamerica.com/review/fall98/lastdays.html

[1635] For a brief description of the process, Nat Hentoff, "The Sons and Daughters of Liberty' All of Us Are in Danger'," *The Village Voice* June 21st, 2002 3:30 PM http://www.villagevoice.com/news/0226,hentoff,35949,6.html

[1636] http://www.villagevoice.com/news/0249,hentoff,40279,6.html

[1637]Nat Hentoff, "A salute to Patriot Act reformers: Changes would make law comply with Bill of Rights," *ternet* , Monday, Dec. 5, 2005. http://www.google.com/firefox?client=firefox-aandrls=org.mozilla:en-US:official

[1638] Passed unanimously by the Council on May 2, 2002. Upon the Recommendation of Council President Michael Bardsley.

[1639] For a copy of the original resolution, see http://www.newrules.org/gov/civilrights.html For a copy of the petition, see "Petition To Northampton Officials" http://www.bordc.org/involved/northpetition.php

Whereas, the City of Northampton houses a diverse student and working population, including non-citizens, whose contributions to the community are vital to its character and function; and

Whereas, the City of Northampton has with gratitude for their supreme sacrifice memorialized those in the Armed Forces who have died in battle protecting these same cherished rights and liberties; and

Whereas, the City Council of Northampton, motivated by the commitment to "uphold the human rights of all persons in Northampton and the free exercise and enjoyment of any and all rights and privileges secured by our constitutions and laws of the United States, the Commonwealth of Massachusetts and the City of Northampton," passed an ordinance in 1998 which established the Human Rights Commission of the City of Northampton; and

Whereas, several acts and orders recently enacted at the Federal level, including sections of the USAPA and several Executive Orders, now threaten these fundamental rights and liberties:

- Freedom of speech, religion, assembly and privacy;
- The rights to counsel and due process in judicial proceedings; and
- Protection from unreasonable searches and seizures;
- All guaranteed by the Constitution of the Commonwealth of Massachusetts, and the United States Constitution and its Bill of Rights;

Therefore, we the City Council of Northampton, Massachusetts, acting in the spirit and history of our community, do hereby request that:

1. Local law enforcement continue to preserve residents' freedom of speech, religion, assembly, and privacy; rights to counsel and due process in judicial proceedings; and protection from unreasonable searches and seizures even if requested or authorized to infringe upon these rights by federal law enforcement acting under new powers granted by the USAPA or orders of the Executive Branch;
2. Federal and state law enforcement officials acting within the City work in accordance with the policies of the Northampton Police Department, and in cooperation with the Department, by not engaging in or permitting detentions without charges or racial profiling in law enforcement;
3. The U.S. Attorney's Office, the Office of the Federal Bureau of Investigation and Massachusetts State Police report to the Northampton Human Rights Commission regularly and publicly the extent to and manner in which they have acted under the USAPA, new Executive Orders, or COINTELPRO-type regulations, including disclosing the names of any detainees held in western Massachusetts or any Northampton residents detained elsewhere;
4. Our United States Congressman and Senators monitor the implementation of the Act and Orders cited herein and actively work for the repeal of the parts of that Act and those Orders that violate fundamental rights and liberties as stated in the Constitutions of the Commonwealth and the United States.

Philosophical Foundation and Policy Issues

There are very few in-depth analyses of the content and philosophy BORDC – anti-Patriot resolutions.[1640]

[1640] Kelly Sechrengost, "Understanding Opposition to USAPA" *Stadium,* Vol. 6 (2005), pp. 4 – 37 http://www.csuchico.edu/pols/studium/PDFs/Studium2005.pdf

Anti-Patriot resolutions were adopted by communities to address[1641] some very specific and pressing local concerns when confronted with post 9/11 federal – state counter-terrorism efforts.[1642] Specifically issues being raised with the implementation of the USAPA in the local community,[1643] including:[1644]

[1641] Lauri Apple, "Will Council Take a Stand on PATRIOT Act?" *Austin Chronicle* AUGUST 15, 2003 (Mayor Will Wynn of Austin Texas is supportive of the resolution philosophical, i.e.,, but "requested evidence that the PATRIOT Act has directly affected the way city departments run -- particularly the Austin Police Dept. and the Austin Public Library -- and had an impact on the city budget." http://www.austinchronicle.com/gyrobase/Issue/story?oid=oid%3A173089

[1642] See Avram Bornstein "Antiterrorist Policing in New York City after 9/11: Comparing Perspectives on a Complex Process," *Human Organization*, 64(1), 52-61 (Spring 2005) (Federally sponsored anti-terrorism has direct impact on police priority, activities and resource deployment, e.g., FBI enlisted NYPD to conduct 80 investigations immediately after 9/11 and NYPD officers were authorized to enforce immigration laws. It has indirect impact on police-immigrant community relationship, e.g., racial profile destroys trust and dry up information, and public perception and reception of police, e.g., various grassroots political organizations joint hand to fight the City hall and oppressive government); Jerome H. Skolnick, "Democratic Policing Confronts Terror and Protest," 33 *Syracuse J. Int'l L. and Com.* 191 (2005) (Federal influence of municipal functions after 9/11 can be more effectively effectuated through professional association and social connections, more so than by means of formal legal authority or administrative process. After 9/11, NYPD Police Commissioner hired Cohen, a long term senior spymaster with the CIA (p. 196) and Michael Sheehan, a former Department of State Ambassador at Large for Counter Terrorism as Deputy Commissioners in charge of the for Counter Terrorism.) See also William J. Stuntz, "Local Policing After the Terror," 111 *YALE L.J.* 2137 (2002) http://www.yalelawjournal.org/archive_abstract.asp?id=334

[1643] Section 215 of the USAPA allows federal agents to obtain "any tangible things" that is deemed necessary "for an authorized investigation . . . to protect against international terrorism or clandestine intelligence activities." ACLU – "What is Section 215"? http://action.aclu.org/reformthepatriotact/215.html Section 215 has been used by FBI to obtain library records, raising concerns with library librarian's role in protecting patron's privacy and duty to obey state and local law projecting release of such and other information. For role and duties, see American Library Association, 1996. *Library Bill of Rights* (January 23, 1996) (Librarian should promote intellectual freedom (Art. 1) and resist "abridgment of free expression and free access to ideas") http://www.ala.org/ala/oif/statementspols/statementsif/librarybillrights.htm.
American Library Association, *Code of Ethics of the American Library Association* (June 28, 1995) ('III. We protect each library user's right to privacy and confidentiality with respect to information sought..."). For impact of USAPA on library, see Leigh S. Estabrook, Edward Lakner, Lidan Luo, and Anita Michel, *Public libraries and civil liberties: A profession divided* (January 22, 2003) (Federal and local law enforcement officials visited at least 545 libraries") (http://alexia.lis.uiuc.edu/gslis/research/civil_liberties.html. Norman Oder, "FBI has visited about 50 libraries: Also, ALA to sponsor an FBI–approved study on Patriot Act," *Library Journal*, volume 128 (11): 17-18 (2003).

[1644] Issues of federalism in law enforcement predated 9/11 and the USAPA. The FBI, DEA, US Attorney's office has worked with state and local police since 1970s in the areas of drugs, guns and gangs through joint task forces. Federalism issues were avoided through inducement, e.g., availability of federal resources to state and local government, or cooptation, e.g., deputizing of local officers in enforcing federal laws. Malcolm L. Russell-Einhorn, "Fighting Urban Crime: The Evolution of Federal-Local Collaboration," NIJ Research in Brief (Dec. 2003)("To illustrate the growth of collaboration during the past 20 years, there were 12 DEA State and local task forces in 1978; there are about 179 today. In 1994, the FBI's Safe Streets Violent Crime Initiative had 19 task forces; these increased to 164 by 1999. From 1984 to 1999, OCDETF investigations increased from 213 to 1,484." (n.7). See also Daniel Richman, "The Changing Boundaries Between Federal and Local Enforcement." In Boundary Changes in Criminal Justice Organizations, Vol. 2 of *Criminal Justice 2000* (National Institute of Justice, NCJ 182409, July 2000). (There has been an explosion of federal criminal law beginning in 1900 (pp. 83-90). Though formally and doctrinally federal criminal laws preempt state law, informally and practically effectiveness of federal law is dependent on and determined by local cooperation obtained through negotiation and not with imposition. This resulted from the fact that federal, as compared to state and local, suffers from a lack of human resources and street level intelligence (p. 93). The federalization of crime, by pre-emption or through negotiation, created issues of federalism hereafter discussed, e.g., local police now can escape state law restrictions (as with evidentiary rule) or local executive control (deputizing local officials as federal officers) (p. 102). The federalization of crime and policing, ultimately raises issues of local political control of crime policy and police activities (p. 97). http://www.ncjrs.gov/criminal _justice2000/vol_2/02d2.pdf

(1) How to secure local autonomy from federal government's encroachment? [1645]

(2) How to protect civil rights and liberties of community members from being violated by federal law and executive orders?[1646]

(3) How to avoid pre-emption of state law and local ordinances by federal law? [1647]

(4) How to make federal officials follow state laws and local ordinance?[1648]

(5) How to discourage local officials from cooperating with the federal law enforcement?[1649]

(6) How to protect local officials for refusing to enforce federal laws? [1650]

(7) How to make sure that local resources[1651] are not commandeered[1652] for federal use?[1653]

[1645] Statement of State Representative Dan Blue, Jr., President of the National Conference of State Legislatures, Before the Committee on Governmental Affairs Of the United States Senate Regarding Federalism and Preemption of State Law (May 5, 1999) ("One of the advantages of federalism is that allows for greater responsiveness and innovation through local self-government. State and local legislatures are accessible to every citizen. They work quickly to address problems identified by constituents. The large number of state and local legislatures encourages innovation")

[1646] Many resolutions were precipitated by perceived ill treatment of local residents. For example: David Weigel "When Patriots Dissent" *Reason Online* November 2005. http://www.reason.com/news/show/33167.html (In March 2004, Sami Omar Al-Hussayen, a native of Saudi Arabia and graduate student in Computer Science at the University of Idaho, was arrested and later deported for maintaining a web site for Islamic Assembly of North America. He was accused of conspiracy to provide material support to terrorists, and violating immigration law, i.e., visa fraud. He was found not guilt but was deported by the INS. The incident galvanized the Idaho public to pass anti-Patriot resolutions.) The first ever municipal resolution at Ann Arbor resulted from the arrest and deportation of a beloved Muslim social activist. The resolution called for due process and non-discriminate treatment for ALL people by law enforcement officials. Jon Dean, "Grassroots Opposition to Rights-Infringing Antiterrorism Tactics: Why the ACLU's Model Resolution Is Dangerous and Should Be Revised," *Findlaw* 9/12/03 ("This movement started when residents of Ann Arbor, Michigan learned of the arrest and detention of certain Arab-American and Muslim men, who were denied bond and open hearings.").

[1647] "Intellectual Freedom Committee: USAPA" Colorado Association of Librarians (Has the Act overturned all state laws on privacy? No, these laws are still in force. However, as a federal law, the Act will supersede any state privacy law in the case of a FISA search warrant. State and local law enforcement agencies are still subject to state and local privacy laws.) http://www.cal-webs.org/if_patriot1.html

[1648] Section 215 of the USAPA allows FBI to request library registration and borrowing records. However 48 of the 50 states have privacy law against release of such information without consent, including: Alabama, Alaska, Arizona, Arkansas, California, Colorado, Connecticut, Delaware, District of Columbia, Florida, Georgia, Hawaii, Idaho, Illinois, Indiana, Iowa, Kansas, Kentucky, Louisiana, Maine, Maryland, Massachusetts, Michigan, Minnesota, Mississippi, Missouri, Montana, Nebraska, Nevada, New Hampshire, New Jersey, New Mexico, New York, North Carolina, North Dakota, Ohio, Oklahoma, Oregon, Pennsylvania, Rhode Island, South Carolina, South Dakota, Tennessee, Texas, Utah, Vermont, Virginia, Washington, West Virginia, Wisconsin, Wyoming. For example, TITLE 41. STATE GOVERNMENT, CHAPTER 8. ALABAMA PUBLIC LIBRARY SERVICE, § 41-8-10. Confidentiality of registration records: "Any other provision of general, special or local law, rule or regulation to the contrary notwithstanding, the registration and circulation records and information concerning the use of the public, public school, college and university libraries of this state shall be confidential"; TITLE 40. PUBLIC RECORDS AND RECORDERS, CHAPTER 25. INSPECTION AND COPYING OF PUBLIC RECORDS, Sec. 40.25.140. Confidentiality of library records: "the names, addresses, or other personal identifying information of people who have used materials made available to the public by a library shall be kept confidential, except upon court order ..."

[1649] Huyen Pham, "The constitutional right not to cooperate? Local sovereignty and the federal immigration power," 74 *U. Cin. L. Rev.* 1373-1413 (2006). http://www.law.uc.edu/lawreview/uclaw74pdf/082906pham.pdf

[1650] Joel Mathis, "City plans careful criticism of Patriot Act: "Commission to balance voicing its disapproval with upholding law" (Lawrence City Commission seeks way to discourage police officers from cooperating with FBI.)

[1651] For a breakdown of post 9/11 anti-terrorism and homeland security cost items and amount, see We have received a document containing some post-9/11 costs for Austin's homeland Security compliance. See your tax dollars at work.. http://www.deveritas.com/AustinBORDC/docs/Post911FinancialCosts.gif

(8) How to make sure that local resources are not used to violate local, state or federal law?

(9) How to keep local officials politically accountable and administratively responsible?

Political Debate

The anti-Patriot movement provides the nation with a rare opportunity to debate the nature of our political union,[1654] and acts as a referendum on the proper conduce of war on terror and appropriateness of USAPA:[1655] What does freedom and liberty mean in time of war?[1656] What is the extent and limits of the President's war powers? What is the role of legislators vs. judiciary in checking against executive powers in the face of menacing terrorism?[1657] What is the relationship between local, state and federal government in protecting individual rights and protecting its own interests?[1658]

Two major issues are at stake here. First, how to balance between security vs. liberty in time of national emergency?[1659] Second, how might check and balance of government

[1652] The commandeer doctrine holds that "the Federal Government may neither issue directives requiring the States to address particular problems, nor command the States' officers, or those of their political subdivisions, to administer or enforce a federal regulatory program." Printz v. United States, 521 U.S. 898, 935 (1997).

[1653] Raleigh City Council USAPA Resolution Update," March 9, 2004. (In recent years, the Council has been reluctant to take up federal issues, but the Coalition appealed to the Council because these federal measures focus on joint cooperation with and enforcement by local city and state law enforcement and intelligence units.) Printz v. United States, 521 U.S. 898 (1997). The Brady Handgun Violence Prevention Act requires "chief law enforcement officer" (CLEO) to check the legality of handgun transfer in local communities. The Supreme Court held that the Federal government cannot commandeer local police resources for enforcement of federal law.) See Ann Althouse, "The Vigor of Anti-Commandeering Doctrine in Times of Terror," 69 BROOK. L. REV. 1231 (2004).

[1654] "National Archives Sponsors debate: The Constitution in a Time of National Emergency," The Nation Archives, September 16, 2006. News Release (Featuring Judge Richard Posner and Geoffrey Stone. "do we balance personal liberty against public safety in the face of grave national danger? Are there inevitable trade-offs, and, if so, when must we let the Constitution bend and when must we insist that it stand firm? Are censorship measures justified in wartime that would not be justified in times of peace? Should "enemy combatants" be indefinitely detained without a hearing? Should executives be able to restrict civil liberties for reasons of national necessity, as President Lincoln did when he suspended habeas corpus during the Civil War? How can constitutional law best remain responsive to current events?") http://www.archives.gov/press/press-releases/2006/nr06-138.html

[1655] "ACLU of Massachusetts Applauds Massachusetts Congressmen for Unanimous Vote Against the USAPA" March 8, 2005. http://www.aclum.org/news/03.08.PATRIOT.pdf

[1656] Attorney General John Ashcroft Testimony Before the House Committee on the Judiciary September 24, 2001 ("Just as American rights and freedoms have been preserved throughout previous law enforcement campaigns, they must be preserved throughout this war on terrorism.") http://www.usdoj.gov/ag/testimony/2001/agcrisisremarks9_24.htm

[1657] Opening Statement of Senator Patrick Leahy, Chairman, Senate Judiciary Committee "DOJ Oversight: Preserving Our Freedoms While Defending Against Terrorism" November 28, 2001. ("Rather than respect the checks and balances that make up our constitutional framework, the executive branch has chosen to cut out judicial review in monitoring attorney-client communications and to cut out Congress in determining the appropriate tribunal and procedures to try terrorists.") http://leahy.senate.gov/press/200111/112801.html

[1658] The same kind of debate happened some 200 hundred years ago. Wayne D. Moore, "Reconceiving Interpretive Autonomy: Insights from the Virginia and Kentucky Resolutions," 11 CONST. COMMENTARY 315 (1994).

[1659] "Liberty vs. Security: An NPR Special Report: A 'Virtual Roundtable' of Experts' Opinions" NPR (The roundtable participants: Michael Chertoff, now the Secretary of Homeland Security; Philip Heymann is James Barr Ames Professor of Law at the Harvard Law School; Kate Martin is director of the Center for National Security Studies; Sen. Patrick Leahy (D-VT) chairs the Judiciary Committee ; Sen. Orrin Hatch (R-UT) is the ranking Republican on the Senate Judiciary Committee.)

powers in time of war be obtained, horizontally (between branches of government)[1660] and vertically (between levels of government)?[1661] As observed by Herman:

> "The war on terror has precipitously shifted a tremendous amount of power to the executive branch of the federal government and minimized the role of Congress and the courts, at the risk of undermining the United States Constitution's horizontal system of checks and balances. These joint federal and state/local enterprises might be viewed as weakening the vertical structures of the United States Constitution by collapsing previously autonomous spheres."[1662]

More pointedly, which of the two governing philosophy should be adopted in time of war (against terrorism): "Those Who Sacrifice Liberty For Security Deserve Neither"[1663] vs. "Constitution is not a suicide pack."[1664]

Analysis of BODDC Resolution

The Northhampton resolution is a resolution of the people and by the people. The resolution aims at protecting individual rights and promoting local community interests. It seeks to advance political ideal of autonomy and localism. It is democracy at work.

Read closely, the preamble clauses make a compelling case for taking action against the USAPA by a local community:

The first clause of the resolution makes clear that civil rights and liberties are very much a personal issue and local concern, philosophically,[1665] historically[1666] and functionally. To achieve maximum freedom Madison argues in *The Federalist No. 10*:

[1660] The "horizontal" check and balance issue raised here is the extent to which the executive branch of government should be placed over and above that of the legislative and judicial branches, in time of war. The "vertical" check and balance issue raised here is that of federalism, i.e., and pre-emption vs. local autonomy?

[1661] Susan N. Herman, "Laboratories of Democracy: Federalism and State Law Independency: Article: Collapsing Spheres: Joint Terrorism Task Forces, Federalism, and the War on Terror," 41 *Willamette L. Rev.* 941 (2005) (In 1798, Thomas Jefferson and James Madison drafted the Virginia and Kentucky Resolutions of 1798 to challenge the impositions of the Alien and Sedition Acts of 1798 on the states by the federal government, rehearsing yet once again the admonition of the anti-Federalists: "Jefferson (drafter of Kentucky Resolutions of 1798) observed a year earlier: "that the States retain as complete authority as possible over their own citizens." When the federal government exceeded its mandate, he added, its acts were "unauthoritative, void, and of no force.")

[1662] *Id.*

[1663] Benjamin Franklin. http://en.wikiquote.org/wiki/Benjamin_Franklin

[1664] Richard A. Posner, *Not A Suicide Pact The Constitution in a Time of National Emergency* (Oxford University, 2006) (Judge Posner, a pragmatic Constitutionalist opined: "it would be odd if the framers of the Constitution had cared more about every provision of the Bill of Rights than about national and personal survival.") For a review, and counter points, see Peter Berkowitz, "Freedom at War Civil liberties in the age of terrorism" The Weekly Standard Volume 12, Issue 01, 09/18/2006. http://www.weeklystandard.com/Utilities/printer_preview.asp?idArticle=12667andR=111EA5CB8 For debate over war time power of the President, see William H. Rehnquist (1998). *All the Laws but One: Civil Liberties in Wartime* (William Morrow and Co., 1998). Geoffrey R. Stone, "Civil Liberties in Wartime" *Journal of Supreme Court History* 28 (3), 215–251 (2003) (Looking back at history: in 1798, the Civil War, World War I, World War II, the Cold War and the Vietnam War – we as a people over reacted to national crisis, preferring to restrict civil liberties over constitutional protection.)

[1665] This raises issue of the extent of personal freedom vs. degree of state governance. Hobbes postulated that: ""The absence of *externall impediments,"* is all that we mean by "Liberty" (n. 91) and Berlin suggested negative freedom is measured by "the area within which the subject . . . is or should be left to do or be what he is able to

"The smaller the society, the fewer probably will be the distinct parties and interests composing it; the fewer the distinct parties and interests, the more frequently will a majority be found of the same party; and the smaller the number of individuals composing a majority, and the smaller the compass within which they are placed, the most easily will they concert and execute their plans of oppression. Extend the sphere, and you take in a greater variety of parties and interests; you make it less probable that a majority of the whole will have a common motive to invade the rights of other citizens.[1667]

State (and by extension local) government has both a duty and responsibility to protect the rights and liberties of the people from encroachment,[1668] even from the federal government. The clause is an invitation to revisit the nation's political history and governing philosophy. It stands for the ideal that civil rights belong to the people and to be achieved locally. The message is clear: protection of civil liberties is everyone's business and very much a local government's charge.

More significantly, the protection of civil rights it too important a task to be delegated to the government and achieved with the use law, alone. Collective vigilance and grassroots political action is every bit as important as Constitutional protection and state action. As Michael Traynor, President to The American Institute argued, that even though the Constitute did not provide for the duty of a citizen,[1669] citizens should keep faith to what President Kennedy preached: "Ask not what your country can do for you - ask what you can do for your country."[1670] He further opinioned that "there are many things citizens can do to resist deception, intrusion, and secrecy, as well as contribute to the debate over values and how best to combat terrorism"[1671], including:

"Become informed and vigilant; Participate in various venues of community of opinion and debate, such as the Internet, thereby contributing one by one to a growing consensus in the country and in the world; Mobilize city councils and state legislatures to speak and act for liberty; Serve on local boards and commissions and in nonprofit organizations, and help recruit good people for government and civic service; Vote, and urge neighbors, friends, relatives, and coworkers to register and vote; Educate ourselves about threats and terrorists and how to deal with them; Train and enlist to help others, such as signing up in advance to be a neighborhood watch captain, a first-aid provider, or a stretcher-bearer, for example; Ask our press and other media to be inquiring and perseverant, not lazy in their reporting; Demand due process for both citizens and resident aliens, and at the very least rudimentary fairness for

---

do or be without interference by other persons." (note 21). J.L. HILL, "The Five Faces of Freedom in American Political and Constitutional Thought," 45 *B.C. L. Rev* 499 (2004)

[1666] The city of Northhampton boasts a long history of civil disobedience, organized resistance, and fugitive assistance in the days of David Ruggles, one of the great unsung heroes of the anti-slavery struggle. For example, Ruggles was "the most visible conductor on the Underground Railroad. Ruggles claimed to have helped 400 fugitive slaves during the 1830s." Historical Northhampton http://davidrugglesinflorence. blogspot.com/

[1667] J.L. HILL, "The Five Faces of Freedom in American Political and Constitutional Thought," 45 *B.C. L. Rev* 499, n. 343 (2004)

[1668] "Dual federalism" give vent to this ideal of equal sovereignty. "Federalism: A Historical Perspective". http://www.cas.unt.edu/~jryan/FederalismTwo.html

[1669] *Id.* ("The Thirteenth Amendment prohibits slavery, but overall, the Constitution, including its amendments, is not structured to address the duties of citizens. (N. 126).

[1670] See *Id.* note 134, page 24. John F. Kennedy, Inaugural Address (Jan. 20, 1961), at http://www.bartleby.com/124/pres56.html

[1671] Michael Traynor (President, The American Law), "Address: Citizenship in a Time of Repression," 2005 *Wis. L. Rev.* 1 (2005).

nonresident aliens;Demand that our senators and representatives repeal the pernicious provisions of the PATRIOT Act; Tell the president that he is wrong to demand renewal of the PATRIOT Act."[1672]

While the first clause makes the case for grassroots participation in national civil rights debate and argues for local community involvement in the protection of civil liberties, clause two makes clear that local community has compelling interests, and indeed a duty, to protect and promote local interests, identity and character. "Diversity" defines (the character issue) and sustains (the functional argument) Northampton. [1673] Tolerance of differences and incorporation of aliens is the ideal form of community sought by the people of Northampton.

To express its commitment to human rights and put its ideal in practice, the City of Northampton established the Human Rights Commission[1674] of the City of Northampton in 1998. [1675] This set up a classical case of conflict of law problem pitting local ordinance with federal law (USAPA). This conflict must be resolved to protect local residents from deprivation of rights and to support local officials in their exercise of duties.[1676]

Finally clause three makes clear that individual rights are important in securing our form of government and defining our way of life. As observed by Hill, individual rights, liberties and autonomy is democracy, incarnated:

> "Three political values dominate the discourse of self-individuating liberalism, and each has an important function in the discovery, development, and expression of the self. Privacy provides the self shelter from the storm; it gives the nascent self the breathing space to develop, and the developed self a personal realm to exist as it is, free from the prying eyes and corrosive influences of society. Autonomy, or self-determination, is the condition by which the individual is able to direct his own life; it is valued both as an expression of individual choice--we value self-determination intrinsically, as the sine qua non of living freely--and for its active capacity to foster self-development. Finally, self-expression is, as one commentator has put it, "not the whole of freedom, but its soul."

[1672] Id.

[1673] Local government is best situated in the defense of local interests, functionally. This view is best argued by proponents of localism.

[1674] "Statement on the Commemoration of the Daley and Halligan Bicentennial'. Human Rights Commission of Northampton.June5,2006.http://www.historicnorthampton.org/Articles/213/resources/1987375//HRCDaleyHalligan Statement2006.pdf

[1675] Human Rights Commission Ord. of 8-20-98 (Amended 12-15-05) http://www.northamptonma.gov/gsuniverse/httpRoot/hrc/uploads/listWidget/4174/HRCordinance2005.pdf

[1676] The Constitutional issue raised here is one of local autonomy vs. federal preemption vs. check and balance. On the one hand it is observed that local municipalities are chartered communities, it enjoyed no sovereign rights to stand up the federal government. This argument does not destroy the claim that individuals' have natural rights before the formation of any government, local, state or federal. Nor does it address the issue of proper limitation of power (through check and balance) between federal vs. state vs. local government. On the other hand, it is observed that federal government has no more powers than delegated by the people. Finally, the debate over sovereignty, balance of powers, and pre-emption does not exhaust and should not eclipse the debate over functionality, i.e.,, which governmental unit stands best to represent the welfare of the people and interests of the community. "Localism" argues for local involvement of the people vs. centralization of control by government. http://www.newrules.org/gov/civilrights.html

Broadly defined, self-expression is the active capacity of the individual to project one's self into the social and political worlds. It is thus the complement to privacy. Through self-expression, in all of its myriad facets, the personal truly becomes the political.[1677]

As the first in the nation, the BORDC success story was widely publicized[1678] and commonly used as a case study[1679] of how such an anti-Patriot Resolution drive can be successfully organized and effectively conducted, from coalition building to public promotion to private lobby to resolution drafting.[1680]

Strategies[1681]

Social movement required planning – organization and strategy. As observed:

> Social Mobilization, as defined by UNICEF, is a broad scale movement to engage people's participation in achieving a specific development goal through self-reliant efforts. It involves all relevant segments of society: decision and policy makers, opinion leaders, bureaucrats and technocrats, professional groups, religious associations, commerce and industry, communities and individuals. It is a planned decentralized process that seeks to facilitate change for development through a range of players engaged in interrelated and complementary efforts...Mobilizing the necessary resources, disseminating information tailored to targeted audiences, generating intersectoral support and fostering cross-professional alliances are also part of the process." [1682]

Strategies are defined by mission and directed towards goals. In the case of BORDC, its missions include:

(1) educating public to the importance of Bill of Rights;
(2) informing the public about the threats of USAPA;
(3) mobilizing the public to fight against infringement of rights;
(4) organizing the public in repealing/revising the USAPA.

To fulfill its education and information missions, the BORDC provides for education resources on the web and organizes public debate about the USAPA. In order to mobilize the public, the BORDC, working with other coalitions, organizes mass rallies in the street, collects signatures for petitions and sends letters to legislators.

[1677] J.L. HILL, "The Five Faces of Freedom in American Political and Constitutional Thought," 45 *B.C. L. Rev* 499 (2004)

[1678] Nat Hentoff, "Ashcroft Watch: Grassroots Patriots," *The Progressives* http://www.progressive.org/node/1521

[1679] "Will rights be restored?: This wasn't supposed to happen here," *Issues and Views* July 1, 2002. http://issues-views.com/index.php/sect/21000/article/21038; "Patriot Act Puts All of Us in Danger," *Peace Talk* Autumn 2002 http://www.peaceactionme.org/september2danger.html;

[1680] "Tips and Tools for Organizing Resolutions in Defense of the Bill of Rights," http://web.mit.edu/jakebeal/Public/BORDC/Tools.pdf

[1681] "Dissent Is Patriotic," The Bill of Rights Defense Committee's e-mail newsletter December 18, 2002, Vol. I, No. *2* http://www.bordc.org/newsletter/bordcnews1-2.php

[1682] "The ICEC and Global Social Mobilization," http://www.tulane.edu/~icec/socmob.htm

Finally, as to cultivating and organizing public, the BORDC lends its expertise and experience in helping with organization effort in communities all over the nation, including making available model resolutions for adoption and formatted letters to legislators.[1683]

When drafting resolutions, BORDC calls for forceful and specific languages, in order to protect constitutional rights and prompt legislative actions. Forceful languages, usually in principled form and universal terms, demonstrate convictions. Specific languages make things clear and allows for easy implementation. For example:

On June 17, 2002, Cambridge City Council, Massachusetts passed Cambridge City Council Resolution condemning USAPA for violating civil liberties in the strongest of language: "Whereas, we believe these civil liberties are precious and are now threatened by the USAPA..." The USAPA violations of rights were considered so blatant and egregious that "Cambridge's representative in Congress Michael Capuano, along with his Massachusetts colleagues, Representatives Frank, McGovern, Oliver, and Tierney, found the USAPA inappropriate and dangerous enough to join 66 other representatives in voting against it." It further points to the need to enlist Federal and City authorities to voice its concerns:

> *Whereas,* in Zadvydas v. Davis this past session the U.S. Supreme Court affirmed that "the Due Process Clause applies to all 'persons' within the United States, including aliens, whether their presence here is lawful, unlawful, temporary, or permanent"; and
>
> *Whereas,* a 1985 City Council resolution declared the City of Cambridge "A Sanctuary City" in which city departments and employees are committed to protect refugees from:
>
> - Requests for information about, or conditioning receipt of city services on, citizenship status;
> - "Investigations or arrest procedures, public or clandestine, relating to alleged violations of immigration law..."; and
> - Deportation and dangerous returns to their homelands...

In the end the Resolution leaves a clear impression that USAPA is in violation of federal constitution, state law and city ordinances.

Similarly, Takoma Park City Council, Montgomery, Maryland passed Civil Liberties Revolution NO. 2002-82 on October 28, 2002 calling for specific actions in clear and unmistakable terms:

> 3. The U.S. Attorney's Office, the Office of the Federal Bureau of Investigation, the Maryland State Police, and any other Federal, State or local law enforcement officials with any such information report to the Takoma Park City Council regularly and publicly the extent and manner in which they have acted under the USAPA and new Executive Orders, including but not limited to disclosing:

[1683] "Fundamentals of Building a State Resolution - Optimum Conditions" ("Regular schedule of citizen lobbyists at the legislature and two to three Lobby Days; Major endorsements from labor, religious, library, school, political parties, and other groups like the League of Women Voters; Group of grassroots representatives from various parts of the state who can organize day to day; Endorsing groups let you use their email lists to contact people throughout the state for various events; Well-organized Phone Tree; Statewide petition with thousands of signatures; Statewide coalition made up of representatives from each part of the state, who have met at least once in person to begin to build trust.") http://www.bordc.org/involved/states/fundamentals.php

- the names of any detainees held in the area or any Takoma Park residents detained here or elsewhere, the circumstances that led to each detention;
- the charges, if any, lodged against each detainee;
- the name of counsel, if any, representing each detainee;
- the number of search warrants that have been executed in the City of Takoma Park without notice to the subject of the warrant pursuant to section 213 of the USAPA;
- the extent of electronic surveillance carried out in the City of Takoma Park under powers granted in the USAPA;
- the extent to which federal authorities are monitoring political meetings, religious gatherings or other activities protected by the First Amendment within the City of Takoma Park;
- the number of times education records have been obtained from public schools and institutions of higher learning in the City of Takoma Park under section 507 of the USAPA;
- the number of times library records have been obtained from libraries in the City of Takoma Park under section 215 of the USAPA;
- the number of times that records of the books purchased by store patrons have been obtained from bookstores in the City of Takoma Park under section 215 of the USAPA.

The said resolution makes clear what is expected of the local, state, or federal officials. While there is a question whether the resolution is enforceable as against state and federal officials, it nevertheless shows the directed law enforcement officials that Takoma Park City Council expects the resolution to be followed.

To make sure that resolutions are properly enforced and duly implemented BORDC asks that resolutions' contain implementation clauses detailing what actions are expected and who is responsible.

V. VARIETIES OF RESOLUTIONS

There are many kinds of USAPA resolutions.[1684] They can be analyzed in terms of process, e.g., sponsorship, and support; or content, e.g., length, specificity, complexity, forcefulness, action. In terms of form and nature, resolutions can be long vs. short; simple vs. complex; legalistic vs. plain; single focus vs. multiplex considerations; strong vs. weak; vague vs. specific, affirmative vs. condemning, principled vs. action oriented.

Some resolutions are written in layman terms with simple demands.[1685] This is especially the case with small towns. The resolution adopted by Woody Creek Caucus (Colorado) – population 404 - on March 31, 2006 falls into this gem:

> "Woody Creek Caucus resolution calling on government officials at all levels to reaffirm their official oaths to protect and defend the U.S. Constitution."[1686]

[1684] http://www.bordc.org/news/cities_urge_restraint_in_fight_against_terror.php
[1685] John Colson, "Woody Creek now a 'Bill of Rights Defense Zone'" Aspen Time March 31, 2006. http://www.aspentimes.com/apps/pbcs.dll/article?AID=/20060331/NEWS/103310052andtemplate=printart
[1686] The actual Resolution was considerably longer. See Woody Creek Caucus. U.S. and Colorado "Bill of Rights Defense' Resolution. March 30, 2006.

The resolution asked of the Caucus member to re-affirm their vote[1687] and clarify their policies[1688] to protect people's rights and follow the Constitution. In the meantime they should hold fact findings hearings to see how the USAPA might infringe upon citizens rights and privacy.[1689]

Definition, Purpose and Effect of Resolution

"Resolution" has been defined as: "A formal expression of opinion or decision, other than a proposed law, that may be offered for approval to one or both houses of the legislature by a member of the house or senate."[1690]

Resolution expresses opinion, espouses conviction and more generally registers the sense of a legislative body towards a matter or issues: "The effect of a typical resolution is merely to express the opinion of one or both houses or to take some action short of enacting a law that is within the province of one or both houses. Also, a resolution is typically temporary in character."[1691]

Resolutions are not law. Usually they have no binding legal effect. In most cases, resolutions carry symbolic meaning and real consequences. For example, open challenge of resolution provisions might attract the displeasure of the legislators and resulted in disciplinary actions, e.g., adverse political, administrative and fiscal consequences.

The Basis of Resolution

A resolution is structured in two parts: The preamble clause (WHEREAS clause) and resolution clause (BE IT RESOLVED clause).[1692] The preamble sets forth the basis – justification or rational – of the resolution.

Many of the Patriot resolutions started with one or more of the following observations or assertions, as a foundation for the Resolutions:

(1) The U.S. Constitution and State Constitution guarantee citizens fundamental rights – due process, free speech, privacy - that are inalienable. These rights should be upheld, even in the face of terrorists attack.

(2) The local community has a proud tradition of and is committed to protecting citizens' rights. For example, the Resolution of Ann Arbor passed of July 7, 2003 reads in

---

[1687] *Id.* "2. Oath reaffirmation, signing statements; office policy clarifications." To be executed on or before July 4, 2006.

[1688] *Id.*

[1689] "3. Local officials' Joint public hearings on Bill of Rights Defense concerns." To find out why federal officials "use secret, warrantless searches, seizures and surveillance" against U.S. citizens; or jail U.S. citizens as "enemy combatants" without due process; or "conduct surveillance and investigative practices that chill" citizens' exercise their Bill of Rights freedom. (4 (a) to (d).

[1690] "Legislative Glossary" Texas Legislature Online. http://www.capitol.state.tx.us/tlo/resources/glossary.htm

[1691] Illinois Legislative Glossary, Illinois General Assembly. http://www.ilga.gov/legislation/glossary.asp. See "A resolution is the formal expression of the opinion, sentiment or will, of one or both Houses of the General Assembly." Glossary of Legislative Terms, State of Delaware. http://www.legis.state.de.us/Legislature.nsf/Lookup/Legislative_Terms?open

[1692] http://www.se.lcms.org/second%20level/2006convention/overtures.html

pertinent part: "WHEREAS, The City of Ann Arbor is proud of its long and distinguished tradition of protecting the civil rights and liberties of its residents and knows that these rights and liberties are essential to the well-being of a democratic society."[1693]

(3) The local community has a diverse (immigrant) population and equal protection of the law is important. For example, the Ann Arbor Resolution of July 7, 2003 reads in part: "WHEREAS, The City of Ann Arbor has a diverse population, including recent immigrants and students from other nations, whose contributions to the community are vital to its economy, culture and civic character."[1694]

(4) The community should do all it can to protect its citizens from discriminatory treatment.

(5) The federal government has the right and duty to protect the nation from further terrorists' threat. There should be a deliberate effort to balance the need for security and liberty in fighting terrorism.

(6) The USAPA should be carefully and narrowly designed to protect the nation without infringing on citizens' rights and liberty.[1695]

Purpose and Goals of Resolutions

The purpose and goals of a resolution, beyond general admonition to protect "the civil rights and liberties of the people"[1696] and guarantee the sanctity of the Constitution of the United States, admits to great divergence and subtle differences. These differences are as much driven by political ideology of people involved, e.g., conservatives vs. liberals, as it is dictated by material interests affected, e.g., privacy in library vs. academic freedom in universities vs. immigrants in community. Local history and culture of the community, philosophy and identity of organization, and personal experience and outlook of life of the organizers invariably play a part.

[1693] "Resolution to Protest the Eroding of Civil Liberties Under the USAPA (Public Law 107-56) and Related Federal Orders Since 9/11/01: R-281-7-03" (July 7, 2003) http://www.bordc.org/detail.php?id=18

[1694] *Id.* There were two Resolutions. This is the second one. "The first Resolution: Resolution in Support of Due Process for All Members of the Ann Arbor Community: R-18-1-02" (01/07/02) is an equal protection and due process kind of resolution. It was precipitated by the arrest and deportation of a well regard Islamic community leader and cleric for raising money for terrorists. "Whereas, It is an important matter that our country to seek a balance between national security and the prevention of discrimination based on race, religion or nationality in the constitutional rights afforded all individuals; and Whereas, The recent arrest and detention of individuals without bond or open hearings has caused great concern within the Ann Arbor community." http://www.bordc.org/detail.php?id=18

[1695] "WHEREAS, federal, state, and local governments should protect the public from terrorist attacks, such as those that occurred on September 11,2001, but should do so in a rational and deliberative fashion in order to ensure that security measures enhance public safety without impairing constitutional rights of infringing on civil liberties." Unified Government of Wyandotte County and Kansas City (Resolution No R-111-04) (11/4/04) Wyandotte County, Kansas.

[1696] RESOLUTION NO. 2003-28: "A Resolution of the City of Bainbridge Island, Washington, to protect the civil rights and liberties of the people of Bainbridge Island, Washington." ACLU http://www.aclu.org/safefree/resources/17239res20030530.html

Bainbridge Island, WA

On May 28, 2005, the City Council of Bainbridge Island, WA, passed unanimously the "Resolution for the Protection of Civil Rights and Liberties of the people of Bainbridge Island, Washington." A visit to the web site BIBORDC found that BIBORDC was formed in March 2003 in response to the USAPA. Bainbridge Island is a liberal[1697] and well to do city.[1698] The BIBORDC shared a website with Bainbridge Neighbors for Peace; a liberal group devoted to peace and justice issues. To the Bainbridge peace activists, the USAPA is found objectionable not only because of its constitutional flaws and civil rights issues, but also because it destroys peaceful community relations and intimate ethnic bonds. Thus, we observed that the resolution opened with the observation:

> *"WHEREAS*, the people of Bainbridge Island, Washington, are acutely aware that over 200 of our neighbors of Japanese descent were forcibly removed from their homes and our community to be interned in camps during World War II, thus denying them the civil liberties guaranteed by the State of Washington and the Constitution of the United States of America..."[1699]

The City is constantly reminded of the dark history of having sent the first Japanese to the WWII internship camp.[1700] Since then, it has made a commitment itself to remind the nation (and the world) that in time of war the rights and welfare of the minority are often sacrificed in the name of communal order and national security.[1701]

> *"WHEREAS*, it is clear to the people of Bainbridge Island, Washington, that parts of the USAPA and other related acts and legislation particularly target students, immigrants, naturalized United States' citizens and foreign nations, but could affect any one of us in the United States who legally acts and speaks against government policy; and that the Executive

---

[1697]   76% of the Island voted for John Kerry in the 2004 presidential election. http://en.wikipedia.org/wiki/Bainbridge_Island,_Washington Senator Maria Cantwell (D – WA) is on the record against the USAPA. "Cantwell Urges Swift Senate Action on SAFE ACT" http://cantwell.senate.gov/news/record.cfm?id=243146and Representative Inslee (D- First Congressional District) is concerned with protecting the privacy rights of citizens in the terror war. "Inslee Raises Privacy Concern Over the Pentagon's Total Awareness Program." http://www.house.gov/inslee/issues/security/homeland_security.html

[1698] The median household income is $70, 110. The family income is $83,415 in 2000. http://en.wikipedia.org/wiki/Bainbridge_Island,_Washington

[1699] http://www.aclu.org/safefree/resources/17239res20030530.html

[1700] http://en.wikipedia.org/wiki/Bainbridge_Island,_Washington " Florangela Davila "Debate lingers over internment of Japanese-Americans" *The Seattle Times*, September 26, 2004. ("It was here that 227 men, women and children of Japanese descent boarded a ferry at the Eagledale dock March 30, 1942, and were sent to the Manzanar War Relocation Center in the California desert, under the orders of President Franklin D. Roosevelt.") http://seattletimes.nwsource.com/html/localnews/2002027639_bainbridge06m.html

[1701] *Ibid*. Internment relics and history is on display at the local museum. Children are taught that internment is wrong and should never be repeated. See also "WWII Intern Curriculum Protested" *NPR* http://www.npr.org/templates/story/story.php?storyId=4186189 The debate over the necessity and propriety of the war time internship still lives. See recent debate in Column: University of Washington Alumni Magazine debate. (March 2006). (Readers' letter reacting to: "Stolen Years, Part I and II") The titles to some of the letters tell the story; of lessons painfully learned and vividly lived: "We knew it was wrong"; "It happened in America"; "Never again"; "Good men, bad decision"; "Prejudice, fear, anger, stupidity, and hysteria." http://www.washington.edu/alumni/columns/march06/content/view/73/1/

Order on secret military tribunals undermines the US government's ability to denounce atrocities carried out in secret by military tribunals elsewhere in the world..."[1702]

The resolution thus makes clear that racial discrimination is not an acceptable national policy even in time of war. It challenges Bainbridge community's core values, and open old wounds.

Ann Arbor, Michigan

Ann Arbor resolution tells a different story. Ann Arbor was the first in the nation to pass an anti-Patriot resolution.[1703] Ann Arbor City Council in fact passed two resolutions. The first resolution: "Resolution in Support of Due Process for All Members of the Ann Arbor Community: R-18-1-02" was passed on January 7, 2002, and the second, "Resolution to Protest the Eroding of Civil Liberties Under the USAPA (Public Law 107-56) and Related Federal Orders Since 9/11/01: R-281-7-03" was passed on July 7, 2003. Ann Arbor remains to be the few cities which have passed two different versions of anti-Patriot resolution.

The passage of two resolutions, 16 months apart, allows us to compare and contrast purposes and goals, process and dynamics of the two resolutions.

The very first resolution, without ever mentioning the USAPA, was actually against what the Act stood for, i.e.,, indiscriminate abuse of police power in the name of fighting terrorism. The resolution was drafted in direct response to the arrest a well regarded community activist - Rabbih Haddad, on minor immigration charges.

Before 9/11, Haddah was a well respected and much loved member of the community. After 9/11 Haddad was looked up to for his unrelenting effort in speaking out against terrorism and reducing backlash against the Muslim community. The U.S. Government however singled Haddad out for sanction because of his ethnicity, i.e., being a Muslim, belief, i.e., being a cleric, association, i.e., being associated with terrorists, and speech, i.e., being the organizer of Global Relief Foundation.

On December 14, 2001, he was arrested by INS in front of his family. He was held in secret. He was confined in solitude. He was finally deported on July 14, 2003. Throughout the whole process, Habbah was treated in the most uncivilized manner (arrest before family) and inhuman way (solitary confinement). His treatment violated all constitutional protection in a democratic society (secret hearing, lengthy detention, without notice, lack of representation). Ann Arbor, a progressive community, was as perplexed as it was angry with this gross abuse of rights. They decided to come to Habbah rescue. They started a grass roots movement to set Rabbit Haddad free, starting with street rallies and ending with a resolution.[1704] The effort resulted in "Resolution in Support of Due Process for All Members of the Ann Arbor Community: R-18-1-02".

[1702] http://www.aclu.org/safefree/resources/17239res20030530.html

[1703] The Ann Arbor resolution even predated the first BORDC resolution, and before the grass roots movement caught on. The next resolution was that of the Denver City Council: "Expressing the Commitment of the City and County of Denver to Civil Rights and Liberties: Resolution No. 13, Series of 2002" (March 18, 2002). All told 22 resolutions were passed in 2002, i.e., about two every months, with the first and the second lapsing by 2 months and 11 days, and 216 resolutions in 2003, or about 17.26 resolutions every month.

[1704] "Information on Rabih Haddad" http://aa- peacemaking.quaker.org/haddad.html

The resolution was as short as it was direct: it accused the government of denying people in the community their due process rights under the Constitution:

> "*Whereas,* The due process and equal protection clauses of the 5th and 14th Amendments to the United States Constitution guarantee certain due process and equal protection rights to all residents of the United States regardless of citizenship or immigration status"
>
> "*Whereas,* The recent arrest and detention of individuals without bond or open hearings has caused great concern within the Ann Arbor community."

More significantly, Ann Arbor considered the discriminatory and abusive use of police power an over-reaction to 9/11, and should never be allowed to happen:

> "*Whereas,* It is an important matter that our country seek a balance between national security and the prevention of discrimination based on race, religion or nationality in the constitutional rights afforded all individuals…"

If the first resolution is a petition to protect (minority) citizens' rights, the second resolution is a resolution to restrict government's post 911 powers. The community is unhappy with how the Ann Arbor Police Department disposed of themselves after 911. The two nemeses to this debate were: Michelle J. Kinnucan, who called for more limited government and police accountability, [1705] vs. AAPD Chief Oaks, who asked for more police power and less legal restrain,[1706] post 9/11.

AAPD Chief Oaks came to Ann Abhor after being a (21 year) veteran of NYPD. He rose through the ranks to become the deputy police chief in charge of intelligence. Because of his professional experience (intelligence gathering) and personal conviction (NYC could be spared of 911), he vowed to do anything to prevent anther 9/11 from happening; to make amend the past, to prepare for the future. Chief Oaks believed that has the FBI and NYPD worked together collaboratively in the past, to collect strategic and tactical intelligence, 9/11 would not have happened. As a result, he has argued for post 9/11 reform to intelligence gathering philosophy and policy, structure and process including: (1) Championing for intelligence policing. (2) Enhancing cooperation between FBI and NYPD, especially in the area of intelligence gathering, analysis and sharing; (3) Allowing NYPD to share in FBI (and other related Federal agencies) data base. (4) Making NYPD an extension of the FBI in gathering intelligence and implementing counter-terrorism operations. [1707] (5) Removing legal[1708] and cultural[1709] barriers that stop FBI and NYPD from working with each other in gathering intelligence and fighting terrorism. Were Oakes to be successful, AAPD would have conducted intelligence operations resembling of that of Denver, Colorado.

[1705] Michelle J. Kinnucan, "Domestic Spying and the Global Intelligence Working Group." *The Public Eye* (2003) http://www.publiceye.org/liberty/repression/big-broth-kin.html

[1706] David Katz and Louie Meizish, "We could have done more: Ann Arbor Police Chief Daniel Oates, former head of the New York Police Department''s Intelligence Division, tells David Katz and Louie Meizlish of The Michigan Daily," *The Michigan Daily*,11/20/01 http://media.www.michigandaily.com/media/storage/paper 851/news/2001/11/20/News/We.Could.Have.Done.More.Ann.Arbor.Police.Chief.Daniel.Oates.Former.Head. Of.The.N1405931.shtml?sourcedomain=www.michigandaily.comandMIIHost=media.collegepublisher.com

[1707] "Police Spying: The Local Connection--AAPD Chief Dan Oates,"http://www.assatashakur.org/forum/ showthread.php?t=7135; From the Desk of Chief Oates. CRIME WATCH: A Publication of the Ann Arbor Police Department – 2003, Vol. 18, No. 1.

[1708] http://aacaw.org/oates%20thanks.htm

[1709] David Katz and Louie Meizish, supra.

Michelle J. Kinnucan, and others of her conviction, is of the firm belief that local police should not be working with FBI to spy on the citizens. Structurally, the vertical separation of power between federal vs. state vs. local government is as important as the separation between legislative vs. executive vs. judicial powers at the federal level, to keep government abuses of power. What has been achieved at the federal level with the USAPA, i.e., doing away with the separation of power and breaking down the walls between agencies, i.e., FBI vs. CUA, should not be allowed to happen at the local level.

Reading "Resolution to Protest the Eroding of Civil Liberties Under the USAPA (Public Law 107-56) and Related Federal Orders Since 9/11/01: R-281-7-03"[1710] in this light, this second resolution specifically find that: "WHEREAS, The US Attorney General has stated that the federal government may ask local police departments to enforce federal immigration law…" Nothing this concern, the second resolution specifically requires the AAPD not to cooperate with federal officials in violation of people's rights, especially in intelligence gathering operations in violations of citizens' rights.

1. "Continue to limit local enforcement actions with respect to immigration matters to penal violations of federal immigration law (as opposed to administrative violations) except in cases where the Chief of Police determines there is a legitimate public safety concern and in such public safety instances, to report the situation to the City Council no later than 60 days after the incident.
2. Continue to refrain from covert surveillance of and/or collection and maintenance of information on individuals or groups based on their participation in activities protected by the First Amendment, such as political advocacy or the practice of a religion, without a particularized suspicion of unlawful activity.
3. Affirm the existing practice, as required by Michigan state law, of providing simultaneous notice of the execution of a state court search warrant to any resident of the City of Ann Arbor whose property is the subject of such a warrant, except in cases of anticipatory search warrants.
4. Report to the City Council any request made by federal authorities for the Ann Arbor Police Department to participate in any activity under the USAPA, to the extent the Chief of Police has knowledge of such request."

Focus and Scope

A few of the resolutions made their resolutions more limited in scope or with a specific focus. For example, In Ann Arbor, Michigan, the focus of the first resolution was *on discrimination and profiling:*

"Whereas, The due process and equal protection clauses of the 5th and 14th Amendments to the United States Constitution guarantee certain due process and equal protection rights to all residents of the United States regardless of citizenship or immigration status ….

RESOLVED, That the City of Ann Arbor reject racial profiling of any group within our community…"[1711]

[1710] http://justpeaceinfo.org/res-aa-cc-7july2003.html
[1711] Resolution in Support of Due Process for All Members of the Ann Arbor Community: R-18-1-02. Approved by: Ann Arbor City Council. Date Passed: 01/07/02. http://www.bordc.org/detail.php?id=18.

In Westford, Massachusetts, the focus of the resolution was *on library and privacy*:[1712]

"We strongly protest those provisions (Sect. 215/218) in the Act of Congress called "The Patriot Act" (Oct. 25, 2001) which permit the Federal Government to seize and inspect the library's records of books our patrons have borrowed and of internet websites they have consulted. Especially as no patron may be informed of an investigation of his/her borrowing or internet records, the chilling effect of this Act is all the more destructive of free access to our library's resources."[1713]

In the City of Englewood,[1714] the focus of the resolution[1715] was *on equal protection for immigrants:*

"NOW, THEREFORE BE IT RESOLVED that the City Council of the City of Englewood, Bergen County, New Jersey, reaffirms its strong support for the rights of all citizens and immigrants and opposes measures that discriminate against individuals for legal scrutiny based on their country of origin or ethnicity; reaffirms its strong support for racial equality and opposes measures that single out individuals based on race; reaffirms its strong

---

[1712] Other Massachusetts resolutions passed in 2004 were not alike in focus: ACTON -- April 12, 2004 ("Affirms the town's strong opposition to parts of the Patriot Act that weaken or destroy civil liberties. Urges Massachusetts congressional delegation, the president, and attorney general to monitor impact of the act and to repeal provisions that infringe on civil liberties.") ARLINGTON -- June 11, 2003 ("Urges elected officials and public employees to preserve residents' civil liberties and rejects racial profiling. Urges Congress to monitor impact of the act and to repeal provisions that infringe on civil liberties.") CARLISLE -- May 3, 2004 ("Requires the town administrator to report to annual Town Meeting any information regarding implementation of the Patriot Act in town. Also urges Congress to monitor impact of the act and to repeal provisions that infringe on civil liberties.") CONCORD -- May 3, 2004 ("Requires the town manager to report to annual Town Meeting any information regarding implementation of the Patriot Act in town. Also urges Congress to monitor impact of the act and to repeal provisions that infringe on civil liberties.") GROTON -- May 11, 2004 ("Urges Congress to monitor impact of the act and to repeal provisions that threaten civil liberties.") LEXINGTON -- April 12, 2004 ("Affirms opposition to provisions of the Patriot Act that infringe on constitutional rights and civil liberties. Requests town police to refrain from some provisions of the law, such as enforcement of immigration matters, racial or religious profiling, and surveillance of people based on political advocacy or religious practice.") LITTLETON -- May 4, 2004 ("Urges Congress to monitor impact of the act and to repeal provisions that threaten civil liberties.") WESTFORD -- Oct. 18, 2004 ("Resolution by the trustees of the J.V. Fletcher Library protests provisions of the Patriot Act that permit seizure of library's records regarding patron's use of books and websites.") Source: Bill Of Rights Defense Committee. http://www.boston.com/news/local/articles/2004/11/14/patriot_act_resolutions?mode=PF

[1713] http://bordc.org/detail.php?id=233 For Small Town Meeting Minutes of October 18, 2004. See www.westford-ma.gov/generalinfo/townmeeting/101804 STM Minutes.pdf

[1714] Englewood originated as a settlement form Dutch West India Company in the 17th century until it was surrendered to the British in 1667. Through the years people from all walks of life and many ethnic complexity find economic opportunities here. Thus, Englewood is a racially and economically mixed city. In 2000, there were 26,203 people representing 9,273 households, and 6,481 families residing in the city, make up of 42.49% White, 38.98% African American, 0.27% Native American, 5.21% Asian, 0.05% Pacific Islander, 8.50% from other races, and 4.50% from two or more races. 21.76% of the population were Hispanic or Latino of any race. The median income for a household in the city was $58,379, and the median income for a family was $67,194. Many residents of the cities are young professionals (23.9% under the age of 18, 7.4% from 18 to 24, 30.5% from 25 to 44, 24.9% from 45 to 64, and 13.3% who were 65 years of age or older) working in the Wall Street, NYC or local hospitals. "History of Englewood" http://www.cityofenglewood.org/history.htm "Englewood, New Jersey" From Wikipedia, the free encyclopedia. http://en.wikipedia.org/wiki/Englewood,_New_Jersey

[1715] WAYNE PARRY, "15 NJ towns, 2 counties oppose Patriot Act provisions," The Associated Press (As of May 20, 2005, the follow cities and counties in NJ has passed Resolution: Englewood, Ewing, Franklin Township in Somerset County, Highland Park, Keansburg, Lawrence Township, Montclair, Mullica, New Brunswick, Paterson, Phillipsburg, Plainfield, Princeton Borough, West Windsor and Willingboro have passed such resolutions, as have the governments of Mercer and Passaic counties)

support for freedom of religion and opposes measures that single out individuals based on religious beliefs...."[1716]

Content of Resolutions

In terms of content of resolutions, they are of five broad types, i.e., resolutions of clarification, resolutions of condemnation, resolutions of affirmation, resolutions of monitoring, and resolutions of repeal and resolutions of non-cooperation.

A resolution usually falls into one or more of the categories, e.g., local council would condemn the USAPA as it affirms importance of Bill of Rights.

Resolutions of Clarification

Resolutions of clarification is drafted for one simple reason: educate the people to the perils of the USAPA; constitutional offensive provisions and rights encroaching characteristics. In so doing, the BORDC hopes to realize one of the main objectives of a democratic grassroots movement, i.e., rekindle constitutional spirit and rejuvenate democratic tradition: inform and educate people of their rights and obligations, empower them to act as a responsible citizen, in holding the government accountable. The other instrumental objective is the lack of transparency to the USAPA legislative process and secrecy in its implementation process. Thus in one of the more detailed resolution, the Baltimore City Council (Maryland, pop. 651,154) passed the "Civil Liberties Resolution-USA Patriot Act" on May 19, 2003, finds that:

> "*WHEREAS* federal policies adopted since September 11, 2001, including provisions in the USA PATRIOT Act (Public Law 107-56) and related executive orders, regulations and actions threaten fundamental rights and liberties by:
>
> a) Authorizing the indefinite incarceration of non-citizens based on mere suspicion, and the indefinite incarceration of citizens designated by the President as "enemy combatants" without access to counsel or meaningful recourse to the federal courts;
>
> b) Limiting the traditional authority of federal courts to curb law enforcement abuse of electronic surveillance in anti-terrorism investigations and ordinary criminal investigations;
>
> c) Expanding the authority of federal agents to conduct so-called "sneak and peak" or "black bag" searches, in which the subject of the search warrant is unaware that his property has been searched;
>
> d) Granting law enforcement and intelligence agencies broad access to personal medical, financial, library and education records with little if any judicial oversight;
>
> e) Chilling constitutionally protected speech through overbroad definitions of "terrorism";

[1716] City of Englewood Resolution 26,203, 09/29/04. Dem. http://bordc.org/detail.php?id=280 Englewood is home to Bergen Action Network (PO Box 5202, Englewood, NJ 07631), a social, economic, political justice grass roots for the young and dispossessed. http://www.bergenaction.net/about_us.php

    f)   Driving a wedge between immigrant communities and the police that protect them by encouraging involvement of state and local police in enforcement of federal immigration law;

    g)   Permitting the FBI to conduct surveillance of religious services, internet chat rooms, political demonstrations, and other public meetings or any kind without having any evidence that a crime has been or may be committed…"[1717]

Resolutions of Condemnation

According to Merriam-Webster dictionary, to condemn is to: "to declare to be reprehensible, wrong, or evil usually after weighing evidence and without reservation."[1718] A resolution of condemnation is one which declares the USAPA to be wrong or wrongheaded. Such resolutions take a principled stance against how USPA is worded, passed, or applied. For example, on April 24, 2000, the Town of Amherst (34, 874) passed a "Civil Rights and Civil Liberties" resolution condemning the actions of Attorney General and DOJ for violating citizens' rights under the constitution:

> "The citizens of Amherst are concerned that actions of the Attorney General of the United States and the U.S. Justice Department since the September 11, 2001 attacks pose significant threats to Constitutional protections in the name of fighting terrorism. *Such undermining of basic civil rights and liberties run the serious risk of destroying freedom in order to save it.*"[1719] (Italic supplied)

Another more apt example is "A Resolution of the City of Santa Monica Affirming the City's Strong Commitment to Civil Liberties, Opposing the USAPA and Related Orders and Directives, and Supporting Unabrogated City Protection for Constitutional Rights" passed by Santa Monica City Council (CA, pop. 84,084) on February 11, 2004. The resolution condemns

> "Department of Justice interpretations of this Act and Executive Orders under the Act appear to particularly target Muslims, people of Middle Eastern and South Asian descent and citizens of other nations, thereby encouraging racial and ethnic profiling; and … the PATRIOT Act (for) significantly expands the government's ability to access sensitive medical, mental health, financial and educational records about individuals, lowers the burden of proof required to conduct secret searches and telephone or internet surveillances, increases federal law enforcement authority to obtain library records and prohibits librarians from informing patrons of monitoring or information requests…"[1720] (Italic supplied)

[1717] http://www.bordc.org/detail.php?id=235
[1718] http://www.m-w.com/cgi-bin/dictionary?book=Dictionaryandva=condemn
[1719] http://www.bordc.org/detail.php?id=194
[1720] http://icujp.org/PATRIOTrepeal_SM.html

Resolutions of Affirmation

Resolutions of affirmation basically affirm, categorically, the importance of the U.S. Constitution to our nation in protecting the rights of the citizens. As such they should not be tampered with, not even in time of national emergencies. If it is necessary to do so, denial of rights in the name of security should be sought in a reflective[1721] and balanced way.

This is one of the most popular and widely adopted kinds of resolution. In adopting this kind of resolution local government is taking a balanced stance and yet sending a clear message and strong signal to the federal government that the basic principles of constitutional government should be upheld after 9/11. Fighting terrorism should be done without unduly disturbing the delicate balance of power between federal vs. state vs. local government. For example:

On March 17, 2003, the Town Council of Los Gatos (Pop: 28,592), Santa Clara, California passed "A Resolution Relating to the USAPA and the Protection of Civil Rights and Liberties of Los Gatans." The resolution, after detailing the importance of constitutional rights, affirms that "all members of this community are governed by and enjoy certain fundamental rights granted under the United States Constitution, including the Bill of Rights, and the California State Constitution." The resolution also makes clear that: "the Town of Los Gatos adheres to the principle that no law enforcement agency, or any other city agency, may profile or discriminate against any person solely on the basis of ancestry, race, ethnic or national origin, color, age, sexual orientation, gender, physical or mental disability, or religion, political views, economic circumstances" and "the Town of Los Gatos wants to recognize the commitment it has to uphold the legal and human rights of its residents."

Finally the Town of Los Gatos affirms its unwavering commitment to protect constitutional rights of its residents:

> "NOW, THEREFORE, BE IT RESOLVED by the governing body of the Town of Los Gatos that it has been, and remains, firmly committed to the protection of civil rights and civil liberties for all of its residents, to the equal treatment of all its residents, regardless of their ancestry, race, ethnic or national origin, color, age, gender, sexual orientation, religion, physical and mental capability, economic circumstance, political background or views, and affirms its commitment to embody democracy and to embrace, defend and uphold the inalienable rights and fundamental liberties granted under the United States and the California State Constitution; (Italic supplied)

Usually this kind of resolution is also accompanied by other more forceful clauses, e.g., clauses calling non-cooperation with USAPA enforcement on the one and monitoring and repealing of USAPA on the other. For example, in Los Ganta, the resolution finishes off with calling for the repeal of the USAPA:

> "BE IT FURTHER RESOLVED that our Federal legislative delegation is petitioned to actively monitor the implementation of the USAPA, any new legislation, or related Executive

---

[1721] "WHEREAS, federal, state, and local governments should protect the public from terrorist attacks, such as those that occurred on September 11,2001, but should do so in a rational and deliberative fashion in order to ensure that security measures enhance public safety without impairing constitutional rights of infringing on civil liberties." Unified Government of Wyandotte County and Kansas City (Resolution No R-111-04) (11/4/04) Wyandotte County, Kansas.

Orders, and actively work for the repeal of those portions that violate the guaranteed civil liberties enumerated in the Bill of Rights".[1722]

Or, in the case of Syracuse Common Council, the resolution[1723] urges universities, colleges and schools within Syracuse to provide written notice to students as follows:

> "WARNING: Under Section 507 of the Federal USAPA public law 107-56, educational records may be obtained by federal law enforcement agents. This educational institution may be prohibited from informing you if your records have been obtained. Questions about this policy should be directed to: Office of the Attorney General, Department of Justice, Washington, DC 20530 – Attention: John Ashcroft."[1724]

Resolutions of Monitoring

This type of resolution calls for monitoring of the implementation and application of the USAPA. Such resolutions seek accountability through openness of the implementation process, e.g., open up of immigration hearings and publication of result, e.g., how many libraries visited by the FBI.

Typical of this kind of resolutions is that of: "Local Referenda Directing the Rhode Island Congressional Delegation to Monitor the USAPA (Federal Public Law 107-56) (Non-binding)" of November 4, 2003 by Middletown Voters, RI.[1725]

> "Shall the Rhode Island congressional delegation be *directed to monitor the implementation of the USAPA* (Public Law 107-56), and related executive orders and regulations, in order to prevent the unfair infringement on fundamental rights and liberties guaranteed by the Constitution of the United States?"[1726] (*Italic supplied*)

Resolutions of Re-Examination, Repeal and Revision

The type of resolutions implores the national law makers to have another look at the USAPA because the: "actions authorized by the USAPA and related Executive Orders may call into question fundamental Constitutional protections, such as due process, the right to privacy, the right to counsel, protection against unreasonable search and seizures, and basic First Amendment freedoms."[1727]

[1722] "A Resolution Relating to the USAPA and the Protection of Civil Rights and Liberties of Los Gatans. " Los Gatos Town Council, Santa Clara, California. 03/17/03. http://www.bordc.org/detail.php?id=131

[1723] Resolution Addressing the Preservation of Civil Liberties and Civil Rights of All Individuals Living in Syracuse, New York in Response to the USAPA. Syracuse Common Council. September 8, 2003.

[1724] http://www.bordc.org/detail.php?id=320

[1725] The Resolution was supported by 1,160 and opposed by 893 who disagreed. "Rhode Island Voters Weighed In On State Representative Race, Local Contest" http://www2.whdh.com/news/articles/local/A28904/

[1726] http://www.bordc.org/detail.php?id=342

[1727] "Resolution in Defense of the Bill of Rights and Civil Liberties," Approved by Charlestown Town Council (December 9, 2003). http://www.bordc.org/detail.php?id=341

On November 18, 2003, the City of Bethel, Alaska, passed a resolution[1728]: "A Resolution of the Bethel City Council Affirming Civil Rights and Liberties; Requesting Immediate Review of Federal Measures that May Infringe on Civil Liberties: Resolution #03-34" calling for the Federal government and national legislators to revisit the USAPA. The resolution, in its preamble, recognizes the necessity to protect the nation from terrorism, but is of the opinion fighting terror should be done without impairing rights:

> "WHEREAS, federal, state and local governments should protect the public from terrorist attacks such as those that occurred on September 11, 2001 and should do so in a deliberate fashion to ensure that any new securities measures will public safety without impairing constitutional rights or infringing on civil liberties..."

The resolution also recognizes that it is necessary to take speedy, resolute and forceful action to protect the national from further and unexpected terrorists' attacks:

> "WHEREAS, in light of the horrific act of terrorism against the U.S. citizens and numerous other nationalities on September 11, 2001, it was a natural response on the part of the government to take actions to prevent such acts of terrorism in the future..."

The resolution maintains a neutral stance as to the necessity or utility of USAPA. It is quick to point out that no one is to be blamed: "WHEREAS, the intent of this resolution is not to undermine the efforts of our elected officials to protect its citizens, nor to criticize the valiant men and women in law enforcement or military service..." However, it is the purpose of the resolution to take stock and seeking improvement to the USAPA:

> "*WHEREAS*, there is growing concern across the nation that language in the U.S. PATRIOT Act has expanded the government's power to use eavesdropping, surveillance, access to financial and computer records and other tools to tack terrorist suspects in ways that were not fully understood by the public or elected officials at the time of its enactment..."

Specifically, the resolution calls for the federal and local legislators to re-examine the USAPA after public consultation:

> "NOW, THEREFORE, BE IT RESOLVED that the Bethel City Council *requests members of the U.S. Congress to immediately re-examine the US PATRIOT Act* that it passed in October 2001, amending any portion of it that infringes upon the civil rights of US citizens. This sweeping legislation required intense public review and comment before it was passed and enacted."[1729] (*Italic supplied*)

Another more recent example is the resolution passed by the Town of Bristol, Rhode Island, passed on July 20, 2005. Typical of this kind of resolutions, it: "recognizes and upholds the United States Constitution and its Bill of Rights and the Rhode Island Constitution" but also give "full recognition ... of the serious nature of the current threats to the United States and its citizens which prompt dynamic actions to defend ourselves and our

---

[1728] http://www.bordc.org/detail.php?id=98

[1729] Be it Further Resovled that the Bethel City Council urges Congress not to re-authorize any provision in the US PATRIOT Act or enact the propose US PATRIOT Act 2 without thorough public review of these Acts.

way of life." The resolution was passed to "to insure that the PATRIOT ACT and related executive orders do not significantly erode our fundamental constitutional protections..." With this purpose in mind, the Council Resolved: "that the Council, while not condemning the PATRIOT ACT, urges its federal delegation to review and work toward revision and/or repeal of those sections of the PATRIOT ACT that may limit or violate the fundamental liberties granted to Americans by the Constitution and Bill of Right."[1730]

Resolutions of Non-Cooperation

Resolutions of non-cooperation actively resist the USAPA enforcement powers. It instructs local officials – police, libraries – not to cooperate with federal officials. For example, City of Richmond (Pop: 99,216) passed a "Resolution to Support the U.S. Constitution and the Bill of Rights" on February 25, 2003, stating:

> "BE IT FURTHER RESOLVED that, to the extent possible, *no City employee or department shall officially assist in or voluntarily cooperate with investigations,* interrogations or arrest procedures, public or clandestine, that are in violation of individuals' civil rights or civil liberties as specified by the U.S. Constitution and the Bill of Rights. (*Italic supplied*)
>
> BE IT FURTHER RESOLVED that the Richmond City Council calls upon all private citizens and organizations, including residents, employers, educators and business owners to demonstrate similar respect for civil rights and civil liberties, especially but not limited to cooperation with investigations and conditions of employment." [1731]

Similarly, on March 4, 2003, the Town of Marlboro (Pop: 976), Windham County, Vermont, passed "A Resolution of the Voters of Marlboro, Vermont: Article 21." The resolution: "resolved that the voters of the town of Marlboro, Vermont, call on local government to defend state and federal Constitutions from threats imposed by the USAPA, the Homeland Security Act, and orders and rules of the executive branch" it specifically instruct local and state police, the local U.S. Attorney's office, and the FBI to: "2. Not participate, to the extent legally permissible, in law enforcement activities that threaten civil rights and civil liberties such as surveillance, wiretaps, and securing of private information, which the Acts and Orders authorize..."

Actions of Resolutions

Affirmation of constitutional duty. Most if and all the resolutions call for locally elected and appointed officials, including police officers, to re-affirm their oath of office under the U.S. and State Constitutions, specifically to honor due process of law and protect civil liberties. This kind of resolution makes clear that the Federal, State and local officials are

---

[1730] The resolution was a compromise between the Bristol Town Council and the vocal East Bay Citizens for Peace (EBCP), an anti-war group. The EBCO wanted to whole USAPA condemned. The Council Balked. *Eastbayri.com* August 8, 2005. http://www.eastbayri.com/story/336622830080680.php

[1731] "Resolution to Support the U.S. Constitution and the Bill of Rights." City of Richmond. (2/25/03). http://www.bordc.org/detail.php?id=140

equally responsible and accountable to the U.S. Constitution. It also reminds the federal as well as local officials that obedience to rule of law and U.S. Constitution is personal. The way the local official can fulfill its oath of office is to stand between the long arm of USAPA and local residence. While legally the local officials cannot stop USAPA from being enforced, practically the local officials can abstain from helping the federal officials on their own accord.

Freedom of information request. Some resolutions require the local officials find out about the implementation policy, process, practice and outcomes of USAPA, by means of Freedom of Information Request. In so doing, the resolutions put into issue the secrecy of how USAPA was implemented. It reminds the federal officials that democratic government IS open government. While mostly symbolic,[1732] this kind of resolutions reminds the local officials that there are legal means to compel government officials to live up to America's espoused democratic ideal. This kind of resolution is best exemplified in "A Resolution of the City of Eugene Defending the Bill of Rights and Civil Liberties: Resolution No. 4743."[1733] The resolution asked the U.S. Attorney's Office, the Office of the Federal Bureau of Investigation, the Oregon State Police, and any other law enforcement to provide the Eugene City Council and Human Rights Commission with enforcement information related to USAPA and related Executive Orders, including: arrests made, persons detained,[1734] search warrants issued,[1735] electronic surveillances conducted,[1736] political monitoring done,[1737] educational records reviewed,[1738] book purchase[1739] and library records inspected[1740] and subpoenas issued.[1741]

Withholding local revenue. Some resolutions seek to withhold local tax revenue from being used for the enforcement of USAPA. This kind of resolutions points out the impact of

---

[1732] Scott Martelle, "New Breed of Patriots Speaking UpGrass-roots efforts to rein in the anti-terrorist USAPA gain support. Eugene, Ore., and other cities formally oppose aspects of law," *Los Angeles Times* December 8, 2002. (Local government resolutions have little to no impact on federal legislative actions, but it has important symbolic effect. The drafter of the resolution observed: "The most important aspect is to build a national consortium, a groundswell, and by making these somewhat symbolic resolutions cities are taking a stand …"You do what you can to slow these things down."

[1733] A Resolution of the City of Eugene Defending the Bill of Rights and Civil Liberties: Resolution No. 4743 . Approved by: Eugene City Council. Date Passed: 11/25/02. The resolution was the brain child of a retired secretary Hope Marston who felt that: "We don't know how many people have had their homes searched, or their library or bookstore records checked.." and people ought to be able to know and do something about it. Scott Martelle, "New Breed of Patriots Speaking UpGrass-roots efforts to rein in the anti-terrorist USAPA gain support. Eugene, Ore., and other cities formally oppose aspects of law," *Los Angeles Times* December 8, 2002. http://www.commondreams.org/headlines02/1208-02.htm

[1734] "1.1 The names of any detainees held in the area or any Eugene residents detained here or elsewhere, the circumstances that led to the detention; 1.2 The charges, if any, lodged against each detainee; 1.3 The name of Counsel, if any, representing each detainee…"

[1735] "1.4 The number of search warrants that have been executed in the City of Eugene without notice to the subject of the warrant pursuant to section 213 of the USAPA…"

[1736] "1.5 The extent of electronic surveillance carried out in the City of Eugene under powers granted in the USAPA…"

[1737] "1.6 The extent to which federal authorities are monitoring political meetings, religious gatherings or other such activities within the City of Eugene …"

[1738] "1.7 The number of times education records have been obtained from public schools and institutions of higher learning in the City of Eugene under section 507 of the USAPA…"

[1739] "1.9 The number of times that records of the books purchased by store patrons have been obtained from bookstores in the City of Eugene under section 215 of the USAPA…"

[1740] "1.8 The number of times library records have been obtained from libraries in the City of Eugene under section 215 of the USAPA…"

[1741] "1.10 Subpoenas issued to Eugene citizens through the United States Attorney's Office without a court's approval or knowledge."

USAPA enforcement on local revenue. In so doing, it makes clear that local government has a right and duty to pass judgment on how local revenue is to be spent:

> "Section 2. We resolve that, to the greatest extent legally possible, *no city resources*, particularly administrative or law enforcement funds, *will be used for unconstitutional activities* conducted under the USAPA or recent Executive Orders which permit activities listed above." [1742] (*Italics supplied*)

Sanctioning cooperation A few local governments passed ordinances prohibiting cooperation with federal officials and/or enforcing the USAPA, in violation of local ordinances, with threat of legal sanctions. The first such ordinances passed on April 2, 2002. The City of Aracata (Humboldt County, California, pop. 16,300), a liberal city[1743] and student town,[1744] passed an ordinance[1745] – An Ordinance of the City Council of the City of Arcata Amending the Arcata Municipal Code To Defend the Bill of Rights and Civil Liberties: Ordinance No. 1339 – to protect civil liberties of local residents,[1746] namely SEC. 2191: No Unconstitutional Detentions or Profiling:

> "No management employee of the City shall officially engage in or permit unlawful detentions or profiling based on race, ethnicity, national origin, gender, sexual orientation, or political or religious association that are in violation of individuals' civil rights or civil liberties as specified in the Bill of Rights and Fourteenth Amendment of the United States Constitution." [1747]

The resolution further outlaws unconstitutional cooperation with federal officials with "SEC. 2192: No Unconstitutional Voluntary Cooperation":

> "No management employee of the City shall officially assist or voluntarily cooperate with investigations, interrogations, or arrest procedures, public or clandestine, that are in violation of individuals' civil rights or civil liberties as specified in the Bill of Rights and Fourteenth Amendment of the United States Constitution."[1748]

Conversely, the Municipal Code makes ample clear that the government will provide "legal defense to any management employee who is criminally charged by another entity for his or her actions in compliance with this Ordinance."[1749]

[1742] A Resolution of the City of Eugene Defending the Bill of Rights and Civil Liberties: Resolution No. 4743 . Approved by: Eugene City Council. Date Passed: 11/25/02.

[1743] Arcata is the first city in the United States to elect a majority of its city council members from the Green Party.

[1744] Arcata hosted California State University: Humboldt State University system with 1/3 of the student living there

[1745] The City has passed a resolution on January 15, 2003: "Resolution of the City Council of the City of Arcata to Defend the Bill of Rights and Civil Liberties" making clear that "fundamental rights granted by the United States Constitution are threatened by actions taken at the federal level, notably by passage of sections of the USAPA, the Homeland Security Act and several Executive Orders" and affirms its "firm" commitment to constitutional principles and protection of civil rights. http://www.arcatacityhall.org/pdf%20forms/patriot_resolution.pdf

[1746] http://www.bordc.org/detail.php?id=119

[1747] http://www.bordc.org/detail.php?id=119

[1748] http://www.bordc.org/detail.php?id=119

[1749] "SEC. 2194: Defense. The City shall provide legal defense to any management employee who is criminally charged by another entity for his or her actions in compliance with this Ordinance." http://www.bordc.org/detail.php?id=119

Ordinance No. 1339 becomes the first anti-Patriot local law[1750] with specific prohibition and real sanction, though it has never been invoked, tested in the court, and very likely illegal.[1751]

All told there are seven city ordinances nation wide which provide for legal or administrative directives and sanctions to city employees or federal agents.

Process[1752]

Sponsorship

Some Resolution was sponsored by the city government as instigated by citizens[1753] or tabled by human rights commission.[1754] Many of the resolutions resulted from concerted efforts of national – local BORDC and coalitions of social activist, the likes of ACLU.[1755]

Adoption

Most anti-Patriot resolutions were co-sponsored by various interest groups. Resolutions are passed as a result of coalition of a number of groups, each with their own political agenda. Many of the co-sponsors are groups with liberal agenda and radical orientation. For example, in the case of Lowell, MA, the resolution[1756] was filed by City Councilor Rithy Uong on behalf of Greater Lowell for Peace and Justice. Uong is a Cambodian refugee. He is the first Cambodian-American to win a seat on the city council in Massachusetts. Greater Lowell for Peace and Justice has four missions: "Pursue non-military solutions to international conflict; Allocate resources to meet human needs; Defend and preserve our civil liberties; Foster Democracy."[1757] Uong objected to the USAPA because as a refugee – immigrant from South East Asia, he is very much against government repression in the name of security: "A lot of people like me came here to escape the Khmer Rouge. America is supposed to be the place of

---

[1750] "Town criminalizes compliance with Patriot Act," CNN.com May 18, 2003. http://www.cnn.com/2003/US/West/05/18/patriot.act.ap/index.html

[1751] Kevin Fagan, "Arcata the defiant Town ordinance penalizes officials who cooperate with Patriot Act, but law may not stand up in court," *S.F. Chronicle* Sunday, April 13, 2003. (The law is illegal. Local law and concerns cannot stands in the way of federal law and interests.) http://www.sfgate.com/cgi-bin/article.cgi?f=/c/a/2003/04/13/BA283270.DTL

[1752] Benjamin Shepard, "A Post-Absurd, Post-Camp Activist Moment Turning NYC into a Patriot Act Free Zone," *Counterpunch* February 5, 2004. (How anti-Patriot Act ordinance, Resolution 909, was ushered through NYPD City Council.) http://www.counterpunch.org/shepard02052004.html

[1753] MINUTES ALHAMBRA CITY COUNCIL Regular Meeting, October 11, 2004. PATRIOT ACT – F2M4-40, F2M4-7, R2M4-37 (At the August 23, 2004 meeting, the City Council considered a resolution which had been prepared by the City Attorney pursuant to Mayor Talbot's direction at the July 2004 meeting. The idea of a Resolution was instigated by a few neighbors who wanted the city to take a stance on the Constitution and civil rights issues) p. 5.

[1754] Jennifer Van Bergen, "100th Anti-Patriot Act Resolution Passed In Broward, Florida," *t r u t h o u t* May 7, 2003 (The resolution was submitted by the Broward Human Rights Board and supported by the Broward Bill of Rights Defense Coalition.)

[1755] 'Raleigh City Council USAPA Resolution Update," March 9, 2004. (Wake County Chapter of ACLU and the Raleigh PATRIOT Act Resolution Coalition requested the Raleigh City Council to adopt a PATRIOT Act resolution.)

[1756] A Resolution Regarding the Protection of Civil Rights and Civil Liberties (Nov. 16, 2004) http://www.bordc.org/detail.php?id=59

[1757] "City urged to back revised Patriot Act," *Boston Globe* Nov. 14, 2004.

hope and freedom. This is an invasion of rights and privacy." [1758] However, conservation groups also represented.

Oppositions to the BORDC Resolution

Anti-Patriot resolutions have many detractors. Even supporter are not all in total agreement as to the need, focus, scope, content or language of a resolution. The most common objection is that such a resolution it is not necessary. The strongest objection it that such resolutions are outside the charter and beyond the reach of local town councils. Otherwise it is in appropriate, illegal, or powerless for local government to tell the federal government what to do. There are a few who support the resolutions in principle but find the language of USAPA to be objectionable. Finally, there are people who find that a specific resolution does not go far enough.

(1) In the case of Eugene, Oregon (11/25/02), [1759] four out of eight of the Eugene City Council members decided not to vote for the resolution. Some Council members suggested that instead of passing an official Council resolution, it is best to send personal letters to the law makers. The major concerns were two. First, the resolution is an act in futility. Such a resolution would have little, if any, impact on the USAPA. It is totally a symbolic gesture. Second, the USAPA is not a municipal business, and thus outside the ambit of the Council authority. Council member Scott Meisner expressed the sentiment very well:

> "This does not change the law …Psychologically, I hope it reduces some people's fears. But I don't have a great deal of faith this will mean anything. I hope we don't stop with getting the city of Eugene to make a symbolic statement. I want effective action, not symbolic action." [1760]

(2) In the case of Burlington, Vermont, the resolution (11/30/02) met with overwhelming support. [1761] But Republican city councilor Kevin Curley (Ward 4) resisted the resolution on the following grounds: First, the resolution is a product of progressive politics as usual. Second, the resolution serves dominant (democratic) Party agenda. Third, the resolution "play on peoples' fears and emotions." Fourth, there is nothing to fear about the USAPA: "The truth of the matter is that how many people are really going to be looked into? Probably some people with some just cause. And what's the percentage of folks that have just cause to be looked at? I would think in the city of Burlington that's such a minute number, and maybe it's warranted for the minute number that's there."

(3) In the case of Ann Arbor, Michigan some proponents felt that the resolution was not clear enough and did not go far enough to control local police powers and/or in resisting

---

[1758] Id.

[1759] Joe Mosley, "USAPA Earns Council's `No' Vote," The Register-Guard, Eugene, Oregon, November 26, 2002. http://www.unitedstatesgovernment.net/usapa-novote.htm

[1760] Id. Scott Martelle, "New Breed of Patriots Speaking UpGrass-roots efforts to rein in the anti-terrorist USAPA gain support. Eugene, Ore., and other cities formally oppose aspects of law," Los Angeles Times December 8, 2002. (Eugene, Oregon Police Department was amongst the few in the nation to refuse cooperating with FBI to round up 5,000 Muslim decent in the City.)

[1761] "Patriot Act Stirs Opposition In Burlington," Channel 3, Burlington, Vermont -- November 30, 2002. http://www.wcax.com/Global/story.asp?S=1032124.

federal encroachment. Objections to the Resolution Adopted on July 7, 2003 (R-281-7-03)[1762] included:

a) The language of the resolution: "RESOLVED, That the Ann Arbor City Council, as a matter of public policy, directs the Ann Arbor Chief of Police, to the extent permitted by law, to..." does not make clear whether the resolution also applies to the Police Department and its officers.[1763] If not, the scope and effectiveness of the resolution is much too limited. More importantly, there is an issue as to who is to decide the legality of police action, i.e.,, what is or is not permitted by law.

b) The resolution requires the Chief of Police to "[c]ontinue to limit local enforcement actions with respect to immigration matters to penal violations of federal immigration law (as opposed to administrative violations)." This provision gives the police wide discretion to enforce immigration law in all federal immigration cases.[1764]

c) The resolution allows Chief of Police to enforce federal immigration law "in cases where the Chief of Police determines there is a legitimate public safety concern...." This gives the Chief of Police too much power to interpret the "public safety" exception, e.g.,, not all "public interest concern" is equally important to the public. The "public security" concern exception allows the Chief of Police to invoke federal immigration law to deal with local law and order problems, expanding federal law jurisdiction in the process. The community will be able to use federal authority to deal with powerless minority or aliens. This federalization of local law and order problems need to be resisted.

d) The resolution calls for the Chief of Police to "Continue to refrain from covert surveillance of and/or collection and maintenance of information on individuals or groups based on their participation in activities protected by the First Amendment, such as political advocacy or the practice of a religion, without a particularized suspicion of unlawful activity." As written, the resolution is objectionable, because: First, it only prohibits the police to "refrain from *covert* surveillance" and not *all* surveillance, e.g.,, taking photos of peaceful demonstration, in the open. Second, it allows for surveillance of any and all kinds of participation in unlawful activity, no matter how tangential or slight, e.g.,, people who helps with the distribute objectional materials by e-mail. Third, it allows for surveillance of protected relationship, e.g., lawyers and clients. Fourth, it allows for surveillance even without "particularized" suspicion. Fifth, it covers violent as well as non violent, major as well as minor, crimes.

[1762] Resolution to Protest the Eroding of Civil Liberties Under the USAPA (Public Law 107-56) and Related Federal Orders Since 9/11/01: R-281-7-03

[1763] A Draft Resolution Circulated in April 2003 provides: "Therefore be it Resolved that the Council of the City of Ann Arbor ... Directs the Police Department of the City of Ann Arbor to..." http://www.aabordc.org/analysis.html

[1764] *Id.* [R]efrain from participating in the enforcement of federal immigration laws."

e) The resolution does not foreclose the use of electronic monitoring devices, e.g.,, mounted video camera.[1765] This allows police to conduct electronic surveillance where personal (covert) surveillance is not allowed, e.g., bugging, concealed TV.

f) The resolution asks the Chief of Police to: "Affirm the existing practice, as required by Michigan state law, of providing simultaneous notice of the execution of a state court search warrant to any resident of the City of Ann Arbor whose property is the subject of such a warrant, except in cases of anticipatory search warrants." The notice of execution of search warrant clause only applies to state warrant execution, not federal criminal warrant execution.[1766]

g) The resolution does not address the legality of profiling,[1767] a major concern with the USAPA.

h) The resolution requires the Chief of Police to: "Report to the City Council any request made by federal authorities for the Ann Arbor Police Department to participate in any activity under the USAPA, to the extent the Chief of Police has knowledge of such request." This language is objectionable, because, first, it only applies to USAPA, not other federal investigative activities. Second, it allows the Chief of Police to claim a lack of knowledge. Third, it does not apply to each and every police in the police department.[1768]

Objections in Their Own Voices

The BORDC and anti-Patriot movement is a highly charged political movement, and each resolution is a political high drama fought out in the backstage. As might be expected, there are as many detractors to the anti-Patriot movement as there are supporters for the USAPA. A systematic and careful examination of such opposing views allows us to see clearly and understand better what the anti-Patriot movement is all about; its controversy and issues, problems and prospect. Often, it is better to see ourselves in through the eyes of our enemies; however unflattering and unpleasant such sight and sound it.

[1765] A Draft Resolution Circulated in April 2003 provides: "[R]efrain from establishing a general surveillance network of video cameras, and refrain from deploying facial recognition technology or other unreliable biometric identification technology within the City of Ann Arbor;"

[1766] *Id.* "[P]rovide advance or simultaneous notice of the execution of a search warrant to any resident of the City of Ann Arbor"

[1767] *Id.* "[R]efrain from the practice of stopping drivers or pedestrians for the purpose of scrutinizing their identification documents without particularized suspicion of criminal activity."

[1768] *Id.* "[R]eport to the City Council any request by federal authorities that, if granted, would cause agencies of the City of Ann Arbor to exercise powers or cooperate in the exercise of powers in apparent violation of any city ordinance or the laws or Constitution of this State or the United States."

Table 1. Before and after: The Making of Ann Arbor's 2003 Civil Liberties Resolution[1769]

	A. Draft Resolution Circulated in April 2003	B. Resolution Adopted on July 7, 2003 (R-281-7-03)	C. Comments
1.	Therefore be it Resolved that the Council of the City of Ann Arbor ... directs the Police Department of the City of Ann Arbor to:	Resolved, That the Ann Arbor City Council, as a matter of public policy, directs the Ann Arbor Chief of Police, to the extent permitted by law, to:	"Police Department of the City of Ann Arbor" (AAPD) was changed to "Ann Arbor Chief of Police". Does the resolution, thus, apply to police officers other than the Chief?* If so, how? (cf. sects. 8.B. and 8.C. below). Observe, too, that the qualifying phrase "to the extent permitted by law" was added. Who decides what is/is not permitted by law? The Chief? The City Attorney? A court? *For the sake of brevity only, the commentary in the sections below assumes that the resolution does apply in some instances to other AAPD officers.
2.	[R]efrain from participating in the enforcement of federal immigration laws;	Continue to limit local enforcement actions with respect to immigration matters to penal violations of federal immigration law (as opposed to administrative violations) except in cases where the Chief of Police determines there is a legitimate public safety concern and in such public safety instances, to report the situation to the City Council no later than 60 days after the incident.	"[P]articipating" has been dropped. Note, too, the addition of the phrase "penal violations." What if the AAPD is only assisting another agency in enforcing "administrative violations" of immigration law? That would, apparently, be permitted. Also, the AAPD can enforce any immigration law whatsoever so long as the Chief "determines" there is a "legitimate safety concern." See also the letter from Kary L. Moss, ACLU of Michigan.

Table 1. (Continued)

	A. Draft Resolution Circulated in April 2003	B. Resolution Adopted on July 7, 2003 (R-281-7-03)	C. Comments
3.	[R]efrain from engaging in the surveillance of individuals or groups of individuals based on their participation in activities protected by the First Amendment, such as political advocacy or the practice of a religion, without particularized suspicion of criminal activity unrelated to the activity protected by the First Amendment; [R]efrain, whether acting alone or with federal or state law enforcement officers, from collecting or maintaining information about the political, religious or social views, associations or activities of any individual, group, association, organization, corporation, business or partnership unless such information directly relates to an investigation of criminal activities, and there are reasonable grounds to suspect the subject of the information is or may be involved in criminal conduct;	Continue to refrain from covert surveillance of and/or collection and maintenance of information on individuals or groups based on their participation in activities protected by the First Amendment, such as political advocacy or the practice of a religion, without a particularized suspicion of unlawful activity.	"[S]urveillance" is replaced with "covert surveillance," narrowing the scope of the resolution. Overt surveillance, often used to intimidate actual or potential activists, is not addressed. Also, if a plain-clothes police officer infiltrates a lawful political advocacy group with the intent to conduct surveillance but also to reveal her identity if asked, is she then conducting covert or overt surveillance? Also, regarding the "collection and maintenance of information on individuals or groups" based on First Amendment activities, the phrase "directly relates to an investigation of criminal activities" has been dropped and "reasonable grounds" is replaced with "particularized suspicion." Note, too, that nonviolent civil disobedience would satisfy the resolution's threshold for the AAPD to conduct covert surveillance and other intelligence activities against otherwise law-abiding religious and political activists.
4.	[R]efrain from establishing a general surveillance network of video cameras, and refrain from deploying facial recognition technology or other unreliable biometric identification technology within the City of Ann Arbor;		The ACLU and other civil liberties groups have documented, and pointed out the real dangers of, the proliferation of private and government video surveillance across the US. Nonetheless, this section was omitted entirely from the resolution as adopted.

	A. Draft Resolution Circulated in April 2003	B. Resolution Adopted on July 7, 2003 (R-281-7-03)	C. Comments
5.	[P]rovide advance or simultaneous notice of the execution of a search warrant to any resident of the City of Ann Arbor whose property is the subject of such a warrant, and refrain from participating in a joint search with any law enforcement agency absent assurances that such notice will be provided to such individuals during the operation of the search;	Affirm the existing practice, as required by Michigan state law, of providing simultaneous notice of the execution of a state court search warrant to any resident of the City of Ann Arbor whose property is the subject of such a warrant, except in cases of anticipatory search warrants.	"[S]earch warrant" is replaced with "state court search warrant"; thus, the resolution no longer addresses federal 'sneak and peak' or 'black bag' searches. The door is seemingly left wide open for the AAPD to assist and participate in such searches by federal agencies.
6.	[R]efrain from undertaking or participating in any initiative, such as the Terrorism Information and Prevention System (TIPS), that encourages members of the general public to spy on their neighbors, colleagues or customers;		Months before Congress blocked funding for TIPS, John Ashcroft announced a related initiative to be managed by the same program--Citizen Corps--that would have run TIPS. The plan is to double the number of Neighborhood Watch Programs (NWP) by 2004 and expand their mission to make participants "a critical element in the detection, prevention and disruption of terrorism." The NWP effort has proceeded apace--there are now more than 10,000 programs. See also the letter "From the Desk of Chief Oates ...," "AmeriSnitch" by Bill Berkowitz in The Progressive, and *"Sheriffs Rounding Up Neighborhood Leaders for Counterrerror Watch Patrols"* by Alice Lipowicz in *CQ Homeland Security.*
7.	[R]efrain from the practice of stopping drivers or pedestrians for the purpose of scrutinizing their identification documents without particularized suspicion of criminal activity;		This might have been a good opportunity to address persistent accusations of racial profiling by the AAPD. However, this section was omitted entirely from the resolution.

Table 1. (Continued)

	A. Draft Resolution Circulated in April 2003	B. Resolution Adopted on July 7, 2003 (R-281-7-03)	C. Comments
8.	[R]eport to the City Council any request by federal authorities that, if granted, would cause agencies of the City of Ann Arbor to exercise powers or cooperate in the exercise of powers in apparent violation of any city ordinance or the laws or Constitution of this State or the United States;	Report to the City Council any request made by federal authorities for the Ann Arbor Police Department to participate in any activity under the USAPA, to the extent the Chief of Police has knowledge of such request.	According to the Ann Arbor News, "[AAPD Chief] Oates said federal agencies have several methods to obtain information, and the resolution only applies to those used under the Patriot Act." He is correct, references to other potential legal or constitutional violations have been dropped. The use in the resolution of the phrase "to the extent the Chief of Police has knowledge" admits of the possibility that other police officers may be asked to "participate in … activity under the USAPA" without the Chief's knowledge. These other officers would apparently not be required to report such activities to the City Council (cf. sect. 1.B. and 1.C. above).
9.		Refrain from participating in informational interviews conducted by federal authorities similar to those conducted by the Federal Bureau of Investigation (FBI) in early 2002 in Ann Arbor of individuals not suspected of criminal activity, unless the interviewee has specifically requested the presence of an AAPD official.	This is the only section that did not appear in the April draft resolution. On June 11, 2003, at a public library forum, Nazih Hassan, president of the Muslim Community Association of Ann Arbor, told the crowd that the AAPD's participation in the 2002 interviews was problematic because it gave interviewees a false sense of security. This practice is now official city policy.

Table 2. Varieties of dissenting voices to anti-Patriot resolutions

Concerns	Voices
USAPA not a local concern	Flagstaff Mayor Joe Donaldson: "The city has no business dabbling in federal issues."[1770]
The public is not affected, interested or concern.	Flagstaff City Councilman Joe Haughey: "I find it embarrassing that the city of Flagstaff passed the resolution. ...My feeling is, the majority of citizens are not worried about the PATRIOT Act."[1771]
The resolution is too polarizing and divisive.	Flagstaff City Councilman Joe Haughey: "It began polarizing different groups in the community..."[1772]
USAPA power is not offensive. Innocent people have nothing to worry about.	Flagstaff City Councilman Joe Haughey: "My main point about the PATRIOT Act is, if you're not doing anything wrong, what are you worried about?"[1773]
The sponsors of resolution are anti-Bush	Rick Krug: "the Peace and Justice Coalition is supported by the Communist Party, whose express purpose is to overthrow the government of the United States."[1774]
People should respect the legislative process	Rick Krug, political director of the Coconino County Republican Party thought the resolution is "disrespectful ... (of federal representatives) ... And it wasn't pushed through like people say. I have enough faith in even the liberal congressmen and senators that they're not going to let someone push them. I think they're smarter than that. I don't think there's any idiots in Washington."[1775]
USAPA becomes political battlefield of patriotism vs. liberalism.	Timothy Lynch, director of the Project on Criminal Justice at D.C.'s Cato Institute: "The law has taken on symbolic proportions over and above the nitty-gritty impact of its actual provisions...On the one end of the spectrum, you have protesters chanting that Ashcroft is Hitler. On the other end, you have an administration that responds to critics by questioning their patriotism."[1776]

[1770] Heidi Walters, "Acts of patriotism: Flagstaff's struggle to define its rights revives democratic roots," *Las Vegas Mercury*. Thursday, July 03, 2003. (Reporting on Flagstaff, Arizona (pop: 52,894) resolution process. The Flagstaff City Council passed "A Resolution Reaffirming the City of Flagstaff's Commitment to Civil Liberties" passed on 12/17/2002.) http://www.lasvegasmercury.com/2003/MERC-Jul-03-Thu-2003/21647310.html

[1771] Heidi Walters, "Acts of patriotism: Flagstaff's struggle to define its rights revives democratic roots," *Las Vegas Mercury*. Thursday, July 03, 2003. http://www.lasvegasmercury.com/2003/MERC-Jul-03-Thu-2003/21647310.html

[1772] *Id.*
[1773] *Id.*
[1774] *Id.*
[1775] *Id.*
[1776] Vanessa Blum, "Pitching the Patriot Act: In the ongoing debate over the merits of the anti-terror law, it's easy to get carried away," *Legal Times* August 3, 2004

Table 2. (Continued)

Concerns	Voices
The resolution is not supported by true public opinion	DOJ spokesman Mark Corallo: "These are cookie-cutter ACLU resolutions … In most cases, the city council is presented with a resolution, usually from the ACLU, and they pass it without conducting any meetings or hearing any input from their local U.S. Attorney." [1777]
There are misconceptions about USAPA	Buchanan, who heads the Executive Office of U.S. Attorneys: "When we started talking to people in the community about the Patriot Act, we realized there were a number of serious misconceptions ….I've accepted any offer to debate whether it's a town hall meeting, a university, a Rotary Club, a local television network." [1778]

[1777] Id.
[1778] Id.

Finally, in as much as the anti-Patriot movement and resolutions is a battle for the hearts and minds of the people, and ultimately a struggle to find the soul of a nation, the debate over its symbolic meaning is at least as important as its substantive merit, i.e., who said what to whom in what forum and manners are all important.

VI. TWO CASE STUDIES

(A) Coalition Building:[1779] The Case of Madison, Wisconsin (October 15, 2002)

Madison, Wisconsin

On October 15, 2002 Madison City Common Council passed a civil liberties resolution against the USAPA.[1780] It was the tenth in the nation and the second largest city (pop: 208,054) at that time to have done so. The largest city to have passed an anti-Patriot resolution at the time was Denver, Colorado with a population of 554, 638 as of March 18, 2002.[1781] The anti-Patriot movement in Madison was spearheaded and orchestrated by two local activist groups: the Madison Area Peace Coalition (MAPC)[1782] and Students for an Informed Response (SIR).[1783] This is a case study of how the two groups work together to pass the anti-Patriot resolution, focusing on their respective mission and vision, divided role and responsibility. Such coalition building process was replicated all over the country during the life span of the Patriot movement. This case study illustrates how such a coalition works.

The Constitution of MAPC

MAPC was formed right after 9/11 on September 25, 2001 by 200 people and a number of organizations in and around Madison, Wisconsin in reaction to 9/11.[1784] "The mission of the Madison Area Peace Coalition (MAPC) is to organize a broad-based movement to inform public opinion and promote US government policies that truly further peace, justice, and freedom in the world. Specifically, three organization values were stressed: Peace and justice, not war and revenge; Unity and respect for diversity: Stop scapegoating and harassment; Protect human rights and civil liberties at home and abroad."[1785]

[1779] Abby Scher, "When Adversaries Become Allies: The Fight Against the Patriot Act and the Surveillance State," *The Public Eye Magazine* - Vol. 20 (1) (2006) (Coalition building is important for the anti-Patriot movement. In Washington, Republican and Democratic Senators are working together to defeat the re-authorization of the USAPA. . Russell Feingold (D-WI) were 42 Democrats and Senators Larry Craig (R-Idaho), Chuck Hagel (R-NE), Lisa Murkowski (R-Alaska) and John Sununu (R-NH). In terms of interest groups, ACLU was working with Gun Owners of America to put police under control. At the state level liberals and conservatives worked closely on citizens' rights issues. In Texas and in Idaho, Green Party was working with Gun Owners.) http://www.publiceye.org/magazine/v20n1/scher_allies.html

[1780] http://madison.indymedia.org/front.php3?article_id=7755andgroup=webcast

[1781] See "Chronology of Civil Liberties Resolutions or Ordinances (as of 9/17/03)" Bill of Right Defense Committee. http://www.bordc.org/Chronology.pdf

[1782] http://madpeace.org/

[1783] http://sir.cakdesign.com/

[1784] See "Madison Area Peace Coalition" Flyer, 9/25/01 prepared by Rae Vogeler http://www.wnpj.org/pdf/mapc06.pdf

[1785] "Madison Area Peace Coalition: Mission Statement" http://madpeace.org/?q=node/17

Operationally, MAPC subscribes to the following goals: (1) Build an effective organization; (2) Legitimize dissent;[1786] (3) Oppose the use of US force; (5) Reduce military spending. (6) Encourage international conflict resolution; (7) Change public consciousness; (8) Mobilize public opinion to build a movement.

In terms of strategy, MAPC seeks reform/repeal/revision of government policies and legislation by peaceful mean and through grassroots action, i.e., communications, outreach, legislative initiatives, and direct political actions. Its declared political action strategy include building an effective organization, legitimizing dissent, changing public opinion/consciousness, mobilizing public opinion to build a movement, and finally changing public policy.[1787] Judging by internal communications and external efforts, MAPC was predominantly concerned with issues of war and peace, i.e., stopping war in Iraq and providing humanitarian assistance to Afghanistan.[1788] Comparatively little organizational effort and resources was devoted to promoting civil liberties at home.

MAPC was led by a 12 person "Coordinating Committee."[1789] Its role and functions include developing strategies, setting policies, coordinating activities and making decisions.[1790] Representation on the "Coordinating Committee" is based on organizational diversity and sexual balance. The day to day activities of the MAPC is run by seven committees or working groups, i.e., Media, Actions/events, Policy, Outreach and education, Communications, Arts, Music, Theatre, Visual, and Cultural, Finance/ Fundraising.[1791] A reading of the internal communications informs that the MPAC functioned on a purely democratic and equalitarian fashion.[1792]

As a budding organization, MAPC confronted many novel problems and difficult issues. The learning curve was steep. The pitfalls were many.

As a growing organization, it has to confront problems of growing pain, from experiencing identity crisis, e.g., what does being a "non-violent" organization means?[1793] How should it manage its image, e.g., should MAPC engage in "civil disobedience"?,[1794] How to deal with burn out syndrome?[1795] As it becomes more effective, it has to deal with problems of legal exposure and political sabotage.[1796]

[1786] "Legitimize dissent against the open-ended so-called "war on terror" and against curtailment of civil liberties. Provide support and a safe haven for those afraid to speak out against government policies."

[1787] See MAPA Mission Statement and Goal. http://madpeace.org/mission

[1788] Starting with October 19, 2001 the MAPC policy committee was devoted entirely to the introduction and passage of a peace resolution in the Madison Common Council. See "The Madpeace-policy Archives" (October 2001) http://lists.opensoftwareservices.com/pipermail/madpeace-policy/.

[1789] "Coordinating Committee" in "Minutes of the Founding meeting of the Madison Area Peace Coalition, 9/25/01 prepared by Rae Vogeler" http://madpeace.org/Wiki/MAPCSept25

[1790] "Coordinating Committee Mission - Approved 11/13/2001," http://madpeace.org/Wiki/Coordinating%20Committee%20Mission

[1791] "Working Groups/Committees" in "Minutes of the Founding meeting of the Madison Area Peace Coalition, 9/25/01 prepared by Rae Vogeler"

[1792] See "The Madpeace-media Archives" (April 2001 – September 2003) http://lists.opensoftwareservices.com/pipermail/madpeace-media/ and "The Madpeace-policy Archives" (October 2001 – September 2003) http://lists.opensoftwareservices.com/pipermail/madpeace-policy/

[1793] "Madison Area Peace Coalition - *General Meeting Notes - April 2, 2002*" (*A discussion over whether "non-violent" should be a part of Mission and Goal of MAPC.*) http://madpeace.org/Wiki/MAPCApr02

[1794] "MeetingOct21" http://madpeace.org/Wiki/MeetingOct21

[1795] "8. State of CC" in "Coordinating Committee Meeting Minutes 04/14/2002" (people are bring out. People are not coming to the meeting. People are not communication. There are more administration than coordination.) http://madpeace.org/Wiki/CCMeetingApr14

[1796] "5. Legal issues" in Coordinating Committee Meeting Minutes 04/21/2002" ("Do we need some kind of strategy to keep us out of trouble? We need to avoid having any reasonable excuse for "them" to go after us.

Being an entrepreneurial organization, there were difficulties with finding adequate finance for its activities, proper allocation of resources and stringent accounting of income/outlay, e.g., how to raise funds? Where to spend the limited resources? What accounting method should be used?[1797]

Given the democratic nature of the organization, there were disagreements and conflicts over leadership, strategy and management, e.g., who was to lead the MAPC? Was there any limit to what MAPC can or should do? How should MAPC dealt with non-participating members?[1798]

As a loosely copulated coalition, it has to deal with many inter and intra organizational stress and strain, e.g., how to accommodate the needs of associated coalition member?[1799]

All these factors affected MAPC's ability to successfully mount, led and coordinate a social movement, i.e., anti-Patriot campaign.

MAPC consisted of no less than 53 loosely associated organizations,[1800] each joined at a different time and for various reasons.[1801] Not every one was in support of MAPC on the anti-Patriot resolution, nor were those in support in total agreement with each other on the objectives sought, strategies used, steps taken.

We need to avoid giving them ammunition of any sort. ... We need to know what our rights are as a group...")
http://madpeace.org/Wiki/CCMeetingApr21

[1797] See "Coordinating Committee, Meeting Minutes, 11-19-01" http://madpeace.org/Wiki/CCMeetingNov18

[1798] See "Coordinating Committee Meeting Minutes 11-11-01" http://madpeace.org/Wiki/CCMeetingNov11 (There were issues being raised as to unclear role and mandate of the coordinating committee, lack of a clear mission and strategy, and problems with inconsistent participation and contribution ("what is democratic?") See also "MAPC Meeting Minutes 09/09/2003" http://madpeace.org/Wiki/MAPCSep09 (Two years later, MAPC still afflicted with organizational – line of authority problems.)

[1799] The student caucaus felt that they were not being respected and treated as co-equal by the old folks. There was a generation gap in the making. "MeetingOct08" http://madpeace.org/Wiki/MeetingOct08

[1800] A Room of One's Own Bookstore, Beyond Terrorism, Colombia Support Network, Community Action on Latin America, Dane County/Apartado Sistership, Democratic Socialists of America - Madison Chapter, East Timor Action Network/Madison, First Unitarian Society Social Justice Council, Food Not Bombs: Madison chapter, Four Lakes Green Party, Health Writers, International Socialist Organization, Industrial Workers of the World - Madison Chapter, Islamic Community of Madison Area, Jews for Equal Justice, Lakeside Press, Left Turn, Madison Arcatao Sister City Project, Madison-area Urban Ministry, Madison Community Co-Ops, Madison Friends Meeting, Madison Hours Coop, Madison Rafah Sister City Project, Madison Women for Peace, Madison World Federalist Partners, Mad Town Liberty Players, Mifflin Street Community Co-Op Muslim Student Association, National Lawyers Guild - Madison chapter, Palestine/Israel Peace and Justice Alliance, Peace and Action to Change Tomorrow, Peace Economics Peoples' Church, Physicians for Social Responsibility - Madison, Progressive Dane, Quakers - Monthly Meeting of the Religious Society of Friends, Rainbow Bookstore Cooperative, Rainbow Family Gathering for World Peace and Healing, St Paul's University Catholic Center Peace and Social Justice Council, Social Justice Center, Socialist Party of South Central Wisconsin, Solidarity - Madison Branch, Solidarity Truckers, Inc., South Central Federation of Labor, The South-West Asia Information Group, Stop The War! - Madison Students/Youth, United Faculty and Academic Staff, AFT Local 223, UW Infoshop, UW-Madison Green Progressive Alliance, Veterans For Peace, Madison/Clarence Kailin chapter. Contact: peacevet@terracom.net, Veterans of the Abraham Lincoln Brigade, War Tax Resisters League - Madison Chapter, Women's International League for Peace and Freedom.

[1801] The following organizations signed joined MAPC on September 25, 2003 (others have signed on since):Chrysalis East Timor Action Network; Four Lakes Green Party; Health Writers Industrial Workers of the World - Madison Chapter; International Socialist Organization; Jews for Equal Justice; Left Turn; Madison Arcatao Sister City Project; Madison Community Coops; Madison Urban Ministry Madison War Tax Resister's League; Mifflin Street Coop; Mr. James and Cullney - New Yorker; Peoples' Church; Rainbow Bookstore Cooperative; Rainbow Family Gathering for World Peace and Healing Socialist Party of South Central Wisconsin Solidarity Truckers, Inc.; Solidarity: a Socialist/Feminist Organization; Stop the War UW Student Organization; U.S. Out Now Veterans of the Abraham Lincoln Brigade; Women's International League for Peace and Freedom. See "GROUPS THAT JOINED THE COALITION" http://madpeace.org/Wiki/MAPCSept25

Students for an Informed Response (SIR)

Students for an Informed Response (SIR)[1802] originated as an extra-curricular activity[1803] at the Madison West High School, Wisconsin.[1804] SIR was formed after 9/11 by the students "to encourage political literacy, discussion, and activism pertaining to this subject." SIR organized such activities as "teach-in" and "fund drives" for Afghan Refugees. With regard to the USAPA it held a very successful Youth for Civil Liberties rally in the spring of 2002.[1805] Madison West High School student Alix Gould, one of the organizers stated the purpose of their organizational effort:

> "We are protesting the infringements the government has made on our civil liberties in the wake of the September 11 attacks ... Right after the attacks, the government passed this amendment in a very short time, and there are several things in it that groups have found fault with."[1806]

Another organizer, Sol Kelley-Jones, a student at Madison West High School, spoke at mass rallies to promote moral responsibility and political activism.

> "At a time when common dialogue is more important than ever, our government is taking away that right and saying it is being done in the name of defending democracy ...The U.S.A. Patriot Act creates a climate chilling to speech, dissent and debate." [1807]

Kelley-Jones urged high school students to get more involved. SIR helped drafted the resolution.[1808] "We may not have the right to vote, but we have a responsibility to think critically."

[1802] The WWW site of S.I.R. is http://sir.cakdesign.com/

[1803] "Club and Activities" http://www.madison.k12.wi.us/west/activity.htm (Visited September 20, 2003). S.I.R. is amongst 30 extracurricular organizations and 70 extramural activities being offered.

[1804] Madison West High School, with a student body of 2160, is a highly acclaimed and academically achieved high school near by University of Wisconsin (Madison). It was awarded a "School of Excellence" award in 1985 by the U.S. Department of Education. SAT and ACT scores of WHS are above national average. For 2002, WHS vs. National Verbal Mean is 607 vs. 506, and WHS vs. National Math Mean is 633 vs. 516. See WHS Profile, http://www.madison.k12.wi.us/west/profile.htm

[1805] Taniquelle Thurner, "High school students protest Patriot Act," *The Badger Herald* Monday, May 6, 2002. http://badgerherald.com/news/2002/05/06/high_school_students.php

[1806] *Id.*

[1807] *Id.*

[1808] Civil Rights Defense Resolution: Expressing the Commitment of the City of Madison to Civil Rights and Liberties.

WHEREAS, following the attacks on the United States of September 11, 2001, the Congress passed the USAPA (PL107-56) on October 26, 2001; and

WHEREAS, the provisions of the USAPA expand the authority of the federal government to detain and investigate citizens and non-citizens and engage in electronic surveillance of citizens and non-citizens; and

WHEREAS, many people throughout communities across the nation, including Madison, are concerned that certain provisions in the USAPA threaten civil rights and liberties guaranteed under the United States Constitution; and

WHEREAS, the City of Madison has been, and remains, committed to the protection of civil rights and liberties for all people as expressed in the United States and the Wisconsin Constitutions; and

NOW THEREFORE, BE IT RESOLVED BY THE COUNCIL OF THE CITY OF MADISON:

Section 1. That the City of Madison has been, and remains, firmly committed to the protection of civil rights and civil liberties for all people.

Section 2. That the City of Madison affirms the following principles: (1) every person has the right to be free from unreasonable search and seizure, (2) neither stops nor arrests may be made without establishing reasonable suspicion or probable cause that a crime has been committed or is about to be committed, (3) every person has

MAPC and USAPA

MAPC Goals

One of MAPC goals is to [1809]"Protect civil liberties." Specifically, to seek the "repeal of the USAPA and other repressive legislation that violates the Bill of Rights and other civil liberties" as a working objective.[1810] In a May 14, 2002 MAPC General Meeting, MAPC further elaborated and prioritized on its *"Mission and Goal" statement concerning civil liberties:*

Table 3. Prioritization of "Protect civil liberties" sub-goals and clarification of strategies of MAPC"[1811]

Sub-Goals	Priority	Statement
1	B	GOAL: Educate the public (and ourselves) about government and corporate racial profiling, and infringements on civil liberties STRATEGY: (1) Hold educational events, e.g., forums and teach-ins. (2) Disseminate literature and information about the Patriot Act, civil liberties violations, and racial profiling.
2	A	GOAL: Work for local and federal legislation that protects civil liberties. Work to repeal legislation that infringes on civil liberties

a right to equal protection under the law and the right not to be deprived of life, liberty or property without due process of law, and (4) every person has the right to free speech and freedom of association as provided for under the First Amendment of the United States Constitution and court opinions thereon.

Section 3. That when the City of Madison engages in public safety intelligence gathering as a part of law enforcement and of national security, the City of Madison intends that such intelligence gathering comply with the following policy: No information about political, religious or social views, associations, or activities should be collected unless the information relates to public safety concerns or suspicion of criminal activity or the potential for criminal activity. Currently held information shall be thoroughly and carefully reviewed by the City Attorney or other appropriate City official to be designated by the Mayor, for its legality and appropriateness, using the United States and Wisconsin Constitutions and the established Madison Police Department policy as guides.

Section 4: That the City of Madison affirms its strong opposition to terrorism, but also affirms that any efforts to end terrorism not be waged at the expense of essential civil rights and liberties of the people of Madison, the United States and the World.

Section 5. That the Clerk of the City of Madison attest and affix the seal of the City of Madison to this resolution.

[MAPC-discuss] Fwd: Students for an Informed Response Resolution. Barbara Smith smithbarbara20 at hotmail.com *Mon Sep 16 15:13:59 CDT 2002*

[1809] The full statement of MAPC goal in this area is: "Protect civil liberties Protect civil liberties that are threatened by government actions such as military tribunals, intelligence gathering, and infiltration and disruption of political groups. We oppose racial/ethnic profiling and discrimination, whether corporate, governmental, or societal. We call for the repeal of the USAPA and other repressive legislation that violates the Bill of Rights and other civil liberties." The full range of MAPC goals are: (1) Build an effective organization, (2) Legitimize dissent, (3) Oppose the use of US force, (4) Protect civil liberties, (5) Reduce military spending, (6) Encourage international conflict resolution, (7) Change public consciousness, (8) Mobilize public opinion to build a movement. See http://madpeace.org/mission

[1810] http://madpeace.org/mission

[1811] The MAPC prioritized within goals but fail to do so between goals, unless the importance of goals follow sserial order, i.e., "(1) Build an effective organization" being most important and "(8) Mobilize public opinion to build a movement" being least important. View in this way "Protect civil liberties" is right in the middle.

Table 3. (Continued)

Sub-Goals	Priority	Statement
		STRATEGY: (1) Organize to repeal the USAPA. (2) Organize to pass the federal "End Racial Profiling Act of 2001" (3) Organize to pass Wisconsin A.B. 489/S.B.238 of 2001.
3	C	GOAL: Organize activities in coordination with other groups to raise public awareness about civil liberties infringements and racial profiling. STRATEGY: Plan demos, street theater, marches, and rallies[1812]
4	D	GOAL: Publicize attacks on civil liberties and racial profiling in the media STRATEGY (1) Write letters to the editors about these issues. (2) Find other ways to get this information into the media, such as contacting sympathetic reporters to write articles on these issues.
5	F	GOAL: Provide support to those who are victims of civil liberties abuses and racial profiling STRATEGY (1) Ensure that the Arab community and other communities of color have a base of support. (2) Provide support and defense, as needed, with other organizations to create solidarity. (3) Support youth of color.
6	E	GOAL: Promote coordinated efforts to track civil liberties abuses and racial profiling STRATEGY (1) Find out if there is a national clearing-house for tracking civil rights violations and racial profiling. (2) Contact the ACLU and other organizations about civil liberties violations and racial profiling incidents.

Source: Table constructed from "MAPC General Meeting - 05/14/2002 Meeting Minutes" http://madpeace.org/Wiki/MAPCMay14 and "Goals 3 and 4" http://madpeace.org/Wiki/Goals%203%20and%204

[1812] The original sub-goal statement was: "Work for local and federal legislation that protects civil liberties. Work to repeal legislation that infringes on civil liberties" (This is a duplication of B, an obvious mistake).

The Process

MAPC was against the USAPA from the start. It staged the very first national protest against H.R. 2975,[1813] the House version of the final USAPA, within days after it made it through the House Judiciary Committee and long before it was incorporated into the USAPA and became the law of the land.[1814] MAPC was on the record objecting to many of its oppressive provisions when it was being deliberated in the House, including: allowing for indefinite detention of non-citizen, minimizing judicial supervision of electronic surveillance of citizens, expanding the government's authority and ability to conduct secret searches, allowing the Attorney General and the Secretary of State to designate domestic groups as terrorist organizations, granting the FBI broad access to sensitive personal and business records without showing criminality, making possible large-scale "intelligence" investigations of American citizens.[1815] It warned, forebodingly: "Ten years from now, our fear is that the American public will look back to this legislation and say, 'this is where we crossed the line to a surveillance society."[1816]

Diane Farsetta, a member of the MAPC Policy Committee, first floated the idea of an anti-USAPA campaign on March 25, 2002 in an internal e-mail.[1817] She proposed following Denver in passing an anti-Patriot resolution.[1818] The Denver resolution made clear: "Section 5. That the City and County of Denver reaffirms its support for the government of the United States of America in its campaign against global terrorism, but also reaffirms its commitment that such campaign not be waged at the expense of essential civil rights and liberties of the people of Denver and the United States."[1819]

MAPC planned and organized a number of well publicized and public profile public assemblies to energize the group and mobilized the public to their causes. For example, on April 27, 2002,[1820] a Racial Profiling Demonstration[1821] *was organized. It was well attended and endorsed by a number of like minded organizations; including AFSCME 171; Student*

[1813] H.R. 2975 was entitled "Provide Appropriate Tools Required to Intercept and Obstruct Terrorism (PATRIOT) Act of 2001. H.R. 2975 was introduced by Rep. Sensenbrenner on October 2, 2001. The Committee on the Judiciary was reported out of the House Judiciary by a vote of 36-0 on October 3, 2001. It passed the House on October 12, 2001 by a vote of 337 - 79, 1 Present (Roll No. 386). H.R. 3162, the USAPA, H.R. 2975 and S. 1510, which passed the Senate on 10/11/2001. For a legislative history, see http://www.gop.gov/committeecentral/docs/bills/107/1/bill.asp?bill=hr2975

[1814] "Protect our Civil Liberties" October 6, 2001. http://madpeace.org/Wiki/PR10062001

[1815] "Protect our Civil Liberties" October 6, 2001. http://madpeace.org/Wiki/PR10062001

[1816] Quoting Laura W. Murphy, Director of the ACLU's Washington National Office.

[1817] [MAPC-policy] FW: Denver opposes anti-terrorism provisions - when will others do so? Diane Farsetta policy@madpeace.org Mon, 25 Mar 2002 12:08:13 -0600 http://lists.opensoftwareservices.com/pipermail/madpeace-policy/2002-March/000233.html

[1818] "Denver Officials, Citing Civil Rights, Decide to Bow Out of War on Terror," Tuesday, March 19, 2002 (Reporting that Denver passed an anti-Patriot resolution on March 18, 2002) http://lists.opensoftwareservices.com/pipermail/madpeace-policy/2002-March/000233.html

[1819] See "Resolution No. 13, Series of 2002, Expressing the Commitment of the City and County of Denver to Civil Rights and Liberties." http://www.denvergov.org/admin/template3/forms/RES013-02.pdf

[1820] MAPC-Announce] April 27 - Anti-Racial Profiling Rally Channa Camins cbcamins@students.wisc.edu *Sat, 13 Apr 2002 16:52:10 -0500 http://lists.opensoftwareservices.com/ pipermail/madpeace-mapc/2002-April/000543.html*

MAPC-Announce] We Need You Now!!! APRIL 27 Demonstration Leafleting and Postering on Sunday Channa Camins cbcamins@students.wisc.edu *Sat, 13 Apr 2002 17:38:16 -0500http://lists. opensoftwareservices.com/pipermail/madpeace-mapc/2002-April/000544.html*

[1821] [MAPC-Announce] Defend Civil Liberties and End Racial Profiling (4/27 Demonstration Email Announcement) Channa Camins cbcamins@students.wisc.edu *Sun, 7 Apr 2002 19:09:16 -0500.* See also[MAPC-Announce] How Can You Help? 4/27 Demonstration on the Wisconsin Capitol Channa Camins cbcamins@students.wisc.edu *Sun, 7 Apr 2002 19:38:01 -0500.*

Labor Action Coalition; Addison Area Peace Coalition; Muslim Students Association (UW-Madison); Jewish Voices Against the Occupation; South Central Federation of Labor; Coalition of Black Trade Unionists; The Urban League of Greater Madison; Progressive Dane; Palestine Right of Return Coalition; United States Students Association; CMA Islamic Community of Madison Area NAACP Milwaukee Chapter; Task Force On Money, Education and Prisons; United Council of UW Students; Rainbow Bookstore Collective; The Progressive Magazine; ISO; A.E. Havens Center; IWW; Solidarity; Asian and Pacific American Council (UW-Madison); Generation 2008; Asian Freedom Project; ASM Diversity Committee (UW- Madison); SIR - Students for an Informed Response; US Out Now.

SIR Political Activism

On May 4, 2002, SIR held a "Youth For Civil Liberties Rally"[1822] on the Library Mall beginning at 2PM. The focus of this event was to promote youth political action. The rally was a cooperative effort with student representatives from each of the Madison high schools.[1823] About 120 attended, marched in the rain from Brittingham park to Library Mall to the Capitol. Speeches were moved to the rotunda due to the rain. The press attended but did not have anything to report. There were speakers of different ethnicities.

The resolution was supported by American Civil Liberties Union, Wisconsin Association of Academic Librarians, Progressive Dane, the Four Lakes Green Party, Communities United, Bill Keyes, Matt Sloan, Mike Verveer, Judy Olson, Jean MacCubbin, Todd Jarrell, Carol Carstensen, Bill Clingan, Juan Lopez, Ruth Robarts, and Rep. Terese Berceau, among others.

With the resolution drafted,[1824] notice was distributed for people to show support on 9/17/02.[1825] The voting of the resolution was later delayed from 9/17/02 to 10/15/02.[1826]

Joining Hands: The October 15, 2002 Meeting

In addition to MAPC, SIR, and Ald. Brenda Konkel, the resolution was co-sponsored by the Wisconsin Association of Academic Librarians, Communities United, Progressive Dane, the Greens, Madison School Board President Bill Keyes, Ald. Matt Sloan, Ald. Mike Verveer, Ald. Judy Olson, Ald. Jean MacCubbin, Ald. Todd Jarrell, school board members Carol Carstensen, Bill Clingan, Juan Lopez, and Ruth Robarts, and State Rep. Terese Berceau.

MAPC and SIR organized people to speak at the meeting. Representing SIR, West High sophomore Sol provided the keynote:

> "We believe that our cherished civil liberties are under attack through the implementation of the USAPA ...Passing this resolution will put our city on record as standing firm in the defense of the U.S. Constitution."

[1822] MAPC-Announce] May 4: Youth For Civil Liberties Rally Ted M kinbote@charter.net *Wed, 1 May 2002 16:26:42 -0500*

[1823] http://lists.opensoftwareservices.com/pipermail/madpeace-mapc/2002-May/000590.html

[1824] [MAPC-Announce] MAPC draft resolution to defend the Bill of Rights and Civil Libertieshttp://lists.opensoftwareservices.com/pipermail/madpeace-mapc/2002-September/000727.html

[1825] [MAPC-Announce] Come to City Council Tues. Sept. 17 Barbara Smith smithbarbara20@hotmail.com *Fri, 13 Sep 2002 22:22:07 +0000* http://lists.opensoftwareservices.com/pipermail/madpeace-mapc/2002-September/000728.html

[1826] [MAPC-Announce] Postponed: Civil Rights Resolution in City Council Barbara Smith smithbarbara20@hotmail.com Mon, 16 Sep 2002 21:56:35 +0000. http://lists.opensoftwareservices.com/pipermail/madpeace-mapc/2002-September/000730.html

"As young people gathered here tonight, we understand that we need to do more than be passive observers of history, because the decisions being made right now are our future...We need to ask questions about our world, to critique what the government and the media tell us, to become a part of the political debate, whether at school or in our community.... Since the tragic events of September 11th, our treasured freedom, has come under attack--not from terrorists, but from our own leaders in the Congress and the White House. Laws like the USAPA were passed in the name of freedom, but what they really do is take away our freedom to fully participate in our nation's democracy."

"Our government wants to scare youth away from our constitutional right to protest...The Patriot Act means government surveillance of our school, library and Internet activities without our even being told. Even reading certain books or researching certain topics, both constitutionally protected activities, are now grounds for criminal investigation. For many of you in this room who were active in the civil rights movement of the '60s, you 've been down a similar road before, and for my generation it's a road we don't want to go down again."

"Further, the Patriot Act is causing an escalation of racial injustice and creates a climate of 'us' vs 'them.' Groups who have already faced systematic oppression in our country are being furthered exiled today ...This kind of injustice is against everything Madison stands for."

"As we gather tonight, across the generations, we understand the importance of our activism to protect our rights, because if democracy is weakened, it won't be because of terrorists.... It will be because we stood by and let it happen ...Now more than ever, our voices of courage can make a difference. In passing The Defend the Bill of Rights and Civil Liberties Resolution tonight you will be reaffirming our city's commitment to the founding principles of this great nation. And together we can bring the heart and soul back to democracy."

There were heated debates – Madison style – over the purpose and language, necessity and appropriateness of the Resolution:

Madison Police department officials were concerned with the restrictive language of the resolution. They further assured the Council members and citizens at the meeting that MPD has been a leader in regulating traffic stop profiling. It has no interest in indiscriminate investigation of persons of Middle Eastern descent.

Some Council members were of the opinion that the USAPA has little or local effect. It is thus inappropriate for the Common Council to get involved. This was challenged by Ald. Paul Skidmore, who sat on the committee overseeing the city's library services. He noted that the Act has grave impact on local libraries. It is a topic of grave concern and much discussion n his committee.

There were times that the resolution seemed destined to fail. The long hour and lateness of the meeting brought out personal animosity and partisan antagonism. Ultimately, Alderman Ken Golden saved the day by reminding his colleagues of the need to keep focus on the main issue at stake, i.e., threat posed by the USAPA. Alderman Kent Palmer asked his colleagues to "to keep watch on the watchers." In the end, Alders from both parties - Holtzman and Bruer, and Jarrell and Powell – finally ended up supporting the resolution.[1827]

[1827] John Quinlan, "Resolution to Defend the Bill of Rights and Civil Liberties" Passes Madison Common Council With 17 of 20 Supportive Votes." http://lists.madimc.org/pipermail/mapc-announce/2002-October/00801.html

(B) Opposition Rendering: Meridian Township Board (September 16, 2003)

The Anti-USAPA Movement

According to the minutes of Meridian Township Board, the first time signs of opposition to USAPA surfaced on May 6, 2003 as a "Business Information" item agenda for the May 7, 2003 Board Meeting.[1828] Two persons spoke against the USAPA at the meeting, Stacy A. Hickox and Melanie Jaramillo. Hickox asked the Board to pass a resolution against the USAPA.[1829] Jaramillo told the Board how that might be done with examples around the nation.[1830]

Hickox, chairman of Capital Area Freedom Defense Coalition, led the anti-USAPA campaign. She is a law professor at MSU. She is a lifetime human rights activists.[1831] She has long time association with the ACLU, starting being selected as its Weinberg Fellow in 1988 in Philadelphia, Pennsylvania. She later acted as the President of ACLU Knoxville Chapter.

Jaramillo was an Information System Analyst working for the State Bar of Michigan.[1832] Both of them have done work for the legal aid. Hickox represented legal aid clients for free since 1985. Jaramillo volunteered on the Michigan Legal Service Computer Committee.[1833]

Hickox wanted to rein in the power of the local police. The Capital Area Freedom Defense Coalition was asking the Meridian Township Police Department to provide advance notice before executing a search warrant; to conduct investigative stops based on particular and articulate suspicion; to stop profiling based on religion, ethnicity or national origin grounds; and to assist federal law enforcement (such as immigration) "only when such law enforcement would further local law enforcement goals."[1834] Hickox and the Coalition picked Meridian Township because of past police abuses – racial profiling and illegal investigation.[1835]

There was no immediate discussion of the subject matter at the meeting on record. The battle has just begun.

Stacy kept the issue alive by registering her opposition as a "Business Information" item at the May 20, 2003 meeting.[1836] Again the proposition did not draw any support or discussion for the next two meetings, i.e., June 3 and June 7, 2003.

[1828] "2). Board Information (BI): BI-7 Stacy A. Hickox, 4291 Indian Glen Drive, Okemos; RE: Support of a Meridian Township resolution against the USAPA" "Agenda - Charter Township of Meridian Township Board Regular Meeting May 6, 2003 6:00 P.M." http://www.meridian.mi.us/meetings/tb/agenda050603.htm6

[1829] "4. Public Remark....Stacy A. Hickox, 4291 Indian Glen Drive, Okemos, requested support for a Meridian Township resolution against the USAPA and in opposition to several provisions of said act." "Charter Township of Meridian Township Board Regular Meeting–Approved and Amended ...Tuesday, May 6, 2003, 6:00 P.M." (May 6, 2003 hearing) http://www.meridian.mi.us/meetings/tb/minutes050603.htm

[1830] "4. Public Remark....Melanie Jaramillo, 2080 Ashland Avenue, Okemos provided additional information regarding various methods nationwide of addressing the USAPA." May 6, 2003 hearing. http://www.meridian.mi.us/meetings/tb/minutes050603.htm

[1831] See resume of Hickox http://www.dcl.edu/faculty_staff/hickoxs.pdf

[1832] See "Finance and Administration" State Bar of Michigan, Melanie Jaramillo, Information System Analyst mjaramillo@mail.michbar.org http://www.michbar.org/directory/whowhat.html

[1833] http://www.mplp.org/technology/LSCC/lscc.htm

[1834] Danile Sturm, "Broad challenge to USAPA underway," City Pulse.com http://www.lansingcitypulse.com/030827/030827patriot.html

[1835] Danile Sturm, "Broad challenge to USAPA underway," City Pulse.com http://www.lansingcitypulse.com/030827/030827patriot.html

[1836] "Agenda Charter Township of Meridian Township Board Regular Meeting May 20, 2003 6:00 P.M." http://www.meridian.mi.us/meetings/tb/agenda052003.htm

The first sign of public support for the opposition movement came on the July 1, 2003 meeting. Jean Nicholas, 6232 Brookline, East Lansing, spoke in support of Board adoption of a resolution against the USAPA.[1837] Jean Nicholas was an Associate Professor Emeritus professor at MSU.[1838] Her support was followed by that of Richard Harrington.[1839] The oppositions at the meeting were spontaneous. They were not listed on the agenda.[1840]

The demonstrated public support and expressed community interest for an anti-USAPA resolution on July 1, 2002 called for a more formal/focused community discussion regarding USAPA enforcement issues, e.g., Township policies and procedures towards USAPA. The Police Chief was invited to address the Board on how Township policies bear on the issue of the rights of Township citizens on July 17, 2003.[1841]

The first formal "community" discussion of anti-USAPA resolution was planned for July 17, 2003 meeting.[1842] There were robust opposing voices. All told nine people spoke out on three separate occasions, three of them twice: Richard Harrington, 820 Piper Road, Haslett; John Veenstra, 320 Piper Road, Haslett; Harold Schmidt, 4086 Dobie Road, Okemos; Dolly Schmdit, 4086 Dobie Road, Okemos; Eldon Clark, 2415 Sapphire Lane, Okemos; William White, 4695 Okemos Road, Okemos; Dorean Koenig, 6365 W. Reynolds, Haslett; Stacy Hickox, 4291 Indian Glen; Mark Rilling, 6365 W. Reynolds, Haslett.

The overwhelming interests shown by the public attending the meeting caused Supervisor McGillicuddy to arrange for a new meeting to discuss the USAPA at the August 19th Board Meeting.

The anti-USAPA resolution was formally put on the Meridian Township Board agenda s a "Discussion ITEMS" on August 19, 2003. The notice called for public comments and Board discussion of how USAPA might be in conflict with existing Township policies.[1843]

At the August 19 meeting more people spoke out against the USAPA.[1844] Jean Nicholas, 6232 Brookline Court, East Lansing, spoke in opposition to provisions in the USAPA[1845] Haslett, President of the Lansing Branch of the Michigan ACLU, spoke of his experience with FOIA request in obtaining copies of police policies on civil liberties protection. Robert Wasserman, 2796 Buglers Way, East Lansing, read a segment from the August 19, 2003 Lansing State Journal editorial concerning the USAPA. The editorial supported a Meridian Township resolution to protect civil liberties of local citizens. Shrikumar Poddar, 2601

[1837] See "4. Public Remarks," "Charter Township of Meridian Township Board Regular Meeting–Approved and Amended …Tuesday, July 1, 2003, 6:00 P.M." (July 1 Meeting) http://www.meridian.mi.us/meetings/tb/minutes070103.htm

[1838] http://www.msu.edu/unit/romclang/fci/faculty/nicholas.htm_(517) 332-4372 devoted to humanitarian causes. She denoted to Michigan Humanities Council. http://search.yahoo.com/search?p=Jean+Nicholas%2C+Lansingandsub=Searchandei=UTF-8andfr=fp-top

[1839] "'Richard Harrington, 820 Piper Road, Haslett, spoke in support of a Board resolution in opposition to the Patriot Act." See "4. Public Remarks," (July 1 Meeting) http://www.meridian.mi.us/meetings/tb/minutes 070103.htm

[1840] "Agenda Charter Township of Meridian Township Board - Regular Meeting July 1, 2003 - 6:00 P.M." http://www.meridian.mi.us/meetings/tb/agenda070103.htm

[1841] "5. Reports/Board Comment/New Worries" (July 1 Meeting) http://www.meridian.mi.us/meetings/tb/minutes070103.htm

[1842] No agenda found.

[1843] "11. "Discussion Items/endsθ (ORCHID) - Public Comment A. Township Policies/Patriot Act" "Agenda Charter Township of Meridian Township Board Regular Meeting August 19, 2003 6:00 P.M" http://www.meridian.mi.us/meetings/tb/agenda081903.htm

[1844] "Charter Township of Meridian Township Board Regular Meeting - Approved …Tuesday, August 19, 2003, 6:00 P.M." http://www.meridian.mi.us/meetings/tb/minutes081903.htm

[1845] "4 Public Remarks" August 19, 2003 meeting. http://www.meridian.mi.us/meetings/tb/minutes081903.htm

Cochise Lane, Okemos, spoke against the USAPA. He cited examples from two (2) other states where he alleged law enforcement violation of civil liberties. Katherine Guins, 4496 Dobie Road, Okemos, spoke in support of a resolution against the USAPA.

It was the Board's turn to discuss about the USAPA.[1846] Trustee Woiwode requested clarification for issues raised by Henry Silverman with respect to his FOIA request. Treasurer Hunting reported that Mr. Fedewa has contacted U.S. Senators Debbie Stabenow and Carl Levin to voice his opinion and concerns with the USAPA.

Afterward at the "Discussion" session [1847] Supervisor McGillicuddy opened up the floor for further public comments/discussions. Seven people spoke, including Stacy Hickox, the original opposition leader. All of them have spoken against the PATRIOT ACT before, except William White who was worried about the implication of local oppositions to a federal law. He too has spoken before.

(1) Dolly Schmidt,[1848] 4086 Dobie Road, Okemos spoke in support of an anti-USAPA resolution.

(2) Stacy Hickox, 4291 Indian Glen spoke in favor of open govern and against secrecy embodied in the USAPA.[1849]

(3) Rex Harrington, 820 Piper Road, Haslett commented on the possible purchase of four cameras at Haslett and Okemos intersection, with funds from a section in the USAPA.

(4) William Tyler White, 4695 Okemos Road, Okemos voiced concern with local implications of the USAPA.[1850]

(5) Joan Guy, 1083 Woodside Drive, Haslett spoke in opposition to the USAPA. She thought that the Act was an important local issue.

(6) Henry Silverman, 1099 Woodwind Trail, Haslett and President of the Lansing Branch of the Michigan ACLU, spoke in support of a resolution against the USAPA.

(7) Harold Schmidt, 4086 Dobie Road, Okemos, voiced his admiration of the Board's work and his desire to hear from the Police Chief on local police application of authority under the USAPA.

After all the town's people were given an opportunity to air their opinions one more time, the Police Chief Gibbons was asked to address the Board and community about current Township polices, especially how USAPA might have an adverse impact on Meridian police operations and practices. Chief Gibbons first explained to the Board about the law enforcement functions of the Meridian Township Police Department. He then made clear that the Meridian Police Department is committed to following nationally recognized standards and constitutional principles in enforcing the law. The department's SOP is recognized by the Commission on Accreditation for Law Enforcement Agencies (CALEA).[1851] Through the

---

[1846] "5. Reports/Board Comment/New Worries" August 19, 2003 meeting. http://www.meridian.mi.us/meetings/ tb/minutes081903.htm

[1847] "11. Discussion Items/Ends" August 19, 2003 meeting. http://www.meridian.mi.us/meetings/tb/minutes 081903.htm

[1848] Dolly Schmidt, a board member of the Lansing ACLU

[1849] Prepared statement in Official Minute Book.

[1850] Prepared statement in Official Minute Book.

[1851] "Purpose of the Commission: The Commission was formed for two reasons: to develop a set of law enforcement standards; and to establish and administer an accreditation process through which law

accreditation process the Township Police Department has demonstrated that it has written directives and practices in place to protect the constitutional rights of citizens.[1852] Chief Gibbons defended the Meridian Police Department thusly:

> "We require officers to protect the rights of all persons by strictly prohibiting biased profiling in traffic contexts, and other discretionary actions. Stops and enforce protect the rights of all persons by strictly prohibiting biased profiling in traffic contexts, and other discretionary actions. Stops and enforcement activities must be based on conduct, and supported by reasonable suspicion."

After Chief Gibbon's presentation, the Board Members and staff discussed issues about passing a motion against the USAPA. Issues discussed, included issues with resolution drafting, issues with police cooperation, and issues with police liability protection. The major concern was in how to reconcile federal laws and local policies. More specifically, how might such federal vs. local conflicts in law, and law enforcement policies and priorities affect the police operations and liabilities.

Trustee Woiwode agreed with the Police Chief that asking the local law enforcement officials to choose between local law enforcement and protecting the Constitution is difficult if not impossible: "our police officers might not be equipped to make that choice." Woiwode invited Chief Gibbons to work with her over a draft resolution acceptable to the police in the next two weeks.[1853]

The public was once again asked to comment on the USAPA.[1854] Supervisor McGillicuddy opened the floor for Public Remarks.

Eldon Clark, 2415 Sapphire Lane, East Lansing, asked that the Police Chief be given an input on any draft resolution regarding the USAPA. John Veenstra, 320 Piper Road, Haslett supported of a resolution in opposition to the USAPA.

The debate over USAPA carried on. On September 2, 2003, the first opposition to an anti-USAPA appeared on record as an agenda item in the "Business Information" section.[1855] The Board discussion has also moved to such a stage that the origin opposing anti-USAPA resolution proponent, Stacy Hickox, offered the Board a sample resolution to consider.[1856]

enforcement agencies could demonstrate voluntarily that they meet professionally-recognized criteria for excellence in management and service delivery.' http://www.calea.org/newweb/accreditation%20Info/Accred %20Program%20Info.htm

[1852]"A. Township Policies/Patriot Act" August 19, 2003 meeting. http://www.meridian.mi.us/meetings/tb/minutes 081903.htm

[1853] Danile Sturm, "Broad challenge to USAPA underway," City Pulse.comhttp://www.lansingcitypulse.com/ 030827/030827patriot.html

[1854] "13. Public Remarks" August 19, 2003 meeting. http://www.meridian.mi.us/meetings/tb/minutes 081903.htm

[1855] "(1). Board Information (BI): "BI-4 Charles Pratt, 3640 East Arbutus Drive, Okemos; RE: Opposition to the Capital Area Freedom Defense Coalition's request for a Board resolution against the USAPA" "Agenda Charter Township of Meridian Township Board" "Regular Meeting September 2, 2003 6:00 P.M." http://www.meridian.mi.us/meetings/tb/agenda090203.htm

[1856] "(1). Board Information (BI): BI-2 Stacy Hickox, 4291 Indian Glen Drive, Okemos; RE: Sample Board resolution to protect civil liberties "Agenda Charter Township of Meridian Township Board" "Regular Meeting September 2, 2003 6:00 P.M." http://www.meridian.mi.us/meetings/tb/agenda090203.htm

On September 16, 2003, a motion for opposing the USAPA was put on the agenda of the Meridian Township Board.[1857] It passed unanimously a resolution in opposition to the USAPA.

VII. DISCUSSION:
UNDERSTANDING ANTI-PATRIOTISM AS A SOCIAL MOVEMENT

Anatomy of a Social Movement

The success of the BORDC – anti-Patriot movement resulted from a convergence of a number of factors.

A Constitutional Crisis in the Making

9/11 changed America, drastically, fundamentally and resolutely. In the name of security, the Bush administration launched one of the most serious attacks on the nation's Constitution. The USAPA and other counter-terrorism measures suspended many key provisions in the Constitution and do away with most of its established safeguards. Many non-citizens are detained without trial routinely, and more than a few are tortured secretly. Citizens have their e-mail searched and phone monitored without warrant and notice. The legislative branch was denied of information to supervise the executive. The judiciary was divested of legal authority to adjudicate government acts and omissions. Overnight, the United State turned into a nation security state with a despotic if paternalistic imperial President at its helm. A Constitutional crisis is looming.

There are many factors which make this Constitutional crisis that much more threatening and foreboding:

First, America has a long tradition and strong commitment to democratic governance, fortified by constitutionalism, rule of law and individual rights. Such democratic ideal and ideas are permanently inter woven into U.S. national ethos and viscerally stamped onto American's personal character. So much so that constitutional principles, legal rules and individual rights are consider sacrosanct, unquestioned and unquestionable. View in this light, the anti-Patriot war is a battle fought over the soul and ethos of the nation and hearts and mind of the people.

Second, the Bush administration intimated that the war of terror would likely to last forever. While Bush did not tell the nation when the war would end, he was clear that it would not stop until every terrorist threat is eliminated, for all time. Since terrorism is a war of and on ideology, and since ideas cannot be killed, war on terror is here to stay until everyone thinks and acts like the U.S. This is not likely to happen. Taking this into consideration, the war on terror, will last indefinitely. In the meantime, there is a de facto suspension of the Constitution.

[1857]"Agenda Charter Township of Meridian Township Board Regular Meeting September 16, 2003 6:00 P.M". http://meridian.mi.us/meetings/tb/agenda.htm

A Universal Ideal[1858]

The BORDC was able to frame the debate in universal terms that the man in the street can understandable.

In terms of successful mobilization, a social movement needs to attract, retain, energize and mobilize like minded social reformers and political activists to do battle. It also needs to attract (human) resources and cultivate (political) networks. A key ingredient to organizational success is to adopt a broad based coalition with an all inclusive strategic. This entails embracing an ideological claim that most can identify with. This means engaging in a discursive practice and participating process which most people in the social movement or political coalition can feel comfortable with, i.e., without having to sacrifice ones ideological integrity, institutional authority and strategic control. [1859] The challenge is: "How do incumbents maintain legitimacy for their dominant ideology during periods of attempted dislocation in fields? ...In short, what strategies do incumbents and challengers typically deploy to mobilize collective support for their potentially antagonistic archetypes?"[1860]

BORDC did so by mobilizing an ideological base, i.e., by promoting a set of common values and mutual interests which helps in the construction of shared reality, through discursive practices and boundary setting. This allows internal members and external groups to communicate and identify with each other, over shared aspirations and with convergence of interests, however transitory or partial. In so doing, BORDC was able to organize their political interests in a comprehensive with a view of shaping a strategy of collective action.

A Common Enemy

The Bush administration's zealous war on terror generated policy and rhetoric which resulted in the growth of grassroots constitutionalism. Bush's radical politics, divisive policy, monopolization of (executive) power and secretive rule assured that he attracts loyal followers and incites hated detractors. From the far right to the radical left, Bush is a person they love to hate.

Tangible Injuries

In the case of anti-Patriot movement, it started with a national crisis that is threatening (loss of liberty), a universal ideal that can be easily identified (protect the Bill of Rights), a common enemy that is menacing (national security state), and wide spread harm that is real and tangible (Muslims being deported, citizens' phone being tapped).

Assessment of a Social Movement

How effective is the anti-Patriot movement in achieving its objectives, either in educating the public about the perils of the Bush's anti-terrorism policy or demonstrating the problems with the USAPA? There is no systematic and comprehensive, much less scientific study, of

---

[1858] Gibson, "Public Goods, Alienation and Public Protest: The Sanctuary Movement as a Test of the Public Goods Model of Collective Rebellious Behavior," Working Paper 90-5, Conflict Resolution Consortium, University of Colorado. (People joint social movement because of desire to promote public goods.) http://www.colorado.edu/conflict/full_text_search/AllCRCDocs/90-5.htm Muller, Edward and Karl-Dieter Opp. 1986. "Rational Choice and Rebellious Collective Action." APSR, Vol. 80. No.2. June: 471-487

[1859] Manuel Hensmans, "Social movement organizations: A Metaphor for strategic actors in institutional fields," *Organization Studies* May-June, 2003

[1860] Id.

aspects of anti-Patriot resolutions. There are many claims and still more hope about what such resolutions can achieve. For example, the BODRC has claimed the following:

> This movement of bottom-up grassroots democracy has markedly expanded the national level of awareness about current and forthcoming legislation that directly threatens civil liberties, and has given U.S. citizens and noncitizens a means to act locally and to demonstrate to Congressional representatives that their constituents care deeply about the rights and liberties guaranteed by the Constitution and Bill of Rights. We have seen that when grassroots groups work toward a common goal, they can make their voices heard on a statewide and national level.[1861]

According to the BORDC, there are the following objectives to be achieved, and judge, the success and failures, achievements and failings of individual resolutions and the movement as a whole:

> "The movement's ultimate goals are to ensure that: Civil liberties and rights outlined in the Constitution and Bill of Rights are understood, restored, observed, and protected; and
> Proposed laws and policy changes that may impact rights and liberties are subject to rigorous, open national debate." [1862]

The above espoused goals and objectives can be reduced to one, i.e., promoting and restoring democratic values in America. In terms of substantive achievements, the individual anti-Patriot resolution and national movement can be measured in two observable dimensions:

(1) Whether the resolutions/movement has contributed to the "understanding" of the Bill of Rights?
(2) Whether the resolutions/movement has contributed to the "restoration" of the Bill of Rights?

On Understanding of Constitution and Bill of Rights

How might it be said that the anti-Patriot resolution(s)/ movement contribute to the understanding of Bill of Rights and Constitution? There are two types of evidence, i.e., first, quantity and quality of information made available to the public on the USAPA. Second, the extent to which people have gained a deeper understanding and renew appreciation of the Constitution and Bill of Rights, in terms of threats posed or protection afforded.

In terms of the first kind of evidence, it is clear that the local and national anti-Patriot resolution campaign have generated substantial and continue media interests, reaching every levels of government and penetrating different sectors of society. Judging by the number of resolutions passed alone,[1863] 409 communities, large vs. small, East vs. Midwest – West, red

---

[1861] http://www.bordc.org/involved/conf-purp.php
[1862] http://www.bordc.org/involved/conf-purp.php
[1863] This figure does not take into account of those resolutions efforts which were aborted, failed or underway still. In terms of informational and educational value, the fate and disposition of a resolution hardly matter. Indeed, it can be argued that a resolution which goes down in fame perhaps achieve more publicity, spark more controversy and engender more debate than one that passes smoothly without objections. It is interesting to

vs. blue, the nation has come together to argue and deliberate and over the propriety and wisdom, and effectiveness and efficacy of the resolutions. Each of these processes afforded the citizens and community an opportunity to engage the Constitution and Bill of Rights and to debate the pros and cons of the USAPA. Judging by media interests, the fight over USAPA attracts media attention and captures audience interests with fierce confrontation, black-white issues, diabolic nemesis,[1864] locally and nationally, in print, TV or blog.

One such media event is that the Attorney General Ashcroft's 18 states, 16 cities tour and media campaign in defense of the legitimacy, necessity and effectiveness of the USAPA.[1865] The tour was not successful in changing minds and attracting converts. But it did more to publicize the cause of BODRC and educate the public to the facts and issues surrounding the USAPA debate, than any one can hope for. For example, the Attorney General Ashcroft courted a fight with the librarians with following ill conceived and most inflammatory statement:

> "You might, for instance, believe the hysteria behind this claim: "Your local public library is under siege by the FBI."..."Why were you at the library? What were you reading? Did you see anything suspicious? Just the facts, ma'am. Just the facts." This image is fanciful, but the hysteria behind it is very real. The fact is, with just 11,000 FBI agents and over a billion visitors to America's libraries each year, the Department of Justice has neither the staffing, the time nor the inclination to monitor the reading habits of Americans. No offense to the American Library Association, but we just don't care."[1866]

On Restoration of Constitution and Bill of Rights

In assessing the achievement of this goal, it is necessary to find evidence of gains in Constitutionalism, i.e., a personal belief, government culture and national ethos that subscribe to the view that: "Government in which power is distributed and limited by a system of laws that must be obeyed by the rulers."[1867]

---

note that the BORDC does not keep track of its failures. In this regard, a comprehensive and competent assessment of the anti-Patriot movement cannot be completely achieved.

[1864] "Attorney General John Ashcroft's Assault on Civil Liberties (Updated September 2003) (10/30/2002)" (The AG accused of "Bold and Regressive Steps to Violate Civil Liberties in the Wake of September 11," "Undermining the Effective Enforcement of Civil Rights Laws," and other misdeeds, e.g., "Continues to use demagoguery to intimidate those who would question his policies." http://www.aclu.org/safefree/general/17658leg20021030.html

[1865] "Ashcroft kicks off campaign to defend Patriot Act," CNN.com Tuesday, August 19, 2003 Posted: 3:08 PM EDT (1908 GMT). http://www.cnn.com/2003/LAW/08/19/ashcroft.patriot.act/index.html Ashcroft tour was reported by all major media outlets, generating its own controversy. Jackie Northam, "Ashcroft Praises Patriot Act Successes." *NPR.* August 19, 2003; Timothy Lynch, "Patriotic Questions: Addressing the Patriot Act." *NOR.* August 21, 2003, 3:30 p.m.; Chuck McCutcheon, "Reno Criticizes Ashcroft's Tour for Patriot Act," *Cleveland Plain Dealer*, Tuesday, August 26, 2003; Sarah B. Miller, "In Defense of the Patriot Act," *Christian Science Monitor* August 20, 2003; Michael Isikoff, "Ashcroft's Campaign to Shore Up the Patriot Act," *Newsweek* August 25, 2003; Declan McCullagh, " Ashcroft stumps for Patriot Act,"The attorney general embarks on an unusual nationwide tour to drum up support for the controversial USAPA. *CNET News.com* August 20, 2003, 4:35 PM PDT; "Bill of Rights Defense Committee and American Muslim Voice Challenge Ashcroft to Publicize His Appearances and to Engage in Open Debate With Critics," *American Muslim Voices* September19, 2003.; Kevin Johnson and Toni Locy, "Patriot Act at heart of Ashcroft's influence," *USA TODAY* September 15, 2003.

[1866] Remarks of Attorney General John Ashcroft, "Protecting Life and Liberty," Memphis, Tennessee. DOJ. Press Release. September 18, 2003. http://www.usdoj.gov/archive/ag/speeches/2003/091803memphisremarks.htm

[1867] http://education.yahoo.com/reference/dictionary/entry/constitutionalism, See also "Constitutionalism" Stanford Encyclopedia of Philosophy (SEP). http://plato.stanford.edu/entries/constitutionalism/

In terms of objective measures, again one can adduce two kinds of evidence. First, 5 years on, there are increasing evidence that constitutional values and rights taken away by the USAPA and related counter-terrorism measures are being successfully restored. In this regard, one can point to the successful establishment of "civil liberties safe zone" all across the nation. Alternatively, and more directly, one can point to successful litigations in rolling back USAPA and effective legislation in restoring people's civil liberties. Lastly, with the change of Party in Congress after the 2006 election, Congressional committees are again demanding accountability from the Bush administration and Inspector Generals of DOJ are begin to compile reports on FBI's failing.

On a still larger compass, we can look at how people's faith in constitutional government is being restored.

In this last regard, the public welcome the thought that their grassroots efforts received national attention.

First, advocates of the anti-Patriot resolutions hope that the resolutions will speak directly to the U.S. Congress and their representatives, informing them of the wishes of the people and the gravity of the concerns. For example, in the debate leading up to the passage of the one of the resolutions, activist Norm Wallen observed that "it was important for cities to show that a great many people oppose the stuff in the PATRIOT Act and it is an effective way to get laws changed--if you have enough cities pass resolutions, Congress has to listen."[1868]

Second, there are some evidences that the anti-Patriot movements are affecting the voting pattern of legislators. The first kind of evidence is supplied by voting records of federal lawmakers. As it turns out legislators from "civil rights free zone" with anti-Patriot resolutions is more likely to support effort to abolish or revise the USAPA, upon renewal.[1869]

Legitimacy of Anti-Patriot Movement

The last issue to be discussed is whether the anti-Patriot resolutions and movement is a legitimate exercise of people's power. Clearly the Congress has spoken and the judicial branch has relented. Equally clear, a war time presidency has been established. What rights do the local communities possess in resisting the USAPA, openly?

In the course of constitutional history, there are repeated attempts by lawyers, judges, scholars and laypersons to find legitimacy in institutional players – executive, judicial, legislative branches – to make and enforce laws. All agree that government cannot long survive without some semblance of legitimacy and authority.[1870]

[1868] Heidi Walters, "Acts of patriotism: Flagstaff's struggle to define its rights revives democratic roots," *Las Vegas Mercury*. Thursday, July 03, 2003

[1869] "Patriot Act Resolutions Affect Congressional Votes." *NYTBORDC* August 15, 2005 http://www.nycbordc.org/index.php?option=com_contentandtask=viewandid=95andItemid=44 (Of the 171 House members who opposed part or whole of the H.R. 3199, the USA PATRIOT and Terrorism Prevention Reauthorization Act of 2005 represented 301 communities with resolutions. Only 85 resolution communities were represented by 257 members who supported the bill. If we further look at the House votes on a motion to recommit the bill H.R. 3199 which called for reinstatement of sunset to 16 controversial provision, we find that "a total of 312 resolutions had passed in the districts of the 209 who voted in favor of the motion, compared to 74 resolutions in the districts of the 218 who voted against it.") http://www.nycbordc.org/index.php?option=com_contentandtask=viewandid=95andItemid=44

[1870] Normal Lefstein, Vaughan Stapleton and Lee Teitelbaum, "In Search of Juvenile Justice: Gault and Its Implementation," *Law and Society Review*, Vol. 3(4): 491 – 562 (1969) (Tacit non-compliance with Supreme Court mandate resulting from lack of legitimacy.) Richard J. Medale, Leonard Zeitz and Paul Alexander, "Custodial Police Interrogation in Our Nation's capital: The Attempt to Implement Miranda," 66 *Michigan Law Review* 1347 p 1422 (1968).

To describe he USAPA as legitimate is to concede the authority of the Congress and Court to regulate the nation's affairs; a legitimate political authority is one which has a right to command respect and demand obedience, to be secured by force, if need be.

How might it be said the anti-Patriot movement is a legitimate challenge to USAPA? Doctrinally, it has been suggested that state illegitimacy allows the citizens to ignore the social contract, in seeking passive civil disobedience, if not active militant rebellion. H.L.A. Hart implied that much in his formulation of the "secondary rule" as a condition precedent to the establishment of valid government laws and regulations.[1871] Rawls are more circumspect. He made clear that civil disobedience should not be engaged in lightly, and only resorted to in limited cases when fundamental moral principles are breached and no remedies are available.[1872] Finally while Aristotle argued for strict obedience in the name of moral obligation to follow disagreeable rule of a state,[1873] Marx proposed a right to rebel in the name of class justice.[1874] There are thus ample political theories justifying challenges to USAPA, individually and collectively.

But what of collective resistance to formally promulgate laws? How can "illegitimate" laws, the likes of USAPA, be challenged, by groups like BORDC?

The answer rests in a renew understanding of Constitution norm. The classical view is that, the established meaning of the Constitution – as interpreted by the Court (in opinion) or applied by the Congress (as legislation) – enjoys presumptive validity, until being successfully challenged and formally changed by the people.

But do the anti-Patriot activists have the right to refuse to obey a law (USAPA) that has passed Congress, be it under the most usual circumstances?

The answer rests in our understanding of Constitutionalism. First to observe is that Constitutionalism as the culture of a nation and habits of a people, is not the same as Constitutional rules. Same can be observed of the distinction between rule of law and rule by law. People should follow the Constitution, if and only if it is agreeable with the fundamental percepts embedded in Constitutionalism.

> Constitutionalism is the idea, often associated with the political theories of John Locke and the "founders" of the American republic, that government can and should be legally limited in its powers, and that its authority depends on its observing these limitations[1875]

Ultimately, it is the people's idea and action which determine whether certain Constitutional norm is considered legitimate and worth following. Here whether the Constitution has changed so much after 9/11 that it can no longer be said compatible with the people's understanding of Constitutionalism, from limited government to open governance?

How do the people decide? The Constitution, as a living document detailing the relationship between the govern and the governed, must reflect the metamorphosis of such a relationship; defining anew every moment and reflecting people's changing idea and ideal of

---

[1871] H.L.A. Hart, *The Concept of Law* (London: Oxford University Press, 1961), Chapter 2.

[1872] John Rawls, "The Justification of Civil Disobedience." In Richard E. Flathman (ed.) Concepts in Social and Political Philosophy (New York: McMillan, 1974).

[1873] Plato, "The Crito'. In *The Last Days of Socrates* (Penguin Classics, 1969), pp. 28-9

[1874] Marx-Engles, *The Communist Manifesto* (1848) ("Law, morality, religion are to him (the proletarian) so many bourgeois prejudices, behind which lurk in ambush just as many bourgeois interests.").

[1875] "Constitutionalism." The Stanford Encyclopedia of Philosophy First published Wed Jan 10, 2001; substantive revision Tue Feb 20, 2007.

what that relationship entails and portents. In fact, the Constitution must be fine tuned to the developing needs and changing aspirations of the people in point of time and within given circumstances. In theory if not in practice, a constitutional convention should be held continuously to monitor the constitutional sentiments of the people, much like the NYSE index gauging the economic pulse of the nation.

In pursuing grass-roots resistance all across the nation, the resisters have earned their legitimacy by defeating the USAPA in 408 communities, large and small, one by one, all over the country. The people have spoken. It is now the government's turn to listen. That is what democracy is all about.

Chapter 8

USAPA: A PRELIMINARY ASSESSMENT

"Recommendation: The burden of proof for retaining a particular governmental power should be on the executive ..."

9/11 Commission (2004)[1876]

I. INTRODUCTION

The USAPA was a controversial piece of legislation right from the start and down to the last detail. Everything about the Act in its short life - from how it was enacted, e.g., speed, to how it was implemented, e.g., secrecy, to how it was promoted, e.g. fear, to how it was received, e.g., grassroots resistance, spells trouble for our constitutional democracy. The ensuing USAPA debate revisits, as it redefines, old constitutional issues, revives, as it recasts, entrenched political divisions and renews, as it reinforces, bitter ideological conflicts. A new constitutional order is in the making. As public intellectual and one time Presidential hopeful Pat Buchanan observed:

> "As polarized as we have ever been, we Americans are locked in a cultural war for the soul of our country. What is it all about? As columnist Sam Francis writes, it is about power; it is about who determines "the norms by which we live, and by which we define and govern ourselves." Who decides what is right and wrong, moral and immoral, beautiful and ugly, healthy and sick? Whose beliefs shall form the basis of law?" [1877]

Looking back at history, the promulgation and reception of USAPA resembled that of other war time legislations and emergency measures, such as U.S. Sedition Act (16 May, 1918) during WWI;[1878] Palmer Raids (1918 – 19210) in the war against Communism;[1879]

[1876] Chapter 12: "What to do? A global strategy," *911 Commission* (2004).

[1877] Patrick J. Buchanan, "The Cultural War for the Soul of America," September 14, 1992. http://www.buchanan.org/pa-92-0914.html For a conservative critique of liberalism, see Robert Bork, *Slouching towards Gomorrah* (Harper Collins, 1996).

[1878] "The Montana Sedition Project." A project of the University of Montana School of Journalism Project Director: Professor Clemens P. Work.

Japanese Internment (1942 – 1945) in WWII; [1880] McCarthyism (1952-4) during the cold war.[1881] View in this historical context, USAPA does not really create a new constitutional threat, as much as it gives vent to recurring constitutional problems.

As a conclusion, this final chapter investigates into four major issues: (1) Can the quick passage of the USAPA be explained? (2) Is the USAPA necessary? (3) Is the USAPA effective in fighting terrorism? (4) Lastly and most important, on the balance, is the USAPA worth the price?

This chapter is organized into seven sections. After the "Introduction", Section II ("More questions than answers") contextualizes this study by summarizing, in brief, some of the arguments for and against the USAPA. Section III ("How was the USAPA enacted?") explains the quick passage of the USAPA in contextual, procedural and substantive terms. It concludes that the legislative process while flawed is not unusual given established legislative protocol in place and dire circumstances of 9/11 of the time. Section IV addresses the issue: "Is the USAPA necessary?" It observes that the USAPA is not necessary to address many of the 9/11 related security problems raised. Section V studies the "The Effectiveness of USAPA". It finds that the USAPA has not been properly applied and enforced. Section VI: "Moral Calculus" discusses and debates the cost of the USAPA. Finally, Section VII: "Conclusion" summarizes the book, concluding with the observation that more studies are needed to fully understand the impact and implications of the USAPA to our constitutional culture, political system, judicial process and social life, i.e., on every aspects of American way of life.

II. MORE QUESTIONS THAN ANSWERS

At a public forum on November 18, 2003, [1882] U.S. Attorney Randy Chartash made the following, all too familiar and well rehearsed[1883] arguments in support of the USAPA:[1884]

(1) The USAPA is legal. It passed the Congress by wide margins. The USAPA passed the House on October 24, 2001 by a vote of 357 to 66, and passed the Senate the next day, October 25, 2002, by a vote of 98 to 1.

(2) The USAPA is constitutional. It has not been declared unconstitutional by any federal court, thus far.[1885]

[1879] A. Mitchell Palmer, "The Case Against the Reds," Part III: "Peacemaking, 1919-1920," *Radicalism and the Red Scare, World War I At Home: Readings on American Life, 1914-1920.* (John Wiley and Sons, Inc.: New York, pp. 185-189.

[1880] For background of Japanese Internment, see *Toyosaburo Korematsu* v. *United States* (323 U.S. 214, 65 S. Ct. 193 (1944).

[1881] Ellen Schrecker, *The Age of McCarthyism* (Bedford Books of St. Marvin's Press, 1994).

[1882] "Patriot Act: Trading Liberty for Security?" co-sponsored by Atlanta Press Club and the Internet and Public Policy Project of Georgia Tech's School of Public Policy (November 20, 2003.) Panelists include: Bob Barr, Former Congressman from Georgia and Randy Chartash, U.S. Department of Justice.

[1883] Under Karl Rove, the Bush administration is a well oiled propaganda machine. The Department of Justice has adopted a certain contrived, rehearsed and synchronized approach the defense of the USAPA.

[1884] Hear audio debate: "Patriot Act: Trading Liberty for Security?"www.IP3.gatech.edu

[1885] Since then the federal courts have struck down part of the USAPA in two instances. Dan Eggen, "Key Part of Patriot Act Ruled Unconstitutional Internet Providers' Data at Issue," *Washington Post.* Thursday, September 30, 2004; Page A16. For court judgment in the case, see *Doe and ACLU v. Ashcroft et al.,* No. 04-CIV-2614 (Judge Victor Marreo, Southern District of New York, prohibited the use of "National Security Letters" to

(3) The USAPA powers have not been abused by the government. For example, Senate Feinstein (D-CA) office reported receiving 21,434 letters complaining about the USAPA. Over half of those complaints are not with provisions related to the USAPA.

(4) The USAPA is necessary. Particularly, the FBI and CIA need to share criminal information and foreign intelligence bearing upon terrorists' identity, intent, capacity, plan and where about.

(5) The USAPA needs to keep up with change. It updates Title III wiretapping law and electronic surveillance law to keep pace with technological advancement, e.g., "roving wiretap" is necessary to deal with disposable mobile phones and "routing and addressing" is necessary to "track and trace" internet messages' origination and destination.

(6) The USAPA powers are not new. For example, criminal investigators have used "sneak and peek" (delay notice) warrants for decades to investigate organized crimes and grand jury has power to subpoena "business documents" including library records.

(7) The USAPA provides for ample check and balance. For example, in order to obtain a Section 215 order, the government needs judicial approval.

Former Congressmen Bob Barr argued the case against USAPA:

(1) Post 9/11 counter-terrorism measures, including USAPA, marks a fundamental shift in constitutional culture in this country.

(2) The USAPA allows for the investigation of a suspected terrorist based on a *mere* suspicion.

(3) The USAPA powers are not necessary. 9/11 happened because the government failed to share and utilize the information they have on the terrorists.

(4) The Bush administration is using 9/11 as an excuse to grab more power. The neo-con use 9/11 to move pass such laws.

The issues raised by U.S. Attorney Randy Chartash and Congressman Bob Barr above are not likely to be resolved in the short term, if at all. The debate over the USAPA is going to last for a long time, if not forever. More research and reflection on the wider influence, deeper impact, longer implications and lasting meaning of the USAPA on America, is necessary. As intimated by the heading of this section, five years since 911, there are more questions than answers. Particularly, we know far too little about the legislation and implementation, performance and utility of the Act. To some of these questions and issues we now turn.

---

obtain ISP customer and business records without judicial oversight. The court also found USAPA gag provision to be an "unconstitutional prior restraint" on free speech.")

III. How Was the USAPA Enacted?

After 9/11, there was panic in the nation,[1886] pandemonium in the Capital[1887] and shock and awe around the world.[1888] Soon after, panic transformed into solidarity, pandemonium turned into resolve, and shock and awe became sympathy and empathy.

9/11 united the nation and mobilized a people[1889] for an epic war of good vs. evil against terror.[1890] In the process, 9/11 was expropriated by the Bush administration to campaign for a national security state at home[1891] and exploited by the neo-conservative[1892] to revive an American empire abroad.[1893] The passage of USAPA is to be understood in this larger social (emotive) and political (utilitarian) context.

USAPA Is Supported by the Public

It is important to begin with a basic fact – a majority of the public[1894] supported most aspects of the USAPA.[1895] Since 9/11 survey after survey shows that the public are willing to

---

[1886] Mark A. Schuster, Bradley D. Stein, Lisa H. Jaycox, Rebecca L. Collins, Grant N. Marshall, Marc N. Elliott, Annie J. Zhou, David E. Kanouse, Janina L. Morrison, and Sandra H. Berry, "A National Survey of Stress Reactions after the September 11, 2001, Terrorist Attacks," *New England Journal of Medicine*, Volume 345 (20):1507-1512 (November 15, 2001) (The nation wide survey conducted 3-5 days after 911 found that 44% experienced substantial stress and 90 % with some stress. 47 percent were worried about safety of themselves or love ones. They coped with 911 through talking (98 %), religion (90 %), collective activities (60 %), and donations (36 %). For similar study in NYC, see Galea, S., Ahern, S., Resnick, H., et al. March 2002. "Psychological Sequelae of the September 11 Terrorist Attacks in New York City." *New England Journal of Medicine*. Volume 346:982-987 (March 28, 2002) (In a more localized survey of people in NYC, the stress level was found to be acute. A survey conducted two months after 911 showed that those who lived in and around WTC suffered from Post Traumatic Stress Disorder (PTSD). 7.5% of those who lived further away in northern Manhattan experienced symptoms of PTSD and 9.7 reported symptoms of depression.)

[1887] "Chronology of anthrax events," Sun-Sentinel http://www.sun-sentinel.com/sfl-1013anthraxchronology.story There were suggestions that the anthrax attacked was manufactured by domestic power brokers to create an environment of fear to usher in the USAPA. Richard J. Ochs, "Government By Anthrax," Free from Terror (revised June 9, 2002) http://www.freefromterror.net/other_articles/gov_anthrax.html#_edn13.

[1888] For a rejoinder: "The Economist (September 15, 2001) describes the terror attacks on the World Trade Center as "the day the world changed." But the real world we are living with has not changed as a result of the tragedy. The biggest problems and challenges our mankind is facing, such as poverty, pollution, old and new epidemics are only getting worse.... everyone is telling American stories even though these stories are irrelevant to their life." See "Abstract" to Li Xiguang and Lu Yanan, "From "Our war" to "their war" - The impact of 911 journalism on Chinese press," Center for International Communications Studies, Tsinghua University Beijing , China , 100084. International Conference on SARS and Bird-flu, Beijing, August 20-22, 2004. http://www.media.tsinghua.edu.cn/iwpc/print.php?ID=82andcId=7

[1889] Charles M. Madigan, "War on Terror. A Survey: It made us cry and united us, - Taking the pulse of the Chicago area after Sept. 11, a study finds prayer, patriotism, pride, support," *Chicago Tribune*, October 14, 2001. http://www.chicagotribune.com/news/nationworld/chi-011013survey.story?coll=chi-news-hed

[1890] Mat Coleman, "The naming of 'terrorism' and evil 'outlaws': geopolitical place-making after 11 September," *Geopolitics* Volume 8 (3): 87 – 104 (2003); R.L. Ivie, "Evil Enemy Versus Agonistic Other: Rhetorical Constructions of Terrorism," *The Review of Education Pedagogy and Cultural Studies*, Volume 25 (3): 181 – 200 (2003).

[1891] C. William Michaels, *No Greater Threat: America After September 11 And The Rise Of A National Security State* (Algora Publishing 2002).

[1892] "Neoconservatism." Wikipedia, the free encyclopedia

[1893] The American Empire Project. http://www.americanempireproject.com/americanempireproject.htm

[1894] James Jay Carafano and Paul Rosenzweig, "A Patriotic Day: 9/11 Commission Recognizes Importance of the Patriot Act," WebMemo #480, April 15, 2004. Heritage Foundation. http://www.heritage.org/ Research/HomelandDefense/wm480.cfmJohn Hawkins, "The Security And Freedom Trade-Off" January 20,

do what they can to support the government in fighting terrorism. For example, on November 12, 2001, NPR/Kaiser Family Foundation/ Kennedy School of Government conducted a national survey on Civil Liberties. The following question was asked:

"25a. In order to reduce the threat of terrorism in the US, would you support or oppose giving law enforcement broader authority to do the following things? Would you support or oppose giving them broader authority to (Insert each item)?"

The survey question elicited the following responses.

Five years later, the public are still very much behind the USAPA. For example, according to a survey conducted by CNN/USA Today/Gallup Poll. Between Jan. 6-8, 2006 with 1,003 adults nationwide (MoE ± 3), only 7% think that USAPA should be eliminated altogether:

"Based on what you have heard or read about the Patriot Act, do you think all of its provisions should be kept, that it needs minor changes, that it needs major changes, or that it needs to be eliminated completely?" (1/6-8/06). All should be kept (13%). Needs Minor Changes (50%). Needs major changes (24%). To be eliminated entirely (7%).[1896]

Upon a closer inspection, it appears that the overwhelming public support for the USAPA might have resulted from mass ignorance and blind patriotism.[1897] There is mounting evidence to suggest that the public supported the USAPA without critically examining the content of the law or rationally reflecting upon the consequences of the Act. They did so based on blind faith.[1898] For example, Gallup Poll shows that in 2003 around 47% to 50% of the public knows very little about the USAPA. In 2005, the ignorance rate jumped to 57%.

2006. http://www.rightwingnews.com/ The Republicans support Bush's war on terror on political – ideological ground. The, general public finds Bush's "zealotry and "bigotry" refreshing and mesmerizing. However, it is also true that the conservatives are breaking ranks. See Bob Bar, "Patriot Act Games" *American Conservative Union* (August 19, 2003). http://www.conservative.org/columnists/barr/030819bb.asp The liberals are against the USAPA because it infringes on people's rights while the conservatives are against the USAPA because it expands the powers of government. Conservative Voices Against the USAPA (4/15/2004) http://www.aclu.org/safefree/general/17244res20040415.html

[1895] "War On Terrorism". *PollingReport.com* http://www.pollingreport.com/terror.htm

[1896] *Id.*

[1897] There were suggestions that the Bush administration generated public fear and induced mass ignorance with deceptive government propaganda and inflammatory political rhetoric. While such facts are rarely in dispute, e.g. watering down of FIOA or hyping of terrorism, the attribution of intention and charting of the impact rarely is. Stephen Kiehl, "Secrecy on the rise: In post-911 era, many public records aren't very public," *Baltimore Sun*, March 13, 2005.

[1898] To describe the constitutional choices made by uninformed and emotive public as based on "blind faith", while unassailably true empirically, is nevertheless objectionable on political - philosophical grounds. One can hardly question the decision of the majority in a constitutional democracy if one does not agree with the result! In a democracy, most argument over policy issues result from a disagreement over facts and differences of values. A legitimate question is raised as to whether a functional deliberative democracy requires an informed public engaging in *rational* debate, before public choices can be deemed too be politically legitimate and morally correct, attracting deference and entitling respect.

Table 1. Post 911 public opinion survey on empowering law enforcement to reduce terrorism

	Support	Oppose	Don't know
a. Wiretap telephones	69	29	2
b. Intercept e-mail	72	23	5
c. Intercept ordinary mail	57	39	4
d. Examine internet activity	82	15	3
e. Detain suspects for a week without charging them	58	38	3
e. Detain terrorist suspects indefinitely without charging them	48	48	4
f. Examine students' education records	76	22	2
g. Examine telephone records	82	17	1
h. Examine bank records	79	20	1
i. Track credit card purchases	75	21	4
j. Examine tax records	75	24	1

Source: Adapted from National poll conducted by NPR/Kaiser Family Foundation/ Kennedy School of Government on Civil Liberties.

More tellingly, a national survey conducted between December 2001 and January 2002 shows that librarians' awareness and understanding of the USAPA were very low. The survey shows that barely 50% (57.7%) of the respondents have "read or heard" about the USAPA. The correct understanding of different issues about the USAPA was still lower. Understanding ranges from a low of 20.8% (allow delayed execution of warrant to consult with lawyer) to a high of 47.6% (allow access to record without warrant).[1899] This is

---

[1899] Leigh S. Estabrook, "Public Libraries' Response to the Events of September 11th, A National Survey Conducted by the Library Research Center at the University of Illinois Graduate School of Library and Information Science." January 22, 2003. Library Research Center, Graduate School of Library and Information Science, University of Illinois at Urbana Champaign. January 22, 2003 http://www.lis.uiuc.edu/gslis/research/national.pdf

troublesome. If the librarians, who were interested in and capable of understanding the USAPA were not informed of the content of the law, the public should fare worse.

Table 2. Public knowledge of USAPA: August 2003 – April 2005

What do you know about the USAPA?				
Date	A Lot	Some	Not Much	Nothing
Aug 25-26 2003	10%	40%	25%	25%
Nov 10-12 2003	12%	41%	25%	22%
Feb 16-17 2004	13%	46%	27%	14%
Apr 13-16 2005	13%	28%	28%	29%

Public support of the USAPA also appeared to be driven by blind patriotism instead of informed consent. Even Dan Rather, a committed journalist and true liberal, broke down in tears twice when interviewed by Letterman right after 911, proclaiming: "George Bush is the president...He makes the decisions, and . . . wherever he wants me to line up, just tell me where."[1900]

As time goes by, putting some much needed distance between the raw emotion of 911 and cold reality of Bush war on terror, the public become increasingly concerned about the impact of the USAPA on civil liberties and their lives. However, the public is still very much confused as to what stance to take on liberty vs. security trade offs.[1901] For example, a February 16-17 of 2004 survey of 501 people shows that 71% disapprove of secret search by law enforcement officials under the USAPA. [1902] According another USA TODAY/CNN/Gallup Poll, people are increasingly concerned that the government is going too far[1903] with the indiscriminate use of USAPA to fight terrorism:[1904]

The USAPA is also a most difficult piece of legislation to comprehend. The structure and content, length and complexity, application and interpretation of the law is not easily accessible to the people, comprehensible to policy makers, and agreed to experts. The USAPA can only be deciphered after extensive research and in depth analysis; a feat that could not have been completed within the time allotted for debate.[1905]

[1900] John Powers, "The Other Texan: Dan Rather's *Evening News* exit," *LA Weekly* March 11 – 17, 2005. http://www.laweekly.com/ink/05/16/on-powers.php

[1901] Toni Locy, "Patriot Act blurred in the public mind," *USA Today.com* Posted 2/25/2004 4:34 PM Updated 2/26/2004 9:32 AM

[1902] http://www.usatoday.com/news/washington/2004-02-25-patriot-main_x.htm

[1903] See "Democrats call for investigation of NSA wiretaps," *CNN* Monday, December 19, 2005 http://www.cnn.com/2005/POLITICS/12/18/bush.nsa/ and Seymour M. Hersh, "Torture at Abu Ghraib: American soldiers brutalized Iraqis. How far up does the responsibility go?" *New Yorker* Issue of 2004-05-10.

[1904] USA Today/CNN/Gallup Poll results. 5/20/2005. http://www.usatoday.com/news/polls/tables/live/2004-02-25-patriot-act-poll.htm

[1905] A typical section looks like this: "Section 5341(b) of title 31, United States Code, is amended by adding at the end the following: (12) Data Regarding Funding of Terrorism- Data concerning money laundering efforts related to the funding of acts of international terrorism, and efforts directed at the prevention, detection, and prosecution of such funding.' See Jon Thibault, "Patriot Act 101" *FrontPage Magazine. com* April 1, 2004. http://www.frontpagemagazine.com/Articles/ReadArticle.asp?ID=12801

Table 3. Based on what you have read or heard, do you think the Patriot Act goes too far, is about right, or does not go far enough in restricting people's civil liberties in order to fight terrorism?

	Too far	About right	Not far enough	No opinion
2004 Feb 16-17	26	43	21	10
2003 Nov 10-12 ^	25	45	20	10
2003 Aug 25-26 ^	22	48	21	9
^ Asked of a half sample.				

Table 4. Does the USAPA go too far?

Date	Too Far	Not Too Far[*]
Aug 25-26 2003	22%	69%
Nov 10-12 2003	25%	65%
Feb 16-17 2004	26%	64%
Apr 13-16 2005	45%	49%
[*]Responded as it is a Necessary Tool, About Right, or Not Far Enough		

Finally, the Bush administration "demanded" that the USAPA be passed quickly. Legislators were told to be patriotic. They were threatened political consequences if they fail to vote for the Act. An agreed version of the USAPA in Congress was jettisoned only to be substituted with a White House version in the ninth hour. Many of the lawmakers have no opportunity to read the USAPA before voting![1906]

Laboring under this set of exceptional circumstances and one of a kind emergency situation, the regular legislative process was suspended and the role of Congress redefined. Instead of representing the will of the people, the Congress answered to the command of an imperial President. Instead of providing check and balance to the executive branch of government, the Congress aided and abetted a dictatorial President. Instead of defending the rights of the people, the government helped turned the country into a national security state.[1907] In so doing, the Congress has relegated its legislative responsibility to vetting 9/11 related legislation actions. Instead, the Congress has passed numerous post 9/11 legislative measures without examination or debate.[1908]

In the first four months, a total of 91 Congressional actions were taken, 41 or 45% in the first day alone and 53 or 58.2% within the week. During the first months after 91/1, the Congress passed five major pieces of remedial legislations/actions: Airport Security -

---

[1906] Chapter 2: "Legislative Process".

[1907] Bernard Weiner, "America Two Years After 9/11: 25 Things We Now Know," *Scoop.com* Monday, 18 August 2003, 7:04 pm http://www.scoop.co.nz/stories/HL0308/S00130.htm

[1908] "Congress Since 9/11" *Congress Weekly Column* November 21, 2001 (Notwithstanding the fact that there was heightened security around the U.S. Capitol building – National Guard, troops at the doors, barricades in the streets, anthrax alarms in offices, absence of incoming mail" - "we are doing our part.") http://www.house.gov/petri/weekly/nov21_01.htm

Aviation and Transportation Act of 2001; The PATRIOT Act; 2001 Emergency Supplemental Appropriations Act for Recovery From and Response To Terrorist Attacks on the United States; The Air Transportation System Stabilization Act; Authorization for Use of Military Force, all without critical examination.[1909] This is an "enviable" legislative record, compare to normal time.

Table 5. The number of 9/11 legislative actions acted upon within six (6) months*

Bills/ Res.	1 D	2 D	1 W	2 W	3 W	4 W	1 M	2 M	3 M	4 M>	Total (%)
No.	41*	8	4	10	6	3	1	9	5	4	91 (100%)
%	45%	8.8%	4.4%	11%	6.6%	3.3%	1.1%	9.9%	5.5%	4.4%	
Total	45%	53.8%	58.2%	69.2%	75.3%	78.6%	79.7%	89.6%	95.1%	99.5%	

*Including 19 floor amendments
Source: Extracted from Margaret F. Klemm and Albert C. Ringelstein, "Congressional Response to the September 11, 2001 Terrorist Attacks," *extensions. A Journal of Carl Albert Center* (Fall 2002).

Still, the passage of the USAPA can be defended and justified on contextual, procedural and substantive grounds.[1910]

Legislative Context

Contextually, 911 was the first major "military' attack on American soil, since Pearl Harbor, except perhaps the bombing of WTC in 1993.[1911] America was at war.[1912] The magnitude, prospect and consequence of a future attack were unknown,[1913] and worse yet unknowable.[1914]

After 911, the American people were shell shocked.[1915] The nation needed to act quickly and resolutely;[1916] to close ranks and prepare for domestic defense,[1917] and to demonstrate

---

[1909] Margaret F. Klemm and Albert C. Ringelstein, "Congressional Response to the September 11, 2001 Terrorist Attacks," *extensions. A Journal of Carl Albert Center* (Fall 2002).

[1910] See DOJ, Preserving Life and Liberty web. http://www.lifeandliberty.gov/subs/h_patact.htm

[1911] Matthew V. Storin, "While America Slept: Coverage of Terrorism from 1993 to September 11, 2001." The Joan Shorenstein Center on the Press, Politics and Public Policy, Working Paper Series. 2002 – 7, Harvard University. http://www.ksg.harvard.edu/presspol/Research_Publications/Papers/Working_Papers/2002_7.pdf

[1912] U.S. Congress. Joint Resolution to Authorize the Use of United States Armed Forces against Those Responsible for the Recent attacks Launched Against the United States. (2001Public Law 107-40)

[1913] J.A. Boscarino, C.R. Figley, R.E. Adams, "Fear of terrorism in New York after the September 11 terrorist attacks: implications for emergency mental health and preparedness," *Int J Emerg Ment Health*. 5(4):199-209 (Fall 2003). (A survey of 1,001 New Yorkers in the community one year after the September 11 attacks showed that New Yorkers were fearful of future terrorist attacks, especially with WMD.)

[1914] This posed problems for risk managers and policy makers, i.e., how to cater for unknown risks.

[1915] Barbara Behrendt, "Finding lessons in rubble of tragedy," *St. Petersburg Times*, September 8, 2002 (Memory still fresh about 911, a year hence.) If one cares to look beyond the mainstream media and willing to dig below the surface, public opinions right after 911 were incredibly diverse, complex and nuanced, with some calling for retribution (from the enemy) and others contribution (from the U.S.), almost all called for a more critical re-examination of U.S.'s role in the world, starting with U.S. foreign – middle east policy, in order to stop the senseless cycles of violence. "Tuesday's tragic events are still unfolding. But it is already clear that our world has changed. We want to provide a forum for Common Dreams readers to express themselves." *CommonDreams* http://www.commondreams.org/911a.htm (Author's note: Since the Common Dreams is a

solidarity[1918] in the face of an invisible enemy and ill defined war.[1919] The USAPA is the first major legislation after 911 to show America's unity and resolve, to itself and the world. Any delay was deemed unacceptable. Any dissent was considered unthinkable.[1920]

Any assessment of the USAPA must not only focus on the substantive merit of the Act but also attend to its symbolic and psychological significance. For example, Attorney General John Ashcroft was very much concerned with sending the wrong message to our enemies if the Congress started to interrogate the USAPA in minutia or failed to pass the USAPA in one clean sweep:

> "To those who pit Americans against immigrants, citizens against non-citizens, to those who scare peace-loving people with phantoms of lost liberty, my message is this: Your tactics only aid terrorists for they erode our national unity and diminish our resolve …Charges of kangaroo courts and shredding the Constitution give new meaning to the term 'fog of war."
> [1921]

The nation's reaction to 911, including the quick passage of the USAPA, must be viewed in this light.

Legislative Procedure Is Not Flawed

Procedurally, contrary to conventional wisdom, the drafter of the USAPA Professor Viet Dinh argued that the Act had gone through a deliberate, all be it compressed and expedited, legislative process. "It is like sitting down and reading War and Peace in one or two sittings[1922] rather than reading one page in a thousand sittings, which is the normal legislative

---

progressive political forum, one would expect to find more diversity of opinions, and with it left to center ideas.) John Lukacs, *Democracy and Populism: Fear and Hatred* (Yale University Press, 2005)

[1916] Bush told the Congress: "Americans are asking: How will we fight and win this war? We will direct every resource at our command …to the disruption and to the defeat of the global terror network." "Address to a Joint Session of Congress and the American People" White House, September 20, 2001. http://www.whitehouse.gov/news/releases/2001/09/20010920-8.html

[1917] "Congress, N.Y. reaffirm solidarity," *Los Angeles Times*, September 7, 2002 (300 of the 535 of House and Senate members held a solemn joint meeting in New York's Federal Hall to pay tribute to 911.)

[1918] U.S. Congress. Joint Resolution Expressing the Sense of the Senate and House of Representatives Regarding the Terrorist Attacks Launched against the United States on September 11, 2001 (Public Law 107-39) (Condemnation of the September 11 attacks, condolences to the victims, thanking foreign leaders and individuals who have expressed solidarity, support for the determination of the President, and a declaration that September 12, 2001, shall be a National Day of Unity and Mourning.)

[1919] William Hamilton, "Bush Began to Plan War Three Months After 9/11: Book Says President Called Secrecy Vital," *Washington Post*, Saturday, April 17, 2004; Page A01. (Bush: "To me the big news is America has changed how you fight and win war, and therefore makes it easier to keep the peace in the long run.")

[1920] Bush said of the war on terror: "Over time it's going to be important for nations to know they will be held accountable for inactivity … You're either with us or against us in the fight against terror." See "You are either with us or against us," *CNN.com* November 6, 2001 Posted: 10:13 p.m. EST (0313 GMT)

[1921] "Ashcroft: Critics of new terror measures undermine effort," *CNN.Com* December 7, 2001 Posted: 9:58 AM EST (1458 GMT)

[1922] Whether *War and Peace* can be read in a short time and in one setting is precisely the issue. Professor Paul N. Edwards recommends reading a book three times; "each time for a different purpose and at a different level of detail …An awful lot of thinking and processing goes on when you're not aware of it…Your ability to comprehend and retain what you read drops off dramatically after a couple of hours….Therefore, you should read a book in several short sessions of one to two hours apiece, rather than one long marathon."). "How to

process." [1923] In essence, there was no short circuiting, but speeding up, of an otherwise slow, tedious and, to most informed insiders and critical outsiders, a seriously defunct legislative process.

As to the accusation that the law was not read by most before passage, Dinh has this to say: "how normally most laws are made and how often or seldom legislators actually read the laws or provisions they pass upon simply because they trust the process that result in the fine work on which they pass judgment." [1924]

If the account of USAPA legislative process by the key drafter of the Act (Dinh) and one of its major sponsors (Senate Hatch) were to be believed, USAPA was not rushed through Congress only for political gain, i.e., advancement of neo-conservative political philosophy and Republican - Bush legislative agenda. [1925]

Putting things in context, the legislative process leading to the passage of the USAPA can best be described as normal rather than abnormal and typical instead of atypical; exceptional for sure as compared to legislations in peace time but not extraordinary given the circumstances. After all, the USAPA is not the first emergency terrorism legislation where the legislative process has been shortchanged. There was the 1995 Oklahoma City bombing which necessitated the abandoning of regular Committee rule (Rule 14) in favor of legislating from the desk instead of on the floor. [1926]

As a rejoinder and reminder, Congressional leaders are quite conscious of the problems with rushed legislation. Thus quite apart from necessity with "compromised" emergency legislation process, there are persistent calls for legislative process reform, including those by the Republican Leadership Task Force on Deliberative Democracy which advocated for a more rational and deliberative process in 1993, "A bill that cannot survive a 3-day scrutiny of its provisions is a bill that should not be enacted. . . . The world's most powerful legislature cannot in good conscience deprive its membership of a brief study of a committee report prior to final action." [1927]

What then does a normal legislative process looks like, in the Congress and during normal legislative sessions? According to Brian Baird, a House representative (D - Washington State), the legislative process in Congress, even without a 911 crisis, is very much politicized, partisan and a flawed one:

In addition to this latest abuse of power, prominent examples from the 108th Congress include the Medicare prescription drug bill, the energy bill, the intelligence bill and the defense authorization bill. These important pieces of legislation total more than 2,900 pages

---

Read a Book: Guidelines for Getting the Most out of Non-Fiction Reading" (2000) School of Information, University of Michigan, http://www.si.umich.edu/~pne/PDF/howtoread.pdf

[1923] Topic: USAPA; Interview Subject: Viet Dinh; Film: The Cost of Freedom - Civil Liberties, Security and the USAPA; Interviewer: Alison Rostankowski/Chip Duncan; Transcripts: Troy Avdek © 2004 The Duncan Group, Inc. http://www.duncanentertainment.com/interview_vietdinh.php Senator Orrin Hatch, *Square Peg: Confessions of a Citizen Senator* (Basic Books, 2004)

[1924] *Id.*

[1925] Sut Jhally and Jeremy Earp, "Hijacking Catastrophe 9/11, Fear and the Selling of American Empire" (DVD) (Domestically, the President used 911 to consolidate his conservative base and secure political cowing over the liberals.)

[1926] Statement of Senator Patrick Leahy The Uniting And Strengthening of America Act Of 2001" ("USA ACT") (October 9, 2001) http://leahy.senate.gov/press/200110/100901a.html para. 13.

[1927] *Id.*

of text and authorize more than $1 trillion of spending. Yet, collectively they were available to members for less than 48 hours total for reading. [1928]

A *Boston Globe* investigative report (2004) provided further evidence to vindicate Dinh's factually well supported, all be it politically self-serving, observation. The report found that the legislative process in Congress is often bypassed, compromised and exploited by the Party in power for political gain. In the Bush era (as with Clinton time), the Republican Congress (2000 to 2006) has monopolized and manipulated the legislative process to pass legislation and consolidate power:

First, the House Rules Committee sometimes rewrote key passages of a bill reported out of committees to foreclose any debate or amendments on the house floor to secure passage. [1929]

Second, the Rules Committee commonly held late night sessions - nickname "the Dracula Congress" - as a strategy to keep opponents (democrats) in the dark. This secured passage of laws without consultation, participation or opposition from Democratic Party members.

Third, Republican Congressional conference committees added a record 3,407 "pork barrel" projects to the budget appropriations bill, without debate, vote or knowledge of the House and Senate.

Fourth, bills were crafted behind closed doors, e.g., the Medicare and energy bills, with few Democrats participating in key conference committee meetings.

Fifth, the number of legislative sessions and amount of time allotted for debate and reading of bills has dropped substantially, More and more bills are being passed under "emergency" procedures without in depth examination and lengthy debate. [1930]

Working under this inherited and inherently flawed legislative process and protocol, the Bush administration with the help of the Republicans and acquiescence of the Demarcates was able to rush the USAPA through Congress with little public consultation and minimal floor debate. [1931] The USAPA was drafted and agreed on by both Parties' ranking members and senior leadership. This was mainly achieved through behind the scene negotiation and off the record compromises. Clock room discussion, hall way negotiation and tit for tat exchanges is how business are conducted inside the beltway of Washington everyday. [1932]

[1928] Brian Baird, "We Need To Read The Bills." *Washington Post*, Saturday, November 27, 2004; Page A31

[1929] Susan Milligan, "Back-room dealing a Capitol trend GOP flexing its majority power," *Boston Globe*, October 3, 2004. (Republicans and Democrats on the House Judiciary Committee negotiated and compromised on key languages of the USAPA bill. However, the Rules Committee rewrote the bill to give the government more power, e.g., "sneak and peak", without further consultation with the House leadership. The House was then given one day to debate the mater.)

[1930] Susan Milligan, "The Globes major Findings," *Boston Globe*, October 3, 2004.

[1931] This raises a most interesting legal – constitutional question, i.e., whether a flawed legislative process can be effective challenged for lack of "legislative due process", procedurally and substantively. Particularly, when such lack of a process is attributable to dubious practices by the ruling party in the Congress. Hart L. A Hart argued that only law that has been passed in accordance with "secondary rule" (or law of laws) is considered law. Philip P. Frickey and Steven S Smith, "Judicial Review and the Legislative Process: Some Empirical and Normative Aspects of Due Process of Lawmaking" *UC Berkeley Public Law Research Paper* No. 63. http://ssrn.com/abstract=279433

[1932] Susan Milligan, "Back-room dealing a Capitol trend GOP flexing its majority power," *Boston Globe*, October 3, 2004. (The Republican controlled Congress, through procedural maneuvers in the Rules Committee denied the democrats full opportunity to read, digest, debate, and if need be amend, important bills before coming up for a vote, e.g., House members were given one day to examine and vote on a 400-plus-page Right of Patients bill.) http://boston.com/news/nation/articles/2004/10/03/back_room_dealing_a_capitol_trend?pg=full

USAPA Content Is Dated

Substantively, the USAPA is not altogether a brand new piece of legislation.[1933] Many of the provisions and most of the related issues have been proposed and discussed before, some of them several times. Specifically, many of the provisions in the USAPA have been proposed and defeated, in the 106th Congress (2000 – 2001). For example, President Clinton's proposed legislation sought to: (1) expand the scope, reach, and severity of Computer Fraud and Abuse Act (CFAA), the Wiretap Act, and the Cable Act; (2) streamline electronic surveillance through standardizing wiretap, pen register, and other information-gathering procedures for all types of communications.[1934]

Senators Hatch and Schumer proposed "Internet Integrity and Critical Infrastructure Protection Act of 2000"in order to federalize computer crimes (e.g., making unauthorized access of protected computer a federal crime without the $5000 damages/benefits threshold), enhance penalty structure (e.g., doubling of penalties, i.e., to 10 years for first offenses and from 10 to 20 years for subsequent offenses), authorize juvenile prosecution (i.e., without consulting state authorities for deferrals), expand wiretapping authority (i.e., adding terrorism as predicate offense) and lower privacy protection (e.g., allowing Pen registers/Trap and Trace Device without meaningful judicial oversight.)[1935]

Many of the law enforcement powers proposed by the USAPA already existed. In fact, many of the Act's powers have been routinely used to investigate organized crimes and drug offenses, e.g., "pen register" device, "track and trace" procedure and "sneak and peak" warrant. This has led Michael B. Mukasey, Chief Judge of the U.S. District Court in Manhattan, in defense of the USAPA to observe:

> "The electronic surveillance provisions give investigators access to cable-based communications, such as e-mail, on the same basis as they have long had access to telephone communications, and give them access to telephone communications in national security cases on the same basis on which they already have such access in drug cases…

[1933] President Bush, Attorney General Ashcroft, Viet Dinh and others. See for example, "Remarks by President George W. Bush at Signing of the Patriot Act, Anti-Terrorism Legislation." (October 26, 2001) ("Current statutes deal more severely with drug-traffickers than with terrorists. That changes today.") *Preserving life and Liberty Web.* http://www.lifeandliberty.gov/subs/speeches/p_bush_102601.htm

[1934] See for example, Clinton White House proposed legislation" "Enhancement of Privacy and Public Safety in Cyberspace Act, August 1, 2000" (S 3038 of 9/20/00 by Sen. Patrick Leahy (D-VT) "by request") For a the text of Clinton's proposed Enhancement of "Privacy and Public Safety in Cyberspace Act," see http://www.cdt.org/security/000801cybercrime_bill.pdf For "White House proposed legislative history: Enhancement of Privacy and Public Safety in Cyberspace Act." (August 1, 2000), see http://www.cdt.org/security/000801cybercrime.pdf For a textual analysis, see "CDT analysis of Clinton Administration proposed changes to Federal computer crime law." (Oct. 4, 2000) http://www.cdt.org/security/000801cybercrime.pdf

[1935] See also "Internet Integrity and Critical Infrastructure Protection Act of 2000" (S2448 of April 13, 2000 by Senators Hatch (R-UT) and Schumer (D-NY) (For a copy of the Hatch-Schumer Bill (S. 2448) (Apr. 14, 2000) see Hatch-Schumer Bill (S. 2448) Apr. 14, 2000. http://www.cdt.org/security/000414Hatch-Schumer.pdf For a section by section analysis, see "Hatch-Schumer S. 2448, "Internet Integrity and Critical Infrastructure Protection Act" http://www.cdt.org/security/000518leahyanalysis.shtml See also See Minority Staff Report-for Permanent Subcommittee on Investigations, Hearing on Private Banking and Money Laundering: "A Case Study of Opportunities and Vulnerabilities," 9th November, 1999; Minority Staff of the Permanent Subcommittee on Investigations, Report on Correspondent Banking: "A Gateway for Money Laundering." (5th February, 2001). See also "The USAPA: Preserving Life and Liberty" *DOJ – Life and Liberty* ("The Patriot Act allows investigators to use the tools that were already available to investigate organized crime and drug trafficking.") http://www.lifeandliberty.gov/ (Visited October 15, 2003)

The statute permits agents to delay disclosure of their presence to the person who controls the premises, again with court authorization. Here too, the logic seems obvious: If you leave behind a note saying "Good afternoon, Mr. bin Laden, we were here," that might betray the existence of an investigation and cause the subjects to flee or destroy evidence. There are analogous provisions that were in existence long before the Patriot Act permitting a delay in notifying people who are overheard on wiretaps, and for the same reason."[1936]

The purpose of USAPA, as Rep. Sensenbrenne viewed it, is not to give the FBI more authorities but to revise old investigative powers in light of new technology: "It brings the basic building blocks of a criminal investigation, pen registers and trap and trace provisions, into the 21st century to deal with e-mails and Internet communications."[1937] If true, the objections to the USAPA are much to do with nothing. The debate is not whether we should invent new counter-terrorism powers to hunt down terrorists but whether we should update our old police powers to keep up with terrorism, which have evolved, mutate and transformed with the change of time and improvement of technology. This recalls the controversy over constitutional "originalism" vs. "interpretationism" debate.[1938]

The observation of a flawed legislative process, leads necessarily to the question of whether the USAPA was well intended and appropriately designed to serve the nation's security interests and anti-terrorism needs, post 911.

Finally, we come to the debate over the necessity of USAPA: First, is it necessary to fight terrorism, e.g., does the FBI need more powers? Second, is it worth the social costs involved, e.g., should we trade liberty for security?[1939]

IV. IS THE USAPA NECESSARY?

Before 911, there were a plethora of independent commissioned studies, e.g. Bremer Commission (2000),[1940] government reports, e.g., DOS – Inspector General or GAO, and

---

[1936] Michael B. Mukasey, "'The Spirit of Liberty' Before attacking the Patriot Act, try reading it," *Wall Street Journal*, Monday, May 10, 2004 12:01 a.m. EDT http://www.opinionjournal.com/editorial/feature.html?id=110005059

[1937] 147 Cong. Rec. H7196 (daily ed. Oct. 23, 2001) (statement of Rep. Sensenbrenner). See also "The USAPA: Preserving Life and Liberty" *DOJ – Life and Liberty* ("The Patriot Act allows investigators to use the tools that were already available to investigate organized crime and drug trafficking.") http://www.lifeandliberty.gov/ (Visited October 15, 2003)

[1938] See Judge Richard A. Posner's *Overcoming Law* (1995). MARSH v. CHAMBERS, U.S. Supreme Court 463 U.S. 783 (1983) (Decided July 5, 1983) vs. GRISWOLD v. CONNECTICUT, U.S. Supreme Court, 381 U.S. 479 (1965) (Decided June 7, 1965) For a summary of the arguments, see "Theories of Constitutional Interpretation," *Exploring Constitutional Conflicts Web* http://www.law.umkc.edu/faculty/projects/ftrials/conlaw/interp.html

[1939] Report of an AAUP Special Committee: "Academic Freedom and National Security in a Time of Crisis" The American Association of University Professors (October 2003) http://www.aaup.org/statements/REPORTS/911report.htm See also Mark S. Hamm, "The USAPA and the Politics of Fear." In Jeff Ferrell et al., eds. *Cultural Criminology Unleashed*. (London: Glasshouse Press, 2004) (Meaningful research into the USAPA suffers from data availability problems. There is also difficulty in assessing the success or failure of the Act and whether it erode civil liberties), p. 19.

[1940] 2000: Countering the Changing Threat of International Terrorism, a report from the National Commission on Terrorism (Bremer Commission); 2001: Road Map for National Security: Imperative for Change, The Phase III Report of the U.S. Commission on National Security/21st Century (Hart Rudman Commission); 2001: The Advisory Panel to Assess Domestic Response Capabilities to Terrorism Involving Weapons of Mass Destruction (Gilmore Commission) (Third Annual Report); 2001: Deutch Commission on Weapons of Mass

Congressional hearing records, e.g., Senate Select Committee on Intelligence and the Congressional Research Service, addressing homeland security and counter-terrorism issues.[1941] Many of the reports pointed to resource limitations, structural weakness, procedure loopholes, capacity inadequacy and performance problems with the U.S. anti-terrorism regime before 911. For example, the Public Report of the Vice President's Task Force on Combatting Terrorism (1986),[1942] the National Commission on Terrorism: Countering the Changing Threat of International Terrorism (2001),[1943] and Roadmap for National Security: Imperative for Change - The Phase III Report (2001),[1944] all pointed to a defective and dysfunctional anti-terrorism system in the U.S., existing as far back as 1980s. They all called for major overhaul and drastic reforms of the homeland security structure and process to secure our nation against "new" terrorism threats, looming ominously ahead. They were most concerned with the discovery of WMD as a terrorist weapon of choice. Some of the recommendations in these studies and reports made it into the USAPA, e.g., breaking down of the criminal vs. terrorist intelligence "wall". Prophetically, there were suggestions that it would take a catastrophic event to mobilize the nation to its defense. Empathetically, they called for concentration of focus and double up effort, instead of more legal authority or less constitutional supervision, to fight terrorism.

Is the USAPA well (narrowly and appropriately) designed to address specific and concrete 911 risks? The answer is no one knows. It turned out that the issue of necessity and appropriateness of the USAPA has never been adequate addressed and satisfactory resolved by the White House or the Congress. There was simply no effort in that direction, before and even after[1945] the passage of the USAPA.[1946] Specifically, there was no study on what caused the lapse of security on 9/11 that required fixing, *before* the drafting of the administration's Anti-terrorism Act of 2001.[1947] This has led some skeptics to conclude that 911 was staged[1948] and USAPA was ready to go.[1949]

Destruction; 2002: A Review of Federal Bureau of Investigation Security Programs, (Webster Commission); 2002: HPSCI Subcommittee on Terrorism Study.

[1941] GAO Reports on Homeland Security (229 items as of January 22, 2006) http://www.gao.gov/docsearch/featured/ homelandsecurity.html; GAO Reports on Terrorism (229 items as of January 22, 2006, dating back to 1979) "What Is Being Done To Protect the U.S. Diplomatic Community From Terrorism," ID-79-3, April 18, 1979. http://www.gao.gov/docsearch/featured/terrorism.html

[1942] Public Report of the Vice President's Task Force on Combatting Terrorism (February 1986). http://www.population-security.org/bush_report_on_terrorism/bush_report_ on_terrorism.htm

[1943] Established by the Congress pursuant to Pub. L. 227, 105th Congress with the mandate to study law, policies and practices in fighting terrorism directed against America.

[1944] Report of the US Commission on National Security for the 21st. Century. (02 Feb 2001) (Warren B. Rudman and Gary Hart Report).

[1945] There more efforts to reassess the USAPA during the re-authorization of the Act, and after the 2006 election.

[1946] . There was a host of reports on the causes and remedies to 9/11, including: Combating Terrorism: Selected Challenges and Related Recommendations GAO-01-822, September 20, 2001 (The first and most systematic analysis of our nation's anti-terrorism preparedness published after 9/11, but compiled before.); Congressional Reports: Joint Inquiry into Intelligence Community Activities before and after the Terrorist Attacks of September 11, 2001 (December 2002) (The controversial Congressional investigation into 9/11 that was initially barred by the President from being published.) The official and most comprehensive investigation of 9/11 is *The 9-11 Commission Report: Final Report of the National Commission on Terrorist Attacks Upon the United States* (Official Government Edition 2004)

[1947] Anti-terrorism Act of 2001, first proposed on September 19, 2001, was the blueprint for the USAPA.

[1948] John Kaminski, "911 Was Staged To Defame Muslims,"skylax@comcast.net. Special to the Yemen Times.

[1949] Jennifer Van Bergen, "The USAPA Was Planned Before 9/11," *t r u t h o u t* (May 20, 2002. The law enforcement community and foreign intelligence agencies have long sought powers under the USAPA. The

In fact there is little evidence to support the contention that more law enforcement powers would have prevented the tragic incident. Conversely, there are amply evidence to show that US counter-terrorism system and efforts needs fixing. It lacks centralized leadership, e.g., no focal point, prior planning, e.g., formal risk assessment, enhanced capacity, e.g., human intelligence, and improved domestic preparedness, e.g., coordination of first responders.[1950]

More significantly for our purpose, there is no systematic and comprehensive effort to assess current achievements, document past impact and understand future implications of the USAPA.[1951] The verdict is as clear as it is disturbing: as a nation we do not know how we failed and what can be done, before we rushed to pass news laws.

This highlight the need to understand USAPA in context, i.e., historically, how does the USAPA fits into a pre-existing counter terrorism framework? Functionally, how do USAPA legal measures compliment and supplement existing counter-terrorism scheme.

A systematic and comprehensive examination of our anti-terrorism philosophy, policy, system, program, process and practices before 911 would have revealed that our national security and terrorism defense system was dysfunctional and broken to the core. However, the problems observed have little to do with lack of legal authority or too much constitutional liberties.

Presidential Study

The U.S. government started to develop counter terrorism policies some 30 years ago, mainly through the use of Presidential Decision Directives, as augmented by Congressional legislation and agency guidelines. The development of a coherent US terrorism policy dated back 30 years,[1952] i.e., since 1970s. In September 1972 President Nixon formed a Cabinet Committee to Combat Terrorism after Palestinian commandos murdered 11 Israeli athletes at the Munich Olympic Games. In May 21, 1975, a sub-group was formed to study WMD.[1953]

President Regan was the first to study and later confront international terrorism head, in a comprehensive manner. The Task Force on Combating Terrorism conducted the first national preparedness study: *Public Report of the Vice President's Task Force on Combatting Terrorism* (February 1986).[1954] The Task Force was organized as a result of actual threat of terrorism worldwide (Table 3) and perceived vulnerability to terrorism domestically (Table 4). The first set of major counter terrorism policy appeared in 1982:[1955] The National Security Decision Directive (NSDD) Number 207 of January 20, 1986 was based on such a study.

Act   was   put   on   the   self   waiting   for   something   like   911   to   come   along.)
http://www.ratical.org/ratville/CAH/PAplndbefore.html

[1950] *Combating Terrorism: Selected Challenges and Related Recommendations* GAO-01-822 (September 20, 2001) http://www.gao.gov/new.items/d01822.pdf

[1951] National security concerns, real or imagined, prompted the Bush administration to hide information from the public and the journalists. See *Homeland Confidential How the War on Terrorism Affects Access to Information and the Public's Right to Know Reporters Committee for Freedom of the Press*, Fifth Edition. Reporters Committee for Freedom of the Press. (9/1/2004)

[1952] For a historical overview of U.S. terrorism policy, see "The United States and Terrorism, 1968–2002: Threat and Response," *Digital National Security Archive* http://nsarchive.chadwyck.com/terr_essay.htm

[1953] Frank Bass and Randy Herschaft, "U .S. Foresaw Terror Threats in 1970's," *AP* Jan 25, 2005.

[1954] Public Report of the Vice President's Task Force on Combatting Terrorism (February 1986). http://www.population-security.org/bush_report_on_terrorism/bush_report_on_terrorism.htm

[1955] National Security Decision Directive 30, *Managing Terrorist Incidents*, April 30, 1982. Secret.

In 1985 there were a total of 812 terrorist incidents worldwide, resulting in 23 Americans dead and 160 wounded. Domestic terrorism was not considered to be a major threat then. But the Task Force predicted that one day U.S. would be vulnerable to attacks; a prophecy came true in 1993 with the blowing up of the WTC in NYC.

Table 6. Significant terrorist incidents involving U.S. citizens in 1985 internationally

Date	Place	Incident	American Injury
2/2/85	Greece – Athens	Athens: nightclub frequented by U.S. servicemen was bombed with 78 people injured.	69 (I)
4/12/85	Greece – Athens	TWA Flight 847 was skyjacked by Shiite terrorists. 145 passengers including 104 Americans on board.	1 (D)
6/12/85	Spain-Madrid	A family restaurant was bombed with 18 people killed and 37 wounded.	7 (I)
6/19/95	El Salvador -San Salvador	Shooting at an outdoor café with 13 people killed.	6 (D)
6/23/85	Atlantic Ocean	An Air-India flight exploded killing everyone aboard.	4 (D)
8/8/85	W. Germany – Frankfurt	Car bomb exploded at the U.S. Rhein-Main Air Base.	3 (D) 15 (I)
10/7/85	Mediterranean Sea - Near Egypt	The Italian cruise ship Achille Lauro was hijacked by Palestinian terrorists.	1 (D)
11/23/85	Greece – Athens	Egyptair Flight 648 enroute to Cairo was skyjacked. A total of 60 persons were killed during the rescue effort.	1 (D) 2 (I)
11/24/85	West Germany	A U.S. military shopping mall in Frankfurt was bombed, wounding 32 people.	23 (I)
12/27/85	Italy – Rome	Rome airport was attacked by terrorists. armed with grenades and automatic rifles. Seventy-three people were wounded, 15 are killed.	5 (D)
12/27/85	Austria, Vienna	Vienna Airport was attacked by terrorists. Three were killed and 41 wounded.	2 (I)
12/31/85	Lebanon	Six American citizens were held hostage.	6 (hostages)

Source: "Significant 1985 Terrorist Incidents Involving U.S. Citizens" *Public Report of the Vice President's Task Force on Combatting Terrorism* (February 1986).

Table 7. Terrorist Incidents in the United States: 1980-1985

Date	Total Incidents	Killed	Injured
1980	29	1	19
1981	42	1	4
1982	51	7	26
1983	31	6	4
1984	13	0	0
1985	7	2	10

The Report concluded with this observation:

"International terrorism is clearly a growing problem and priority, requiring expanded cooperation with other countries to combat it. Emphasis must be placed on increased intelligence gathering, processing and sharing, improved physical security arrangements, more effective civil aviation and maritime security, and the ratification and enforcement of treaties.

It is equally essential, however, that our defense against terrorism be enhanced domestically...

The Task Force's review of the current national program to combat terrorism found our interagency system and the Lead Agency concept for dealing with incidents to be soundly conceived. However, the system can be substantially enhanced through improved coordination and increased emphasis in such areas as intelligence gathering, communications procedures, law enforcement efforts, response option plans, and personal and physical security."[1956]

The basic organizational framework and overall strategic principles in dealing with terrorism was enshrined in (NSDD) Number 207, which survives until today.

The NSDD made clear that terrorism is a national security issue. Terrorism is not tolerated. The United States will not negotiate with or make concession to terrorists. The nation will bring all national resources at its disposal – legal, economic, military, diplomatic – to prevent, e.g., removal of root cause, deter, e.g., preemptive attack, defend, e.g., airport security, manage the crisis, e.g., first responders, and consequences, e.g., attack site clearance, of terrorism attacks. The nation will deny resource support and state sanctuary to terrorists. Counter-terrorism effort will be organized under a lead agency (as organizer and coordinator) concept, i.e., the State Department for international terrorism, the Justice Department for domestic terrorism, and the Federal Aviation Administration for hijackings within the United States.

It also established and specified the role and functions of a number of White House/executive branch groups to deal with specific terrorism threats, such as the Terrorist Incident Working Group to deal with crisis and Interdepartmental Group on Terrorism to deal with coordination.

NSDD 207 gave shape to an emerging counter-terrorism regime, defining its structure, i.e., interagency collaboration under centralized co-ordination, concepts, e.g., lead agency,

---

[1956] *Id.* "Part 3: Task Force Conclusions and Recommendations"

and strategy, e.g., denying terrorism of sources of support. NSDD was relied upon and refined by later PDDs to give us the national counter-terrorism regiment we have today.

The clearest and boldest manifestation of the nation's counter-terrorism regime is that of PDD 39 of June 1995. PDD 39 (1995)[1957] declares that terrorism is a national security risk. The U.S. will use all resources at its disposal to deter, defeat and response to terrorism at home and abroad. The basic principles informing U.S. counter terrorism strategy are: no negotiation with and concession to terrorists; assisting democratic states and pressuring sponsoring states; treating terrorists as criminals and attack them under rule law.[1958]

The overall counter-terrorism strategies are: (1) reduce domestic vulnerabilities through assessment and fortification; (2) prevent and deter terrorism from happening; (3) plan and prepare for crisis management; (4) apprehend and punish terrorists; (5) organize and coordinate consequence management. Structurally, it endorsed the multi-interagency effort under a lead agency approach.

Finally, PDD-62[1959] established the Office of the National Coordinator for Security, Infrastructure Protection and Counter-Terrorism. The National Coordinator was in charge of overseeing counter-terrorism efforts, protecting critical infrastructure, preparing for crisis and consequence management in case of WMD attacks. The National Coordinator would work within the National Security Council and report to the President through the Assistant to the President for National Security Affairs. He was responsible for producing an annual Security Preparedness Report.

As is evidence from the findings of *Public Report of the Vice President's Task Force on Combatting Terrorism* and related counter-terrorism policy statements, then and afterward, the major obstacles in fighting terrorism have *not* been a lack of legal authority. The problems have always been a lack of leadership and coordination. [1960] That remains to be true at the time of 9/11 and now, five years later.

Commission Study

The Gilmore Commission produced a total of five annual reports from 1999 – 2003. The First Annual Report summarized what need to be done to prevent and response to terrorism.[1961]

The First Annual Report as the subtitle suggests – "Assessing the Threat" – focused on describing the danger posed by new terrorism and lethality of WMD.[1962] Of most interest to

---

[1957] PDD-39, "United States Policy on Counterterrorism," signed June 21, 1995. (Federal Bureau of Investigation (FBI) to serve as the lead Federal Agency for "crisis management" and the Federal Emergency Management Agency (FEMA) to serve as the lead Federal Agency for "consequence management.")

[1958] The USAPA Bush's counter-terrorism doctrine treats terrorism not as criminal conducts but as acts of war. In so doing it deals with terrorism outside the confine of the law in two senses. First, terrorists are not entitled to the protection of the Constitution or rule of law. Second, the President, as the Commander-in-Chief, exercises war powers without the Constitutional structure and process.

[1959] Presidential Decision Directive-62 (PDD-62), "Protection Against Unconventional Threats to the Homeland and Americans Overseas," (May 22, 1998) http://biotech.law.lsu.edu/blaw/general/pdd62.htm

[1960] The Report was noted for this observation.

[1961] Testimony of James S. Gilmore, III, Chairman, Advisory Panel to Assess Domestic Response Capabilities for Terrorism Involving Weapons of Mass Destruction Before the Joint Hearing of the U.S. Senate Select Committee on Intelligence And the House Permanent Select Committee on Intelligence On the Joint Inquiry into the September 11 Attacks, October 1, 2002. http://www.rand.org/nsrd/terrpanel/testimonies/Gilmore10-01-02.pdf

our discussion here is the review of the problems and issues with U.S. anti-terrorism structure and preparedness. [1963] The First Annual Report made the following observations and assessments of the United States' anti-terrorism programs and posture:

First, a sound anti-terrorism policy depends on understanding of the nature of terrorist threats faced by the nation, realistically and continuously.[1964] Threat and risk assessment should be conducted on low probability – high consequences risks (e.g., WMD attack) as well as high probability – low consequences threats (e.g., suicide bomber). The one size fits all worse case scenario approach should be abandoned and discouraged.[1965]

Second, a national strategy should be built upon a competent assessment of terrorism risks and the nation's vulnerability to prioritize missions, distribute resources and concentrate efforts.[1966] In this regard the Attorney General's "Five-Year Interagency Counterterrorism and Technology Crime Plan" (December 1998) does not suffice as a Federal Government Strategy because it fails to provide for a national leadership structure and process as it neglects to integrate and coordinate state and local resources and efforts.[1967]

Third, the nation's anti-terrorism efforts are carried out by a myriad of overlapping and duplicative anti-terrorism programs, operated and controlled by a variety of federal government agencies in a complex and intricate way. Such arrangements are neither comprehensible to the insiders, nor accessible to the outsiders.[1968]

Fourth, the authorization, appropriation, and oversight of anti-terrorism programs and efforts are controlled by a multitude of Congressional committees and sub-committees, with different jurisdiction and mandate, interests and concerns. [1969] Such a Congressional committee system led to turf fighting over policy direction, funding priority and oversight standard.[1970]

[1962] First Annual Report, pp. 1 – 52.

[1963] *Id.* pp. 52 – 62.

[1964] *Id.*p. 52. Quoting p. 3 to Combating Terrorism: Need for Comprehensive Threat and Risk Assessments of Chemical and Biological Attack (GAO/ NSIAD- 99- 163, Sept. 7, 1999), at note 183.

[1965] *Id.* p. 54.

[1966] See "Threat Assessment and Analyses." *Id.* 55.

[1967] See "A National Strategy." *Id.* pp. 54-56, 56.

[1968] See "Complexity of Federal Structure", p. 56.

[1969] Currently, there are no less than 40 stakeholder committees and subcommittees having independent authority over counterterrorism spending, including 11 Senate committees and 13 house committees, and numerous subcommittees. See Daniel J. Kaniewski, "Create a House Select Committee on Homeland Security and Terrorism," *Homeland Security Journal.* February 2002. ("According to the Gilmore Commission's 2nd Annual Report, the stakeholder committees for terrorism involving weapons of mass destruction are the Agriculture Committee (House and Senate), Appropriations Committee (House and Senate), Armed Services Committee (House and Senate), Budget Committee (House and Senate), Commerce Committee (House and Senate), Energy and Natural Resources Committee (Senate), Resources Committee (House), Foreign Relations Committee (Senate), International Relations Committee (House), Governmental Affairs Committee (Senate), Government Reform Committee (House), Health, Education, Labor, and Pensions Committee (Senate), Science Committee (House), Judiciary Committee (House and Senate), Transportation and Infrastructure Committee (House), Ways and Means Committee (House), Select Committee on Intelligence (Senate), and Permanent Select Committee on Intelligence (House).") http://www.homelandsecurity.org/journal/articles/ kaniewskilegislative.htm

[1970] See "Congressional Responsibilities." Second Annual Report, P. 57

Government Accounting Office Study

The GAO report – "Combating Terrorism: Selected Challenges and Related Recommendations", prepared before 9/11 and rleased shortly thereafter (September 20, 2001, provides one of the most comprehensive analysis and assessment of the nation's counter-terrorism capacity, vulnerabilities and readiness.[1971]

The GAO report found that the nation's anti-terrorism structure and process, first espoused in PDD 30 and later revised in PDD 62, to be fragmented and in disarray.[1972] There was a noticeable lack of leadership and lapse of responsibilities. There were multiple and overlapping accountability lines.[1973] In order to ratify the situation, President Clinton issued PDD 62 to concentrate all anti-terrorism policy formation, implementation and coordination functions in the NSC.[1974]

Clinton's attempt to centralize all terrorism policy functions in the Office of the National Coordinator for Security, Infrastructure Protection and Counter-Terrorism however caused more fragmentation and confusion in anti-terrorism policy than it was designed to solve. This resulted from a failure to clearly define the role and functions, authorities and responsibilities, reporting line and communication process of the National Coordinator. The NC turned out to compete against and conflict with other agencies playing a leading role in the management of terrorism response, i.e., FBI as the lead agency in domestic terrorism – crisis management and FEMA as lead agency domestic terrorism - consequence management. Other long neglected problems observed include lack of risk analysis, lack of a nation strategy, and program coordination and implementation across myriad agencies.[1975]

In order to solve the long observed leadership vacuum and coordination void, GAO and the Congress[1976] has repeatedly recommended a focal point to lead and coordinate all counter-terrorism effort in the Untied States.[1977] It was recommended that the focal point should reside within the executive office of the President and have full responsible to plan, develop, and plan for the terrorism prevention, crisis management and consequence management.[1978]

[1971] *Combating Terrorism: Selected Challenges and Related Recommendations* GAO-01-822 (September 20, 2001) http://www.gao.gov/new.items/d01822.pdf onducted pursuant to section 1035 of the Floyd D. Spence National Defense Authorization Act for Fiscal Year 2001 (P.L. 106-398, Oct. 30, 2000) in reviewing the nation's strategies, policies and programs in fighting terrorism particularly with respect to WMD.

[1972] *Combating Terrorism: Spending on Governmentwide Programs Requires Better Management and Coordination* (GAO/NSIAD-98-39, Dec. 1, 1997); *Combating Terrorism: Combating Terrorism: Linking Threats to Strategies and Resources* (GAO/T-NSIAD-00-218, July 26, 2000); *Comments on Bill H.R. 4210 to Manage Selected Counterterrorist Programs* (GAO/T-NSIAD-00-172, May 4, 2000); *Combating Terrorism: Issues in Managing Counterterrorist Programs* (GAO/T-NSIAD-00-145, Apr. 6, 2000);

[1973] Michael Scardaville, "The New Congress Must Reform Its Committee Structure to Meet Homeland Security Needs," Backgrounder #1612, November 12, 2002. ("Indeed, the White House has identified 88 committees and subcommittees that currently exercise authority over homeland security policies.) See also "Making America Safer: Reforming Congress for the post-9/11." February 15, 2005, AEI.

[1974] Combating Terrorism: Comments on Counterterrorism Leadership and National Strategy (27-MAR-01, GAO-01-556T). ("No single entity acts as the federal government's top official accountable to both the President and Congress. Fragmentation exists in both coordination of domestic preparedness programs and in efforts to develop a national strategy").

[1975] *Id.* p. 10.

[1976] On March 21, 2001, Representative Thornberry introduced H.R. 1158, the National Homeland Security Act, which advocated the establishment of a National Homeland Security Agency to lead homeland security activities.

[1977] *Id.* P. 11.

[1978] *Id.* P. 39 – 40.

Table 8. Organizations Currently Responsible for Key Interagency Leadership and Coordination Functions for programs to Combat Terrorism

Key Interagency Leadership and Coordination	Current organization responsibility for the functions
Act as the top official accountable to the President	NSC (National Coordinator for Security, Infrastructure Protection and Counterterrorism), as appointed by the President in PDD 62.
Act as the top official accountable to the Congress.	Numerous officials (Including the Attorney General, Director of the FBI, Secretary of State, and Secretary of Defense) who testify before the Congress on these matters.
Overall a national threat and risk assessment.	FBI
Lead the development of a national strategy	Attorney General (other officers also have discussed doing this).
Set priorities within a national strategy	OMB, on behalf of he President, is required to identify priorities in it annual reports; to date, it has not done so.
Coordinate and monitor international programs	Secretary of State (via Coordinator for Counterterrorism).
Provide liaison and assistance to state and local governments.	Department of Justice (the Office for State and Local Domestic Preparedness Support and the National Domestic Preparedness Office) and FEMA.
Monitor budgets across federal agencies	NSC and OMB.
Develop and monitor overall performance measures	No agency assigned to do this overall task.
Coordinate overall research and development	NSC (via the Preparedness Against Weapon of Mass Destruction Research and Development Subground).

Source: Adapted from Combating Terrorism: Selected Challenges and Related Recommendations GAO-01-822 (September 20, 2001), p. 34.

Table 9. Proposals to Create a Focal Point for Overall Leadership and Coordination of Programs to Combat Terrorism

Source of proposal	Focal point for overall leadership	Scope of responsibilities	Location of focal point
H.R. 4210 (original version)	Office of Terrorism Preparedness	Domestic terrorism incidents involving weapons of mass destruction	Executive Office of the President
H.R. 1158	Cabinet-level head of proposed National Homeland Security Agency	Homeland security (including domestic terrorism, maritime and border security, disaster relief, and critical infrastructure activities)	Lead executive agency (National Homeland Security Agency)
H.R. 1292	Single official to be designated by the President	Homeland security (including anti-terrorism and protection of territory and critical infrastructure from unconventional and conventional threats by military or other means)	To be determined based upon the President's designation
Senate Report 106 – 404	Deputy Attorney General for Combating Terrorism	Domestic terrorism preparedness (crisis and consequences management)	Lead executive agency (Department of Justice)
Gilmore Panel	National Office for Combating Terrorism	Domestic terrorism preparedness (crisis and consequences management)	Executive Office of the President
Hart-Rudman Commission	Cabinet-level head of proposed National Homeland Security Agency	Homeland Security (including domestic terrorism, maritime and border security, disaster relief, and critical infrastructure activities)	Lead executive agency (National Homeland Security Agency)
Center for Strategic and International Studies	Assistance to the President or Vice President for Combating Terrorism	Homeland Defense (Including domestic terrorism and critical infrastructure protection)	Executive Office of the President

Source: Adapted from Combating Terrorism: Selected Challenges and Related Recommendations GAO-01-822 (September 20, 2001), p. 34.

V. THE EFFECTIVENESS OF USAPA

The Attorney General has acknowledged that he was not sure how effective the USAPA might be in contributing to the nation's security:

> "It—there is absolutely no guarantee that these safeguards would have avoided the September 11 occurrence...Nor can I assure this Committee that we won't have terrorist attacks in the future. The mere fact that we can't do everything should not keep us from doing what we can do, and I believe these each are constructive, valuable tools to be used in the fight against terrorism." [1979]

In essence, after 9/11, we need to do everything we possibly can to prevent terrorism, even of we do not know the impact of such counter-terrorism measures.

The Attorney General candid assessment of the utility and effective of anti-terrorism measures to keep America secure was much welcomed by some[1980] and often repeated by others. As Senator Leahy of the Judiciary Committee observed:

> Let me be clear: No one can guarantee that Americans will be free from the threat of future terrorist attacks, and to suggest that this legislation – or any legislation – would or could provide such a guarantee would be a false promise. I will not engage in such false promises, and those in the Administration who make such assertions do a disservice to the American people.[1981]

Two years after the passage of the USAPA, many of the USAPA powers have either not been invoked or did not result in any major terrorist arrests. The DOJ – FBI self-reported terrorism convictions rates were in the low hundreds, before as well as after 9/11, being 124 (1998), 262 (1998), 173 (1999), 249 (2000),225 (2001), 373 (2002).[1982] DOJ – US Attorney Office (USAO) reported data shows that terrorism conviction rates to be in the teens[1983] - being 13 (1998), 44 (1998), 59 (1999), 30 (2000), 29 (2001), 156 (2002).[1984] A closer

---

[1979] *Administration's Draft Anti-Terrorism Act of 2001* Hearing Before the Committee on the Judiciary House of Representatives. One Hundred Seventh Congress, First Session, September 24, 2001. http://commdocs.house.gov/committees/judiciary/hju75288.
000/hju75288_0.HTM
Thus far there are only scattered and anecdotal evidence that the USAPA was useful in tracing down terrorists. For example, Christopher A. Wray, head of the Justice Department's Criminal Division, along with Virginia U.S. Attorney Paul J. McNulty and Illinois U.S. Attorney Patrick J. Fitzgerald, testified before a Senate panel that the USAPA was invaluable in investigating important terrorism cases, including breaking up of a terrorist cell in Portland, Ore., and an investigation of the murder of Daniel Pearl, a Wall Street Journal reporter, in Pakistan. Susan Schmidt, "Patriot Act Misunderstood, Senators Say Complaints About Civil Liberties Go Beyond Legislation's Reach, Some Insist," *Washington Post* Wednesday, October 22, 2003; Page A04. http://www.washingtonpost.com/wp-dyn/articles/A61591-2003Oct21.html

[1980] See Bob Barr, "Patriot Act Games," *bobbarr.org* Aug. 19, 2003. http://www.bobbarr.org/default.asp?pt=newsdescrandRI=440

[1981] "Statement of Senator Patrick Leahy The Uniting And Strengthening of America Act Of 2001 ("USA ACT")" (October 9, 2001) http://leahy.senate.gov/press/200110/100901a.html

[1982] *Justice Department: Better Management Oversight and Internal Controls Needed to Ensure Accuracy of Terrorism-Related Statistics.* GAO-03-266, January 17, 2003. http://www.gao.gov/new.items/d03266.pdf at Table 1, page 9.

[1983] *Id*

[1984] The 2002 jump in conviction reflected a change in USAO classification rather than USAO activities, i.e., making USAO classification more conforming to FBI's classification scheme.

examination shows that many of the cases prosecuted are not terrorism crimes at all, if they are they are not serious cases. More disturbingly the USAPA has been used creatively and expansively in purse of conventional criminals and political dissidents.

The data provided by Transactional Records Access Clearinghouse (TRAC)[1985] at Syracuse University suggests possible misuse or abuse of the USAPA for undetermined reasons.

Judging by federal criminal enforcement, terrorism and anti-terrorism prosecution referral and conviction rates jumped by wide margin before (10/1/99 – 9/10/01) and after 911 (9/11/01 – 9/30/03): terrorism and anti-terrorism referral cases acted upon increased by 6 times (from 594 to 3,555) and conviction increased by 8 times (110 to 879) during the period. In the case of terrorism referrals and convictions, they increased by 3 (544 to 1,778) and 3.5 (142 to 748) times respectively. Clearly, this set of enforcement data shows that the FBI and other federal agencies have changed their law enforcement posture, from common criminality to terrorism crimes. It is also of interest to note that the growth in referral rates for all terrorism offenses lagged far behind their conviction rates, suggesting that the federal courts were also more inclined to convict, this is particularly the case with international terrorism cases where the increase in referral vs. conviction was 5 vs. 7.5 times.

Table 10. Criminal Enforcement Before and After 9/11/01 Attacks

Federal Terrorism Programs	Two Year Cohorts*		
	Before 9/11	After 9/11	Change
Terrorism and Anti-Terrorism: Referrals acted on	594	3,555	increase 6 times
Convictions	110	879	increase 8 times
Terrorism (excluding Anti-Terrorism): Referrals acted on	544	1,778	increase 3 times
Convictions	96	341	increase 3.5 times
International Terrorism Only: Referrals acted on	142	748	increase 5 times
Convictions	24	184	increase 7.5 times

* "Before 9/11" cohort covers referrals for prosecutions received under federal terrorism programs from October 1, 1999 thru September 10, 2001.

"After 9/11" cohort covers referrals for prosecution received under federal terrorism programs from September 11, 2001 thru September 30, 2003.

In the two years since 911 (September 11, 2001 - September 30, 2003) about 6,400 terrorism cases were investigated. There were 2845 cases or 44.5% still pending closure, release or prosecution. The total cases acted upon were 3, 555. The prosecution rate was 56.3% or 2001 cases and decline to prosecute rate was43.7% or 1,554 cases. To be expected

---

[1985] "The purpose of TRAC is to provide the American people -- and institutions of oversight such as Congress, news organizations, public interest groups, businesses, scholars and lawyers -- with comprehensive information about federal staffing, spending, and the enforcement activities of the federal government." http://trac.syr.edu/aboutTRACgeneral.html.

there were more prosecution of international terrorism cases than domestic terrorism cases, i.e., 44.4% vs. 34.5%.

Except with anti-terrorism prosecution (71.5%), the prosecution rate of all terrorism cases lagged behind other federal criminal cases prosecuted during the same year, i.e., 56.3% vs. 67.7%. This observed low referral - prosecution rate for terrorism crimes became much more pronounced when we compared it with prior year, i.e., 2000 – 2001. In October 2000 to September 2001 the US Attorney's office handled 118, 978 suspects, of which 72.9% or 86,728 were prosecuted. [1986] The prosecution rate for regular criminal crime is near double of that of prosecution for domestic terrorism in 2001. This low prosecution rate with terrorism referrals, especially with domestic terrorism (34.6%), perhaps reflected the minor nature of the terrorism activities charged or lack of evidence in support of referrals, or both.

Table 11. Terrorism and Anti-Terrorism Programs: Actions by Federal Prosecutors on Referrals for Prosecution Received: September 11, 2001 - September 30, 2003

	Total Acted On	Prosecution Filed	Prosecution Declined	Percent Prosecuted
All	3,555	2,001	1,554	56.3%
Terrorism:				
International	748	332	416	44.4%
Domestic	700	242	458	34.6%
Finance	330	156	174	47.3%
Subtotal	1,778	730	1,048	41.1%
Anti-Terrorism	1,777	1,271	506	71.5%
All Federal Programs*	285,896	193,473	92,423	67.7%

* FY 2002-2003 Only. Copyright 2003, TRAC.

A look at reasons given by federal prosecutors for declining prosecution, we find the following dominant reasons: Lack of evidence of criminal intent (31.8% anti-terrorism, 18.2 % terrorism); Weak or insufficient admissible evidence (14.6%, 15%); No federal offense evident (6.7%, 11%); Suspect to be prosecuted by other (9.7%, 10.2%); Reasons not given (8.8%, 8/9%).

One more observation before we leave this subject. A full 2% or 22 of the terrorism suspect died before successful prosecution, as compared with anti-terrorism suspect of only 0.2%. The disproportionate among of death before prosecution needed to be carefully investigated, especially when deaths were in custody and from unnatural causes. This might implicate police abuse or human rights violations.

[1986] Federal Criminal Case Processing, 2001: With trends 1982-2001, Reconciled Data, Bureau of Justice Statistics. http://www.ojp.usdoj.gov/bjs/abstract/fccp01.htm

Table 12. Reasons Given by Assistant U.S. Attorneys for Declining to Prosecute Number of Terrorism/Anti-Terrorism Referrals for Prosecution Declined: September 11, 2001 through September 30, 2003

Declination Reason	Number			Percent		
	Anti-Terrorism	Terrorism	Total	Anti-Terrorism	Terrorism	Total
Total	506	1,048	1,554	100.0	100.0	100.0
Reasons pointing to possible weakness in investigation: Lack of evidence of criminal intent	161	191	352	31.8	18.2	22.7
Weak or insufficient admissible evidence	74	157	231	14.6	15.0	14.9
No federal offense evident	34	115	149	6.7	11.0	9.6
Minimal federal interest or no deterrent value	11	29	40	2.2	2.8	2.6
Other Reasons: Agency request	27	128	155	5.3	12.2	10.0
By Action of the Grand Jury	1	1	2	0.2	0.1	0.1
Civil, admin or other disciplinary alternatives	6	15	21	1.2	1.4	1.4
Declined per instructions from DOJ	4	4	8	0.8	0.4	0.5
Defendant similarly charged in subsequent instrument	8	1	9	1.6	0.1	0.6
Department Policy	3	-	3	0.6	-	0.2
Dism: by govt from District Court w/ DOJ authorization	1	-	1	0.2	-	0.1
Dism: by govt from District Court w/o DOJ authorization	3	6	9	0.6	0.6	0.6
Dism: by govt from Magistrate Court w/o DOJ authorization	-	2	2	-	0.2	0.1
Final order of forfeiture-asset substituted	-	2	2	-	0.2	0.1
Jurisdiction or venue problems	3	12	15	0.6	1.1	1.0
Juvenile suspect	-	8	8	-	0.8	0.5
Lack of investigative resources	4	5	9	0.8	0.5	0.6
Lack of prosecutive resources	13	43	56	2.6	4.1	3.6
No known suspect	9	49	58	1.8	4.7	3.7
Offenders age, health, prior record, or personal matter	7	15	22	1.4	1.4	1.4

Table 12. (Continued)

Declination Reason	Number			Percent		
	Anti-Terrorism	Terrorism	Total	Anti-Terrorism	Terrorism	Total
Office policy	5	7	12	1.0	0.7	0.8
Operation of Law (District Court)	-	1	1	-	0.1	0.1
Rule 20 (District Court)	-	1	1	-	0.1	0.1
Rule 20 (Magistrate Court)	-	4	4	-	0.4	0.3
Rule 40	3	1	4	0.6	0.1	0.3
Staleness	-	6	6	-	0.6	0.4
Statute of Limitations	13	1	14	2.6	0.1	0.9
Suspect a fugitive	1	-	1	0.2	-	0.1
Suspect being prosecuted on other charges (e.g.,, UFAPs)	14	14	28	2.8	1.3	1.8
Suspect deceased	1	21	22	0.2	2.0	1.4
Suspect deported	5	4	9	1.0	0.4	0.6
Suspect serving sentence	1	2	3	0.2	0.2	0.2
Suspect to be prosecuted by other authorities	49	107	156	9.7	10.2	10.0
Suspects cooperation	-	2	2	-	0.2	0.1
Witness problems	-	2	2	-	0.2	0.1
Reason not given	45	92	137	8.9	8.8	8.8

Copyright 2003, TRAC Reports, Inc.

When we compare how terrorism cases vs. other criminal cases were handled, we find two salient differences: First, there were many decline in prosecution of terrorism cases (68%) vs. criminal cases (34%). Second, the reasons given for legal insufficiency (legally insufficient includes: lack of criminal intent, weak or insufficient admissible evidence, no federal offense evidence, minimal federal interest or no deterrent value) was twice as high with terrorism cases (37%) than criminal cases (16%). Putting these two observations in perspective suggest that the quality of the cases referred for prosecution were not as solid as they otherwise could be. This might be deal to difficulty in prosecuting terrorism cases, where evidences are hard to come by, e.g., overseas, or it could be deal to zealous enforcement or investigation, i.e., lowering of evidentiary standards. Or it might just be a case of better safe than be sorry mentality. Finally, the criminal justice process might be used to incapacity or punish terrorists. In any event, may terrorism suspects have to go through the ordeal of the criminal justice system before being exonerated.

Of those who were prosecuted, i.e., 2001 cases, 1127 cases or 56.3% were completed, of which 234 cases or 20.8% were dismissed. About 75% (879 or 75.33%) of the cases were convicted. A few, less than 2% (1.24% or 14) were found not guilty. In 2001, 77,143 defendants were prosecuted in federal courts of which 68,533 were convicted for a conviction rate of 88.8%. The dismissal and non-conviction rates were 9.9% and 1.3% respectively. While the finding of "not guilty" in terrorism cases (1.24%) followed "not conviction" rate nation wide for common criminal cases (1.3%), the large rate of dismissal is disconcerting (20.8% - all terrorism vs. 9.9% criminal). The difference is still higher with terrorism vs. criminal cases (24% vs. 9.99%)

Table 13. Handling Terrorism vs. Other Criminal Referrals for Prosecution

	Terrorism Referrals		All Criminal Referrals	
	Number	Percent	Number	Percent
Referrals where Prosecution Decision Made	1006	100%	645,709	100%
Prosecution Filed	326	32%	423,218	66%
Prosecution Declined	680	68%	222,491	34%
All Reasons Prosecution Declined	680	68%	222,491	34%
Legally Insufficient*	368	37%	103,014	16%
Other Reasons	312	31%	119,477	18.5%

* legally insufficient includes: lack of criminal intent, weak or insufficient admissible evidence, no federal offense evidence, minimal federal interest or no deterrent value.

Table 14. Criminal Enforcement Activity: Federal Terrorism and Anti-Terrorism Programs: September 11, 2001 - September 30, 2003

Referrals	6400	*
Pending	2845	*
Declined	1554	**
Prosecution Filed	2001	
Prosecution Filed	2001	
Pending	874	
Completed	1127	**
Prosecution Completed	1127	
Dismissed	234	
Not Guilty	14	
Convicted	879	
Convicted	879	
No Prison	506	
Prison	373	
Prison	373	
1 day - < 1 yr	250	
1 yr - < 5 yrs	100	
5 yrs - < 20 Yrs	18	
20 yrs – life	5	

* These numbers are estimates.

** Completed: Total (2,681) = Declined (1,554) + Prosecution Completed (1,127).

This set of data reinforces the above findings in referral and decline for prosecution data, i.e., quality of cases brought up for prosecution in terrorism cases was low overall. This means that many of the cases were either hastily brought (without sufficient investigation) or poorly investigated (without competent investigation) or failed for investigation (no sufficient evidence found).

Table 15. Criminal Enforcement Activity: Federal Terrorism — Not Including Anti-Terrorism - September 11, 2001 - September 30, 2003

Referrals	3500	*
Pending	1722	*
Declined	1048	**
Prosecution Filed	730	
Prosecution Filed	730	
Pending	276	
Completed	454	**
Prosecution Completed	454	
Dismissed	109	
Not Guilty	4	
Convicted	341	
Convicted	341	
No Prison	121	
Prison	220	
Prison	220	
1 day - < 1 yr	155	
1 yr - < 5 yrs	49	
5 yrs - < 20 Yrs	12	
20 yrs – life	4	

* These numbers are estimates.
** Completed: Total (1,502) = Declined (1,048) + Prosecution Completed (454).

Some evidence for poorly investigated cases can also be found by examining the international terrorism decline prosecution rate. Except for 2001, where it appeared that the decline for prosecution rate dipped to 33%, the decline for prosecution rate remained to be high in all years before and after 911, from 79% in 1997 to 68% in 2000 to 61% in 2002.

Lastly, perhaps the most telling sign of the low quality of the terrorism cases came from the disposition of convicted terrorists. First to observe is that terrorists as a whole did not received heavy punishment with the courts, in absolute terms. The median prison time of sentences for all terrorism cases was 0 days, being international 14 days; domestic – 3 months, finance – 4 months and anti-terrorism – 0 days.

Second, the severity of punishment for terrorists, declined sharply in relative terms before and after 911. For example, cases with no prison term for terrorism and anti-terrorism offenders have gone up substantially from 18 to 506 cases.

Table 16. International Terrorism: FBI Referrals Acted Upon: Prosecuted orDeclined - Fiscal Years 1997 – 2002

Fiscal Year	Referrals Acted Upon		
	Number Filed	Number Declined	Percent Declined
	8		79%
	6	9	60%
	26	26	50%
	8	17	68%
	53	26	33%
	38	60	61%

* Covers first six months only (October 2001 - March 2002).

Table 17. Federal Prison Sentences Before and After 9/11/01 Attacks

Federal Terrorism Programs	Two Year Cohorts*		
	Before 9/11	After 9/11	Change
Terrorism and Anti-Terrorism: No prison	18	506	up sharply
1 day to less than 1 year	11	250	up sharply
1 year to less than 5 years	56	100	Up
5 years to life	25	23	Down
Total Convicted	110	879	
Terrorism (excluding Anti-Terrorism): No prison	15	121	up sharply
1 day to less than 1 year	8	155	up sharply
1 year to less than 5 years	49	49	no change
5 years to life	24	16	Down
Total Convicted	96	341	
International Terrorism Only: No prison	3	80	up sharply
1 day to less than 1 year	1	91	up sharply
1 year to less than 5 years	14	10	Down
5 years to life	6	3	Down
Total Convicted	24	184	

* "Before 9/11" cohort covers referrals for prosecutions received under federal terrorism programs from October 1, 1999 thru September 10, 2001.

"After 9/11" cohort covers referrals for prosecution received under federal terrorism programs from September 11, 2001 thru September 30, 2003.

Table 18. Prison Sentences under Federal Terrorism Programs Referrals Received from September 11, 2001 through September 30, 2003

Federal Terrorism Programs	Number of Convictions	Prison Sentence (1 day or more)		Median Prison Time
		Number	Percent	
International	184	104	56.5%	14 days
Domestic	117	90	76.9%	3 months
Finance	40	26	65.0%	4 months
Anti-Terrorism	538	153	28.4%	0 days
Total	879	373	42.4%	0 days

Copyright 2003, Transactional Records Access Clearinghouse, Syracuse University.

Another way to understand how the USAPA was used is to look at some of the cases prosecuted with the help of the Act.

In many instances the USAPA was liberally and creatively used to investigate conventional crimes.

The reason for and utility of the USAPA is put in doubt. Still the question is whether the USAPA is worth the costs. To the issue of social costs of the Act we now turn.

VI. MORAL CALCULUS[1987]: WHAT PRICE SECURITY?

There are a number of social costs associated with the passage of the USAPA. These include:

Unsettling Constitutional Balance

First, the USAPA unsettled the delicate constitutional check and balance in place. Overnight the Act changed the U.S. from a democratic nation to national security state, with the executive branch holding the balance of power against the Congress and judiciary. For example, the Bush administration has openly and blatantly challenged Congressional constitutional supervisory function and judicial legal oversight powers over USAPA. The administration's blatant rejection and resentment of Congressional oversights started when the Attorney General Ashcroft rebuked the Congress for asking questions about the impact of the USAPA on civil liberties. On December 6, 2001, Attorney General Ashcroft lectured the Senate Judiciary Committee thusly: "To those who scare peace-loving people with phantoms of lost liberty, my message is this: Your tactics only aid terrorists, for they erode our national

---

[1987] The term "moral calculus" was first used by Bentham, the moral philosopher, who gave us utilitarianism. "III. Bentham and the Early Utilitarians." In *The Cambridge History of English and American Literature*, 18 Volumes (1907–21).

unity and diminish our resolve They give ammunition to America's enemies and pause to America's friends." [1988]

On July 25, 2002 the Attorney General was asked by the Senate Judiciary Committee at the "Oversight Hearing of the Department of Justice" to provide written answers to questions on the implementation of Section 215 of the USAPA. The Attorney General did not provide the information.[1989] The non-cooperative attitude led Senator Patrick J. Leahy (D-VT) to remark, in anger: "Since I've been here, I have never known an administration that is more difficult to get information from that the oversight committees are entitled to."[1990]

With respect to the judiciary, the administration in the name of war on terror, has reduced the courts' Constitutional check and balance role into one of knowing accomplices of unfettered exercise of Presidential powers.

Encroaching on Civil Liberties

Ultimately, USAPA propriety and utility debate is one of national security vs. civil liberties. As Morton Halper put it:

> "International terrorism is rapidly supplanting the communist threat as the primary justification for wholesale deprivations of civil liberties and distortions of the democratic process. Once governments, guerilla movements, and individuals disliked by the US government are labeled 'terrorists,' measures such as warrantless searches and wiretaps, restrictions on the right to travel, speak, and receive information ... often become acceptable."[1991]

As of May 1, 2007, there are eight states and 406 communities all over the nation which have adopted anti-Patriot resolutions to defend the civil liberties of 85,140,029 people.[1992] Beyond this grassroots resistant movement, the public knows very little about the true cost – impact or implication of the USAPA.

What little we know about the implementation and impact of the USAPA came from a few surveys by ALA and anecdotal accounts. For example, in October of 2002, Leigh S. Estabrook, Director, The Library Research Center, University of Illinois at Urbana-Champaign conducted a national survey on the impact of USAPA on libraries. The survey was conducted on 1,505 of the 5,094 U.S. public libraries serving populations of over 5,000, with a response rate of 60.2%. The survey found that federal and local law enforcement

---

[1988] See Testimony of Attorney General John Aschroft. Senate Committee on the Judiciary December 6, 2001. http://www.usdoj.gov/ag/testimony/2001/1206transcriptsenatejudiciarycommittee.htm

[1989] Dan Eggen, "Aschroft Assailed On Policy Review: Lawmakers Say Oversight Is Blocked," *Washington Post* August 21, 2002; Page A02.

[1990] Adam Clymer, "Justice Dept. Balks At Effort to Study Anti-terror Powers," *New York Times*. Aug. 14, 2002.

[1991] See Morton H. Halperin and Jeanne M. Woods, "Ending the Cold War at Home," *Foreign Policy*, winter 1990–1991, p. 136. See also Frank J. Donner, *Protectors of Privilege: Red Squads and Police Repression in Urban America* (Berkeley, CA: University of California Press, 1990); David Wise, *The American Police State: The Government Against the People* (New York: Random House, 1976); Frank J. Donner, *The Age of Surveillance: The Aims and Methods of America's Political Intelligence System* (New York: Alfred A. Knopf, 1980); and Cathy Perkus, ed., *Cointelpro: The FBI's Secret War on Political Freedom* (New York: Monad Press, 1975). For an overview of the issues see Stephen Marrin, "Homeland Security Intelligence: Just the Beginning," *Homeland Security Journal* November 2003.

[1992] Bill of Rights Defense Committee, http://www.bordc.org/OtherLocalEfforts.htm (Visited November 14, 2005).

officials visited at least 545 (10.7%) libraries to ask for their records, as compared to 703 visits (11.8%) a year before 9/11; 178 libraries (3.5%) received visits from the FBI; 15 were unable to answer because of legal prohibition (gag order); 362 (7.1%) libraries reported that patrons have expressed concerns about their privacy rights under the USAPA; 433 libraries (8.5%) reported that they were more likely to monitor checked out materials than before; 209 libraries (4.1%) have voluntarily reported patron records or behaviors to authorities in relation to terrorism; 423 libraries (8.3%) have received patrons' report of suspected terrorist activities;59.9% of librarians thought that the secrecy provision is an abridgement of First Amendment rights. Finally when asked: "Do you think the U.S. government should remove information from its websites that might potentially help terrorists, even if the American public has a right to know" Public response 67 % vs. librarian response 35.3%.

There are anecdotal evidences that the FBI and local police has been looking for terrorist related information in the library. For example, on September 15, 2001, Kathleen Hensman, a research librarian at Delray Beach Public library, Florida, called the local police to report seeing 9/11 suspects using a library computer. Hensman also volunteered to search the library records for any further match between known 9/11 suspects and the library's computer sign-in sheets.[1993]

On March 31, 2003, Scott Shafer, Director of Lima Public Library sent an e-mail [1994] to his colleagues protesting the removal of "sensitive but not classified" library materials from his library by the Allen County Emergency Management Agency (EMA).[1995] The facts of the case are not in dispute:[1996] The Local Office of Homeland Security appeared at the Lima Public Library to "update" "The Allen County Hazardous Materials Emergency Plan." They were checked for ID and given the loose leaf binder by the Reference Staff. When the Reference Staff checked the binder back, they found that the entire contents of the manual was removed and replaced with a page referring all inquiries to the EMA office. The same scenario was repeated at the Spencerville branch.

The USAPA also affects the nation's education and research in many ways. The Act makes research more difficult by placing restrictions on possession and transfer of Centers for Disease Control (CDC) controlled biological agents and toxin. It places limitations on research activities of international students and other so-called "restricted persons." It imposes regulation on "sensitive but unclassified information," or "homeland security information."[1997] Lastly, it precludes non-U.S. citizens from getting involved with classified data on government funded or contracted scientific projects. Finally, the government discourages the publication of "sensitive but not classified information" by scholarly journals. There is a steady rise in the number of defense-related research contracts that require prior

---

[1993] John Holland, Jennifer Peltz and Robin Benedick, "Library links Investigated Computer Use by Suspects Reported to FBI," *South Florida Sun - Sentinel* September 16, 2001. p. 8.A.

[1994] See "Homeland Security and the removal of library materials" Ohio Citizen Action. http://www.ohiocitizen.org/campaigns/library/lima.html

[1995] Norman Order, "Security Officials Pull PL Document," *Library Journal.* May 1, 2003. http://libraryjournal.reviewsnews.com/index.asp?layout=articleandarticleId=CA292617anddisplay=searchResultsandstt=001andtext=fbi

[1996] There is a dispute as to whether the local Homeland Security officials have instructed the librarians to report upon any suspicious activities at the library.

[1997] Andrea M. Hamilton, "Faculty fear Patriot Act threatens research, civil liberties," Stanford Report, November 13, 2002. (Stanford and other research institutions, faced problems posed by the Patriot Act and Public Health Security and Bioterrorism Preparedness and Response Act) http://www.stanford.edu/dept/news/report/news/november13/patriot-1113.html.

DOD approval before publishing research findings on electronic bulletin boards, sending them over unsecured e-mail systems, or posting them elsewhere on the Internet is allowed.

VII. CONCLUSION

The USAPA is a controversial piece of legislation. In assessing USAPA a number questions can be raised: how could the USAPA legislative process be satisfactory explained? whether the USAPA is effective in dealing with terrorism? what are the costs of the USAPA to our society? Is USAPA worth the cost?"

In terms of necessity, this research argues that USAPA powers – "sneak and peak", "track and trace", etc. - are not necessary to fight terror.

First, 9/11 happened not because of a lack of power, but in spite of it. In common parlance, the drafters USAPA were "barking up the wrong tree." All pre-9/11 studies and reports point out that we need more effective leadership, coordination and administration of counter-terrorism programs more legal authority. More frontline powers do not automatically translate into effective central leadership nor help with inter-departmental cooperation. In fact, the expansion of power without effective control invites abuse of power, from mission creep[1998] to power leaks, and added authority without cooperation leads to jurisdiction disputes and operational chaos.[1999]

Second, the government already has the powers to secure the nation before 9/11, but has failed to prevent or stop the hijackers. This is "barking up the wrong tree" II - more frontline powers to do not automatic translate into better – efficient and effective - use of use of such powers, old and new. For example, before, and even after 9/11, GAO reports and FAA inspections have repeatedly warned that the nation's airport security was not safe.[2000] Specially, in May of 2000, GAO agents were able to gain access into airport secured areas with fake law enforcement IDs and credentials. In June of 2000 airport screeners failed to detect threat objects on passengers and luggage, planted by FAA.[2001] In 1987, 20% of such dangerous objects were routinely missed. As it turned out, the problem with lack of or slack in aviation security was one of certification, training and turnover of screeners, not lack of legal authority.

Third, 9/11 could not have been stopped with or without the USAPA. There are seven variants to this argument. (1) Security system is designed to be perfect, but it never functions perfectly because it is a human system. Humans, unlike machine, makes mistakes; routine,

---

[1998] "Newsbrief: Federal Prosecutors in Seattle Use Patriot Act in Marijuana Case." (8/6/04) http://stopthedrugwar.org/chronicle/349/creep.shtml

[1999] See Mark Riebling, *Wedge: The Secret War Between the FBI and the CIA* (New York: Knopf, 1994). Hulnick, Arthur S. "Intelligence and Law Enforcement: The 'Spies Are Not Cops' Problem." *International Journal of Intelligence and Counterintelligence* Vol. 10 (3): 269-286 (1997).

[2000] Since June of 1986, GAO has issued 68 aviation security reports, 40 of those before 9/11. The earliest FAA airport screening security exercise was conducted between September and December of 1986. Detection rate ran from 99% to 34 percent, i.e., x-rate was 84%, metal detector was 82%, and search was 81%. *Aviation Security: FAA Needs Preboard Passenger Screening Performance Standards* RCED-87-182, July 24, 1987, p. 11.

[2001] *Aviation Security: Terrorist Acts Demonstrate Urgent Need to Improve Security at the Nation's Airports.* (GAO-01-1162T, September 20, 2001) and *Aviation Security: Terrorist Acts Illustrate Severe Weaknesses in Aviation Security* (GAO-01-1166T, September 20, 2001.

fatigue, incompetence, miscommunication, or sheer apathy, etc.[2002] (2) Perfect functioning system is prohibitively expensive for the society, in financial or transactional terms. Perfect security means a total lockdown, security with no liberty. (3) There is only so much we can do with die hard – motivated and committed - adversaries.[2003] Terrorists are not are not afraid to die and cannot be deterred. [2004] (4) Terrorist attack is unstoppable. There too many soft targets.[2005] (6) There is only so much we can do to hunt down the terrorists and prevent terrorist attacks, without transforming the nation to a police state or terror regime.[2006] (7) In overacting to the treat of terrorism, the terrorists have won.

As to utility, more security powers means less it is argued that the citizens' rights. A security state threatens the sanctity and integrity of our constitutional system of government. There are three versions to this thesis. (1) The marginal utility of the USAPA in preventing or interdicting 9/11 is speculative at best and non-existence at worse In utility calculus, the marginal safety derived is far outweighed by the economic, e.g., burden on air transport, social, e.g., discrimination from racial profiling, legal, e.g., violation of civil rights, and moral, e.g., end justify means, costs incurred. (2) The USAPA has the effect of encroaching on the fundamental rights of citizens and violating the foundational constitutional norm of the country. (3) The USAPA has put the nation on a wartime footing with the creation of a police state with an imperial President at the helm, unchecked by Congress and not supervised by the Court. Given the indefiniteness of terror war, which is likely to last forever, and indeterminacy of the terrorism, as a shifting concept, government power cannot be checked. In effect, if not by intent, the war on terror, has transformed United States democratic form of government.

On a broader constitutional compass and larger socio-political context, the research raised two fundamental issues that should be reflected upon:

First, at variant with the purpose of this book, there is a distinct possibility that more public debate over the USAPA might *not* have contributed much to the better understanding of the Act. This is more than borne out by the ideological and cultural war of words between the liberals (e.g., ACLU) and conservatives (i.e., Bush administration) over the propriety, appropriateness and utility of the USAPA. The crossing of swords generates more fire than heat, more smoke than light, and in the end more talking but less understanding. In context and as a result, the merits of USAPA are less important than the ideological posturing, political negotiation, power struggle of ideological camps and interested parties. In the ultimate analysis liberals and conservatives are using 9/11 to fight for power and influence, interest and value, on higher grounds and as rally point, in the name of security vs. liberty,

---

[2002] *The 9-11 Commission Report: Final Report of the National Commission on Terrorist Attacks Upon the United States,* Official Government Edition (2004) (Four of 13 the terrorists on one plane were selected by the Computer Assisted Passenger Prescreening System for further check. They were all led go, p. 1) http://www.gpoaccess.gov/911/.

[2003] Fareed Zakaria , "America's New World Disorder," *Newsweek* (US Edition) September 15, 2003. http://www.fareedzakaria.com/articles/newsweek/091503.html

[2004] Adam Wolfson, "Demystify It: How to defeat suicide terrorism." *National Review.* 9/16/03. http://www.nationalreview.com/comment/comment-wolfson091603.asp.

[2005] "FBI Concerned About Terrorism At Political Conventions." *Terror Analysis* March, 26 2004. http://www.terroranalysis.com/story/40156.html

[2006] Rep. Cynthia McKinney, "War on Terrorism or Police State?" *CouterPunch* July 25, 2002. http://www.counterpunch.org/mckinney0725.html.

democracy and justice.[2007] If that should be the case, political pundits and policy advocates are not looking for facts and arguments to enlighten and enliven an open debate but opinion and authority to support preconceived principles and positions.

Second, how might constitutional democracies be able to effectively check government in time of a national crisis, when people are consumed by present threat and politicians are pandering to public fear? In what way can it be said that the public are making informative and deliberate choices? How can it be said the Congress has dutifully discharged its duty when it is overwhelmed by catastrophic events, the magnitude of which is not contemplated by a peace time Constitution?[2008] It was Chief Justice William H. Rehnquist who once said: "While we would not want to subscribe to the full sweep of the Latin maxim -- *Inter Arma Silent Leges* -- in time of war the laws are silent, perhaps we can accept the proposition that though the laws are not silent in wartime, they speak with a muted voice." [2009] If we were to accept Rehnquist's proposition that the Constitution is avoided and law becomes mute in time of war, what is there to hold the country together in time of war besides raw passion and heated patriotism that bind a people? This invites tyranny of the majority and makes possible abuse of power in name for security for all.

Finally, a caveat on how to read and consider the observations to this research is in order. This study offers a preliminary assessment of the USAPA. The USAPA is too new (only five years old) and the war on terror has yet to mature (with no end in sight) to allow for definitive judgment on the state of our constitutional union. For example, the lament about disturbing constitutional democracy, e.g., changing the constitutional balance and institutional relationship between the three branched of government and state vs. public relationship is at best premature and at worse over-reacting. In reality, the democratic process has yet to work its full course, e.g., It takes a long, lone time to right the wrong of Japanese internment. In the end the Constitution is vindicated and strengthened.

There is also the larger issue of how our constitutional form of government *should* evolve into. The infinite wisdom of the forefathers – a Lincoln or Franklin – notwithstanding, the Constitution is a living and dynamic document which registers and resonance the dreams and aspirations of a nation. If perchance the people of the United States, under terrorism, wants the Constitution to be rewritten through practice and trial and error and not through constitutional amendment. The people should be and will be able to do so. In essence, America might be witnessing an epochal change in the structure (e.g., relative powers of three branches of government), process (e.g., meaning of due process) and substance (e.g., meaning

---

[2007] Patriotism silences any criticism of the war effort, in the name of unity ("divided we fall") and love for country ("my country right or wrong"). The larger context of course is the ascendancy of conservatism and the demise of liberalism as a political ideal, and the remaking of the nation, in Gods image. Aimee Carrillo Rowe and Sheena Malhotra, "Chameleon Conservatism Post - 9/11 Rhetorics of Innocence," *Poroi,* 2, 1, August, 2003. ("Conservative agenda has achieved its hegemony' through cultural reproduction of its main claims – right to life, reverse discrimination, in creating "chameleon conservatism") http://inpress.lib.uiowa.edu/poroi/papers/ rowe030816.html John Lukacs, *Democracy and Populism: Fear and Hatred* (Yale University Press, 2005) (For as long as we can remember and since the founding of the Republic, we consider anti-liberal as anti-intellectual.) Bob Moser, "The Crusaders (Christian evangelicals are plotting to remake America in their own image)" *rollingstone* Apr 11, 2005 (The Christian fundamentalists are reclaiming American's heart and soul and remaking America in the image of God.) (http://www.rollingstone.com/politics/story/_/id/7235393

[2008] Albert Gore Jr., "US Constitution in Grave Danger," *t r u t h o u t* | Speech Monday 16 January 2006. http://www.truthout.org/docs_2006/011606Y.shtml

[2009] Remarks of Chief Justice William H. Rehnquist 100th Anniversary Celebration of the Norfolk and Portsmouth Bar Association Norfolk, Virginia, May 3, 2000. http://www.supremecourtus.gov/publicinfo/speeches/sp_05-03-00.html

of privacy rights) of the Constitution. The analysis and assessment of this book should not be embraced without a healthy sense of criticalness, even cynicism.

As the content of this book attests, there are more questions to answer, and more questions than answers. More research is required to answer some of these troubling questions, and raises new one.

Some Afterthought

It is hoped that the findings and observations of this study summarizes in this last chapter, can contribute to the ongoing national dialogue, and in time helps with rendering a historical judgment, about the problems and issues, performance and utility, impact and implications of the USAPA.[2010] While not intended, this study, of necessity and by extension, will influence people's assessment on the conduct and merit of the war on terror. While not definitive, this study should help in laying a necessary foundation in animating and defining an emergent, but yet to be fully explored, field of study.

As intimated above, there is a grave need to assess the impact and chart the implications of the USAPA; to inform policy makers, to enrich academic study, to provide for meaningful oversight, or simply to establish an historical account and public record. Some, including the Bush administration, argued that it is grossly appropriate to play politics with war, lest it emboldens the enemy. Others, including scholars and public intellectuals, observed that it is simply too early to pass judgment on the USAPA, an emergency legislation barely 5 years old in a war without end. But to most people – journalists, democrats, public, there is not only an abstract right to know, but a real need to be informed, as citizens and patriots.

[2010] Charles Doyle, "USAPA Sunset: Provisions That Expire on December 31, 2005,"*CRS* Updated June 10, 2004. RL32186 (Subsection 224(a) of the USAPA (the Act) indicates that various sections in Title II of the Act are to remain in effect only until December 31, 2005.

INDEX

B

G

H

I

N

O

P

Q

T

U

U.N. Security Council, 3
U.S. history, 193, 206
U.S. military, 107, 109, 119, 363
UK, 22, 112, 115, 257
uncertainty, ix, 2, 11, 163, 169, 213, 243, 262
undergraduate, 143
unemployment, 279
UNICEF, 299
uniform, 113, 119, 125, 182, 217, 233, 241, 284
Universal Declaration of Human Rights, 18
universities, x, 6, 7, 11, 12, 13, 14, 69, 78, 86, 129, 130, 132, 136, 140, 145, 147, 150, 151, 152, 153, 154, 155, 157, 168, 169, 171, 172, 173, 175, 181, 182, 186, 187, 196, 303, 312
university community, 7, 8, 12, 14, 15, 128, 131, 144, 145
unreasonable searches, 292
updating, 134
USA Patriot Act, i, iii, ix, 191, 192, 196, 256, 309
users, 141, 146, 152, 164, 165, 166, 167, 171, 173, 185, 191, 224, 231, 241, 245, 247, 254, 257, 258, 271

V

vacuum, 367
validation, 5, 156
validity, 151, 182, 345
values, 6, 15, 25, 34, 57, 86, 99, 124, 143, 144, 190, 195, 216, 245, 261, 279, 286, 287, 297, 298, 305, 327, 341, 342, 344, 351
Vermont, 56, 81, 83, 225, 229, 281, 282, 283, 294, 314, 318
victims, 1, 45, 67, 68, 73, 93, 102, 103, 285, 332, 356
video surveillance, 322
Vietnam, 69, 75, 109, 110, 218, 226, 281, 286, 296
violence, 24, 126, 201, 205, 355
Virginia, 82, 192, 195, 236, 263, 266, 286, 294, 295, 296, 370, 383
visas, 8, 9, 10, 13, 127, 128, 131, 132, 133, 136, 173, 176, 209
vision, 97, 111, 143, 237, 259, 284, 327
voice, 51, 76, 81, 118, 300, 338, 383
voice mail, 76
voicing, 256, 294
voters, 101, 192, 314
voting, 54, 66, 260, 281, 300, 334, 344, 354
voting record, 281, 344
vulnerability, 5, 41, 123, 125, 126, 261, 362, 366

W

Wall Street Journal, 234, 236, 269, 360, 370
War on Terror, ix, x, 1,2, 3, 4, 20, 24, 25, 26, 27, 28, 32, 35, 45, 49, 57, 59, 62, 76, 81, 89, 90, 99, 100, 107, 109, 110, 111, 113, 122, 123, 124, 125, 126, 189, 190, 191, 192, 193, 195, 197, 198, 199, 208, 209, 214, 216, 217, 221, 229, 237, 261, 265, 269, 276, 278, 284, 290, 295, 296, 328, 333, 340, 341, 351, 353, 356, 362, 379, 382, 383, 384
warrants, 32, 81, 83, 212, 238, 247, 250, 258, 301, 307, 315, 320, 323, 349
watershed, 49
weakness, 34, 361, 373
wealth, ix
weapons, 12, 26, 52, 197, 205, 233, 366, 369
weapons of mass destruction, 12, 52, 366, 369
web, 11, 45, 54, 55, 58, 62, 79, 94, 96, 132, 134, 138, 139, 140, 141, 152, 160, 161, 163, 167, 168, 169, 173, 181, 185, 238, 246, 263, 269, 284, 294, 299, 304, 355
websites, 205, 308, 380
welfare, 45, 101, 136, 143, 172, 187, 215, 283, 298, 304
well-being, 15, 303
White House, 1, 2, 3, 4, 5, 9, 10, 36, 38, 39, 40, 57, 61, 63, 64, 77, 87, 96, 99, 100, 102, 104, 105, 106, 111, 119, 120, 124, 189, 203, 279, 335, 354, 356, 359, 361, 364, 367
wholesale, 48, 218, 268, 379
winning, 96, 125, 198
winter, 62, 252, 379
wiretaps, 58, 69, 94, 104, 121, 314, 353, 360, 379
Wisconsin, 69, 70, 73, 82, 92, 141, 147, 149, 152, 153, 154, 226, 255, 258, 268, 273, 280, 284, 294, 327, 329, 330, 331, 332, 333, 334
witnesses, 207, 221
WMD, 3, 31, 98, 105, 111, 230, 355, 361, 362, 365, 366, 367
women, 86, 119, 275, 304, 313
workers, 27, 31, 68, 200, 202, 258, 262
working groups, 328
working hours, 71
working population, 292
workload, 128, 139, 147, 155, 183
workstation, 269
World Trade Center, ix, 1, 50, 81, 85, 122, 123, 131, 246, 350
World War I, 69, 75, 218, 296, 304, 348
World War II, 69, 75, 218, 296, 304
writing, 107, 178, 269
WWW, 330